MOBILE HOME WEALTH PART 2

HOW TO BECOME EVEN WEALTHIER INVESTING IN MOBILE HOME PARKS

Zalman Velvel

Zalman Velvel Inc.

זלמן וועלוועל

The strategies presented in this book are based upon the research and experiences of the author in his many years as a real estate professional. As you make your own investments, the author, the publisher, and the owner of the copyright strongly suggest consulting appropriate professionals in the fields of law, real estate, and finance.

Because no investment strategy is foolproof, the authors and publishers are not responsible for any adverse consequences resulting from the use of any of the strategies discussed in the book. However, the publisher believes that this information should be made available to the public.

EDITOR: Karen Anspach
TYPESETTING AND COVER DESIGN: Gary A. Rosenberg
INDEXING: Kitty Chibnik

Zalman Velvel Inc.
602 Center Road • Fort Myers, FL 33907
(239) 768-1234 • (866) 799-1234
www.ZalmanVelvel.com

Library of Congress Cataloging-in-Publication Data is on file with the Library of Congress.

ISBN: 978-0-9823531-0-3

Printed in the United States of America.

10 9 8 7 6 5 4 3 2 1

Contents

PART THREE

Reap Your Profits

This book is dedicated to my wife, Fran;
our children Holly, David, and Amy;
our extended family, Charlie and Andrea;
and our grandchildren C.J., Emmy, Samson,
Jazzy, Jakey, and the one soon to come.

Acknowledgments

Once again, I want to thank the real estate investors and colleagues who I have come in contact with over the years, and the professionals who assisted them, for their help and knowledge. I also want to thank the management and trainers at the Wealth Intelligence Academy, and their support personnel, who multiplied all our efforts. And Russ, who trained me on how to train and taught me by his example.

I would also like to recognize Karen Anspach for her editorial assistance and Gary Rosenberg for his typesetting and layout skills.

And last, I would like to thank the people I have trained and taught, from whom I have learned so much.

Introduction

Mobile Home Wealth Part 2 is the sequel to *Mobile Home Wealth.* This book, as well as the previous one, is intended for people seeking financial independence, people who are tired of living paycheck to paycheck. Both books are intended for people who are worried that the company they work for might "downsize" them onto the unemployment line, or worse, that their job might not even exist in the future.

This book is written for people who have little or no experience investing in income producing real estate, or have read *Mobile Home Wealth* and want to go to the next level. We are going to delve into the exciting and lucrative field of investing in mobile home parks, which is an overlooked part of the real estate market, usually hidden from the average investor. This book will take you by the hand and show you how to make a good secure living, or a fortune (your choice), by using proven success formulas for investing in mobile home parks.

ROAD MAP TO $100,000 EXTRA INCOME AND 1 MILLION NET WORTH

In the first book, we gave a road map to adding $100,000 a year to your income, part-time, while you continued to work at your present career. That same goal will be continued in this book because most people need to keep their current job while they create a new real estate investing career, so we are going to assume the same need for you. When you work the plan and the plan works for you, and you feel secure, then you can decide whether you want to remain a part-time investor, or quit your job and go full time into investing in mobile home parks and affordable housing.

In this book, we are going to establish a second goal—adding $1,000,000 to your net worth. We want every reader to become a millionaire by investing in mobile home parks, and then multiply that wealth into becoming a multimillionaire. You will be shown formulas on how to accomplish that.

As in the previous book, you will receive real-life examples to follow and train on. There will be no "smoke and mirrors," or "motivational rah rah" where you are told repeatedly, "if you think it, or imagine it, it will happen." Yes, it helps to have a positive attitude, and you will be encouraged to have one because it will energize you for the success you want. However, along with a good attitude you must have focused actions and a plan. Without effort on your part, all the motivation in the world isn't going to deliver the concrete results you want—more money in your pocket, and more quality time for the important people in your life.

FORMULAS FOR SUCCESS

Throughout my first book, *Mobile Home Wealth,* we introduced simple formulas, which we called *formulas for success.* In this book we are also going to share the *formulas for success* for mobile home parks, which only involve simple math. When you follow them, you are practically guaranteed positive results. Formulas are the foundation for estimating costs, and then the resulting profits, in almost every profession.

Don't believe it when someone tells you they have no formulas and just "fly by the seat of their pants" when figuring out how much to bid or pay in their profession. If that were true, they would fail due to the lack of predictability of their income. The real reason many successful people don't like to share their success formulas is they don't want to make their business easy for competitors to copy. I'm not concerned with that. There are thousands of mobile home parks, and hundreds of thousands of individual mobile homes, for sale at any one time. There are plenty to go around for everyone.

The formulas given to you in *Mobile Home Wealth* are very similar to the ones given in this book. However, you will learn in the coming pages that *there is a basic difference between how you price a mobile home park versus how you price a single mobile home.* When you buy a group of mobile homes in a mobile home park the method of evaluating them changes.

YOU ARE BUYING A SMALL TOWN WHERE YOU ARE THE MAYOR

Another primary difference between buying a mobile home park and a single mobile home has to do with the way a mobile home park is set up. When you buy a mobile home park, you are buying a small town where you are the mayor. The nice part is you don't have to run for office and play politics. You merely have to do a good job and you will be paid handsomely for your efforts, without the threat of being voted out of office. You don't have to go begging in front of a town council for a raise either. You just have to improve the income of your small town and you automatically merit and receive a raise.

A major part of every small town is its infrastructure, which is just a fancy word for the water and sewer system, the electric and gas transmission lines, the roads, and any common areas and amenities available to the residents, like swimming pools, shuffle board courts, tennis courts, golf courses, and water and snow sporting equipment, etc. You will need to study the infrastructure before you buy a mobile home park, since you will be responsible for maintaining and repairing it. This book will help you understand and evaluate the infrastructure of mobile home parks to limit your risks and maximize your profits.

SO WHAT EXACTLY IS A MOBILE HOME?

Mobile homes are built in a factory and then transported and set in place for people to live in. The attractive home pictured here was built in a factory in two sections, and then each section was towed down the highway and fit together on-site. The home can be detached and moved again if the owner decides to change where he wants to live, hence the word *mobile.* Recently, manufacturers have wanted to give a more permanent feeling to people residing in their products and not focus on their mobility, so they have coined a fancy new word, "manufactured housing."

However you refer to them, as mobile homes or manufactured housing, *they are the most affordable form of housing.* There is a huge demand for affordable housing, and there always will be—you are entering a field where you won't have to worry about the Internet, or a computer, eliminating your career. You also don't have to worry about a new single-family home or townhouse subdivision opening up down the street and under-selling you—they will not have more affordable housing than you.

To show you just how affordable mobile homes are, think about this: recently the median-priced home sold in the United States was worth approximately $200,000. That means there were just as many homes sold above $200,000 as there were that sold below that number. In simple terms, the number is similar to the average price. The median price for a new mobile home (without land) was around $50,000. That is a quarter of the price! If you are impressed by that number, then you should be even more impressed when *I show you how to buy good used mobile homes for $10,000 or less.*

SO WHAT EXACTLY IS A MOBILE HOME PARK?

A mobile home park is just two or more mobile homes on the same piece of property or on adjoining properties. The picture on the left is an aerial photo of one of our parks which contains 120 mobile homes and 50 RV lots.

If you have read *Mobile Home Wealth,* you've read our discussion about investing in mobile homes one at a time, in various locations. In this book, we are going to explore *buying many of them at one time,* in one location. Rule number two in the six rules of wisdom that you will be given at the end of this book applies mightily here—if one mobile home is good, two mobile homes is even better, and three is even better still . . . and so on . . . and so on.

Furthermore, as a bonus for those of you who have a creative streak, in Chapter 15 you will be shown how to set up your own mobile home park, starting with just a vacant piece of land.

HOW MUCH MONEY WILL YOU NEED TO GET STARTED?

It would be beneficial if you could start out with some savings to invest, and good credit, but if you don't, you won't be left out. If you have no money to get started with (other than the purchase price of this book) and no credit, or even bad credit, don't worry. Several tried and true "no money down" and "no credit" strategies have also been included to get you started, so you don't have to have any money or any credit to get started. That's totally different than if you were buying a franchise, like MacDonald's or Burger King.

MOBILE HOME PARKS ARE A PROVEN FRANCHISE, BUT WITHOUT THE FEES

Investing in mobile home parks has all the positive elements of a franchise. There are millions of customers out there who need affordable housing, as much or more than they need a Big Mac or Whopper. Also, like a franchise, this book will give you proven management and marketing techniques to insure your success in finding your customers, meeting their needs, and getting paid a healthy profit for doing so. However, unlike a franchise, no one will be siphoning 10 percent or more of your income each month. Instead, you will be acquiring assets—land and buildings and infrastructure—that produce income and you get to keep *all* of the profit. You also get to own the land and buildings and infrastructure, which appreciate in value, unlike tables and chairs and grills and fryers, which depreciate and go down in value.

LET'S GET TO KNOW ONE ANOTHER

If you read my first book, we already know each other, so you can skip ahead to the next heading. If you didn't read that book, then stay right here, because at this point you might be wondering about this author's credibility. If you are, then good for you! Anytime someone promises to deliver important changes in your life, and wants money beforehand, you should ask about their qualifications. So let's get to know one another.

I have been actively investing in real estate for more than twenty-seven years, and in mobile homes in particular for more than sixteen years. Currently we own eleven mobile home parks, some big and some small, worth millions of dollars. We've made millions investing in mobile homes and mobile home parks, and I'm going to unlock the secrets so you can, too. I'm also going to be upfront and honest about some of the pitfalls, to protect you from making mistakes that might take some of the wind out of your sails.

Another benefit to you is my more than twelve years experience working as a real estate trainer. Along the path of my investing career, I met the owner of one of the largest real estate seminar companies in the world, which was located in the same county where I live. We clicked immediately. As a result, I taught three courses for his company as an independent contractor.

The first course already had a curriculum, which I enhanced. I created the curriculum and manuals from scratch for the other two courses. This book is based upon my years of experience teaching the curriculum of those three courses, which now cost $4,500 each for three days of live training or six weeks of "distance learning" on the Internet.

After training literally thousands of people to invest in real estate, from just about every walk of life and every age group, from all around our great country, you can be sure the strategies and techniques you're going to receive actually work. Some strategies may work better than others in your area, so in that case, you will just have to choose which are the most profitable and most interesting to you.

If you would like more information about my credentials, then let me add that I have also acquired a CCIM designation, which is billed as "the PhD of commercial real estate." Along with that designation, I have an active real estate brokerage license, a mortgage broker license, and an auctioneer's license. For many years, I also had a real estate appraisal license, but had to give it up when the continuing education requirement took up too much of my time. My auctioneer's license will prove to be very useful to you because, after selling hundreds of properties at auction, it put me in contact with thousands of investors. During negotiations I learned the strategies of the most successful ones, and they are also included in this book.

Okay, at this point, I have completed our introduction and we have gotten to know one another. I hope you're not thinking, *Zalman is special, and I can never do what he does.* It would not be accurate to believe that. Instead, you should think, *if Zalman can do it, then so can I.*

Now, let's talk briefly about the three basic ways people like to learn, because this book is geared toward all three.

THE THREE WAYS PEOPLE LEARN

The most common way people learn is by *watching an expert* do something. Then they copy the expert, performing on their own, building confidence along the way. We have included case studies with pictures to train you this way.

The second most common way to learn is to watch the expert, and then include lots of *facts and figures and manuals.* This is for people who believe *they must know every possible thing about a subject, so if anything ever goes wrong in the future, they will know how to fix it.*

Please keep in mind that while it is a healthy goal to have as much information as possible before you start something new, many of the people who learn like this unfortunately develop "paralysis of analysis." Their mind is so cluttered with remembering facts that they lose sight of their basic strategies. In other words, they wind up doing nothing because the goal of knowing everything that can possibly go wrong is not achievable. You will learn a different way of looking at problems here—that they are just another part of your investing process. You shouldn't be afraid of them—when unexpected problems happen, and they always do . . . it's okay! When you learn how to overcome problems—and you will here—these situations will point the way to *more* strategies for making money. Then you will actually go out and try to find the same problems to create a good deal for yourself. You become a part of the solution and get paid handsomely for your effort!

The last type of student and their learning path is nothing short of thrilling. I refer to them as *Type-3's*. Type 3's are people who just want a brief outline of what they need to do before they jump in and do it. They learn while they are doing, and they don't want to be bogged down with facts and figures. In other words, they like combining learning and making money with adrenaline. They're the kind of people who like to jump into the deep end of the pool to learn how to swim. As a trainer, I enjoy these students, because I know they are going to use my training. But I also have to warn you that many times these students have entered my training all set to repeat the same mistake they made before—when they jumped in without checking first to see if it was the right swimming pool for them to be in.

This book is going to help all three kinds of learners. You're going to learn as we take you by the hand and show you from examples. Those of you who need to know as much as possible before you get involved are going to get formulas and facts, but not so much data that you get bogged down and don't do anything at all. And for those who like the adrenaline rush, you are going to get road maps to follow so you can quickly get into the action without jumping into a pool with no water in it. That way, you won't get hurt or waste your time trying to climb out of a mess.

HOMEWORK

You will get homework. What's that? I can almost hear you groaning from here, *"Oh no, not homework!"* Yes, homework. And you will be expected to do it, not because of a mark a teacher puts on a piece of paper you hand in, but because the homework you will be given *will make you money*. You will be encouraged to have fun while you are doing it. Your grade will be what you add to your wallet and your balance sheet.

HOW THE BOOK IS SET UP—A LOGICAL LEARNING PROCESS

There are three major parts to this book. Each part builds on the previous one, filling in new, skills that are vital but simple. We will begin with a funny story called "The Second Adventure," which describes the opportunity that led to my start in investing in mobile home parks. The first adventure, which I described in my first book, was about the opportunity that led me to invest in my first mobile home.

Then, in *Part One* of the book, you will be introduced to *The Magic Formula,* the pricing model for mobile home parks. The Four Basic Profit Strategies and each strategy's *Formula for Success* will follow. You will learn how to think and act like a successful mobile home park investor, determining your profit *before* you even own a property.

In *Part Two,* you will learn how to *Get the Deal Right,* using the Five Green Fs. These are good "Fs" because they are the color of money—green (not red, like the bad "Fs" given out in school). You will be shown where to *find* your mobile home park deals; how to *figure* out what they're worth; how to set your *flag* on the park like a pro, with an offer that fully protects you and negotiate the best deal for yourself; and how to inspect the property to recognize defects in the infrastructure, so you'll know in advance what you will have to *fix.* Careful attention will be paid to "due diligence," which is studying the property before you buy it. Due diligence is extremely important when you buy mobile home parks, and this book has one of the most complete discussions on how to perform this to protect yourself against mistakes and being taken advantage of by sellers. If the four previous "Fs" are a "go", you will be shown the fifth "F," how to *finance* the park.

In *Part Three,* you will learn how to *Reap Your Profits.* You will be shown how to close the deal, manage your mobile home park, and build a Power Team of professionals that will enable you to do it over and over again. You will also be shown how to protect your assets and save on taxes. In this part, you will learn how to develop your own mobile home park from scratch. You will also learn advanced strategies for creating wealth using mobile home parks, and finally the *Three Secrets of Long Term Wealth,* which will teach you how to provide for you and your loved ones for generations to come. The three secrets are told in an amusing way, but don't be misled because of that. They are very powerful. For many of you, they will reveal a whole new way of thinking.

Your Road Map is the final chapter of the book. This is a plan that will let you earn an additional $100,000 per year, part-time, and increase your net worth by at least $1,000,000 while you continue to work at your present career. After you follow the plan, you can decide whether to remain a part-time mobile home park investor or go full-time into your new career. The choice will be yours.

I hope you are excited to begin, because I sure am. Let's get going!

The Second Adventure

My first adventure happened in 1992, when I was introduced to mobile homes after never having owned one before. It is described in my first book, *Mobile Home Wealth*.

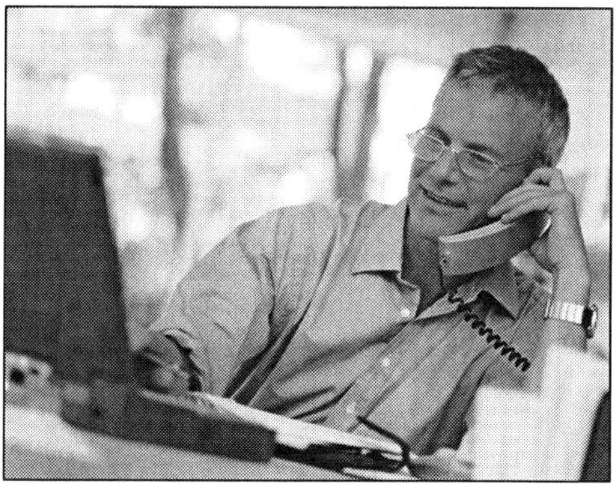

The second adventure began eight years later, in the winter of 2000, during the first morning of a three-day training course I was teaching on how to become a millionaire by investing in real estate. A group of forty people from all around the United States were sitting in front of me, listening and taking notes. The first day of class began at 7:00 A.M. and went to 7:00 P.M. We allotted the first two hours for an overview of the course material and to introducing the students to each other. By 9:00 A.M. we were ready to get down to business.

I was standing by a desk in the front of the room. On the desk was a phone equipped with a loud speaker so the class could hear both sides of any phone conversations. Next to the phone was a copy of the local *Pennysaver* or *Thrifty Nickel* type newspaper, which in Southwest Florida is called *The Shopper.* Ads that looked like they might be a good deal were circled. Off to the right of the desk was an easel with a large blank pad and black marking pens on its ledge.

For the next two hours, I was going to make phone calls to sellers whose ads I had circled. The class would listen to me interact with sellers and learn how I began a search to purchase investment property. As I spoke to the sellers, I wrote on the easel, fitting each property into one of the two basic success formulas I was teaching—flippers and keepers—which you will learn about shortly. When I found a good deal, I made an appointment with the sellers to see their properties the next afternoon. At that time, the class and I would board a tour bus and go out and view the properties and make offers. We called it "reality training," like the reality TV shows that became popular years later.

I had just finished calling ads about duplexes listed for sale in the $50,000 to $60,000 range, which gave around $200 per month in positive cash flow, with little or no down payment. The intent was to *keep* the duplexes and receive the cash flow. When an investor owned enough of them, he or she would achieve financial independence and not be dependent on a weekly paycheck. Then the investor could quit his or her job (if he or she wanted to) and invest full-time in real estate, and become wealthy.

I also called on single-family homes listed in the $40,000 to $75,000 range. The intent there was to buy houses for big discounts because they were run down and needed sprucing up. We would then fix them and make them look pretty, and *flip* them for quick profits, which would be used for additional investing capital or simply to enjoy life a little more.

While I was scanning the ads in *The Shopper,* I came across a listing in the mobile home section that advertised: *"Mobile for Sale—$1,200."* After "running numbers" on duplexes in the $50,000 to $60,000 range, and homes in the $40,000 to $75,000 range, a property priced at $1,200 was irresistible. I dialed the number in the ad and this is how the conversation went:

"Hi, I'm calling from an ad in *The Shopper* listing a mobile home for sale. Is it still available?" I asked.

"Yes," the woman answered.

"Can you tell me where it is?"

"It's in North Fort Myers, in the Happy Trails Mobile Home Park." (Note: Since we may still own some of the parks in this book, we wanted to give privacy to the residents living there, so we have changed the names of people and parks from this point on.)

"Do the residents in the park own their own lots, or do they pay lot rent?"

"They have to pay lot rent. It's $285 per month."

"I see," I said. "And how many bedrooms and baths does your mobile home have?"

"It has one bedroom and one bath."

"One bedroom and one bath," I repeated. "Well, I'm an investor and I would be interested in putting a tenant in it and renting it out. What do you think I could I rent it out for . . . by the way, my name is Zalman." I figured it was time to introduce myself.

"Hi, Zalman. I'm Peggy. I'm not an investor," she replied, "but I think the investors around here are getting around $500 per month from tenants."

I've learned not to rely solely on the rental information I received from sellers because many were not experienced landlords. However, from my own experience as a landlord, I knew $500 per month was a reasonable number for rent, so I wrote $500 on the top of the easel pad for the monthly income coming in. Then I subtracted $285 for the monthly lot rent, $50 for monthly repairs, maintenance, and vacancy (10 percent of the rent), and $15 for insurance and yearly tags. There were no real estate taxes because the mobile home was on a rental lot, and the owner of the park paid the taxes. That left $150 in positive cash flow, like so:

	$500 Monthly Rental Income
–	**$285 Lot Rent**
–	**$50 Repairs, Maintenance, Vacancy (10 percent of the rent)**
–	**$15 Insurance and Tags**
	$150 Positive Monthly Cash Flow

Now it was time to test the seller's price and flexibility.

"Peggy, I see you have it listed for $1,200. Is that the best you can do on the price?" I asked, winking at the class. $1,200 was already ridiculously cheap, and some of the students recognized this and giggled.

"Well, for a quick cash deal, I might be able to let you have it for $1,000," she said, after some hesitation.

"Is that the absolute best you can do?" I replied. Once again, some of the students giggled at my audacity to bargain down an already great deal.

"Well . . . " she said after an even longer pause. "If you buy them all, I could give you a package deal."

I hesitated here and considered her reply. Then I asked, "All? How many mobile homes do you have for sale in the park?"

"Five."

"Five? Peggy, why are selling five mobile homes in the same park?"

"The owner just did a cleanup in the park. He kicked people out who didn't pay their lot rent or didn't follow the rules. Then he gave the mobile homes they abandoned to me. I fix and clean them, and then sell them."

"You mean the owner of the park *gave* you five mobile homes?" I asked.

"Sure. He doesn't want to get involved in fixing them. He is only concerned with getting the lot rent, and I get them back on the rent roll in a month or two. So Zalman, if you want to buy all five, I'll give you a really good deal."

"What's a really good deal?" I asked.

"How about $800 a piece?" Peggy asked.

The class was on the edge of their seats. I wrote down the following:

5 Mobile Homes × $800 for Each Home = $4,000 Total Price
$150 per Month in Positive Cash Flow × 5 Homes = $750 per Month

Then I showed that if an investor put the five mobile homes on a credit card, thus buying them for *no cash money down,* the investor could have all five mobile homes paid off in about six months, including $500 interest, like so:

$750 per Month in Positive Cash Flow × 6 Months = $4,500 Cash Flow
$4,000 Purchase Price + $500 Credit Card Interest = $4,500 Total Price

After using the first six months of cash flow to pay off the credit card for the homes, there would be an annuity of $750 per month coming in.

I put my phone on mute, so Peggy couldn't hear me, and asked the class:

"How many of you have a credit card with them, and would like to have five *free* mobile homes after six months, and earn $750 per month after that?"

Almost every hand in the room went up. Now I decided to be cute. I unmuted the phone.

"You know, Peggy," I continued, "if I'm going to buy five mobile homes in one park, I might as well own the park." I winked and the class giggled.

"It's funny you should mention that," she said. "I heard the owner of the park just put it up for sale."

The class became dead quiet. I was speechless, my mouth hanging open.

"Hello?" Peggy said.

"Uh . . . well . . . I see . . . so Peggy, how do I get in contact with the owner?"

"Well, I don't know the owner's phone number, because I only talk to the park manager, Billy. Would you like his number?"

Peggy gave me Billy's number. I made an appointment to see Peggy the next day and then hung up. Next I called Billy, and he verified that the park was up for sale. He didn't know any of the details, but he gave me the name and number of the owner.

I didn't call the owner right away. I wanted to visit the park and see what it looked like, and whether I would be interested in owning it or not. When the class and I visited the park the next day, the first mobile home she showed us looked like the picture below. It was small and old, but in decent condition after Peggy got finished cleaning and painting it. When we visited the park, I liked what I saw. It was crowded with older mobile homes, on four and one-half acres, on the corner of two busy roads. The land was very valuable, which was a good thing.

A typical mobile home.

I knew nothing about mobile home parks and that was not a good thing. But I figured, what the heck, now might be a good time to learn, so I called the owner. He explained the basic financials of the park, that it had around ninety lots, but only sixty-six had homes on them, paying $285 per month in lot rent. It also had a corner store paying $450 per month in rent. I discovered in our conversation that the owner was retiring, and he and his investment partners just sold their *whole portfolio* of mobile home parks for a profit of around $40,000,000. That's right, forty million dollars. This was the last mobile home park they had left to sell, the runt of the litter. This is how the important parts of the conversation went, which was not in front of the class.

"So, Mr. Seller, how much do you want for your mobile home park?"

"We would like to get $800,000," he answered.

"Yes, that would be nice," I replied, not knowing anything on how to price mobile home parks. "But what is the least you would take?"

"Make me an offer," he replied.

"How about $650,000?" I said.

"Put it in writing and fax it over to me. I'll present it to my partners."

"So would you take $650,000?" I asked, surprised.

"Put it in writing and fax it over and I'll present it."

"But would you take $650,000?" I repeated.

"Zalman, how many times do I have to say this? Send over your offer."

The line went dead then. I assumed that when a seasoned investor just made 40 million dollars in profits, he had the right to be impatient with amateur mobile home park investors like me who kept repeating the same foolish question.

I faxed over an offer for $650,000 to the seller. In my offer, I asked for sixty days to inspect the property. Then, if everything was in accordance with my expectations, I would have an additional sixty days to get a mortgage. I was going to borrow $450,000 from a local bank, and I wanted the seller to give me a $200,000 second mortgage. In other words, my offer constituted a "no money down" deal for me.

	$650,000 Purchase Price
–	**$450,000 First Mortgage from Local Bank**
–	**$200,000 Second Mortgage from Seller**
	0 Money Down

I heard nothing from the seller for the next three days, so finally I called him. This is how the conversation went:

"Mr. Seller, did you receive my offer?"

"Yes, Zalman. I'm sorry for not calling back, but I've been very busy."

Yeah, I'm sure, I thought. When you just made 40 million dollars, six hundred and fifty thousand was nothing to get excited about.

"So what is your answer?" I asked.

"Well, we're okay on the price."

My heart almost leaped out of my chest, but I remained quiet and listened.

"But the second mortgage is a deal killer, Zalman. My partners want nothing to do with giving out financing. When we sell, they want to cash out—period. They are all older, in their late seventies and even eighties, and not interested in burdening their estate with a second mortgage down in Florida. They don't know what tomorrow will bring—some don't even buy green bananas anymore."

"I see," I said, missing the joke. I really wanted to buy the park for no money down, holding back our cash for unforeseen problems while we learned how to manage a mobile home park, something we never did before.

"And Zalman," the seller continued, "I would advise you to not wait too long. There is another buyer who also made us an offer."

"Okay, Mr. Seller, I'll rework the numbers and get back to you."

I did not get back to the seller and rework the numbers. I found another deal in the meantime that I felt more comfortable with. It was a package of fourteen individual mobile homes located on fourteen separate lots on four different streets in a subdivision of several hundred homes that was about two miles from the Happy Trails Mobile Home Park. The seller wanted $420,000, or $30,000 per mobile home, and was willing to give financing with almost 20 percent down. This is the way the owner wanted to sell:

	$420,000 Purchase Price
–	**$340,000 First Mortgage from Seller**
	$80,000 in Cash from Me for Down Payment

While I liked the prospect of not having to go to a bank for financing and pay the bank's closing costs, I was definitely not thrilled with putting down $80,000. I asked the seller if he would reduce the down payment to $20,000 but he was definitely not interested in doing that. So taking all this in, this is the way I countered back on the fourteen individual mobile homes:

$400,000 Purchase Price
– $300,000 First Mortgage from Local Bank
– $100,000 Second Mortgage from Seller

0 Money Down

The seller was still not interested. He did not want to take back such a large second mortgage. While we were negotiating, I brought in a young partner with whom I purchased a nearby motel a year before. His name was Gershon, but I referred to him, affectionately as Crazy Gersh. In our partnership, I find the deals, arrange the financing, and manage the books. Crazy Gersh's job is to oversee the properties on a day-to-day basis and fix any problems that arise with the buildings, infrastructure, tenants, or our property managers.

I call him Crazy Gersh because he has at least one crazy idea every day. But the wonderful thing is this—during the period of a year, at least two of his crazy ideas are absolutely brilliant. My job in our partnership is to weed through the 363 crazy ideas and find the two brilliant ones. (Warren Buffet, arguably one of the best investors ever, has said that all you need is one or two "big ideas" in your whole business career to become wealthy.)

Don't think Crazy Gersh believes only two of his ideas are brilliant each year. He won't give up on an idea just because I *say* it's crazy. I have to *prove* to him that the idea is unworkable with cold hard facts, because he is as persistent, tenacious, and stubborn as he is crazy. (Persistence is also a very important attribute when it comes to being successful, by the way.)

Gersh was solid behind buying the mobile home park, and uneasy about the fourteen separate mobile homes. This is how our conversation went:

"Gersh, let's buy the fourteen homes," I argued. "At least we know about managing individual mobile homes. They're just like single family houses."

"But Zalman, we have little control over the neighborhood," he argued. "We'll own fourteen homes on four different blocks. If one or two of the neighbors let their places run down, or rent to druggies, we're going to have problems. When we buy the mobile home park, we control the whole neighborhood because we own it. And in this park, we control ninety lots, not just fourteen."

"But we don't know anything about managing mobile home parks, Gersh!"

"How much did we know about motels before we bought our first one?"

"Nothing," I reluctantly agreed.

"And we're averaging $4,000 per month in positive cash flow with almost no money down. I'll bet running a mobile home park is easier than a motel."

I found myself unable to refute Gersh's logic at this point. "That's the . . . best idea you've had in the last six months, Gersh," I replied.

This is how both investments stacked up:

COMPARISON OF 14 MOBILE HOMES VERSUS HAPPY TRAILS MOBILE HOME PARK

	14 Mobile Homes	Happy Trails Park
Cost	$420,000	$650,000
Down Payment	$80,000	0
Number of Lots	14	90
Potential Gross Rents	$8,400	$26,000 per month??
Potential Cash Flow	$4,000 per month	0–10,000 per month??
Management Time	5–10 hours per week	A few hours per week??
Control of Neighborhood	Little control	Tight control

One of 14 individual mobile homes.

Happy Trails mobile home park.

The mobile home park seemed like it was better. We were buying more lots with a smaller down payment, greater gross rents, and greater control over the neighborhood. However, we were not sure of three of our conclusions—the ones with the "??". We didn't know how we were going to fill the twenty-four empty lots (90 total lots – 66 rented lots = 24 empty lots) to increase the gross rents, how much our positive cash flow was going to be afterwards, and how much time it was going to take to manage it, all of which are extremely important criteria.

The cash flow could have been anywhere from zero to $10,000 per month, depending on how many vacant lots we could fill up, and how we managed our costs. The management time was supposed to be lower because the park came with a manager who was supposed to take care of everything.

You may be wondering how I arrived at the zero down payment for the mobile home park. While Gersh and I were considering both investments, I completed negotiating a deal with the owner of the park for a price of $650,000 with no owner carry back financing. During the sixty day inspection period for the mobile home park, I spoke to a few local banks about borrowing all the money for the loan, and one agreed to give us a loan for the whole purchase price if I pledged additional collateral.

This was one of the most difficult investment decisions I made up to this point in my career. That $650,000 was a lot of money to me in 2001, and each day I wavered between buying and not buying the park. It was definitely "outside my box" and caused me a great deal of worry. There were no books or seminars on investing in mobile home parks at the time.

But, what the heck, I thought. The terms were good and Gersh was persistent. In June 2001, with Crazy Gersh pushing me every step along the way, we bought our first mobile home park. We borrowed the whole purchase price of $650,000 from a local bank and I pledged $150,000 in additional collateral, which was two duplexes I owned free and clear. I also arranged a provision in the loan so the lien on my duplexes would be released when the park's net operating income, the NOI, reached $100,000. (You'll learn about NOI in the pages coming up.)

In keeping with our partnership agreement, Gersh got involved in the day to day "hands on" management of the park, and I took care of the marketing, accounting, and paperwork. Together, we climbed the learning curve, one step at a time. We created our management style based upon our experience running this mobile home park.

The park looked like the picture in the comparison chart *after* it was fixed up by us. It was one of the ugliest mobile home parks in three counties at the time we purchased it. Worse, it had no positive cash flow for the first six months we owned it. Whatever money we took in went out for expenses and the mortgage. It looked like we put a millstone around both of our necks, and I violated my cardinal rule about being a landlord: ***If you have to wake up to tenants, you need to be paid for the privilege.***

> ***Remember:***
> *If you have to wake up to tenants, you need to be paid for the privilege.*

The experience had a very happy ending, however. By the start of 2003, after a year and a half, we had all ninety lots rented out and $10,000 per month or more in positive cash flow after all the bills were paid, including the mortgage payment. The bank released their lien because we exceeded $100,000 NOI.

After seven years of ownership, the park has made in excess of $10,000 in positive cash flow per month. As of this writing, it's worth in excess of $2.2 million dollars, a profit of $1.5 million dollars if we want to sell it, which as of this writing, we don't.

When I show this example to people at the mobile home trainings I conduct, I ask the class, "Let me see a show of hands: how many people would like to buy a mobile home park for no money down and then get $10,000 per month or more in positive cash flow from it a few years down the road?"

Every hand goes up.

Then I ask, "Who could retire with a smile if they had one of these?"

Again, every hand goes up.

Then I finish with, "Who would like to leave this to their children?"

And again, every hand goes up.

I am going to teach you how we did this, so you can do it when you buy your own parks.

By the way, crazy Gersh and I went on to buy two more mobile home parks together. He bought two more small parks by himself, and I bought eight additional mobile home parks by myself, some big and some small. He and I are still on the lookout for more.

SUMMARY

You should feel better about adventures after reading this chapter, because you are sure to have your own as you learn and invest in affordable housing. With the right attitude on your part, you can turn those adventures into your own personal money making strategies. You may also be lucky enough to find a partner like Crazy Gersh. Gersh thinks "outside the box" more consistently that just about anyone I have ever met.

HOMEWORK

First, I want you to go out and buy a spiral or bound notebook (not a loose-leaf binder). This is going to be a diary of how you got started in the great field of mobile home park investing—something to review and smile at later. It's easier to keep bound notebooks than loose-leaf binders, which lose their pages and take a beating over the years, so that's why I am insisting on something bound. You may want to give this to your children, if they join you in this great endeavor. My children have, and someday I hope my grandchildren will, also.

Second, I want you to list on page one some of the adventures that have come your way, how you reacted to them, and how you could have used them as opportunities. If getting this book was an adventure, list it there right up front. Don't spend too much time on this—it's just a brainstorming session.

Third, let's start on your roadmap. You need to go out and look at mobile home parks in your area. Check the classifieds, call brokers and FSBOs (for sale by owner properties), look in the yellow pages under "Mobile Home Parks," and just drive around and keep your eyes open. Later on, I'll show you how to find thousands of mobile home parks for sale, but for now, I want you to "window shop" to get familiar with where mobile homes parks are in your area and what they look like. Think of it as a scouting trip or an adventure. Write in your notebook about the properties you saw and your first impressions of them. You might be surprised by what you find.

For those of you in the third group of learners, you Type 3's who like to add adrenalin to your experiences, *please* don't buy anything yet. I know it's going to be hard to restrain yourself. If you want to have some fun, go into the manager's office of the mobile home parks you find and ask to speak to the owner. Don't tell the manager why you want to speak to the owner, just say it's personal and important. (Some managers do not want their parks sold because they like things just the way they are, good or bad, and don't want any changes or to risk losing their job.) When you contact the owner, ask if he or she would like to sell their park, and at what price. Say you'll get back to them with an offer. *Please* finish reading this book before you do give them an offer.

COMING ATTRACTIONS

We're going to start Part One of your training. You're going to be introduced to The Magic Formula, and the Four Basic Profit Strategies, and each strategy's *formula for success.* You are going to learn a simple way to figure out *before* you buy a mobile home park whether you will make a profit *after* you own it, so you can remove the guesswork. We're also going to take you by the hand and show you specific examples of how to apply each strategy, so you can repeat the process for yourself where you live. Most of the examples were chosen for their humor, so you can continue to learn when you aren't expecting it, and you won't be so tense about learning.

Why do we get so tense when it comes to learning?

Part One

The Four Basic Profit Strategies + The Magic Formula

Being a mobile home park investor is an exciting career when you think of it as an adventure. You can apply your own individual talents and personality as you explore the world of affordable housing and start on your own path toward wealth. When you set off on your path, you will have to get your business mind and actions going in the right direction by doing two things:

1. Prospecting for good deals

2. Managing the parks you own for maximum cash flow

Number one above means that you are going to go out into the real estate market as often as you can, to look at mobile homes parks for sale. When you look at each one, you are going to ask yourself the question, *"If I buy this property, what am I going to do with it afterwards—does it fit any of the four basic ways I make money?"*

Number two above means that you will be upgrading the management of the parks you already own to give you maximum income and minimized expenses, which will result in greater profits and greater price appreciation (you will learn about this shortly when we discuss The la). You will also be trying to minimize the time you spend roblems" associated with the residents on your mobile home lots, or with tenants renting your mobile homes. This will be discussed in Chapter 13, when we discuss management of mobile home parks.

The Magic Formula is your starting point for determining the value of a mobile home park opportunity that you discover. It is the basic formula you will use to compute the price of a mobile home park, given its current yearly net income (its profit), and the degree of risk and management intensity it requires in order to attain that income. Once you understand The Magic Formula, you will compute the current price of the park and then turn to your *Four Basic Profit Strategies* to see which, if any, is best for the park you are looking at Each of the four strategies for making money also provides a simple *formula for success.* Before you buy any park you will plug the park into that strategy's *formula for success* to see how it performs. In other words, these profit formulas will tell you what your current profit will be, and will also help you arrive at an estimate of your future profit potential, so you can greatly reduce your investment risk. *The Four Basic Profit Strategies* are:

1. **Keepers**—mobile home parks that you hold onto because they provide you with a continuous *monthly cash flow* and, in the future, price appreciation. If you move the income of your parks up, you will also move the price of the parks up. Then you can do a *Refi Bonanza* to take your profit out, tax-free, without selling the property. Keeper strategies are explained in Chapters 2 and 3.

2. **Flippers**—mobile home parks that you *buy and then sell* for a profit. Your goal here is to make fast cash to use to build your business and to enjoy your life more. In my first book, *Mobile Home Wealth,* I listed this profit strategy first because it is uppermost for most beginning investors, who want to buy one mobile home at a time. They want to create a stockpile of cash to give them some breathing room from living paycheck to paycheck. I listed flippers as number two in this book because I have found most mobile home park investors are more interested in creating steady monthly positive cash flow. Five flipping strategies are explained in Chapter 4.

3. **L/Os**—mobile home parks that you *lease with an option* to buy in the

near future, in the next year or two or three, and then either sell for a profit to another investor or put on permanent financing and keep for yourself for the cash flow. It is a combination of a flipper and a keeper, and will be explained in Chapter 5.

4. **BBs**—mobile homes that you buy or set up on empty lots in your mobile home park and then sell to residents and take back financing. You will *be* the bank, hence the name BB. The main goal of this strategy is to buy older mobile homes, still in good shape, at big discounts, and sell them for full retail price by giving financing. You will be able to make money three ways by doing this in your own park: on the mobile home itself, on the lot rent, and on the price appreciation of the park. For that reason, it becomes a *Triple Zotz,* which will be explained in Chapter 6.

When you apply each of these profit strategies to the mobile home parks you are looking at, you will be using the *formula for success* associated with each strategy. Some parks will fit nicely into one of the four strategies. You should make an offer then, an offer in which both you and the seller gain something. This is called a win/win situation. Some parks will fit into two or more of your strategies, which is even better for you because you will have greater flexibility and more ways to win. Of course, you should also make an offer then, too.

Some parks won't fit easily into any of the profit strategies unless you make a more one-sided, win/slightly-win type of offer. I use the term "slightly-win" because whenever a seller sells his mobile home park, whatever the price and terms, he still has won something because the property is no longer on his mind, and that can be considered a "slight win" to him. Don't underestimate the importance of having peace of mind to a nonprofessional or accidental investor in real estate, or on the other end of the spectrum, the vice president of a bank foreclosure department, who needs to get properties "off the books" for bank regulators.

In the case of the win/slightly-win, where the mobile home park doesn't fit easily into any of the Four Profit Strategies, you could either move on and make no offer, or make a one-sided offer and then move on if it's turned down. It is better to make an offer if one can work for you. Make it nicely—not apologetically, but nicely—by explaining that you are an investor and this is the only way the property can benefit you. If you are turned down, then you can move on. However, if your offer is accepted even though the transaction is more one-sided, you just struck gold. It's a free country with a mostly free enterprise system and you are entitled to hit the jackpot every now and then.

MAKING OFFERS

After I had been a real estate trainer for a little more than a year, doing two to three classes per month, forty people on average per class (if you do the math, that comes to more than a thousand people per year), I was handed a message. A student from one of my previous classes had called the main office and needed to speak to me right away. I called during a lunch break, and here is how the conversation went (as mentioned earlier, names have been changed to protect people's privacy throughout this book):

"Could I please speak to Patty?" I asked.

"Zalman, is that you?"

"Yes."

"I'm so glad you called me back. Do y'all remember me, honey?" Patty had the sweetest southern drawl, and when she said "y'all" and "honey", it made me smile.

"Sure I remember you, Patty. Didn't you sit up front with your husband, Earl? Wasn't he a roofer, and he had a bad back from a fall . . . and weren't you a manager at a 7-Eleven?"

"That's us, Zalman."

There was a pause now in our conversation.

"Well, what can I do for you, Patty? Your message said it was important."

"Oh, it's very important, Zalman . . . to us. First, I want you to know that when my husband and I left the training, we were very excited. We felt like you gave us the keys to success, and sometime soon, Earl and I would both be able to quit our jobs and work for ourselves. As soon as we got home, we hit the ground running. We called brokers, called the classifieds like you did in class, and rode around in our car looking at for-sale–by-owner properties. I want you to know we looked at over a hundred properties . . . all because you were such an inspiration to us."

I felt like a big compliment was coming my way, and I was getting excited to hear it. Besides being paid very well as an independent contractor when I trained, there was also a strong element of "giving back." I put my heart and soul into teaching and helping people improve their lives. I liked to hear when it was effective.

"Well, I'm glad I inspired you, Patty."

"Oh, you inspired us, all right. We told everyone we know about this great real estate trainer we met and how what he taught us was going to turn our lives around."

I was blushing now.

"Well, thank you, Patty."

"So I wanted to call you and let you know that what you taught us . . . "

It was coming, now. She was going to tell me I was the greatest thing since sliced bread.

". . . yes, what you taught us, Zalman . . ." she paused and then she said in her cute southern drawl, "was the biggest load of *crap* we ever heard!"

I pulled the phone from my ear and stared at it.

"I d . . . d. . . . d . . . don't understand," I stammered.

"What is there about the word 'crap' that y'all don't understand? It don't work, honey. The only place it does work is in your imagination. We looked at over a hundred properties and didn't buy even one! A hundred properties! When I think of all the time we wasted, and the money for the course, I could just scream! Earl and I, we want our money back, and I mean a full refund, plus our plane fare and room and board while we took your useless class."

I was dumbfounded. I didn't know what to say. I figured the best thing to do was to ask a few more questions, and maybe she could help me figure out what went wrong.

"I'm sorry, Patty, but I still don't understand. You say you looked at a hundred properties?"

"Yes, honey. Up and down and over and under and all around."

"And you didn't buy one?"

"Nope, not a one."

"Well . . . how many offers did you make, Patty?"

"Oh, we didn't make any offers, honey."

"You didn't make any offers?! Why not, Patty?"

"Because the sellers were always asking too much."

Hello?! This Is Your Wake Up Call, Zalman!

Patty's problem was a wake-up call to a gap in the training, and I closed that gap right away. Ever since then, I make every class repeat the following, at least three times:

If I'm not making offers, I'm not making money.

Go ahead and repeat it out loud right now. I'll wait.

I told Patty to go back out and take the ten best properties she and her husband saw, and find a price that fit the property into one of the Basic Profit Strategies, and then *make an offer . . . on every one of the ten.* I told her to not accept the price the seller placed on the property. I explained that sellers will usually ask too much for their properties because they pick a price that only works for them. Patty needed to offer a price that worked for her and Earl.

Patty changed on me then. She became worried about what they would do if all ten of their offers were accepted. I told her she should be so lucky, but not to worry—they could just activate the inspection contingency clause in their offers and only choose the best of the best. There was even a more exciting alternative: they could wholesale the properties they choose not to keep to another investor. You will learn about both of these options soon.

If I'm not making offers, I'm not making money.

Go ahead and repeat it out loud again. I'll wait.

Guess who is one of the worst examples of forgetting that statement? That's right, yours truly. Many times in my real estate career, people have asked me, "How's the real estate market?" Many times, my answer was, "It's a little slow right now." Guess who was slow? Me. I wasn't making offers. As soon as I got back out into the market and started making offers, business picked up. The phone started ringing again, and money started rolling in.

If I'm not making offers, I'm not making money.

Go ahead, repeat it one more time. It's worth it.

By the way, this story had a happy ending. Patty called back two months later, excited "as all-get-out," because she and Earl bought three out of the ten properties, two flippers and a keeper (a good ratio in the beginning) and they were working on five more offers! I congratulated her and mentioned that she might want to slow down a little and sell the two flippers before she bought any more, so she could get a little more feedback from the market.

For those of you who are positive thinkers, and statistically about 40 percent of you are, you can make the same statement in a positive fashion, like so:

For every offer I make, the richer I get.

Go ahead, make that statement out loud. See if you can motivate yourself in a positive direction by saying it.

For every offer I make, the richer I get.

One last time, for good luck. There is a principle of human nature behind Patty's experience. Let me give it to you in nice bold letters so you can take it to heart. I have discovered this principle after hundreds of flips and more than two decades in real estate: ***You won't usually take a good deal—you will have to make a good deal.***

> *You won't usually* ***take*** *a good deal—you will have to* ***make*** *a good deal.*

The way you *make* a good deal is by starting the process and making an offer that works for you. We're going to return to the subject of making offers in Chapter 8, when I show you how to appraise a mobile home park so you can figure out what it's worth, and from there, figure out what a good deal on the property is. In Chapter 9, you are going to learn how to construct an offer so you can lock up the good deal for yourself and how to protect yourself from making mistakes by inserting contingencies. You will also learn how to negotiate—which will change your whole outlook on life for some of you. You are going to learn how to get what you want without creating antagonistic situations and defensive opponents. This will be useful in many areas of your life, and also can be fun.

SUMMARY

You've learned how to think and act like a mobile home park investor. As an investor, you will go out and look at mobile home parks for sale and will try to fit each of them into one of your Four Basic Profit Strategies, which you've already been given brief descriptions of in this chapter. You will make either a win/win offer or a win/slightly-win offer, because you know that if you are not making offers you are not making money. Along with that, you also know that you will be *making* a good deal much more often than you will just be *taking* a good deal someone hands you. Also, when you buy a park that is a keeper, you will manage it for maximum profit and minimum people problems.

HOMEWORK

We're going to continue with your roadmap. Go out again and look at mobile home parks in your area, after checking the classifieds, brokers, FSBOs (for sale by owners), and mobile home parks. Keep driving around and go "window shopping" for mobile home park investments. I want you to write down now in your notebook the different areas you visited, your impressions of them, and the price ranges of the mobile homes located there.

I want you to imagine what you will do with the first $100,000 you make. Write it down in your notebook. Then I want you to imagine what you will do with the first $1,000,000 you make. Write that down in your notebook.

COMING ATTRACTIONS!

In the upcoming chapters, you are going to learn at least five ways of making a million dollars on one mobile home park. That's right, one million dollars on one deal. (Typically, that will involve buying a park with 100 or so lots.) I hope you're excited, because you should be.

Now, let's learn the basic formula for evaluating mobile home parks. I call it The Magic Formula because it will pave the way to great wealth for you, once you understand it.

1

The Magic Formula

In this chapter you are going to learn an exciting but simple formula that mobile home parks are valued by. I call it The Magic Formula because of its magical effect on your net worth and yearly income once you understand it. You must learn this formula first so you can apply the Four Basic Profit Strategies for your maximum benefit.

There is no sleight of hand or witchcraft involved with the formula. It is not a potion that you mix and then drink and suddenly your effect on the world is different. Instead, it is a very down-to-earth concept. When you understand and apply it you can earn hundreds of thousands more in yearly income, and add millions more to your net worth. A formula that has that effect is indeed magical.

Buying Groups of Mobile Homes Changes Things

If you have read my first book, *Mobile Home Wealth,* you would have learned that the formula for pricing a single mobile home is the same method used to price a single family home. Recent sales of other single family homes—in this case, mobile homes—in the same neighborhood are analyzed. These are known as comparable sales, or simply as "comps." Then the value of the property being appraised (the subject property) is adjusted relative to the comps to arrive at a consistent amount. In other words, the value of the home as a shelter is the ruling component. How big the home is, how many bedrooms and bathrooms it contains, how large the lot is, and how nice the area is, are important determinants of value. How much rent the individual mobile home generates is not taken into account.

When it comes to pricing a mobile home park, the net income the park produces is paramount. Investors do not purchase mobile home parks for their value as a shelter. They are not moving in. They are buying mobile home parks for their current income now and/or the income they will produce in the future.

The net income that a mobile home park produces is a tangible number and is easy to calculate. You add up the total yearly rents received, subtract the expenses paid out, and voila, there it is. This figure is called the net operating income, or NOI. After the NOI is calculated, the current investment rate that the average investor wants to earn on that type of park is introduced. You then plug these two numbers—the NOI and the investment rate—into the simple formula I call The Magic Formula to arrive at a price for the park.

The good news is that The Magic Formula for pricing mobile home parks is also used to price almost all other income-producing properties like duplexes, apartment buildings, warehouses, industrial complexes, shopping centers, offices, retail stores, etc., as well as mobile home parks.

The good news continues. Dollar for dollar, mobile home parks produce one of the highest incomes of just about any form of income-producing real estate, with the least amount of risk, if you learn how to manage and improve them. When run right, they become "cash cows." This book will show you how to manage a mobile home park for maximum income and minimum management expense and risk.

The good news continues even further. You probably already know The Magic Formula. I learned it from my father when I was a young boy, but I didn't know I was learning it at the time.

THE SAVINGS ACOUNT FORMULA

My Dad did a surprising thing when I was a youngster. He called me, my sister, who was a year older than me, and my brother, who was a year younger, to the dining room one Sunday afternoon. This worried us. We wondered what we did wrong, because our serious family discussions always took place around the dining room table during Saturday night dinner. Now, there was no food to distract us, but there were three things on the table that did. One was my father's wallet and the other two were a pad and pencil.

Dad saw the worried looks on our faces.

"Relax, kids," he started out. "This is going to be a good discussion, not a painful one."

Upon hearing that, there were three sighs of relief. Dad explained we were all growing up, and it was time to experience the rewards and responsibilities of being mature. He started first with the rewards.

"All of you kids are going to get an allowance now, and it's going to be the same, one dollar per week each," Dad stated. Then he opened his wallet and gave each of us a dollar bill, which thrilled us—this was serious money back in the 1950's, when a gallon of gas or a pack of cigarettes were only twenty-five cents. To us kids, a candy bar was five cents, a Superman comic book was fifteen cents, and a ticket to the movies on Saturday afternoon was thirty-five cents. Dad continued on, having captured our complete attention.

"You can spend that dollar bill you're holding now any way you see fit after our discussion. And your future paydays will not be Sunday afternoon, but Friday afternoons, after you've completed your responsibilities during the previous week." Dad could see the puzzled looks on our faces after he said the word responsibility.

"Your responsibilities are going to be your individual jobs—your weekly chores." Dad then handed out our chores. My chores were mowing the lawn in the summer, raking the leaves in the fall, and shoveling the snow off the sidewalk and driveway in the winter. My younger brother's chores were taking the trash cans from the house out to the curb on Monday and Thursday nights, and bringing the empty cans back in on Tuesday and Friday mornings after the sanitation men emptied them. My sister's chores were setting the table for family dinners, which were only on weekends, followed by rinsing the dishes and putting them in the dishwasher, adding soap, and turning it on. After the dishwasher went through its cycles, she was to put the clean dishes and silverware back into the cabinets.

"I want to teach you three about work, and how it is a good thing to do work, and get paid for it," Dad stated.

While we were mesmerized by our dollar bills, my father explained that in addition to learning about the value of work and getting paid, he wanted to teach us two more things—how to save and how to invest. He repeated we could spend the dollar bill immediately as we saw fit or we could save them up to buy something bigger. My brother and sister listened, but not with great interest. They were more interested in how much candy or toys they could buy right then.

I listened intently as my Dad explained about banks and saving. I knew banks were where you put your money to be safe, and after it accumulated, you took it out and bought big things like cars and boats.

"If you kids decide to put your allowance in the bank," Dad continued, "I will double the amount, and put in *two dollars* each week into your bank account instead of only the one dollar in your hand. If you leave that money in the bank for a year, you can take out the money and it's yours to spend whatever way you want. If, however, you want to take the money out before the year is over, then I will withdraw two dollars from your bank account for each dollar you want, give you one, and take back the extra dollar." He said this was to teach us to have the discipline to save, and reward us for being able to wait to spend our money.

In retrospect, this was both wise and somewhat misleading. It was wise because my Dad instilled in me a strong motivation to save. This is a difficult motivation to instill because we live in a world that dangles instant gratification in front of us like a carrot in front of a horse, and saving goes counter to the impulse of "Buy it now!" It was misleading because a savings account does not double your money yearly. You must invest that savings well to become wealthy. Savings account interest rates are low, historically 5 percent or less, and the interest income is taxed at high personal income tax rates at the end of the year, reducing it. You will be shown in the coming pages how investing in mobile home parks at 10 percent and more each year will make you wealthy.

Next, my Dad picked up the pad and pencil on the table and explained about interest. He said if we put our money in the bank each week, except for two weeks each year, at the end of the year we would each have $100:

50 Weeks × 2 Dollars Each Week = $100

If we left the money in the bank for the whole next year, the bank would pay us 5 percent interest, which would be $5 on $100. He wrote these numbers down:

$100 × 5% = $5

and then he wrote the savings account formula out in words:

Money in the Bank × Interest Rate Paid by Bank = Interest Income

I asked my Dad what interest was, and he said, "It's money the bank *gives you* for putting your money in their bank." I asked him why the bank would give me this *free money*, and he explained, "The bank lends your money to other people at 10 percent, twice the rate they pay you, so the bank makes as much money as they pay you for the use of your money."

I had a worried look on my face and my Dad saw it. He asked me if I was wondering what would happen to my money if the people the bank lent it to did not pay the bank back, and I said yes. Then he explained that the federal government, the people who printed the dollar bills we were holding, *insured* my money. I would always be able to get it back from the bank, no matter what, even if the people who borrowed it did not pay it back.

This conversation changed my world. Earning $5 per year in interest, which was *free money*, was the same as five weeks allowance, and that was no small amount of money to a young boy. Sitting with a pencil and paper afterwards, I proceeded to figure out what would happen if I saved all my allowances for ten years, which was when I graduated high school:

$100 per Year × 10 Years = $1,000

If I had $1,000 in the bank at 5 percent interest, it would give me:

$1,000 × 5% = $50 per Year in Interest

This was almost a dollar per week, *which was a free yearly allowance*! I would then be able to spend my free allowance from interest while I continued to save twice my allowance that Dad paid me, and then put it away in my savings account, causing me to make even more money. I would become rich by saving money!

I was fascinated by this free money called interest and having my savings insured by the federal government, the same people who printed our dollar bills in the first place. My dreams of riches were cut down to size by the time I graduated middle school, because by then I realized that $1,000 in the bank would not make me rich and having a free dollar each week to spend would not be a lot of spending money. By the time I graduated high school and entered college, I adjusted my dream upward like a young adult should. Now *I wanted to save one million dollars,* and earn 5 percent interest.

$1,000,000 × 5% = $50,000 per Year in Interest Income

I didn't know how I was going to earn one million dollars, but I knew once I had it, I would receive $50,000 per year in income for the rest of my life, or almost $1,000 per week, without working or doing any chores.

$50,000 per Year in Interest Divided by 52 Weeks
= $1,000 per Week (Approximately)

There was a lot of safety and little risk in my dream. Once I had the million dollars in the bank, the FDIC would insure it as long I put my nest egg in $100,000 deposits in ten separately named accounts, or ten separate banks, and no one could ever take my dream away from me. (As a side note, my roommate in college laughed when I told him my goal of *saving a million dollars.* He said that I wanted to be as useless as possible at an early age, so I could just spend my time playing while withdrawing interest as I needed it. I have come to agree with him. Work should not be just a chore you perform for someone else and thus avoided. It has been my experience that when you find work that energizes you, in a field of endeavor that uses your God-given talents, it makes your life more meaningful and satisfying as well as richer. I have met people who have had all their money needs taken care of and don't perform any meaningful work, and they tend to be unhappy. Sometimes, they resort to drugs or alcohol to give their life an artificial meaning they lack.)

As you can see, this was my very first glimpse of *investing* money, because putting money in the bank and earning interest is probably one of simplest ways of being an investor, and one of the safest. It is the benchmark by which all investments are judged and calibrated, because it is so easy and so safe. You don't have to do anything other than withdraw the interest each week or each year. When you place your savings in other forms of investment, you have to evaluate the risks and the time you will have to spend on that investment, and whether the return on your money is worth the time and risk, versus just putting your money in a savings account.

THE MAGIC FORMULA

The good news is that most of you already know The Magic Formula. It is the same as the savings account formula we discussed above, except we need to change the names of the terms. The net affect and the principles are the same. So first, let's start with the savings account formula:

Money in the Bank × Interest Rate Paid by Bank = Interest Income

The first term, "Money in the Bank," represents just one choice. You have many other choices where you can invest your money. Yes, you can put your money into a savings account at a bank, or you can buy an income property, like a mobile home park. Let's assume you purchase a mobile home park. In this case you would substitute "Money in the Bank" with "Purchase Price of a Mobile Home Park."

Next, let's change "Interest Rate Paid by Bank" to the *yearly rate of return the average investor expects to earn on that type of mobile home park.* The fancy term for this is *Capitalization Rate,* or *Cap Rate,* which just means the rate of return the average investor expects, expressed as a yearly interest rate. The good news is that this rate of return historically has averaged around 10 percent, which is twice what you would earn in a savings account.

There is a reason why the historical rate of return is double for a mobile home park versus a savings account. A savings account is a *passive* investment and requires little time to manage it, and has no risk as long as you keep the amount less than $100,000 per separate account, which is the current limit for the FDIC. A mobile home park is an *active* investment and requires management time from the investor, and there will probably be some problems to solve along the way, along with some risks.

Now, we will change the right side of the savings account formula, the "Interest Income" from your savings account each year, to *the net income the mobile home park produces in a year's time.* This number requires more effort to arrive at than the previous two terms. To calculate this number, you must add up all the mobile home park rents and other income for the year and subtract all the legitimate expenses during the year. The result is your net income or what is commonly called *Net Operating Income,* or *NOI.* Keep in mind two important principles are assumed when calculating the NOI. These two assumptions are necessary to make The Magic Formula a universal formula that is useful to everyone. They are:

1. You don't take into account any mortgage payments and interest paid on mortgage loans—it is assumed all cash was paid for the park.

2. There is a manager who oversees the park and maintenance personnel who maintain it, and their salaries and repairs are normal, legitimate expenses.

The first assumption, that we are ignoring any mortgage payments and interest, is necessary because some investors pay all cash, most invertors put something down, and some buy with no cash down at all. The amount of financing is not included in the formula to set a level playing field. Keep in mind—there is an important *formula for success* you will learn about in Chapter 2 when we discuss keepers. This is called the *Cash Flow Formula.* The Cash Flow Formula does take into account the mortgage and borrowing costs of the purchase price of a mobile home park and the net positive cash flow you receive from the mobile home park after *all expenses are paid,* including mortgage interest. For many people, the Cash Flow Formula is more critical to their investing decision, but *before* you can use the Cash Flow Formula you have to come up with a value for the mobile home park, and that is done by using The Magic Formula.

The second assumption about management and maintenance costs is also important. Some investors manage their parks themselves and perform all the maintenance and repairs with no outside help, other investors have a part-time manager who performs some of the duties of a manager, and still other investors are entirely hands off and have a manager and maintenance people who completely take care of their parks. The Magic Formula assumes there is a manager who receives a fair wage for the day-to-day management of the park and maintenance people are paid to repair it.

The second assumption is extremely important when you advance from buying mobile homes one at a time to buying them in groups, many at one time. When you buy an individual mobile home the price is based strictly on the comparable sales of other individual mobile homes. This is the shelter value, and there are no management fees assessed in the valuation.

When you buy a park, it is assumed that a manager and maintenance people will be paid to run it, and these expenses are every bit as important as real estate taxes, insurance, and utility bills. This can be a strong motivation to move upward from investing in individual mobile homes to mobile home parks. When you have someone else spending their working hours taking care of your property, and paying them is a universally acceptable expense, this becomes a wonderful wealth acceleration tool—you are multiplying your best efforts through other people.

Now that you understand the terms, this is The Magic Formula:

> ***THE MAGIC FORMULA***
> **Price of Mobile Home Park × Cap Rate = NOI**

Understanding and Applying The Magic Formula

The Magic Formula can be used two ways, depending on whether a buyer or a seller is using it:

1. For a buyer, the formula will be used to determine the validity of the asking price of the park. The buyer has been given the price, and he plugs in a cap rate that he believes is realistic, and then calculates what the NOI should be. Then the buyer inspects the park's accounting statements to see what the NOI actually is and whether it justifies the purchase price chosen by the seller.

2. For a seller, the formula will be used to arrive at a fair selling price by taking the NOI and dividing by a generally acceptable cap rate.

The first method, to determine the validity of the asking price of the park, comes from using the formula as it sits, multiplying price times cap rate to come up with the NOI. This is the most common use of The Magic Formula for buyers because most sellers and their agents are amateurs, not professionals. They choose a price that the seller wants for his property, regardless of any justification, and then hope the buyer will not justify it. They do not price the park as in #2 above, but rather by picking a number out of thin air.

When a prospective buyer does try to justify the price, he will run the purchase price through the formula and see *what NOI should be produced by the park.* Then the prospective buyer calculates *the actual NOI* from the accounting statements to see if the results match. Typically, the buyer will then change his offer to match the actual NOI.

First Example: Applying The Magic Formula for a Buyer

Let's assume that the price of a mobile home park is $100,000 and the generally accepted cap rate for that particular park is 10 percent. You would apply the formula like so:

Price of Mobile Home Park	×	Cap Rate	=	NOI
$100,000	×	10% (0.1)	=	NOI
$100,000	×	0.1	=	$10,000 NOI

In other words, the mobile home park with a cap rate of 10 percent should produce $10,000 in NOI when it is priced at $100,000. The prospective buyer then adds up the actual rental income, subtracts the actual expenses of the park, and sees if $10,000 is the NOI. If the buyer winds up with an actual NOI of $12,000, $2,000 more than should be expected, then the buyer should believe the park is a good deal. If the buyer winds up with $8,000 for the NOI, $2,000 less than should be expected, then the buyer should think the park is not a good deal, and should adjust the price to $80,000.

Second Example: Applying The Magic Formula for a Seller

This is the formula used by professionals to come up with a justifiable price for a park. By using simple algebra, the professional seller or broker would change the formula around to divide the NOI by the cap rate to come up with a purchase price, as follows:

Price of Mobile Home Park	=	NOI	÷	Cap Rate

To demonstrate this using numbers, the professional starts with the

NOI of the mobile home park, which we'll say is $100,000 per year. Then the professional uses a generally acceptable cap rate for that kind of park. The professional might even call an appraiser and ask what the generally acceptable cap rate is in the area. For our example, let's continue to use 10 percent. Then the professional determines the price of the park like so:

Price of Mobile Home Park	**=**	**NOI**	**÷**	**Cap Rate**
	=	**$100,000**	**÷**	**10% (0.1)**
	=	**$1,000,000**		

It is very important to understand that when you calculate the purchase price of a park, it is an absolute number with no opinion attached to it. It is just an amount of money. That's it. However, the two terms you use to derive and justify the purchase price—the NOI and the cap rate—contain actual calculations and *opinions* that determine their amounts. We will discuss this at the end of the chapter.

Third Example: A Quick Application of The Magic Formula for a 10 Percent Cap Rate

As a result of training thousands of people, I know that the key to understanding this all-important formula comes when students apply it to the real world. So, to start, we are going to assume that the average mobile home park investor wants to earn 10 percent on the mobile home parks we will discuss now, and that this will also be the generally accepted cap rate an appraiser will arrive at. As I explained before, this is historically a popular rate.

There is also a mathematical simplicity in choosing 10 percent as a cap rate. If you fix the cap rate at 10 percent, then all you need is one of the two terms, NOI or Price, to figure out the other in your head without needing a calculator. It is as simple as moving a decimal point one way or the other. Let's look at a few calculations so you can visualize this:

Let's assume you are driving along looking at mobile home parks in your area, and there is a For Sale sign in front of a cute mobile home park just thirty minutes from your home. You stop your car and get out, walk up the front office, and a middle-aged woman is sitting as a desk, counting daily receipts. This is the way the conversation might go:

"Hi. I saw the For Sale and would like to speak to the owner."

"Here is the owner's phone number. Her name is Sally," the middle-aged woman replies.

You thank the woman and walk around the park, inspecting it, while you dial the Sally's number on your cell phone. After a few rings, the call is answered.

"Hello, my name is _____," you begin. "I was driving on Country Oaks Drive and I saw a For Sale sign in front of a mobile home park. I stopped and went inside the office and the manager gave me this phone number. Are you the owner?"

"Yes, I'm the owner of the Country Oaks Mobile Home Park. My name is Sally Smith. What can I do for you?"

"Well first, Sally, can you tell me how much you are asking for your mobile home park?"

Sally says, "$250,000."

You write down that number on a piece of paper and then do the following calculation because we are going to assume a 10 percent cap rate:

$250,000 Purchase Price × 10% (0.1) Cap Rate = $25,000 NOI

Because we are using 10 percent as a cap rate for simplicity, *all you have to do is the move the decimal point one place to the left on the purchase price to get the appropriate NOI.*

Then you ask, "Can you tell me how much the NOI is, Sally?"

If Sally only owns this one park, chances are she is an amateur investor and she is going to respond by saying, "The N.O. what?"

You should be prepared to give a simple definition of NOI to owners that you meet. Many of them will not be sophisticated and may not even have an understanding of how to price their property. Your explanation will go something like this:

"Well, Sally, if you add up the yearly rents you receive and then subtract your expenses, without taking into account mortgages, then . . ."

Sally may interrupt you and say:

"There is no mortgage. My husband paid that off years ago before he passed away and left the park to me."

"Okay, Sally," you continue. "If you add up rents and subtract all your expenses, how much is left over for you at the end of the year?"

Sally will probably hesitate at this point, you will hear some scratching of pen or pencil on paper, and then she might say:

"There is $35,000 left over for me."

Once you knew what the price was, you wrote down that a 10 percent cap rate would result in $25,000 NOI. Sally said it had a $35,000 NOI. At this point you should become very interested because the park is throwing off $10,000 in excess of what a 10 percent cap rate would produce. The mobile home park should have been priced at:

Price of Mobile Home Park	=	**NOI**	÷	**Cap Rate**
	=	**$35,000**	÷	**10% (0.1)**
	=	**$350,000**		

By using a little simple algebra to transform the formula, we knew that the price of the park really should be $350,000, or it is $100,000 undervalued. *Since we used a 10 percent cap rate, all we really had to do was take the NOI, and move the decimal point one place to the right to get the price.*

As you can see, by using a 10 percent cap rate, if you are given the price of a park, you just have to move the decimal point one place to the left to get the NOI that should be produced by that price at a 10 percent cap rate. Compare this to the NOI you are given to see whether the price is high or low or okay.

The same principle applies if you are only given the NOI of a park. Then you take the NOI and move the decimal point one place to the right, that will tell you the correct price at a 10 percent cap rate. You can compare that price to the price you are given to see if it is a bargain, overpriced, or fair.

If you want to figure out what the actual cap rate is for a park, you would use some more simple algebra. You would rewrite The Magic Formula like so:

NOI	÷	**Price of Mobile Home Park**	=	**Cap Rate**
$35,000	÷	**$250,000**	=	**14% (0.14)**

This tells you that the park is priced using a 14 percent cap rate, which is a higher return, whereas the market generally accepts 10 percent on that type of park. We're going to do a few more examples so you get the hang of The Magic Formula and how to determine quickly whether a park is priced fairly, too high, or a bargain.

Unlike the example above, there will be many times when a park will be overpriced. The owner is in love with his own inventory and picked a nice round number that excited him, something like one million dollars.

If you probe deeper into the property, you might also discover that the owner deducted little or nothing for management and/or maintenance expenses, because he was managing and maintaining the park himself and assigned little or no value to his time. It's okay for the owner to voluntarily take on the full time job of manager and maintenance man in his own park, but it's not okay for you, nor is it okay when the owner expects you will do the same. You might find that when you subtract the cost of normal management and maintenance expenses the NOI is reduced even further and the price becomes even more over-inflated. In a case such as this, where you encounter an owner with such extreme pride of ownership, you should make an offer that reflects what the market price should be and then walk away nicely if the owner refuses to accept reality.

We're going to do one more example, this time how a pro does it.

Fourth Example: How a Professional Applies The Magic Formula

You have become a professional mobile home park investor, and you bought the Country Oaks Mobile Home Park formerly owned by Sally. After five years, you've decided it's time to sell the park. You may have one of many reasons for this—you want to exchange it for a bigger park closer to your home, you are moving and don't want to look back, or for any of the other reasons people have for doing anything.

Since you are now a professional, you will work from the NOI forward to arrive at an offering price. During your tenure owning the County Oaks Mobile Home Park you increased the NOI from $35,000 to $45,000 by using some of the methods you learned in this book. Further, you believe that the generally accepted cap rate has not changed for the average investor looking to purchase this type of mobile home park—it is still 10 percent. Applying The Magic Formula, you get:

Price of Mobile Home Park	**=**	**NOI**	**÷**	**Cap Rate**
	=	**$45,000**	**÷**	**10% (0.1)**
	=	**$450,000**		

This price is exciting because it indicates you will make a profit of $200,000 on the Country Oaks Mobile Home Park (before closing costs).

Anticipated Profit	**=**	**$450,000 Sales Price**	**–**	**$250,000 Purchase Price**
	=	**$200,000**		

Since you are a professional, when a buyer inquires about the park, you will have all the facts and figures available on how you arrived at the NOI, and thus the cap rate, and the price.

The Effect on Price of Raising or Lowering the Cap Rate

So far in this chapter, we assumed a normal cap rate of 10 percent for the mobile home parks we discussed. Now it's time to discuss the effect on the cap rate when we are not dealing with an average park, because not all cap rates are 10 percent. Some are higher and some are lower.

The cap rate has an inverse relationship to the price. That's a fancy way of saying as one goes up, the other goes down. This means that as the cap rate increases for a park, the price of the mobile home park will go down, and vice versa—as the cap rate decreases for a park, the price will go up. Let's look at this mathematically so you will understand it.

Let's take three mobile home parks, all with the same NOI of $50,000. This means that each park is putting out the same amount of profit each year—$50,000—but investors make a distinction about the rate of return they expect for each the parks. The parks are as follows:

1. Park A is cute and pretty, with mostly newer mobile homes, and a waiting list for new residents. It is in an age-restricted community for retirees who take excellent care of their lots and are cooperative and easy to deal with. Investors believe the cap rate for this park should be 8 percent.

2. Park B is an average park occupied by working-class families, with some older homes as well as newer ones. Some of the lots are well cared for and some are a little messy. There are occasional problems with children and domestic disturbances, but nothing out of the ordinary. Investors believe the cap rate for this park should be 10 percent.

3. Park C is a run down and occupied by low-income families, some of whom are out of work and haven't paid their lot rent in months. It contains older homes and only a few of the lots are well cared for. There are constant problems with the residents and the police are called once or twice each month. Investors believe the cap rate for the park should be 15 percent.

If you apply The Magic Formula to each park, you will find the following prices will result:

Price of Mobile Home Park	**=**	**NOI**	**÷**	**Cap Rate**		
Price of Mobile Home Park A	**=**	**$50,000**	**÷**	**.08**	**=**	**$625,000**
Price of Mobile Home Park B	**=**	**$50,000**	**÷**	**.10**	**=**	**$500,000**
Price of Mobile Home Park C	**=**	**$50,000**	**÷**	**.15**	**=**	**$333,000**

Do you see what happened to the prices? All the parks had the same NOI, $50,000, but investor expectations were different for each park. This was reflected in each park's cap rate and made the purchase prices different. Given the same NOI, as we raise the cap rate, the prices of the parks went down.

Investors paid $500,000 for the average park, Park B, with the average cap rate of 10 percent. Investors were willing to pay $125,000 more, or $625,000, for Park A, which had less risk and the least management problems, and they expressed this with a lower cap rate of 8 percent. Investors were only willing to purchase Park C if it was priced $167,000 less that the average park, or $333,000, because the park had greater risk and greater management problems, and a cap rate of 15 percent reflects that. If you look at the numbers the cute park is almost twice the price as the troublesome one, but the income is the same at the end of the year.

Advanced Discussion of Cap Rate

We started by defining the cap rate as the average investment rate that the average investor wants to earn on a particular type of mobile home park. That is a good start to understanding the term. You should have seen from the previous discussion on cap rate and price that cap rate is a term that is rich in meaning and variable factors. Now we are going to discuss some of the more advanced aspects of cap rate, because the cap rate includes judgments about risk as well as other considerations within its definition. Some of these are:

1. Accounting for the risk that the park may or may not generate the same rental income in the future.

2. Accounting for the risk that the current expenses will not remain constant in the future.

3. Accounting for time involvement and difficulty in managing the park.
4. Accounting for the effect that the rate on borrowing mortgage money has on cash flow.

As the risk of predicting future income and expenses increases, so will the cap rate—there will be a factor in the cap rate to cover the unpredictability of the NOI. For example, let's assume you are looking at a possible purchase of a mobile home park that is located near an Army base. Many of the residents work there, but the Army base is slated to close. This will have a strong impact on the occupancy of the mobile home park as residents lose their jobs and many are forced to move away to seek other employment. This will lower the future rental income and thus the NOI. In this case, you might want to substantially raise the cap rate on the park—or avoid buying it all together until the Army base closes and a more accurate assessment of NOI can be compiled.

There also might be a case where a mobile home park has many vacancies now, but a new Toyota plant is opening down the road and will be bringing in a thousand new jobs. Many of those new employees will need affordable housing that is near the new plant. In that case, an investor might want to offer a lower cap rate on the park to take into account the increasing rents and higher occupancy that will result when the plant is completed.

Management intensity is another characteristic that is embedded in the cap rate. The average small to medium-sized mobile home park (10 to 100 units) is easy to manage, and the property manager will not be stressed. As a property manager's problems and stress increase, so does the rate the average investor wants to earn on that mobile home park (or on any income producing real estate investment for that matter). It is not unusual to see cap rates go into the high teens or above 20 percent in the worst cases.

Current interest rates on mortgage money also strongly affect cap rates. Most investors want at least a 1.5 to 2 percent difference between their borrowing cost and the cap rate of a mobile home park that they are considering for purchase. In other words, if investors can borrow from lenders at 8 percent to finance their purchase of a mobile home park, they will usually want at least a 9.5 to 10 percent cap rate on the mobile home parks they buy. Recently, borrowing rates went down to historically low levels, like 5 percent, so cap rates on the better quality mobile home parks went down to 6.5 to 7 percent. Then as borrowing rates rose again, so did cap rates, until eventually they returned to the historically common 10 percent.

Even with the above four determinants of cap rates—risk on income, risk on expenses, management intensity, and interest rates available on borrowing—there are usually three different cap rates for every mobile home park:

1. The cap rate the current owner of the park believes is realistic.
2. The cap rate that current buyers for the park believe they are entitled to.
3. The cap rate the general market accepts as realistic for that particular type of park, i.e. the rate a licensed appraiser will determine from his evaluation of the sales of other comparable mobile home parks in the area.

You can see from the above discussion that the cap rate is both an objective and subjective term. It is arrived at from both opinion and facts, unlike the other two terms in The Magic Formula, NOI and price, which are just amounts of money. Cap rate is a reflection of the risk, and contains elements of scientific formulation and subjective opinion. It is similar to how appraisers refer to their profession, as both an art and a science.

Advanced Discussion of The Magic Formula

As a trainer, experience has shown me to keep the discussion on The Magic Formula simple in the beginning. The vast majority of mobile home parks conform easily to this simple version. There will be times you encounter a park that is more complicated or unusual, but we will postpone that discussion until you are comfortable with the basic investment category. Some of these more complex situations are:

1. Using a pro forma NOI based on the future versus the actual NOI today.
2. Unusual mortgage financing.
3. Accounting for empty lots when calculating the NOI.
4. Accounting for mortgage payments *received* on mobile homes you buy along with the park when calculating the NOI.

5. The effect on price for "park-owned" mobile homes that are rented along with the land.
6. Accounting for the highest and best use of the land today when it differs from its current use as a mobile home park.
7. Accounting for the value of excess land.

We will discuss the first situation in Chapter 8, and the remaining situations in Chapter 17, as you become more comfortable with the fundamentals of mobile home parks. There is little value in complicating this wonderful investment category so early on and possibly confusing you.

SUMMARY

You are now equipped with the first major tool in your tool kit for being a mobile home park investor, as well as an investor for the many other types of income properties like apartments, warehouses, stores, offices, etc. Everyone involved in the income property business uses the same Magic Formula—whether they are buyers, sellers, lenders, or appraisers.

It should also be apparent to you that *what rules in the formula for pricing a mobile home park is the NOI, the net income the property produces.* Cap rates are difficult to have control over—they are set by the market place and interest rates. When interest rates on borrowing come down, cap rates come down. When interest rates on mortgages go up, cap rates go up. Once the cap rate is set, the price of a property is then determined by the NOI, not the reverse. When you increase the NOI, either by creating more rental income or lowering expenses, you automatically increase the value, and therefore the price, of the property. You can increase the price of a property arbitrarily but that does not mean it is justified. Unless the NOI increases proportionally, all you are doing is overpricing the property. Therefore, *if you want to become wealthy investing in mobile homes parks, you need to increase the NOI of the parks you own,* and that is what the next chapter is going to show you how to do.

HOMEWORK

It's time to put The Magic Formula to work in your area. Of all the mobile home parks you have looked at so far, take the ones that were for sale and call to find out the price the seller wants, the NOI, and the resulting cap rate. Draw a grid in your notebook for parks and their cap rates, and write down next to the cap rate each is offered at what *you think* is the appropriate cap rates for the various kinds of parks based up the size of the park and quality of the residents.

For those of you that are not Type 3's, I want you to try something bold—something I asked the Type 3's to do in their homework at the end of the section titled "The Second Adventure." I want you to take the list of parks you looked at that weren't for sale, and go in and ask the manager for a contact number for the owner. Say you would like to discuss something important and private with the owner, and nothing more. Then, when you speak with the owners, ask if they would be willing to sell their park, what price they would want, and their current NOI. You might be surprised at your results—you might uncover a motivated seller and a good deal.

Type 3's—please relax and don't buy anything yet. There is more to learn, I promise you. After you absorb the important points, you might be ready within a month or less. I realize that a month is a very long time to a Type-3, but buying the wrong property and being saddled with it for years is an even longer, more painful time, so please be patient.

COMING ATTRACTIONS

Investors in mobile home parks want cash flow. They want to build their own ATM to achieve financial independence, and that involves keepers. The next chapter will show you how to do just that—how to invest in mobile home park keepers. Think about how you'll feel when you close your eyes at night or when you look in the mirror in the morning and know that you have a safe and secure cash flow each month for you and your loved ones.

Think of what it'll be like when you don't have to depend on a boss or a job in someone else's company. Think of what it'll be like to control your own financial destiny, bound only by your ability and energy when it comes to getting paid and earning a living. Think about how you can make a ton of money in one big chunk without ever selling the park, and without paying any taxes to boot. Think about that as you turn the page.

2

Keepers: Creating Your Own ATM

Welcome to the world of being a property owner, where you will hold onto and *keep* the mobile home parks you buy. This is a good world when you understand the principles involved and have the right attitude. You've already learned that when you own a mobile home park, you own your own little town where you are the mayor, like the gentleman on the right. But you are not running for office and you are automatically elected when you buy the park. In addition, you control your salary and reelection.

You are also responsible for the citizens in your little town, and the infrastructure that helps them live their lives on a daily basis. Fortunately, your little town should come equipped with a manager and maintenance personnel who are responsible for keeping it running smoothly. The expenses of having a manager and maintenance personnel are considered normal legitimate expenses of the mobile home park, just like real estate taxes and insurance. Your job as mayor is to oversee and manage your personnel, not do their daily work. Owning a mobile home park as an investment is not a full-time job if you understand how to buy your little towns, manage them, and turn them into "cash cows."

Once you gain knowledge about how to buy, maintain, and improve mobile home parks, you will realize that investment real estate is a great way to accumulate and hold onto wealth, if you are a good caretaker of the real estate you own. Income-producing property can provide you with a stable income for life and then continue to do the same for your loved ones in the future. Keepers are the meat and potatoes on your table of real estate investing. Let's define a keeper, the first of the Four Basic Profit Strategies:

DEFINITION OF A KEEPER

A keeper is a property that will give you a positive return on the investment you make and will continue to do so for the foreseeable future. A keeper will pay its own way by providing enough income to pay all the expenses associated with it: taxes, insurance, and loans, as well as the maintenance and repairs of any buildings and infrastructure situated on it. The best keepers provide a healthy profit after all expenses are paid, and continue to do so.

Therefore, in order to decide if a property is a keeper or not, we need a *formula for success* that shows if the property can pay its own way. This is known as The Cash Flow Formula. We will discuss this formula shortly, after we introduce a few new concepts. First, we'll separate mobile home parks into two kinds of keepers:

1. Parks that are *close by*—you can be there *in 3 hours or less.*

2. Parks that are a *long distance*—it will take *longer than 3 hours to get there.*

If you assume your average visit to a park might take a few hours, then you will spend about a half a day or more whenever you visit one that is close by and a full day or more when it is long distance.

We will further separate both close by and long distance types of parks into two more categories:

1. Turnkey mobile home parks.

2. Turn-around mobile home parks.

Turnkey parks are properties where all you have to do is change the ownership, the name on the deed, to your name. The park is running smoothly and gives you instant profit. It is just like the turning on the key in a smooth running car that takes you where you want to go with a minimum of fuss and hassle. In a turnkey park, there are few, if any, management problems to overcome and very few vacancies that demand immediate occupancy. Turnkey parks should generate excellent returns, but not as much as the next category.

Turn-around parks are parks with problems that need solving when you buy them. This category of park may or may not give you profit right away (in the more extreme cases, they may generate losses in the beginning.) You will have to spend time fixing these problems—and you should get paid handsomely when you do. *Turn-around parks should generate fantastic returns once they are turned around and become a turnkey park.*

The reason we separated parks by their distance from where you live and their degree of management intensity is because some investors will have the flexibility and free time to be able to buy a long-distance turn-around park, while other investors will not have that flexibility. They must restrict themselves to turnkey parks that are close by. This will become apparent later when we discuss finding deals in Chapter 7.

THE POSITIVES AND PITFALLS OF INCOME PROPERTY

My experience in training people has shown me that it's very important to deal with the positives as well as the pitfalls about income property right at the start, because some people have emotions and preconceived notions that can interfere with the learning process. First, the positives.

A New Relationship With Your Mailbox

When you own income property, you develop a whole new relationship with your mailbox. Instead of approaching it with a frown on your face each day because you think of it mainly as a source of bills and junk mail, it will become your own personal ATM and you will walk up to it with a smile and affection. You may even hug it from time to time. What will change your attitude?

Checks. There will now be lots of envelopes in your mailbox each month (or each week) containing checks made out to you. The more mobile home parks you own, the more checks you will receive. This is hard to understand until it happens to you. When you own keepers, be prepared to fall in love with your mailbox.

Where do these checks come from? Well, the most common way that property provides income is by renting it to someone so that means you will be a landlord and have tenants to manage. In other words, you are renting your mobile home lots, and possibly the mobile homes on those lots, to people and this is the point where investors who are just starting out tend to have misinformation and misunderstandings. My goal here is to clear up this misinformation, and explain your rights and duties as a landlord and how much power you have as a landlord—which is a lot.

At the three-day seminar I taught on the general principles of becoming a millionaire using real estate, there usually would be a substantial portion of the class who did not want to deal with tenants. In some classes that portion was as many as a third of the students. These students just wanted to flip and flip and then flip some more until their net worth reached seven or eight figures. Then they figured they would put their profits in bank certificates of deposit and live off the interest. (Sound familiar?)

No matter what I said, this group refused to see anything positive in having tenants because of all the prevailing wisdom they received from people who were not experienced or competent landlords. I used to love it when the owner of the seminar company, a world-class speaker, would tell the class they'd better get training on being a landlord, because sometimes a "flipper don't flip" right away, and then they'd wish they'd learned how to put a tenant in the property so they could collect rent to offset their expenses. He also suggested they learn how to do a lease-option to get a flipper sold (this is the third Basic Profit Strategy, which we will discuss in an upcoming chapter).

At the three-day seminar I taught on mobile home investing, the student's attitudes were different. The majority of the class wanted to be landlords, understood the value of a steady monthly cash flow, and wanted to dress up their mailboxes and make them more attractive and welcome when their checks arrived each month.

There is no doubt that when you are an income property owner, you will have to manage some short-term problems with your customers, who we will now refer to as *renters*. When you look at the problems other businesses have with their customers, renter problems can be *easier* to deal with. If a MacDonald's customer is upset about a Big Mac because there wasn't enough special sauce on it, or it has too many onions, or it was cooked too much or too little, or for any other reason, he or she can simply drive over to Burger King or Wendy's.

Your customer/renters, on the other hand, are dependent on you for shelter, and cannot switch their business so lightly. You should accept the responsibility of the long-term landlord/renter relationship and act accordingly. However, if one of your customer/renters gets upset for an irrational or unimportant reason, moving out takes a lot more time and can negatively impact their credit and finances (I'll explain this in Chapter 13).

When I first became a landlord, in Staten Island, New York City, other people warned me about renters. None of these people were experienced landlords, but I paid attention to the prevailing wisdom they imparted anyway. It went like this: "Renters?! Oh no, thank you very much, I don't want any part of them or being a landlord! I've heard the first month's rent is the last rent you ever get, it takes years to get the courts to evict tenants when they stop paying you, and when they finally leave, the property is trashed and they steal your refrigerator and stove."

This "prevailing wisdom" about renters worried me, so one of the first things I learned when I became a landlord was how to do an eviction. I discovered that I could do one myself, because the Clerk of the Court provided all the right forms. The forms were not complicated to fill out, the judges were fair, and it took forty-five days on average before the marshal put a nonpaying renter out on the street, not the months and years I had been warned about. In New York City, I had two months of deposits—a month's security deposit *and* the last month's rent, so I had backup funds when it came time to evict a renter, and the renter was quickly replaced because there was a shortage of affordable housing (this shortage continues to this day). By the way, in New York City we had our renters supply their own fridge and stove, so we didn't worry about them stealing their own appliances.

When we moved to Florida, we found the eviction process was faster than New York City, and we could usually get a nonpaying tenant out in thirty days. We also discovered there was still a strong demand for affordable housing, but we did have to start supplying appliances.

The point of this discussion is that many inexperienced people think a landlord is a "patsy" when it comes to collecting rent. If these people ever saw the end result of an eviction, they would not think that way.

They would see a nonpaying renter standing at the curb by the street, after being escorted out of their rental unit by a sheriff with a gun on his hip. They would also see all of the renter's belongings being carried from the rental and being placed out on the curb. If the tenant had to leave the curb for any reason, their neighborhood "friends" would steal their property.

An eviction can be devastating to renters, ruining their credit and their security. They are literally left "out on the street." Many times, I have helped my own renters move before they are subjected to this painful experience. I'm referring to mothers with children who have been abandoned by their husbands, renters with emotional problems who stopped taking their medicine, and renters who lost their jobs and couldn't make ends meet on unemployment, to name a few situations. Instead of being a "patsy" when you are a landlord, you will discover that you have incredible police power behind you. My advice is to exercise this power judiciously.

Please take this to heart: *You can eliminate the vast majority of your problems with being a landlord by choosing your renters carefully in the first place, and then managing them correctly once you choose them.*

Mobile Home Parks Have Two Kinds of Customers

Mobile home parks are unique in the field of income producing real estate because they have two kinds of customers/renters:

1. Tenants

2. Residents

It is important to make a distinction between these two different kinds of customers so you can choose wisely between having residents or tenants.

Tenants are customers/renters who rent both the mobile home and the land underneath it from you. The units they live in are referred to as *Park-Owned Units,* and this is another important buzzword for you to highlight. Tenants have no ownership in the mobile home and, usually no responsibility for repairs and maintenance. This is the most common way residential real estate is leased, and most investors take it for granted that this is the only way it can be—until they purchase their first mobile home park that is a land-lease community. Then they get spoiled by the next kind of customer: residents.

Residents are customers who own their own mobile homes and take care of the maintenance and repair problems inside and immediately around it. They rent the land, or lot, that the mobile home sits on from you. You take care of the infrastructure: the roads leading up to the lots (unless they are government maintained), the common areas in the park (like club houses and swimming pools, if any), and utility connections going to their lot (water, sewer, electric, and gas, if they are not government maintained). While it may seem that infrastructure requires a lot of maintenance, in actual practice, maintenance and repair problems are limited. Mobile home parks that only lease the lots and don't own the individual mobile homes are called *Land-Lease Communities*. It is a good word to know, so highlight it now.

Having residents is one of the best ways to own income property. They have the following advantages over tenants:

1. They maintain and repair their own homes.
2. They own their homes so they exhibit pride of ownership.
3. They have greater stability during periods of recession and high unemployment.

The first advantage of having residents is that there are no more calls to unclog toilets, fix dripping faucets, or repair roof leaks. These problems are the resident's responsibility, not yours. Also gone are the frantic calls on Thanksgiving morning when an oven is not working and the renters need to cook a turkey. (The same oven that stopped working two months previously and they "forgot" to tell you.)

The second advantage is due to human nature. Since residents own their own mobile homes, the way it looks reflects upon them as a person. "Pride of ownership" flourishes when there is ownership instead of a leasing relationship.

We were not aware of the last advantage, rent stability, until the housing downturn at the end of 2005. We were practically immune to national recessions and unemployment in our area of South Florida for decades, because of our constant growth in population and jobs along with retirees moving down and bringing their wealth. We were unpleasantly surprised when we were hit by an unexpected and nasty recession and high unemployment and our tenants, who had no ownership in either the mobile home or the lot, suddenly moved away to find employment elsewhere. Our residents, on the other hand, had a much stronger tendency to remain in their mobile homes and continue to pay lot rent rather than give up and leave the area. Why? Because they owned their mobile home and in many cases, it was the only real thing of lasting value they owned, and they didn't want to give it up. The rents we received from our land-lease communities remained remarkably stable while tenants who rented both the mobile home and the land moved away at the first sign of employment distress, leaving us with an unprecedented amount of vacancies to fill. For all of the above reasons, most experienced mobile home investors gravitate towards parks with residents, or land-lease communities after they experience the ease of management and stability of rents. If you are used to being a landlord for tenants, you might find yourself singing, "Free at last! Great God Almighty, free at last!" when you own and operate a land-lease community.

Even given the advantages and disadvantages noted above, most beginning mobile home park investors buy parks with tenants rather than residents. In other words, they buy parks with almost all park-owned units, where they own the mobile homes and the land and are responsible for maintaining them. They do this because mobile home parks with park-owned units are usually smaller and less expensive to purchase, and their income is greater—they have higher cap rates. But make no mistake about it, when you have to maintain the mobile homes in addition to the infrastructure in the park, you will earn every extra dollar you make.

Now let's introduce your first *formula for success:*

UNDERSTANDING THE CASH FLOW FORMULA

While it may look like this formula is complicated and contains many terms, in practice it is usually simple to calculate. The most common way of figuring your cash flow is to start with an accurate NOI and then just subtract your total yearly mortgage payments—the principal and interest. Here's how it looks simplified:

NOI – Yearly Mortgage Payments (P + I) = Yearly Cash Flow

Remember from the previous chapter on The Magic Formula that *NOI does not include the mortgage payment.* That was because we need a universal formula for pricing a mobile home park that levels the playing field between the different financing options that investors use. Now, we are calculating a very individual formula that represents your success with a specific mobile home park—*how much money is left over for you at the end of the year.* This is your own particular cash flow and is strongly dependent on how much you borrow and the terms of the loan. Let's start at the top of the formula and explain the different terms.

The Total Yearly Rent and How You Figure It

This is the most important number, and it is critical to your success. It is best to use the actual rent collected and deposited by the current owner

The Cash Flow Formula

Start with the total yearly rent, then add income from other sources, such as:

1. Laundry, vending machine, and propane gas income.
2. Rents from additional commercial or residential buildings.

Then subtract expenses, on a yearly basis:

1. The mortgage payments.
2. Real estate taxes and sales taxes.
3. Insurance—liability, casualty, wind storm, flood.
4. Utilities—water, sewer, electric, gas, heat, trash *if* you pay for it.
5. Management, maintenance, and repair expenses.
6. Vacancy and lost rent expense—pick a fair number, 2–10 percent.
7. Reserves for replacements (roofs, streets, electric, etc.).
8. Miscellaneous expenses—other expenses unique to the property.

What's left is your yearly positive cash flow.

of the park. If for some reason, that number is not available, you can just multiply the total number of lots that are actually rented by the average rent received per lot. This will give you the monthly total rent, which you can then multiply by twelve to get the total yearly rent.

Total Yearly Rent = Total Lots Rented × Monthly Lot Rent × 12

I have seen some real estate brokers do something different. They used the above formula but they substituted the total number of lots rented with the total number of lots, rented or not. They then subtracted a vacancy factor between 5 and 10 percent. Both ways were used when the seller of the park did not have an accurate number for the total rent actually collected and their brokers tried to approximate it. If either calculation is the only number available, you can use it, but it is more accurate to use the actual rent collected.

Once you are an experienced mobile home investor in an area you will know what the average acceptable lot rents are and/or the rents for park-owned units. For mobile home parks in our area of South Florida, ranked by the quality of the park, with one star being the lowest quality and five stars being the highest quality (we will discuss park quality ratings in greater detail in Chapter 7), the lot rents currently are:

1. One Star Park = $300 per Month
2. Two Star Park = $350 per Month
3. Three Star Park = $400 per Month
4. Four Star Park = $450 per Month
5. Five Star Park = $500 per Month

As you can see, we start at $300 per month per lot for the lower-quality parks and then add $50 per month for each improvement in quality rating. That's what *we* get for lot rents in our area, but how do you find out how much *you* will get when you are first starting out in an area? What you need to do is just imagine that you want to be a resident in a mobile home park and buy a mobile home for sale there. How would you figure out how much to budget for your monthly lot rent?

The answer is—you would get the local newspapers and look in the classifieds under Mobile Homes for Sale for mobile home parks that are land-lease communities and also in the local *Pennysaver,* or *Shopper,* the weekly paper in your area that has lots of inexpensive ads. Go do that now. Get your classifieds and *Pennysavers.* I'll wait . . .

Once you have the classifieds and/or a *Pennysaver,* then you would make phone calls to sellers or their brokers who specialize in selling mobile homes in various land-lease mobile home parks in the area. You would find out the particulars, like how much the lot rent is for each mobile home listed for sale, who pays for what in terms of utilities and yard care, and then you would ask for an address so you could take a ride by and see if the mobile home and the neighborhood fit your needs. When you take your ride by and view what the resident dollar buys in terms of lot rent, you should fill out a list like I did above to understand what the rental differences are between a one-star park and a five-star park. While you are driving the different areas, call the phone numbers on any mobile home parks that have a For Sale sign for the whole park. You might discover a good deal by accident, which is perfectly fine.

If you are buying a park with park-owned units, you will use the same process to figure out what the rents are, but you will start by figuring the monthly rent on both the mobile home and the lot. In our area of South Florida, this is the way the market accounts for rents on single-wide mobile homes with one bathroom in a one-star park when the lot rent is included in the total monthly rent:

1. One Bedroom = $500 per Month
2. Two Bedroom = $600 per Month
3. Three Bedroom = $700 per Month
4. Four Bedroom = $800 per Month

As you can see, a one bedroom single-wide mobile home rents for the lowest amount and we add $100 per month for each extra bedroom. To factor in the effect on rent for a second bathroom, we would add $50 per month. A double-wide would add $50 to $100 per month, and for a higher-quality park, we would add $50 per month for each star above one star.

To see this in practice let's assume you are looking at a park-owned three-bedroom, two-bath doublewide unit in a three-star park:

Three-Bedroom, One-Bath Single-wide, One-Star Park = $700 per Month
(from table above)

Second Bathroom	=	**Add $50 per Month**
Double-wide	=	**Add $100 per Month**
Three-Star	=	**Add $100 per Month**
Total Monthly Rent	=	**$950**

Again, you will have to do your own market research by using the classifieds and *Pennysaver* to call sellers and brokers of park-owned units in your area to figure out these numbers, just like you did above for lot rents. Then you will construct a table of values in your area. You should discover that there usually is a logical basis for the rents being charged.

Collecting Rents Monthly versus Weekly

For park-owned units, you may have noticed that some rents in your area are quoted monthly and some are quoted weekly (the monthly rent divided by four). Why is that? Let me list for you the advantages, and disadvantages of each method of collection:

Advantages of collecting rents weekly

1. Tenants are paid weekly, and many live from paycheck to paycheck.
2. You get an extra month's rent each year.

Disadvantages of collecting rents weekly

1. Collecting weekly takes more time.
2. You may be carrying around a lot of money at a set time each week.

Advantages of collecting rents monthly

1. Less time to collect.

Disadvantages of collecting rents monthly

1. Many tenants don't have the discipline to save up for a month.
2. You are slower to see how your property is treated and/or vacated.
3. You get the normal amount of rent, and not one extra month.

We will talk more about collecting rents and how to eliminate the disadvantages of collecting rents weekly when we discuss managing tenants in Chapter 13.

Washing Machine, Vending Machine, and Propane Gas Income

Washing machines and dryers bring in additional monthly income in many parks, especially parks that cater to the RV industry. In some cases, this income can approach hundreds or even thousands of dollars each month. Soda machines and candy machines can do the same. I looked at buying an RV park that brought in more than $1,000 each month in profit from propane gas sales to the residents. It is reasonable to include this income with the rents when it is a repeatable and continuing source of income that is likely to remain into the foreseeable future.

Video machines and pinball machines can also bring in additional income, but there is a downside: when you have video machines you will have children hanging around them day and night, and they result in an increase in vandalism and management headaches. We didn't install them in our parks for this reason. There also was a time when we installed pay phones, but we found that cell phones and pay-as-you-go cards have replaced them, and they no longer are a reliable income source.

Additional Rents from Commercial or Residential Units

Many mobile home parks have additional rental units like houses, duplexes, apartment complexes, stores, warehouses, etc. Again, it is reasonable to include this income with the rents when it is a repeatable and continuing source of income and is very likely to remain so into the foreseeable future. You must remember that this is probably *tenant* income, not *resident* income, so you will be making repairs to these units and their management and maintenance expenses will be higher.

What Not to Include in Rental Income

You should not include in the rental income any profits that will not be a continuous source of income into the foreseeable future. These are things like:

1. Profits received from sales on existing mobile homes.

2. Commissions received from sales on new mobile homes.

3. Profits from convenience/retail stores operated by the park.

4. Mortgages and/or option payments received by the park on units the park used to own that were sold to residents with financing taken back (BBs, which are discussed in Chapter 6).

Profits received from sales on existing mobile homes

In some mobile home parks, the owners buy and sell units in their park and make money on the profits generated from this activity. They then add the profit to the NOI, which in a 10 percent cap rate park *effectively increases the price of the park by ten times the amount of profits.* Since there is no way of knowing how long this income source will continue, or if it even will, it must be removed from the lot rents. In only the most stable cases should it be treated the same as income from a business, like a pizza shop or convenience store. And, in those cases where it is considered, the future profits would be multiplied by two or three times (not ten times) and added to the price of the park as "good will."

Commissions received from sales on new mobile homes

Commissions received from the sale of new units in the park should be treated in the same manner because, again, there is no way of knowing how long this income source will continue.

Profits from convenience/retail stores operated by the park

There are parks with convenience stores, gas stations, bait stores, equipment rental stores, etc. This usually happens when the park is on a lake or river, in other recreational settings, or on a main highway. This is an impediment if you are looking to own turnkey parks, because retail stores require additional management time and theft can be a serious problem. Sellers like to add this income to the rental income, because in a 10 percent cap rate park, *it effectively increases the price of the park by ten times the amount of profits.* I treat this income the same way as mobile home sales and remove it from the lot rents, since there is no way of knowing how long the income source will continue or if it even will. Instead, I figure out what the net rent from the stores would be when it is rented to an entrepreneur who would run the business and pay you rent. Then I add only that net rent to the NOI. I do not want to run stores—I want to manage mobile home parks with the least amount of management problems and the least amount of risk from unpredictable rents and expenses. If you do want to keep running the business, then in the most stable cases you can multiply the profits by two or three times (not ten times) and add it to the price of the park as good will.

Mortgages and/or option payments received by the park on units the park used to own that were sold to residents, with financing taken back

The fourth category of income that should not be included with rental income is mortgage or lease-option payments from units that the park used to own and then sold to residents and took back financing. You will learn more about this excellent strategy when we discuss BBs in Chapter 6. It is not correct accounting when sellers include this income along with rents and then multiply it by ten in a 10 percent cap rate park. The income will certainly stop in the future when residents pay off the mobile homes. Most professional mobile home investors separate out the units that are paying mortgages or lease-options to the park owner and discount the remaining principal balance of the mortgages heavily—in some cases, 50 percent or more. In other words, let's say there is $100,000 in remaining principal in mortgages on mobile homes in the park. These mortgages are held by the current park owners and each year the mortgage payments are $15,000. A new buyer will subtract the $15,000 in mortgage payments from the NOI and come up with a price that is $150,000 lower (based upon a 10 percent cap rate). Then the buyer might allow only $50,000 in added value for the mortgages, discounting it by 50 percent, and add this to the price of the park. (See the discussion in Chapter 17 under advanced topics, for a method on how to determine the fair price for a park with park-owned units when you turn it into a land-lease community.)

As you can see, it is important that you go over the income that is placed into the NOI to distinguish what is repeatable and less risky—and therefore appropriate for the NOI—from the more risky types of income noted above.

Understanding Expenses

You were told before that the money you actually have in your pocket at the end of the year, the cash flow, can usually be determined from two numbers: the NOI minus the total yearly mortgage payments (P&I). That statement came with the caution to use it when you are given an accurate NOI. However, many times you will be given an NOI that is less than accurate, either intentionally to inflate the price to the mobile home park or unintentionally by someone who is not professional or experienced. Therefore, you need to understand mobile home park expenses in depth so you can calculate your own true NOI.

Mortgage Payments

The secret to getting rich in real estate is using leverage, or borrowed money. This is commonly referred to as OPM, Other People's Money. Real estate is unique in that investors can use OPM to create enormous leverage for themselves. This leverage is the reason so many people choose real estate as their preferred form of investing. For instance, in the stock market, you can usually only borrow 50 percent of the value of the stocks you buy, so you must put down half from your own savings, if you have it. In real estate, you can put from 20 percent down to nothing down—0 percent. Zero percent down means no money down, and that is infinite leverage. Buying with no money down means you can buy as much property as you want, limited only by your ability to manage the property you buy. How's that for an unlimited horizon?

Now it stands to reason when you use OPM, you will have a mortgage loan, and this translates into monthly mortgage payments and debts. Technically, when calculating your cash flow, you should only subtract the interest paid out over the year, and add back the principal that was paid down on the mortgage. I don't do this and I won't do it for the remainder of this book for two reasons:

1. You can't spend the principal paydown until you refinance or sell the park.

2. I treat it as a secret savings account coming some time in the future.

Some people have misconceptions about debt, and this necessitates a discussion now on the different types of debt—which type of debt is good, and which is not. When we complete our discussion about debt, you will get a simple formula for estimating your monthly mortgage payments if you don't have a mortgage calculator handy.

Good Debt and Bad Debt

What distinguishes a good debt from a bad debt is the answer to the following question: "*Can I earn money by borrowing this money after I make the repayment on this debt?*"

For instance, let's assume you want to buy new furniture for your house, and it costs $20,000. You borrow the money for five years at 10 percent interest. If you put the terms into a mortgage calculator, the payment is $435 per month. So if you borrow the money to buy the furniture, you will have a $435 per month payment going out. Besides the better feeling this new furniture gives you, what additional income is coming in each month as a result of this debt? Answer—*nothing*. Therefore, this is classified as *consumer debt*. Consumer debts are loans you take out for sports cars, vacations, clothing, boats—anything you can put on a credit card to satisfy the raging consumer inside of you, who wants to acquire things and is willing to mortgage your future paychecks to get it. This raging consumer is manipulated by advertising that convinces you to buy now, forget about tomorrow, and live paycheck to paycheck.

> ***Remember:** Debt is good when you borrow money on appreciating assets with positive cash flow, because then you are worth tomorrow what you owe today, as long as you have been a good caretaker of the property in the meantime.*

Now let's talk about a different kind of debt, called *investment debt*. This is money you borrow to buy an investment, and the investment gives you monthly income, in addition to the monthly repayment of the debt. If you calculate all the expenses of owning this investment, including the monthly repayment of the debt, and the rent is greater than all the expenses, then the debt generates a positive cash flow and it is a good debt.

Let me give you a simple example of the most basic kind of good debt on a parcel of real estate. Years ago, I met Abe, a railroad conductor from Boston who was thirty-five. Abe was a down-to-earth guy with a simple dream—he wanted to retire a millionaire. At the time, he had only one investment and that was all he wanted. It was a twenty-unit apartment building, for which he paid a million dollars, and it was worth exactly that, no more and no less. Abe borrowed all the money on a thirty-year loan, so he also owed a million dollars. Therefore, when he started out, Abe's net worth was zero. Let me demonstrate this:

	$1,000,000 =	Purchase Price of Apartment Building
–	$1,000,000 =	Mortgage Loan on Building
	0 =	Increase in Abe's Net Worth

Abe owned a million dollar building, and he owed a million dollars on it. The NOI on the apartment building was $10,000 per month, and the mortgage payment on building was $10,000 per month. When Abe did his cash flow calculation, the apartment building broke even, and there was nothing extra each month.

NOI	–	Mortgage Payment	=	Cash Flow
$10,000	–	$10,000 Mortgage (P + I)	=	0 Cash Flow

Abe didn't care about cash flow—he made enough from working on the railroad to take care of his and his family's needs. He figured, if the rents kept up with expenses, which they did, and he put away the required money as reserves for repairs and maintenance, which he did, at the end of thirty years, when he was ready to retire at sixty-five, he would be a millionaire. How? *The mortgage would be paid off.* If the building was still worth what he paid for it thirty years before—and the chances of that were very, very good—then he would be worth one million dollars!

	$1,000,000 =	Purchase Price of Apartment Building
–	0 =	Mortgage Loan on Building
	$1,000,000 =	Increase in Abe's Net Worth

Even better, he would be able to keep that monthly mortgage payment he had been paying for thirty years, so he would have an extra $10,000 per month when he retired, plus his pension and social security. Abe figured the extra $10,000 would make his retirement years easy.

$10,000 NOI – 0 Mortgage Payment (P + I) = $10,000 Monthly Cash Flow

When I asked Abe if he was a little panicky about owing a million dollars, he said he had been in the beginning, but that he then told himself the following every month, when it came time to send in the mortgage payment:

"I am worth tomorrow what I owe today."

Please think about Abe's simple statement and the wisdom it implies. When you borrow money on income-earning real estate and the property pays off the monthly mortgage payment and all the expenses, then when the mortgage is finally paid off, you are worth on that tomorrow what you owed in the beginning, as long as you have been a good caretaker of your property in the meantime, which is not difficult.

If Abe had bought a mobile home park, the same would have been true after thirty years. If he had read this book first, he would have chosen a park that gave him positive cash flow every month and did not just break even. Then he would have made money each month while he was waiting to be worth a million dollars, using the Landlord's rule:

If you wake up to tenants, you should be paid NOW for the privilege.

This point is this—not all debt is bad. Consumer debt can be bad if it is not kept in check. Consumer debt attacks your paycheck, makes you poorer, and makes you mortgage your tomorrows with assets that are wasting away. There is debt that is good, called investment debt, which pays itself off, and afterwards the asset is still there, smiling at you, helping you even more. Abe, the railroad conductor bought a neutral, break-even investment. You are not being encouraged to do that. You should find investments with positive cash flow that puts extra spending money in your pocket each month, while the assets appreciate to be worth even more in the future.

Now that you gotten your mind and attitude focused correctly about debt, let's learn how to figure this expense quickly, when no calculator is handy.

How to Find Your Monthly Mortgage Multiple

You need a simple way to figure your monthly mortgage payment on a mobile home park. This involves a new term called your *monthly mortgage multiple.* To figure out your monthly mortgage payment you take your monthly mortgage multiple and multiply that number by how many thousands you are borrowing:

Thousands Borrowed × Monthly Mortgage Multiple
= Monthly Payment (P + I)

Here is a list of interest rates and their related monthly mortgage multiples for thirty-year loans:

- 7% = 6.6 times
- 8% = 7.3 times
- 9% = 8. times
- 10% = 8.7 times
- 11% = 9.5 times
- 12% = 10 times

For instance, let's assume you are borrowing $25,000 at 8 percent for thirty years. Well, $25,000 is 25 thousands, and from the table up above, the monthly mortgage multiple for 8 percent for thirty years is 7.3. Therefore:

Thousands Borrowed × Monthly Mortgage Multiple
= Monthly Payment (P + I)
25 × 7.3
= $182 per Month Payment

Let's do another example. Let's assume you are going to buy a small mobile home park for no money down for $50,000 at 9 percent interest for thirty years. Looking at the table, 9 percent interest for thirty years has a multiple of 8:

Thousands Borrowed × Monthly Mortgage Multiple
= Monthly Payment (P + I)
50 × 8
= $400 per Month Payment

If you want to simplify the calculations even more, just take the interest rate that you can borrow at and subtract one, and that is a loose approximation of the monthly multiple for thirty years.

Ultra-Simplified Monthly Mortgage Multiple Formula for Thirty-Year Loans
Interest Rate − 1 = Monthly Multiple

So for 9 percent interest, you would use a monthly mortgage multiple of 8, and for 10 percent interest, you would use a monthly multiple of 9, etc.

How will you find *your* monthly multiple? Again, let's use common sense. Let's assume you want to buy a mobile home park from a real estate broker. A broker's livelihood depends not only on writing contracts to sell mobile home parks, but also on making sure that buyers can get financing to close the deal. For this reason, they normally know which lenders are the easiest to borrow money from. Therefore, the best way to find lenders is by calling real estate brokers who specialize in selling mobile home parks. You will know which brokers specialize in mobile home parks because they have the most listings, the most ads, and the most signs. After you get a list of lenders from the brokers, go to at least three mortgage brokers and/or direct lenders in your area who specialize in lending for mobile home parks. We'll talk more about this in Chapter 11 when we discuss financing.

When you get the average rate and terms you can borrow at, get a mortgage calculator and figure out the monthly payment for $1,000 at the average interest rate and terms. For instance, let's assume you can borrow at 7.5 percent for thirty years in your area. When you put in $1,000, you will come up with:

$1,000 at 7.5% for 30 Years = 6.9 Dollars per Month per Thousand

Now, whenever you want to convert an amount you are borrowing to a monthly mortgage payment, you multiply the number of thousands by 6.9. I personally would round it off to 7 so I could do the math easier.

Taxes, Insurance, Utilities

Since you own the land under the mobile homes in your park, you will have to pay *real estate taxes.* Figure out how much the real estate taxes are in your area, as a percentage of the property appraiser's assessed value. In our area, real estate taxes are 2 percent of the assessed value, so a mobile home park that is assessed for $300,000 would have taxes of $6,000 per year, or $500 per month. Sales tax is not collected in our area unless you lease a mobile home or RV for less than six months. If you do, you are forced to collect an extra 11 percent of the weekly or monthly rent in sales and bed taxes! For this reason, we try to make our leases for six months plus one day whenever we can.

Insurance has changed dramatically in our area, and probably in your area, too, if you have had hurricanes come through and do damage. If you haven't had hurricanes, then your insurance is like ours used to be—you have one company that gives you one bill per year to insure your mobile home parks for everything. Now, in our hurricane-prone area, our insurance is broken up into four parts, and some of our properties have four different insurance companies to cover each of the parts. *Liability insurance* protects you when someone sues you—for instance, if someone trips and falls—and it is the least expensive insurance and the easiest to get. *Casualty insurance* protects you when there is a fire, theft, or similar damage, and it is more expensive. *Windstorm insurance* covers your property when there is damage from hurricanes and tornadoes, and this is the most expensive. *Flood insurance,* which is usually a federal program, protects property in low-lying areas that are prone to flooding. If you don't have flood insurance and your mobile home park is damaged by a flood, chances are you will have no insurance coverage at all from the other three forms of insurance either. Some residents of New Orleans suffered total losses when their property was damaged when the levees broke from Hurricane Katrina and they had no flood insurance. Therefore, flood insurance can be very important if you are in a flood-prone area.

Utility expenses are for water, sewer, electric, gas, heat, trash, and so on. We try to have each of the lots in our mobile home parks separately metered for each of these utilities, but if that isn't possible, then you as the property owner might be responsible for them, and you must account for it in your expenses. A few notes here. When the tenant is paying for water, he tends to be impatient about our handyman's arrival to stop a leak, even when there is just a little drip. However, when we pay for the water, I have seen toilets run for months and waste hundreds of our dollars before a tenant will call and ask for it to be fixed. Also, when we have a few mobile homes on one meter, we put in the leases that each tenant is responsible for an equal share each month. For instance, if there are four mobiles on one water meter, then we bill each of the tenants a quarter of the bill. We have had very little problem with doing this, so you might want to give it a try in your area.

Management, Maintenance, and Repairs

One of the advantages of buying mobile home parks is that the expense of an on-site manager is considered a normal business expense and is discounted from the NOI. Management expenses also include advertising, office expenses, and accounting expenses, and usually run 8-10 percent of the total rents. If you hire a management company to manage one of your mobile home parks, they usually charge a fee that is 8-10 percent of the total rents collected.

Maintenance and repairs can sometimes be difficult to estimate. Some mobile home parks, especially land-lease communities, get very few calls for repairs, are always rented, and remain in excellent shape. In others it may seem like the list of repairs is never ending and the tenants are on a merry-go-round, moving in and moving out. As you learn how to select tenants in Chapter 13, you will reduce your expenses for repairs, maintenance, and vacancy. A good estimate for repairs, maintenance, and vacancy on park-owned units is 10 percent of the monthly rent. This is easy to figure by moving the decimal point one place to the left on the monthly rent. For instance, if the monthly rent is $600, allot $60 per month for repairs, maintenance, and vacancy.

Let me give you some notes here on what we do to keep our repair and maintenance bills in line on park-owned units. *First,* we try to make the tenants responsible for repairing all the appliances—fridges, stoves, A/C's, heaters, dishwashers, and the like, and they must leave working appliances when they leave or we will subtract it from their security deposit. *Second,* we try to make the first $100 of any repairs each month the responsibility of the tenant. *Third,* we have the tenants mow their own lawns. We hope someday to carry this to its logical conclusion and rent out park-owned mobile homes like we rent out commercial buildings, on a triple-net basis. This means the tenant is responsible for all repairs and maintenance, except the roof, and all expenses, including real estate taxes and insurance.

Also, you should take snow removal into account as a separate expense if your mobile home park is located in a colder climate that gets varying amounts of snow. In some parks this can be a significant amount of money, in the thousands or even tens of thousands. A park on ten acres may have half of a mile of roads to plow, so if it doesn't come with a snowplow, be prepared to pay thousands of dollars to snow-plowing companies every time it snows.

How to Pay for a Full-Time Handyman in the Beginning

When we started investing in residential income property, I took care of the tenant maintenance and repairs myself. However, after our first twenty rentals I needed a prompt, reliable, *part-time* handyman, and that was not easy to find. Most handymen want the security of a full-time job and the full-time paycheck that goes along with it. We decided to hire a handyman full time, rather than on a call-by-call basis. On the positive side, that meant we controlled when a repair was made and we lowered our costs, because repairs cost half as much as an independent contractor who charged on a call-by-call basis. On the negative side, a good full-time handyman can handle around fifty rental units, so if you have ten or twenty units, the handyman will be sitting around idle much of the time. We believed it would take us years to build up to those numbers with careful and conservative growth, so we needed to do something productive with our handyman's unused time, something that would bring in extra income. Can you think of what that was?

Our answer was to use our handyman's extra time to fix and add value to our flipper properties—about one property per month. The hundred thousand dollars or more it added to our profits each year made it easier to buy more rentals and provided the money for his full-time salary. It worked well for us and I recommend it heartily to others based upon our positive experience.

Vacancy and Lost Rent Expenses

In a land-lease community, vacancy and lost rent, or collection expenses, is usually a low number on a turnkey park—in the range of 2–10 percent of the gross collectable rents. It could be a large number—20–50 percent or more—on a turn-around park. You will have to determine what a reasonable vacancy rate is based upon the individual park and what other similar mobile home parks in the area are experiencing.

Reserves for Replacements (Roofs, Streets, Electric, and Such)

When you are determining reserves for replacements, you are estimating when the major components of the mobile home park are going to wear out and what it will cost to replace them. You then add these numbers to your yearly expenses. You will be looking at expensive replacements: the roofs on common element buildings, the paving of the streets, the electric meter boxes, and the motors on lift stations and on-site water wells and sewage-treatment plants.

For instance, let's assume the mobile home park office has an A/C that will need to be replaced in five years and will cost $2,000. Let's also assume that the roof on the manager's building will need to be replaced in ten years for $3,000. Therefore, you must add the following to the park's yearly expenses:

Yearly Reserve = Cost of Replacement ÷ Years of Life Left
= $2,000 New AC ÷ 5 Years = $400 per Year Reserve
= $3,000 New Roof ÷ 10 Years = $300 per Year Reserve

Miscellaneous Expenses

Miscellaneous expenses don't fit into any of the above categories and are unique to that mobile home park. For instance, there may be a special tax on mobile home clubhouses or individual septic systems, or things of that nature. In our area we have to pay for street lights in our parks, and we also have to pay for yearly permits for the water and sewer systems and a license to run a mobile home park. These would all be considered miscellaneous expenses.

Three Additional Questions the Pros Ask

At this point, we have completed our discussion on the Cash Flow Formula. Again, let me remind you that the most common way to calculate your monthly cash flow on a keeper is usually very simple. You start with a reliable NOI and subtract the yearly mortgage payments, only the principal and interest. It looks like this:

NOI – Yearly Mortgage payments (P + I) = Yearly Cash Flow

However, pros do not accept that the current numbers they calculate for a keeper are carved in stone and will never change. They also ask the following questions about the future:

What is the likelihood of the income changing? Throughout history rents have gone up. However, there have been rare times when they have not increased and even when they went down slightly. This almost always depends on the population and job trends. If population and jobs are increasing, rents will go up with the increasing demand—there are more people needing rentals and fewer rentals available. If jobs and population remain stable, then rents will remain stable and adjust only to inflation. However, if you are buying in an area where an Army base is closing down or large manufacturing plants are leaving town, then population and jobs are going to decrease. As a result vacancy rates are going to increase and rents may drop in price, because fewer people will be living there and more rentals will be available. Check with the Chamber of Commerce and the local Planning Commission about the population and job trends.

What is the likelihood of the expenses changing? Expenses have gone up throughout history, because of inflation, and rents have increased to keep up with the expenses. Property owners will stop renting if renting is not a positive investment, and then builders will stop building rentals. Here, the pro looks to make sure there are no unusually high expenses coming up in the future, like large water and sewer assessments or hookup fees, or exorbitant increases in real estate taxes or insurance. Florida was hit hard from 2004 through 2007 with real estate tax increases due to increased property values and large insurance increases due to hurricane damage, but rents had also risen to absorb the additional costs.

How much of your time is it going to take to fix the problems and then manage the property? You should estimate how much time and how much money it will cost to fix a property before you buy it. My advice is to keep away from major rehabs in the beginning unless the monthly cash flow is going to be a necessary addition to your yearly profit. Management time is also critical, because some areas attract renters that are easy to take care of, and some areas have renters that require a lot more attention. This is your decision to make, because it is your time that you are spending. In the beginning, cash flow will probably be uppermost in your mind and you won't mind the extra time some properties will take to manage as long as the return is good. As you get wealthier and more appreciative of your spare time, you may change your outlook and sell off the more management-intensive mobile home parks because you want more spare time and don't need as much cash flow from any one property.

First Example: Happy Trails—Our First Mobile Home Park

We're going to return now to the first mobile home park we purchased, "Happy Trails," the one we described briefly in the first section titled "The Second Adventure." Below are the more complete characteristics of the park:

HAPPY TRAILS MOBILE HOME PARK	
Price	$650,000
NOI	$65,000
Cap Rate	10%
Down Payment	0
Terms of Mortgage Loan	$650,000, 9%, 25 years, $5,400/month
Lots rented	66
Free Vacant Mobile Homes	5
Total Usable lots	90
Current Lot Rent	$285/month
Utilities	County water and sewer, $5,000/mo
Trash Pickup	Private company, $700/mo
Who paid for Utilities + trash	Mobile home park owner
Corner Store	$450/month rent—poor condition
Manager's House	Occupied by manager, no rent received

In terms of NOI and cap rate, The Magic Formula shows the following:

Purchase Price	×	Cap Rate	=	NOI
$650,000	×	10%	=	$65,000

In other words, we purchased the park for $650,000, with a 10 percent cap rate, and received $65,000 per year in NOI. We didn't know it at the time, but this park was burdened with unreasonably large expenses, specifically the water and sewer expenses of the park were outrageous at $5,000 per month.

If you remember from our discussion of The Magic Formula in Chapter 1, we calculated the price of mobile home parks with the assumption there was no mortgage on the property. Then, in this chapter, you learned the Cash Flow Formula for keepers, showing how much money you had left after you paid the mortgage. You were told that this was a very important number, and it is.

You can see from the figures above that the terms of our mortgage

Street scene at Happy Trails mobile home park.

were $650,000 at 9 percent for twenty-five years (no money down). The mortgage payment was $5,450 per month, or approximately $65,400 per year, which we'll round off to $65,000. Using the simple *formula for success* for cash flow:

Cash Flow	=	**NOI**	–	**Yearly Mortgage payments**		
Cash Flow	=	**$65,000**	–	**$65,000**	=	**0**

No, your eyes are not deceiving you. *There was no cash flow!* (It is not unusual to have little positive cash flow when you buy a mobile home park for no money down, and there is a narrow spread between the cap rate of the mobile home park (in this case, 10 percent) and the rate on the mortgage money you borrowed to purchase the park (in this case, 9 percent.)

You also know that this park violated the first law of being a landlord, which is *"if you have to wake up in the morning to tenants, you should be paid for the privilege."* In this case, we were not being paid for the privilege of managing sixty-six tenants.

We had a tentative plan of what we wanted to do. We had ninety total usable lots, of which only sixty-six were occupied, and five free mobile homes that were vacant. (The woman I called from the class did not sell any because she left the park due to personal circumstances.) Our top priority was to sell and get lot rent on the five free mobile homes and then rent out as many of the nineteen vacant lots as we could.

The park was at the intersection of two arterial roads, with about 30,0[illegible] cars driving by each day, and it already had two little signs that advertised mobile home and RV lots available for rent. To take advantage of the high traffic count, we added a small sign that offered for sale the mobile homes we inherited with the park. We only asked $2,000 for some of them but we had no takers. Nobody who drove by and saw the sign seemed to have $2,000 in cash. Further, we only had one or two people inquire about moving their mobile home onto one of our nineteen vacant lots.

At this point, we became creative. We changed our sign to advertise our mobile homes for sale with *owner financing.* The terms were $500 down and $95 per month until the note was paid off. Naturally, the people who bought the mobile homes also had to pay lot rent of $285 month while they were paying off their notes, which was the prize in the transaction for us. Before we offered to take back financing, we went down to the Department of Motor Vehicles (DMV) and inquired about the repo (repossession) procedure when someone defaulted on the note on a mobile home that we sold to them.

We discovered, to our great surprise, that a repo on a mobile home was the same as for a car—it was practically instantaneous. We simply went down to the DMV and filled out an affidavit that we were not paid on the note, and the mobile home was titled back in our name. We have since discovered that a few states (Texas being one of them) are not as easy as Florida when it comes to repossessing mobile homes. In that

Corner store at Happy Trails mobile home park.

'd do lease-options with new buyers. We will discuss n Chapter 6.

n we put up made a dramatic difference in the cash flow of y Trails Mobile Home Park—so much so that we called it the Magic Sign. It looked like this:

MOBILE HOMES
$500 & UP
OWNER FINANCING
LET'S TALK! 995-6442

Within a few months, the Magic Sign enabled us to sell the five free mobile homes, with us taking back owner financing. Besides having $500 down payments, we now had $95 coming in extra each month from mortgage payments we received on mobile homes we got for free and used to own, and lot rent of $285 coming in on each of the five lots. This was the start of our positive cash flow. (If you are going to copy the sign, I would recommend that you change the "& UP" to "DOWN" after the $500.)

Meanwhile, the signs advertising vacant lots available in the park were a failure. Maybe one person called each month and we only rented one space to an RV owner for a few months. Since we had such a positive experience selling our own free mobile homes and taking back financing, Gersh and I decided to buy inexpensive used mobile homes and RV park models from outside the park, set them up in Happy Trails, and then sell them. We spent $1,000 to $2,000 apiece, and we offered them for sale at $500 down, $95 per month, at twice what we paid, including setup costs. We financed the mobile homes and RV park models with an investor using the BB, which you will learn about in Chapter 6. The price we asked was almost irrelevant, since the buyers only cared about how much down and how much per month they would have to pay, and were thrilled they didn't have to walk into a bank and be subjected to all the fees and paperwork.

For the first six months we owned the Happy Trails the park threatened to *take money from us.* When there is no positive cash flow after mortgage payments, any extra unforeseen expense will cause you to hit your savings. My daughter, who I was teaching to manage the park, came to me with any unexpected expenses and we worked them out by waiting a week or two to pay some bills until more rents to come in.

However, after a little more than a year of ownership, she came to me with a scared look on her face. I said, "What's the matter, honey?"

She said, "Dad, there is almost $20,000 in the checking account, and I don't know where it came from."

We sat down and went over all the checks and deposits, and low and behold, the $20,000 was correct. Where did it come from? The additional twenty-four units we put on the rent roll, as we went from sixty-six paying residents, to ninety paying residents. I figured that approximately $200 of the $285 in lot rent was profit, and the remaining $85 was for the water, sewer, and trash expenses the park paid.

$285 Lot Rent – $85 Expenses per Lot
= $200 Profit per Additional Lot Rented

We increased our paying lots from sixty-six to ninety lots, which is twenty-four additional lots, or:

$200 Profit per Lot × 24 Additional Lots = $4,800 per Month Extra NOI

I looked at my daughter and smiled. "I guess what we're doing is working!" I said. We held $10,000 for the next improvement we were contemplating, and divided up the remaining $10,000 between Crazy Gersh and me. (It is my intention to leave the bulk of my estate to my children and/or charities run by them. Therefore, I want to teach my children how to take care of the property I leave to them before I depart this world. In the case of my daughter, I told her I would give her 25 percent of my half of Happy Trails positive cash flow if and when we had positive cash flow. I added that when she was able to manage the park entirely on her own, with less than a few hours assistance from me each week, I would give her 50 percent of my half of the positive cash flow. As soon as I made the first partner disbursement of $10,000, my daughter's motivation and responsibility increased. Within three more months she was able to manage Happy Trails with almost no help or time from me, which she continues to do to this day.)

Filling Empty Lots—One of Your Most Important Strategies

This strategy, filling empty lots with BBs, is extremely important. There are four methods for doing this:

1. Bring in mobile homes yourself and sell them (and possibly take back financing—do BBs.).
2. Have a mobile home dealer set up homes in your park, sell them, and arrange financing, or the dealer sells them from his mobile home dealership and moves them in.
3. Advertise the empty lots and wait for owners to move in their own homes and finance them.
4. Investors move in homes and sell them (and possibly take back financing—do BBs).

The first method, the BB, is the route we usually take because it is the most reliable, and we have ways of financing that we will discuss later. The second method is excellent if you find a reputable and hard-working mobile home dealer and he or she can find financing for your potential residents. You will have to give free lot rent if the dealer sets up units on vacant lots in your park, until the dealer sells the units, but that is a small price to pay—you aren't earning anything on them anyway. The third method is the slowest and least reliable. Most potential owners of mobile homes don't have the $2,000 to $4,000 it can take to move in and set up a mobile home in someone else's park. The fourth method, having other investors move in units to your park and sell them (or possibly take back financing in a BB) is not that common, but is a welcome advantage.

Some aggressive mobile home park owners will advertise directly to residents in competing parks. They will offer to pay all or part of the moving expenses, and give discounts on lot rent to any owners who move to their park. I personally wouldn't do this because it feels a little too cutthroat. If a resident of another park were to come to us, unsolicited, because they were unhappy elsewhere and they needed help with moving and setup expenses to move to our park, then we might negotiate.

Submetering, Another Powerful Strategy to Increase NOI

When we purchased the Happy Trails Mobile Home Park, the water and sewer bill was $5,000 per month. After we added the twenty-four new paying residents, it was close to $6,000 per month. There was one master water meter for the park and the sewer bill was calculated directly from the water bill. We wanted to *submeter,* which means install individual water meters on each lot, read them once a month, and bill the residents for their individual usage.

Since we bought Happy Trails, we had been receiving two mobile home magazines, the *Manufactured Home Merchandiser* and *The Journal.* While reading them, I saw an article where a mobile home park owner submetered a park in New York, and the residents sued him in court to take them away and have the owner continue to pay for the water and sewer. I didn't want that to happen to us, so we checked with the local water company and the State of Florida Department of Professional Regulation (DPR) that regulates mobile homes, and found there was no law preventing us from submetering.

Next, we went shopping for individual water meters and were very pleasantly surprised to learn the heavy duty brass water meters the water company used were only $35 a piece when bought in bulk. We figured that two of our less-skilled handymen working for $10 per hour could put in at least five per day, and this was how we estimated our costs for installing them:

	$35 per Water meter
+	**$25 Additional Plumbing Parts (on Average)**
+	**$40 Labor ($100 per Day Each Man × 2 Men; divided by 5)**
	$100 Total Cost per Lot

90 Lots × $100 per Lot = $9,000 Total Cost to Submeter

The actual cost was very close to that number. For some mobile homes, we installed an inground plastic box for the meter. For others, we simply cut the water-supply line to the mobile home that came up out of the ground, attached some PVC pipe so the water meter could be mounted on the outside skirting, and then reconnected the supply line into the home.

The residents saw us doing this and wanted to know what was happening, so we sent around a notice to everyone in the park. In that notice we explained we were going to raise the rents, for the first time since we owned the park, to $300 per month. This amounted to an increase of $15 per month per resident. Then we added that in two months we would be lowering the rent to $275 per month. *That's right, we would be lowering the rent $25 per month*!

Can you guess what the lowering of the rent would be accompanied by? That's right—we were going to bill the residents for their individual water and sewer usage. We explained if they were thrifty with their water usage and spent $15 to $20 per month on water and sewer, the net affect of the change would be less than $300 ($290 to $295 per month for lot rent + water and sewer usage).

We also ran a "shake-down cruise" for almost two months. We read everyone's meter, which started from 0 when they were installed, and let them know every two weeks how much water they were using and how much their bills would be. For the people who were using in the range of $25 or more of water and sewer *every two weeks*, we paid our handymen to go inside the homes of our residents and fix dripping faucets and running toilets. That's right. We paid to have our residents' plumbing fixtures repaired so their water bills would not be too high. This earned us good will with the residents and it was not a lot of money, because the average mobile home had one kitchen and one bathroom and that was only two sink faucets, one bath faucet, and one toilet. We had everyone up and running efficiently in less than a month with perhaps an additional $1,000 in parts and labor, which put us right on target for spending $10,000 for the project.

It's interesting to note a few things here:

1. There were quite a few residents who would have had to pay $100 per month or more because of dripping faucets and running toilets, but not after we were done. (Guess who was paying those bills before and didn't know it.)

2. There was one resident with a small family who was using $500 per month with no leaking plumbing fixtures. It turned out that there was a water supply pipe underneath the trailer that leaked into the ground and was unseen because it was right below the trailer. We crawled underneath and repaired it, and then wondered how many thousands of dollars it cost us and the previous owner.

3. We charged everyone $4.95 each for our manager to read meters each month. This was added to the water usage bill and was still $5 less than the water utility charged for this service. This meter-reading income added $450 a month to our NOI and only took about two hours of the

manager's time and about two hours of clerical time in the office to input all the readings into a program that calculated the bills.

The final note is positively amazing. *The water and sewer usage of the park went down 66 percent.* That's right—the bill was one-third of what it used to be, now that the residents paid their fair share.

What effect did this have on our cash flow? An amazing effect. We lowered our lot rents to $275, but then we added almost $5 for reading water meters each month, so we reduced our total income by very little from the $285 it was before. However, our net income was raised by the removal of a major cost—the $5,000 per month water and sewer bills that existed when we bought the park. When you add the $4,800 increase in gross rents we got by adding twenty-four residents to the $5,000 we saved each month on water and sewer:

$4,800 Additional Rent from 24 New Residents + $5,000 Water and Sewer Savings = $9,800 per Month Positive Cash Flow

We can round up the $9,800 to $10,000, and now you can see how we went from a park that had no positive cash flow to a park that gave us $10,000 per month. We all thought this was a wonderful accomplishment every month, when I distributed the $10,000. My partner Gersh was thrilled to get $5,000 every month, which was the total amount of money he previously made from two jobs—one with the city, and the other from his small lawn mowing business where he worked in the hot Florida sun and torrential rains. My daughter was thrilled to get half of my half, or $2,500 each month as a bonus, to pay for her day-care bills and other expenses. I felt this was a gift from above. My family had other investments that gave us more than enough to live on, so I donated my whole share to a local charity, and have been doing so ever since, and continue to do so as of this writing.

We are not finished with how we improved our cash flow at Happy Trails, but these two techniques, filling vacant lots and submetering, provided the bulk of the increase.

Maximizing Income on Other Rental Units

Some mobile home parks also come with additional rental units, like houses, stores, warehouses, and storage units. Happy Trails had a corner store and a nice two-bedroom home that was used by the previous owner's manager. We hired a new manager, who was bilingual and could communicate better with the 80 percent of our residents who were Spanish. We paid him a normal salary with benefits and gave him free rent in an additional mobile home we placed inside the park.

We then rented out the house for $600 per month, which brought in an additional $7,200 per year into Happy Trails. We raised the rent on the corner store from $450 per month to $1,750 per month, increasing our NOI by $1,300 per month or $15,600 per year. Further, the following year we passed along the expenses for trash pickup by billing each tenant $9.95 per month for their part of the bill.

The following is a chart of how we increased the NOI at Happy Trails from the original numbers when we purchased it:

Action	Montly Increase NOI	NOI Yearly Increase
Added 24 Units	+ $4,800 per Month	+ $57,600 per Year
Submetered	+ $5,000 per Month	+ $60,000 per Year
House Rent	+ $600 per Month	+ $7,200 per Year
Store Rent Increase	+ $1,300 per Month	+ $15,600 per Year
Trash Bill Charge	+ 900 per Month	+ $10,800 per Year
TOTALS	**+ $12,600 per Month**	**+ $151,200 per Year**

Remember that we purchased Happy Trails for $650,000 with $65,000 in NOI at a 10 percent cap rate, and there was no positive cash flow because our mortgage payment was equal to our NOI. When you look at the chart above, you are looking only at the *increase* in NOI on a monthly and yearly basis. *We went from a park that we purchased for no money down and gave us no money at the end of each month to a park that gave us $12,600 per month to distribute in profits—a $151,200 per year positive cash flow.*

Since we started with $65,000 in NOI, and we increased it $151,200, we created more than a triple-fold increase in NOI over when we started:

$65,000 Starting NOI + $151,200 Increase in NOI
= $216,200 Current NOI

Ask yourself, what is Happy Trails Mobile Home Park worth now? Well, if we continue to use a 10 percent cap rate, you should remember from the previous chapter on The Magic Formula that you simply move the decimal point one place to the right to convert from NOI to price:

\$216,200 NOI ÷ 10% Cap Rate = \$2,162,000 Market Value

That's right. We increased the value of the park by \$1,512,000, from \$650,000 to \$2,162,000. That is an increase of slightly more than \$1.5 million dollars:

\$2,162,000 Current Value − \$650,000 Original Cost = \$1,512,000 Profit

We are not dealing with imaginary, pie-in-the-sky, smoke and mirrors profits here. The cash flow is a fact and the checks we have been writing ourselves for the past six years don't lie. Let's consider a concrete, realistic way of proving that the park is worth 2.16 million dollars—putting it up for sale. Let's assume Gersh and I did just that and put a sign out front saying, "Mobile Home Park for Sale" along with our phone number.

Now let's assume you or another mobile home park investor was driving by and saw the sign, and either stopped in at the office and spoke to our manager or called the phone number on the sign. Either way, when you asked what the price of the Happy Trails Mobile Home Park was, you would be told \$2.16 million. When you inquired about the NOI, you would be told \$216,000. You would then do a quick calculation and discover that a cap rate of 10 percent on a 2.16 million dollar park would be the NOI we gave you. If you agreed that 10 percent was a realistic cap rate you might write a realistic offer on the park for \$2.16 million.

Then you or the investor would take that contract to a bank, and the bank would send out an appraiser, and guess what he would ask us, the sellers of Happy Trails? What is the NOI, and could we substantiate it, which we have demonstrated here that we could. You or the investor would do your own research on our NOI, and we would substantiate that also. The checks and the deposits don't lie.

The bottom line is, everyone is using The Magic Formula—buyers, sellers, banks and appraisers—and as long as the NOI is accurate and the cap rate is appropriate, there is usually agreement about price. *This case study proves what I told you in the beginning of the book: that you are going to learn techniques where you can make a million dollars in profit on one property.* In the next chapter we are going to prove it again.

The question you might now be asking yourself is, given your belief in the new value of Happy Trails, "How do I get my hands on this profit?"

Getting Your Hands on the Profits

There are three ways to get your hands on your profits after you improve the NOI on your mobile home park:

1. Sell the property.
2. Do nothing other than just enjoy the additional cash flow.
3. Do a cash-out refinance—harvest the profit in a *Refi Bonanza.*

Sell the Property

Selling the property is the simplest way of getting your hands on the profit. Keep in mind, however, that you will also be killing the goose that lays the golden egg—losing a good income source you fully understand. You might have to pay commissions and closing costs when you sell, which could amount to 10 percent, or $200,000. You will also have to pay capital gains tax on the million and a half profit minus the closing costs, which at a tax rate of 15 percent also comes to around $200,000.

You could try a 1031 exchange to avoid the taxes, but not the closing costs. In that case, you would sell the park and then replace it within six months with another real estate investment of equal or greater value and with equal or greater mortgage financing on it. However, if you decide to keep some of the cash from the sale, you will have to pay tax on it, as it is considered *boot.* I will go into the ramifications of a 1031 exchange later in the book, when we discuss taxes and asset protection.

Do Nothing Other Than Enjoy the Additional Cash Flow

This is what we did with Happy Trails because we liked the additional cash flow. We had enough savings to buy more mobile home parks so we had no need of additional capital. When the time comes that another excellent mobile home park presents itself, we will use the next technique.

Do a Cash Out Refi—Harvest the Profit in a Refi Bonanza

This is the best alternative for accesing the profits in your park. Here, you will go to your bank or another bank and apply for a loan to refinance the park. The bank will send out an appraiser, and given the new NOI and the typical cap rate, will come up with a value like we described. However, the bank will only lend 80 percent of the new value of $2,162,000 and come up with a loan for approximately $1,730,000. We'll round it to $1.7 million dollars after closing costs.

$2,162,000 Park Value × 80% Loan Value
= $1.7 Million (After Closing Costs)

When you go to the loan closing, you will pay off the old loan of $650,000, sign for a new loan of $1.7 million, and receive a check for $1,050,000.

$1.7 Million (New Loan) – $650,000 (Original Loan)
= $1.05 Million Cash Out

You will be looking at a check for a million dollars! Think about what that will be like. You will not have to pay any taxes on this money because refinances are not taxable. You can do anything you want with it. A good strategy is to keep some for a rainy day (perhaps $100,000), spend some to reward yourself (perhaps another $100,000)—for those of you that believe in tithing or giving charity, you could give what is appropriate—and use the balance to buy another mobile home park or two that could be fixed up to give you even more income and wealth. When you get to this stage, you will enjoy being an investor even more because now you have a track record, and even better, you have cash to put down on the next park when you need it. Let's face it, having cash to put down is better than having no cash.

As I mentioned above, the reason we have not refinanced Happy Trails is that we did not need the additional capital. Let's assume that another large mobile home park that is close by presented itself and we needed the capital to buy it. If that happened we would also have a higher mortgage payment on Happy Trails after we refinanced. Let's assume we refinanced with a mortgage at 7.5 percent interest over thirty years.

In this case the monthly mortgage multiple is 7, so our new mortgage payment on Happy Trails would be:

$1,700,000 (1700 Thousands) × 7 = $11,900 per Month New Mortgage

Our old payment was $5,400 per month, so we would have:

$11,900 (New Mortgage) – $5,400 (Previous Payment)
= –$6,500 Cash Flow

In other words, we would be losing $6,500 per month in cash flow on Happy Trails after we refinance, increase the mortgage, and take the $1.05 million dollars in cash out. Our cash flow would then go down to:

$12,600 Cash Flow Before Refi – 6,500 Additional Mortgage Paid out
= $6,100 per Month

We need to get an increase of $6,500 per month or more on the next mobile home park we buy to keep our monthly cash flow from changing. Let's assume we found another park that costs $5 million and we purchased it with our $1 million Refi Bonanza money from Happy Trails. Let's assume the new park had a 10 percent cap rate and gives $500,000 a year in NOI.

NOI = Price × Cap Rate = $5 Million × 10% = $500,000 Year
= $500,000 Year ÷ 12 = $41,600 per Month

Let's assume we put down 20 percent, the $1 million from the refi, and borrowed the remaining $4 million at 7.5 percent for thirty years, with a 7 mortgage multiple. The mortgage payment and cash flow on the new park will be:

Mortgage Payment = Thousands Borrowed × Monthly Mortgage Multiple
= $4,000 ($4 Million) × 7 = $28,000 per Month

Cash Flow from New Park = NOI – Mortgage Payment
= $41,600 – $28,000 = $13,600 per Month

Cash Flow Increase = Cash Flow from New Park – Lowered Cash Flow on Happy Trails = $13,600 – $6,500 = $7,100 per Month

You see now that we add $13,600 in cash flow to our earnings by buying the new park and we sacrifice $6,500 in cash flow on Happy Trails to do it, but the net result is that we increase our cash flow by $7,100 per month, which is $85,000 in extra profits per year.

The Difference Between Turnkey and Turn-Around

Now, what kind of park was Happy Trails? Was it close by or long distance? Was it a turnkey or turn-around? The answer is Happy Trails was close by—it was only twenty minutes from my house, which made it easier to add twenty-four residents and do submetering and the other improvements, and therefore it was also a turn-around park.

It's important to realize that there is a difference between a close by turn-around park and a long distance turn-around park. Turning around a park takes additional time and effort. Someone has to buy all those mobile homes and RV park models, supervise their installation, and then sell them to new residents and do the paperwork. Someone has to supervise any improvements made to infrastructure. A park manager is typically not suited to do all this work. It must be done by you, the owner, or your partner, an entrepreneur, both of whom have an ownership position for motivation. Gersh was my partner and fellow entrepreneur, and I could not have turned around Happy Trails without the time he spent on-site overseeing the improvements.

SUMMARY

You should not be thinking how smart, or lucky, this writer is. That is not my intention and it serves no useful purpose. Instead, you should be thinking how you can take the powerful techniques I showed you—filling vacant lots, submetering, and maximizing additional rental income from nonmobile home property—and how you would apply them to mobile home parks that are available for you to buy.

You should also recognize that a turn-around park will give you fantastic profits and cash flow after you turn it around. If you are limited in the time you can spend improving a turn-around park into a turnkey park, then it is much easier to do this when the park is located close by. If you don't have a lot of time but are interested in buying a turn-around park located a long distance from you then you will need a partner who has an ownership in the park to do it for you.

Last, but not least, you should see how Keepers give you steady money for a long time, and how when you effect a major change in the NOI, a mobile home park can act also like a Flipper. This is when the increase in the NOI, and thus the value of the park, gives you a big tax-free payday through the Refi Bonanza.

HOMEWORK

Go back and visit all the mobile home parks you have looked at so far, but only the ones that were either openly for sale or the ones where the owners agreed to put it up for sale when you contacted them. Write down the price the seller wanted, the NOI, and the resulting cap rate. Now, I want you to see if you can apply the new techniques you learned: filling in vacant spaces with owner financed units, and turning utility costs over to the residents through submetering and the other methods described above. See what effect this has on the NOI of the park and the resulting price. Write down your ideas in your notebook.

Also, I now want you to classify the parks you see as either close by or long distance, and then as either turnkey or turn-around. If you are limited in time, I want you to think about how you will be able to buy turn-around parks.

Type 3's: continue to relax and don't buy anything yet. There is still more to learn and my promise still holds true. You might be ready within a month or less if you read carefully and absorb the important points. I realize a month is forever to a Type-3, but the wait will be worth it.

COMING ATTRACTIONS

In the next chapter you are going to get more actual case studies of mobile home parks we purchased and a little more advanced discussion. One of the parks we bought is giving us an even greater return than Happy Trails! Stay tuned.

3

Keepers Continued

"All beginnings are difficult."

That is a popular Israeli saying, and it is so true here. By the end of the first six months of owning Happy Trails Mobile Home Park, we weren't sure if we made the right decision investing in mobile home parks, and definitely weren't sure if we ever wanted to buy another mobile home park. Why? Because there was little or no cash flow up to that point. We were still climbing up the learning curve on mobile home parks one foot at a time. There was almost no educational material available on mobile home parks that we were aware of, not like you have now with this book.

After a year of owning Happy Trails, when half of the potential cash flow started to materialize, Gersh and I began to *consider* buying more parks. At the year and a half point, January 2003, the cash flow was pouring in on Happy Trails to the tune of $10,000 per month and rising. Any problems that surfaced were handled. We were gung ho on owning more mobile home parks, but we waited a little more just in case there were unforeseen problems. By the middle of 2003, we were ready to buy more. There were not many turn-around mobile home parks for sale at reasonable prices in our area, however. South Florida is a popular destination for mobile home park investors, and our real estate market was overheated and appreciating in record amounts each month. There were many long-distance parks for sale, but we did not feel comfortable about investing out of our area yet.

My family decided to sell off most of our duplex and triplex apartments and exchange the proceeds into mobile home parks when they became available after seeing how easy it was to manage a mobile home park with an on-site manager, and experiencing the wonderful cash flow. We had a lot of capital to invest at this time, and Gersh didn't, so we bought our next park, the Jefferson Mobile Home Park, without him.

As a side note, you may find that when you are partners with someone on a mobile home park, or any kind of investment for that matter, there is a tendency to feel that you must remain partners on *all* future investments. Bad feelings can result when you don't partner up, similar to straying outside a marriage. However, Crazy Gersh is a great human being and generous to a fault, which is why he is my best friend and I love him. He understood my family's need to invest capital and gave his blessing on the next mobile home property that we bought without him. (To this day, he even helps out when problems arise at the Jefferson, though he has no ownership position in the park. A few years later, Gersh had a similar family situation and needed to invest capital, so I sold two small parks to him from my flipping inventory: the Washington Street Mobile Home Park and the Meandering Lane Mobile Home Park. I gave his family a wholesale price that still resulted in a reasonable profit to my family, as you will see when we discuss the Washington Street and Meandering Lane mobile home parks in the next Chapter on flipping.)

Six months after I bought the Jefferson without Gersh, Gersh and I did a Refi Bonanza on our motel, the first property we purchased together. We took out several hundred thousand dollars in cash and used it to develop a large rental storage yard and to purchase two more mobile home parks, The Palm Frond and Las Casas. If you remember from our discussion in the previous chapter about what to do when you have a profit on your mobile home park, you will see that we did what I recommended—we took out our profits in a refinance and bought more turn-around mobile home parks close by.

In this chapter we will begin by discussing the Jefferson Mobile Home Park, the first park my family bought by ourselves and then Las Casas Mobile Home Park, the second park Gersh and I bought together. (We will discuss the Palm Frond Mobile Home Park in the chapter on due diligence and infrastructure.) Once again, you should concentrate on the techniques you will be learning to improve NOI (net operating income), which will increase your monthly cash flow and, as a result, raise the price (value) of the park. Please do not concentrate on how much money we made. It's far more important for you to take away techniques to improve *your* wealth and *your* life, and not a greater appreciation of my luck or skill (however you decide to look at it).

THE JEFFERSON MOBILE HOME PARK

This mobile home park was next door to a property we owned called the Northwood Center. The owner of the Jefferson Mobile Home Park had called me a few years earlier to see if we wanted to sell the Northwood Center to him. We briefly discussed some numbers but nothing came to fruition. On a hunch, I called the owner of the Jefferson back and asked if he was still interested in buying Northwood. He said no, that he had no need to buy the Northwood anymore since he was selling the Jefferson Mobile Home Park. He added that he just recently had a contract but it fell through. I asked him for the details on the property and this is what he told me:

1. NOI $175,000
2. 116 mobile home lots—only 96 occupied
3. Seven apartments that were vacant 75 percent of the time

Aerial views of Jefferson mobile home park.

4. 55 RV lots—only rented four months of the year
5. Lot rent $205 per month—rents not raised in five years
6. Ten-acre mobile home park and vacant two-acre tract next to it—total 500,000 square feet

This is how the conversation went after I received the above information:

"How much do you want for the Jefferson, Mr. Neighbor?" I asked.

"I want $2.2 million for the park," Mr. Neighbor answered. "The previous contract was for $2.2 million, and one week prior to the closing the buyer suddenly wanted a $100,000 discount. I told him to go spit in the wind. If you offer me anything less than $2.2 million, Zalman, I will tear up your offer and refuse to talk to you again."

I said, "I understand. Are you willing to do any financing?"

Mr. Neighbor said, "It has to be all cash. I have partners and we need to cash out and split up. We have no interest in doing financing of any kind. Forget about creative financing or no money down. $2.2 million in cash better hit the closing table or we have no deal. Do we understand one another?"

There is a chapter in this book on negotiating that you will enjoy and should be very useful to you on your path to greater wealth. I must humbly admit that some people consider me a seasoned negotiator. This is how this seasoned negotiator responded to the owner's aggressive posture:

I said, "OK, you got a deal." And that was that.

I faxed over a contract entitling me to sixty-day inspection period, and if I approved the inspections I had forty-five days to secure financing, putting down a minimum of 20 percent in cash. (Remember, I had the cash from the sales of our duplexes and triplexes.) And, oh yes, I offered full price, $2.2 million.

Why did I do that? The Jefferson was a 10 percent cap rate park, and the cap rate he was offering me was approximately:

NOI	÷	Sale Price	=	Cap Rate
$175,000	÷	$2.2 Million	=	8%

The price at the appropriate cap rate of 10 percent would have been:

NOI	÷	Cap Rate	=	Price
$175,000	÷	.10	=	$1.75 Million

In other words, on the surface *it looked like I was paying $450,000 too much for the Jefferson Mobile Home Park.* ($2.2 million vs. $1.75 million) Why would I do such a thing? I will tell you why, shortly, but let me give you some more disappointing numbers.

I was going to put down $500,000 and borrow $1.7 million at 5.5 percent, amortized over twenty years, with a seven-year balloon. (Yes, I was scared. It was the most money I ever borrowed and the most money I ever put down. But the South Florida market was boiling hot, and we had profits to invest from the sale of our duplexes and triplexes.) Here is what the mortgage payment, cash flow, and cash-on-cash return (the ratio of annual before-tax cash flow to the total amount of cash invested) were going to be. We will be rounding the numbers to make it easier. (Remember that you need a mortgage calculator to figure out monthly mortgage multiples.)

Mortgage = $1.7 Million at 5.5% for 20 Years
= Monthly Mortgage Multiple of 7

1700 (Number of Thousands Borrowed) × 7 (Multiple)
= $12,000 per Month × 12 = $144,000 per Year

Cash Flow	=	NOI	–	Mtg Payments for Year
$31,000 Year	=	$175,000	–	$144,000

Cash-on-Cash Return	=	Cash Flow per Year	÷	Down Payment
6.2%	=	$31,000	÷	$500,000

Okay, why was I willingly making such a poor investment? It was overpriced, had a lousy cash flow, and a poor cash-on-cash return. A good cash-on-cash return will be greater than the cap rate you are buying the park at, in this case more than 8 percent. We put down $500,000, and only received $31,000 in yearly cash flow, or $2,500 per month, which was half of my half on Happy Trails—and we bought Happy Trails for no money down. The reason we were willing to overpay was because there were many ways of increasing the NOI of the Jefferson to yield far more than an 8 percent cap rate, as I will explain.

The reason the cash flow and cash-on-cash return were poor is because the mortgage was paying itself down quickly, and the amount of the principal paydown does not show up in our numbers. The pay-down was $48,000 the first year alone, and then increased from there. This paydown was on mortgage principal, since it was not received as cash to me and did not go into the cash flow calculation or the cash-on-cash return. Some people include this figure in their calculations, and if we did, then the following would result:

Cash Flow	=	NOI	–	Mtg Payments	+	Mtg Paydown
$80,000 (Rounded)	=	$175,000	–	$144,000	+	$48,000

Cash-on-Cash Return	=	Yearly Cash Flow Payment	÷	Down Payment
16%	=	$80,000	÷	$500,000

Now, a 16 percent cash-on-cash return is more like it. It is a real return because the mortgage has been paid down with $48,000 real dollars. However, we are going to continue to eliminate the yearly mortgage paydown in our future calculations because I want the cash flow and cash-on-cash return to be as conservative as possible, considering only the dollars that are really in your hand, and able to be spent, at the end of the year.

The following was my step by step plan and the actual results:

Step 1: Filling in Vacancies on Mobile Home Lots

This picture is a street scene at the Jefferson Mobile Home Park. There were 116 total mobile home lots in the park but only 96 were occupied and paying lot rent, leaving 20 vacant mobile home lots. We purchased twenty used mobile homes from a park that was closing down, moved them to the vacant lots, and set them up. We had an investor who paid the $5,000 cost for each mobile home and then sold them for $10,000

Street scene at Jefferson mobile home park.

and gave owner financing with easy terms to each purchaser. We could get higher prices for these units then we were getting at Happy Trails because the Jefferson had bigger lots and bigger mobile homes. We completed this within the first year and the mobile homes sold quickly.

The effect on the bottom line was dramatic because all the mobile home residents paid their own utilities at the Jefferson. It was already submetered for electric, water, and sewer, and after a while we also charged the trash cost to the residents. Therefore, there was no additional cost involved in filling these lots, and we calculated that $200 of the $205 lot rent went right into profit and NOI. This was the effect on the NOI:

20 Lots × $200 per Month Additional Lot Rent × 12 Months = $48,000

We added $48,000 to the NOI per year. Since we started with $175,000, what was the effect on cap rate and cash flow?

New NOI	**=**	**Starting NOI**	**+**	**Increase in NOI from Filled Lots**
$223,000	**=**	**$175,000**	**+**	**$48,000**

Cap Rate	**=**	**NOI**	**÷**	**Price**
10% (Rounded)	**=**	**$223,000**	**÷**	**$2.2 Million**

In terms of cash flow and cap rate, we increased the cash in our hands by $48,000, which was the same as the principal paydown of $48,000. If we go back to the previous discussion about calculating the cash-on-cash return conservatively, without adding in the principal paydown, we can substitute the NOI increase that resulted from filling in the vacant lots for the mortgage paydown and achieve the same cash flow of $80,000, a 16 percent cash-on-cash return.

What happened here? We essentially forced the cap rate to where it should have been in the first place, 10 percent, and saw a corresponding increase in NOI and cash flow. But if this was the only strategy I had to increase the performance of the Jefferson, then it still would have been a poor investment. Why?

It takes time and energy—which means work—to move in twenty additional mobile homes. Someone has to find them, inspect them, oversee moving them in and setting them up, sell them to a new resident, and arrange for financing. Someone has to do all the paperwork with each new resident. It doesn't make sense to perform all that work just to get a park to a 10 percent cap rate. We could have bought a park somewhere else that already had a 10 percent cap rate, a turnkey that needed no extra expenditure of time and energy.

However, there were more strategies available to improve the figures at the Jefferson.

Step 2: Filling in Vacancies on the Seven Apartments

This is another example of a mobile home park that had rental units in addition to mobile homes. The Jefferson also had two buildings, with four efficiencies in one and three in the other. Some apartments were very small, containing only one room and a bathroom. The kitchen, bedroom, and living room were all part of the one room. A few of the apartments had two rooms: a kitchen and living room in one room and a separate bedroom.

Efficiencies at Jefferson mobile home park.

The reason these apartments were vacant 75 percent of the time is that the previous owner didn't care about the Jefferson. He didn't want to do anything to improve it, and didn't want to spend one dollar more than he had to. He said he had problems with his partners, and surmising from that, he probably didn't want them to get a "free ride" from any increased effort on his part. He told the manager not to spend any money on advertising or repairs and to try to rent out the apartments in their deplorable condition. As a result the manager had to wait for people to stop in and ask about renting an apartment. She then had to do the best she could when the tenants complained about the lack of repairs. Because of this the manager could not hold onto tenants and they left after a short while, usually owing rent.

This was an easy renovation for us. We were used to apartments and the apartment rental business. We spent $2,000 per apartment, or $14,000 for all seven, fixing them up. We took the money for repairs from the park's cash flow profits. The apartments rented quickly as soon as they were painted and repaired, after we placed a small ad in the classifieds. We advertised $400 per month for the one-room apartments and $500 per month for the two-room apartments, including all utilities. Each building had only one water and electric meter, and based upon the bills, we netted approximately $300 per month on each apartment. The effect on the NOI was:

7 Apartments × $300 per Month Net × 12 Months = $25,200
75% of $25,200 Increase = $18,900, or $19,000 (Rounded)

Since the apartments previously were rented 25 percent of the time, we increased the income by 75 percent of the total yearly rental amount, or $19,000 per year. This meant that within seven months we were paid back the $14,000 it took to renovate the apartments and get long-term tenants. After that, we were money ahead forever. This now made the Jefferson worth slightly more than the 10 percent cap rate we achieved with the previous technique of adding mobile homes to vacant lots, and was our first glimpse of a "profit" over a normal purchase of a 10 percent cap rate park.

Step 3: Filling in Vacancies on Fifty-five RV Lots

The fifty-five RV lots at the Jefferson were rented three to five months of the year, during "tourist season"—December, January, February, March, and sometimes April. I took the most conservative approach and used four months as my estimation because the previous records for the RV rentals were not easy to understand and it was difficult to separate the RV rentals from the total collected rents.

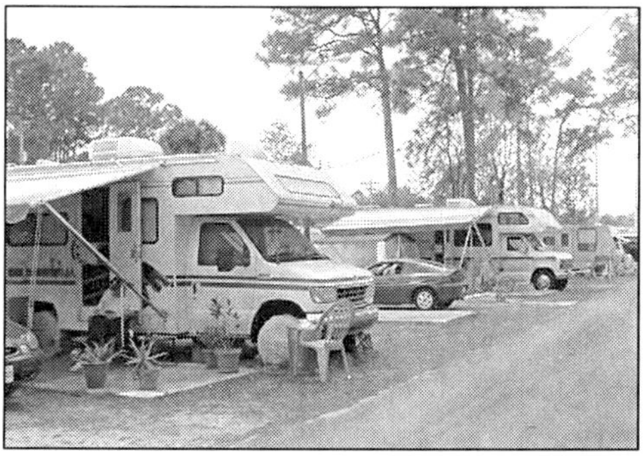

RVs at Jefferson mobile home park.

My strategy was to move in good used RV park models, sell them with owner financing at easy terms (which we secured from the same outside investor), and then turn the RV lots into year-round rentals, instead of renting them for only four months of the year.

Perhaps you are wondering what an RV park model is? RVs, or recreational vehicles, used to be only separated into two types: the pull-along variety that is hitched behind a car or pickup truck to be towed around the country, and the motor coach, which has its own engine and the living quarters are behind the driver's seat. The problem is that both types used to be eight feet wide, and people complained that the walls and the ceilings started to feel like they were closing in on them after they lived inside them for a few weeks or months. Manufacturers realized there was a market for a wider RV with higher ceilings that could be towed to an RV lot and just left there so someone could live in it year round, like a home. They called them "park models" because they were meant to be left in the park.

The park models looked like small thirty-five foot-long mobile homes. They were built to the same standard as a tow-behind RV or a motor coach, so zoning departments could not complain they were not RVs and not allow them on an RV lot. However, the manufacturers listened to their customers and made them twelve to fourteen feet wide, so they feel more spacious on the inside than older RVs. At first they were built with "tip outs", which are three- to four-foot-wide pop-out extensions for the living room and bedroom. (Manufacturers put the same extensions in motor coaches a few years later so their sides could be extended through a cranking system when they were parked.) Later park models were built to be twelve to fourteen feet wide so tip outs were not needed.

We discovered we could buy good used RV park models and install them semipermanently on an RV lot for a cost of $1,000 to $2,500 each, and then sell them for $3,000 to $5,000, with owner financing and the same easy terms as our mobile homes, which provided excellent returns to the investor. We did not need permits as long as we did not add porches.

We were not sure of the success of this strategy because we weren't sure if there were enough people in our area who would live in an RV park model year round. Our results were excellent the first year, with almost half of the RV lots filled. We were within a year of completing this strategy when the county undertook a massive construction project on the road in front of the Jefferson, widening it and adding two more lanes. The project was supposed to take one year, but because of delays it stretched to two-and-a-half years. That's when we learned that whenever there is long-term construction on the road in front of a commercial enterprise that depends on drive-by traffic and retail customers (and a mobile home park is a commercial enterprise) the businesses on that road typically can't survive and go under. People find a different resource for their needs that is less of a hassle. Remember this if you ever buy any enterprise on a major road. The rule is: *customers will take the path of least resistance when they want to purchase something, so you have to make it easy for them to come to you to buy.*

Our customers for the RV park models took the path of least resistance as soon as the road project began, and went somewhere else. The sales of RV park models slowed down dramatically. As of this writing, we were able to convert thirty of the fifty-five RV lots to year-round residents. This added eight months of rent to the previous four months. The following is the result to the NOI:

30 Year-Round RV Lots × $200 per Month × 8 Months = $48,000

This was still one of the most important strategies, and while it hasn't been 100 percent successful yet, it was successful enough to add $48,000 to our cash flow, a very welcome addition.

Step 4: Raising the Rents

In the twenty-seven years I have been investing in real estate, I can only remember a few times when a broker or a seller did *not* say, "The rents are low and can be raised." Sellers and real estate sales people know that raising rents is an important benefit to investors so they almost always state it. Let me also state that it was rare that the rents on the properties I was looking at weren't already at market rates, and I would have to wait for either inflation or supply and demand to catch up before I could increase rents.

Such was *not* the case at the Jefferson. The lot rents were indeed very low at $205 per month. We purchased the Jefferson after we had owned Happy Trails for three years, and we had raised the rents there to $295 per month with the residents paying for all utilities. The Jefferson was only a mile and a half from Happy Trails, and it was a superior mobile home park with bigger lots and less traffic noise, so there was no reason the rents at the Jefferson could not be equal to those at Happy Trails, or even a little higher.

In my opinion, raising rents at a mobile home park should be done gradually and smoothly, taking into account human nature. The lot rent at the Jefferson could have been raised $90, from $205 to $295 per month, and still have been competitive. However, it would anger the residents to do that in one jump, and possibly could have resulted in a rent strike and legal battles. I wanted to do it over three years, averaging $30 per year, to bring it into line with other mobile home park lot rents in our area.

There was a problem, however, unique to Florida. There is a law in Florida that establishes an anniversary date for every land-lease mobile home park, and lot rents can only be raised on that date each year. The date for the Jefferson was November 1st. As part of that same law the owner of the park must give all the residents written notice of the lot rent increase ninety days before the anniversary date. In the case of the Jefferson, that meant on or before August 1st every year we would have to give all the residents written notice we were raising the rent on November 1st.

The problem was we bought the Jefferson on August 1st, so the only way we could raise the rents that year would be by immediately sending a notice to all the residents the first day we owned the park. It would be too late on August 2nd. Think about what kind of message that would have sent the residents. First, they get a new owner for the park, which shakes them up because they don't know what kind of owners we'll be. Then the first thing the new owners do is raise the lot rent. Not exactly an endearing start.

When I teach my classes, I pause here and ask, "How many people would raise the rent anyway as the first act of buying the Jefferson?" Usually only 20 percent of the students agree that raising the rent would be a smart move. Then I write down for them what it meant to us in terms of money. We had 146 mobile home and RV park model residents paying lot rent at the Jefferson, so delaying a $30 increase the first year meant:

149 Lots × $30 per Lot × 12 Months = $52,000 per Year (Rounded)

By delaying the first lot rent increase until we owned the Jefferson for one year, we were losing $52,000 in lot rent, and this was money we would never see again. Now that I have framed the question in dollars and cents, I take a recount on the vote from the class. Usually almost 80 percent—four times as many—think I should have raised the lot rent as my first act of being the new owner.

Well, we didn't do that.

We kept the lot rent the same for the first year, taking a long view regarding management of the park. The next year we raised it $40, to $245 per month. The year after that we raised it $30, to $275 per month, and then $295 per month after the third year. The following is the effect the rent increases had on our NOI

146 Units × $90 per Lot Increase = $13,140 per Month
$13,140 × 12 Months = $158,000 per Year Increase in NOI (Rounded)

That is a big number. When you study that number, you should realize that at a 10 percent cap rate, the price of the park just went up 10 times that increase in NOI, or $1.6 million. That's right, 1.6 million dollars, more than we made on the Happy Trails.

How to Raise Lot rents

Here is my recommendation on how to handle raising rents. It is what we did before every lot rent increase in every park we have owned:

1. *Send a letter explaining to every resident when and how much the lot rent will increase, as is mandated by law.* Florida law requires that we send around a letter ninety days before the date of the increase detailing how much and when the lot rent will increase. Find out what it is for your state and local area.

2. *Include a second letter listing other parks that have a higher lot rent, showing their rates.* In the worst case show other parks with equal lot rents. We do not include any parks with rents that are lower.

3. *Explain in the second letter how the lot rent increase is needed to maintain the park in a professional manner.* Mention that you don't want anyone to leave, but if they want to they have the right to do so. You can also add, as we do, that you might be interested in buying their mobile home if they want to sell.

4. *Have a meeting to discuss the increase at 7:00 P.M. for one hour, on a weekday.* Again we list the neighboring parks that are charging more for lot

rent and that we will understand if anyone wants to leave, and we might even be interested in buying their mobile home if they insist on leaving. We make these meetings last no more than one hour. We have our manager there and we take questions and complaints, and even ask for suggestions about what types of reasonable improvements the residents want. If there was a previous meeting, we list all the improvements we made since the last meeting. It is important to cut the meeting off at one hour, because when no time limits are given they can easily turn into long "gripe sessions" instead of productive meetings.

5. *Do some inexpensive and easily visible improvements to the park.* A few weeks before the meeting, we plant flowers at the entrances and exits to the park, plant bushes, clean up common areas, paint the clubhouse, etc. to enhance the overall appearance of the park and to give the impression that the lot rent increase will go for improvements in the park rather than into our own pockets to enhance our own lifestyle.

I believe the letter and the meeting are both important. The letter gives the residents a reason for the increase and fills them in on what the competition is charging (only if it is more, or the same). The meeting is important because the residents get to meet you face to face, as a human being, not some absent, resented authority figure.

Collecting For Trash and Meter Reading

After the second year of owning the Jefferson, we started to collect $9.95 per month from every resident for trash, and $4.95 each month to read the water maters. These charges were generally accepted, but a few people resented the trash charge. First, they said they would carry their trash to the dumpster themselves. We explained we were not charging for labor, but for the trash itself. They then insisted that they would throw their trash out elsewhere, and refused to pay. We explained, nicely, that we would dislike evicting them from the park just for $9.95 per month, but we would do it if we had to. After a few more months everyone was on board. Our profit from this was:

146 Units ×	**$9.95 Trash**	**× 12 Months**	**=**	**$17,500 per Year (Rounded)**
146 Units ×	**$4.95 Meter Reading**	**× 12 Months**	**=**	**$ 8,500 per Year (Rounded)**

Now you can see why we paid too much for the Jefferson in the beginning. We believed it would be an impressive investment when it was turned around. Specifically, it developed into a 20 percent cap rate, gave off more than $25,000 per month in cash flow, and was worth $2.5 million more than when we bought it. We are earning 66 percent on the money we invested in it, our original $500,000 down payment. Those are pretty impressive returns, don't you think?

What about the downside and risk? What if we were wrong, and every technique failed to yield results? Then we would have only earned an 8 percent cap rate on the Jefferson, which was okay. Keep in mind that there was 500,000 square feet of land in the Jefferson, located on a major arterial road that was worth six dollars per square foot, or three

Summary of the Jefferson Mobile Home Park

Action	NOI Increase
Add 20 Mobile Homes	+ $48,000 per Year
Renovate Apartments	+ $19,000 per Year
Add 30 RV Park Models	+ $48,000 per Year
Raise Rents $90 per Month	+ $158,000 per Year
Trash Fee	+ $17,500 per Year
Read Water Meters	+ $8,500 per Year
Total Increase	**$300,000 per Year (Rounded)**
Original NOI	**= $175,000**
NOI After Increases = $175,000 + $300,000	**= $475,000**
Price Paid	**= $2.2 Million**
Value at New NOI	**= $4.75 Million**
Increase in Value = $4.7 – 2.2	**= $2.5 Million**
Down Payment	**= $500,000**
Cash Flow = $31,000 + $300,000 Increase	**= $331,000**

Cap Rate at New NOI = 475 (Thousands) ÷ $2.2 Million = 21.5%

Cash-on-Cash Return = 331 (Thousands) ÷ $500 = 66%

million dollars just for the land. This was $800,000 more than the price we paid for it. So, again, please don't look at the Jefferson as a testament to our luck or talent, but as an example that you can copy in your area with similar turn-around mobile home parks.

ANOTHER KEEPER EXAMPLE: LAS CASAS MOBILE HOME PARK—PARK-OWNED OR LAND-LEASE?

This park came to us from Bill, one of my assistants at the seminar company. It was close by and a turn-around park. I told Bill that I would give him an assignment fee of $2,000 and take over his contract if he could not complete his purchase for some reason. Well, it turned out Bill could not raise the capital to buy the park, so he offered the deal to me.

The park contained two acres of land and was zoned for sixteen mobile homes, which it used to contain. The previous owner threw nine mobile homes away because he didn't want to renovate them and he didn't like being a landlord. When we contracted to buy the property, it had only seven mobile homes left: four that were salvageable and occupied but in poor condition, and three that were vacant and too far gone to fix. It was located on the corner of two arterial roads in an up-and-coming area of South Florida. Across the street was a commercial node. One day this property would find its highest and best use as a commercial site, and that was what interested me.

When a property goes from a residential use to a commercial use, the land is evaluated on a per square foot basis instead of a per acre or per mobile home lot basis. In order to appreciate what that means to your wealth creation, *you need to know that there are 43,560 square feet in an acre.* Please highlight that number and try to commit it to memory, because it will serve you well someday in the future. Since we were buying two acres, the total square feet of land was:

2 Acres × 43,560 Square Feet per Acre = 87,120 Square Feet

In our area, it is not unusual for a commercial corner to go for $10 to $20 per square foot. This is what it would be worth at both extremes:

87,120 Square Feet × $10 per Square Foot = $871,200
87,120 Square Feet × $20 per Square Foot = $1,742,400

When that would happen is anyone's guess, but we like owning mobile home parks that have an excellent upside potential for the land, but still give a great cash flow while we are waiting for the appreciation. (Happy Trails contains 4.6 acres of land, a little more than 200,000 square feet, and is located on a corner of two heavily traveled arterial roads.)

LAS CASAS MOBILE HOME PARK	
Price	$300,000
Gross Rents (4 Units at $500 Month Each)	$24,000
Expenses	
Real Estate Taxes	$6,000
Insurance	$2,000
Repairs, Maintenance, Vacancy ($50 per Month x 4)	$2,400
Manager ($200 per Month)	$2,400
Total Expenses	**$12,800**
NOI (Current)	$11,200
Cap Rate (Current)	3.7%
Down Payment	$60,000
Terms of Mortgage Loan	$240,000, 6.5%, 25 Yrs, $1,600 Month
Mobile Homes Rented	4
Mobile Homes to Throw Away	3
Total Usable Lots	16
Current Rents	$500 per Month for Mobile + Lot
Utilities	County Water and Sewer—Tenant Paid
Trash Pickup	Private Company—Tenant Paid

The NOI and the cap rate for the current state of Las Casas were terrible. There were only four mobile homes earning rents and they needed renovation. It even had a negative cash flow:

Cash Flow = NOI − Mortgage Payments
= $11,200 − $19,200 = −$8,000

What was important was how much money it would take to turn-around the park, and what the return on our investment would be when we were finished. Since we were dealing with a park that was 75 percent vacant (twelve of the sixteen lots were empty), we had two options:

Option A: Create a small, sixteen-lot, land-lease community

Option B: Have sixteen park-owned units generating monthly or weekly rents

No matter which option we picked, we needed to put a fence around the park and upgrade the electric and plumbing services for the nine vacant lots. We would also have to rehab the four units that were occupied but in poor condition. After those improvements, we would have to throw out the three mobile homes that were not worth fixing. If you look at the table below, you will see that all these costs added up to $24,000. The final step was to bring in twelve used mobile homes and set them up, and then either rent all the homes out as park-owned units or let an investor take them over and offer owner financing on them as BBs.

IMPROVEMENTS NEEDED WITH EITHER OPTION	
9 New Electrical Hook-ups	$9,000
9 New Plumbing Hook-ups	$3,000
Fence around Perimeter	$9,000
Dispose of 3 Unusable Mobile Homes	$3,000
Total	**$24,000**

Las Casas mobile home park.

IMPROVEMENTS NEEDED WITH OPTION B: PARK-OWNED UNITS	
Buy 12 Used Mobile Homes ($5,000 Each)	$60,000
Renovate 4 Free Mobile Homes ($5,000 Each)	$20,000
Total	**$80,000**
Cash Needed	
Option A: Renovation Cash + Down Payment = $24,000 + $60,000 = $84,000	
Option B: Renovation Cash + Down Payment = $104,000 ($24,000 + $80,000) + $60,000 = $164,000	

Option A: Turn the Park into a Land-Lease Community

If we chose this option, when we were done there would be sixteen residents who owned their own mobile homes and were paying a monthly mortgage payment of $195 per month to an investor. They would also pay us lot rent, and utility and trash costs, which were just pass-through fees. Assuming the lot rent was $300 per lot, (the same as Happy Trails at that point in time) this is the way Las Casas looked as a land-lease community:

LAS CASAS MOBILE HOME PARK AS LAND-LEASE	
Price (Cost + Improvements)	$300,000 + $24,000 = $324,000
Gross Rents (16 Lots at $300 per Month Each)	$57,000 (Rounded)
Expenses:	
Real Estate Taxes	$6,000
Insurance	$2,000
Repairs, Maintenance, Vacancy (10% Gross Rent)	$5,760
Total Management (10% Gross Rent)	$5,760
Land-Lease 40% Expense Factor	$3,530
Total Expenses	**$23,000 (Rounded)**

NOI = Gross Rents − Expenses = $57,000 − $23,000 = $34,000
Cap Rate = NOI ÷ Price = 34,000 ÷ 324,000 = 10.5%

Cash Flow = NOI – Yearly Mortgage Payment
= $34,000 – $19,000 = $15,000

Cash-on-Cash Return = Cash Flow ÷ Cash Put In
= $15,000 ÷ $84,000 = 18%

To get to our results, we assumed that the management expenses would be 10 percent of the gross rents, and the repairs, maintenance, and vacancy would be 10 percent. Then we added in a factor we called the 40 percent land-lease expense factor, which I will explain when we discuss the second option. (Suffice it say for the moment that this factor made the calculations conservative and realistic.) When we did this, the NOI was calculated by taking the gross rents, $57,000, and subtracting the total yearly expenses (without mortgage payments) of $23,000, to come up with $34,000. It is useful to see that at a 10 percent cap rate, Las Casas would then be worth $340,000, which was $16,000 more than our original cost plus fix up of $324,000. This was not a generous profit, but it was sufficient for our means. (All the calculations are *pro forma,* an important term that you will see a lot of when you invest in parks. Pro forma means "in the future if everything goes according to plans.)

Also, we can calculate the cash flow that should go into our pockets every year by taking the NOI, $34,000, and subtracting the mortgage payments of $1,635 per month for twelve months, or $19,000, to come up with a positive cash flow of $15,000 per year.

The cash-on-cash return, a healthy 18 percent, was figured by taking the $15,000 cash flow coming out of the park at the end of each year and dividing it into the cash put up in the beginning, which is the down payment of $60,000 plus the necessary park renovations of $24,000. This cash-on-cash return was more than three times what we would have earned if we put the money in a savings account at 5 percent. Of course, we would have to work a little harder to get this higher return, but it would be worth it. Why? Because down the road we have a second payday waiting, called the highest and best use of the land. When the land at Las Casas becomes a viable commercial site, it should be worth a minimum of $10 per square foot, or $871,200. At that point we would help the residents move their mobile homes to another of our parks and then sell off the land. Our profit would be more than half a million dollars:

Profit = Price at $10 per Foot − Cost = $871,200 − $324,000 = $547,000

Option B: Turn Las Casas into All Park-Owned Units

We haven't discussed the management differences between investing in land-lease communities where residents own the mobile homes and lease the land under it, versus having all park-owned units where you own the homes and have tenants who lease both the mobile home and the lot and you maintain and repair the mobile homes. As you will see from the numbers, having all park-owned units was a cash intensive option, but we had the cash.

LAS CASAS MOBILE HOME PARK AS ALL PARK OWNED	
Price (Cost + Renovation Expenses)	$300,000 + $104,000 = $404,000
Cash Outlay = Down Payment + Renovation Expenses	$164,000
Gross Rents (16 Lots at $150 Week Each)	$124,000
Expenses:	
Real Estate Taxes	$6,000
Insurance	$6,000
Repairs, Maintenance, Vacancy (10% Gross Rent)	$12,480
Total Management (10% Gross Rent)	$12,480
Park Owned 50% Expense Factor	$25,440
Total Expenses	**$62,000 (Rounded)**

NOI = Gross Rents − Expenses = $124,000 − $62,000 = $62,000

Cap Rate = NOI ÷ Price = $62,000 ÷ $404,000 = 15%

Cash Flow = NOI − Yearly Mortgage Payment
= $62,000 − $19,000 = $43,000

Cash-on-Cash Return = Cash Flow ÷ Cash Put In
= $43,000 ÷ $164,000 = 26%

Once again, we used a factor—this time the park-owned 50 percent expense factor—to make the calculations conservative and realistic. As you can see from the numbers, we received a lot more cash flow by turning the park into all park-owned rentals, $43,000 versus $15,000. In order to do this, we had to outlay a lot more capital: $164,000 versus $84,000 for the land-lease community. The cash-on-cash return for this option was a whopping 26 percent! Yes, we would have additional management time maintaining and repairing the mobile homes because we had tenants instead of residents, but we had the manpower to do it and do it efficiently, because the park was close by. So we proceeded with the second option. We would not have chosen this option if we had been limited on cash. Also, we probably would not have bought Las Casas in the first place if this was a long-distance park. There was too much work to do, and it was not worth it without a partner who was on-site to take care of it.

Our overall game plan on Las Casas was to invest a windfall of cash we received on a refinance, get a great return on it—26 percent—while we waited for the land under the mobile home park to appreciate in value to $870,000. How long could we wait? If you were earning 26 percent each year on an investment, how long could you wait for your original cash outlay to double? Our answer was forever. And what if we were wrong, and the land never would have a commercial use? Our answer to that question was, "So what." A 26 percent cash-on-cash return is a great return.

The 40 Percent and 50 Percent Expense Factors

As noted above, we added an additional expense in the calculations for both options for Las Casas. It is extremely important for you to remember these expense factors as rules of thumb. They will become very useful to you in the future when you receive the initial information on a possible mobile home park investment. The chart on page 117 shows how these expenses are broken down for land-lease communities.

The rules of thumb are:

1. On land-lease communities of eighty units or less, the rule of thumb is the expenses are usually 40 percent of the gross collected rents.

2. On park-owned communities of eighty units or less, the rule of thumb is the expenses are usually 50 percent of the gross collected rents.

Are both of those hard-and-fast rules carved forever i
They are merely the averages determined after researching
home parks and coming up with accepted standards in our industry. Will there be mobile home parks with greater or lesser expenses? Of course. But both of these rules of thumb are excellent places to start when testing the truthfulness of the NOI you are given on a mobile home park.

For instance, if you are looking at a mobile home park that is a land-lease community and the seller or the Realtor listing it states, "The gross

MOBILE HOME PARK EXPENSES TABLE

Categories	% Gross Revenues*
Administrative Expenses	
Management Fee	5.0
Wages	4.5
Administrative Costs	2.5
Telephone	0.5
Advertising	0.5
Operating Expenses	
Supplies	0.5
Heating	0.5
Electric	1.0
Water/Sewer	9.0
Maintenance Expenses	
Repairs	5.0
Wages	3.0
Taxes & Insurance	
RE Taxes	6.5
Other Taxes, Licenses	0.5
Property Insurance	1.0
Total Annual Expenses	**40.0**

*Percentages based on a model by Lawrence Allen, MAI, author of *How to Find, Buy, Manage, and Sell a Manufactured Home Community.*

rents are $100,000 and the total expenses are $10,000, so the NOI is $90,000." When the Realtor or seller states the expenses are $10,000, he is claiming the expenses are:

$10,000 Expenses ÷ $100,000 Total Rents = 10%

Since the average expense ratio is 40 percent, you would expect expenses of four times what was given:

$100,000 Gross Rents × 40% Normal Expense Factor = $40,000

And thus there is a good chance some expenses have been left out. For communities that are park-owned, there are repairs and maintenance, so an additional 10 percent is factored in. Keep in mind, the rents in a park-owned community will likely be twice or more what the lot rent is, so the 50 percent you are taking for expenses is based on a much large number than would result if the community were run as land-lease.

Why the Cash-on-Cash Return Is Much More than the Cap Rate

You might have noticed that the pro forma cap rates on the land-lease and park-owned options, 10.5 percent and 15 percent, were lower than the cash–on-cash returns of 18 percent and 26 percent. Why is that? It's because of the leverage of using borrowed money at relatively low rates, in this case, 6.5 percent. Furthermore, the greater the difference between the cap rate of the park and the rate at which you borrow, the bigger your cash-on-cash return will be.

Conversely, if your cap rate and your mortgage interest are the same, there will be little or no cash flow unless you put down a large down payment. In the extreme case, when your cap rate is lower than your borrowing rate, you will have a negative cash flow and will have to take money out of your savings to hold onto the park (unless you put down a large down payment.)

Let's demonstrate this. Let's assume you are looking at a park that costs $500,000, and you are going to buy it for no money down and borrow the whole $500,000. The park has the average cap rate of most parks, 10 percent, and you are borrowing at 10 percent in an interest-only mortgage. What will your cash flow be? First, you can calculate the NOI:

Price of Park	×	Cap Rate	=	NOI
$500,000	×	10%	=	$50,000

Then you calculate your interest only yearly mortgage payment, as:

Amount Borrowed	×	Interest Rate on Mortgage	=	Interest Paid Out
$500,000	×	10%	=	$50,000

NOI	–	Mortgage Payments	=	Cash Flow
$50,000	–	$50,000 Mortgage Interest	=	$0

So, when the cap rate and mortgage interest rate are the same, there is no cash flow when you borrow all the money to buy the park. What if the mortgage rate, say 8 percent, is lower than the cap rate, say 10 percent? Well, the NOI and cap rate are the same, but the mortgage payments are lower.

Amount Borrowed	×	Interest Rate on Mortgage	=	Interest Paid Out
$500,000	×	8%	=	$40,000

NOI	–	Mortgage Payments	=	Cash Flow
$50,000	–	$40,000	=	$10,000

Now there is a positive cash flow of $10,000 per year. What if the interest rate is 12 percent on the mortgage?

Amount Borrowed	×	Interest Rate on Mortgage	=	Interest Paid Out
$500,000	×	12%	=	$60,000

NOI	–	Mortgage Payments	=	Cash Flow
$50,000	–	$60,000	=	(–$10,000)

Now there is negative cash flow of $10,000, which means you will have to take money from your savings until you get the cap rate of the park up to the same rate, or greater, than your mortgage interest rate.

What can we summarize from this discussion? *Try to buy parks with as high as a spread as possible between the cap rate of the park and your borrowing rate on the mortgage. 1.5 to 2 percent should be the minimum difference between the cap rate on the park and your borrowing rate for a turnkey park.* If you are buying a turn-around park, it would be best to buy on this spread also, but on a serious turn-around you may not be able to. In that case you will have zero or even negative cash flow in the beginning when the initial cap rate is less than your borrowing rate. The spread between the two should become better as you improve the NOI, and thus the cap rate, of the park, but in the meantime, plan for cash going out from savings when you estimate your cash needs in that situation.

SUMMARY

With the Jefferson, you learned two powerful techniques for increasing cash flow in a land-lease community: raising the rents and turning RV lots into year-round rentals with RV park models. You also saw a reapplication of three of the powerful techniques you learned in the previous chapter: filling in vacant lots with mobile homes, renovating other rental property for maximum rents, and passing along trash bills and meter-reading costs.

Of these, the three most powerful techniques are filling in vacant lots, raising lot rents, and moving in RV park models, but in order to use them you must buy a park with vacant lots and low lot rents to begin with. Again, I would not have attempted to buy a park like the Jefferson if it was long-distance from where I lived unless I had a partner living locally, who could do all the work involved in turning the park around and increasing the cash flow.

With Las Casas, you learned the difference between a park that is land-lease versus one with all park-owned units. Remember that buying a park with all park-owned units usually will give you more cash flow and a greater return on your money. In the beginning of your investment career, you will probably make the choice to buy small mobile home parks with all park-owned units for just that reason—greater cash flow, but you will pay for that greater cash flow with greater management intensity.

HOMEWORK

Go back and visit all the mobile home parks you have looked at so far, but only the ones that were either openly for sale or where the owners agreed to put it up for sale to you. Also, see if you can find some new mobile home parks for sale. (If you are having difficulty finding parks for sale, then it would be all right to skip ahead to Chapter 7 and discover other places to find more parks for sale, and then return here.) Write down the price the seller wants, the NOI, and the resulting cap rate. Now, I want you to see if you can apply the two new techniques you learned: raising lot rents and converting RV lots into year-round lots with RV park models. You are going to have to compare the parks for sale with parks around them in terms of lot rent, amenities offered, and location to figure out if you can raise lot rents, and by how much. These will be your comparable rents and they are very important.

I also want you to go visit mobile home dealers and look at RV park models to familiarize yourself with them. When you are at the mobile home dealer, ask for the names of mobile home movers and installers. Contact them and ask how much it costs to move a mobile home from one place to another and set it up. Also find out about buying good used mobile homes.

COMING ATTRACTIONS

Your meat-and-potatoes as an investor is building your own ATM, and that involves mobile home park Keepers. Now you have the knowledge on how to do that. Coming up are Flippers, the dessert on your table of mobile home investing. Flippers provide quick cash, and everyone loves that, too. The next chapter will show you how to get it.

4

Flippers: Fast Cash

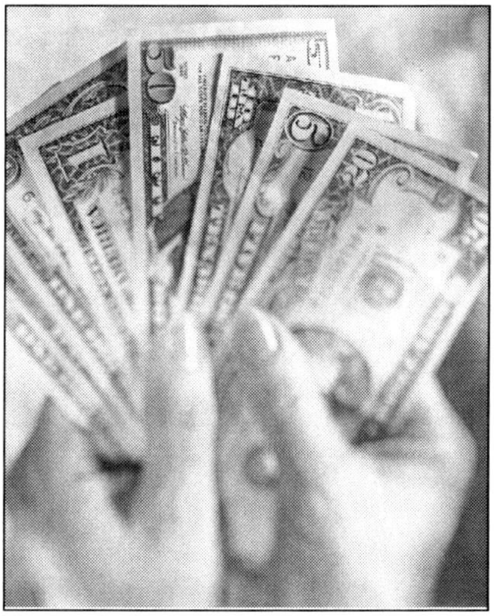

In this chapter you are going to learn the second of the Four Basic Profit Strategies: flipping, or if you would like to call it by a fancy name, "quick turning." The strategy puts cash in your pocket right away, and many people want that cash in the beginning to get some breathing room. It's feels good to have $10,000 to $100,000, or more, in the bank. It puts a smile on your face in the morning, especially when you are used to living paycheck-to-paycheck and having the worries that comes with that. Then there is also the thrill of selling your old clunker of a car and buying a shiny new Lexus that your friends and neighbors gawk at. Yes, fast cash has a beauty and style all its own. Those of you who like immediate gratification are going to love the art of flipping.

DEFINITION OF FLIPPING

Flipping is buying a property and then selling it quickly for a profit. What distinguishes this strategy is that there is no intention to hold onto the property any longer than needed. The goal here is to buy the property as cheaply as you can, with the best terms you can, and then sell it as fast as you can, for as much profit as you can, spending as little time and money as you can in between buying and selling.

Understanding the Flipping Formula

The beauty of this formula is that *you are starting at the end of the transaction and working backwards.* (There are people who believe you should look at all goals in life this way: start at the end result and trace the steps back that will make it happen.) When you look at a property, figure out what the final retail price will be and then take off a little discount so it will sell quickly. Depending on the market and the price, the discount may be anywhere from 5 to 10 percent of the price. Now that you have the price you are going to sell it for, you need to subtract all of the costs you will incur on your way to getting it sold, including your expected profit.

To understand flipping, it helps to picture yourself in a videorecording being played in reverse. For instance, at the end of the transaction you're sitting at a closing table, so you will subtract your closing costs. At that point you will pay any real estate commissions, title insurance, documentary stamps, title search fees, and so on. You should contact a title company to get an exact list of costs and their percentages. We

The Flipping Formula

Start with the *final price* that will *sell quickly,* and then:

- Subtract closing costs when you sell—commissions, title insurance, documentary stamps, and other such expenses. Use 10 percent of the selling price if you're not sure of these costs.
- Subtract clean-up and fix-up costs, if any. Be generous with this figure, because most surprises are unpleasant.
- Subtract holding costs—interest, loan costs, insurance, and advertising.
- Subtract your intended profit.
- The remainder is what you can pay for the property.

commonly use 10 percent for closing costs because real estate commissions alone can be 6 to 7 percent, and 10 percent is easy to figure out—you take the decimal point on the final selling price and move it one place to the left, and that is your closing cost. (This calculation is just like the one you learned when we discussed The Magic Formula, when you converted a price to an NOI using a 10 percent cap rate.) For instance, let's assume $100,000 is your final price:

$100,000 Final Selling Price – 10% Closing Costs = $10,000 Closing Costs

If you don't plan on using a real estate broker, you can cut your closing costs dramatically, to 5 percent or less, but then you will have to do all the work that a broker does, which is considerable. We will talk more about this in a later chapter, when we discussing selling.

Now, continue rewinding. You are backing away from the closing table and walking around the property in its cleaned and quickly fixed-up condition. You will subtract the costs that got the property into the improved condition that interested the new buyer. You should be as generous as possible in figuring these costs because there can be surprises, and the surprises can be unpleasant, so leave a little "give" in your estimate of what it will take to do this work.

Next, picture yourself borrowing the money to buy the property and writing the mortgage checks each month while you held onto it. Subtract your mortgage payments and your holding costs while you were waiting for a buyer, and also include your loan closing costs when you bought the property, your insurance payments while you owned it, any advertising you did, and any other expenses.

Finally, we are at the beginning of the videotape—when you first saw the property. You knew it was going to take some of your time to flip it, and you wanted to be paid handsomely for your efforts. Subtract your expected profit now—what is left is what you should pay for the property.

How much profit you want to make is up to you. In the beginning I liked to make at least $10,000 on a $50,000 property, which was 20 percent of the final price. Now I vary the amount of profit I expect and the percentage of selling price depending on how much time the property will take to flip, how much money it will need for improvements, how busy I am, and how many flipper properties are available in the market.

The more that are available, the higher my profit percentage, the fewer that are available, the more aggressive I am. We will discuss each type of flipping now, and look at examples of each one.

THE FIVE BASIC TYPES OF FLIPPERS

There are five basic types of mobile home park flippers:

1. Quick Wholesale Flip
2. Added-Value Flip
3. Pie Flip
4. Resident Flip
5. Land Flip to Higher and Better Use

Each type of flipper is distinguished by how much effort you expend and who the buyer you are going to "flip it" to is.

1. Quick Wholesale Flip

In a *quick wholesale flip*, you buy a park below value, do little or nothing to it, and then sell it to another investor for a profit. You buy it below value because the current owner is not aware of its true worth or is highly motivated to sell quickly by his or her poor financial situation. Usually, you will buy parks below value because they are run down and in disrepair, have a high vacancy rate, and/or rents that are below market values, and the only way they can attract an investor is by a low price. In other words, the parks were poorly managed. What distinguishes this type of flip from the added-value flip is that any changes you make, if you decide to clean up or do repairs, are completed cheaply and quickly—they cost less than $10,000 and take less than a few weeks.

In any case, whatever the reason the park is priced below value, you will turn around and sell these flippers to other investors who will usually keep them, manage them properly, repair the infrastructure, fill vacant lots, raise rents, and enjoy the positive cash flow and additional appreciation in value. Typically, when you wholesale property you will try to do no more than write contracts—first buying and then selling. The ultimate wholesale flipper is a property you never even take title to.

Beginning investors love this type of flipper because it's the least amount of work, takes the least amount of time, needs the least amount of money up front, and has the least amount of risk.

Usually this type of flipper starts with an older property that looks distressed, but it can be done with any property that you get under contract at a great price. You find the current owner and you write a contract to buy his property at a "wholesale" price, closing in sixty to ninety days. You put an escape clause (also known as a *contingency* clause) in the contract so you don't have to buy the property if you can't arrange financing or if a further inspection reveals defects that render it unusable. You will learn how to write these clauses in Chapter 9, when you learn about writing offers.

Then, after locking the property up for yourself with the contract, and before the closing, you advertise the property for sale in order to sell it to someone else at a higher price than you have contracted to pay. Wholesalers usually maintain a large investor list with hundreds or even thousands of names, because the new buyer will be *another* investor, and the nice thing about investors is that they are repeat customers. They will continue to buy properties from you over long periods of time. The new investor is going to fix up the property and then either keep it and rent it out for cash flow, or flip it themselves for a higher price—the retail price—to an investor who wants a turnkey park. With modern methods of communication, real estate wholesalers can send out hundreds, or even thousands of faxes and emails to their investor list at a low cost, either for free or just a few dollars, after they "tie up" a property with a contract.

If you are starting out with just a little cash, timing can be very important here. If you don't have enough money to pay for the property at closing, you will want the new buyer to close and pay for the property on the same day you are supposed to close with the current owner. If you schedule the closing this way, the new buyer doesn't know what your cost was, or how much profit you are making, because there is nothing recorded. All you have is a contract to buy the property, which the new buyer won't have a copy of. This is called a *simultaneous closing*, which I will explain shortly.

You can also sell the property another way. In this case you "assign" your contract to another investor, say for $5,000 up to $20,000 extra or more, depending on the deal. You write out a simple one-page *assignment of contract* that assigns all your rights in the contract with the seller to the new buyer for a specified sum (see the Appendix for a sample), so the next buyer effectively steps into your shoes. You collect all your profit upon the signing of the assignment, before the closing, then the new buyer shows up for the closing instead of you. I don't do this as much, because I have found that when the new buyer sees how much profit I am making, which is the assignment fee, they try to chisel me down to almost nothing. They don't like the fact that I am making so much money for just writing a contract and doing an assignment. In reality what profit I am making, or not making, is irrelevant to the next buyer. What is relevant is how much money he is going to make after he owns the property at the price I sell it to him for.

Let me give you some examples of wholesaling to make the concept clearer. Please bear in mind, the purpose here is not for you to be impressed by me, but for you to copy what I did, because in actuality, what I have done in each case is *make* a good deal. The main talent you will need is common sense: you will need the good sense to recognize the possibility of a good deal when you see it and then harvest it by writing an offer.

First Example: Splendor in the Tall Grass

I borrowed this example from my first book, *Mobile Home Wealth*, because it illustrates wholesale flipping so well. I became aware of this property while I was driving around in a "redneck" area. The grass was six feet high, which is not that unusual because we get so much rain in the summertime in Southwest Florida that you can almost watch the grass grow in front of your eyes.

It looked like some abandoned mobile homes were hiding in the back of a two-acre lot, but I couldn't tell for sure because the tall grass obstructed my view. It looked like the picture on page 129 *after* it was fixed up. If I had a picture of what it looked like before, you would only see some very tall grass.

I poked around and found three mobile homes in the rear of the property. They were wide open, full of trash, and in terrible shape. Windows were broken, the bathrooms and kitchens needed remodeling, and the floors had holes in them because roof leaks caused the particle board on the floors to weaken and fall apart. We did not have the time to fix

Splendor in the Tall Grass.

this property, as we were involved in three other flips and all our handymen were maxed out.

I wrote down the address of the property and then looked in the property appraiser's records to find the name and address of the owner to whom they sent the tax bills. I discovered the owner lived in another state—which was good—some of the best deals come from owners who live far away from their property, because fixing problems and managing property becomes more difficult long distance. I called information, got the owner's phone number, and called him. His name was Clyde, and right away he gave me his tale of woe about what it was like to be an absentee landlord. Clyde told me how the last three tenants trashed the property and he didn't have the money to fix it. He didn't know what to do because he was four months behind on his mortgage payments, and his brother-in-law, who managed the property for him, just divorced Clyde's sister and moved away, leaving him with no manager and no replacement.

We worked out a deal on the phone in which I was going to pay Clyde $18,000 for the property. We arrived at that price because it enabled Clyde to pay off the two mortgages he had on the property and still walk away with about $5,000 cash. We needed to close in thirty days because Clyde was afraid he was going to lose the property on the courthouse steps if he didn't pay the mortgages off. I faxed Clyde a contract detailing what we worked out and he signed it and faxed it back. Now we were off to the races! I called a local lawn-maintenance contractor, and for $200, he agreed to bush hog the two acres of six foot high grass so you could see the property and the mobile homes. Then I put the following ad in the classifieds:

Handyman Special
3 Mobile Homes on 2 Acres
$35,000

Over the next two weeks, I received about twenty calls, but no offers. My thought was, "Time is a wastin'." If no one steps up to the plate, we'd have to buy it ourselves, which at the time, would have depleted our cash reserves. Then one investor stepped up to the plate—Billy. He said he already owned twenty-three mobile homes in the area and he was a cash buyer, so he could close very quickly, like in a week. I gave Billy the address, and asked what time he wanted to meet me there for his inspection. He said it was okay, he didn't need anyone holding his hand and he would fend for himself.

I didn't hear anything for about a day or two and then Billy called back. He started to tell me how much work the mobile homes needed, and I stopped him after a few sentences. I said, "Don't waste your breath, Billy. I already know the place is a mess, so why don't we just get down to business?"

He said, "Okay . . . I'll pay you twenty-five." I said, "Twenty-five?! The land alone is worth the $35,000 offering price, so the three mobile homes are free." He said, "Free is more than they're worth. I have to haul them off to the dump, and that will cost about $5,000." I said, "I'll save you the dump fees and the trouble of hauling them off. I'll call the fire department and they'll do a practice fire and burn them down to the ground for free."

At this point, there was a lull in the conversation, and I waited. Then I finally added, "Come on, Billy. You and I are pros. If I wasn't so bogged down with other rehabs, I would keep the property, fix it up, and rent the mobiles out, which is what you're going to do, and we both know it. It's going to be a cash cow, and you're the guy who knows how to milk it. You just want to see how much pain I can tolerate, and twenty-five is too much pain. You have to make this easier on me. I want you to get rich, just not all at once, and not just from me."

I waited for an answer, and the answer I got was laughter. He laughed, and then I laughed, and then I knew we were going to do business. I said, "Billy, I like your style, and because I like you, I'm going to give you a big discount. You can buy the property from me for $31,000." I figured I would let him chisel me down to thirty, and then I'd give in. Instead, he said, "I'll meet you halfway at twenty-eight, and that's it . . . because I like *your style.*" So I met him halfway at twenty-eight. We drew up a cash contract with no contingencies, and I set up the closing for ten days later, which made it a *simultaneous closing.*

Simultaneous Closings

The process of a simultaneous closing will be helpful to you throughout your investing career. Setting up a simultaneous closing meant I arranged for both my purchase from the current owner, Clyde, and my sale to the new owner, Billy, to take place at the *same title company, at the same time.* Since Clyde lived out of state, the title company overnighted him the closing papers along with the deed from him to me. He signed the papers, had them notarized, and then overnighted them back to the title company. The title company held the deed from Clyde to me in escrow, which meant they put it safely aside. Then we closed on my sale of the property to the new buyer, Billy. When Billy paid $28,000, the title company took $18,000 out for Clyde and cut me a check for the difference, $10,000. I actually netted a little less, around $9,000 when we subtracted the bush hogging, the classified ad, and some closing costs (like title fees and so on.).

$28,000 Sale Price – $18,000 Cost
– $1,000 (Bush Hogging, Ad, Closing Fees) = $9,000

Not a bad day's pay, when you consider all I did was have the grass cut, place an ad, answer the phone, and write two contracts. Billy did keep the mobile homes, as I figured he would. He did a good job of rehabbing them and then finding tenants.

Second Flipper Example: Meandering Lane— Five Units on Two and One-Half Acres

This property was introduced to me through a combination of networking and reputation, which is how more properties are being introduced to me nowadays. It wasn't always like that. I do not have talent for net-

Meandering Lane: Aerial view (left), mobile home (top right), and house (bottom).

working. Many of you reading this are probably better at meeting people who will become important in your investing career.

On the positive side, I have been an investor for twenty-two years in our area of South Florida, with a reputation for treating people fairly and acting ethically. In one sentence that means, "Do what you say, and say what you do." I do not make commitments rashly because promises mean something. I don't say things like, "I changed my mind," when a commitment becomes difficult to complete. When I make a commitment, it makes no difference whether it is in writing or just my word. Either one is binding. I have business relationships with others who operate in the same way and I value them. For those of you reading this book: I would not assume this quality in others until it is proven. Until then you should get all your commitments in writing.

The owners of this property, Danny and Sherry Lee, bought their previous home from me. I made the purchase easy by giving them a second mortgage so they could buy it for no money down. There were a few times when they had a problem making the second mortgage payments and I treated them with patience and understanding.

One day, out of the blue, Danny called me and described his small mobile home park to me—four mobile homes plus a house, on two and one-half acres, all park-owned and maintained. It was on Meandering Lane and, ironically, I had just bought and sold a mobile home right across the street the month before. The total rent on Danny's park was excellent—$900 per week, or close to $4,000 per month. After expenses, it netted around $3,000 per month. This is how the conversation went:

"Zalman, what do think my property is worth?"

"Well, Danny, I haven't seen it up close and personal, but judging by what you described and how it looks here on the property appraiser's website, I would say it is worth $200,000."

"And how long would it take to get that?" he asked.

"Anywhere from six months to three years."

After I said that I waited, and then he started laughing.

"Danny, I'm being serious." I said.

"I know you are, Zalman. Everyone tells me it's hard to find buyers right now."

"Danny, I just sold the mobile home on one acre across the street from you. I had only two phone calls on it during the two months I had it in the paper and in the MLS. I had to give 80 percent of the price in seller financing to get it done. If you'd like, I'd be glad to list your property for $200,000 as a broker, with a 6 percent commission, or you can try to sell it yourself. You could get lucky and sell it in six months, or it could take three years or more if you insist on cash, in this market."

"Zalman, if I needed to move quickly, what price do you think it would it take to make my property sell fast?"

"Well, Danny, you know I'm also an investor. Right now I have $100,000 in my savings account. It's giving me no trouble. It just sits there and cranks out 5 percent interest, and I don't have to do anything. If you want me to step into your shoes, I'm willing to give you my $100,000 and buy your property, after I inspect it first, of course. I realize that is only half, but in this slow market, I'm not interested in buying a property for $200,000 that is worth $200,000. I would just as soon leave my money in the bank."

There was a long pause and then Danny asked, "How long would it take you to close, Zalman?"

Remember, when you hear that question after you've made an offer, it means your offer is being seriously considered by a seller.

"I can close in two weeks, Danny. I'll need a week to have the property inspected and then, if everything looks okay, I can have the title company get the papers ready the following week."

"Let me get back to you, Zalman,"

"Danny, please remember I'll do whatever suits you best. If you want me to list it for $200,000, I'll be glad to do that. If you want a quick cash deal, I'm also willing to use my hard-earned cash, but at a price where there is an opportunity to make some money for the risk I am taking in this slow market."

"I understand that, Zalman."

When he hung up, I went about my business, thinking no more on the subject. A week later, Danny called me again.

"Zalman," he started out. "Do you still have that $100,000?"

"Yes," I answered.

"Why don't come on out here and take a look, and bring a contract with you. Sherry Lee and I want to get out of here ASAP. We're moving to North Carolina to be with our kids and grandkids, and we need some quick cash for the home we want to buy up there, one the missus already has her heart set on."

I met him out at his mobile home park the next day, with a contract written exactly the way I described the deal on the phone—one week for inspections, and if inspections were okay, closing the following week for $100,000 cash.

On the last day of the inspection period, I bought Crazy Gersh out to Danny and Sherry Lee's property and introduced him as my partner. After we walked around and inspected it, I offered Gersh the property for $150,000. I did this because Gersh's wife wanted to become more involved in real estate investing, and we both agreed this would be a good property for her to learn on and make money from. The fact that it was at least $50,000 cheaper than the retail price was not lost on Gersh either. I didn't tell Gersh what I was paying for the property, but I did tell him I was making money on the sale to him. If he was uncomfortable about that, I would understand and he didn't have to buy it. I felt reasonably certain I could get at least $175,000 for the property, $25,000 more than I was offering it to Gersh for, while I earned $3,000 a month in cash flow waiting for the next buyer. Keep in mind, the two and one-half acres the park was situated on was worth at least $100,000, without the four mobile homes, the house, and the swimming pool. Oh yes, I forgot to mention it had a small swimming pool at the largest mobile home, which had four bedrooms, two baths, and a fireplace.

Gersh knew it was a good deal and brought out his wife to look at it after we inspected it. Gersh's wife agreed it was a good deal. I wrote an *as-is* contract selling it to Gersh and his wife. I didn't need a contract with Gersh because his word and my word are good enough, but the title company and the bank would need paperwork detailing our agreement.

I worked out a deal with a local banker to finance the property for Gersh and his wife for no-money-down, if they used the equity he had in another investment home as additional collateral. While we were waiting to close, I asked Gersh if he wanted to include another little park I owned, three mobile homes on Washington Street, for $75,000, and he and his wife agreed. You will find out about Washington Street when we discuss rehabs later in this chapter.

The bank's appraiser valued Meandering Lane for more than $200,000 and he appraised Washington Street for $86,000, which proved that Gersh and his wife were getting a good deal on each of them. The bank took longer than they were supposed to close the deal, so in the meantime, I had my best handyman paint and fix all the mobile homes on Meandering Lane with the cash flow I received from it. I didn't have to add value to the park because I sold it as-is, but I wanted Gersh's wife to have as few problems as possible when she bought her first two small mobile home parks, and I wanted them to look good, too.

As you can see, I made $50,000 on just the Meandering Lane part of the transaction:

$150,000 Sale to Gersh and Wife – $100,000 Purchase Cost from Danny and Wife = $50,000 Profit

Why did Danny sell the park to me for such a great price? This was not a case of not knowing the value. I told him I thought the value was $200,000, twice what I paid him. It was a case of a seller needing cash quick, and willing to give a discount to get it quick. By the way, at closing, Danny and his wife thanked me profusely when I purchased Meandering Lane from them. And Gersh and his wife thanked me profusely when I sold it to them at more than $50,000 below the appraisal price..

2. Added-Value Flip

This is the most common form of flipping, in which you buy a park that is in poor condition. You will receive a healthy discount because it looks bad and requires time and money to repair it, so that fewer *end users* (buyers) are interested in investing in it. Usually these are older parks but sometimes there are newer ones that are also in poor condition.

After you buy the park, you will add value and *force the price up* by having it cleaned and fixed. Then you will sell the property to an investor who is going to keep it and rent it out. Obviously you want to sell it for more than you paid, including repair costs to improve the park's condition, plus a nice profit.

I have done this on many different types of real estate for more than twenty-seven years, and continue to do so now. This is a very safe and secure form of investing for two reasons:

1. You don't depend on and wait for the market to go up in value to give you a profit. You have a profit going in, as long as you've calculated your flipping *formula for success* correctly.

2. You purchase the property wholesale at a discount, so if there is market weakness when it comes time to sell, you have a "margin of safety" as Warren Buffet likes to refer to it, or simply, a low cost.

When you specialize in the profit strategy of adding value, you are really in two businesses—the real estate business and the renovation business (like a contractor)—but you are making more than the average contractor. If you have the skill to do the rehab yourself, all the more power to you. Along with two helpers, I did all of our rehabs at the beginning of my real estate investment career. I did it myself for two reasons: I wanted to keep my costs down, and I wanted to learn how to estimate and perform repairs.

If you don't have the skill to rehab, then you will need to either hire your own salaried handymen (which is what we did after the first five years) or hire subcontractors ("subs"). If you hire subs, plan on getting three different bids on your jobs to keep them competing with one another to give you the best price. Some subs like to become friends and then slowly raise their prices when they assume you are no longer getting bids and making them compete for your jobs.

Whether you fix it yourself or hire it out, you must learn how to figure how much time it will take, and what it will cost, to fix up the various things that go wrong with property. If you are using your own handymen, trips to Lowe's and Home Depot will educate you on costs, and watching your handymen work will help you estimate the time. If you are using subcontractors, ask them how they figured their bid to you so you can use that calculation in the future and save them the trip out to your properties to give you their bid estimate. Almost all subcontractors price jobs by the square foot, and the reputable ones don't mind disclosing to you how much per square foot they charge. They simply measure how many square feet they are painting, siding, roofing, or flooring, and then multiply that figure by a number, their own special number, which includes their profit, to get the total cost to you. That's why the estimators carry a tape measure with them.

When you are a value-added flipper, there are three types of renovations. Each is distinguished by how much time, money, and effort you will expend:

1. The cosmetic rehab
2. The serious rehab
3. The career rehab

The Cosmetic Rehab

The cosmetic rehab is the most sought-after flipper because it involves the least amount of time and money. You will be cleaning up the property, throwing out the trash inside park-owned mobile homes, and picking up trash on the park grounds. Let me say a few words now about trash: *get used to it* if you are in the flipping business. Trash and distressed properties go hand-in-hand. Get used to buying heavy duty contractor trash bags by the twenty-count box, and filling up tens, or even hundreds of them, at flipper properties.

When we got seriously involved in flipping, we bought an eight-foot wide by sixteen-foot long open trailer. It's been filled with trash, hauled to the dump, and emptied by hand countless times. Eventually we bought a dump trailer, which has a bed that lifts up and dumps out the trash, because we spent so much time emptying our other trailer by hand at the dump. We try to make detrashing more interesting for our handymen by allowing them to keep whatever good stuff they find, and they always find a bunch of good stuff. If you don't want to handle trash there are site clean-up companies who will clean up your flippers at a reasonable price.

After you get the property back to square one in terms of cleanliness, you are now ready to paint the outside, or the inside, or both, and mow the lawns, and improve the landscaping. Because the cosmetic rehab is the most popular kind of rehab and the easiest, you will usually have the most competition from other investors interested in buying properties like this. Don't worry, there are plenty to go around.

Example: Washington Street—Three Mobiles on Three Contiguous Lots

The Washington Street Mobile Home Park came to me, again, as a result of networking and reputation. I was in my office when I received a phone call from Frank. He identified himself as a good friend of another investor, Oliver, from whom I had purchased twelve mobile homes on individual lots in a subdivision I liked. Frank said he wasn't as rich as Oliver, but he had three mobile homes, one next to another, on three separate lots in another subdivision I was familiar and comfortable with. He offered them to me for $50,000.

"Is that $50,000 for all three, Frank?" I asked. "A total of $50,000?"

"Yes, of course. A total of $50,000," he replied. Then he added, "But I need a cash deal, like you gave Oliver."

I understood the significance of Frank needing cash, but he did not understand the significance of my question. This was at the top of the market in South Florida, and there were some mobile homes selling for *$50,000 apiece* in the subdivision where Washington Street was located.

"I might be interested, Frank. What is the condition of the mobile homes?"

"Let me say this, Zalman, they're all rented at $450 per month, so they must be livable."

I made an appointment to visit Frank's property the next day, and brought a contract with me. While I inspected the units, we talked. The mobile homes were in below-par condition—not terrible, but they needed cosmetic repairs like painting, repairs to the flooring and skirting,

Three mobile homes on Washington Street.

bathroom cosmetics, and so on. The three pictures you see above were taken "before."

I negotiated with Frank for a price of $45,000, to take into account $5,000 in repairs, with a closing in two weeks. We signed a contract on the hood of my car. When I bought the property, I did not know what I was going to do with it, but every choice was a good one. I could keep it, raise the rents to $150 per week, the market rent at the time, and get the following as cash flow:

$650 per Month Rent per Mobile Home
– $50 per Month Real Estate Taxes
– $50 per Month Insurance
– $65 per Month Repairs and Vacancy (10% of Rent)

$485 per Month net Profit per Mobile

$485 per Month Net × 3 Mobile Homes × 12 Months = $17,460 per Year NOI

Cash-on-Cash Return = NOI ÷ Cash out of pocket = $17,470 ÷ $45,000 = 39%

If we want to be conservative, we could use 50 percent of the gross rents as the average expenses for park owned mobile homes. In this case, that would reduce the NOI and cash flow to:

$650 per Month × 50% = $325 per Month per Mobile Home NOI

$325 per Month per Mobile Home × 3 Mobile Homes × 12 Months = $11,700 NOI per Year

Cash-on-Cash = Cash Flow ÷ Cash Down = $11,700 ÷ $45,000 = 26%

A 26 percent return on cash invested is still a great return. So if we kept the property, it would give between a 26 percent and a 39 percent return on our money.

We could also flip the property for a $100,000 sale price and a $50,000 profit.

$100,000 Price – $5,000 Closing Costs (5%) – $45,000 Cost = $50,000 Profit

We didn't come to a decision on what to do, so we used the cash flow to rehab the properties while we made up our minds. One of the tenants moved out about a month after we bought Washington Street, so we rehabbed that trailer. Then we moved a family from one of the other trailers into that one. We rehabbed the next empty trailer and moved in new tenants rather than disturbing the other tenants, who were fine where they were.

When I offered Washington Street to Gersh and his wife for $75,000, it was a good deal for them. If we assume all the income from the trailers went to rehabbing and closing costs, then we made:

$75,000 Sale Price – $45,000 Cost = $30,000 Profit

Why did we flip Washington Street? I wanted to raise some cash for another mobile home park that we could have our son manage. He had been managing our park-owned units—a total of seventy-five—in a subdivision I liked, and I wanted him to experience the ease of management of a land-lease park as a reward for his hard work.

Why did this deal work? Because the previous seller was an older man who was tired of managing tenants and park-owned units. He also needed cash, and knew from one of his best friends that I was a cash buyer and a man of my word. We did not have to pay all cash on this deal; we could have gone to a bank and financed it easily with 20 percent down.

By the way, the seller paid only $10,000 per mobile home many years before, and had enjoyed great cash flow. It was time for him to harvest his money and a $5,000 profit per mobile home and move on. He did have a "For Sale" sign on the property--a one-foot-square piece of cardboard nailed to a tree—that said it was for sale for $50,000. He had no takers until he called me because no one could see the sign.

Once again, at the closing, the seller thanked me when I bought it, and then later on Gersh and his wife thanked me when I sold it to them at a wholesale price.

The Serious Rehab

The serious rehab needs some or all of the fixes that the cosmetic rehab needed, but also requires fixes to the infrastructure and remodeling of the park-owned units. Costs for remodeling park-owned units can begin at a few hundred dollars each and rise to \$5,000 to \$10,000 or more per unit when replacing bathrooms, kitchens, floors, and major roof repairs are involved. We average around \$3,000 to \$5,000 on a serious rehab of a park-owned unit, using our own handymen. The time it takes us to complete a serious rehab is around two to three weeks per unit if we put one good man on the project full-time.

Example: Airey Drive—3 Mobile Homes on 1½ Acres

This property came to us from a foreclosure on the courthouse steps. When I drove up and looked at it right before the sale, there were three mobile homes that looked vacant and abandoned and lots of trash around them.

At the foreclosure sale I spoke to the lawyer who was representing the mortgage holder of the property, the previous owner, who had given owner financing to the current owner. The final judgment was in excess of \$38,000, but the attorney told me that, considering the condition of the property, the mortgage holder would stop bidding at \$29,000. I was prepared to pay \$38,000, so this was a welcome piece of information.

The property contained an acre and one-half of land, in two parcels, and at that time was worth at least \$75,000 as vacant land without any other improvements. Since almost all of the foreclosure investors in our county are unfamiliar with mobile homes, no one else bid. I bought the property for \$29,001, one dollar more than the attorney bid.

I drove directly to the property after the sale on the steps. I discovered, to my surprise, that the mobile homes were not vacant and abandoned. Instead, there was a family living in each one. The tenants were just very messy people and left trash and discarded things outside. The

Aerial view of three mobile homes on Airey Drive.

owner of the property continued to collect rent from them up to the day before the sale, even though he was not paying the mortgage payment or real estate taxes.

I knocked on the doors and met each tenant. I handed them a copy of the certificate of sale showing I was the new owner. Then I told them their rent would remain the same, at $150 per week, or $650 per month. When you multiplied the rent by three mobile homes, there was almost $2,000 per month in total rents coming in.

We planned to use the rents to fix the mobile homes and then sell the property. We took on a partner for this project who was going to supply his labor for $15 per hour to fix each of the mobile homes inside, paint them, and get the property looking neat and clean outside. When it was sold, we would split the profits. Sometimes we like to take on a working partner for a flip. This is someone who is extremely trustworthy and has all the skills of a seasoned flipper, but is not as good as we are at finding deals and doesn't have the cash to make the deal happen quickly.

In this case, I found the deal, paid for it, and then had my working partner take care of everything. I didn't have to spend any more time on the property other than to show up at the closing when it was sold and get a check for 50 percent of the profits. All the costs of fixing up the property, plus the purchase price, would be refunded to me before any profits would be split.

We spent longer on this rehab then I figured, almost six months (because we wound up buying even more flippers), and didn't sell it for four months after that, but there was rent coming in from at least two of the mobiles at any time. When the first mobile home became vacant, we fixed up the inside and moved one of the other tenants into it. We then rehabbed the mobile home they moved from. We arranged for the third tenant to rehab his own unit for a $50 per week reduction in his rent.

When it came time to sell the property, I did something I rarely do—I sold it to one of the students from a three-day training. The student was middle aged, living in New York and retiring soon and moving to Florida. He came to me and asked if I had anything that was a good deal. I mentioned this little park, which I had listed for $100,000. Since he was a student, I offered it to him a discount, and priced it at $85,000. He liked the idea of almost $2,000 per month gross rents and an $85,000 selling price, which was cheap compared to New York prices. I met him at my office and drew up a contract.

The contract called for a closing in two months, but I wound up giving him an extra month to get his financing completed. During that extra month, I offered to give him a $2,000 quick profit to walk away from the contract, but he wouldn't take it. He even asked me if I was using a new selling technique, called "seller's remorse" by offering the buyer money to NOT buy my property. I wasn't using any new technique. The market had gone up on mobile homes and acreage, and I could not replace the little park I was selling to him for anywhere near an $85,000 price. Even so, our profit was excellent on this deal. Here's how it stacked up:

	$85,000 Sale Price
–	**$ 8,000 Closing Costs + Past Due Real Estate Taxes**
–	**$22,000 Fix-up Expenses**
–	**$29,001 Cost**
	$26,000 Profit on Sale
+	**$13,000 Net Rents Collected**
	$39,000 Total Profit

I wrote a check to my partner for $19,500, half of the total $39,000 profit, and we both went smiling down the road. I would rather have held onto the property as a keeper, though, because as of this writing the student who bought it from me has it for sale for over $200,000.

The Career Rehab

In a career rehab, you are essentially rebuilding the mobile home park in place. You are doing many of the same things needed in the serious rehab, but in addition you may have to add new water or sewer systems or new natural gas transmission lines, repave roads, and perform other very expensive repairs. You can spend from $50,000 up to millions of dollars on these infrastructure repairs, depending on the seriousness of the problem and the size of the park. A mobile home park career rehab may take years, which is why I call it a *career rehab*—it feels like you are spending your whole real estate investment career fixing it up. You should avoid mobile home park career rehabs.

You may also face career-type rehabs on some or all, of the park-owned mobiles homes, if there are any. On park-owned units, you may have to gut the mobile home inside, which means taking it down to the wall studs and then replacing wiring, plumbing, floor joists and/or roof joists, as well as some or all of the exterior siding. The question that arises when you have to do a serious or a career rehab on a park-owned mobile home is this: "Does it make more sense to throw away the mobile home that is on the property now and move on a good used one?" To figure this out you first have to make sure the current home is basically sound and worth fixing. If it is sound, you still will need to compare the total repair costs to the total replacement costs—which include the cost to detach the mobile, haul it to the dump, buy a replacement, acquire its permit, and have it set up. In our county, these are the average costs to replace a single-wide mobile home with another good used one:

1. $1,000 to detach old mobile home and haul it to the dump
2. $1,000 to $3,000 to buy a good used older replacement mobile home, or $5,000 to $15,000 for a later model repo
3. $4,000 to permit and set up the replacement mobile home ($500 for an RV park model)

As you can see, the least it will cost is $6,000 to $8,000 to move in an older replacement or $10,000 to $20,000 for a newer repo, versus $7,500 for us to do a serious rehab on the existing one (double all costs for double-wide models). Our serious rehab will be in better condition than the average replacement because the wiring, plumbing, floors, bathrooms, and kitchens will be checked and fixed, but will not be better than a late model repo because of improved advanced construction standards.

Example of Career Rehab: Palm Frond MHP—64 Units on 2 1/2 Acres

We tried to buy the Pond Frond Mobile Home Park for two years, either from a broker when it was listed, or directly from the owner when the listing expired. We were aggressively pursuing it because it was right across the street from Happy Trails. Happy Trails was 100 percent occupied with a waiting list, and we could have our manager manage both parks for only a slight additional cost. The Pond Frond was badly managed and had only a 50 percent occupancy on the sixty-two RV lots and two apartments. The owner could not meet the expenses of the park and was in both foreclosure and bankruptcy.

The real estate market was in a buying frenzy and prices were going up each month during the two years I tried to purchase the Palm Frond. The owner kept raising his listing price from $400,000 to over $700,000. At the end of the two years, I had it under contract for $650,000, but the title was a mess because of the bankruptcy and all the liens on the property. As a result, we could not get a bank interested in lending on it.

Just before our contract expired, I noticed a group of plain white pickup trucks at the Palm Frond, which usually meant some county agency was inspecting a problem. When I called the owner, he said everything was okay and I thought nothing further about it.

We waited and sure enough, the Palm Frond came up for foreclosure again, after the bankruptcy court freed it up and gave the bank permission to recover its loan. Gersh and I teamed up with a father and son I had partnered with many times before on foreclosures and tax deeds, and we purchased the Palm Front on the courthouse steps for $640,000.

The bad news started as soon as we bought it. I received a phone call and then registered letters from the Health Department, telling us we had to disconnect and fill in the sixteen malfunctioning septic tanks in the park, and hook up to the county sewer system immediately, as required by law. If we didn't do that within ninety days, the Health Department threatened to close down the Palm Frond Mobile Home Park and evict everyone living there. The Health Department attorney said the previous owner knew about the problem and should have told us. (Yes, that was the reason all those plain white pickup trucks were there that day.)

We asked three underground utility companies to give us bids for putting in new sewer pipes and connecting to the county system through

Aerial view of Palm Frond mobile home park.

our neighbor's parking lot. The neighbor allowed us to install pipes under his parking area in exchange for about $150,000 worth of work clearing trees, connecting his septic lines to the county system, collapsing his old tanks, and repaving his parking lot when we were finished. Each bid for the new sewer system was higher than the next, starting at $500,000 and escalating to more than $600,000 for just *part of the job!* In other words, the Palm Frond was about to cost us more than twice what we paid for it, and at $1.3 million, it was sure to lose money with any kind of reasonable financing.

We spent years getting postponements from the Health Department on hooking up to the county sewer system, during which they allowed us to keep the Palm Frond open. Finally, during a brainstorming session with the county sewer engineer and our engineer, we arrived at a different way of doing the sewer system that would still make the Health Department happy. We had our engineer design a system with small, inexpensive lift stations on every lot, and we arranged for an easement from a different neighbor for only $2,000 to hook up to the county sewer system. As of this writing, almost three years later, we finished the new sewer system for a cost of around $60,000. We then submetered the sewer and the water. After all this effort, the Palm Frond is finally turning a profit, which we will use to repave the roads and fix the roofs on the two apartments. When we are done we will have spent $100,000 in repairs, which is a far sight better than $500,000 to $600,000 for only part of the job. We are now at 65 percent occupancy, and after the final improvements, we should have it up to 100 percent and earn a nice profit.

And yes, after three years, it feels like I spent most of my real estate career rehabbing the Palm Frond. I imagine after another year, I will feel this way even more. Am I sorry we bought the Palm Frond? No. We learned a lot about fixing sewer systems and persistence. However, we don't plan on buying any more career rehabs without much better due diligence on the infrastructure before hand and a much bigger profit margin afterwards.

Our total cost on the Palm Frond Mobile Home Park will be around $750,000 and it will be worth around $1.4 million. It should have a cash flow of $94,000 per year, and after taking into account our total cash outlay of $238,000, we should have a 38 percent cash-on-cash return after financing.

3. Pie Flip

A *pie flip* is where you buy a park, and then sell off parts of it in slices, like a pie, for a sum greater than the whole that you paid for it. I call it a pie flip because it is like buying pie in your favorite restaurant. If a whole pie costs the restaurant $8, then the restaurant will usually charge $12 to $16 to buy the complete pie, which is a 50 to100 percent markup. However, if we order only one slice at the table, and the pie has been divided into eight slices, then the restaurant will usually charge $3 per slice, a 200 percent markup. The cost of a slice of pie to the diner or restaurant is still only $1 per slice, but now they will make $24 for the whole pie to take into account the extra handling costs.

The same principle applies to subdividing land. If you buy a large parcel of land and split it up into slices, you can usually charge two to three times per acre for the smaller slices compared to the price per acre of the whole parcel. You can do the same with a mobile home park. There are many mobile home parks around the country that contain single family houses, commercial buildings, apartment buildings, or excess vacant land in addition to the mobile homes. In a pie flip, you separate out the nonmobile home park properties and sell them to another investor who specializes in that kind of investment, and then sell the park to a mobile home investor. When you split it up that way, you can usually realize a much greater profit than selling the park as one complete unit, the way you bought it.

The most prevalent form of pie flip involves a single family house and a mobile home park. These parks usually started out as a home with excess land. The owner wanted to create an additional income stream by setting up mobile homes on the excess land, and kept bringing them in until all the excess land was gone. It's usually a simple matter to separate the original home along with a reasonable plot of land, surround it with a six-foot stockade fence to give it privacy, and then sell the home for a nice profit to someone looking to buy a house. Many times, the park manager was living in this home, so after the sale, the manager will be housed in a mobile home inside the park at a much lower cost.

Example: Pie Flip—Happy Trails Front Building

Happy Trails had a former gas station in the front corner of the park. When we bought the park, we separated the corner building from the purchase of the park and took title to it on a separate deed. The corner building was not included in the $650,000 loan for the whole park. The bank knew this and allowed it because just the Happy Trails mobile home park, without the corner building, appraised for more than the loan, and I added two duplexes for additional collateral.

We separated out the corner building because if we ever wanted to sell it we could get a much higher price than was allotted to it from our original purchase. Remember, the corner property only produced $450 per month in rent. After real estate taxes and insurance it netted less than $300 per month, and at a 10 percent cap rate, this is how much the corner store cost us:

Price	=	NOI	÷	Cap Rate
$36,000	=	$3,600	÷	10%

In other words, the cost of the corner store was only $36,000 when you broke it out from the NOI. However, with all the traffic that goes past it, and with the current rent of over $2,000 per month, *we could sell it for $200,000 or more today,* if we wanted to. We don't want to do it just yet.

4. Resident Flip

In a *resident flip,* you buy a park and then sell it to the residents living there. It is similar to the pie flip in that you are buying the whole pie and

The front corner building at Happy Trails.

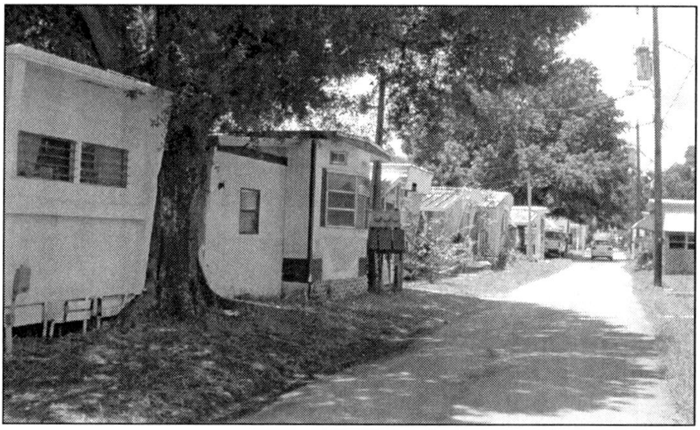

Street scene at Happy Trails.

then cutting it into pieces with a much higher cost per slice than for the original whole pie.

There are two basic ways of cutting up a park. If the zoning department gives their approval to subdividing it, then you simply call in a surveyor and cut it into as many slices as are feasible with separate deeds. Sometimes, however, zoning departments do not give their approval to subdividing. If that is the case, you would keep it as one common property, turn it into a cooperative, and then sell off individual shares to the residents. Each share would be represented exactly like a surveyed lot in the case above, but there would be shares in a co-op instead of individual deeds.

Example: Calm Lake Mobile Home Park—100 Mobile Homes on a Lake

I found this park by searching on the Internet. A broker's website listed a 100-unit mobile home park in the center of Florida, about two hours from our home. The park had sixty mobile home lots and forty RV lots. There were ten mobile home lots and ten RV lots right on the lake. The remaining eighty lots had access to the lake via a boat ramp. I wanted to buy a waterfront park so the family would have fun fishing, swimming, and boating there.

I met with the owner and his wife, and they reduced the price from $1,400,000 to $1,000,000 for a quick deal. The park's cash flow was limited and it barely broke even at a discounted price of $1,000,000, but that was not going to be my strategy. I knew from looking in the real estate classifieds and the MLS in the area that lakefront lots were worth upwards of $50,000 apiece, whether they were occupied by a mobile home or an RV. Nonwaterfront mobile home lots went for $20,000 apiece, and nonwaterfront RV lots went for $15,000 apiece. This is how the park would stack up when it was split up and sold to the residents:

20 Lake-front Lots	**×**	**$50,000 per Lot**	**=**	**$1,000,000**
50 Nonwaterfront Mobile Lots	**×**	**$20,000 per Lot**	**=**	**$1,000,000**
30 Nonwaterfront RV Lots	**×**	**$15,000 per Lot**	**=**	**$450,000**
Total Sales	**=**	**$2,450,000**		
Closing and Sales Costs	**=**	**$245,000**		
Original Price	**=**	**$1,000,000**		
Profit	**=**	**$1,200,000 (Rounded)**		

That's right. There was a potential profit of more than $1 million!

However, there is a law in the state of Florida that allows existing mobile home park associations the first right of refusal to purchase their park at the same terms as a new buyer, as long as they do it within forty-five days of the signing of the contract. The seller sent the association for Calm Lake Mobile Home Park the terms of our contract, and forty-five days later, the association bought the park right out from under me. (I am not aware of any other states that have this first right of refusal to purchase their park, but you should check the laws in your state to see if there is one.) The story still had a happy ending. Since I am a real estate broker, the contract called for me to receive half of the commission on the sale of the park, and since the park did sell (although not to the company I set up to buy it) I received a $15,000 commission check. I would rather have bought the mobile home park, but $15,000 was a nice consolation prize.

5. Land Flip to Higher and Better Use

A *land flip* is when you buy a park for its development potential. This is where the underlying land in the park can be changed to a higher and better use, rather than being used as a mobile home park. The residents will be asked to leave, the mobile homes will be removed, and then a new real estate development will be built in its place, like a town home or condominium subdivision or even better, a shopping center or commercial complex. In this kind of flip, you will especially be looking for parks located on high traffic roads, waterfront, or just plain well located land.

First Example: Sunny Mobile Home Park

I was driving down the main arterial road in our area and saw a for sale sign on an old mobile home park that was located right on the main shopping corridor. I called and the ex-husband of the woman who owned the park answered the phone. I knew this man well and after exchanging pleasantries, we got down to business. The Sunny Mobile Home Park contained almost nineteen acres of land, approximately 800,000 square feet, with almost one thousand feet of valuable road frontage. There were 200 mobile homes on the property paying $350 per month in lot rent, which could easily be raised to $400 per month right away, and then to $450 per month in the next two years. The location was fantastic—right in the middle of everything. The price was $8 million.

The land was easily worth $20 per foot as a commercial shopping center, or would support 400 units in a condominium or townhouse development. This is how the land stacked up either way:

Commercial Use: 800,000 Square Feet × $20 per Square Foot = $16,000,000
Condominium or Townhouse Use: 400 Units × $40,000 per Unit = $16,000,000

What was my plan? I was going to get together a group of investors and buy the park with a $1 million down payment and a $7 million mortgage. At those terms, the lot rents paid for the mortgage and the park threw off a 10 percent cash-on-cash return right away. This is how the NOI was calculated:

Gross Rent = 200 Lots × $350 per Month per Lot × 12 Months = $840,000 per Year
NOI = Total Gross Rent × 70% (30% Expenses)
$840,000 × .7 = $600,000 NOI (Rounded)

I assumed 30 percent expenses instead of 40 percent because the park was 200 units, 100 percent rented with a waiting list, efficiently run, and had submetered utilities. As the number of units increase from 80 in a land-lease community, the percentage of expenses decreases to around 30 percent due to "efficiencies of scale." The NOI was $600,000 (rounded). At a cap rate of 7.5 percent, which was the current cap rate at that time for such a park, the price was:

Price	=	NOI	÷	Cap Rate
$8 Million	=	$600,000	÷	7.5%

In other words, *the park was worth $8 million as a mobile home park, and had a land value of twice that, or $16 million.* If we borrowed $7 million at 6 percent interest for thirty years, the current borrowing rate at the time, the cash flow on the park was:

Mortgage Payment = Amount Borrowed in Thousands × Monthly Mortgage Multiple
$7 Million Loan = $7,000 × 6 = $42,000 month × 12 = $500,000 per Year (Rounded)

Cash Flow = NOI – Yearly Mortgage Payment
$600,000 – $500,000 = $100,000

Cash-on-Cash Return = Cash Flow ÷ Cash Down
$100,000 ÷ $1,000,0000 = 10%

The park threw off 10 percent right away, and when we sold it for twice what we paid for it, we would divide up the $8 million in profit between four partners, including myself, who put up $250,000 apiece for the down payment. In other words, we would receive 10 percent on our money until the park was sold, and $2 million each in profit when the park was sold.

Normally on a land investment, the investors put up a down payment and then make mortgage payments until the property is sold—creating negative cash flow in the extreme. The beauty of this investment was that there was no negative cash flow, even if the park did not sell quickly. The mobile home lot rents were paying the mortgage from the point the park was purchased and still giving a 10 percent cash-on-cash return. Within two years, when the lot rents were increased by $100 to $450 per month, this increase would have gone straight to the bottom line, and the cash-on-cash return would have been:

200 Lots × $100 Lot Increase = $20,000 per Month × 12 Months = $240,000

$240,000 per Year Additional Cash Flow + $100,000 Original Cash Flow = $340,000 Cash Flow

Cash-on-Cash Return = $340,000 Cash Flow ÷ $1 Million Down = 34% Cash-on-Cash Return

The investment looked good no matter what!

I sent them an offer for $7 million, and the ex-husband told me, "Zalman, they want full price, $8 million."

I sent them another contract, for $7.5 million, using the old "let's split the difference" negotiating strategy. The ex-husband once again told me that his ex-wife rejected the offer and wanted full price.

I sent them another offer for $7.75 million.

"Zalman," the ex-husband replied. "We're not communicating here. She wants $8 million and not a penny less."

So, once again, I sent in an offer, this time for full price, $8 million.

I didn't hear a thing for almost two weeks. I didn't want to appear too eager, so I didn't call right away. Finally, I called and this is what I was told:

"There is another offer on the table, Zalman, for more than full price. If you really want the property, I would suggest you offer $8.25 million."

I didn't believe the ex-husband and refused to pay above the listing price. As a result, the park really did sell to another investor for $8.2 million. In retrospect, I should not have let an additional $250,000 stand in the way of $8 million in profit, but it was difficult for me to pay above listing price after so many years of negotiating hard to get the lowest price I could.

This episode had a twist. The new buyers were condominium developers, and while they were applying for the zoning to build condominiums, they evicted all the residents and removed their mobile homes. Then the market for condominiums collapsed. The new owners called me and offered the now-vacant land for $1 million less than they paid, but without the mobile homes paying lot rent, we weren't interested in negative cash flow land.

Second Example of Higher and Better Use: The St. Pete Spectacular

This example was told to me by my attorney, David, who works with the biggest investors in mobile home parks in the state of Florida. I did not personally witness it, but David handled the closing and I have no reason to expect anything other than the truth from this exceptional lawyer.

Two entrepreneurs contracted to buy a mobile home park in St Petersburg, Florida. It had a $600,000 NOI and at a 7 percent cap rate, it priced out at $8.5 million. The buyers offered the owner $12 million, *$3.5 million more than it was worth,* as soon as all the residents were vacated from the park. The owner accepted the generous offer, and then offered the park to the residents' association, as required by law. The association did not exercise their first right of refusal, stating that the price was too high. Then the owner gave all the residents notice that they had six months to move out, which was required by law.

When the last resident moved out, the buyers did a simultaneous closing. They purchased the park for $12 million from the seller, and then flipped it to a developer of high-rise condominiums and marinas for $22 million, *and walked out of closing with $10 million profit*!

Did I forget to mention that the park contained waterfront property with marina rights, and beautiful views for a high rise condominium?

SUMMARY

An excellent overall strategy is to buy medium to large mobile home parks for cash flow, keep them, and occasionally do a Refi Bonanza to pull cash out. While you are maintaining your keepers, you also flip individual mobile homes, or small parks, for quick profits. Please consult my first book, *Mobile Home Wealth,* for ways to do this.

As you can see from preceding examples, flipping can be very profitable, has a simple formula, and requires mostly common sense. You can also expect there are going to be many mobile home flipping deals where you have to add value. When you get in your car and drive around blue-collar areas with mobile homes, you will find many examples of properties that are not taken care of and look distressed. I started this chapter with a section on wholesaling because if you are going to be a mobile home flipping specialist, there will be times when you have too many deals in the hopper and you will be too busy to fix up a property quickly. You don't have to pass up a deal because you are too busy or strapped for cash. You just get the "extra" deal under contract and then wholesale it to another investor, as I showed you in the first two examples. The new owner will either fix it and retail it out, or keep it for cash flow. If you happen to free up some time and cash before you flip it, you can add the value yourself, as in the later examples I showed you.

Flipping is the dessert on your dinner table of mobile home investing. When you add value to flipper properties and then sell them you can add $100,000 or more each year to your cash reserves, so that you can eventually buy flippers with all cash. When you can pay cash for your flippers you cut your holding costs down dramatically, and you have an advantage when it comes to buying quickly from motivated sellers. Fast cash and a guaranteed closing are extremely valuable to distressed sellers. Also, buying foreclosures or tax deeds at big discounts, which you will learn about in a later chapter, often require all-cash strategies.

HOMEWORK

Once again, go back and visit the mobile home parks you have looked at, but only the ones that were either openly for sale or ones the owners agreed to sell to you after you contacted them. Also see if you can find some new mobile home parks for sale. (Remember, if you are having difficulties finding parks for sale, then it would be all right to skip ahead to Chapter 7 and discover other places to find more parks for sale and then return here.) Write down the price the seller wants, the NOI, and the resulting cap rate.

Now, I want you to write down into your notebook the five new flipping techniques you learned: the quick wholesale flip, added-value flip, pie flip, resident flip, and land flip to higher and better use; see if you can apply any or all of these to the parks you have seen for sale. Use the Flipping Formula to see if there is any profit to be made around the listing price, and then adjust the price so you can make a reasonable profit.

COMING ATTRACTIONS

The next technique, the lease option, is a fantastic way to buy mobile home parks with little money down. Once you buy them you can either flip them or keep them. Lease options are also a great technique for selling a mobile home park when the market becomes slow or difficult to operate in. It is another very powerful arrow to have in your investment quiver, and will one day make you wealthy.

5

L/Os: Fast Cash + Cash Flow

L/O is the abbreviation for *lease option,* the third Basic Profit Strategy. It is a combination of the first strategy, keepers, and the second strategy, flippers, with a few additional features all its own. It is a powerful, flexible strategy, and a great addition to your investment tool box. In this chapter, you are going to learn how to harness the power of lease options to increase your wealth.

Lease options serve three major purposes to the mobile home park investor:

1. They allow you to acquire keepers with less risk.
2. They entice buyers when you want to sell a park
3. They act as a no-money-down flipping strategy with a sandwich L/O.

There are two parties to an L/O transaction: the current owner of the property, who is on the deed, whom we will refer to as the *owner,* and the holder of the lease option, who has a right to buy the property from the owner, whom we will refer to as the *optionee.* Let's define L/Os with respect to these two parties.

DEFINITION OF A LEASE OPTION

A lease option has two parts. The first part of an L/O is a *lease* that entitles the optionee to rent the property for a specified monthly rent for a specified length of time. Part of the rent may be set aside by the owner of the property as a credit toward the optionee's purchase of the property, and that is called the monthly *rent credit.*

The second part of an L/O is an option contract that entitles the optionee to the right, but *not* the obligation, to buy the property on or before a specified date in the future, called the *expiration date,* at a specified price, called the *option price.* The optionee has the choice of buying or not buying the property in the future, but the owner has no choice—he must sell the property to the optionee if the optionee wants to buy it on or before the expiration date. Along with the option to buy the property, the optionee pays the current owner a nonrefundable consideration fee, called an up-front *option deposit.* This deposit is applied to the purchase of the property when the optionee closes on the property, or is forfeited to the owner if the optionee does not buy the property by the expiration date.

The above definition of L/Os contains five important terms, shown in italics. Some of them may be new to you, but this strategy is not as complicated as it may seem. L/Os are simply a combination of two strategies and some additional factors. If you don't feel comfortable with L/Os initially, that's okay! Read this chapter anyway, and if you are still not comfortable with L/Os when you are done, come back to them later in your investment career. You can still make plenty of money with keepers and flippers without ever doing an L/O. But once you understand these terms L/Os will make sense, and using the terms will become second nature. Let's discuss the five terms in detail.

The L/O Lease

You probably already understand what a lease is, since many of you have already rented a place to live and signed a lease at some time in your lives. However, when you rented it, it probably did not occur to you that you could, or should, arrange to buy it at some time in the future, either to keep or to flip it to someone else for a profit. An L/O lease is not materially different from a regular lease, except that some of the terms that are fixed and taken for granted in a regular lease may be made flexible and negotiable in an L/O lease—specifically, the *duration* (length of time) of the lease, the ability to *sublet*, who pays for the *repairs and maintenance*, and the *security deposit*.

The *duration* of a residential lease is usually for one year or less, with one year being the most common length of time. When you are buying using an L/O lease, you will want to make the term as long as you can—if possible two or three years, or even longer, to give yourself the most flexibility and control. The opposite is true when you are selling using an L/O. Then you will want to make the term as short as you can for the optionee—one year or even just six months—again to give yourself the most flexibility and control.

The right to *sublet* means the optionee has the right to turn over possession of the property to another tenant and rent to them at whatever new terms the optionee and the new tenant agree to, as long as those terms do not conflict with the optionee's agreement with the owner. When an optionee is allowed to sublet, the optionee becomes a secondary landlord on the property.

Most landlords don't like to give tenants the ability to sublet, because they wind up with a new tenant that they have not selected, and tenant selection is one of the most critical components of running a good rental property management system. What most owners don't realize is that a tenant automatically has the right to sublet unless the lease specifically states that subletting is *not* allowed. When you are an optionee using an L/O to acquire a keeper, you will want the ability to sublet. When you are an owner using an L/O to sell a property and entice an optionee to buy it, you will probably not want to allow the optionee to sublet.

As we saw earlier, *Repairs and maintenance* are major costs of keepers. However, when you are an owner using an L/O to sell a property, the optionee can be made responsible for maintaining the property and doing all the repairs, and this is one of the strong points of L/Os. When you sell using an L/O, you should either make the optionee accept the property *as-is*, with all faults, or put the property on a "shake-down cruise" for the first month of the lease. During this first month you will fix whatever is reasonable, and then afterward it's the optionee's responsibility to maintain the property. Explain that you are training the optionees to be owners, like you. When you have a problem with your mobile home parks, you take care of it or pay the expenses involved with fixing it—you don't have anyone else to hand the problem over to. Make it plain that you are helping them create a rare opportunity to own their own mobile home park, and along with that opportunity comes responsibility. Most people understand and accept that principle, and if they don't, then they probably won't make a good optionee and you are better off selecting someone else.

The *security deposit* for an L/O is usually included as part of the up-front option money, and as such is nonrefundable. When you buy using an L/O option, you should try to make the deposit you are paying out as small as possible. When you sell to an optionee using an L/O you should try to make the deposit you are receiving as large as possible. Either way, the deposit on an L/O is not refundable, unlike with a regular lease, where the security deposit is refundable as long as the tenant returns the property in the same condition at the end of the lease as it was in the beginning, subject to normal wear and tear, after paying all the monthly rents that were due.

The Rent Credit

The rent credit is unique to L/Os. A set portion of each monthly rent can be applied as a credit towards the purchase by the optionee. If the optionee buys the property, all the monthly credits are added up from the rents that have been paid and that amount is subtracted from the final price. If the optionee does not buy the property, the monthly credits evaporate and are forfeited. This is one of the prime motivations for the optionee to purchase the property—the monthly credits help the optionee save for a down payment, and act like a savings account for when the optionee applies for a mortgage loan to close the transaction.

While it is not absolutely necessary to give the optionee a monthly rent credit when you are offering an L/O, it is strongly advisable—it acts a further enticement for the optionee to close on the property and buy it. One of the basic emotional hooks of an L/O is the following principle:

The Principle of Buyers Chasing After Their Own Money

This is the basic emotional hook for life insurance, lay-away-plans, funeral insurance, mortgage loans, car loans—and L/Os, too. It is the basis for anything purchased under an installment plan. The buyer puts down a deposit and makes a monthly payment for a property, which can be either real estate or personal property (such as a boat or a car). With each monthly payment, the buyer builds up credits to pay off the original loan, until the day when the loan is completely paid off, there are no more payments, and the buyer fully owns the property.

If the buyer stops making monthly payments before the property is paid off, the buyer loses his deposit and his monthly credits, and the property reverts back to the original seller. In effect, the buyer does not have complete ownership until he has made all the payments. Therefore, between the first payment and the last payment, the buyer is *chasing after his own money*. The buyer will lose the property and all the money he has previously paid in if he defaults on the installment payment program. For this reason you should give a healthy and generous monthly rent credit, if you want to give the optionee in an L/O a strong motivation to complete the L/O and buy the property. People feel a fifh to a third of the rent is realistic, but when it comes to mobile home parks, *I would recommend a fifth to a third of the positive cash flow only* (based upon a mortgage for 80 percent of the purchase price).

The Expiration Date

The *expiration date* of the lease is usually the same as the expiration date of the option. This is the last date by which the optionee can purchase the property and the last date the optionee can lease the property. This "buying on time" is a major part of what makes the L/O so powerful—the optionee has a chance now to own his or her mobile home park while getting his or her business affairs in order. During the time period up to the expiration date, optionees may save up money for a down payment, fix their credit, complete the sale of another property, decide if they want to continue to own the property, or do any of the things that people need to do in order to feel comfortable before they commit to a mobile home park purchase.

An L/O is based on the "puppy dog" closing technique. This strategy is used by smart pet shop owners when they see a customer becoming affectionate with a cute little puppy in their store. They tell the customer they can put the cost of the puppy on their credit card and take it home over the weekend and play with it. If on Monday morning the customer is unhappy for any reason, they can bring back the puppy for a full refund, no questions asked. How many people do you think take advantage of the refund after playing with, and falling in love with, an adorable puppy over the weekend? Not many.

The "puppy dog" close is also used effectively by car salesmen. When I was looking to buy a Corvette, the salesman handed me the keys to a beautiful new red convertible that was sitting on the lot and told me to take it home over the weekend. He said we would fill out the papers but not sign them until Monday morning—or tear them up then if I didn't want to buy. I smiled and handed the keys back. I said, "I want a little more time to think about it," which are dreaded words to salespeople everywhere. When I made puppy noises as I walked out, the salesman smiled.

When you give a future buyer an L/O, each day until end of the expiration period they will wake up to a mobile home park that they want to make theirs. They are living like an owner, feeling like an owner, and they will want to continue to hold onto that "little puppy" and pay for it before they lose it after the expiration date.

The Option Price

This is the price the optionee will pay during the time period that the option is in force, should the optionee decide to buy. A few things must be said about the pricing of L/Os. First, most optionees are not price sensitive. They are usually so thankful to get the opportunity to buy a mobile home park that they don't want to "kill the deal" by trying to negotiate a discount. In most areas, there are not many L/Os offered and there are many buyers who need them and can not own a park any other way. Most investors who use L/Os to sell property will pick the "full retail" price of the park as the option price—they use L/Os to get top dollar, and reduce their holding costs to nothing while doing so, because the optionee will repair and maintain the park.

Second, as the length of the expiration period increases, usually an owner experienced in giving L/Os will also increase the option price and rent. The amount of the increase usually reflects the market appreciation that mobile home parks in the area have been experiencing over time. This could be anywhere from zero percent to upwards of 10 percent, depending on the real estate market. For instance, let's assume you live in a market that has experienced 10 percent average price appreciation each year over the last ten years, and you are giving an optionee an L/O to buy your mobile home park for $1,000,000. You offer to L/O the park for $10,000 per month (including the mortgage payment), with a $1,000 monthly credit, for one year, at the option price of $1,000,000. The L/O optionee likes the terms but says she may need two years to get her financial house in order. You say you can agree to two years, but if the optionee does not purchase the property from you during the first year, you want $11,000 per month in rent payments during the second year in order to give the same $1,000 monthly credit, and you want a price of $1,100,000 during the second year, both of which are a 10 percent increase over the first year. It looks like this:

L/O 1st Year = $10,000 Monthly Rent, $1,000 Monthly Rent Credit, $1,000,000 Price
L/O 2nd Year = $11,000 Monthly Rent, $1,000 Monthly Rent Credit, $1,100,000 Price

If the optionee complains, you can simply say, "At the end of the first year, given the way parks have been appreciating 10 percent per year, I should be able to get $1,100,000 and $11,000 per month from the next optionee. If you want to keep the appreciation for yourself, then you should buy it before the first year is over and put the 10 percent increase in your pocket instead of mine."

The Option Deposit

The *option deposit* is the carrot on the end of the stick for the owner. The owner is now holding a nonrefundable deposit for agreeing to give an optionee the right, but not the obligation, to buy his property in the future. No matter what happens, the owner will at least get the option money. If the optionee goes on to complete the transaction and purchase the property, the option deposit will be a credit toward the price. If the optionee does not complete the transaction by the expiration date, the deposit will belong the owner, along with all the rents and monthly rental credits.

A note should be mentioned here about who should hold the option deposit. When I am an optionee, I prefer to have a title company or an attorney hold the deposit in their escrow account and not release it until the expiration date or the closing, whichever comes first. I don't want to worry about an owner disappearing off the face of the earth with my deposit and rental credits. However, when I give an L/O, I hold the deposit because I am not worried about my ethics, which are sound. It's other people's ethics that I want to be protected against.

Now that we have defined all our terms, let's learn how to make money with L/Os. A good L/O will put money in your pocket each month when you use it like a keeper. A good L/O will also give you more profit when you sell a property if you want to use it for a flipper. Therefore, we have to have three *formulas for success* in order to decide if a property is a good L/O or not.

1. One formula that determines if an L/O will make money as a keeper if you are the optionee.
2. A second formula that shows whether giving an L/O to an optionee will be profitable if you are the owner.
3. A third formula for a sandwich L/O.

Don't worry, the first two L/O formulas are practically the same as the previous formulas we used for flippers and keepers—they just have few commonsense modifications that we will emphasize and note. The third formula is just a combination of the first two L/O formulas.

THE FIRST L/O FORMULA—USING AN L/O TO ACQUIRE KEEPERS

It helps to think of the benefits to each party in this first L/O application. Here, you would ask the question, "*Why would a buyer want to use an L/O to acquire a keeper*?" Why doesn't the buyer just buy the property right now, and eliminate the hassle of waiting and the doubt as to whether the sale will close or not? The three most common cases when buyers want to be an optionee in an L/O deal are:

1. The optionee wants a keeper today, but needs time to arrange a loan.
2. The optionee wants time to assess the park as a long-term keeper.
3. The optionee wants an almost riskless way of flipping the property to a second optionee, by doing a sandwich L/O, which will generate immediate cash out, positive cash flow, and no money down, or the optionee wants to flip it immediately to a cash buyer.

The L/O Cash Flow Formula

Arrange the lowest *monthly rent* from the owner. Then arrange for the lowest *option price* and *up-front money,* while getting the highest *monthly credit* and the longest *expiration date.* You may want to take over making the mortgage payments to make sure they remain current while you are optioning the park. You should receive higher rents from the residents in the mobile home park than your monthly rent to the owner, including your costs for repairs, maintenance, and expenses. If the owner continues to make the mortgage payments your cash flow formula is:

Monthly Cash Flow = Monthly NOI – Your L/O Rent

If you take over the mortgage payments, your monthly cash flow formula is:

Monthly Cash Flow = Monthly NOI – L/O Rent
– Mortgage Payment

You must decide whether to keep the property, sell it to someone else, walk from the deal, or sandwich it by expiration date of the L/O. If you keep it or sell it to someone else, your profit is:

Value at Time of Closing – Option price = Market Appreciation
+
Monthly Credits × Number of Months Rent Was Paid
+
Monthly Positive Cash Flow × Number of Months Rent Was Paid

If you decide to walk away from the option, your profit/loss is:

Monthly Positive Cash Flow × Number of Months
– Up-front Option Money

The optionee or second optionee in each of these three cases will take care of all the repairs and maintenance of the property and foots those bills. The owner receives a monthly income while waiting to sell, a deposit in case the property does not sell, and a good price for the property when it does sell. Keep in mind that now *we are dealing as astute investors when we are optionees, and changing the negotiable terms to our benefit.* That means we try to adjust all negotiable terms in our favor as the buyer: we want the lowest monthly rent, the lowest up-front money, and the lowest option price. We also look for the longest lease and expiration date and the biggest monthly credit possible.

For the *first case,* you know the benefits of the park as a long-term keeper and you just need time to arrange a mortgage or get your affairs in order.

In the second case, you're not sure if you want to keep the property and you'd like time to assess it to decide whether to keep it or let the option expire. You're not sure yet if you want the risk of taking out a long-term loan and being obligated to manage the property for an extended period of time. You gain experience and knowledge while you hold the property during the L/O lease term, and then you can decide whether to hold onto it or not. If the long-term outlook of holding the property is good, you will keep it. If the long-term outlook is not good, then you can either sell the property to someone who has a different outlook or let the option expire. While you hold onto the property, it would be nice if the positive cash flow totaled as much or more than the up-front option deposit, so you won't lose money.

In the *third case,* you want to buy the property and eventually sell it, doing a sandwich L/O. You option the property and then turn around and give someone else an option to buy the property from you—even though you don't own it yet and only have an option on it. This is one of the most powerful flipping techniques there is! You have put no money down, you *get cash out up front,* while arranging positive cash flow. We'll go over this advanced technique after we go over the *second case.*

Understanding the L/O Cash Flow Formula

Let's start at the top, while keeping in mind that we are either looking to keep the property as a rental or to salvage our deposit and credits and sell it to someone else. Either way, you will be managing the mobile home park and collecting rents, so you need to negotiate the lowest rent, the lowest price, and the lowest amount of up-front money, while also getting the highest monthly credit and longest expiration date.

You want to fill up as many vacant spaces as possible, so you will have to advertise lots or mobile homes for rent, either with classified ads, signs, or both. You might want to raise rents so that you have an even greater positive cash flow. You will take over all the repairs and maintenance for the park. Each month the residents will pay you rent and you will pay the L/O monthly rent to the owner, keeping the difference. You may also make the mortgage payments, with a correspondingly lower L/O monthly rent.

After a period of time, if you decide to keep the property, you will seek long-term financing and exercise the option to buy. When you buy, you will pay the option price you negotiated minus the deposit and any rent credits. If you don't want to keep the property, you can flip it to another investor at a higher price than your option price. In this case, your profit will be the increase in value from your option price, plus all your credits and positive cash flow.

There is one major pitfall when you buy using an L/O, and it must be discussed now so you can prevent it from happening to you.

A Warning About L/Os—Good Title and Recording

In order to exercise the option to buy you must be able to get good title to the property. You don't want to be an optionee on a property that you can't buy later or sell to someone else because the title is not marketable, which means there are problems with the title, such as liens or questionable ownership. Without a clear title you aren't going to be able to borrow against the property, which means you aren't closing until the problems are fixed . . . if ever.

Do not spend a lot of your own money improving an L/O before you get title to it. If there are any problems getting title, or unpleasant occurrences like the owner skipping town, disappearing, or dying with estate problems, then you might be out the money you spent fixing up a property that you might never own. If you are persistent in seeking good title in this kind of situation, you might have to hire an attorney and pay high attorney fees trying to acquire title through a "quiet title suit."

Like a good prize fighter, you should always follow the rules, but protect yourself at all times against someone who doesn't. The way you protect yourself when you are an optionee is by getting a title insurance company to give you an Owners and Encumbrance (O&E) report before you sign the papers for an L/O. An O&E report costs between $100 and $150, and it will show all the liens outstanding against the property that have to be cleared up before title is marketable—which means there are no outstanding problems on the title and you will be able to get title insurance, then a mortgage, and close. The O&E will also show the current owners on the property and therefore who needs to sign the L/O. You want to make sure everyone who owns the property agrees to the terms of the L/O.

In addition to getting an O&E, you will also want to protect your L/O by recording it in the public records, giving notice to the world that you have an option to buy the property. You could use the Memorandum of Contract form in the Appendix of this book.

This is another duality in L/Os. As an optionee you want to record the L/O to protect your rights. However, when you are an owner giving an L/O, you specifically *do not* want the optionee to record the L/O. If the L/O is recorded and the optionee does not buy the property, the title will be "clouded" by the L/O. Unless another instrument called a Release (also in the Appendix) is also recorded, you as the owner will not be able to give marketable title to someone else in the future.

Don't throw out L/Os because of this pitfall. The vast majority of L/Os have good title and the owners are all present and agree to the terms of the L/O. Also, rest assured that if in spite of all your precautions you still run into a title problem, there is a legal way of clearing up title defects through a quiet title suit. You will need an attorney to do this, and it will take from three months to a year or more, and it could cost from five hundred up to several thousand dollars, depending on how many liens there are to clean up. But at the end of the process you should have a property that can be financed.

I have known a few people in my twenty-seven-year real estate investment career who created an L/O without doing a title check, or recording their L/O, and their L/O could not be executed. In these cases, the owner had liens of greater value than the option price and the owner couldn't come to closing and write a check to clear them up. These problems would have been avoided up-front with an O&E report, and the optionee could have found a different property that had marketable title.

Example: The Oasis Motel

I have not used an L/O to buy a mobile home park, but I have helped friends who used an L/O for their purchase of keepers. This example is one of the more interesting L/Os I have seen. My friend, Bobby, wanted to establish a half-way house for people with alcohol and drug problems. Bobby was a recovering alcoholic himself, and he wanted to help others recover from their addictions. He asked me if I was familiar with a property where he could do this, and I brought him to the Oasis Motel.

The Oasis had four separate buildings with a total of thirty-eight rooms. One of the buildings was uninhabitable and needed a complete rehab. The motel had been for sale for years, with no buyers. The owner of the Oasis was a widow who needed to sell because the motel lost money every year, which she had to borrow from a friend. This friend came to me because the value of his loans was soon going to be greater than value of the motel, otherwise known as being "upside-down," and he wanted me to buy it before that happened. I didn't want to buy it because it was too management intensive, needed too much rehab, and had too many vacancies during the seven-month off season. I had other projects that had more profit potential. However, this looked like it could be a marriage of convenience between Bobby and the owner of the motel and her friend.

Bobby and the motel owner worked out an L/O that was a win/win for both parties. Bobby got an L/O to buy the motel over the next year at a good price. During that year, Bobby got exclusive control of one of the good buildings and the uninhabitable building. He could bring in customers that were released from treatment programs, needed a half-way house to stay in, and had personal money or funds coming from the

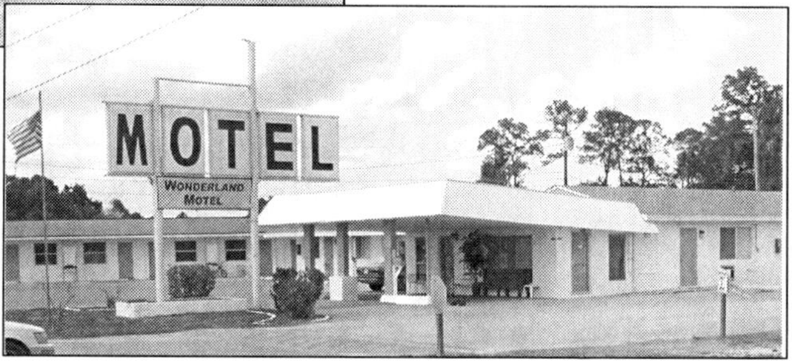

The Oasis Motel, before (above) and after (right).

state of Florida for their living expenses. Bobby would supervise them closely. Like the first group of alcoholics who started AA, they would live together and help each other overcome their addictions. His idea was to have them renovate the uninhabitable building as part of their recovery and therapy, which was a great idea. All the rents that came in from Bobby's good building, less the pro-rata share of the expenses for that building, would go to Bobby to use for materials to fix up the uninhabitable building, and whatever they were short Bobby planned to get donated. Bobby only had to come up with $5,000 option money, and they gave him two months to do that *after* the option began and he had control of the two buildings.

This was a good deal for Bobby because he was dealing with a highly motivated seller. Bobby's plan was brilliant, with everyone benefiting —the widow who owned the motel was selling a property she could not manage and lost money on every year, her "lending friend" would get paid back the money he lent her, Bobby would be creating an income for himself, and he was helping people recover from addictions. During the two months Bobby had to come up with the up-front money, he used the rental profits to start fixing up the uninhabitable building and to pay his own living expenses. He tried to the best of his ability to find someone who would lend him the 20 percent down so he could buy the motel, and not forfeit his time and work and deposit. Sad to say, he couldn't find anyone. Bobby did not put up the $5,000 option money, so after two months the option defaulted.

The story does have a happy ending. Bobby licked his wounds, became stronger in his own recovery, and now he is helping people all over the world recover from their addictions, rather than just running a small motel that was converted to a halfway house in South Florida.

The friend who lent the money to the widowed owner of the Oasis Motel came to my office months later. He literally begged me to buy the motel, and I told him no, it was too much work for too little return. He kept insisting I buy it, and I kept insisting I shouldn't. Finally we worked out a deal where I put down less than 10 percent of the purchase price, and they gave me the remainder in owner financing. The deal was subject to me finding a young, hardworking partner who had the time to be on-site and supervise the renovation and management of the motel. I found such a partner, Crazy Gersh, and together we fixed the Oasis and developed the excess land in the back into a storage facility. It went on to give us $10,000 per month in positive cash flow—but that is another adventure, better told at another time.

Theoretical Example: The River Mobile Home Park

While the previous example is real, it was not a mobile home park, and we didn't take into account many of the features of a mobile home park. For the rest of this chapter we are going to consider the features of a mobile home park I wanted to buy, using rounded numbers to make it easy to understand. A broker presented this property to me on a Friday morning, and as I was writing an offer over the weekend, the seller accepted another offer, one that involved a lease option.

The broker and I were surprised that the seller accepted a lease option rather than wait for a cash offer from me, but that goes to show how a lease option can be a viable strategy for some sellers. In this case, the seller was very price conscious, needed some immediate cash, and wanted out of the management of the park as soon as possible because of a health crisis in her family. The lease optionee offered full price, came up with fast cash for the option, and was willing to take over management of the park immediately.

The park was located on a narrow river in western North Carolina. It contained 120 lots, of which only 100 were rented for $220 per month per lot. The following were the rounded and approximate financials of the park:

THE RIVER MOBILE HOME PARK	
Number of Lots:	120, Only 100 Rented
Monthly Lot Rent:	$220 per Month
Yearly Gross Income:	$264,000 ($22,000 per Month)
Total Yearly Expenses:	$120,000 ($10,000 per Month)
NOI:	$144,000 ($12,000 per Month)
Listing Price:	$1,400,000
Cap Rate:	10.28%
Outstanding Mortgage:	$1,000,000
Monthly Mortgage Payments:	$7,000 P&I

The lease optionee offered to lease option the park at full price, $1,400,000 for two years. He put down $25,000 as an option deposit, which he allowed the seller to take right away. The approximate details of the lease option are:

THE RIVER MOBILE HOME PARK LEASE OPTION	
Option Price:	$1,400,000
Nonrefundable Option Deposit:	$25,000
Length of Lease:	2 Years
Monthly Lease Payments (Including Mortgage):	$10,000 per Month
Monthly Credit to Buyer:	$500 per Month
NOI per Month:	$12,000 per Month
Mortgage Payment:	$7,000 per Month
Monthly Positive Cash Flow to Seller	$3,000 per Month
Monthly Positive Cash Flow to Buyer	$2,000 per Month

You should see from the above that each month the lease optionee collected total rents of:

Total Monthly Rent = Rented Lots (100) × Lot Rent ($220 per Month) = $22,000

Then the optionee paid the monthly expenses and lease payment, which included the mortgage:

Cash Flow (Monthly)	=	Total Rent	–	Expenses	–	Lease Payment
$2,000	=	$22,000	–	$10,000	–	$10,000

Remember, the $10,000 lease payment of the optionee included the $7,000 per month mortgage payment, so the seller took the $10,000 lease payment, made the mortgage payment of $7,000, and kept $3,000 while the lease optionee ran the park. The lease optionee collected $2,000 per month in positive cash flow, so at the end of two years or twenty-four months he would have taken out $48,000 in profits. If, at the end of the two year lease, the optionee decided not to buy the park, he would have made back his forfeited $25,000 up-front deposit and had an additional

$23,000 for his effort. I was not entirely privy to the details of this transaction and I am not sure if the lease option details changed in the second year, so I am presenting this example in the simplest way possible.

I have assumed that the lease optionee's goal was to raise rents to $260 per month at the end of two years, which would have brought in an extra $40 per month per lot, or:

Additional Cash from Lot Rent Increase = Number of Rented Lots × Price Increase = 100 × $40 per Month = $4,000 per Month

When the optionee took title to the park at the end of two years, he could do BBs (which you will learn about in the next chapter) and fill the remaining twenty empty lots from his profits over the next two years. At the end of four years, he could have expected to have all 120 lots rented at a lot rent of $300 per month, and a park that now did the following:

Gross Rent = Number of Rented Lots (120) × Lot Rent ($300 per Month) = $36,000 per Month

If he expected his expenses to increase no more than 5 percent each year with inflation (and utilities were submetered so they were not an additional cost), there would only be a 20 percent total increase in expenses, which would go from the $10,000 per month to $12,000 per month. The NOI would be:

NOI = Gross Rent − Total Expenses
= $36,000 − $12,000 = $24,000 per Month
× 12 Months = $288,000 per Year

The park would be worth, at a 10 percent cap rate, $2,880,000, twice what he paid for it! He would have made a $1.4 million profit. The beauty of this option plan is that if he was wrong, he could have walked away from the deal with little or no risk, and if he was right, there was a bonanza waiting for him. What the optionee saw (and I did too) was that the lot rent was a little low for a nonwaterfront park at $220 per month, but it was extremely low for a waterfront park. Other waterfront mobile home parks were charging $260 per month or more at the time he optioned The River Mobile Home Park. It was reasonable to assume the other waterfront park lot rents would increase $10 per year to $300 by the end of four years.

How often do you get a chance, using simple strategies, to double an investment, and make over a million dollars? That being said, let's introduce you to the second part of the L/O *Formula for Success* where you are the owner of a property and want to use an L/O to help you sell it.

THE SECOND L/O FORMULA—USING AN L/O TO SELL YOUR PARK

Again, when you are dealing with investment strategies, it usually helps to think of the benefits to each party in the transaction. In this case, you would ask the question, "*Why would an owner want to give an L/O?*" Why doesn't the owner sell for cash right now, and eliminate the hassle and the doubt as to whether the sale will close or not?

The two most common reasons an owner gives an L/O are:

1. There are few or no cash buyers around willing to pay as much or more than the option price, and the owner wants to limit his management time and keep the holding costs of the property down while he is waiting to sell, or

2. The opposite is true—there are many buyers that need L/Os and few L/Os are available. The owner can find buyers without the help of real estate brokers because of this, and not have to pay a commission.

In each of these cases, the optionee will take care of all the repairs and maintenance of the property and foot those bills. The owner receives a monthly income while waiting to sell, a large deposit in case the property does not sell, and a good price for the property when it does sell.

There are other reasons for an owner to give an L/O. The owner may want to delay the sale for income tax reasons, or he wants or needs the highest price possible for the property but does not need to sell right away, or he does not need or want a fast sale.

(Human nature being what it is, I must mention that some investors have taken this wonderful strategy and abused it. They have concocted L/Os where the optionee can't possibly comply with the terms and are in default as soon as they sign the option. The investor's goal here is *not* to sell the property, but rather to keep the up-front deposit from the current optionees, evict them as soon as possible, and then turn around and do another L/O and get another up front deposit, which they will also keep. Please check with the Attorney General in your state to see if there have been limitations placed on L/Os because of the unscrupulous behavior of these investors.)

Prequalifying the Optionee

When you are an owner giving an L/O to an optionee, your optionee has to close by the expiration date if you are to reap your total harvest. This usually means that the optionee has to qualify for and obtain a mortgage loan, although there are some cases where the optionee is waiting for a sale of another property, or waiting for large amount of cash to come in. If the optionee needs a loan, you should send her to your mortgage broker or lender to get prequalified before you enter into an L/O. The mortgage broker or lender will check the optionee candidate's credit and income qualifications and then report back to you on whether the optionee candidate has a good chance of securing a mortgage for your property or if the optionee candidate has too many challenges to overcome. If the mortgage lender feels confident that he can arrange a loan, write up the L/O with the optionee. If the lender feels the optionee is a poor mortgage candidate, then you should find another optionee. The mortgage broker or lender will usually prequalify your optionees for *free* if you assure him that he will get first chance at doing the mortgage loan.

Understanding The L/O Flipping Formula

As you can see, the L/O Flipping Formula is a combination of the previous Cash Flow Formula and Flipping Formula, with some slight modifications. That is the reason L/Os were introduced after keepers and flippers—so you could use what you learned from the first two Basic Profit Strategies and build upon them to apply them to this powerful strategy.

We started with the Lease part of the L/O so we could use the monthly positive cash flow to figure out the monthly lease payment and monthly credit. This is the principle of having the optionee "chase after his own money." This will be used as a forced savings by the optionee, when he wants to close and needs a down payment and closing costs for his mortgage.

The L/O Flipping Formula

For the Lease part of the L/O Flipping Formula, figure out your monthly positive cash flow using the Cash Flow Formula in Chapter 2. Use a mortgage payment for 80 percent of the current value, or 80 percent LTV (loan-to-value) if there is no mortgage or the mortgage is small. (The LTV is the percentage arrived at when the mortgages are divided by the value of the property.).

Total Cash Flow/Month = NOI/Month – 80% LTV Mtg Payment

Determine a reasonable cash flow to the optionee, and subtract that from the total cash flow. Let's use half as a start:

Reasonable Cash Flow to Optionee = 50% of Total Cash Flow per Month
Cash Flow to Owner = 50% of Total Cash Flow per Month

The monthly lease payment, including the mortgage payment, will then be:

Monthly Lease Payment = 80% LTV Mortgage Payment + Cash Flow to Owner

To determine the monthly credit, you can use 20 percent of the cash flow to the optionee as a place to start. This is a negotiated amount with no hard-and-fast rules.

Monthly Credit = 20% Cash Flow to Optionee

To figure out your final profit for the Option part of the L/O:

1. Use the Flipping Formula in Chapter 4, *substituting* the option price for the final price.
2. Subtract the closing costs you will incur when you sell—the commissions, title insurance, documentary stamps, and so on—use 10 percent if not sure and *modify* if no commissions are due.
3. Subtract your original cost + fix up costs + holding costs in the property until you gave the L/O.
4. Modify by subtracting the total L/O monthly *rent credits you gave.*

5. Modify by adding the total L/O monthly cash flow received by the owner (figured out in the first part of the L/O Flipping Formula).
6. The remainder is your profit.

Next, we worked on the Option part of the L/O. Our first modification was to start with the full retail price as our option price rather than a price that would sell quickly with a discount. Next we subtracted our closing costs. You will modify your closing costs if you found the optionee by yourself without a broker and did not have to pay out any commissions—L/Os are scarce, so you may not need to use a broker. Then we subtracted our cost in the property up to the point we did the L/O; we added up our original cost, fix up costs, our holding costs, and so on. Next we subtracted the total monthly rental credits we would have to give out at closing. Then we added our total monthly cash flow while we were waiting for the optionee to close. The remainder was our total profit from doing the flipper by using an L/O.

Example: Selling the River Mobile Home Park Using an L/O

Let's use The River Mobile Home Park again, only we are going to assume we own the property, and we're working out an L/O with a prospective new buyer:

THE RIVER MOBILE HOME PARK	
Number of Lots:	120, Only 100 Rented
Monthly Lot Rent:	$220 per Month
Yearly Gross Income:	$264,000
Total Yearly Expenses:	$120,000 ($10,000 per Month)
NOI:	$144,000 ($12,000 per Month)
Listing Price:	$1,400,000
Cap Rate:	10.28%
Outstanding Mortgage:	$1,000,000
Monthly Mortgage Payments:	$7,000

THE RIVER MHP—WE GIVE 1-YEAR LEASE OPTION	
Option Price:	$1,400,000
Nonrefundable Option Deposit:	$25,000
Length of Lease:	1 year
Monthly Lease Payments (Include Mortgage):	$10,000 per Month
Monthly Credit to Buyer:	$500 per Month
NOI per Month:	$12,000 per Month
Mortgage Payment:	$7,000 per Month
Monthly Positive Cash Flow to Seller	$3,000 per Month
Monthly Positive Cash Flow to Buyer	$2,000 per Month

Now let's follow the L/O formula, step-by-step:

1. The current monthly cash flow is the NOI – mortgage payment, or $12,000 – $7,000 = $5,000 per month. We decided to give the optionee 40 percent of the positive cash flow, or $2,000 per month, and keep $3,000 per month for ourselves. Further, since the property makes $2,000 per month in positive cash flow to the optionee, we decided to give 25 percent of this as a monthly rental credit towards purchase, or $500 per month. Since we are giving the L/O, we would allow one year as the expiration date, not two years. If two years were needed, we would negotiate new higher terms for the second year, as we discussed before.
2. We picked an option price of $1.4 million, which is the full retail price for the park. This is a reasonable expectation for a seller on an L/O. We did not escalate it because only one year is being given on the L/O.
3. Subtract closing costs, our original cost, and fix-up and holding costs.
4. If the optionee buys the property, there will be twelve monthly lease credits of $500 per month, a total of $6,000, to subtract from our profit.
5. If the optionee buys the property on or near the expiration day, there will also be the twelve months of positive cash flow collected by seller, at $3,000 per month, or $36,000, to add to our profit.

If the optionee does not buy the park at the end of the year we will keep the $25,000 nonrefundable option deposit and wipe out the $6,000 in monthly rental credits. Then we will look for another lease optionee, potentially at a higher price and higher monthly lease payment.

THIRD L/O FORMULA—MAKING A SANDWICH

A *Sandwich L/O* is when you contract to buy a property as an optionee using an L/O, and turn around and give someone else an L/O to buy it from you. This is a powerful, advanced strategy that doesn't require money down, or even taking title.

You are using your experience and training as a real estate investor to negotiate the best deal for yourself as an optionee using the L/O to buy a keeper. Then you are using your expertise again when you turn around and flip the property by giving a *second optionee* an L/O, as in the second application above. When you do this correctly, you will have three paydays. This may sound a little complicated, but it will be made clear in the success formula below and then illuminated by the example of a sandwich L/O.

Like the successful prize-fighter you have become, you will also protect yourself on both sides of the sandwich L/O. *On the buy side,* you will get an O&E to make sure the title is clear and will not prevent the deal from closing. You will make sure you have the right to sublet, and you will record a Memorandum of L/O in the public records to give notice to the world you have a claim on the property. *On the sell side,* you will prequalify the second optionee to make sure she can complete the transaction. You will also not allow the second optionee to record the L/O and "cloud" the title if she does not close.

Understanding the Sandwich L/O Formula

Let's start by understanding the concept of three paydays. The *first payday* is fast cash right away from the difference in up-front deposits between what you pay the owner and what the second optionee pays you. Your *second payday* is the monthly positive cash flow from the difference in rents between what you pay the owner and what the second optionee pays you while you wait for the second optionee to complete the transaction. Your *third payday* is when the transaction closes and you make a profit from the difference in option prices and monthly credits. If you have a long expiration period, you can repeat the first and second

The Sandwich L/O Formula

On the buy side, arrange L/O with the owner for the lowest *monthly rent, option price,* and *up front money,* and highest *monthly credit* and longest *expiration date.* You will pay for repairs, maintenance, and all expenses, but you will be turning these over to the second optionee.

On the sell side, you will sublet the property using an L/O to the second optionee at a higher *monthly rent, option price,* and *up front money,* and smaller *monthly credit* and *expiration.* The second optionee will pay for repairs, maintenance and all expenses.

The Three Paydays: Your first payday is the difference in up-front deposits:

Deposit From Second Optionee – Your Deposit to Owner
= First Payday

Your second payday is the monthly positive cash flow:

Rent From Second Optionee – Your L/O Rent to Owner
= Second Payday

Your third payday is the final flipping profit:

Second Optionee Price – Your L/O Price
+
Your Monthly Credits – Second Optionee Credits
= Flipping Profit

If the second optionee does not complete their L/O, you can repeat the first and second paydays above with the extra time you negotiated on the buy side:

Your Option Time – Second Optionee Option Time
= Amount of Repetitions

paydays with another second optionee. Let's run through an example, to bring everything to light.

Example: A Sandwich L/O on The River Mobile Home Park

THE RIVER MOBILE HOME PARK— YOUR TWO-YEAR LEASE OPTION WITH OWNER	
Option Price:	$1,400,000
Nonrefundable Option Deposit:	$25,000
Length of Lease:	2 years
Monthly Lease Payments (Include Marketing):	$10,000 per Month
Monthly Credit to Buyer:	$500 per Month
NOI per Month:	$12,000 per Month
Mortgage Payment:	$7,000 per Month
Monthly Positive Cash Flow to Seller	$3,000 per Month
Monthly Positive Cash Flow to Buyer	$2,000 per Month

These are the same terms on a lease option that I assumed the investor who took the deal from me received. Now you are going to find another investor, a second optionee, who will accept the following terms:

THE RIVER MOBILE HOME PARK— THE ONE-YEAR LEASE OPTION GIVEN TO SECOND OPTIONEE	
Option Price:	$1,500,000
Nonrefundable Option Deposit:	$50,000
Length of Lease:	1 Year
Monthly Lease Payments (Include Mortgage):	$11,000 per Month
Monthly Credit to Buyer:	$500 per Month
NOI per Month:	$12,000 per Month
Mortgage Payment:	$7,000 per Month
Monthly Positive Cash Flow to Seller	$3,000 per Month
Monthly Positive Cash Flow to First Optionee (You)	$1,000 per Month
Monthly Positive Cash Flow to Second Optionee	$1,000 per Month

If the second optionee buys the property at or near the end of the first year, the following will be your three paydays:

Your first payday is the difference in up-front deposits:

First Payday = Deposit from Second Optionee – Your Deposit to Owner
= $50,000 – $25,000 = $25,000

Your second payday is the monthly positive cash flow:

Second Payday = Rent from Second Optionee – Your L/O Rent to Owner
= $11,000 – $10,000 = $1,000 per Month × 12 Months = $12,000

Your third payday is the final flipping profit:

Flipping Profit = Second Optionee Price – Your L/O Price – First Payday
+
Your Monthly Credits – Second Optionee Credits
= $1,500,000 – $1,400,000 + $500 per Month – $500 per Month
= $100,000 + 0 (Rental Credits Given vs. Received same)

So, when you complete the sandwich L/O, you will have:

Total Profit = First Payday + Second Payday + Third Payday
= $25,000 + $12,000 + $100,000
= $137,000 – $25,000 Additional Deposit Given Back
= $112,000

A profit of $112,000 in one year is great, with no money down, no management time, and little or no risk. It is not as much profit if you purchased the property as a keeper and, after four years, achieved all the goals we established before, and it was worth $2.8 million. Then you could have done a Refi Bonanza and pulled out more than $1 million in tax free profits. Even so, this strategy is worth considering when you find a good deal but don't have the time, the money, or the inclination to own the property yourself.

Note, if the second optionee does not complete their L/O, you can repeat the first and second and third paydays above with the extra time you negotiated on the buy side as opposed to the time you gave the second optionee, two years versus one year. This would give you another $112,000, plus the additional $25,000 forfeited from the first deposit, or

$137,000, for a total profit of almost $250,000! You can have even more repetitions if you negotiate an even longer expiration date with the owner:

Your Option Time – Second Optionee Option Time = Amount of Repetitions

Arranging a Sandwich L/O with Little Risk

In order to do a sandwich L/O with as little risk as possible you need to close with the owner on his L/O on the same the day the second optionee closes with you. You would arrange this the way you arrange simultaneous closings, which you learned when we discussed wholesaling in Chapter 4 on flipping.

Basically, you will get a long enough inspection period from the owner, with sixty days being a comfortable time, so you can arrange to find a second optionee for the park. You will mention to the owner that you will need to do a thorough inspection of the mobile home, to make sure there are no serious problems that will hit your pocketbook hard.

Remember to call your title company and get an O&E to make sure the owner you spoke to does indeed own the park, and that any liens on the property are not greater than your option price. Once you have completed and approved the mobile home park inspections, you will start marketing for a second optionee under the terms we figured above.

Since there are few L/Os being offered in your market, and plenty of buyers who need them, you will get a lot of phone calls. After you show potential investors the mobile home park, you will send those who appear the most eager and the most qualified, to your mortgage lender, who prequalifies them. You and your mortgage lender will select the investor with the best credit out of the three best candidates. (Keep in mind, if you find a buyer who wants to close right away and doesn't want a lease option—all the better.)

After you find a second optionee, you will have the owners sign and notarize the L/O agreements (samples are in the Appendix). You will add your notarized signature, and the title company will hold the papers in escrow. Then you will have your second optionee sign your set of L/O papers. You collect his or her option deposit and first month's lease payment and then you send the option deposit and first month's lease payment to the owner. You will record a Memorandum of your L/O with the owner, but *not* the second optionee's L/O.

In the unlikely event you could not find a second optionee, you would let the transaction pass due to problems with your inspection. This would not be unethical. There were hidden problems—there was no market in that area for buyers needing L/Os, which is a rare, but possible occurrence. You would be out any money you spent cleaning and advertising, benefits the owner would have for free. If the sandwich L/O is signed on both sides, but the second optionee does not close by his expiration date, you would not have your third payday. When you find another second optionee, you would receive another first and second payday and then hopefully the third payday. Even if you walk away at the end of the second sandwich lease option, you will still have four paydays.

Remember, at least two months before the end of the first year, you should call the second optionee and recommend that they get their mortgage in motion with the lender they prequalified through. You send both L/Os to the title company—the one you signed with the current owner, and the one you signed with the second optionee. The title company will prepare all the closing documents and arrange a simultaneous closing between the second optionee and the owner. You never take title, but you collect checks.

HOW TO PRESENT AN L/O TO AN OWNER

After seeing how powerful a sandwich lease-option is, you might want to do a passel of them. The main ingredient, as you can see, is getting an owner to give you a lease option. For that reason, you will usually need to find highly motivated sellers.

Reasons that might make sellers highly motivated include divorce, a death in the family, a need to relocate, or a job loss, among others. In the best case, you want someone who simply wants to get the monthly mortgage payment off his or her neck.

The way to present your offer to L/O is to give the owner two options:

1. You will buy the property at your price and with the owner's terms
2. You will buy the property at the owner's price and with your terms

Buying at your price means the lowest price possible—the wholesale price, which may be a shocker to the owner, but at the owner's terms, which means cash at closing. The result is that, at your price, the cash at closing is minimized for the owner. This will motivate the owner to choose the second option, which is what you want anyway.

The second choice is for you to buy at the owner's price, which means close to the retail price but at your terms—the owner gives you a long-term L/O to buy the property, with the understanding that you may turn around and place a good second optionee in it who will eventually buy it and pay off the outstanding loan.

Once you have an L/O from the current owner, it is usually very easy to find someone else—a second optionee—to pass along the L/O to, and your sandwich is created.

SUMMARY

As you can see, lease options can be used for flippers, keepers, or sandwiches. They are a great for waking up buyers in a sleepy market or for selling for maximum dollar in a hot market. They are also a great way to accumulate property in a hot market with no or low money down or to buy property in a slow market while you wait for prices to rise before you close.

If you are familiar with stock options, you will see real estate L/Os have many similarities. The terms expiration date, option price, and upfront money mean essentially the same thing for both. However, there is no monthly rental credit in a stock option like there is in a real estate option, and the leverage is much greater in real estate lease options. You can do L/Os for little or no money down on large amounts of real estate, whereas stock options must be paid for upfront in cash, or if you are fortunate, 50 percent down. In my opinion, the profit potential is more secure with a real estate L/O.

Let me offer another understanding word to the mathematically challenged at this point. I know from being a trainer that some people may not be comfortable with so many calculations on sandwich L/Os. That's okay. Either find a partner who is or just put sandwich L/Os in the back of your mind for now. You may feel more comfortable with sandwich L/Os later on, after you have more experience with one sided L/Os.

HOMEWORK

Look in the papers and see if there are any L/Os being offered on mobile home parks. Usually there are not many—that's why this technique is so powerful., Go see whatever L/Os you find and talk with the owner about how they are willing to set it up and what forms they use. Write down the L/Os you find in your notebook.

Now go back and visit all the mobile home parks you have looked at so far that were either openly for sale, or that the owners agreed to sell when you contacted them. Also, see if you can find some new mobile home parks for sale. (If you are having difficulty finding parks for sale, then it would be all right to skip ahead to Chapter 7 and discover other places to find more parks for sale and then return here.) Write down the price the seller wants, the NOI, and the resulting cap rate.

Now write down in your notebook how you would offer to lease/option these parks from the owner. Write down how you would turn around and sell the property immediately to an investor and get a big payday. Then set up a sandwich of that lease option with a second optionee. You should be able to make three paydays when you sandwich it: two paydays immediately, and one later on when the second optionee closes on the property and buys it.

Type 3s: continue to relax and don't buy anything yet. I know it looks like you can create a sandwich L/O and make money immediately, but there is still more to learn. My promise still holds true. If you read carefully and absorb the important points, you could be ready within a month or less.

It would be great if you owned a mobile home park and could put an ad in the paper advertising it for sale as an L/O, so you could see the response. I'm willing to bet it would be great.

COMING ATTRACTIONS

Congratulations! Now you understand flippers and keepers and the combination of them—L/Os. The next strategy is just as sweet as the previous three. You can earn returns of 50 percent or more per year. That's right, I said 50 percent or more. We call it *Being the Banker,* or *BBs.*

BBs have an even greater benefit to you when you own your own mobile home park. They are a powerful way of filling empty spaces and giving you a *Triple Zotz.* Yes, that's right—a Triple Zotz.

To learn more about BBs and Triple Zotz's, turn the page.

6

BBs: Being the Bank

This is your Fourth Basic Profit Strategy, and after you understand it you might believe we saved the best for last.

Now, you're going to *Be the Bank*, which means you are going to become the lender on older, but still in fine shape, mobile homes.

You can earn returns of 40 to 80 percent by employing this strategy. It is a powerful strategy for mobile home park investors who want to turn around a park that has vacant lots or, on the other end of the spectrum, for retired investors who want to supersize their retirement income.

You will be employing the BB in three different cases:

1. Existing mobile homes in parks owned by others

2. Existing mobile homes in parks you own

3. Setting up mobile homes on vacant lots in parks you own—creating the *Triple Zotz*

In the first or second case above, whether you elect to do a BB in someone else's park or in your own park, you shouldn't have to do much rehabbing or spend much time, if any at all. You will have to spend more time and do more work if you elect to create a BB in your own park to fill a vacant lot but then you will be the beneficiary of the Triple Zotz, which we will discuss later in this chapter. The Triple Zotz is what powered our fantastic returns in the parks we turned around in Chapters 2 and 3 when you learned about keepers, and it will do the same for you. The BB is the most powerful way of overcoming the most common problem in turn-around parks—filling a vacant lot.

You are going to discover there is a strong demand for older mobile homes that are in good condition, but many banks do not want to lend on them. This stems from a problem of perception that some people have. They believe that since a mobile home has a title like an automobile it must depreciate in value and usefulness like a car. They assume that it is worn out and ready for the junk heap after twenty years. The reality is that mobile homes depreciate more like a house than a car—if you take care of them. Like a house, they can last fifty years or more. I personally own mobile homes that are approaching fifty years in age and are still going strong. Conversely, I have seen mobile homes less than ten years old that were ready for the scrap yard because they were abused.

You will learn how to take advantage of this oversight on the part of lenders in this chapter. This gap in bank lending activity makes this into an opportunity for you to be a smart lender. And don't worry—if you don't have any money to lend, we'll show you how to get some. If you execute this strategy correctly you should be able to find the money you need until you have built up your own capital base.

DEFINITION OF A BB

There are three parties to a simple BB transaction:

1. The *current owner* of the mobile home on a rental lot, who is on the title.
2. The *new buyer,* who needs to borrow money to buy the mobile home.
3. The new buyer will borrow money and sign a note made payable to you, *the banker.* If you need to borrow the money to pay the current owner for his mobile home, there is a fourth party to the transaction:
4. The *OPM lender* (OPM means Other People's Money).

A BB starts when you purchase an older mobile home, still in fine condition, from the *current owner* in a park where the residents rent the land. You offer to pay cash and close quickly, and because of this you buy the mobile home at a large discount, typically half of its value. Then you sell the mobile home to a *new buyer* at the retail price, around twice the price you paid, and give financing to the new buyer as described on the note the new buyer signs. You will collect a down payment and monthly mortgage payments until the note is paid off by the new buyer. You will not do repair and maintenance after the mobile home is sold to the new buyer because you will *Be the Banker.*

If you need to borrow the money to pay the current owner, you will give a second note to an *OPM lender.* You will pledge the mobile home as collateral for the second note. Then, you will collect on the first note signed by the new buyer each month, pay the OPM on the second note, and pocket the difference.

This strategy dramatically lowers or completely eliminates the work and time consuming aspects of the first three Basic Profit Strategies—keepers, flippers, and L/Os—while still taking advantage of their great investment returns.

Like a flipper, you will be adding to your wealth by increasing the price of the mobile homes you buy. Unlike a flipper, you will only be buying very light cosmetic rehabs or mobile homes that require no rehab at all. It's up to you and the market whether you even need to lightly rehab the ones you buy or just leave it up to the new buyer. Because of the need for financing on older mobile homes, buyers (new owners) will go out of their way to clean and repair them by themselves.

Like a keeper, you will be earning great cash-on-cash returns, but you will not have to take care of repairs and maintenance because you will not own the mobile home. You are the banker, and the banker does not come and fix a home after they lend the owner the money to buy it. (The banker's only concern is, "Did you make your mortgage payment?") And like a sandwich L/O, you can do this for low or no money down, have multiple paychecks, and earn great returns while you provide a valuable and needed service to buyers and sellers of older, but still in fine shape, mobile homes.

You should note that in the definition we limited the BB to mobile homes where the owner rents the land underneath it—homes in land-lease communities. You can also use this strategy with mobile homes that are considered real estate, when you own the land. However, because of the additional cost of the land, you will have to give mortgages that are much longer in maturity and the strategy will not yield as high as a return.

That being said, let's introduce the BB *Formula for Success* (see page 191).

UNDERSTANDING THE BB FORMULA

This formula may seem complicated but it really isn't, once you know your way around a mortgage calculator. After we're finished explaining the steps, you'll see it's really based upon common sense. It will become crystal clear—and exciting—once we run through the three different cases and do the examples.

However, if like the lease option, the math seems too challenging to you, stay with it until the end of the chapter. If it still does not feel comfortable, find a partner who is comfortable with it or come back to this strategy later on. If you feel comfortable with L/Os but not BBs you can still use the fundamental basis of this strategy to turn around your own mobile home parks that have vacant lots. Many park owners do lease options rather than BBs. We will discuss the difference between using a L/O or a BB later on in the chapter. If you still don't feel comfortable with L/Os or BBs, you can find BB investors who will move mobile homes into your parks but you won't get a Triple Zotz from them—only a Double Zotz. Life is still good.

Case One: The Mobile Home is on a Lot in Someone Else's Park

In this case you are going to buy an older mobile home that is in excellent shape for about half its value, located in a park where you rent the land beneath the home. This is the strategy you would also use in your own park. You will find these homes for sale in classified ads, on the Internet, by running a Gold Mine Ad, by driving around large rental parks and looking at For Sale signs, and so on. You will learn the many places to find good deals in Chapter 7. Keep in mind, you are looking for homes that need a light cosmetic rehab or no rehab at all, and you will arrange a big discount because you will offer to pay cash and close

The BB Formula

1. Buy a mobile home for approximately half of its value. This is your **Original Cost**
2. Figure your total cost, based on: **Total Cost = Original Cost + Fix-up Costs + Holding Cost**
3. Figure your selling price, based on: **Selling Price = Total Cost × 2**

When you find a new buyer:

1. Select a **Down Payment** of $500, $1000, or $2,000, depending on **Selling Price**.
2. Select a **Monthly Payment** of $95, $195, or $295, depending on **Selling Price**.
3. Select the **Interest Rate** you will charge (for example, 9.9%).
4. Figure the note amount, based on: **Note Amount = Selling Price – Down Payment**.
5. Compute the **Number of Payments** using **Note Amount, Monthly Payment,** and the **Interest Rate** you choose (9.9%).
6. Round the **Number of Payments** up by one if there is a partial month.
7. Refigure the **Monthly Payment** with number of rounded months.

Now, to figure your profit and check your figures:

1. Figure the total collected: **Total Collected = Monthly Payment × Number of Payments**
2. Figure the total out of pocket cost: **Total Out of Pocket Cost = Total Cost – Down Payment**
3. Check: is the **Total Collected at least 2 times Total Out of Pocket Cost?**
4. Figure your profit: **Profit = Total Collected – Total Out of Pocket Cost**

The cash-on-cash return is:

Profit ÷ Total Out of Pocket Cost ÷ Years = Cash-on-Cash Return

> You may choose to collect insurance and yearly title and tag fees, as an extra security that these get paid. If you do this, you should:
>
> 1. Collect the first whole year's insurance payment and pay it.
> 2. Collect the first whole year's title and tag fees and pay it.
> 3. Divide the insurance by 12, and that is what you will collect monthly.
> 4. Divide title + tag fees by 12, and that is what you will collect monthly.

quickly. You will know how to figure what to pay and what to sell for when we discuss appraising in Chapter 8.

When you buy the home, you will use the form in the Appendix titled "Contract for Buying Mobile Homes in Rental Parks." Before you close on the mobile home, apply to the park manager to lease the lot under the mobile home. Wait until the manager approves you and gives you a lease before you pay the current owner in full.

At this point, we should include a word about sales tax, title, and tag fees. We became mobile home dealers in the state of Florida, a fairly simple and inexpensive process, and by doing so we were able to transfer the sales tax, title, and tag fees when we bought a mobile home from the current owner to the new buyer and not pay any of it ourselves. If you are going to be doing a lot of BBs, find out what license you can obtain in your state or county so you can pass along these fees to the new buyer too.

Now you will either call new buyers on your waiting list, or place a sign at the mobile home and an ad in the local *Pennysaver, Uwanna,* or *Shopper* that reads as follows:

3BR Mobile Home
Nice Quiet Park
Owner Finance, No Banks Needed
Let's Talk 555-1234

You can modify the first line as to the number of bedrooms and the second line to give a short statement of the benefits of the park. Leave lines three and four alone except to insert your phone nı three and four are your market tested sales magnets, so plea: with them. "Don't fix something that ain't broke."

MOBILE HOMES
$500 & UP
OWNER FINANCING
LET'S TALK! 995-6442

Please notice the sign that started us on BBs. It is a variation of the ad on the previous page. At the time, we were actually selling some mobile homes for $500 that we got for free when we purchased the park. They were in very poor condition, and we were looking for new buyers who were capable of doing heavy rehabs. I would modify the sign to read $500 Down & UP, rather than $500 & up, if you are not selling mobile homes for $500 as the total price.

When you find a new buyer, prequalify him or her on the phone. Ask questions like how old the caller is and if there are children, in case it's an over fifty-five park. You will also want to know approximately how much money the household brings home in weekly salaries, and how long the family members have been working at their jobs. Last but not least, you need to know how soon the family wants to move in and if they have the down payment available now. If they don't want to move in soon or don't have the down payment now, ask the caller, politely, to call back when they are ready. I would put the caller's name and number on a waiting list and move on. There are too many qualified buyers out there to waste your time on Looky Lou's. (Please don't say that to your callers, but it's okay to think it.)

If the potential new buyers pass your initial prequalification, show them the mobile home. If they like the mobile home and they give you a good feeling about their character so you believe they will pay off a loan to you, work out the terms of the note and explain it to them. Have them fill out an application (listed in the Appendix), then check their references and credit, like we'll show you in Chapter 13. If your market allows it, charge an application fee of $25-$75 for your time. You may decide to refund the application fee if the buyers qualify and go forward with the purchase. If the new buyers check out, take a healthy deposit and fill out a BB Sales Contract (also listed in the Appendix). Give them a few days to apply and be approved by the park manager to lease the lot, if the BB is not in your own park, and give them the name of a good insurance agent who can arrange a comprehensive insurance policy protecting you as the lender in case the mobile home gets damaged, or they get sued and they haven't paid off their loan. If you want to make absolutely sure the mobile homes you lend on are insured at all times and are properly tagged and titled, you can have the new owner pay for the first full year of the insurance, tag, and title fees up front, and then collect one-twelfth of these fees each month. When the insurance policy expires at the end of the first year, you will take the money you have been collecting each month and pay for the next year, just like banks do on their escrow accounts.

When the new buyer is ready, willing, and able to go forward, has been approved by the park, fully qualified by you, and has an insurance policy in hand, you will collect the remainder of the down payment and then fill out a note. (This note is also in the Appendix.). If they refuse to go forward at this point you can keep their deposit and application fee, as is your right for spending your valuable time.

As the Banker, you will hold the original note, and in most states, you will also hold the title to the mobile home with your name listed on the title as the lienholder and the new buyer listed as the owner. Later on, when the new buyer pays off the note, you will give him the original note marked paid, and you will list the lien on the title as paid. Now, let's talk about creating a note, which is what bankers do.

The Note

Since many of you might have signed a note when you bought a car on time payments or a secured a mortgage loan on a home you lived in, you probably already understand what a note is. However, now you are keeping the note, like a bank, and someone else is signing it and obligating themselves to repay it to you.

A note has four terms: the *amount* borrowed, the *interest rate* paid on the outstanding balance, the amount of time or *number of payments* to pay the loan back, and the amount of each *monthly payment. When you know any three of these terms, the fourth term can be calculated using an inexpensive mortgage calculator.* When you went into a bank for a loan in the past, you knew how much you wanted to borrow, how long the bank gave you to pay it back, and the interest rate the bank was going to charge you. You put these three terms into a mortgage calculator, and your monthly payment amount popped out.

Now that you are the Banker, you will learn what bankers know: *Borrowers care the most about how much they have to put down and how much they are paying each month.* Since many bankers have missed the opportunity to lend on older mobile homes, you are going to become more flexible with each of these four terms to maximize your investment while lending on agreeable terms for your customers.

As you know, the *amount* you are lending will usually be twice the price you paid for the mobile home, less the *down payment*. We round up the price we ask for mobile homes to the nearest thousand and we fix the amount we require for down payment to $500, $1,000, or $2,000, depending on the *sales price* we are asking.

Most of the people that borrow are living from paycheck to paycheck, and their savings ability is limited. Therefore, *we accommodate them by taking low down payments that are affordable for them, but large enough so that the emotional pull of chasing after their own money will be there to make them stick to the payment plan.* Notice that the down payment is not one of the terms entered into a mortgage calculator. This is because the down payment is going directly to the Banker at closing. This is how we choose the *minimum* down payments we require of our new buyers:

Sales Price	Minimum Down Payment
1. $1,000–$4,999	$ 500
2. $5,000–$9,999	$1,000
3. Greater than $10,000	$2,000

The *interest rate* we charge is usually 9.9 percent because even when the current borrowing rate on houses was between 5 to 7 percent, we found borrowers are not that concerned about the interest rate they are paying until the interest rate gets into the double digits, i.e. 10 percent or more. So we keep the interest rate at 9.9 percent, just under 10 percent. The difference in the amount of the payment is very slight between 9.9 percent and 12.9 percent, three full percentage points higher, but we have found that buyers get upset about the interest rate being charged, not about the actual dollar difference. For instance, the payment on $5,000 for three years at 9.9 percent is $161.10 per month. The payment for the same loan for the same three years at 12.9 percent is $168.23. The difference is only $7.13 per month, but after you've argued with a buyer over the interest rate for an hour, like I have more than once, and the sale doesn't go through because no matter what you say, the new buyers feel as if they are being taken advantage of if they pay more than 10 percent interest, you might decide to do things our way, also.

When it comes to *monthly payments,* we make the payments slightly less than multiples of $100. You can calculate your notes with payments like $161.10, or do what we do—we come up with payments as close to $95, $195, or $295 per month as we can, depending on how much we are financing. These are the *minimum* monthly payments we usually require of our new buyers:

Sales Price	Minimum Down Payment
1. $1,000–$4,999	$ 95
2. $5,000–$9,999	$195
3. $10,000 or Greater	$295

We use a calculator to determine how many months it takes to finance the amount they are borrowing by using $95, $195, or $295, and then if the months have a partial decimal, we round up to one more month and then do the exact payment calculation. Let me show you how we do this. Let's assume we are looking to finance $5,000 at 9.9 percent with a $195 month payment. We put this in the calculator and it tells us that the number of months is 28.9. We then round up the number of months to the next higher whole number, which is 29, and redo the calculation looking for the payment for $5,000 at 9.9 percent interest for 29 months. This comes to $194.56, and that is what we charge.

By choosing the payment range to be close to $95, $195, or $295 per month, we wind up with different *number of payments* on each loan. We don't fix the term of the loan like traditional bankers do at five, ten, twenty, or thirty years. *The new buyers are usually unconcerned with the number of payments.* They are much more concerned with how much is coming out of their weekly paycheck now, and how much they have to come up with for a down payment. Our experience indicates that to the average buyer, three years feels like forever—so four or five years is just forever plus one or two years, which still feels like forever. Most people who live paycheck to paycheck are used to mortgaging their future for the immediate gratification of their current desires.

Notifying the Park of Your Lien

When you complete the sale, you will want to send a Notice of Mobile Home Lien (see the Appendix) to the park manager and/or owner. This will inform him or her of your note and lien on the mobile home that is sitting on their lot and will request that you be informed immediately when the lot rent is overdue. You might even want to work out an arrangement with the park manager so you collect the lot rent from your mobile home buyer while the note remains unpaid, and then you pay the park manager. This will let you to keep the lot rent current in case the new buyer defaults.

Keep in mind—if the new buyer does not pay the lot rent, that is one of the conditions of default on the note. If this situation is not rectified quickly, you can repo the mobile home and sell it to someone else. We will discuss this shortly.

Case Two: Buying Mobile Homes in Your Own Park

From time to time, your residents might approach you about buying their mobile homes so they can move somewhere else. One of the interesting things I learned about older mobile homes is this:

Older Mobile Homes Ain't Really Mobile.

It costs too much to move them versus the value of the home, and many parks will not allow new residents to move in older mobile homes.

For instance, in our area of South Florida, it costs around $3,000 to $4,000 to disconnect a mobile home from its current lot, tow it to a new location, set it up and tie it down, and pay for permits. If the mobile home is only worth $5,000 or less, it's simply not worth it to spend $4,000 to move it. You will only be saving $1,000 in equity. An owner is better off selling his or her current home for $5,000 and then buying another home for $5,000 in a different park. In addition, many residents of mobile homes can't scrape up $3,000 to $4,000 in cash to move their home, even if they have fallen in love with it and want to keep their home but change the location.

The decision to buy a resident's mobile home in your park is strictly up to you. If you already own more than a few vacant mobile homes for sale in your park, you might not want to add to your inventory. If you have no inventory of unsold mobile homes, it can be a profit center. We have found that most mobile home residents are poor marketing people. They go to Home Depot and buy a $3 paper sign, put it in the front window of their mobile home, and wait. They do no other advertising. We, on the other hand, have a big 4′ x 8′ sign on the park entrance, run newspaper ads, and our managers have a wide network of prospective buyers and/or a waiting list.

Here is how we offer to buy mobile homes in our parks: We send the manager over to inspect the home carefully and then ask our manager what the cash price (the wholesale price) is for the home. This is the price a cash buyer will pay. Our managers know the price because they see sales in the area and the range of values that are paid when cash is offered versus low down payment financing. We take the cash price and subtract $1,000 for our profit, two months lot rent for holding costs, and any fix-up costs, like so:

Price Paid for Mobile = Cash Price of Mobile Home – $1,000 (Profit) – 2 Months Lot Rent (Holding Cost) – Fix-up Cost

We tell the owner the price we will pay, and the following explanation: "We're not going to buy your mobile unless we can make $1,000 on a cash sale, after fixing it up and taking two months to sell it." Then we become very patient. We usually end up buying our residents' mobile homes after a few months, because people don't like paying $300 in lot rent each month while they're waiting to move. They understand that each month their mobile home is not sold means they are getting $300 less on their mobile home.

When we buy the resident's mobile home we put it up for sale at twice the price with the terms described above. If the new buyer wants to pay cash, then we will negotiate to sell it to them at the wholesale price and make $1,000. If the new buyer wants terms—which they usually do—then we sell it at the retail price.

Case Three: The Triple Zotz—Setting Up a Mobile Home on a Vacant Lot in Your Park

Okay, I admit it. I love the sound of the phrase "Triple Zotz." I discovered the Triple Zotz by accident when we were trying to fill up the vacant lots at our first mobile home park, Happy Trails.

There was a sign out front of the park offering vacant lots to people who had mobile homes or RVs. There were more than 30,000 cars driving by that sign each day, yet few called. The park came with free mobile homes, so we put up a new sign that advertised the homes that were for sale. This sign received lots of calls. The sign is the same sign I showed you before and looked like the one on page 193. When I teach the live seminar on mobile homes I refer to it as the Magic Sign, because its effect on the Happy Trails' cash flow was indeed magical.

We figured out within a month or two that very few people had the money or inclination to move *their* mobile home or RV park model into Happy Trails, but there were many people who wanted to buy a mobile home that was already set up and had owner financing.

We also learned something even more impressive—when you move a mobile home onto a vacant lot in *your own mobile home park*, instead of making money only one way through a BB (the first Zotz), you make money three ways by buying and selling it and taking back financing:

1. Buy and sell the mobile home as a BB
2. Collect lot rent on what was previously a vacant lot
3. Value of the park rises because you increased the NOI

Since the payments we constructed for the BB deals in Happy Trails were usually in the $95 per month range, this brought in a nice income. And since the lot rent was in the $300 range, each mobile home we brought to the park added *three times* as much money in lot rent as it did through the mortgage payment, and this was the second part of the Triple Zotz. Then, if we ever looked into refinancing Happy Trails, each additional lot we filled up added *ten times* the yearly lot rent we received to the value, because the NOI is the main factor in pricing a mobile home park. So:

Additional NOI	=	**Additional Lot Rent**	×	**12 Months**
$3,600 per Year	=	**$300 per Month**	×	**12 Months**

Additional Price	=	**Additional NOI**	÷	**Cap Rate**
$36,000	=	**$3600**	÷	**10%**

In other words, for each mobile home we place on a vacant lot in the park, the park appreciated $36,000 in value. *This was the third Zotz in the Triple Zotz.* You can see that while you can make great returns by doing BBs in other people's mobile home parks, you can become even wealthier two more ways by doing BBs in your own mobile home parks.

Keep in mind, you can pull 80 percent of the increase in price out of the park tax free, by doing a Refi-Bonanza. For instance, let's say that after filling ten vacant lots we went to the bank and wanted to refinance our existing loan. When the appraiser comes out to evaluate the park, she is going to discover that our NOI has increased by $3,600 per lot, which reflects a price increase of ten times that at a 10 percent cap rate, or $36,000. Since we filled *ten lots* that were vacant, this is an increase of $360,000 in value. The bank should allow us to refinance 80 percent of that increase, or $288,000—and since money pulled out during refinancing is tax free, we would not have to pay any taxes on it.

The Difference Between Doing an L/O and a BB

We do BBs in Florida because the repossession (repo) process is so simple, and we will describe it in the section after this one. A Repo takes only a few minutes and the title is switched from the owner to you, the lender. In some other states the repo process is not simple and is more expensive and time consuming. In those cases, an L/O is used instead of a BB.

The terms are changed around a little, but the net effect and profit are almost identical with an L/O and a BB. Instead of a *down payment* in the case of the BB, you collect an *up-front non-refundable option deposit* of the same amount for the L/O. Instead of a *purchase price,* which is double your cost, you use an *option price* which is still double your cost. Instead of a *monthly mortgage payment,* you use a *monthly lease/option payment,* which is the same amount. Instead of having a *number of months as the term of the loan* in a BB, you have an equivalent *lease term.* The lot rent is either paid separately or added to the lease payment. There are no monthly credits in a BB, just a pay down on the mortgage. *The complete paydown of the mortgage in a BB is equal to the total monthly credits in an L/O.* In a BB, the title is given right away, subject to the mortgage, and the lender usually holds onto to the title until the loan is paid off. When the L/O is completely paid off, the optionee gets the title, so there really isn't much difference there, either.

There is a difference between a BB and an L/O when it comes to liability insurance, however. In a BB, you will require that the new owner get casualty insurance to protect yourself in case there is a fire or natural disaster, but you don't have to concern yourself about liability arising from the mobile home because you don't own it—the new owner does, and is liable for any casualty problems. You are just the lender.

In an L/O, you will need to get both casualty *and* liability insurance (which the optionee pays for), to protect yourself as the owner, because you still own the mobile home. If there is a law suit your continued ownership of the mobile home in an L/O will incur additional liability. Liability insurance is usually the most inexpensive part of insurance, though, so there is little difference in the costs between a BB and an L/O.

Note Defaults and the Repo Process

We saved the most common objection to doing BBs for last—what happens if the new owner defaults on the note?

If you read the note in the Appendix that the new owner signs, you will see that there are more provisions that create a default than just whether the new owner stops making the monthly payment. The note also states that it is a default if the lot rent is not kept current. It also states that it is a default if the mobile home is moved off the lot before the note is paid off. The bottom line is that the repo process is usually simple if there is any default on the note (except in a few states). There is no land involved, so this is not a lengthy, expensive foreclosure action. The note is on personal property—a mobile home.

In Florida, the repo process is exactly the same as the repo process for nonpayment of a car. We go down to the Department of Motor Vehicles and fill out an affidavit that the note is in default. Minutes later the title gets switched over from the new buyer to the lienholder—and that's us, as the bankers. Now we own the mobile home once again, and we can sell it for a *second profit!* If you are interested in doing BBs, spend some time with an attorney and/or the Department of Motor Vehicles to research what the repo process is in your state or county, so you feel comfortable with it.

In conclusion, it is a good thing for you, as the banker, when a BB buyer defaults on his note, and a bad thing for the person you sold it to. You will get the mobile home back and can then sell it quickly again—only this time, *some or all of your costs have already been paid by the previous owner who defaulted.* We have repo'ed some mobile homes two or three times, and made money each time. It is not something we hope for, however, because we would rather our residents keep their homes. Many times, it is the only asset of lasting value that they have.

Using OPM: Refinancing Your Financing

The second objection I get about the BB is the initial cash outlay involved. Many of the people I train don't have much ready cash, but they do have IRAs. If you have savings or IRA money, BBs are one of the best investments you can make with those funds. The IRA laws have changed, and you are now allowed to invest your IRA in real estate and notes. There is an excellent book written on this subject by Patrick W. Rice called *IRA Wealth*, published by Square One Publishers. When we go through the four examples on the coming pages, you might find yourself becoming eager for the incredible returns you can earn. *But what if you don't have any money to lend, not even an IRA, but want to do BBs and get in on the action?*

The answer is to find investors who have savings or IRAs, and offer them a safe and secure 10 percent return. You will find many people have substantial amounts in their IRAs, and most are barely earning 5 percent from the banks. When you tell them you can double the return to 10 percent, and that the collateral for their investment is worth around twice what they are investing, they might be a little skeptical at first. However, since many BBs usually only involve $4,000 to $6,000, they should be willing to take a chance on you in the beginning. After you perform—and you should perform—they will offer you more money to invest and send their friends and relatives to you, and you will have the money you need.

If you need to use OPM (Other People's Money) to get the money to lend, here is your *Formula for Success:*

UNDERSTANDING THE BB FORMULA FOR OPM

You know how much cash you will need from the OPM—that is the original cost of the mobile home, plus fix-up costs (if any) and holding costs. Now you can take your calculator and figure out the monthly payment

The BB Formula for OPM

First, figure out the amount of cash you will need to get from the OPM:

Total Cash Needed from OPM
= Original Cost + Fix-up + Holding Cost.

Sign a note to your lenders for the OPM for the Total Cash Needed plus 10 percent interest, with the same number of payments that your new buyer's note will have, to get the *OPM Monthly Payment.* Then:

1. Pay the current owner the *Original Cost.*
2. Fix up the mobile home, spending and/or putting aside the fix-up and holding costs.
3. When you find the new buyer, collect the down payment and have them sign a note to you. Use the same number of months for the monthly payment as the OPM payment with 9.9 percent interest, for twice the total cash needed minus the down payment, as you learned to do using the previous BB formula.
4. Keep the down payment from the new buyer—this is your *First Payday.*

To calculate your monthly profit (your *Second Payday*):

Second Payday = Monthly Payment from New Owner
− Monthly Payment to OPM

To calculate your total profit:

BB Profit = Down Payment + Second Payday
× Number of Payments

on the money you borrowed from the OPM based on the Total Cash Needed from OPM at 10 percent interest, divided by the same number of months as the note you intend to give the new buyer. This is the payment amount you will be sending each month to your OPM investor. You will create a new note based on this, that you will sign payable to the OPM investor.

Then you will pay the original cost to the current owner, fix up the home if necessary, and put aside the holding costs. When you find a new buyer, you will collect a down payment, and have them sign a note to you. Figure their monthly payment using the same number of months you used for the OPM payment, at 9.9 percent, for twice the Total Cash Needed minus their down payment, as you learned in the BB formula. *You will put the down payment in your pocket. This is your First Payday.*

Now you will truly *Be the Bank.* Each month you will receive a check from the new buyer and you will deposit it. The new buyer represents the loan you made, which will return from 20 to 78 percent or more. Then you will write a check to the OPM investor for his or her Note, because that investment gave you the cash to buy the mobile home from the previous owner. The OPM investor's note is like a CD that a bank issues to raise money, but instead of paying a paltry 5 percent, you will pay 10 percent. You will make money on the difference between the rate you lend the money out at to the new buyer (who is borrowing double the amound you did) minus what it costs you to raise the money, your OPM payment. You have none of your own money invested. Let me show you how the entire BB process works now by using examples.

Example One: A BB on a Mobile Home Already in Our Park—The Case of the Independent Redneck

Native blue collar Southerners have amongst them some staunch believers in individual rights. Red believed in his constitutional right to follow "whatever damn rules and regulations" he pleased, which meant he didn't get along with his neighbors in one of our mobile home parks. Red liked to drink a case of beer occasionally—like four or five times a week—and then get noisy and rambunctious at 2:00 or 3:00 A.M.

We explained to Red that he had a right to enjoy himself, but he needed to do that without disturbing the people close by who also had the right of quiet enjoyment of their own property. If he couldn't adapt

then he needed to move to a place with more privacy. Red kept doing what he wanted to do anyway, in spite of our warnings, so we served him with eviction papers for noncompliance with the rules, which he ignored. His trailer looked like the picture on the right.

As the eviction progressed, Red hired an attorney, and when his attorney informed him that he was going to get kicked out of our park unless he changed his habits, Red tried to sell his mobile home, but couldn't find anyone to pay $8,000 cash for it right away. His attorney asked us if we wanted to buy it, and we offered $3,000 cash. Red took the money and moved out, hopefully to a place in a more rural area where his neighbors would be cushioned from the noise of his late-night antics.

Red's mobile home needed a very light rehab, a floor repair, a rug in the master bedroom, and some general cleaning, but otherwise it was in good shape. We sold it almost immediately without doing any rehab, so we just doubled the price. Let's follow the BB formula.

We had no fix-up or holding costs, so:

$3,000 Original Cost + 0 Fix-up and Holding Costs = $3,000 Total Cost

We figured the sales price as two times our total cost:

$3,000 Total Cost × 2 = $6,000 Sales Price

We figured the new buyer's note amount as:

$6,000 Selling Price – $1,000 Down Payment = $5,000 Note Amount

Looking at the table on page 195, the down payment on a $6,000 sales price should be $1,000, the monthly payment should be around $195, and the note amount would be $5,000. Putting those three numbers into a mortgage calculator, the number of monthly payments comes to 28.9. Round up the number of payments to 29 and then refigure the monthly payment, which now comes to $194.56.

Therefore we *wrote a note for $5,000 at 9.9 percent interest, for twenty-nine payments of $194.56.*

When we made out the note, we were out-of-pocket:

$3,000 Total Cost − $1,000 Down Payment = $2,000 Total Out-of-Pocket

The monthly payment came back to us for the next twenty-nine months, at $194.56 each month. To figure the total collected over the whole loan:

$194.56 Monthly Payment × 29 Payments = $5,642 Total Collected

We check our figures now to make sure we haven't made a mistake. Since the total collected is $5,642, which is more than two times the $2,000 out-of-pocket (which would be at least $4,000), our calculations look okay.

Now we calculate our total profit:

$5,642 Total Collected − $2,000 Total Out-of-Pocket = $3,642 Total Profit

In other words, we took $2,000 from our savings and we were returned our original $2,000 plus an extra $3,642. To figure our cash-on-cash return:

$3,642 Profit ÷ $2,000 Out-of-Pocket = 182% over 29 Months
29 Months ÷ 12 Months per Year = 2.42 Years
182% ÷ 2.42 years = 75% per Year

Think about this. We invested $2,000 and got back $5,642 in less than two-and-a-half years—a $3,642 profit, for a total return of 182 percent. To figure our return on a yearly basis, we divide the total return by the total number of years. Dividing twenty-nine months by twelve months in a year comes out to 2.42 years. Dividing 182 percent by 2.42 years gives us a yearly *cash-on-cash return of 75 percent!*

Keep in mind—all we are doing when we are the bank is collecting mortgage payments—we are doing no managing, no repairs, no maintenance, and so on. And since we did this in our own park, there was no need to notify the park manager.

If we did not have the $2,000 to purchase the mobile home, this is how we would handle the OPM part of the transaction:

We would collect $3,000 from the OPM investor to use as the payment to Red for his home. We would sign a note to the OPM investor for $3,000 at 10 percent interest for twenty-nine monthly payments of $116.88. When we found the new buyer we would collect $1,000 as the down payment and have him sign a note for $5,000 at 9.9 percent interest for twenty-nine payments of $194.56. We would keep the $1,000 down payment as our first payday. Each month we would receive a check for $194.56 from the new owner and send out a check for $116.88 for the OPM payment. We would keep the difference, $77.68, as our profit:

$194.56 Payment from New Buyer – $116.88 Payment for OPM
= $77.68 Second Payday

Our profit is twenty-nine of these $77.68 second paydays plus the $1,000 down payment:

$77.68 × 29 Months = $2,252.72 Total Second Paydays
+ $1,000 Down Payment = $3,352 Total Profit on BB Using OPM

Not bad for buying a $3,000 mobile home while putting up no money and just swapping checks each month. Let's do this for a slightly larger loan and see how that works, and to see what happens if there is a default.

Example Two: The Triple Zotz—Moving a Mobile Home onto an Empty Lot in Our Own Park

Remember we had twenty empty spaces in the Jefferson Mobile Home Park when we bought it. We found another park owner who changed the use of his park from lots for mobile homes to new townhouses. The previous mobile home residents were given a reasonable amount of time to find new places to move their mobile homes, but many abandoned them. One of them is in the picture shown at right. We bought twenty used single-wide mobile homes similar to the picture for $1,000

apiece and paid a mobile home setup contractor $3,500 each to detach them from the other park, tow them to our park, permit them, and set them up. (In my opinion $3,500 is a lot of money to move a mobile home and set it up. We did this between 2004 and 2006, the boom years in South Florida, when licensed contractors were booked for months in advance and charged exorbitant prices. There are places in this country where you can get a mobile home towed over and set up for $2,000—almost half.) We had another $500, on average, in fix-up and holding costs, so our total cost was:

$1,000 Original Cost + $3,500 Set-up Cost + $500 Fix-up and Holding Costs = $5,000 Total Cost

We had a sign in front of our mobile home park that attracted buyers. Let's run through the BB formula for one of these mobile homes:

We figured the sales price as two times our total cost:

$5,000 Total Cost × 2 = $10,000 Sales Price

Then the note amount was:

$10,000 Sales Price – $2,000 Down Payment = $8,000 Note Amount

Looking at our table for down payments, a $10,000 mobile home would usually require $2,000 down and a monthly payment of $295. Putting these numbers and a note amount of $8,000 into a mortgage calculator, the number of payments comes to 30.82. Rounding up the number of payments to 31 and refiguring the monthly payment gives us a new monthly payment of $293.53.

We wrote a note with the new owner for $8,000 at 9.9 percent interest, for thirty-one monthly payments of $293.53.

Therefore, when we made out the note, we were out–of-pocket:

$5,000 Total Cost – $2,000 Down Payment = $3,000 Total Out-of-Pocket

This money came back to us for the next thirty-one months at $293.53 each month. To figure the total collected over the whole loan:

$293.53 Monthly Payment × 31 Payments = $9,100

We do our check now, to make sure we haven't made a mistake. Since the total collected is $9,100 and it is more than two times the $3,000 out-of-pocket (which would be at least $6,000), our preliminary check looks okay.

Now, let's calculate our total profit:

$9,100 Total Collected – $3,000 Total Out-of-Pocket = $6,100 Profit

In other words, we took $3,000 from our IRA or savings, and were returned our original $3,000 plus an extra $6,100. To figure the cash-on-cash return:

$6,100 Profit ÷ 3,000 Out-of-Pocket = 203% Over 31 Months
31 Months ÷ 12 Months per Year = 2.58 Years
203% ÷ 2.58 Years = 78% per Year

Think about it like this. We invested $3,000 and got back $9,100 in about two-and-a-half years, of which $6,100 was profit, for a total return of 203 percent. To figure our return on a yearly basis, we divide the total return by total number of years. Dividing thirty-one months by the twelve months in a year comes out to 2.58 years. Dividing 203 percent by 2.58 years gets us a yearly *cash-on-cash return of 78 percent!*

Please keep in mind that *as the amount of the BB goes up, the return will go down if the down payment and monthly payment does not rise according.* Realistically, a $1,000 down payment is twice as easy to get as $2,000, and $195 per month is easier than $295 per month to arrange, and we had twenty of these BBs to do all at once. On a few of the more difficult ones to sell, we took only $1,000 down and monthly payments of $195. When you plug these numbers into the BB formula it yields only a 38 percent return over fifty-nine months, but a 38 percent return is still wonderful, compared to 5 percent in the bank. Once again, since we did this in our own park, there was no need to send notices to the park manager.

If we did not have the $5,000 to buy each trailer and set it up, this is how we would have handled the OPM part of the transaction: We would collect $5,000 from the OPM investor and sign a Note. We would calculate the note payments for the OPM for $5,000, at 10 percent interest, with thirty-one monthly payments of $183.69. Then we would pay $1,000 to the other park owner for the mobile home, pay $3,500 to the mobile home setup contractor, and spend and/or hold $500 for fix-up and holding costs.

When we found a new buyer, *we would keep the $2,000 down payment as the first payday.* We would have him sign a note for $8,000 at 9.9 percent interest for thirty-one monthly payments of $293.53. Then each month we would receive a check from the new buyer for $293.53 and we would send a check to the OPM investor for $183.69. We would keep the difference, $109.84, as our profit:

$293.53 Payment from New Buyer – $183.69 Payment for OPM = $109.84 Second Monthly Payday

The total profit is the total of the thirty-one monthly paydays of $109.84 plus the $2,000 down:

$109.84 × 31 = $3,405 Second Paydays + $2,000 Down = $5,405 Total Profit on BB

We made $5,405 profit, put up no money, and just swapped checks each month.

What Do You Do When There Is a Default on the Note?

Okay, all you worriers—which includes me—let's look at the negative possibility. You do a BB, and in spite of your best efforts to qualify the new owners, they default after a year. In this case you would repo the mobile home, put yourself on the title, and remove the new buyer from the title. The note is now worthless unless you want to hire an attorney and try to collect—which would cost more in attorney's fees than it's worth, in my opinion.

It's much easier to keep the $2,000 deposit and the twelve monthly payments of $293.53, which equal $3,522. The total you have already collected:

$2,000 Down Payment + 293.53 × 12 Months ($3,522) = $5,522 Collected

Assuming you have to spend $1,000 on repairs and holding costs, your cost in the trailer is now:

$5,000 Original Cost + $1,000 Repairs and Holding Costs = $6,000 Total Costs

$6,000 Total Costs − $5,522 Collected = $478 New Cost for Mobile Home

Now, when you sell the mobile home again for $10,000 and take back financing, the $2,000 deposit you collected goes directly into your pocket, again. Once you subtract the $478 new cost of the mobile home $1,528 is pure profit and all monthly payments are pure profit to you. *You should almost wish your BBs default so you can make a second and even a third profit on them!* I say *almost,* because ethically and morally it's not right to wish bad tidings to the people you do business with.

Now, how do you handle the OPM if there is a default? You repo the mobile home and continue making the same monthly payments on the note you gave the OPM investor. When you find a new buyer you will keep the down payment once again for a third payday and you will continue receiving payments from the new buyer and sending checks for the OPM. However, once you make the last payment on the OPM note, you will still have twelve more payments from the new buyer and you will keep them all for yourself.

SUMMARY

As you now see, you can earn remarkable returns by Being the Bank for older mobile homes in land-lease parks that are still in good shape. If you are investing your own savings or IRA, you can earn up to 75 percent or more. If you use OPM, you will earn two paydays for yourself that total approximately what you initially paid for the mobile home. You should limit BBs to an initial cost of $10,000 or less—$3,000 to $7,000 is the best range. As the amount of the note goes up, the length of time is greater to pay it back and the cash-on-cash return goes down. Also, it is harder to find buyers as the down payments and monthly payments increase.

You also learned about the Triple Zotz—moving mobile homes onto vacant lots in your own mobile home park and taking back financing to make it easy for the new residents. This enables you to make even more money in two additional ways: with increased lot rents and NOI. This is a powerful solution for the major problem facing mobile home investors on turn-around parks—vacant lots.

You also saw that if there is a default on the note for any reason and you have to repo the mobile home, the process is fast and inexpensive and you will make a second profit with a third and fourth payday. What do you think of being the bank now?

By the way, I understand that some of you are not natural mathematicians and some of these formulas might challenge you. It's okay. If you can't get someone to help you do BBs, just tuck this strategy away for the time being. Flippers and keepers are simpler to figure and will make you lots of money in the meantime. You can add BBs later, after you feel comfortable doing flippers and keepers. It's important to feel comfortable with a strategy before you use it.

Let me repeat again for the mathematically challenged that you really only *need* the first two profit strategies at this point. You can add L/Os and BBs after you get started and feel comfortable with flippers and keepers. I know many active multi-millionaire mobile home park investors that have never done an L/O or a BB and still became quite successful. However, if you buy a turn-around mobile home park with empty lots, you will be missing out on these powerful strategies if you don't do BBs or L/Os.

HOMEWORK

Look in the papers and around town to see who is offering mobile homes in land-lease parks with easy financing. I think you will be surprised at how few people are doing it. Find the sellers that are offering BBs and record their terms and conditions in your notebook.

Go back and visit all the mobile home parks you have looked at so far, again only the ones that were either openly for sale or where the owners agreed to put it up for sale when you contacted them. Also, keep trying to see if you can find other mobile home parks for sale.

Now, I want you to write down in your notebook how you would offer to do BBs in these parks. Then write down how you would turn around and sell them to new residents. If you don't have an IRA or savings account to invest in BBs, network with your family, friends, and business acquaintances to see who is interested in earning 10 percent on their IRA with a high degree of safely.

It would be great if you owned a mobile home park and could put an ad in the paper advertising BBs so you could see the response. I'm willing to bet the response would be great.

COMING ATTRACTIONS

Congratulations! Now you have completed your Four Basic Profit Strategies. You have the mobile home investor mindset—you are going out to look for mobile home parks for sale, plug them into your Four Basic Profit Strategies using your *formulas for success,* and then compute how much profit you will make *before* you buy them, eliminating almost all of the guesswork.

Now it's time to learn where to find good deals and how to set the deal up right, so you can hit the ground running and not waste a lot of time. In the next part of the book you are going to learn the secrets of where to find great deals from someone who has been finding them for more than twenty-seven years.

On with the adventure!

Part Two

Getting the Deal Right: The Five Green Fs

Congratulations again! You've studied the Four Basic Profit Strategies, and in your homework, you ventured out into your area and got comfortable with the mobile home park market. Maybe you've imagined yourself, while you're driving around in your car, to be an explorer setting sail to discover exciting new trade routes that will make you rich.

While you were exploring, you worked on your investor mindset—looking at mobile home parks for sale and plugging them into your formulas for success, to compute how much profit you would make *before* you bought a deal. Even though we're going to look in some hidden and some not-so-hidden places, you still need to place firmly in your investor mindset that the key to *taking* a good deal is *making* a good deal.

Now it's time to get focused on the actions you are going to take that will make the wealth you want a reality. We created a slogan to help you remember the steps you must take: the *Five Green Fs* of Getting a Deal

Right—*Find it, Figure it, Flag it, Fix it, and Finance it.* These are good Fs, so they're green, the color of money. Don't associate them with the bad Fs, the red ones that stood for a failing grade in school. The Green Fs are going to put you on the honor roll in the school of wealth.

Part Two of this book focuses on action. Part One was to "get your mind right." That was essential because you must know the Profit Strategies and their formulas . . . *but it's not enough!* You have to take action and apply the strategies and formulas—*no one is going to deliver a mobile home park to your driveway. You have to go out and find one that will be successful for you.*

Now you are going to learn the right actions to take to do that. It begins with where to *Find* a good mobile home park deal. Once you find it, you have to *Figure* out what it's worth using your Magic Formula and your Four Profit Strategies to assure yourself that it's a good deal. Then you have to write an offer that stakes your claim and sets your *Flag* in front of your park. You will learn how to negotiate the best deal for yourself, like a pro, and write an offer that fully protects you. Next you will be shown how to inspect the mobile home park, do due diligence to discover defects that you will need to *Fix,* if any. Finally, if the deal is a "go" because the first four Fs assure you of greater wealth, then you will learn how to *Finance* the park, even if you have no money or no credit.

To use the analogy of a carpenter, in the first part of this book you learned how to hammer nails, cut wood, and measure. In the second part of this book you will learn how to build walls, floors, and roofs, and then install windows, doors, and finishes to complete the building.

Here is how the second part is set up, on a chapter-by-chapter basis:

Chapter 7: Finding Deals: Find It. We're going to start by focusing your attention on where to find good deals on mobile home parks. We've been finding good deals on real estate for more than twenty-seven years, and we're going to pass the secrets along to you. You will also learn about the different segments of your market and the different types of parks. The Internet will be introduced and various important websites you can use.

Chapter 8: What's It Worth: Figure It. You're going to learn how to appraise mobile home parks so you can figure out what a park is worth and how much you should pay to create a good deal. You also will know how much to sell your park for when it comes time to sell, and you will be able to explain logically how you arrived at your selling price

Chapter 9: Writing Offers and Negotiating: Flag It. Here you will learn how to construct an offer to buy a mobile home park, now that you've found a good deal and valued it. You have to make offers that work for you, based upon your *formulas for success.* You may have to make more than a few offers to get one good deal, and that's okay. One good deal is better than no good deals and a lifetime of living paycheck to paycheck. Your offer will lock up this opportunity for you. You will be staking your claim, setting your *flag* in the ground in the front of the property so no one else can buy it out from under you. At the same time, you will protect yourself so you will be assured of making a healthy profit. If you feel more comfortable having an attorney or real estate broker do this for you, you will still learn how to guide them in setting up your offers and double-check their efforts. Since many of your offers will require give and take, you will also learn how to negotiate like a pro and get the best deal possible. You can then take this negotiating skill and apply it to other areas of your life, because much of life involves negotiation.

Chapter 10: Due Diligence: Fix It. This chapter shows you how to inspect and do due diligence on a mobile home park. This is extremely important because as you know, when you buy a mobile home park, you will be purchasing a small town in which you will be the mayor—you will be responsible for making money, managing the residents, and maintaining the infrastructure. We have put together a method for due diligence taken from our experience and research, and from the experiences of many others we respect, so you will be aware of any hidden defects before you buy and avoid any unpleasant surprises. Yes, you will probably have to fix some things, but don't worry—you will get paid a healthy profit for doing so. You're also going to learn how to set up a mobile home park "from scratch," on a parcel of vacant land wherever that makes sense, so you can create an affordable housing ATM.

Chapter 11: Financing and No Money Down: Finance It. Now that you have your good deal flagged, researched, and waiting for you, you need to pay for it. You will be shown you how to walk into a bank like a professional, borrow the money you need, and then have the banker asking you to bring more deals to finance. If you don't have any money to put down or good credit, you will learn "no-money-down and no credit" strategies. By the way, if you have a lot of money to put down now, no-money-down strategies are still going to be important in your real estate career. You will probably learn, like we did, that no matter how much money you have today, you will eventually spend it all buying good deals tomorrow. Then what do you do when another good deal pops up—which they always do—and you're out of money? We'll show you what to do.

SUMMARY

In Part One you learned the basics of how to think like a mobile home park investor. In Part Two you're going to learn how to act like one. You'll learn what you will need to do to set up your deals and get them right—the Five Green Fs—*Find it, Figure it, Flag it, Fix it, and Finance it.*

HOMEWORK

I'm not going to give you any homework on this part, so keep reading!

COMING ATTRACTIONS

Let's go find some good deals!

7

Finding Deals: Find It

In this chapter you will be shown where to find good deals. This is the foundation of your mobile home park investment career. When you learn how to open the tap on good deals, they will come pouring out. We are going to give you twelve places to look, called the *Wealthy Dozen*. Some may have occurred to you, but many probably have not.

Before you are shown specifically where to look, we are going to expand your horizons about how the mobile home real estate market is set up. You need to be aware of the full width and breadth of this market to be able to take advantage of all of the different types of good deals that are found there.

First, there are *three segments* to real estate markets, and mobile home parks may be found in all three segments: *affordable-, middle-,* and *upper-income areas*. The income we are referring to is not the income coming from the properties located there but the income earned by the residents who live there. Perhaps you thought mobile homes were only located in affordable-, or low-income, areas, but that is not true. They can be found in the other two segment areas as well, and you are going to learn about the different characteristics of each segment.

Second, you're going to learn about the *three different types of parks: family, over-55,* and *RV*. Each has different characteristics that affect investing in them. We are going to be concerned mainly with parks where the mobile home park owner leases the land, or both the land and a mobile home. We are not concerned with parks where the individual residents own the land underneath their mobile homes, which are referred to *resident-owned communities.* This was described in my first book, *Mobile Home Wealth.*

After you learn about the different segments and the different mobile home parks within each segment, you will be in a better position to understand and take advantage of all the good deals that are out there.

THE THREE SEGMENTS IN REAL ESTATE MARKETS

If you've been living in your city or county for a number of years, you probably know where the "lower-income" areas are and where the "rich" areas are, and where the "middle" areas are in between. As much as we try not to be class-conscious in this country, we are still reminded daily of the distinctions that come about from how much money you earn. Now you are going to understand these three areas in terms of how they can make money for you when you invest in them.

The lower-income areas, which we will refer to now, and in the future, as *affordable-income* areas, are in almost every town and city. They contain a large part of the total housing units, usually from a quarter to a third of them. The middle to upper end of these affordable-income areas are where you are usually going to find the most mobile home parks. The breadwinners of these households are blue collar, working in the basic service jobs of the local economy. Every town and city needs these areas, because they are where the people who keep the community running live. They work in the supermarkets, the fast food restaurants, the factories, the shopping centers, and so on. They mow the lawns, fix and clean the houses, and do the labor-intensive jobs in the middle and upper income areas of the community. Because blue collar workers are paid lower wages, they cannot afford to travel long distances to their jobs, and their households must be located within a reasonable commute from the middle- and upper-income areas. The breadwinners in affordable-income areas want the same things for themselves and their families as the families in other income areas—a safe and comfortable place to live and raise their children.

The basic investment characteristic in affordable-income areas is this: *the housing there costs much less than the middle and upper income segments, but the rents charged are not proportionately less.* Therefore, the greatest cash flow returned to an investor per dollar spent is usually in affordable-income areas—they have the highest cap rates and some of the best keepers.

There is a slight downside to investing in mobile home parks in affordable-income areas—there are greater management costs, in the form of higher repairs and maintenance, and greater tenant turnover. When you read Chapter 13 you will learn how to reap the maximum benefits from affordable-income areas while minimizing management costs, making it a valuable source of wealth for you, and at the same time providing a valuable service in your community with healthy and safe affordable housing.

A warning must be given at this point: there may be a small portion of the affordable-income area that is run-down and dominated by very low-income households, and these are sometimes accompanied by a high crime rate and drug usage. (Don't think all of affordable housing is like this, because it is not.) Unless you have experience and expertise working with these types of problems—if you are a police officer, a parole officer, or a corrections officer, or someone in a similar career—*you should avoid investing in these areas.* You can buy ultra-cheap in crime and drug infested areas and earn great income from investments there, but you need to feel comfortable and know how to deal with the problems that go along with them, which most people do not. My recommendation is when you find a great deal on a mobile home park in one of these difficult areas, get it under contract with an inspection contingency and then flip it to an investor who is comfortable investing there. You were shown this technique, called wholesaling, in Chapter 4, when you learned flipping.

The second segment is the *middle-income* area. This is usually the dominant area in most communities. You will find some of your larger mobile home parks in this segment, some catering to retirees and others to families. The cap rates on these parks are usually less than in the affordable-income areas but still can be profitable. On the positive side, investing in mobile home parks in the middle-income segment usually has fewer management costs and less resident turnover.

People are surprised to discoverer there are mobile home parks in *upper-income* areas, the third segment. The land underneath the parks is prime, which is what puts the park in the upper-income area. They typically are located near waterfront or recreational areas or contain golf courses, to name just a few of the possibilities in prime locations. The lot rents are high in upper-income mobile home parks, yet the cap rates are usually lower.

Using the Four Basic Profit Strategies in the Different Segments

How do you put what you just learned about the three different segments to work for you? In your homework, you will be asked to take a map of your city or county and highlight the different areas—affordable, middle, and upper income. Then you will be asked to locate the mobile home parks and determine what kind of parks are within each income segment. You will then decide which areas are going to be your *wealth farms*—where you are going to plant and grow the seeds of your future wealth.

For *keepers*, the best place to invest is the affordable- and middle-income areas, provided you can earn a good cap rate and yearly profit. When it comes to *flippers*, you can make money in all three areas, provided the parks you buy are either managed poorly or priced too cheaply before you buy them. Experience shows that most of your flippers will usually be in the affordable- and middle-income segments, because that's where the most parks are and where the most investors are interested.

There are two different strategies for *lease options*. If you want to buy a keeper using an L/O or you already own a park and want to flip it, then the best place to use a lease option is the same place as for keepers, the affordable- and middle-income segments. If you want to do a sandwich L/O, then all three income areas will work, just as with flippers. Again, your primary goal is to buy a mismanaged and/or underpriced park, no matter what area it is in.

As you know, *BBs* are the powerful strategy you are going to use to fill vacant lots in your parks and get the Triple Zotz. BBs work best in the affordable-income segment and the lower end of the middle-income segment. When you get to the middle and upper end of the middle-income areas and the entire high-income area, the residents usually have enough money and credit to purchase newer mobile homes using a bank. That's okay. As the price of the mobile home goes up, which it does in middle and upper-income parks, your returns on BBs go down.

As you can see from the previous discussion, the most flexible areas for mobile home park investing are the upper end of the affordable-income segment and the lower end of the middle-income segment. If you specialize in those segments you should have maximum results, because all four Basic Profit Strategies work there. We concentrate in those segments, but we have found that we need to remain flexible and not shut our eyes to the other segments. Good deals come from all over, and sometimes the best deal available is in a different segment than the one you want to specialize in.

DIFFERENT TYPES OF PARKS

Not only are there three basic segments when investing in real estate, there are also three basic kinds of mobile home parks in each segment: *family*, *over-55*, and *RV*. The first two are based upon the age of the residents and the last is based upon the type of mobile home the people inhabit.

Family parks, or *all-age communities*, allow people of all ages to live there and are distinguished by allowing children. They look like the picture below and they have the following characteristics: they are easiest to find residents or tenants for, they have the greater turnover and more need for management, they have higher expenses due to damage and carelessness, and the residents are more tolerant of price increases because many of them are working their way up at their jobs and receiving salary increases.

Example of a family park.

Over fifty-five retirement communities, or *age-restricted communities*, are the easiest mobile home parks to manage. In fact, they are one of the easiest of any type of residential income properties to manage, including apartments, townhouses, condos, and so on. They also have the lowest turnover in residential income producing real estate. Around 10 percent of the available over-fifty-five mobile home rental units change hands each year, compared to 50 percent of apartments.

This type of residential income property has the only permitted form of discrimination in this country—age restrictions. For age restrictions to be legal *80 percent of the households must have at least one member who is fifty-five years old or older.* If the community conforms to that definition it can require that all households contain at least one member who is fifty-five or older and not allow children at all. The community does have a choice of whom they want to accept, age-wise, in the remaining 20 percent of the households. For example, they can allow households in which members are less than fifty-five but more than forty.

Age-restricted communities have the following investment characteristics: buyers or tenants are more difficult to find, but turnover is less once they are found. The mobile home parks are easier to manage, and in certain areas, many residents leave for part of the year but still pay for the whole year. Expenses are usually lower than in other types of parks due to less damage and carelessness. However, there is also strong resistance to lot rent increases in over-fifty-five communities because many of the residents are on fixed incomes.

Whenever I show the picture below when I am training, I ask the class, "What hints are there in the photograph that indicate this is probably an over-fifty-five community?" After the class scratches their heads for a few moments, I answer with, "If the flowers are not trampled over, and there are no bicycles and toys on the front lawn, chances are it is an age-restricted community." That usually gets a knowing smile or chuckle from people who have children or grandchildren.

Mobile home in an over fifty-five community.

Two examples of an RV park.

RV Parks are one of the oldest forms of mobile home parks, and they are still evolving as we speak. The original purpose of these parks was to provide a place for vacationing people to unhitch their travel trailers from their cars, hook up the trailer to water, sewer, and electric, and stay for anywhere from a day or two to a four-month season. These parks could be family or over-fifty-five type parks, depending upon the owner's preference.

This original purpose is still served in the majority of RV parks. As you can see from the pictures here, many of the RVs are now self-contained, with the living area and the driving vehicle built together.

There has been a major change in some RV parks recently, in that the residents want to live there year-round. Some RV designs have changed dramatically to accommodate this change and they are called RV park models. These park models look and function like small mobile homes; they are typically twelve to fourteen feet wide, thirty-five to forty feet long, and eight to ten feet high. There is a example of an attractive one with a porch on the left. RV park models are left in place in RV parks where they can be lived in comfortably year-round, if desired. They are too big to be towed behind a car or pickup truck, and but are still considered like pull-behind trailers.

RV park model.

The main features of RV parks for an investor are as follows: they are most difficult to find tenants for unless the location is superior, they have the greatest turnover, large seasonal variations, high management intensity, and higher expenses due to damage and carelessness. In addition, the owner/investor may have to pay for utilities because residents are not there long enough to pay for them. On the positive side, RV park investments are more tolerant of price increases, and you can turn an RV park into year-round residences with park models and then double or triple the income you receive from it.

In the majority of cases, a mobile home park will only be one of the above three classifications. However, as in the case of the Jefferson Mobile Home Park, there are mobile home parks that have a section containing mobile homes and another section containing RVs. They are usually separate sections because the mobile home section does not change occupancy rapidly, while the RV section has transient occupancies with people coming and going more often. There are also mobile home parks which have a section for family households and a separate section for over-fifty-five age households with no children allowed.

WHERE TO FIND DEALS

Finding good deals is the most exciting part of being a mobile home park investor. You can't receive checks until you find a good deal and set up the deal right. You have to focus on the fact that you make money when you buy—you just collect it when you rent the property out or sell it for a profit.

We are now going to give you twelve specific places to find good deals—the Wealthy Dozen (see inset on page 227). We separate these deals into three groups:

1. The highest motivated sellers
2. The bread and butter basics
3. Long-term networking

You should search groups A and B on a daily, weekly, or monthly basis, depending on your level of activity and whether you are a full-time or part-time investor. For many of you Internet websites will provide the most mobile home park opportunities.

Group C are the deals that will come to you over time, as you network

The Wealthy Dozen—Where to Find Good Deals

Group A: The Highest Motivated Sellers

1. Tax deeds and liens
2. Foreclosures—before, during, and after sale
3. Auctions

Group B: The Bread and Butter Basics

4. Internet sites for mobile home parks
5. Driving by your favorite segment areas
6. Calling FSBOs from ads in newspapers and trade magazines
7. Calling Realtors, Realtor magazines, MLS listings and Realtor.com
8. The gold mine ad and your website
9. Mailings to owners, cold calling, and making offers

Group C: Long-Term Networking

10. "I Buy" signs on your car and in favorite segment areas
11. Scouts—mail carriers, FedEx and UPS drivers, lawn and sanitation workers, and code enforcement officers
12. REIAs, CCIM, and CIP

with more and more people who will help you create wealth. Each of the Wealthy Dozen will now be explained in depth. The Internet is listed as a specific resource in categories four and eight, but the Internet may also assist you in any or all of the other ten categories as a business communication medium—of which it is the finest in the history of the world.

Group A: The Highest Motivated Sellers

As the name implies, this group contains property owners who have a strong need to sell, and sell right away. Intuitively, you probably understand that someone who needs to sell, and sell quickly, is likely to give the best deal to a buyer. Some typical high-motivation scenarios are when the owner is behind in mortgage or tax payments or is facing foreclosure, divorce, bad health, a forced job relocation, or a death in the family. On the banking side, you have lenders who have taken property back in foreclosure and now need to sell that property so they can recapture the loan money and lend it again in the mortgage market to earn interest once more.

Tax Deeds and Liens

A *tax deed* is created when an owner does not pay the real estate taxes owed on their property, and the property is forcibly sold by the clerk of the court to an investor who pays the back taxes. In some cases, you can buy tax deeded property for pennies on the dollar—10 to 20 percent of market value. Many people are unaware of this area of investing and the kind of deals you can get. We discovered tax deeds and liens more than ten years ago and have been investing in them ever since.

An investor usually pays between one and three years of back real estate taxes for tax deeds, with two years delinquent taxes being the average. Sometimes, the property is sold by the auction method and other investors can compete to buy the property by bidding above the taxes owed. In all but a few cases, *all the mortgages and liens on the property are wiped out after the tax deed sale* and the investor owns the property free and clear! This is one of the prime motivations for investors who buy tax deeds. Local government liens, like water and sewer assessments, code enforcement liens, and so on, are the only liens that remain after a tax deed sale.

Tax liens are created when an investor pays the delinquent real estate taxes on a property for one year and is offered a high interest rate for doing so. The investor is effectively loaning the property owner the tax money with the hope of getting paid off in the near future, earning a high rate of interest while he or she waits. Statistically, about 90 percent of all tax liens are paid off and no sale of the property takes place. Investors earn between 10 percent to 25 percent on their money per year when the lien is paid off. If the tax lien is not paid off within a certain period of time, the investor can start a legal action and get title to the property through the issuance of a tax deed, again with all the mortgages and liens wiped out.

Tax deed research can be time consuming, but there may be services available in your area for a reasonable monthly fee. There are books and seminars on this subject and it's worthwhile to pursue this type of investment.

Tax Deed Example

This example is a small park with two mobile homes located on slightly more than an acre, with a small swimming pool and a large workshop. Though it is only two units, it still serves as a case in point. Most of the tax deeds we have purchased contain only one mobile home and the land under it, and they have proved to be very profitable. This was one of the few doubles. We purchased it for a net price of $15,000 a few years ago at a tax deed sale. We completely rehabbed one of the mobile homes and replaced the other, adding around $15,000 in additional fix-up expenses, for a total cost of $30,000 ($15,000 purchase + $15,000 fix-up costs).

The two mobiles rented for $650 each per month for a total of $1,300. Monthly expenses such as insurance, taxes, maintenance, and repairs ran about $300 total, so the property netted around $1,000 per month. If you get out your calculator, you will see that the NOI is $12,000 and the cash-on-cash return is $12,000 divided by $30,000 or 40 percent per year.

Foreclosures—Before, During, and After Sale

As you probably already know, foreclosures result when property owners don't make their mortgage payments, and the lender is forced to repossess the mobile home park to get the loan money back. Then the lender sells the mobile home park, gets whatever money back possible from the sale, and lends the money out again. Lenders are not in the property management business, so they do not like to hold onto mobile home parks.

There are three ways to buy foreclosures: *before the sale, at the sale* on the courthouse steps, and *after the sale* when the property goes back to bank and is considered REO (Real Estate Owned). Each way has different investing characteristics with separate rules and different players, cash requirements, inspections, and title risks.

When you buy *before the sale*, or *preforeclosure*, you are dealing with the owner of the property. You can inspect the property and not have to worry about hidden defects. Your goal is to get the owner to give you a deed for ownership of the property and assume the outstanding loans, while you give the owner something for his equity, if any. You then bring the loan current with the bank and stop the foreclosure, and either keep the property or sell it to a new buyer for a nice profit. You, as the investor, only need enough money to bring the loan current and give the previous owner whatever is necessary to get him to sign the deed and give up ownership.

Buying on the day of sale *on the courthouse steps* is the most risky and capital-demanding way to buy a foreclosure. In many cases, you might not be able to inspect the mobile home park and do a complete due diligence because the owner is still there and not in the mood to invite strange investors onto his or her park. Buying at the sale also requires all cash as payment, and in most cases, on the same day as the sale. Last, but not least, there are no guarantees of clear title when you buy this way, so an investor needs to have the title checked in advance or can run into problems. You will see in the upcoming example how buying a park at a foreclosure sale, with the risk of no detailed inspection, lots of cash up front, and possible title questions, came back to haunt us.

The third and last way to buy foreclosures is *after the sale*, from the lender. The property goes back to the lender when no one other than the lender bids on a property or investors do not bid enough and the lender outbids them on the courthouse steps. The technical term for this is REO, which stands for Real Estate Owned by the bank. Buying after the sale is less risky because you can inspect the park carefully, the deal can be subject to financing and not require all cash, and you are guaranteed clear title from the lender. I prefer to buy when the property becomes REO. I like dealing with lending institutions that don't have any emotional attachments to the property. Then it's strictly a business decision for them and for me.

It used to be much easier to deal directly with bank foreclosure departments than it is today, after all the bank mergers. Many of the large money-center banks prefer to give their REOs to approved brokers and not deal directly with investors. When you contact the bank, they will just tell you to contact the listing broker. In this case you should follow their advice. You can still get some great buys by dealing with the brokers for the banks.

The foreclosure departments in the smaller community banks are usually more than happy to talk directly with investors, however, and you can get some great deals there, as well. To find them, go to the yellow pages and look up the local community banks and lending institutions in your area. Call and ask for the vice-president who handles foreclosures. Ask him or her for a list of foreclosures currently on the bank's books.

Foreclosure research is as time consuming as tax deed research, so you can save time by locating a service in your area that provides information on foreclosures for a reasonable monthly fee. Unlike on tax deeds, there are many books and seminars written on this subject, and pursuing it is very worthwhile.

Example: Buying on the Courthouse Steps— The Palm Frond Mobile Home Park

We used this as an example of a career rehab when we discussed flipping in Chapter 4. If you remember, I had been trying to buy this park for a few years. Each time, another investor put in a contract before me, the property was taken off the market for several months, and then the contract did not get completed. Then the owner would put it back on the market for an even higher price. By the time I adjusted to the higher price, someone else put it under contract, and then didn't complete the sale. Finally, the park went into foreclosure, and the owner escaped a sale on the courthouse steps a few times by declaring different forms of bankruptcy, delaying the inevitable.

To review, this was an RV park with several very old, run-down, small mobile homes, in addition to many old, run-down RVs. It contained sixty-two small lots and two apartments, with about forty occupancies and twenty-two vacancies. It was on two and one-half acres on the corner of two arterial roads, so the land was valuable. The aerial is shown on page 232.

We bought the Palm Frond Mobile Home Park on the courthouse steps for $640,000. That's right—$640,000 cash. Because of the large amount of cash required, Crazy Gersh and I teamed up with a father and son with whom I been buying foreclosures and tax deeds for many years. They also owned an RV dealership and were experts in RV and mobile home sales.

As soon as we bought the property, the problems started. The day after the courthouse sale, we were informed by the attorney for the Health Department that the entire septic system was in violation of health ordinances. (The previous owner lied and told us nothing was wrong with the septic system during our negotiations.) The Health Department would not allow us to fix the existing drain fields and demanded that we connect the mobile home park to the county sewer system. Further, the Health Department demanded that we come into compliance within three months or they would shut down the park and make the residents move out. They softened their stance and became more accommodating when they saw how serious we were about fixing the problem, unlike the previous owner, who merely gave them lip service. The Health Department made weekly inspections and insisted we pump out the septic tanks on a routine basis, which ran $1,000 or more some months.

It took us more than a year to engineer a new septic system and get estimates from underground utility contractors to dig up the mobile home park streets, put in new septic lines, and then connect to the county system. It also required obtaining a very expensive easement from one of our neighbors. It was a period of tremendous development and growth in our county, and contractors were backed up with work for six months or more.

Once we could get three contractors to grace us with an estimate for the work, it was for more than $600,000! That amount of money was never in our calculations for the improvements to the park. All of the partners intended to spend a total of around $100,000 extra for a total cost of $750,000 when it was completely occupied. Spending an additional $600,000 to fix the septic system alone would have made the park into a loser with negative cash flow. In that case, we probably would have let the Health Department close the park down and we would have sold it as vacant land. Since it was at the corner of two heavily traveled streets, the land was probably worth what we paid at the courthouse steps, so the transaction would have been either a break even or a slight loss.

The park is proof that buying on the courthouse steps is the riskiest way to buy because of the inability to perform good due diligence. If we had been able to conduct adequate inspections and complete sufficient due diligence, we would have contacted the Health Department and found out about the violations. Then we would have discounted the price of the Palm Frond Mobile Home Park heavily or simply walked away from it. When we discuss due diligence in Chapter 10, you will see that septic system inspections are one of the most important things you must check out. Remember—when you buy a mobile home park, you are buying a town in which you are the mayor, and the mayor is responsible to the residents for the infrastructure.

This experience had a good ending. Through perseverance and the help of the county sewer department, we redesigned a system that cost $60,000 to install. In addition, on the recommendation of the county sewer department, we contacted another neighbor and got an easement across their property for only $2,000. The other easement would have cost us over $150,000 to put into place. I want to mention that wonderful neighbor, Uncle Bob's Storage, a national chain of mini-storage facilities. They charged us only for their legal fees to review the easement and didn't hold it up for ransom. When someone does me a kindness, I remember it, and Uncle Bob's did us a kindness. Thank you, Uncle Bob.

As of this writing, it is three years after we bought the Palm Frond. We have a new septic system in place as well as new water lines and submeters. The occupancy during the three years went down to thirty lots because we didn't want to add new residents until we were sure we solved the septic problem. Now, we are back up to forty rented units and accelerating. We expect the Palm Frond Mobile Home Park to be completely rented within another year by bringing in older park model BBs. This is how the park will perform when fully rented:

INCOME	
62 Lots at $295 per Month per Lot	$18,290 per Month
2 Apartments at $1100 per Month	$1,100 per Month
Total Income per Month	$19,390 per Month
Total Income per Year	$232,680 per Year
Expenses – 40%	$93,072 per Year
NOI (Total Income – Expenses)	$139,608
Price at 10% Cap Rate	$1,396,080
Cost	$750,000
Profit	$646,080
Cap Rate Earned = NOI ÷ Total Cost	**$139,608 ÷ $750,000 = 18.6%**

A few months after we purchased the park, we refinanced $512,000 through a local bank and used that money to repay the partners part of our original purchase price of $640,000. The loan was at 7.5 percent for twenty-five years, adjusting every three years, the payment being $3,783 per month, or $45,396 per year.

Therefore, we have the following cash invested in the Palm Frond:

$750,000 Total Cost – $512,000 Mortgage = $238,000 Cash Invested

Our cash flow will be:

Cash Flow	**=**	**NOI**	**–**	**Yearly Mortgage**
$94,212 per Year	**=**	**$139,608**	**–**	**$45,396**

Our cash-on-cash return will be:

Cash-on-Cash Return	**=**	**Net Yearly Cash Flow**	**÷**	**Cash Down**
38.5%	**=**	**94,212**	**÷**	**$238,000**

The Palm Frond Mobile Home Park will have a profit of $646,000 when we have completed the turn-around and will have a yearly positive cash flow of $94,000, which will be divided among four partners. Each of the partners will have about $60,000 invested in the property and will earn 38 percent on that investment. You could say, "All's well that ends well," but this purchase could have turned out badly were it not for the flexibility of the Health Department and the help we received from the County Sewer Department and Uncle Bob's Storage. It was no fun for two-and-a-half years—receiving the weekly calls from the Health Department inspectors and the monthly calls from the Health Department attorney, while trying to get estimates from underground contractors and engineers who were so busy they couldn't answer their phones.

Auctions

I am an auctioneer, and not only do I enjoy conducting auctions for sellers, I also like buying at auction as an investor. Auctioneers don't hide their auctions—they spend a lot of money promoting them because they know that the better the auction is promoted, the more people will show up and the higher the bids will be. The higher the bids are, the more the auctioneer gets paid, because we are usually paid a percentage of what we sell the property for.

There are two types of auctions: *absolute* and *reserve*. To sell by *absolute* auction means the property is going to sell, regardless of price. Whatever the high bid is on sale day is the price it will sell at. To sell by *reserve* auction means that the seller has the right to reject any bid below their least acceptable price, which is called the reserve. Sometimes the auctioneer discloses the reserve amount, and sometimes the auctioneer does not. Most bidders prefer absolute auctions because they know the property is going to sell, and any research and time they invest in determining what to bid is well spent. Many bidders do not like reserve auctions, especially when the reserve is not published, because they don't know how serious the seller is about selling the property. The bidders' time could very well be wasted by an unrealistic seller who has set an unrealistic reserve.

The bids are usually higher at absolute auctions, however, a fact that is not obvious. Because more people show up at absolute auctions, there are more bidders, and consequently prices are higher. Conversely, the bids are usually lower at reserve auctions because less bidders show up. I attend both types of auctions because you can get good deals at either type of auction. I have gotten many good deals and have sold many good deals at auction.

A word to the wise about auction terms of sale. While auctions have the allure of a good deal, they have very stringent terms. Most auctioneers will require the high bidder to put down a nonrefundable cash deposit of 10 percent of the value of the bid on the day of sale. If the high bidder doesn't close for any reason, the deposit will be forfeited. Also, the vast majority of auction properties are sold as is, with no warranties. Last, most auctions are not sold contingent on the high bidder finding financing. You will lose your deposit if you can't arrange financing and don't have the total price available by closing day.

Let me give you a little tip about how to bid at auctions—something I have never read in any book on auctions—and it is very important. First, you should figure out what you want to bid by using the flipping or the keeper formula. In almost all of the books I have read about auctions, the advice is to stick to whatever bid you came up with before the auction and to not go a penny higher. The advisers are afraid you will get "auction fever" and go to an unrealistically high bid when faced with competition.

The advisors are right. As an auctioneer, my job is to give you auction fever and get you to compete with the other bidders. But here is what you should do. Figure out what you want to pay. Write that number down. Now take 10 percent of your intended profit, if it's a flipper, and write that figure down. That is the most you will add to your bid in case you have competition. For a keeper, you might want to add 1 to 2 percent of the total purchase price onto your bid. Most people bid to a round number, and then stop dead once that round number is reached. This new strategy will help you take advantage of that tendency.

For example, let's assume a mobile home park is being auctioned and it is worth $400,000 as it sits. Most serious investors will stop somewhere between $300,000 and $320,000 if they are going to flip it, or somewhere around $350,000 and $375,000 if they are going to keep it. Let's further assume you want to buy it and flip it, and you are feeling particularly aggressive because the market is strong and your inventory of flippers is low. You are willing to pay $320,000, and make $80,000 in gross profit when you flip it. However, another investor shows up and is bidding against you, and she bids $321,000. Do you stop bidding and go home, like many books advise? I say no. You should allow yourself to bid another $8,000, up to $328,000. This is 10 percent less gross profit for you, but you will still make $72,000 instead of $80,000. That's better than going home empty-handed, isn't it?

If you are going to keep the property and you are feeling aggressive because the market is strong, and the park at auction really is worth $400,000, then you may want to pay just a little more and stop bidding somewhere between $380,000 and $383,000 if you get competition at the auction.

You should be able to find most auctions in the classifieds. Call the auctioneer and ask to be placed on their mailing list or email list. You can also go to the yellow pages again and call all the auctioneers in your area.

Group B: The Bread and Butter Basics

This group of six contains three places you have already looked into while doing your homework: driving by your favorite segment areas, calling from the classifieds, and calling Realtors. Now we are going to introduce three more: the Internet, a gold mine ad (and your own Internet site), and sending out mailers.

Internet Sites for Mobile Home Parks

The Internet has become the place to start doing business when it comes to real estate, and this is even more true with mobile home parks. It is said that more than half of all the people who buy real estate today start their search on the Internet, and I am willing to bet the percentage is even higher for investors looking to purchase or sell mobile home parks. The following are sites that are dedicated to helping investors sell their mobile home parks:

1. LoopNet: www.loopnet.com/

2. Mobile Home Park Store: www.mobilehomeparkstore.com/

3. eBay: www.ebay.com/

4. Craig's List: www.craigslist.org/

LoopNet is the most popular site for mobile home investing, with MobileHomeParks.com a close second. When I was writing this section, LoopNet had 1,300 parks listed for sale and MobileHomeParkStore had 850. The list of websites and each site's popularity changes daily. eBay can be interesting as to the mobile home parks offered for sale and/or auction. Some of my students have also gotten favorable results using Craig's List.

There are also nationwide real estate brokers and regional brokers who have websites that contain mobile home parks for sale. They are:

1. Marcus & Millichap: www.marcusmillichap.com/

2. Sperry Van Ness: www.svn.com/

3. Rochester Commercial: www.rochcomrealestate.com/

4. EMC-Atlanta: www.emcatlanta.com/

5. Gorial Realty: www.gorialrealty.com/

6. Correll Realty: www.usmhc.com/

7. Fortune Real Estate: www.fortunerealestate.com/

8. George Allen: http://mfdhousing.com/gfa/

This list will change as time goes on. I suggest you do your own personal Internet search on Google, Yahoo, MSN, etc. for mobile home parks for sale in the areas of interest to you. I neither endorse any sites nor caution against them, so you will have to decide for yourself how useful they are.

Driving by Your Favorite Segment Areas

You should get in your car and explore your favorite segment areas on a regular basis, at least once a month. You are looking for:

1. Mobile home parks that look vacant or abandoned

2. New Realtor signs on parks for sale

3. New For Sale By Owner signs on parks

We will cover what you should do with new Realtor signs when we discuss calling Realtors in this section. We will cover what you should do with new For Sale by Owner signs in the next section about calling from ads. Calling about vacant or abandoned property is the exciting art that we will discuss now.

There are four steps to making deals on abandoned or vacant property:

1. Figure out what it's worth as it sits
2. Find out what is owed on it to see if there is any "juice in the orange"
3. Find the owner
4. Negotiate a deal with the owner

You must follow the above order or you will be wasting a lot of your time. Steps one and two will tell you if there is any reason to contact the owner at all. For instance, suppose you see an abandoned mobile home park on three acres and it's worth $200,000 as it sits. You look up what's owed on it and find out there is a mortgage of $205,000. There is "no juice in that orange" because you probably won't be able to buy it below $205,000—say at $150,000—because that would mean either the lender will take $150,000 as payment for the $205,000 mortgage (this is called a "short sale," a time-consuming process, but one in much discussion today), or the owner will come to closing and pay $55,000 so you can buy it. Sellers don't usually like going to closings and paying to sell their property—they want to come to a closing and receive a check for their equity. If there is no equity and the seller is "upside down" on the property, you're probably better off pursuing other properties.

We have found that a lot of vacant and abandoned property had little or no "juice" in them; that's why they were abandoned. The seller was either waiting for the lender to foreclose and take the property, or waiting for the clerk sell it as a tax deed due to unpaid real estate taxes. *However,* there are the some great deals on abandoned or vacant property, so it is worth the time to check them out.

Once you have determined that there is "juice in the orange" or equity in the property, it's time to find the seller. You may get lucky and find the owner at the address where the real estate tax bills are sent by the Tax Collector. If that doesn't work, you may find a forwarding address from the neighbors or the post office. If the owner proves to be elusive, which frequently happens, you can hire a private detective to do a "skip trace" on the Internet to locate other addresses or relatives who know the current address of the owner. You may pay from $50 to $150 for the skip trace, but it's worth it.

When you locate the owner, don't appear too eager to buy the property. Usually you will be eliminating an eyesore in the neighborhood, and let the owner know that. Negotiate firmly but nicely, after trying to fit the property into one or more of your four Basic Profit Strategies. The example called "Splendor in the Tall Grass" in Chapter 4 on flipping and wholesaling shows you how I did this.

Calling FSBOs from Ads in Newspapers and Trade Magazines

For the first fifteen years of my real estate career, I did not call much from classified ads. I figured the best deals would only come from foreclosures and tax deeds. When I started training people in real estate investing more than eleven years ago, the owner of the seminar company insisted I call on ads from the classifieds, in front of the class using a speaker phone, so the students could hear both sides of the conversation. That's when I learned how wrong I had been for fifteen years. If you remember in the first section "The Second Adventure," calling on an ad in the classifieds is what got me started buying mobile home parks. While a good percentage of the deals I buy are still foreclosures and tax deeds, I also find good deals in the classifieds.

I do not call on every ad. I narrow the calls down to the mobile home parks that look the most attractive given the market knowledge I have accumulated. In the beginning, you will call on lots of ads until you gain the market knowledge of which areas you want to invest in and what price ranges you are seeking in those areas given the NOI and quality of the park. When it comes to trade magazines, *The Journal* and the *Manufactured Home Merchandiser* are two trade magazines that have FSBO mobile home parks for sale.

When it comes to buying, I concentrate on the *Pennysaver* weekly type of papers, because many of the sellers are not sophisticated investors and it's easier to get a good deal from them. When it comes to selling, I place my ads in the general circulation paper, usually only on Sundays, Wednesdays, and Thursdays. Even though the ads are more expensive, they bring in many more serious buyers. In my experience, the *Pennysaver*-type papers make the phone ring, but most of the buyers are not qualified and "just looking."

Calling Realtors, Realtor Magazines, MLS Listings, and Realtor.com

Realtors have joined together in almost every area of this country and to share their listings with each other. They call this sharing the Multiple Listing Service, or MLS. What that means is this: if Realtor A gets a seller to agree to sell their mobile home park with a 6 percent commission, it will be placed in the MLS. Realtor A will usually get half of the commission, or 3 percent, for writing up the listing and interfacing with the seller, should the property sell during the listing period. Realtor A is thus called the listing broker.

Now if any other Realtor, such as Realtor B, sells the mobile home park by writing a contract with a buyer, and the contract is accepted by the seller, then Realtor B will get the other half of the commission, or 3 percent. Realtor B will be called the selling broker. If Realtor A lists and then sells her own listing, then Realtor A will keep the whole 6 percent. In slow markets, we sometimes give listings on our flippers to other brokers who specialize in obtaining good prices on properties, even though we are a broker. We'll allow the listing Realtor to keep the listing "in their pocket" and not place it in MLS for a week, so they can have a chance to earn both sides of the commission, and be eager to do more business with me. In an active or even hot market, I will remain as the listing broker and only offer 3 percent to the selling broker.

Most local MLS agencies around the country have an agreement with the National Board of Realtors to download their listings onto the Internet to the website www.Realtor.com at the end of each day or week. Any individual can then sign onto Realtor.com and look at listings throughout the U.S. The information on Realtor.com is limited in some respects—it is designed so that serious buyers and sellers will call or email the Realtors who have the listings for more information.

As you know, we specialized in foreclosures in our real estate investment career. We did all our own research, so we did not often use Realtors to help us find deals. Our belief was that if the MLS had any good deals, the Realtors would grab them right away. It followed in our reasoning that all that was left in MLS were listings that were priced at "retail" or higher, and we wanted to buy wholesale, below retail.

Boy, were we wrong! Again, as a result of conducting seminars, I worked with a Realtor who searched the MLS for the best listings, and then he showed these listings to the students during our bus tour of properties. I was amazed at some of the good deals he found. Ever since then I have become a firm believer in searching the MLS to find good deals. Only a small percentage of Realtors invest actively in real estate—

most are more concerned with earning commissions. I encourage Realtors that specialize in listing and selling mobile homes and mobile home parks to call me first when they have a "hot" listing. If they do that, I let them keep the whole commission and treat me like a retail customer, even though I am also a broker. When the deal is right, the extra 3 percent that I could keep from my end of the selling commission is small compared to the money I make on a good deal.

When I drive one of my segment areas and see a new For Sale sign from a Realtor, I'll call to get the details of the listing. If it's a Realtor I'm not doing business with, after I get the details of the listing, I'll tell them the following, which you should put into your own words and also use:

Hi, my name is _________ and I specialize in investing in mobile homes and mobile home parks. I'll buy them with two or three units, or hundreds of units. I don't mind if the mobile home park is cosmetically distressed, it, and in some cases I prefer it. Usually I keep them, but sometimes I fix them up and flip them. I like owner financing, but for the right deal, I can pay cash. Do you have any other listings to show me?

Any Realtor worth his or her salt will take down your name and number and put you on their "must call" list when they get a mobile home park for sale in the future. And don't think you are lying by saying you will pay cash. You will. It will just be someone else's cash if you need to buy with no money down.

I am constantly asked the question, "Should I become a Realtor if I'm going to be an investor?" and my answer is this: "To us, the benefits of being a Realtor have far outweighed any drawbacks. When we buy properties, we get to keep half of the commission because we are the selling Realtor, even though we are selling it to ourselves. When we want to flip or sell properties and list them in MLS, we only pay half the commission to the selling Realtor because we are considered the listing broker and entitled to half of it. Therefore, we have literally thousands of Realtors working for us, and we only have to pay them half of the commission, or 3 percent. We also get unlimited information access to MLS, whereas non-Realtors get only a part of it on Realtor.com."

Last but not least, you'll notice we also included Realtor magazines on the list of things to look at for good deals. In our area of south Florida, there are probably twenty or more of these, published by the largest Realtors with many listings. When I have the time, I look through them as well.

Gold Mine Ad or your Own Website

The *gold mine ad* is an ad that you place in magazines and newspapers that sellers of mobile home parks might read, or on your own website. The beauty of this is that you have sellers calling you. This is how it is worded:

(Wife's name) buys Mobile Home Parks
Any Kind, Any Condition, Anywhere
Quick Closing
Call 555-555-1234
www.ZalmanVelvel.com

We use my wife's name in the ad because one of the students who took our training said that when he put his wife's name in the ad, he got more phone calls. Apparently, he said, people are less intimidated by calling a woman. When people call on the gold mine ad, I tell them my wife is busy, but I can help them also.

Having your own website and email address now is inexpensive and quickly accomplished. There are a number of website creators who will create a simple website for free, as long as you pay them a monthly fee for hosting it. When you have a website, you should put your website and email address on all your signs, cards, ads, brochures, and stationary. It's a great way of letting your market know all the investments you are into. For instance, you can list your flippers, L/Os, and BBs on your website, as well as any vacant mobile homes you want to rent out. You can also put the gold mine ad right on your website.

Updating your website used to be a problem because you had to pay the website creator extra money to do it. Now this has completely changed. Most of the web creators have simple editing programs that allow you to change, update, and add new listings to your website yourself.

It's also important to get your website put in the major search engines, like Yahoo, Google, and Microsoft, to name just a few. The website creators will show you how to do this or do it for you.

Mailing, Cold Calling, and Making Offers Directly to Owners of Mobile Home Parks

This is one of the more adventurous and time consuming ways of finding good deals. It is also one of the best.

You start by getting lists of the mobile home parks in your area, either from the property appraiser, the yellow pages, lists available on the Internet from Mobile Home Park Store, as well as other websites. Then you either send out postcards or phone the existing owners asking them to call you if they are interested in selling. The best way to do this is to continue do it throughout the year, perhaps every four months or six months or so. When the owners are interested in selling, they will call you and give you first chance at buying their parks.

If you want to be even braver, make an offer in your postcard or phone call, based upon the number of units and the type of park. Obviously your offer will be contingent on conducting due diligence on the park.

Group C: Long-Term Networking

These are things you should be doing in the normal course of business to get people to help you create wealth for yourself (and also for them), although they don't have an immediate effect. Networking is another part of the business I overlooked for the first fifteen years of my investing career and have come to appreciate even more as I mature. The value of networking came home when, after spending hundreds of dollars in advertising to sell one of our flippers in a slow market and answering a hundred phone calls, we received a call from a buyer sent to us by a business acquaintance. The deal was wrapped up with both sides being happy within an hour.

The power of networking also became apparent when, after our assistant had been cold-calling for a month prospecting for auction listings and we had spent a thousand dollars on a mass mailer, we received a call from a seller sent to us from a former auction client, and we contracted their auction within an hour. When you have to sell a new client on your services, it's hard work, but when you get a referral as a result of networking, it's like dealing with a friend.

"I Buy" Signs on Your Car and in Favorite Segment Areas

Magnetic signs on your car, or cars, are a wonderful way of getting deals and are very cost effective. Your car and your family's car become moving billboards. What should you say on your magnetic sign? The same thing you have in your gold mine ad is a real good start, but instead of putting your wife's name as the buyer, put "I buy." You will be surprised at the people who stop to talk to you at traffic lights and parking lots when you have a sign on your car that says you buy, sell, or rent mobile homes and mobile home parks. Make sure you put your phone number and website on the sign.

You can also network with the inexpensive eighteen-inch plastic signs that you can stick in the ground or tack up on trees and power poles in your wealth farm. Again, the wording on the sign can be the same as the gold mine ad, only with "I buy" instead of a name, and make sure you put your phone number and website on the signs.

Scouts—Mail Carriers, FedEx and UPS Drivers, Meter Readers, Lawn and Sanitation Workers, Code Enforcement Officers

Wouldn't it be nice if the people that constantly drove your favorite segments areas—your wealth farms—on a daily basis were out looking for deals for you? Well, they will, if you put them on your team. Anyone who delivers mail or packages is a valuable resource for you, like postal workers and UPS and FedEx drivers. Meter readers are another valuable resource as are sanitation workers and landscaping companies. They know your segment areas almost as well as you. They can be your scouts for finding deals.

Introduce yourself and tell them you buy mobile homes and mobile home parks. Give them your card and ask them to call you when they see a property that looks like it has been abandoned or gone vacant. Things like tall grass, junk mail spilling out of the mail box, free newspapers piling up in the driveway, meters being pulled or turned off, garbage cans not being put out, are dead giveaways. Also ask them to call you when they see a new FSBO or Realtor For Sale sign go up.

Now, giving them a benefit to call you can be a little tricky. Some people like good old cash, and you should offer them $100 to $200 when they give you a lead that turns into a deal. That's enough money that they'll be motivated to help, but not too much so they'll get the idea of going into competition with you.

Some people might not be allowed to take rewards or gratuities, or they may get insulted at being offered a tip. In that case, if you see anything other than eagerness on their faces when you offer a reward, change your offer to one of donating the same amount of money, in their name, to their favorite charity or their church or synagogue. That offer will likely melt the hardest of hearts.

You should also include code enforcement officers on your list of scouts. You are a real benefit to them—you will take raggedly-looking properties in their area and convert them to well-maintained properties. Again, cookies, donuts, a bottle of cheer, or a donation to a favorite charity go a long way with government workers,.

REIAs, CCIM, and CIP

Don't you just love initials and acronyms? I remember listening to a speaker recently about a subject in investment real estate, and I had to stop her five times to ask what the acronyms and initials meant that she was using.

REIAs are Real Estate Investment Associations. They have grown up and matured and are now an excellent way to network with other investors and learn more about real estate investment in general. Our local REIA meets monthly and has seminars on different aspects of investing in real estate and networking sessions afterwards where members trade listings and work out swaps on different properties.

You might think you are giving aid to your competitors by joining a REIA, but if the association maintains a real spirit of sharing information, you will reap benefits commensurate with what you share. You can probably find your local REIA in the yellow pages or on the Internet by searching under REIA in your area.

The CCIM organization, which stands for Certified Commercial Investment Members, has state and city chapters. If you are not a CCIM member they still might invite you to attend their meetings. Let the agents who attend know that you are a mobile home park investor looking to buy. Locally, we have a CCIM chapter, as well as a separate CIP organization, which stands for Commercial and Industrial Professionals. The CIP meets twice a month, and about fifty to seventy-five of the most active commercial brokers come in and share listings and listen to speakers with useful information. We have seen quite a few mobile home park listings from them.

YOUR OWN BUS TOUR EACH WEEK

When I am training, we set up a bus tour of properties where we see anywhere from twelve to fifteen properties in four to six hours. You should set up your own tour each week, or every other week, depending on how active you are. On this tour you should put any of the properties that look like they could be a good deal, taken from the previous Wealthy Dozen.

My wife and I did this every Friday for many years. We'd start around 9:00 A.M. after the kids were off to school, and we had the list of properties printed out. We'd have lunch together in the middle of the tour and then work our way back to the house so we could be home for the kids around 4:00 P.M. She was the navigator with the map, giving me directions as we drove around our county. We inspected the properties and figured out what our offer would be. Now with GPS on-board computerized navigators you can program the addresses of your tour and have the computer tell you where to turn, so you don't need a navigator, but it's more fun with your wife or children than a computer, and it involves the family in your adventure.

If Fridays aren't possible for you, then a weekend day would be just as good. Try to make it fun and a family or a relationship experience. What's that? Yes, I know. Some of you don't want to give up part of your weekends to go looking for deals, not matter how much "fun" it is. Well, okay, then perhaps you can suggest another way that you can stop working paycheck to paycheck without doing it?

SUMMARY

You now have an organized twelve-point plan to help you find good deals—ranging from highly motivated sellers to bread and butter exploring to long-term networking. At some point it will occur to you that the most efficient and profitable use for your time as an investor is finding good deals and then making the deals you keep more efficient and profitable. The repairs, the maintenance, and the management of your parks, as well as the selling of flippers and L/Os and BBs can all be done later by people you hire, once you know what they need to do, how to train them to do it, and, of course, have the cash flow to pay them. If you want to become really wealthy, you will want to spend the majority of your time finding and putting together good deals, because that is where real wealth comes from.

HOMEWORK

I want you to start finding highly-motivated sellers. Go to your county clerk's office and see how foreclosures and tax deeds are done. See if there is a foreclosure and/or tax deed service that will do the research for you for a monthly fee. It's worth it, so don't be cheap. Call the local community banks in your area and ask to speak to the vice-president in the foreclosure department and ask for a list of REOs. Look in the newspapers for auctions, and use the yellow pages to find auctioneers in your area and ask to be placed on their mailing or email list. Write all of the above names and phone numbers down in your notebook. You don't have to do this all in one day, but do it.

For your bread and butter basics, you're going to create your wealth map now. Take a map of your city or county and highlight the different areas—affordable-income, middle-income, and upper-income areas. Explore the Internet sites that I gave you and see if there are any mobile home parks for sale close to you. If there are none close, see where the closest ones are. Also, if you can search your county records by property type, then do that for mobile home parks. If your county has a mobile home park association, get a list of parks from them. Put the codes: *fam, 55+*, or *RV* next to each park to note what kind of park they are, and then *LL* or *RO*, for land-lease or resident-owned. Drive around and visit the parks, write your impressions of them in your notebook along with the price ranges and the lot rents for the mobile homes there.

While you are driving around, note the addresses of any vacant properties or run-down properties you see. Find out if they have any profit potential and try to find the owners if they do. If you pass any For Sale signs by Realtors, write down the ones with the most signs and call them. Tell them what I told you tell them in number 7 above. Call on the FSBO signs also to find out what they are and how much they cost. If you think you will be ready within the next month to start buying property place your gold mine ad in the local *Pennysaver* or wherever you believe sellers of mobile home parks will be reading.

For your long-term networking activities, order some "I buy" signs. Put magnetic ones on your cars and plastic ones around your segment areas. Start up a website and get an email address related to the website. Find a local website creator or call the local board of Realtors and see if they can recommend someone, because many Realtors have their own websites and the website creators know this. While you are ordering these things, order some business cards and put your website and email address on them, along with your phone number. Meet your scouts: the mail carriers, the FedEx and UPS delivery people, the lawn and sanitation workers, and the code enforcement people. Give them a business card and offer them a finder's fee or a contribution to their favorite charity. Join your local REIA, CCIM, and/or CIP.

Is this going to be a lot of work and time? *You bet it is!* When you get tired, I want you to imagine again what you will do with the first $10,000 you make and write it down again in your notebook. Then imagine what you will do with the first $100,000 you make, and write that down in your notebook, too. You now have a specific roadmap to becoming wealthy, perhaps the first one you have ever had, along with formulas and profit strategies. Don't blow it by adopting the same attitudes that kept you from wealth in the first place. Come on. Get up off that chair and get involved in your own adventure. You can do it, you know you can.

COMING ATTRACTIONS

Now you know where to find good deals. Next I'll show you how to figure out what the mobile home parks are worth, so you can recognize a good deal or create one for yourself. You will make offers and make money based on your appraisals. You will also learn how to be able to discuss prices intelligently with Realtors, buyers, and sellers, just like a professional.

8

What's It Worth: Figure It

Figuring out what something is worth—*appraising*—is essential to any business that involves buying and selling. The people who do the buying and selling for that business must understand the value of the product or service they deliver to their customers, as well as the value of what they purchase in order to create that product or service. The owners of the business have to make sure there is a difference between the two values that results in a profit.

In this chapter, you're going to learn how to appraise mobile home parks. We are going to apply The Magic Formula you learned in Chapter 1 so you can figure out what a mobile home park is worth before you buy it and what it will be worth after you own it or get ready to sell it. You will figure how much you should pay to create a good deal for yourself when doing a flipper, keeper, L/O, or when using BBs to fill vacancies. When it comes time to sell or rent, you will be able to explain logically how you arrived at your selling price, or rent, to prospective buyers, appraisers, Realtors, tenants, lenders, and so on. You are going to look and sound like a professional when we're finished training you in this chapter, and you will get the respect that a professional creates.

The ultimate question in any appraisal is, "What will a buyer pay for this product or service? What is the market value?"

DEFINITION OF MARKET VALUE

The USPAP, the Universal Standard of Professional Appraisal Practice, defines market value for real estate as follows:

> **Definition of Market Value:** The most probable price which a property should bring in a competitive and open market under all conditions requisite to a fair sale, the buyer and seller, each acting prudently, knowledgeably and assuming the price is not affected by undue stimulus. Implicit in this definition is the consummation of a sale as of a specified date and the passing of title from seller to buyer under conditions whereby: (1) buyer and seller are typically motivated; (2) both parties are well informed or well advised, and each acting in what he or she considers his or her own best interest; (3) a reasonable time is allowed for exposure in the open market; (4) payment is made in terms of cash in U. S. dollars or in terms of financial arrangements comparable thereto; and (5) the price represents the normal consideration for the property sold unaffected by special or creative financing or sales concessions granted by anyone associated with the sale.

Understanding the Definition

The above definition is a real mouthful, isn't it? As you can see, real estate appraisal has gone deep into the exploration of what market value is. The reason is clear—so much depends upon real estate appraisal. A huge part of the wealth in this country is contained in real estate, so a universal way of arriving at value is needed. There is a huge amount of debt placed upon real estate, over 11 trillion dollars in housing alone. Appraisal is critical to banks in order to determine the market value of properties and what the bank wants to lend on them, based upon that value.

Let explore the different parts of the definition so it can help you understand the process of appraising, and then we'll simplify it for you. First, the mindset the buyer and seller is described—they are both "typically motivated." In other words, the seller is willing to sell but is not desperate for money. The buyer is also willing to spend money, but the money is not burning a hole in the buyer's pocket or pocketbook. The intelligence and experience of the both sides is also defined—they are both "well informed and advised." The relationship between the buyer and seller is "at arm's length" in that they have no personal motivation to complete a transaction between each other, and for all intents and purposes they don't even need to know who the other side is. Each is acting in his own best interest. The market exposure is then described as having the property offered for sale in the marketplace for a reasonable amount of time so a reasonable number of buyers can inspect it and judge its value. Neither side should be in a hurry. Last, the sale will be in American dollars, and any extra concessions given in terms of financing or additional personal property are factored out.

If you want to buy good deals—in other words, deals you can buy below market value—it follows from this definition that you want to find a seller who is desperate to sell and in a big rush to cash out, not well informed, selling a property that is not well marketed, and willing to give lots of concessions. It also follows that you want to be a buyer who is in no rush to buy, very well informed, and well advised about what's available in the market and can close quickly for the right deal.

Three Approaches to Value

The three usual approaches to determining the fair market value of a property are: *income approach*, *sales comparison approach*, and *cost approach*. An appraiser will determine which approach is applicable and develop an appraisal based upon information from each individual market area.

Properties that are typically purchased by investors for their rents will give greatest weight to the *income approach*, which computes the gross income coming into a property and subtracts the expenses to come up with the net operating income (NOI) and then capitalizes that income stream by dividing it by a cap rate to get a market value. This approach is the most useful one for our purposes, but it must be combined with the sales comparison approach below to get the cap rate.

The *sales comparison approach* looks at the price of similar properties being sold in the marketplace. These are called comparable sales, or "comps." The sales are analyzed and the sale prices adjusted to account for differences between the comparables and the property being appraised to determine the fair market value of that property. *What we are primarily looking for is a cap rate from comparable mobile home parks that have sold*. This approach is generally considered very reliable if good comparable sales exist. Once we have a cap rate we can determine the price by dividing the cap rate into the NOI.

We are also going to use comps to determine the lot rents in other comparable mobile home parks, so we can determine if the rents in the park we are buying are at market, below market, or above market, and to find the cost of purchasing mobile homes in other comparable mobile parks when we are using BBs to fill up vacant lots.

The *cost approach* is defined as "the land value, plus the cost to reconstruct any improvements, less the depreciation on those improvements." In other words, you add up the cost of the land, the cost of the mobile homes and other improvements, and subtract the amount of value that aging has taken away from those improvements. This approach is most useful when you are developing a mobile home park for the first time on a parcel of vacant land. We will do this in Chapter 15.

A humorous sidebar to all of the above fancy terms and jargon is this: we appraisers call our work both an art and a science. When our appraisal matches what a customer actually pays for a property, we say, "Of course!" because we have produced a scientific product. When our appraisal differs from how a customer values a property or someone disagrees with our estimate of market value, then we also say, "Of course!" because now we are producing an artistic product and art is subjective, not objective. Art or science, when you have to make a living in the real world, your appraisal had better be accurate or you can lose money, and losing money isn't scientific or artistic—it just plain stinks.

You probably noticed I used the words "we appraisers" in the above paragraph. I did that because I held a Registered Real Estate Appraiser license in Florida for about fifteen years. Initially, I took the classes to learn more about how to appraise as many different kinds of property as possible, as an investor and as an auctioneer. As an investor, twenty to twenty-five properties came up for foreclosure each week, and I had to be prepared to evaluate all types of property in every area to see if the foreclosure judgment represented a good deal. As an auctioneer, I was also asked to evaluate many different types of property to estimate what an auction would bring in terms of price. Every two years I had to take forty hours of continuing education to keep the license, and the courses were useful. I kept the license until I could no longer justify spending the forty hours, and then sadly said goodbye to it.

Now that you have an understanding about the complicated parts of appraising, let me show you a simpler approach. Then I'll take that approach and show you how to make money with it.

A SIMPLER APPROACH

Getting past the jargon above, an appraisal boils down to this:

1. Use the most accurate NOI that *you are given* for a park *as it sits.*
2. Decide what cap rate you want to earn on it.
3. Divide the NOI by your cap rate to come up with a price.

Once you have the NOI given to you and the cap rate you want to earn, the price is set by formula. Simple, isn't it? Well, not quite.

More about Actual NOI

Using the most accurate NOI that *you are given* for a park *as it sits* deserves further explanation. The vast majority of mobile home park sellers will supply you with the price they want and the NOI their park produces. Some sellers are honest and will supply an accurate accounting, down to the penny, of their mobile home park's actual yearly income and expenses and the resulting *actual NOI.* When you encounter such a seller, it is a blessed event because it renews your faith in humanity.

When we mentioned NOI above, we italicized *"as it sits."* We did this for two reasons. The first reason is that many sellers understand that the higher the NOI is, the higher the value will be on their mobile home park. Therefore, they give higher, optimistic values to the current income achieved and lower values to the expenses actually paid, which results in a misstated *idealized NOI,* and a correspondingly unrealistic higher price that they hope to get. (It won't help to get angry at this because it is a form of lying and cheating. Like a good prize fighter, you should just protect yourself from it.)

A good way to detect problems in the NOI right from the start is to look at the ratio of current total income received to the current total expenses. If the expenses are much less than 40 percent on a land-lease park, or 50 percent on park-owned units, then that is a red flag that there may be some "fictionalizing" of the NOI. It is possible to have slightly lower expenses than those two rules of thumb, but it is somewhat rare and unusual to have less than 30 percent expenses on land-lease parks and 40 percent on park-owned units. How will you discover when the expenses are misstated? Simply take the valuable chart of average expenses you were given on page 117 of Chapter 3 and compare the percentages on the chart to the percentage of the expenses you were given by the seller or broker. As you compare the two, you might discover some expenses were "forgotten," like management, or repairs, or maintenance.

The second reason we italicized *"as it sits"* is because some sellers and their brokers go a step further and represent a *potential NOI,* using a future *potential gross income* and expenses after all the problems of the park are cured, like vacant or undeveloped lots, raising the lot rent, evicting bad residents and tenants, and possible submetering, etc.. They call this a *pro forma NOI.* The more sophisticated of the sellers will price their park somewhere between the actual NOI and the pro forma NOI in an attempt to raise the price. The sellers who are pure dreamers will only supply the pro forma NOI and price their park using it.

Do not be misled!

When you come up with a final figure for the price of a park, *only use the actual NOI as it sits to come up with a price.* That is the NOI and the corresponding price the bank is going to lend on, and the NOI the appraiser for the bank will use to calculate value. It is possible that after you have a proven track record of turning around mobile home parks and the proven savings and capital reserves to do that, a bank may lend an additional amount based on part of the future potential income, or pro forma, to the value of the mobile home park.

The most important reason to not price a park based on the potential future NOI is because you will not benefit from the time and money you will spend getting the park to perform to that more ideal level. You will, in effect, be using your hard-earned savings and valuable time for free. If the future NOI is tantalizing and easy to attain, you might want to add a part of it to the actual NOI—but only a small part—say 20 percent of the increase or less.

Now, you might wonder why we also italicized the NOI *"you are given."* We would not have added those italics if we were only dealing with small parks, say ten units or less. With smaller parks, you can determine a fairly accurate NOI in a few hours and quickly base your evaluation of the park and your offer on this. We added the italicized *"you are given"* to the NOI because on parks with more units than ten, certainly for more than fifty, it might take you several days to determine for yourself what the actual NOI is. Then, after you have spent all that time, you can compare your NOI to the one supplied by the owner or his or her agent, to arrive at your own accurate representation. The problem is, while you are spending your valuable time checking the information, another buyer could come along and get their offer accepted, and then all your time has been wasted.

This principle applies also to when you are doing the rest of your due diligence inspecting the infrastructure on a park. You will be spending a lot of valuable time doing this, and you don't want to have another buyer come along and scoop the property up while you are doing your research. Therefore, on larger parks you are going to have to use the most accurate NOI that *you are given* by the seller or broker to make an offer. You should not spend hours and days of your valuable time evaluating a park until you first get it under contract. You will find out what to do in Chapter 10 if and when your final actual NOI and the NOI represented by the seller or broker, are materially different.

So, to summarize, use the most accurate actual NOI *you are given* on mobile home parks with more than ten units, and calculate your own NOI on mobile home parks with ten units or less. When you are calculating your own NOI, you will use the chart of expenses in Chapter 3 to make sure all the expenses are accurately stated and accounted for.

More about Cap Rate

You have more control over the cap rate you want to earn on a mobile home park than on the NOI. This is because it is your own number and doesn't depend on the seller's information. If you want to make it simple, you can just pick a cap rate that suits your investment goals, like 10 percent or more (whatever you decide you need) and forget about what the rest of the market thinks.

You can take a more professional approach by determining the appropriate cap rate from comparable sales of mobile home parks in the area, and then adjusting the comparable's cap rates to reflect the differences in the mobile home park you are buying. Remember that there is an inverse relationship between cap rate and price—the higher the cap rate, the lower the resulting price of a mobile home park, given the same

NOI. You can understand that principle by intuition—the more an investor wants to earn on a property, which is represented by a cap rate, the lower the price has to be when he or she buys it.

Remember also from our discussion of cap rate in Chapter 1 on The Magic Formula that the cap rate is a composite of many important factors, like the risk of the NOI remaining same in the future, the management intensity, and the current interest rates on borrowing mortgage money. If any of those factors increase, so does the cap rate. They rise and fall in relation to one another.

However, now you will learn that the size of the park, the quality of the park, and the type of park also figure in the cap rate, but inversely (in the opposite direction). The bigger the park the lower the cap rate, because big investors, like REITs (Real Estate Investment Trusts), are aggressive buyers, but only for large parks, usually around 200 units or more. I have seen REITs buy high-quality large parks at cap rates of 5 and 6 percent, not the average 10 percent.

Also, the higher the quality of the park, the lower the resulting cap rate. Woodall's Rating System, which goes from one to five stars, is the most commonly used measure for quality. The better the quality, the more the stars, and the lower the cap rates get. (See the Appendix for the components of Woodall's quality ratings by number of stars.)

The Appendix also has two historic charts showing how cap rates vary versus the size and quality of mobile home parks. One chart is for age-restricted, 55+ retirement parks, and the other is for family parks. You will see from the charts that age-restricted parks have lower cap rates than comparable family parks, probably because of their easier management and greater income stability. There is no chart available, but you will also find that parks with many park-owned units sell at higher cap rates than parks that are land-lease communities.

Getting the comps for mobile home parks that have sold in the area might be easy or difficult, depending on how many sales there have been and the information available about the NOI on the park. Probably the best way of determining the comparable cap rate is to ask some local appraisers or CCIMs for the comps. If that is not available, you can try a bolder move by calling newer owners of parks in the area, who have purchased within the last year. Introduce yourself and say you are doing an appraisal (which you are), and ask them for the NOI and price of the park, and then calculate the cap rate yourself by dividing the NOI into the price. If the county property appraiser makes sale prices available to the public, then all you will need is the NOI from the current owner.

Remember—comps rule. Current market listings are almost irrelevant to appraisers. They don't care about who is asking what price for such and such a property, unlike most novice investors in real estate. Asking prices of properties that are not yet sold are not very important to appraisers. The actual sales are. To me, as an investor, I always look at current listings, but mostly to see how much competition there is in the segment I am looking to invest in. Current listings are extremely important to me as an investor, however, when the market is rapidly moving up or down, which happens once or twice every ten years. If the market is moving up, I want to see how high my competition has taken prices to. If it's moving down, I want to make sure my competition isn't already priced lower than what the comps show. Recently lenders have influenced appraisers to include current listings in their appraisals because our market has been gyrating wildly due to the subprime mortgage problem.

You should take at least three comps and compare them to the property you want to buy, which we'll now call the *subject property*. In the extremely rare case that a comp and the subject property are exactly identical, then you won't have to make adjustments and the comp and the subject property should be worth the same cap rate. In the much more common case where there are differences between a comp and the subject property, like a different size, age, or quality, you will take the cap rate that the comp actually sold for, and then make *adjustments*, upward or downward, to make it perform like the subject property. If the subject property—your property—has something better than the comp, you will *lower* the value of the cap rate that the comp sold for. If the comp has something better than the subject, you will *raise* the comp's cap rate.

Example of Adjusting Cap Rate to Comparable

Let's assume you are looking at buying a fifty-unit mobile home park that is an all age community and a Woodall three-star in quality, called Family Acres Mobile Home Park. That is your subject property. There is a comparable sale of a 100-unit mobile home park located a few miles from the subject property that is a 55+ retirement community, and a

Woodall two-star in quality, that sold six months ago, called Retirement Living Mobile Home Park. You found out the price of the comparable sale, Retirement Living Mobile Home Park, was two million dollars, and the NOI was $160,000. First you would calculate the cap rate of the comp:

Cap Rate	=	NOI	÷	Sale Price
8%	=	$160,000	÷	$2 Million

Now the comp, Retirement Living, was a 100-unit park, and the subject property, Family Acres, was only 50 units. You talked with an appraiser and found out that cap rates for 50-unit parks are higher than 100-unit parks. You also found out the cap rates for family parks are 1 percent higher than age-restricted parks. Further, you discovered that cap rates for Woodall two-star parks are .5 percent higher than Woodall three-star parks. *Keep in mind that as cap rates go up, prices go down, given the same NOI.* This is how you would adjust Family Acres to the comparable sale, Retirement Living:

Retirement Living Mobile Home Park vs.
Family Acres Mobile Home Park

Cap Rate at Sale for Retirement Living	8%
100 Units for Comp vs. 50 Units at Family Acres	+ .5%
Age-Restricted for Comp vs. Family Park	+ 1%
Woodall 2-Star for comp vs. 3-Star at Family Acres	– .5%
Cap Rate Indicated for Family Acres	9%

Remember, whenever Retirement Living, the comp, is *better than the subject* property you are evaluating, you add a cap rate adjustment for your subject property to make the cap rate of the subject higher. The reverse follows; whenever the comp is lower in quality in any aspect, you will subtract a cap rate adjustment to the make the cap rate lower on the subject property. You are doing this because as the cap rate goes up, the price goes down.

Let's try another comp, called All Age Acres, and the same subject, Family Acres. Let's assume All Age Acres Mobile Home Park, located a few miles away, has only twenty-five units, is a family park, and has a Woodall four-star rating. Let's assume All Age Acres Mobile Home Park sold four months ago for $500,000 and the NOI was $50,000. First you would calculate the cap rate of the comp:

Cap Rate	=	NOI	÷	Sale Price
10%	=	$50,000	÷	$500,000

**All Age Acres Mobile Home Park vs.
Family Acres Mobile Home Park**

Cap Rate at Sale for All Age Acres	10%
25 Units on Comp vs. 50 Units at Family Acres	– .5%
Family Park on Comp vs. Family Park on Subject	+ 0%
Woodall 4-Star on Comp vs. 3-Star on Subject	+ .5%
Cap Rate Indicated for Family Acres	10%

When you find three or more comps, you will perform an analysis on the differences between the comps and the subject and make adjustments on each one, like you were shown here, to come up with a cap rate on the property you want to buy relative to the comps. Then you will have to figure the most probable value the subject is worth. This is called *reconciliation*. In some cases, you can average the results, or in some cases, you will give greater weight to the comps that are closer in look and feel to the subject property. In this case, if we found another comp for another family park that indicated a cap rate of 10 percent for Family Acres, then we might simply use 10 percent as a cap rate, and not average 9 + 10 + 10 to get 9.33 percent, because the last two comps were so similar to the subject property that we decided to give them more weight rather than average all the comps.

You may be wondering how we determined the adjustments in the examples above. If you are, that's good. I estimated the adjustments from my experience in my area of South Florida. You are probably wondering, *how do you know what characteristics to adjust, and how much to make on each adjustment?*

There are two ways. The first, and in my opinion the best way, is by asking a qualified real estate appraiser in your area what types of adjustments she typically makes when appraising a mobile home park, and how she calculates the amount of each adjustment. If you are giving business or are going to give business to this appraiser, you will probably get your answers for free. If you do not contemplate a business relationship, then offer to pay $50 per hour to the best appraiser in your area, with a minimum of two hours, and discuss the typical adjustments in each. The second way to learn about adjustments comes ı experience. After you look at enough mobile home parks enough comps, you will know what to adjust for and by Jnfortunately, it will take you a fairly long time to be able to do that using just your experience and you might miss out on a lot good deals while waiting to learn, so I recommend the first way as better and faster.

There may also be times when you can't find good comps, which means you can not find any sales within the last six months, or within a few miles of the subject property, or sales that differ by a reasonable amount. In that case, you must use whatever comps you can find and then make adjustments for time, distance to subject, and so on.

You may also be wondering, *where do I get my comps from*? That is a great question. One way is to search the county records for sales in the last six months, within a few miles of the subject property, and within a certain range of the assessed value of the subject. In many counties, the property appraiser has a free website and a search engine for you to use. If you are not fortunate to have a good website from your property appraiser, you can try some of the new websites that give comps from all around the country. A few of these websites are:

- LoopNet.com
- MobileHomeParkStore.com
- Zillow: www.zillow.com/
- Net R Online: www.netronline.com/
- First American Real Estate Solutions: www.firstamres.com/

If all of the above don't yield good results, then you can also get comps from Realtors from the MLS, or from title companies. The professional way to assess a cap rate for a park you are intending to buy is to locate comparable sales of mobile home parks in the area, and then adjust the comps' cap rates to get an adjusted cap rate for the mobile home park you are evaluating.

SUMMARY

We have simplified the second step in the Five Green Fs, called *Figuring*. You have learned the appraisal process in this chapter, and you should feel comfortable discussing prices and cap rates and NOI with anyone—buyers, sellers, lenders, and even appraisers.

To figure the realistic price of a park, you first used the most accurate NOI *you are given* on mobile home parks with more than ten units, or calculated your own NOI on mobile home parks with ten units or less. You gave little weight to a pro forma NOI, and used the NOI of the mobile home park as it sits today, not one based on projected improvements.

After you found the NOI, you checked the comps in the area for their cap rates, and learned the typical adjustments to cap rates. The best way to do this was to contact an experienced appraiser and ask her. When you had three comps and their adjustments, you reconciled the cap rates to come up with the best fit for the property you want to buy.

Once you have the NOI and reconciled cap rate, you simply divide the NOI by the cap rate to get the price of the mobile park you are evaluating.

HOMEWORK

It's time to visit the county property appraiser in your area. Find out what information is available to the public from their files and what is available on the Internet. Determine how you are going to get your comps on real estate—from the property appraiser, from the other websites on the Internet, or from Realtors or title companies.

Next, ask around for some referrals for real estate appraisers. You can go to the trusty yellow pages, ask Realtors you have started relationships with, or ask lenders in your area who they respect and use for appraisals on mobile home parks. Contact the appraiser and let them know you expect to be buying mobile home parks and you want to be able to make intelligent offers based upon market value, and you will be recommending that they be the appraiser when it comes time to getting your loans. Then ask them about their most common adjustments and how they do the adjusting.

Now, take the three best deals on mobile home parks you've seen so far and check the NOIs to make sure you have the NOI as the park sits today, not the pro forma NOI. Check the ratio of expenses to the total rental income to see if it is in the 40 to 50 percent range, depending on whether it is a land-lease community or has park-owned units. Go down the chart of expenses to see how the expenses are in relation to the average expenses around the country. Find three comps for each of the parks you believe are the best deals, adjust the comps to come up with a cap rate, and then reconcile the values. Check to see how the offering prices on your best deals differ from your value. Then, using each of the formulas for success—the flipping formula, cash flow formula, and L/O formula—figure what your offer would be so you could make a profit. Write all this down in your notebook.

COMING ATTRACTIONS

Now I'm going to show you how to construct a written offer. Type 3s, we're going to protect you with this offer, and we're also going to lock it up for you so no one else can steal it away, so relax and learn. The time for making money is almost at hand.

We're also going to show you how to negotiate comfortably and successfully, and have a little fun in the process. Some people have said that all of life is a negotiation—well, if that's true, shouldn't you have the best skills possible at it? Read on . . .

9

Writing Offers and Negotiating: Flag It

You learned there are a dozen places to find good deals, and you searched them, heart pounding in expectation. Now you think that you've found one—your first good deal! It's a mobile home park with ten park-owned units on two acres. You inspected it quickly but not completely, because it does not pay to spend a lot of your time and money on inspections until you're sure the property can be yours and no one else can buy it out from under you. In other words, you have to *flag* the mobile home park for yourself, with an accepted offer.

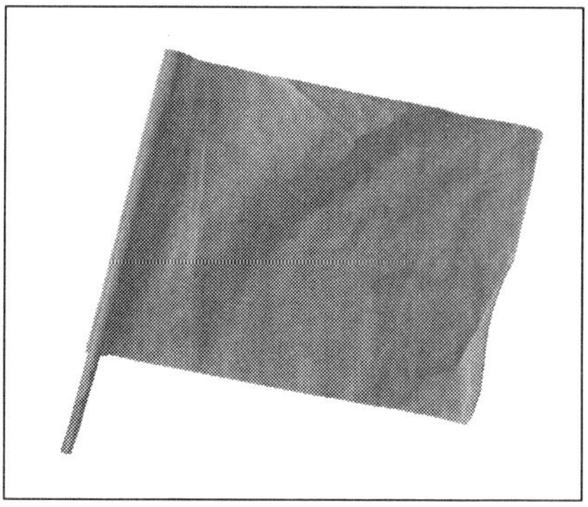

You found three good comps and adjusted and reconciled them. Lo and behold, the comps pointed to a value $25,000 *higher* than the listing price, so your intuition led you to the right place. You ran the property through your *formulas for success* on three of the four Basic Profit Strategies, and because it's in the upper end of the affordable-income segment, it worked well as both a flipper and a keeper, or even as an L/O if you decide to offer one later. However, you want to flip it, and make some fast cash, specifically $25,000 to apply to your credit card debt (which came from another time and place when you didn't know about the two different kinds of debt—investment debt and consumer debt.) In order to net a $25,000 profit, the flipping formula shows you must pay $10,000 less than the listing price to account for closing, holding, and fix-up expenses.

So you make an offer. A written offer, because verbal offers are not enforceable—they're not worth the paper they're not written on. It isn't absolutely necessary to have a written contract to complete a transaction, but if one of the parties, either the buyer or seller, changes his mind or says he understood the terms differently, the agreement must be in writing to be enforceable.

In this chapter you are going to learn how to construct a written offer, an offer that enable you to stick your investor flag on the property so no one else can buy it out from under you. This offer will protect you while you inspect the property and try to secure financing, and determine if the property really "fits" your investment style.

I put quotation marks around "fits" because buying real estate is similar to buying a new suit. You take the prospective suit off the rack and bring it into the dressing room to see if it fits. While you are trying it on, no other buyer can take it out of your dressing room and run up to the cashier and buy it. Other buyers will have to wait in line until you are finished making up your mind. If the suit fits, you will buy it. If it does not fit, you will take the suit off, put it back on the rack so another buyer will have a chance at it, and you won't be penalized for not buying it. Making an offer on a mobile home park property is similar, only the park costs more money than the suit.

Most areas of the country have no limitations on investors; they can make their own written offers when they buy or sell real estate for themselves. However, there are a few areas in the country where lawyers must handle almost all the contracts. Some of you won't feel comfortable unless an attorney or broker does it for you in the beginning even though you have the right to make your own offers, and that's okay. Either way, knowing how to construct an offer is a valuable skill to have, even if you use it only to assist your attorney or your real estate broker.

When I started in real estate in Staten Island, New York City, attorneys prepared our contracts even though I was a real estate broker. When I moved to Florida, I was surprised to find out anyone, including Realtors and investors, could write up contracts, but I still had an attorney write up my first three contracts because I felt more comfortable that way. Now, after more than twenty-two years in Florida and writing literally thousands of contracts, I smile when someone has an attorney write up their offer, because that will usually add a few weeks to the negotiation time. Attorneys—while I admire, respect, and use them more as I grow wealthier—have their own idea of what is and isn't a priority, and how fast to respond to offers.

In this chapter, you are also going to learn how to write offers for prospective buyers of your properties. Many times your buyers won't be experienced investors and they will appreciate it when you give them a hand constructing an offer and have the forms readily available. We usually have buyers come to our office, where we sit down together and help them write out an offer. Before we make the appointment, we explain that the buyers can have their attorney do this or we can try to do it together and save them the legal fees, whichever is their preference. We prefer to meet and negotiate face to face, to get an acceptable deal between both sides as quickly as possible.

We don't take advantage of inexperienced buyers and we hope you won't either. We give them a due diligence period of between a week and a month, depending upon how many units there are in the property. During this time they can inspect the property and if they are not happy for any reason, they can cancel the contract, no questions asked. If they want to cancel, they will be relieved of any obligations and get their deposit back. If they want to proceed and they need financing, we give them a reasonable time to find a loan.

Perhaps you're wondering, "What if your initial offer is not accepted by a seller or a buyer? What do you do then?" Well, many times your offers won't be accepted. Plan on it. We're going to show you how to continue to negotiate and still get a good deal in the second part of this chapter. You will be able to take these negotiation skills and use them everywhere in your life. And if the negotiation still does not get you a good deal, then we're going to show you how to walk away. This is very important. You will learn how to walk away nicely, with respect, with the door still open to doing a deal in the future, should either side change their minds.

THE PARTS TO AN OFFER

An offer is simply an agreement in which a buyer agrees to buy, and a seller agrees to sell, on certain terms. It is not an accepted offer or effective contract until both sides agree to *all* of the terms.

The Parts of an Offer

1. Who the *Buyer* and *Seller* are
2. A *Description of the Property* and its *Location*
3. What *Personal Property* is included and not included
4. The *Offer Price*
5. The amount of the *Deposit, Who holds it,* and *Terms of Refund*
6. *Financing Terms,* if any
7. The *Time for Acceptance* of the offer by both sides
8. The *Closing Date*
9. *Occupancy and/or Renters* and *Condition of the Property* at closing
10. *Inspection Period* and the *Final Walk-through* before closing
11. *Who is Responsible for fixing any Defects,* and up to *How Much*
12. *Who pays for which Closing Costs,* like Title Insurance, and *what to do if there are Title problems*
13. The *Brokers* involved, who they are and who pays for them
14. *Signatures* of all Parties
15. Any *Addendum* spelling out *Additional Terms and Conditions*

While it may look like an offer has so many parts to it that it would be like writing a book each time you want to make one, *the truth is the parts are all commonsense, and are there to protect you.* For the most part, you will just be filling in blanks on a preprinted form, as in the example on page 289 when the mobile homes come with land and are considered real estate. When you are buying one mobile home on a rented lot for a BB, which is considered personal property, you will be filling in a different simple form, as shown on page 290. My offers are entered on those forms, and they contain only one page when there is only one mobile home involved.

When you are buying a mobile home park, you will be given three additional simple sheets, or addendums, to the contract. One is a common list of personal property, and the second is a list of information you want from the seller. Those two are just lists and require little or nothing from you to add. You will tailor the third addendum to your individual inspection and financing needs.

You should use the commonly accepted forms in your area, the same ones the Realtors use. Either have one of your Realtor contacts order you some or go down to the local Board of Realtors and buy them. You should buy a pack of them, with at least three carbon copies. Many Realtors are now getting away from using preprinted forms, instead using computer software to generate an offer. It is an advantage to do this because the contract is stored in the computer and can be changed easily. Unfortunately, in our area, the contract software took a one page form and made it into eight pages, so we stayed with the one page preprinted form for simplicity.

Please don't worry that it will take you hours to write an offer. After you become familiar with the basics, it shouldn't take very long. When we construct offers in front of training classes, we usually complete writing one in ten minutes or less, to show how easy it really is. Then we spend an hour or more explaining all the parts and the important options for each part. It is important to understand the parts of an offer, and those parts are basically the same whether the mobile home is real estate or personal property. You are going to learn about the parts of an offer in the pages that follow. If there are differences depending upon whether the mobile home is real estate or personal property as in a BB, they will be noted. If there are differences based on whether you are the buyer or the seller, they will be noted. also

Generally, as a buyer, you will want as many contingencies as possible to protect you: a small deposit, a low price, a nice comfortable amount of time to decide whether you will buy the property or not, with as many financing options as possible, and as many concessions from the seller as possible. As a seller, you want the opposite—a sure deal, a big nonrefundable deposit, a high price, no contingencies, and a quick cash closing. The offer is a compromise between those two goals. Now, with that in mind, let's examine the parts of an offer:

Who the Buyer and Seller Are

When you are buying real estate, you should look in the property appraiser or county records to find out who the current owners are of the property, so you don't miss any seller's signature and agreement. You might want to take title using different entities other than your name and/or that of your significant other, for asset protection or tax purposes (Chapter 16 talks about protecting your assets). When you are buying mobile homes on leased land or BBs, you will need a copy of the title from the seller so you can verify the make and model as well as the owners of the mobile homes. There will usually be no other way of doing this for a BB.

When you are selling, ask the buyers if they want to take title as joint tenants with rights of survivorship, as most couples do, or as tenants in common. The main difference is that when you take title as joint tenants with rights of survivorship, complete ownership goes to the surviving partner if one partner should die before the other. If buyers take title as tenants in common, then if one person dies before the other, their half of the ownership goes to their estate and not necessarily to the surviving partner.

A Description of the Property, and Its Location

If you are buying real estate, you will need an address and a legal description of the land, which you can get from a copy of the previous deed in the courthouse records. You don't want to have only an address, because there are times when an address is imprecise and will not contain all the land involved. You will also need a copy of all the DMV (Department of Motor Vehicles) titles to any of the mobile homes that are included in the sale, where you will note the VIN number, the manufacturer, the model, the age, and dimensions of the mobile homes on the contract.

If you are buying a mobile home on leased land, like in a BB, there is no legal description, but you will need the make and model, and so on, of the mobile home, and the address where it is located.

What Personal Property Is Included and Not Included

On larger mobile home parks, the list of personal property can be extensive and the value extremely important. That is the reason you want to have a separate addendum called Schedule B (see next page). In a small park, you can fill in this list by hand and place it with your offer. On larger parks, the list will usually be too extensive and take too much time. It won't make sense to spend that time unless you are sure you are

Schedule B: Personal Property and Inventory Checklist Included in Sale

- ❑ ***Computer systems and management and software and databases***
- ❑ ***Website software and Internet website and name***
- ❑ ***Phone number***
- ❑ ***Yellow page ad and/or other advertising listings (voluntary on buyer only)***
- ❑ ***List of office equipment and furniture***
- ❑ ***Mobile home and/or RV dealership license included, if one exists***
- ❑ ***List of mobile homes and RVs to be added to this schedule within one week***
- ❑ ***List of parts to be added to this schedule within one week***
- ❑ ***List of lawn equipment to be added to this schedule within one week***
- ❑ ***List of snow removal equipment to be added within one week***
- ❑ ***List of tools to be added to this schedule within one week***
- ❑ ***List of pool equipment to be added to this schedule within one week***
- ❑ ***List of boats, canoes, kayaks, recreational equip, etc. to be added to this schedule within one week***
- ❑ ***List of golf carts to be added to this schedule within one week***
- ❑ ***List of laundry equipment to be added to this schedule within one week***
- ❑ ***List of vending machines to be added to this schedule within one week***
- ❑ ***In clubhouse, list of furniture, fixtures, and kitchen equipment to be added to this schedule within one week***

buying the park. The list will be completed to your and the seller's satisfaction within a week of agreeing to all the other terms.

You'll notice there are probably many things on this list you may not have thought of. The list has logic to it: the first part describes the office and things that revolve around managing the mobile home park. The second part covers any mobile homes that are included with the park, any parts inventory, and the dealership license. The third part lists the grounds maintenance equipment and recreational features, like pools, boats, recreational equipment, and so on. A golf cart is a big benefit for the manager in parks that are bigger than an acre or two, and they are expensive, so it's important to make sure that the one that is there now is included in the sale. Vending machines and pay-laundry equipment can provide hundreds and even thousands of dollars of extra money each month. Last but not least, if there is a clubhouse, you want all its furniture and kitchen equipment.

The Offer Price

When you are buying, you want to keep this price as low as possible. When you are selling, you want the price to be as high as possible. I told you this is mostly common sense, didn't I?

Amount of the Deposit, Who Holds It, and Terms of Refund

First, whether you're buying or selling, you don't want to give or receive a deposit until you have an accepted written offer from both sides. Wherever the deposit is listed on a contract, add the words "upon acceptance" after it. Life is short, and you don't want to be chasing after deposits.

Second, this deposit is called a "good faith" or earnest money deposit. It is a measure of the buyer's earnestness is purchasing the property. A $50 or $100 deposit does not show that when the property is worth hundreds of thousands of dollars. The following are what we offer as a deposit, depending upon the price of the property:

Offering Price	Amount of Deposit
Up to $5,000	$ 100
$5,001 to $25,000	$ 500
$25,001 to $1 Million	$ 1,000
$1 Million and Up	$10,000

It is not usual for the buyer and seller to agree that the deposit will be increased after inspections are completed and satisfactory, but before the financing has been approved.

As to who holds the deposit, you should *never* allow a seller to hold your deposit when you are buying (unless the seller is a Realtor or attorney with an insured escrow account). If the seller disappears with your deposit, it can cost more in time and attorney's fees to get it back than the original amount of the deposit. We are lucky because we have a brokerage escrow account that is protected by the State of Florida, where we deposit almost all of our earnest money and good faith deposits. We will let a reputable title company or attorney with a longstanding business in our area hold deposits if the seller demands this, but this rarely happens. When we explain to sellers that one of the only insured escrow accounts in the State of Florida is a real estate broker's escrow account, and that in the past some title companies and even some attorneys have run off with escrow deposits—with no insurance protecting the owner of the deposit—we have little trouble. Find out who in your area has an escrow account that is insured for fraud and theft, so they can hold your deposits.

As to the return of the deposit, as a buyer, make sure your deposit is *immediately* refunded if you don't approve of the inspection results, can't get acceptable financing, the title is clouded, or there is any other reason the contract can't go forward. However, when you are a buyer, after you approve of the inspection and approve the financing, you will forfeit your deposit if you fail to close. As a seller, you will want the deposit to be as high as possible and nonrefundable. In an average real estate market, both parties will usually agree to a reasonable and refundable deposit. In a red-hot market, the seller may be able to demand a large nonrefundable deposit that will be kept regardless of whether the deal goes forward or not.

Financing Terms, if Any

This section is very important to both buyer and seller. As a buyer, you want to have as many options as possible and as much time as you need, to get a loan. You will need to find out what is considered an acceptable amount of time to find financing in your area, because it can vary. In our area, sixty days is a reasonable amount of time to get financing for a mobile home park. Keep in mind, even though a mobile home park is a residential development, you will be dealing with commercial lenders and larger amounts on your loans. Large loans usually mean that the lender will need more time to complete the due diligence.

As a seller, you don't want to take your property "off the market" for extended periods of time only to find out the buyer can't get financing. Therefore, when a contract is subject to the buyer obtaining a loan, you as a seller should insert an addendum clause to the buyer's offer requiring that the buyer supply you with a prequalification letter, or "prequal," from their lender within five days of the effective date. You will have to approve this letter or the contract will be null and void. Prequal letters have been abused by lenders. They claim to have done a preliminary analysis of the buyer—so far, so good— *but* that they can not give a "firm commitment" to the loan until they receive additional important information. We follow up on the prequal letter and call the lender to ask what he or she feels are the realistic chances of the loan going through. Based upon what we hear, we either accept the offer, or reject it.

When we discuss addendums, you will be given clauses that you can use to protect yourself as either a buyer or seller when financing is involved. We will also discuss more of this in Chapter 11, when we discuss financing and the concept of no money down.

The Time for Acceptance of the Offer by Both Sides

As a buyer, you don't want to give a seller too much time to make up his or her mind. There is the possibility the seller will take your offer and then "shop it around" by calling other buyers who indicated an interest in the property. The seller tries to get the other buyers into a bidding competition—creating a quasi-auction—to raise the price. If the sellers live locally, you should allow them twenty-four hours to make up their minds. If the sellers live out of town, and a broker is involved, a few additional days might be more practical.

Keep in mind that as a buyer, you can cancel your offer at any time before the seller signs it even if you gave the seller more time. Also, keep in mind that unless the seller and the buyer agree to all the terms, you have an offer/counteroffer situation. There is no effective contract until *both sides agree to all the terms, in writing.*

There is an important term to learn here called the *effective date.* This is the date when both sides agreed, in writing, to all the terms of the offer—after the initial offer has been made and all the counteroffers have gone back and forth and have finally been resolved. You should note on the contract exactly when the effective date is, because the time periods in the contract will usually start from that date, not from the date the initial offer was made.

The Closing Date

First, it makes sense to choose all your time periods with respect to the effective date, as we just discussed. Second, you are going to need two separate time periods when you are a buyer, both to be added together:

1. Due Diligence Period: 30–60 days from the effective date
2. Financing Period: 45–60 days from the end of the due diligence period

The due diligence period is the time you will need to research and inspect the property. The schedule of the due diligence you want from the seller or the broker is given on the next page. As you can see, the due diligence is an involved study. If you are working a full-time job, it will be difficult to do this quickly. You have more flexibility if you are a full-time investor. For a small mobile home park of ten units or less, it may only take two weeks to do it. For a larger park, thirty to sixty days will be needed. Your due diligence is divided up into three areas:

1. The business aspects of the park (NOI)
2. The people who live there and the laws surrounding them
3. The infrastructure

First, you need to know if the park is, or can be, profitable. You then need to know about the people for whom you will be the mayor and the laws surrounding that mayoralty. Last, you need to know about the infrastructure you will have to maintain for your little town.

Once you determine these three areas have a positive outlook you will apply for financing and be asked to pay for the list called "if available due diligence"—the environmental and engineering inspections, property appraisal, survey, and so on. These cost money, and for larger parks will cost in the thousands of dollars ($3,000 to $5,000 or more). It doesn't make sense for you, as a buyer, to spend that money if you have determined from the due diligence period you don't want to buy the park. *Therefore, the finance period comes after the due diligence period and can not be done simultaneously.* You can get a prequal letter from a lender, but it won't really mean anything until the environmental, engineering inspection, property appraisal, and survey are completed and paid for.

As a buyer, you should pick a time period that is comfortable: forty-five to sixty days is a reasonable time period to secure financing, if neither side is in a rush and a third party is doing the financing. If the transaction only involves owner financing the closing can be soon after the due diligence period. When a seller gives you a fantastic price because you are closing fast, then obviously you should pick a date that is sooner rather than later.

As a seller, there is nothing to be gained by pushing a buyer to close too soon, especially if that buyer needs to secure financing from an outside party. All that will happen is that everyone will get upset when the transaction doesn't close as soon as the seller wanted, and then extensions to the contract have to be worked out and more paperwork needs to be created.

Occupancy and/or Renters and Condition of Property at Closing

Occupancy concerns whether or not the park will have someone living in it after the closing date. Since rental income is so important to mobile home parks, there will be a strong tendency on both the buyer's and the seller's part to have as many residents or tenants remain as possible.

Sometimes, if the seller lives on the property, he may want to remain in the property for a set period of time *after* the closing, and this can present complications. Many buyers are worried about this, and what they will have to do if the seller refuses to move out, even though he's supposed to. I have never had the problem, but if I did, I would go through a holdover eviction on the person or persons refusing to vacate. I strongly recommend having a written lease drawn up before closing if you are going to allow the previous seller to remain after the sale, in case you have to appear in front of a judge because the occupant refuses to move out on schedule. In that rare case, you will have a document that protects you, and not each side's self-serving memory.

Schedule C: Due Diligence from Seller

Business Aspects—NOI

- ***Annual Profit & Loss Statements*** (P&L) past three years and ***Monthly P&L*** current year
- ***Current Rent Roll*** with tenants' names, monthly rent, move-in date, expiration, and balance
- ***History of Rent Increases and Legal Procedure to Increase Rents***
- ***Delinquency List*** for last three months
- ***Tax Returns*** of seller for three years (if available)
- ***Title Insurance Policy*** with current O + E showing marketable title and/or exceptions
- ***Hazard & Liability Insurance Policy***—riders, risk assessments, carrier—past claims
- ***Real Estate Tax Bills and/or Assessments***—last three years, tax amount after you buy it
- ***Service or Advertising Contracts Assumed by Purchaser***—trash, extermination, maintenance, laundry, management, commission, union agreements, vending, billboard
- ***Payroll***—list of employees with name, position, wage rate, and entitled benefits
- ***Business License, Occupancy Permit, and/or Dock Permits***
- ***Utility Bills***—water, sewer, gas, electric, trash, street lights—two years monthly statements
- ***Existing Loan Documents***—if you are assuming the loans from seller

People and Laws

- ***All Leases***—entire copies plus any addendum or riders
- ***Security Deposits***—full list
- ***Rules and Regulations and Park's Eviction Procedure***—any prospectus for residents

- ***Litigation History***—any past or pending litigation; if none, affidavit from owner

Infrastructure

- ***Physical Inventory***—furniture, fixtures, equipment, and supplies (see Schedule B)
- ***Sewage Treatment Plant Permit*** and maintenance records—letter from maintenance company on monthly costs, operating problems, lot capacity, capital expenditures needed
- ***Water Supply Permit*** and maintenance records—letter from maintenance company on monthly costs, operating problems, lot capacity, capital expenditures needed
- ***Natural Gas Permit*** and maintenance records—letter from maintenance company on monthly costs, operating problems, lot capacity, capital expenditures needed

If Available Due Diligence

- ***Engineering Reports*** of sewer systems, water systems, gas, roads, electrical, and so on
- ***Environmental Inspection and Survey*** on asbestos, lead paint, underground tanks, wetlands, and so on
- ***Appraisal for bank***
- ***Survey*** (as-built)—with legal description

If you are buying the property as a keeper, and you want to keep all the current tenants, then you need to inspect a copy of the leases to see if you can accept the terms. If you don't want a particular tenant or tenants, then have the closing dependent upon the seller making the tenants vacate the property before the closing date. Having a good, paying, tenant is a real benefit for a keeper, but having a lousy, nonpaying tenant is not.

Typically, you will want the property in broom-clean condition when you take title to it at closing. Most sellers leave the property in good condition and I have had few problems with this. However, some tenants seemed to be entering the "Pig of the Month" contest before they vacated the property.

Inspection Period and the Final Walk-Through Before Closing

We have partially discussed the inspection period, which is also called the due diligence period, when we discussed the time period allowed for closing. There are still a few things to add. First, some people refer to this as the "free look" period. They call it that because the buyer gets his deposit returned at the end of the inspections if he does not want to buy, and it cost him nothing to look at the property. Make sure you let the seller or broker understand it doesn't make sense to apply for financing during the inspection period because the really important things relative to financing—like getting an appraisal, engineering report, environmental study, and a survey—all cost money. Buyers don't want to spend any extra money until they're sure they want to buy the property after the inspection period. Who wants a $3,000 bank appraisal on a mobile home park he didn't buy because the inspection showed too many repairs were needed, and the seller didn't want to pay for them?

If a park has more than ten units, you should hire an engineer to conduct the due diligence on the infrastructure. You should give strong consideration to hiring this service no matter what size your park is, unless you have experience and training on infrastructure. Depending on the size of the park, the engineer is going to take from a few hours to a few days to do the report, and it will cost anywhere from $500 to $2,000 or more. You will want to order the report near the end of the inspection period, after you have found the business and people parts of the due diligence acceptable. Again, why pay for inspections on a park you're not going to buy?

For park-owned mobile homes, we do the inspections ourselves because we feel comfortable doing so after investing in real estate for more than twenty-seven years. But if someone feels uncomfortable about his or her knowledge in this area, there are any number of reputable home inspectors who charge anywhere from $250 to $350 for a single mobile home inspection. You can get referrals from the yellow pages, Realtors, and title companies.

Termites are an everyday problem in South Florida, and the termite inspection is usually done at the same time as the building and park-owned mobile home inspections. If there are termites, most contracts call for the seller to treat for them, up to a certain dollar limit, and most lenders will insist that buildings and park-owned mobile homes be treated before they will lend on the property. In Florida, most buyers are not unduly concerned about termites. The property is routinely treated and any resulting damage is repaired. It doesn't make sense for a seller to avoid fixing and treating this problem. If the buyer walks away from the deal because the seller refuses to treat the termites, the seller will still have the problem, and it will be get worse with time, not better.

The final walk-through inspection is usually done on the morning of the closing or the afternoon of the day before. At this point the property should be clean and all the personal property that is supposed to remain is there. Also, if any homes or buildings were supposed to be vacant but still have people occupying them, that situation needs to addressed.

Who Is Responsible for Fixing Any Defects, and Up to How Much

This is subjective and will vary from case to case. Some sellers sell as is, where they agree to do no repairs at all. Other sellers will fix whatever is reasonable, up to a limit. When we sell, it's always as is, but we tell the buyer to give us a copy of the inspection report at the end of the inspection period, and if there are any "unpleasant surprises," chances are we will agree to fix everything that is reasonable. We do it this way because we don't want to be handed a bloated list of thousands of dollars of discretionary repairs at the closing table, demanded by a buyer who won't close if they aren't fixed.

When we are buying, right after the inspection we hand the seller a list of what needs to be fixed and what it would cost for a contractor to fix the problems. Then we ask for a discount from the selling price. Because we have full-time handymen working for us, we can usually get the repairs done for less. If you have a full-time handyman, you will be able to do the same.

Who Pays for Which Closing Costs, Like Title Insurance, etc., and What to Do if There Are Title Problems

Who pays for different closing costs also varies on a case-by-case basis. In some areas custom determines which side pays for title insurance, documentary stamps, and so on. However, the written contract will supersede whatever is done by custom. As buyers, we try to get the seller to pay as many closing costs as possible. As sellers, we try to shift the burden to the buyer. There is also the question of unpaid prior lot rent and current lot rent. The customary action is to have the seller prorate the current month lot rent received to the buyer. Then any unpaid current month or back lot rent is the responsibility of the new owner to collect and rebate back to the seller. This is a sensitive area and should be approached with tact.

It is not unusual for a buyer to ask a seller to help pay part, or all, of the closings costs when a buyer is limited on cash reserves. When we are buying, we usually ask the seller to do this, and we make it a point of negotiation. When we are selling, we will often pay all, or almost all, of the closing costs for the buyer. However, don't think we are being foolishly generous, because we're not. We just add whatever contribution the buyer wants us to make to closing costs back onto the purchase price.

We learned the above strategy on our first flipper in Florida. We had a property listed for $40,000, and a broker called and said she had a client that wanted to offer us $43,000. My response was, "Is this some sort of IQ test? Why wouldn't we take $3,000 *more* than we are asking?" The broker explained that the buyer had the down payment, but needed help with the closing costs and prepaids. If we would add $3,000 extra to the price and then rebate it to the buyer at closing, we would have a deal. I asked what the downside would be for us if we did this, and the broker said the only downside was that the property had to appraise for $3,000 more. But she had already brought an appraiser by and the appraiser thought the higher price wouldn't be difficult to justify. The transaction was completed without problems.

Therefore, when we are asked to pay for closing costs by the buyer, we just add the total of the closing costs onto the sales price. For example, if we are offering a property for $1 million and the buyer wants to pay $1 million but needs help with the $20,000 in closing costs, we will change the price on the contract to $1,020,000 and we will add a clause to the addendum that states that the seller will give the buyer $20,000 at closing towards the buyer's closing costs. There is no difference in the net proceeds to us; we get $20,000 more in price and then give it back to the buyer as cash at closing for costs. There is no problem as long as the property appraises for the additional $20,000, which it usually does.

Speaking of problems, occasionally—and I mean *very* rarely—there are title problems, meaning the title company can not give marketable title. As a prudent buyer, you should read the "exceptions" page on every title commitment to make sure the exceptions do not make the title unmarketable. If there are title problems, most contracts provide a specific time period for the seller to correct the problems. If the seller can not fix the problems the contract is null and void. Use common sense in such situations. If you are getting a great deal, and the market is stable, then it's probably wise to wait for the title to be fixed. We have waited as long as two-and-a-half years for title to be fixed, and not regretted a day of it.

The Brokers Involved, Who They Are, and Who Pays for Them

In the good old days, the seller always paid the brokers. In these days of buyer brokers and selling brokers and transaction brokers and so forth, this is no longer set in stone. If one broker is responsible for bringing the two sides together, note on the contract who the brokerage firm is, how much they will be paid, and who will be paying them. If the transaction involves both a listing broker and a selling broker—whether they are from two different firms or even the same company—that also needs to be noted on the contract, as well as who is paying each of them. Further, when we are selling directly to a buyer, we always write down on the contract that no commission is due. We don't want to find a distant relative or friend with a real estate license sitting at the closing table with their hand out waiting for some of our profits, though he did nothing to get the transaction completed.

Signatures of All Parties

All parties must sign and date their signatures with the date when the final agreement was achieved as the effective date.

Any Addendums Spelling Out Additional Terms and Conditions

We keep our addendums short. On every mobile home park contract where we are buying, we include three pages after the preprinted forms:

1. The contract addendum, Addendum A
2. The personal property addendum, Schedule B
3. The due diligence addendum, Schedule C

We covered the personal property and due diligence addendums, Schedules B and C. Now we will cover the contract Addendum A (shown on page 284), which references them. If there is something unusual about our offer, we add it to Addendum A because verbal agreements outside of the written contract are not enforceable. This addendum is a basic part of your protection when you set your flag. Addendum A starts out with:

If any of terms of this addendum conflict with the contract, then the terms of this addendum rule. The contract is now modified as to the following terms and conditions:

What this means is that if there is anything on the preprinted contract for your area that contradicts the addendum, then whatever is written on the Addendum A overrules it. This is to protect you against someone hiding a clause in tiny print that you miss.

The first clause of the Addendum A states:

The Buyers will have forty-five days to conduct due diligence, and contract is subject to Buyers' approval of it. The due diligence period will begin when Seller gives Buyers all the items on Schedule B (List of Personal Property) and Schedule C (Due Diligence from Seller) which are necessary for Buyers to secure financing and make an informed decision. By the end of the due diligence period the Buyer will send a written letter to Seller stating whether Buyers wish to continue forward or not. If Buyers do not wish to continue, Buyers' escrow deposit will be returned immediately.

This is worded carefully. As a buyer, you will have forty-five days to do your inspections, and the inspection period does *not* begin on the effective date, but rather on the date the seller gives you everything on the Personal Property Schedule B and Due Diligence Schedule C. This forces the seller to promptly get all the information to you so you can make an informed decision. We did this because most of the information we need to make an informed decision, is in the seller's hands. Once, a seller gave us little or no information on his park during the inspection period and time ran out, wasting our time. That never happened again because of this clause.

At the end of the due diligence period, there are going to three possible outcomes, and you will put in writing which one it is. The first is that you like what you saw and want to continue on with the contract.

Addendum A to Contract

dated ____/____/____ between:

____________________________________, Sellers, and,

____, Buyers

on the Property known as ________________________________

If any of terms of this addendum conflict with the contract, then the terms of this addendum rule. The contract is now modified as to the following terms and conditions:

1) The Buyers will have forty-five days to conduct due diligence, and contract is subject to Buyers' approval of it. The due diligence period will begin when Seller gives Buyers all the items on Schedule B (list of personal property) and Schedule C (Mandatory Due Diligence section) which are necessary for Buyers to secure financing and make an informed decision. By the end of the due diligence period the Buyer will send a written letter to Seller stating whether Buyers wish to continue forward or not. If Buyers do not wish to continue, Buyers' escrow deposit will be returned immediately.

2) If Buyers wish to continue with transaction after due diligence, Buyers will have sixty days from the end of the Due Diligence period to secure Third Party financing, and contract is subject to Buyers' approval of financing terms. If Buyers do not secure financing or do not approve of the terms, Buyers' escrow deposit will be returned immediately.

3) If Buyers approve of Third Party financing, Sellers will give a purchase money second mortgage on the property at the following terms: ____________________ amount of seller financing, ______% interest rate, _____________ amortization years, balloon in ____ years, payable monthly, assumable and non-recourse

4) Seller will pay Buyers closings costs up to $____________________.

All other terms and conditions of the contract will remain in force.

____________________________________ ____________________
Buyer Date

____________________________________ ____________________
Seller Date

____________________________________ ____________________
Seller Date

The second outcome is you don't like what you saw and want your deposit back. The third outcome is you want to negotiate further based upon the information you discovered and what you were given. If that is the case and these negotiations are successful, you will add an additional addendum, Addendum D, describing the new terms that are agreeable to both.

The second clause states:

If Buyers wish to continue with transaction after due diligence, Buyers will have sixty days from the end of the due diligence period to secure Third Party financing, and contract is subject to Buyers' approval of financing terms. If Buyers do not secure financing or do not approve of the terms, Buyers' escrow deposit will be returned immediately.

This clause is activated only after you wish to go forward with buying the park after the due diligence period. Here, you are allowed an *additional* sixty days to secure financing with a lender, and if you don't approve of the terms, you can cancel the contract and get your escrow back. From this point on you will forfeit your escrow deposit to the seller if you do like the terms of the financing but decide to not close for other reasons.

The third clause states:

If Buyers approve of Third Party financing, Sellers will give a purchase money second mortgage on the property at the following terms: ____________________ amount of seller financing, ______% interest rate, _____________ amortization years, balloon in ____ years, payable monthly, assumable and non-recourse

This is for those of you that are down-payment challenged or even if you are not, you want a no-money-down deal. This will be explained further in Chapter 11 on financing.

The last clause states:

Seller will pay Buyers closings costs up to $____________________.

This is to have the seller pay your closing costs. Again, this is to limit the amount of cash you have to come up with.

As you can see, Addendum A is short and sweet and contains clauses we want in just about every mobile home park offer we make. We have them saved in Word format and just print them out and fill them in when we make an offer. One day, we made three offers on mobile home parks and it took us less than an hour to do all three. You will see that it is a simple and easy process after you have done a few of these, and you will feel empowered to do more.

When we are *selling* a mobile home park, and the buyer needs financing, we insert the following clause in Addendum A:

> This contract is subject to the Buyer giving Seller an acceptable prequalification letter within five days of the effective date. If Seller does not approve of the prequalification letter, then contract is null and void. If Seller approves the pre-qualification letter, Buyer will have up to forty-five days after the due diligence period to secure a firm loan commitment from the lender, with no contingencies, i.e. a loan commitment that is clear to close within fifteen days, or Seller may at his own discretion, declare the contract null and void.

Where to Start Your Initial Offer?

The most commonly asked question when I train is: "*What percent off the listing price should you offer when you make your initial offer to buy?*" I answer, "No percent." At which point, the class members scratch their heads and wonder if I mean you should pay full price . . . at which point, they wonder if I have taken leave of my senses.

I purposely answer that way to make the class think. What I mean by "no percent" is that you should not make offers by subtracting a fixed percent from the seller's price. The right way is to appraise the property using the method you were shown in Chapter 8, "What's It Worth: Figure It". Then you should fit that property into your *formulas for success* to find a price that will make the property work for you. When it is less than the listing price, which it usually is, you should decide how aggressive you want to be, depending on your inventory and the market. If you need inventory and feel aggressive, offer a little below the *formula for success* bottom line number, say 5 to 10 percent, to allow some negotiation room. If you have a flood of good deals, then take off a higher percentage from the *formula for success* bottom line number.

If the *formula for success* bottom line price is *higher* than the listing price, which is possible, but very rare, then offer 5 or 10 percent below the listing price, to allow some negotiation room, and then say a blessing for your good luck.

There is something important for you to consider when you are buying and your offer is far below the listing price. With some sellers, a "lowball" offer will shut down the transaction, because the seller either gets upset or thinks you aren't serious, and perhaps doubts your intelligence to boot. When you are far below the listing price, then you should preface your offer as follows: *"I know this is below what you were asking, but I'm an investor, and I'm not moving into the property and running it myself. I'm looking to make a profit on this transaction and this is what I have to pay to make it work for me."* If you still cannot make the transaction work for you, you will learn how to leave it like a pro when we discuss negotiating.

The Genius of Real Estate

I tell this funny story to my classes after I answer, "no percent" to their question about what percentage to take from the listing price when you make your first offer:

When we left New York more than twenty-two years ago, we sold all of our real estate and moved to Florida. We had $1 million in the bank. I thought I was *The Genius of Real Estate* because I started out with nothing and saved a million dollars in fifteen years. We found a new home on the Caloosahatchee River on five beautiful acres covered with oak trees, listed for $300,000. The same home in New York would have cost a million dollars. Someone told me you should offer 20 percent off the listing price, so I offered $240,000. The seller accepted my first offer. I thought, of course the seller accepted my offer, because I was . . . *The Genius of Real Estate.*

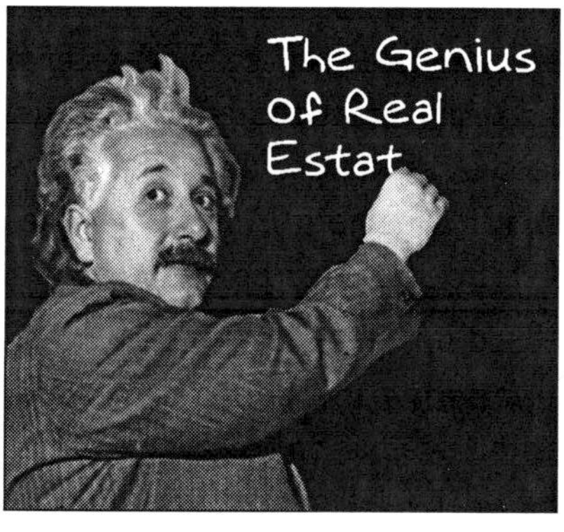

We wanted to pay cash for the property, but were told it was better to borrow some of the money. I applied to a local bank to borrow half of the purchase price, or $120,000. I expected the bank to approve the loan, because I was . . . (I pause so the class can fill in *The Genius of Real Estate.*)

Sixty days later we were sitting at

the closing table. The seller was smiling, and I was smiling. I knew I had a great deal because our new Florida home cost less than half of what we sold our house for in New York, and the Florida home had five times the land and was *on the water!* After the closing, the banker asked if I wanted a copy of the appraisal—I said sure! The banker handed me a big yellow envelope, which I put with the rest of our closing papers. There was no need to read it. I knew the appraiser would be another voice that echoed what I already knew, that I was . . . (At this point, I pause again so the class can say *The Genius of Real Estate.*)

After we finished unpacking at our new home, I saw the big yellow envelope and I opened it, so I could see just how much the appraiser thought the house was worth. Four hundred thousand? Five hundred? Six hundred? Was there any limit because I was . . . (At this point, I paused a third and final time so the class could fill in *The Genius of Real Estate.*) I turned to page two of the appraisal, and on the bottom, it said our house was worth $198,000, *a full $42,000 less than what we paid!* That when I felt like . . . *The Dummy of Real Estate.* The point is this—you don't offer a set percentage below the listing price, because you may find a seller who outplays you at that game.

By the way, the story had a happy ending. Five years later, we sold that house for $278,000, $38,000 more than the $240,000 we paid. By that time, *The Dummy of Real Estate* had learned his lesson.

Example of an Offer on a Mobile Home Park

Let's make a hypothetical offer on a mobile home park so you can see how to apply what you have learned. Let's assume you found a good deal, the Primavera Mobile Home Park, listed at $600,000. It was in the upper-end of an affordable income area, a land-lease community with fifty lots and a lot rent of $250 per month. Only forty of the fifty lots were rented. The owner told you the gross rents were $120,000 per year and the expenses were $50,000, so the NOI was $70,000. You realized the expenses were about 40 percent of the gross rents, so the numbers made sense. You inspected the park quickly, but not thoroughly, and there was nothing that raised negative concerns to you. You found three good comps, adjusted them and reconciled, and the comps pointed to a cap rate of 10 percent for the park, which would have made it worth $700,000, *$100,000 higher than the listing price of $600,000.*

THIS FORM HAS BEEN APPROVED BY THE FLORIDA ASSOCIATION OF REALTORS® AND THE FLORIDA BAR

Contract For Sale And Purchase

FLORIDA ASSOCIATION OF REALTORS AND THE FLORIDA BAR

PARTIES: ____________________ ("Seller"), and ____________________ ("Buyer"), hereby agree that Seller shall sell and Buyer shall buy the following described Real Property and Personal Property (collectively "Property") pursuant to the terms and conditions of this Contract for Sale and Purchase and any riders and addenda ("Contract"):

I. DESCRIPTION:

(a) Legal description of the Real Property located in ____________ County, Florida: ____________________

(b) Street address, city, zip, of the Property: ____________________

(c) Personal Property includes existing range, refrigerator, dishwasher, ceiling fans, light fixtures, and window treatments unless specifically excluded below.
Other items included are: ____________________

Items of Personal Property (and leased items, if any) excluded are: ____________________

II. PURCHASE PRICE (U.S. currency): .... $ ________

PAYMENT:

(a) Deposit held in escrow by ____________ (Escrow Agent) in the amount of .... $ ________

(b) Additional escrow deposit to be made to Escrow Agent within ____ days after Effective Date (see Paragraph III) in the amount of .... $ ________

(c) Assumption of existing mortgage in good standing (see Paragraph IV(c)) having an approximate present principal balance of .... $ ________

(d) New mortgage financing with a Lender (see Paragraph IV(b)) in the amount of .... $ ________

(e) Purchase money mortgage and note to Seller (See Paragraph IV(d)) in the amount of .... $ ________

(f) Other: ____________ .... $ ________

(g) Balance to close by cash or LOCALLY DRAWN cashier's or official bank check(s), subject to adjustments or prorations .... $ ________

III. TIME FOR ACCEPTANCE OF OFFER AND COUNTEROFFERS; EFFECTIVE DATE:

(a) If this offer is not executed by and delivered to all parties OR FACT OF EXECUTION communicated in writing between the parties on or before ____________, the deposit(s) will, at Buyer's option, be returned and this offer withdrawn. **UNLESS OTHERWISE STATED, THE TIME FOR ACCEPTANCE OF ANY COUNTEROFFERS SHALL BE 2 DAYS FROM THE DATE THE COUNTEROFFER IS DELIVERED.**

(b) The date of Contract ("Effective Date") will be the date when the last one of the Buyer and Seller has signed or initialed this offer or the final counteroffer. If such date is not otherwise set forth in this Contract, then the "Effective Date" shall be the date determined above for acceptance of this offer or, if applicable, the final counteroffer.

IV. FINANCING:

☐ (a) This is a cash transaction with no contingencies for financing;

☐ (b) This Contract is contingent on Buyer obtaining approval of a loan ("Loan Approval") within ____ days after Effective Date for (CHECK ONLY ONE): ☐ a fixed; ☐ an adjustable; or ☐ a fixed or adjustable rate loan, in the principal amount of $________, at an initial interest rate not to exceed ____%, discount and origination fees not to exceed ____% of principal amount, and for a term of ____ years. Buyer will make application within ____ days (if blank, then 5 days) after Effective Date and use reasonable diligence to obtain Loan Approval and, thereafter, to satisfy terms and conditions of the Loan Approval and close the loan. Buyer shall pay all loan expenses. If Buyer fails to obtain a Loan Approval or fails to waive Buyer's rights under this subparagraph within the time for obtaining Loan Approval or, after diligent, good faith effort, fails to meet the terms and conditions of the Loan Approval by Closing, then either party thereafter, by written notice to the other, may cancel this Contract and Buyer shall be refunded the deposit(s);

☐ (c) Assumption of existing mortgage (see rider for terms); or

☐ (d) Seller financing (see Standard B and riders; addenda; or special clauses for terms).

V. TITLE EVIDENCE: At least ____ days (if blank, then 5 days) before Closing:
☐ (a) Title insurance commitment with legible copies of instruments listed as exceptions attached thereto ("Title Commitment") and, after Closing, an owner's policy of title insurance (see Standard A for terms); or ☐ (b) Abstract of title or other evidence of title (see rider for terms), shall be obtained by (CHECK ONLY ONE): ☐ (1) Seller, at Seller's expense and delivered to Buyer or Buyer's attorney; or ☐ (2) Buyer at Buyer's expense.

VI. CLOSING DATE: This transaction shall be closed and the closing documents delivered on ____________ ("Closing"), unless modified by other provisions of this Contract. If Buyer is unable to obtain Hazard, Wind, Flood, or Homeowners' insurance at a reasonable rate due to extreme weather conditions, Buyer may delay Closing for up to 5 days after such coverage becomes available.

VII. RESTRICTIONS; EASEMENTS; LIMITATIONS: Seller shall convey marketable title subject to: comprehensive land use plans, zoning, restrictions, prohibitions and other requirements imposed by governmental authority; restrictions and matters appearing on the plat or otherwise common to the subdivision; outstanding oil, gas and mineral rights of record without right of entry; unplatted public utility easements of record (located contiguous to real property lines and not more than 10 feet in width as to the rear or front lines and 7 1/2 feet in width as to the side lines); taxes for year of Closing and subsequent years; and assumed mortgages and purchase money mortgages, if any (if additional items, see addendum); provided, that there exists at Closing no violation of the foregoing and none prevent use of the Property for ____________________ purpose(s).

VIII. OCCUPANCY: Seller shall deliver occupancy of Property to Buyer at time of Closing unless otherwise stated herein. If Property is intended to be rented or occupied beyond Closing, the fact and terms thereof and the tenant(s) or occupants shall be disclosed pursuant to Standard F. If occupancy is to be delivered before Closing, Buyer assumes all risks of loss to Property from date of occupancy, shall be responsible and liable for maintenance from that date, and shall be deemed to have accepted Property in its existing condition as of time of taking occupancy.

IX. TYPEWRITTEN OR HANDWRITTEN PROVISIONS: Typewritten or handwritten provisions, riders and addenda shall control all printed provisions of this Contract in conflict with them.

X. ASSIGNABILITY: (CHECK ONLY ONE): Buyer ☐ may assign and thereby be released from any further liability under this Contract; ☐ may assign but not be released from liability under this Contract; or ☐ may not assign this Contract.

XI. DISCLOSURES:

(a) ☐ CHECK HERE if the Property is subject to a special assessment lien imposed by a public body payable in installments which continue beyond Closing and, if so, specify who shall pay amounts due after Closing: ☐ Seller ☐ Buyer ☐ Other (see addendum).

(b) Radon is a naturally occurring radioactive gas that when accumulated in a building in sufficient quantities may present health risks to persons who are exposed to it over time. Levels of radon that exceed federal and state guidelines have been found in buildings in Florida. Additional information regarding radon or radon testing may be obtained from your County Public Health unit.

(c) Buyer acknowledges receipt of the Florida Building Energy-Efficiency Rating System Brochure.

(d) If the real property includes pre-1978 residential housing then a lead-based paint rider is mandatory.

(e) If Seller is a "foreign person" as defined by the Foreign Investment in Real Property Tax Act, the parties shall comply with that Act.

(f) If Buyer will be obligated to be a member of a homeowners' association, **BUYER SHOULD NOT EXECUTE THIS CONTRACT UNTIL BUYER HAS RECEIVED AND READ THE HOMEOWNERS' ASSOCIATION DISCLOSURE.**

XII. MAXIMUM REPAIR COSTS: Seller shall not be responsible for payments in excess of:

(a) $____________ for treatment and repair under Standard D (if blank, then 2% of the Purchase Price).

(b) $____________ for repair and replacement under Standard N not caused by Wood Destroying Organisms (if blank, then 3% of the Purchase Price).

XIII. RIDERS; ADDENDA; SPECIAL CLAUSES:

CHECK those riders which are applicable AND are attached to this Contract:

☐ CONDOMINIUM ☐ VA/FHA ☐ HOMEOWNERS' ASSN. ☐ LEAD-BASED PAINT
☐ COASTAL CONSTRUCTION CONTROL LINE ☐ INSULATION ☐ "AS IS" ☐ Other Comprehensive Rider Provisions
☐ Addenda

Special Clauses(s): ____________________

XIV. STANDARDS FOR REAL ESTATE TRANSACTIONS ("Standards"): Buyer and Seller acknowledge receipt of a copy of Standards A through W on the reverse side or attached, which are incorporated as part of this Contract.

THIS IS INTENDED TO BE A LEGALLY BINDING CONTRACT. IF NOT FULLY UNDERSTOOD, SEEK THE ADVICE OF AN ATTORNEY PRIOR TO SIGNING.

THIS FORM HAS BEEN APPROVED BY THE FLORIDA ASSOCIATION OF REALTORS AND THE FLORIDA BAR.

Approval does not constitute an opinion that any of the terms and conditions in this Contract should be accepted by the parties in a particular transaction. Terms and conditions should be negotiated based upon the respective interests, objectives and bargaining positions of all interested persons.

AN ASTERISK(*) FOLLOWING A LINE NUMBER IN THE THE MARGIN INDICATES THE LINE CONTAINS A BLANK TO BE COMPLETED.

____________ (BUYER) ________ (DATE) ____________ (SELLER) ________ (DATE)

____________ (BUYER) ________ (DATE) ____________ (SELLER) ________ (DATE)

Buyers' address for purposes of notice ____________ Phone ________

Sellers' address for purposes of notice ____________ Phone ________

Deposit under Paragraph II (a) received (Checks are subject to clearance.): ____________ (Escrow Agent)

BROKERS: The brokers named below, including listing and cooperating brokers, are the only brokers entitled to compensation in connection with this Contract:

Name: ____________ ____________
Cooperating Brokers, if any **Listing Broker**

FAR/BAR-6A 10/01 RIDERS CAN BE OBTAINED FROM THE FLORIDA BAR OR THE FLORIDA ASSOCIATION OF REALTORS®

MOBILE HOME PURCHASE AGREEMENT

Date: ____________________________

The undersigned Seller(s) agree to sell and the undersigned Buyer(s) agree to buy the following mobile home:

Make:____________________________ Year:. __________ ID#:____________________

Located at:____

Total Sales Price: $ ______________________ Deposit Paid: $ ____________________

Additional Payment Due: $ _______________ Due Date: _________________________

Date of Possession by Buyer(s): ____

Appliances and Contents included in Sales Price: ______________________________

____

Unless otherwise noted, Seller(s) warrant that all appliances, AC, electrical service, plumbing and heating system to be in good working order at settlement, which is to be on __________________. Buyer(s) reserve right to a walk through inspection and approval on day of possession and settlement. Seller(s) agree to remove all trash and debris from premises and leave home in clean condition.

Seller(s) certify they are the legal owners of mobile home, appliances, and contents. Unless otherwise noted, Seller(s) certify that no liens exist on home, appliances, or contents. Any existing liens are to be paid and satisfied by Seller(s) prior to settlement and payment by Buyer(s). Upon approval and payment by Buyer(s), Seller(s) agree to deliver to Buyer(s) a clear title to mobile home.

Seller(s) certify that park lot rent is current through ___________ and agree to furnish proof of same prior to settlement. Any delinquent rent or other charges by the mobile home park to be paid by Seller(s) prior to settlement. Seller(s) to furnish proof that all taxes on mobile home have been paid and current through _____________.

If for any reason mobile home is not allowed to remain on present lot, this agreement becomes null and void and Seller(s) agree to return all money paid by Buyer(s) and cancel this agreement.

This agreement is subject to verification of information necessary to complete this agreement, and subject to approval by Business Partner. Otherwise, this agreement becomes null and void and Seller(s) agree to return all money paid by Buyer(s) and cancel this agreement.

Seller(s) verify they have read, understand, and agree to this sales agreement and acknowledge a copy of this agreement.

SELLER:	**BUYER:**
Signature______________________________	Signature______________________________
Print Name ____________________________	Print Name ____________________________
SS# __________________________________	DOB __________________________________
SELLER:	**BUYER:**
Signature______________________________	Signature______________________________
Pnnt'.\ame ____________________________	PrintName______________________________
SS# __________________________________	DOB __________________________________

___ Appliance inventory including serial numbers attached and signed by Seller(s) and Buyer(s).

___ Identification checked and compared with name(s) on title.

From this you realized that this park could either be a keeper, a flipper, or an L/O. You want to keep it, and start on your way to financial independence. Now what do you do? Simple—you make an offer. Let's walk through it:

Who the buyer and seller are:
You are the buyer, and John and Nancy Smith are the sellers.

A description of the property, and its location:
The Primavera Mobile Home Park. *Legal description—Lot 3-10 on Block 2 of Sunny Subdivision, your county. The address is 123 Sunny Court.*

What personal property is included and not included:
You submitted Schedule B along with your contract, and noted that the park had a golf-cart and a complete manager's office with computers and software. There was also a lawnmower and plumbing parts. The clubhouse had furniture and a full operational kitchen.

The offer price:
$550,000—you left $50,000 room for negotiations.

The amount of the deposit, who holds it, and terms of refund:
$1,000. Your attorney holds it after both sides agree to all terms. It is refundable if the buyers do not approve of inspection or financing.

Financing terms, if any:
You will apply at your local community bank, doing No Money Down and the seller giving you a second mortgage for 20 percent of the purchase price.

The time for acceptance of the offer by both sides:
The seller lives near the mobile home park, so you gave twenty-four hours for acceptance.

The closing date:
Forty-five days for inspections and due diligence, plus sixty days additional for financing, all starting from the date the seller supplied everything on Schedules B and C.

Occupancy and/or renters and condition of property at closing:
All residents will stay and the seller will leave the clubhouse and park clean.

Inspection period and the final walk-through before closing:
See the closing date above. Standard walk-though time the day of closing.

Who is responsible for fixing any defects, and up to how much
Sellers will fix any defects up to $25,000.

Who pays for which closing costs, like title insurance, and what to do if there are title problems:
Sellers pay for title insurance and documentary stamps.

Brokers involved, who are they, and who pays their commissions:
Sellers' listing agent is Sally Davis at Century-21. Sellers pay her.

Signatures of all parties:
You signed, and are now waiting for sellers to sign or counteroffer.

Any addendum spelling out additional terms and conditions:
You used Addendum A and the two schedules, which are detailed above. You asked the sellers to contribute $20,000 toward your closing costs.

This is our offer, and we will discuss possible counteroffers and strategy after we discuss negotiation techniques.

NEGOTIATING

Let me start this section by saying some people consider me to be a great negotiator. I don't agree with them. I believe I am a good negotiator, and I know enough about the craft to recognize when others have greater talent and experience. I have a partner who is a world-class negotiator, and when it is called for, I will invite him into a deal and offer him an equal share, just to have him negotiate. I refer to him affectionately as "the Deal Doctor." What qualities make him excel at this craft? I'll tell you about his qualities, which I call the *Three Be's*, in the next section, but for now, let's talk a little more about how I learned to negotiate. This will help you learn from my mistakes, and sometimes they can be the best teacher. I needed a teacher. I was pathetic.

When I first started my real estate investing career, I disliked negotiating with a passion. To me, it looked like a game where each side lied through their smiles, masking their selfish goals and desires. For the first four years, I had brokers do all my negotiating when I bought or sold. I didn't want to get face-to-face, gut-to-gut, belly-to-belly with a buyer or seller, because, I knew I would get angry and ruin the deal if I had to listen to their lies and false pleasantries. I did not suffer liars well, then.

In my fifth year of investing, I bought a book on negotiating and I became even more pathetic. The book said that having the ability to walk away from a deal gave you power, because the sellers would then beg you to buy their property and buyers would pay you more when you were selling. Armed with the knowledge from that book, I started negotiating face-to–face. I walked away from two really good deals. In one deal, I could have bought a large two-family house for $8,000—that's right, $8,000, and in the other deal, I could have sold a fourplex for $97,000, which we had purchased two years before, for $26,000. After I walked away, I did feel more powerful. I also never heard from the other side again. Then I felt pretty stupid, because I had exercised my ability to be stubborn at the cost of accomplishing nothing.

It wasn't until my seventh year in real estate that I had an inkling of what a good negotiator did. It happened after I became an auctioneer, when I had real estate auctions that fell short of getting the reserve price that a seller wanted for their property, In those cases, I chose to give up and move on to the next auction. Then I watched my partner in the auction company make a different choice on his listings. He negotiated between the high bidder and the seller to see if there was a price in between that could get the deal done. I asked my partner why he was wasting his time, and he said, "Wasting my time?! Think of all the hours I spent getting the property to the auction block, writing up ads, creating brochures, answering the phone, and doing showings and open houses. It has to be at least forty man-hours per property, and we still haven't been paid. Isn't it worthwhile spending a few hours more trying to get a compromise, so maybe we can get paid?"

The wisdom of his words was not lost on me. I listened to him negotiate, and then I also set about trying to arrange a price on my auctions between what the high bidder wanted to pay and what the seller needed to have. I learned how to—calmly and patiently—get each side of a transaction to compromise. I was amazed how much could be accomplished by calmly and patiently asking questions and making suggestions.

Now, I find negotiating interesting and sometimes it can even be fun. I do it all the time, whether I'm in a restaurant, checking into a hotel, in a doctor's office, or working out a problem with my wife or children or *grandchildren*. When you learn how to go about it, you'll see it's not difficult. Don't look for perfection in this art, because you won't always be successful, but you will be successful enough that you will consider it important, and at times, enjoyable. Let me show you the easy way to do it, after watching my friend the "Deal Doctor."

Negotiating Simplified

To be a good negotiator, you must learn three simple things, the *Three Be's:*

1. Be nice
2. Be asking
3. Be patient

Being nice is absolutely critical. While you are being nice, it won't hurt to be polite, too. Being nice and polite is the first step toward getting the other side of the transaction to like you. *It is a fact of human nature when the other side of a negotiation likes you, they will have a much stronger tendency to give you a good deal.* How would you like to learn a great technique for getting people to like you, so they will want to give you a good deal? Are you ready? . . . Drumbeat . . . *Like them first.* Find something to like about the person on the other side of the transaction and concentrate on that. Everybody has something likeable about them—find it. Many times we concentrate on other people's faults and imperfections. Instead, you should look at their talents and strengths. Granted, you may have to look deep to find some people's good points, but they're there. When you find something to like in the person you are negotiating with, then you'll also find that it's easier to be nice and polite to them.

Along with being nice, there is an advanced strategy when it comes to getting people to like you, called *mirroring*. When you mirror someone, you take on their style of gesturing and manner of speech. If someone is very demonstrative and uses a lot of hand and body movements, they will feel comfortable with someone who also does that. If someone speaks slowly and distinctly, they won't feel comfortable with someone who talks fast. You shouldn't copy someone exactly, but more in general terms. Keep in mind, when you are nice to people, you can ask them just about anything, which brings us to the Second Be.

Be asking means you must ask questions, lots and lots of questions. The purpose of your questions is to gather information. This is a critical part of being a good negotiator—the ability to gather information about the wants and needs of the other side. The way you do that is by asking questions. We have one mouth and two ears, a cosmic reminder that we should listen twice as much as we speak. There is a rule to the art of the asking—the more difficult and more revealing the question, the *nicer* you have to ask it.

Another powerful part of asking questions is *the ability to make a suggestion sound nonthreatening by putting it in the form of a question, rather than a statement.* If you want to be a good negotiator, you should limit the statements you make, especially the ones that express your personal opinions and value judgments, because they can push people away. For instance, if you quote a few comps to a seller to get him to be more flexible in his price and the seller says he doesn't give a fig about comps, you could say, "You're wrong, Mr. Seller, when you say that the prices of the comps aren't important, because every appraiser thinks differently." This would probably upset a seller, implying he wasn't smart in the pricing of his property. It is better to say, "Did you know, Mr. Seller, that appraisers have told me they consider sales in the area to be the most important criteria in evaluating a property? Further, did you know that if the appraiser in our transaction doesn't agree to our price, I won't be able to borrow money from the bank?"

Another part of asking is asking for compromise. During the negotiation, you should continually be asking the other side, "If I give that to you, will you give me this in return?" There is an innate sense in most people that they should give a little to get a little, and vice versa.

The Third Be, *be patient,* is the ability to take the time to understand the other side, listen, and then respond nicely with your own wants and needs. You will find when you listen to most people, really listen, they will listen to you. Part of being patient is the ability to walk away from the transaction if it is at an impasse, and being willing to wait for the other side to come around more to your way of thinking.

How to Walk Away from a Deal

You must learn how to walk away nicely—the first book I read about negotiating didn't mention this. The author didn't explain that while it's okay to walk away, if you do it nicely, the other side may call you back later when they reconsider. If you walk away badly, the other side may never call you back but instead they will give someone else they like better the same good deal you asked for! Here is the way you should walk away from a deal:

"Well, Mr. or Mrs. Seller, I want to thank you for taking the time to show me your mobile home park. I'm sorry we couldn't come to an agreement, because I really did want to buy it. If in the future you change your mind, I would appreciate it if you'd give me a call, because you'll find I'm very flexible and easy to deal with."

Then shake their hand, give them a business card, and walk away. If you are selling and dealing with a buyer, you should say, "Well, Mr. or Mrs. Buyer, I want to thank you for taking the time to look at my property. I'm sorry we couldn't come to an agreement, because I really did want to see you own it. If in the future you change your mind, I would appreciate it if you'd give me a call, because you'll find I'm very flexible and easy to deal with."

Net Effect to You in Becoming a Better Negotiator

If you look at the result of using the Three Be's, you'll find you'll be nicer and more polite to people you are buying from or selling to. You will search out the good character traits in other people and show them you like them, which will make them like you. You will be a good listener, yet you will be able to lead conversations in the direction you want by asking questions. You will also be patient with other people, and when you can't arrange a win/win type of negotiation, you will walk away nicely, leaving the door open for reconsideration and compromise later on. And when you walk away, you will walk away with the other side respecting you and liking you.

How does that sound? Doesn't it sound like when you become a good negotiator, you're also on the road to becoming a better person, with better character traits? How can that be wrong? And you will be wealthier, too, with relationships and with money, which are both good rewards.

Ethics

There are many people that think lying is okay in a negotiation, as long as you aren't caught at it and it gets you a lower price when you are buying or a higher price when you are selling. As I became more comfortable with being nice to people, liking them before they liked me, asking questions and not giving out value judgments, I became more comfortable with telling the truth. Then I discovered the following:

When I was honest in my negotiations, it felt better, it didn't hurt me, and I still got good deals.

Let me add something else about the truth. When you ask questions, check out the answers you get, so you will know about the other side's character. Many people don't feel the same way about honesty as I do, so as it is for a prize fighter, your first rule must be, "Protect yourself at all times."

Also, if you don't want someone to know something, you don't have to lie. You can simply say, *"If you don't mind, I'm a little uncomfortable about answering that now. Could I get back to you on that later?"* and then let the subject drop. Most people will respect your privacy, as you should theirs. You should also be aware, if you don't answer a reasonable question, that it could indicate you have a trust issue with the other side and they might start to have a trust issue with you in response. Negotiating and trust is a two way street.

Specific Buying and Selling Gambits

If you remember, my evolution as a negotiator began by letting the broker do it all. Then I read one book, and started negotiating myself, perfecting my ability to walk away by acting stubborn. When that didn't work, I read every book I could find, and listened to every tape course I could get my hands on, and added *gambits*, games of ploy and strategy, in order to lower the price when I was buying, or raise the price when I was selling. I am going to describe these gambits now so you will be familiar with them when the other side of the transaction is using them on you. And if you feel that using gambits is the way negotiating really works, you will want to have a variety at your disposal.

In this stage of my negotiating career, I no longer use gambits. I still begin each transaction by writing an offer that works for me after appraising the property and running it through the *formulas for success.*

Then this is how I approach the transaction, depending on whether I am buying or selling:

If I am buying, I explain that I am an investor and am not moving into the property and running it myself. I am going to hire a manager and maintenance personnel. I am looking to either purchase the property to resell it at a later date for a profit or keep it and rent it at a profit. In order to do this, I have a budget that I have to work with. The benefit to the seller in dealing with me is that if the information given to me in the beginning proves to be factual, I can complete the transaction and not waste his or her time. In other words, I offer a sure deal. By the way, the next chapter will show you how to negotiate situations in which you are given information that is not factual or when there are surprises.

We usually offer a little less than our target price to leave a little negotiation room, because many sellers need to express themselves by raising our offering price. If there is a wide gulf between what we want to pay and what the seller wants to be paid, we try to bridge that gulf with reason and logic. If that fails, we walk away, nicely, leaving the door open.

When we are selling, we create a printed color brochure for the property, which we email or fax when we are contacted by a buyer. The brochure has a picture of the mobile home park, our contact information, and a brief description of the property. The description lists the major important details I would want to know if I were buying the park, like the type of park it is, the price, the number of lots, the lot rent, and the total income, expenses, and NOI. If the prospective buyers want more information, we have two more packages—a more detailed NOI and rent roll, and a full due-diligence package from Schedule C. Again, the next chapter will discuss that.

We don't put a For Sale on a mobile home park because residents feel threatened when their park goes up for sale. They become nervous when they think about new owners and negatives changes like increased lot rent, new rules, and possibly being asked to leave. If the residents do find out that the park is for sale, then we send a note to everyone explaining the reason for the sale and calming their fears about changes.

We also have a list of comps ready for when the buyers want to get down to "brass tacks" and negotiate price. We add a small amount to the price for negotiation room, for buyers that feel they must express themselves by lowering the price. When buyers appear interested, we don't act anxious, and we listen attentively to their gambits, should they decide to use them. We also use the Three Be's with the buyers—be nice, be asking, and be patient. We'll discuss additional strategies to use when selling after we cover the gambits that follow.

We are grouping the gambits according to their aggressiveness, from Least Aggressive to Highly Aggressive. We will explain how they are executed, and also how to counter them, because every gambit has a reasonable counter. The gambits are mainly geared towards buying—lowering the price, getting good terms, and extra concessions. Many can be reversed and used by sellers to raise the price and not give concessions.

Fifteen Negotiation Gambits

Least Aggressive

1. It's All the Money I Have Budgeted
2. Meet Me Halfway
3. Absent Higher Authority
4. I Need a Discount Because of My Lender's Charges

Medium Aggressive

5. Decoy
6. It Won't Appraise
7. Space Invader
8. Feel Sorry for Me

Highly Aggressive

9. Flinch
10. Multiple Flinch
11. Nibble and Whine
12. Take It or Leave It
13. Billy the Kid Last-Minute Chisel
14. Crying
15. Attila the Hun Swat Team

1. It's All the Money I Have Budgeted

As already explained, this is our main way of negotiating now, and it's really not a gambit but the truth. We verify that we are investors and make money by reselling or renting at a profit, hence we will be offering a price that makes sense to us. Again, the benefit we offer in the transaction is a sure deal working with an experienced professional.

The *counter* to this is for the seller to be willing to wait for a "retail" buyer who will be willing to pay more. This is similar to when you buy a new car from a dealer but refuse to take their wholesale terms on your trade-in. Instead, you sell your car to a buyer directly, so you can get more money.

2. Meet Me Halfway

This is best used in the final stages of negotiating, after you have moved from your initial offer and the other side has moved also. If half the distance between you and the other side is still a good deal, then consider using this. A nice way of saying it might be, "Why don't we split the difference between us, shake hands on it, and get this deal going?"

The *counter* to this is simply to say that you have come down or up as much as you believe is reasonable, and that any more would be unreasonable.

3. Absent Higher Authority

This is used by many people to postpone making a decision on a transaction. You'll hear, "Well, I have to talk this over with my wife (or husband/partner/father/mother) and I'll get back to you." A more aggressive way of using this gambit is to get the missing higher authority on the phone while someone is negotiating face-to-face, and then to use the absent higher authority as the good guy/bad guy to raise or lower the price and add or take-away concessions.

The way to *counter* this is by not making an appointment in the first place until all the parties on the other side are present. You do this by asking, "Who else is a decision maker in this transaction, and when can we get everyone together?"

4. I Need a Discount Because of My Lender's Charges

This is a way to get the seller to pay for the closing costs of the buyer. It is commonly used, and reasonable. Closing costs are an integral part of what buyers have to contend with when they buy a property.

There are two ways to *counter* this. The first way is the best—to agree to pay the closings costs, after you add the same amount to the purchase price. The second way to counter it is to say that it's not your problem and you'll wait for another buyer who will either pay cash and not have a lender's closing costs or have enough money to put down so that closing costs aren't a problem.

At this point, we are going to transition into the medium-aggressive part of the gambit spectrum. You will start to see honesty and truth being "tweaked" a little here to gain an advantage.

5. Decoy

The Decoy gambit is where someone asks for a lot of little things, wears down the other side by negotiating hard on each item, and then gives in if there is only one major concession made, usually on price. An example of this type of gambit is when a buyer insists on including additional personal property, like the owner's pickup truck, or free park-owned mobile homes. The gambit player uses up a lot of energy on the other side in this process and then offers to give in if the other side will give a price concession.

The *counter* to this as a seller is to explain what terms and concessions you are willing to offer and then stick to it. If you sense the other side is trying to force you to use up a lot of your energy and patience, then you should nicely look at your watch, say you are running short of time, and unless you both can move forward you will have to adjourn the meeting for another time. Before you agree to another meeting, you should verify that the other side is going to drop their previous decoy requests.

6. It Won't Appraise

This is a gambit where the buyer wants the seller to accept a lower estimate of the value of the property, because otherwise the deal will die in the end stage when the bank refuses to loan the necessary amount. The gambit player explains that when the appraiser comes up with a lower value, the bank will require more of a down payment, which the buyer doesn't have—and neither will any other buyer—and the deal will not go through.

To understand this, let's assume the buyer thinks the mobile home park is worth $500,000 but the seller thinks it's worth $600,000. Further, let's assume lenders are only going to lend 80 percent of the value of the property, which is common, and buyers have to come up with the remaining 20 percent for a down payment. If a buyer has 20 percent of $600,000, or $120,000, to put down, and they agree to a price of $600,000, but the lender sends an appraiser and the appraisal comes back at $500,000, the bank is only going to lend 80 percent of the appraisal value, or $400,000. That means the buyer will have to come up with the difference between the $600,000 purchase price and the $400,000 the bank is willing to lend, The buyer will now need $200,000, which he doesn't have. The buyer might add that anyone with $200,000 to put down will not be interested in a mobile home park with a purchase price of $600,000, when they can use that amount to purchase one worth $1 million. Further, why would anyone pay $600,000 for a property that a professional appraiser says is worth $500,000-$100,000 less?

This powerful gambit is *countered* a number of ways. One, both sides can agree to have their own appraisals done and then average the appraisals. They could agree to use that number as the purchase price or do no deal at that point. Two, the seller can share his comps and adjustments, and then offer to write up the contract at his price and wait to see what the appraiser comes up with. Or, three, the seller can simply have an appraisal done by a licensed appraiser before trying to sell the property, list the property at the price arrived at on the appraisal, and refuse to budge from what logically looks accurate. When sellers do this it is a powerful pricing mechanism.

7. Space Invader

This is an interesting gambit. In order to use it for maximum effectiveness, the person on one side waits until there is only one point separating the two sides (usually it's price, but it can be any term), and then steps forward and gets physically very close to the other person—as close as inches away—to create a sense of invading the other side's space. Then he makes his suggestion, pauses, and steps back.

This gambit was introduced to me live, in front of a training class, by a student who considered herself an experienced negotiator. We were role playing on a contract; she was the buyer, I was the seller, and I was not making it easy for her. She stood a safe distance to me and reached a compromise on every point of our theoretical contract—except price. We were $5,000 apart, and I wasn't coming down any more. She paused and looked directly at me, and smiled. Then she stepped forward until she was inches away from my face, looked directly into my eyes, and said in the sweetest voice, "Come on, Zalman. Are you really going to let $5,000 stop us from completing this transaction? Why don't we split the difference—I'll go up $2,500 and you come down $2,500, and we'll get this deal done?" She paused again, smiled, and then stepped back.

I felt more connected with the other side of the negotiation, but at the same time slightly threatened. This combination of feelings got me to think "outside my box" and pushed me over the block I had on price, and I agreed. She didn't touch me in the demonstration, and I wouldn't recommend touching. If executed well this can be an impasse breaker in a negotiation.

The *counter* to this is simple. You stand your ground, smile, and shake your head no after it is executed, or you can move back when the other side steps forward, never allowing him to invade your space.

8. Feel Sorry for Me

In this gambit, the person on one side attempts to get the other side to compromise due to feelings of sympathy for his or her situation, which has nothing to do with the transaction. For instance, a buyer can say she really wants to buy the park because she has always dreamed of being financially independent and having time to spend with her children. Then she pleads with the seller to come down in price to make that dream possible. Or, alternatively, the seller might indicate she cannot come down in price because she needs the money for an expensive medical procedure.

The *counter* to this is, "I sympathize with your situation, but it's outside the bounds of this business transaction. Why don't we get back to discussing the mobile home park, and after we are finished, perhaps we can look at some ways to help you outside of this transaction."

You probably felt that the above four gambits demonstrated a moderate form of aggressiveness on the part of the person using them, and also the possibility that the truth was being manipulated. The next seven gambits are highly aggressive. They culminate with the Attila the Hun

Swat Team, which feels almost illegal. Truth, nicety, and politeness are irrelevant in the next gambits, in which the major focus is price reduction.

9. Flinch

The Flinch is a powerful gambit. One side asks the other for the price of the property and, upon hearing the price, the gambit player flinches and then re-asks, "*How* much?" This can be executed softly or with great exuberance. When it is said softly, the gambit player looks puzzled and confused by the price. When it is said emphatically, the gambit player implies the other side has lost their mind and taken leave of their senses. Either way, the onus is placed on the other side to justify the price from a defensive position. Don't think only a buyer can use the Flinch. A seller can reverse it by saying, "You only want to pay *how much*?!"

The *counter* to this is simple. You smile, repeat the price, and assume the other side didn't hear you and wanted the price repeated. If the gambit player keeps aggressively repeating the Flinch, you can repeat the price until you look at your watch and say, "Well, I have another appointment. Why don't we get back to this discussion at another time?"

10. Multiple Flinch

This gambit is used when the both sides are spending a great deal of time together, like during a property inspection. In this gambit, the buyer uses the Flinch, asking, "*How* much?" After the price is repeated the buyer follows up with, "Is that your best price?" After the second question is asked, and then answered, the gambit player nods. Then the gambit player waits a while, and then initiates the Flinch again, followed again by the question, "Is that your best price?"

This gambit was used against me by Billy the Kid, an eighty-three-year–old-real estate investor who is hard of hearing and wears hearing aids. He is also one of the cleverest gambit players I have ever met. He called me about a house we were selling, and when I met him at the property for an inspection, he employed the Multiple Flinch. In every room of the house, he stopped and asked me to repeat the last price I quoted him, and then asked if it was my best price. Then he followed up with, "Come on, Zalman, you know you can do better than that." Each time he got me to lower the price a few thousand dollars. We started at $129,900, and wound up at $110,000 when he climbed back into his car.

After all that gambit playing, he didn't buy the house. We sold it to someone for more money, but I always the remembered the gambit.

The *counter* to the Multiple Flinch is the same as the Flinch, repeating the price as if the other side didn't hear you. In Billy the Kid's case, I was never sure whether his hearing aids were malfunctioning or he was a tenth degree black belt Flincher.

11. Nibble and Whine

This gambit is employed by a buyer *after* an agreement is reached by both sides, either verbally or in writing. Some imperfection is found in the property, either real or imaginary, and the buyer whines about it and asks for a price concession to take care of it. In effect, the buyer is nibbling away at the price. This happens repeatedly until the nibbling turns into a full banquet at the expense of the seller. Every property has imperfections, so don't think you will be impervious to this gambit if you only sell prime properties.

We have learned over the years that certain cultures believe that written contracts are only the starting point of a negotiation, and the serious negotiations start at the closing table. Americans think that once the contract is written and agreed to, the closing follows with no further discussion. Some other cultures don't think that way. They will ask for concessions even after every condition has been fulfilled on the written contract right at the closing table,. The buyer will nibble and whine, or worse—threaten to walk out of the closing and not pay the seller. If this happens to you, you very likely will feel indignation, even anger. Don't succumb to it.

This has happened to me a few times over the years. The most memorable was a flipper we did on a warehouse property. At the closing table, the buyer was sitting next to his attorney, who had clearly lost his sense of humor decades before this day. We were waiting for them to hand the closing agent their funds, but instead, they handed me an estimate for a $3,000 repair. The buyer said he wanted it taken off the price. The estimate was inflated, because the defect was tiny. I stopped, examined the estimate, and said, "Why didn't you bring this up during the inspection period?" The buyer said, "I didn't see it until a few days ago." I reminded the buyer that the inspection period ended over a month ago and he had agreed to take the property As-Is after that the inspection period ended. The buyer repeated that he wanted the repair taken off the price or he wasn't paying for the property, and he would walk out of the closing. His attorney agreed.

I sighed, looked directly at the buyer, and said, "Well, if that's what you want to do, I can't stop you. I thought you really wanted to buy the property, and if you walk away now, I'm going to be forced to keep your $10,000 escrow deposit to make up for my time and loss, because I had other buyers interested in the property after you and I signed the contract that you are now trying to break." The buyer said I couldn't do that, and he would sue me to get his deposit back. His attorney nodded belligerently. I said, "This is a free country and you are entitled to sue anyone about anything, even when you sign a contract to do something, and then you renege on that contract at closing. I guess you have to do what you have to do." The buyer and his attorney studied me closely and then went into a huddle . . . and then passed their checks over to the closing agent. We completed the contract as originally agreed upon.

To *counter* this gambit, require a large escrow deposit if you sense you are dealing with someone who is a nibbler. If you don't become aware of the nibbling until after you have agreed to a good faith deposit, then take backup offers from other buyers that will go into effect if the first contract falls through. It took a lot of fortitude on my part to take the position we did on the above transaction—we needed the property to close. Our profit was $20,000, and we could have afforded to give up $3,000 rather than put the property back on the market, start all over again, and spend another ninety days trying to find another buyer. At the time, 50 percent of our flipper capital was tied up in this property—but we had a feeling the buyer was nibbling. He needed to buy the property. His primary warehouse was filled to the gills, and was less than 200 feet from my warehouse. The close proximity was valuable to him.

12. Take It or Leave It

This gambit can be used by buyer or sellers. It is an intimidating expression of the other side's ability to walk-away. When someone is buying, she tells the seller she is not changing any part of her offer, and she is indifferent as to whether she buys the property or not because there are many other properties on the market that are just as good. If someone is selling, she tells the buyer essentially the same thing—that there are plenty of other buyers in the market ready, willing, and able to buy the property.

The *counter* to this is to ignore the intimidation and respond the way you normally would without the threat. This gambit was used on me more than twenty years ago when I first came to Florida, by a woman who owned a lot next to six duplexes we owned. She told me on the phone she wanted $22,000 for the lot and she wasn't going to take a penny less. I explained that I bought a similar lot on the opposite side of my duplexes for the equivalent of $12,000, but she just kept repeating she wanted $22,000. She then added, "Take it or leave it."

I mailed her an offer for $17,000 because I didn't want to hear her say, "Take or leave it!" anymore. Along with the offer, I included a copy of the $12,000 contract for the other lot and a very nice letter explaining that I didn't want to offend her, but $17,000 was all I believed the lot was worth. I was shocked down to my socks when the signed contract was returned with all terms accepted. It was a lesson in how to treat this gambit, which is used by many people.

13. Billy the Kid Last-Minute Chisel

This gambit is strictly a buyer's tool. In this strategy, the buyer offers a quick deal, usually for cash, subject to an inspection. The final date for the inspection is chosen as close as possible to the closing date, so the seller is put on pins and needles as to whether the closing will happen or not. Then, at the last possible minute, the buyer requests large discounts for inflated, questionable repairs, or he is not going to close. This works well in a slow real estate market with a motivated seller who needs a quick deal so he can move on to another property.

The *counter* to this is for a seller to take backup offers and be patient, but this can be more easily said than done when a cash deal is staring an impatient seller in the face.

Let me give you an example of how the Billy the Kid Last-Minute Chisel was used against a client of ours when we were acting as a broker. Eighty-three-year-old Billy the Kid taught the seller and me a valuable lesson about time and motivation by using this gambit. (Whenever someone introduces a new and interesting gambit, I name it after them.)

Our clients, the sellers, had a very nice older waterfront home in Cape Coral for sale. The home was on a sailboat-access canal and they wanted to replace it with a larger, newer home on the wide river. We listed it at $169,900, a price that would stimulate interest and get it sold quickly. Billy the Kid called me a few days after we stuck our For Sale in the ground and we arranged a showing. Billy went through the house quickly and offered $160,000, with a $16,000 deposit and a cash closing in two weeks, subject only to a two-week inspection period. Billy set up the closing for the same day as the end of the inspection. The house was in excellent condition, so the sellers and I felt confident and went on a buying expedition to purchase their new home on the river. After a week and a half, we made an offer that was accepted subject to selling their current home. The sellers were excited about moving.

Billy the Kid, on the other hand, still had not completed his inspections. He claimed his contractor was very busy and kept breaking appointments with him. The inspection was finally completed the night before the closing, and Billy faxed me the inspection results at 6:00 P.M. He claimed that contractor would need $20,000 to complete repairs and he wanted this as a discount from the $160,000 contract price. The sellers got angry. Their former home was in excellent condition with little deferred maintenance. Billy insisted he needed the repairs completed or he could not rent out the home, and he would not pay the full $160,000. The sellers asked me what alternatives they had, and I admitted that waiting for another buyer was another alternative, but there were no other buyers in the market who had expressed interest at that time. How long we would have to wait was anyone's guess—perhaps a year, because the real estate market was very slow. The sellers wanted to be done with their previous home and moved into the new one, so I recommended the good old "Let's split the difference." The sellers reluctantly agreed. We offered Billy a generous $10,000 discount, half of $20,000. He countered that he could not accept $10,000, but he would split the difference between $10,000 and $20,000 and accept a discount of $15,000. The closing went through at $145,000, and I named a gambit after Billy.

14. Crying

This gambit has been used on me by both sexes, but more often by women. Crying usually occurs when a seller needs a higher price to help overcome a personal tragedy. A few buyers have also cried when they needed a lower price to help them resolve a tragedy.

The *counter* is the same as the Feel Sorry For Me gambit, which is to listen sympathetically and then say, "I sympathize with your situation, however this is outside the bounds of this business transaction. Why don't we get back to discussing the mobile home park and after we are finished with that discussion, perhaps we can look at some other ways to help you."

I've had a widow cry that she couldn't take my offer because she would not have enough money for food and housing and would be forced to live out on the street as a "bag woman." I've had a mother cry and tell me she if she took my offer she couldn't provide an operation for one of her children. When I mentioned in my training classes that I caved in both times, some of the women rolled their eyes and told me I was a sucker. I don't know if the gambits were true or fabricated, but I still made a profit, even at the higher price.

15. Attila the Hun Swat Team

This last and most aggressive gambit is borderline illegal, and I don't recommend that any one use it, buyer or seller. This gambit takes the good cop/bad cop game and stretches it to the maximum. I mention it here so you will be aware of it when someone unscrupulous is using it on you.

In this gambit, there are three, or possibly more, buyers working in tandem. The first buyer visits the seller and is aggressive and obnoxious like Attila the Hun, and offers half of what the seller is asking. When the seller rejects the offer the buyer says that the seller was lucky to be offered that much and leaves in a huff with the threat that he will never come back.

A few days later, a second buyer shows up and offers *even less* than the first buyer, and is even *more aggressive and obnoxious*. When that buyer's offer is rejected, the same threats are issued. This gambit can be continued with a third or even a fourth buyer until the nice buyer shows up. This final buyer offers 70 percent off the listing price. Now this offer looks good compared to the offers from the Attila the Huns. This gambit works best in slow markets and on properties that have a specialized and smaller interest than other properties.

This gambit can also used by a seller who will pack a mobile home park with phony interested buyers to convince the real buyer that there is a lot of interest in the property and the price is a "steal."

If you suspect someone is using this gambit on you, the *counter* to it is to stand your ground. If you want to be more proactive, get the names and business cards of everyone who visits your property and check them out with the Better Business Bureau or have a private investigator check them out.

Additional Negotiating Strategies When You Are the Seller

After the red-hot seller's markets of the early to middle 2000s, when there were plenty of buyers and not many competing properties being offered, there were additional strategies we learned to employ when we were selling to maximize the sales price. It was a pleasant experience having a strong market for our inventory of mobile homes and mobile home parks, and gave us real power in our negotiations.

As you learned before, gathering information is an important part of negotiating, but in seller's markets you are gathering information on the motivation of buyers. We asked questions about why prospects were buying, when they were prepared to close, and whether their financing was already lined up. If the buyers did not give answers that indicated that they were serious and not "Looky Lou's" we wouldn't give them an appointment to see the property.

If the prospective buyers were neighbors or a relative of neighbor, we were accommodating. Some neighbors are just curiosity seekers, but many are seriously looking to get an investment close to their home and are highly motivated buyers. The following are additional strategies to employ when you are selling. They are not gambits but they have a gambitlike gamesmanship aspect to them.

Always Counter the First Offer Unless Full Price

We have learned over the years to always counter an offer from a buyer, unless it is for full-price. We do this because we have had buyers who were unhappy later on after we accepted their first offer. They got buyer's remorse and didn't go through with the contract. Once we discovered what happens after a buyer makes an offer, we used this strategy.

In almost every buyer's circle of acquaintances, there is a friend or family member who is an "expert" on real estate. When the expert finds out the buyer's first offer was accepted, they tell them he offered too much and he should have offered much less. In other words, any first offer that is accepted by a seller is too much. In their opinion, you have to make an offer that the seller won't accept to find out the seller's boundaries. When the buyer is told by the expert that he paid too much, he feels taken advantage of, and wants to get out of the contract, because now he believes he is paying too much. Therefore, when you are selling counter the buyer's first offer and make the buyer work for every dollar that is discounted off the full listing price. Then the buyer can tell the expert that he did offer less, and the seller wouldn't accept it. He tested the seller's boundaries, fought hard for every dollar, and finally "won" the discounted price.

If you are worried that you will lose a deal because you counter a buyer's initial offer (even though it is something you would like to accept) and that the buyer will refuse to accept your counteroffer and walk away, don't despair. You can always backtrack as a seller, call back the buyer and say you've changed your mind and are willing now to accept the first offer.

This is a very difficult strategy to use because there are times that you will be happy to accept a buyer's first offer because it represents a substantial profit to you. However, if you take the long view, you will find that a quick contract now might lead to no contract later, when the buyer gets "remorse sickness" after talking to an "expert." Giving a counteroffer is the best way to inoculate against this disease.

Don't Respond to a Verbal Offer. Say, "Let's Put It in Writing and See."

This is another difficult strategy to put into action, but we do it anyway. Whenever a buyer makes a verbal offer—even if it is one that we would be very happy, or very *unhappy* to accept—we say, "Let's put it in writing and see." We have learned over the decades that many buyers make verbal offers just to see what the seller will take, even though they have no intention of going through with the transaction. We don't want to waste valuable time on someone who is not really serious about buying, and there is a principle we have learned about this. It goes like this:

Someone's willingness to complete a transaction is directly proportional to the time he or she has invested in it. The more time that is invested, the greater the inclination is to complete the transaction.

A verbal offer and its answer take little time, so there is little motivation to complete the transaction. Demanding that someone spend the time to write up an offer gives you an edge when it comes to negotiating and forces the other side to spend that time or quit wasting yours.

There is a Lot of Interest and I Have Another Buyer in the Wings

Many times buyers have asked, "Have you had a lot of interest in the property?" or "Have you had any offers on the property?" or "How long has the property been for sale?" or "Are there other buyers getting ready to make offers?" If the answer to any of the above questions is negative, some buyers feel it gives them a license to make a low offer. As you know, we don't like to lie in a transaction, so if the answer to any of the above questions is negative we have found that the best way to answer, without lying, is, "Yes, there is a lot of interest in the property," even if the interest is just our own. We might add, "We are expecting another offer any moment," because we're optimistic, and therefore we do expect an offer at any moment.

Lowball Offers

One of the hardest things to do as a seller is not get angry when you get an unjustifiable lowball offer from a buyer. When we sold our home in New York, the broker, a seasoned pro, said something that has stuck with me ever since: ***Buyers are liars, and sellers are yellers.***

If we find ourselves inclined to yell when we get a lowball offer, we stop from getting angry and continue calmly forward. We will ask the buyer, in a soothing voice, "Could you please share with us how you arrived at that price?" There are usually only two answers to that question. The most popular is: "That is what I hear properties are going for in this area." We will then ask, "Could you please share with us which properties you are referring to?" Almost always the answer will be, "No property in particular, just properties in general," which lacks logic. The second explanation we get for the lowball offer is: "That is all I want to pay right now for your property." In response we will ask, "If we could show you comparable sales that indicate a higher price, would you be willing to look at them?" If the buyer says yes, we move forward. If the buyer says no, we give our counteroffer, and if it is rejected, we end the negotiation nicely.

The best way to counter a lowball offer is to remain calm and have your appraisal comps ready. There have been many times that we have converted a lowball offer into an acceptable one by just being nice, polite, and patient, repeating our counteroffer and waiting while the buyers kept raising their offer until it was acceptable.

Example of Counteroffer and Further Negotiation

The offer we made to John and Nancy Smith on their Primavera Mobile Home Park is detailed below. *Our initial offer is in italics* and their counteroffer is in bold italics. If one of the terms of the offer is not carried forward in this example it means they agreed to our initial terms:

What personal property is included and not included?

We asked for the golf cart; the office equipment, computers and software; the lawnmower; plumbing parts; the clubhouse furniture; and kitchen appliances.

The Sellers agreed to include everything but the desk chair in the office and the piano (his grandmother's) in the clubhouse.

What is the offer price?

$550,000—we left $50,000 for negotiating room.

The Sellers countered at $575,000, $25,000 below their listing price.

Who is responsible for fixing any defects, and up to how much?

We wanted the Sellers to fix any defects up to $25,000.

The Sellers will fix defects up to $5,000.

What are the financing terms, if any?

We will apply at the local community bank, doing no money down and want the Sellers to give a second mortgage for 20 percent of the purchase price.

The Sellers countered, offering only 10 percent of the purchase price in a second mortgage.

Are there any addendums spelling out additional terms and conditions?

We wanted forty-five days for due diligence and sixty days after the due diligence for financing. We wanted the Sellers to contribute $20,000 towards our closing costs.

The Sellers agreed to thirty days for due diligence and thirty days after due diligence for financing. They would give $10,000 toward closing costs.

In my opinion, we would be very close to doing this deal. It was already a great deal because it was priced $100,000 below the comps. The additional set of italics below the Sellers' counteroffer show how we would the counter the sellers' counteroffer:

What personal property is included and not included?
We asked for the golf cart; the office equipment, computers and software; the lawnmower; plumbing parts; the clubhouse furniture; and kitchen appliances.
The Sellers agreed to include everything but the desk chair in the office, and the piano in the clubhouse.
We agreed to let the desk chair and piano go, but the seller had to replace them with comparable substitutes.

What is the offer price?
$550,000—*we left $50,000 for negotiating room.*
The Sellers countered at $575,000, $25,000 below their listing price.
We asked the Sellers to split the difference with us at $562,500.

Who is responsible for fixing any defects, and up to how much?
We wanted the Sellers to fix any defects up to $25,000.
The Sellers countered with $5,000.
We decided to wait until after the due diligence was completed to negotiate this. There may only be $5,000 worth of defects.

What are the financing terms, if any?
We will apply at the local community bank, doing no money down and want the Sellers to give a second mortgage for 20 percent of the purchase price.
The Sellers countered, offering only 10 percent of the purchase price in a second mortgage.
We asked the Sellers to meet us halfway, with 15 percent of the purchase price for the second mortgage.

Are there any addendums spelling out additional terms and conditions?
We wanted forty-five days for due diligence and sixty days after the due diligence for financing. We wanted the Sellers to contribute $20,000 towards our closing costs.
The Sellers agreed to thirty days for due diligence and thirty days after due diligence for financing. They would give $10,000 towards closing costs.

We agreed to thirty days due diligence because we had free time to do it. We countered the thirty days after due diligence for financing at the original sixty days and sent a letter from the vice president of the bank stating that the bank would need sixty days to make a loan decision. We accepted $10,000 for closing costs because we had a great deal at a great price and terms.

You should learn an important rule of negotiating from this example: *If you want something, you should ask for it—nicely. The worst that will happen is someone will say no.*

SUMMARY

The process of making an offer should be comfortable now. You will take the best deals, do a light inspection, then figure out what price and terms you want to offer after doing your own appraisal and running the property through your *formulas for success.* You will use the preprinted contract the Realtors in your area use and fill in the blanks. Then you will add to your offer the Addendum A plus Schedules B and C. You will offer somewhat less than the price the *formula for success* suggests, for negotiation room.

If your first offer is not accepted—and many times it will not be—you know how to negotiate. You know the Three Be's of negotiating—Be Nice, Be Asking, and Be Patient. You should feel comfortable about the negotiation process and realize that the way to become a good negotiator is to make enough offers so it becomes second nature to create a successful give-and-take working relationship with others.

HOMEWORK

First, let's get the preprinted forms for real property contracts from your local Realtor contacts or from your local Board of Realtors. You have a contract on page 290 for mobile homes that are on leased land.

Next, I want you to write contracts for the three best properties your have seen so far. As this point, these contracts are still only going to be for practice and are not for real, so don't submit them to the sellers. Type 3s, after you read Chapters 10 and 11, I promise you can go out and make offers. In the meantime, I want you fill out these three contracts and then staple them to a page in your notebook for future reference.

I also want you to find someone to hold your escrow deposits—this can be a title company, your attorney, or a Realtor. Try to find someone with an escrow account insured against fraud and theft.

And last, start using the Three Be's of negotiating in any situation where a negotiation can take place—whenever there is flexibility in your purchasing or selling power because you are purchasing something that doesn't have a fixed price and fixed terms of sale. Try using the Three Be's in your personal life as well, whenever you want to change a situation to be more to your liking.

COMING ATTRACTIONS

We're at the point where you only have two more disciplines to learn before you can start buying property—performing inspections (due diligence) and obtaining financing. We'll discuss inspections first, because if the inspection is unsatisfactory, there is no need to get financing. We're going to show you how to inspect a mobile home park so you will protect yourself from hidden defects and unpleasant surprises.

We're also going to show you how to set up a mobile home from scratch, so you will be empowered to place a mobile home anywhere one is allowed. Think about how much this will advance your investing career when you can turn a vacant lot or a parcel of vacant land into another ATM.

10

Due Diligence: Fix It

Congratulations again! You *found* a good deal on a mobile home park, *figured* the price you wanted to pay, and stuck your *flag* in front of it with an accepted contract so no one else could buy it out from under you.

Now it's time to look at what you will have to do, if anything, to *fix* the park so you can keep it, flip it, or L/O it. You gave the property a reasonable once-over before you got it under contract, but stopped short of a full-blown inspection because it didn't make sense to spend a lot of time and/or money until you were sure it could be yours. Now you are sure it can be yours (after you secure financing, the final step I will show you in the next chapter). The question is: *Do you really want it to own it, after you find out what you have to fix, maintain, and manage?* The answer to that question comes after you research the property and do your due diligence.

Due diligence. Sounds fancy, doesn't it? All it means is inspecting a mobile home park to see if it is really going to be a good investment once you own it. Due diligence should provide you with enough information about the problems you will be buying along with the park, and also a plan for how to fix them and get paid handsomely for doing that. We're going to refer to this process in a humorous way, called *Doin' the Due*

Dilly. You can think of it like a dance with your favorite music playing in the background.

If your due diligence turns up discrepancies between the information you were supplied from the seller or broker when you wrote up your offer and what you discovered, or if there were other surprises, we are going to show you how to continue to negotiate for a good deal, or walk away—nicely. You will also learn in this chapter how to inspect a single mobile home from the roof down to the ground, or, as my son says, "From the roof to the struts, from soup to nuts," when he conducts the bus tours at the live training This will show you how to find defects in any park-owned units you are buying. Last, you will be shown how to replace a mobile home that is worn out, and how to install a mobile home from scratch on a vacant lot. Making a vacant lot come alive to give you the Triple Zotz is an empowering feeling.

THE THREE AREAS OF DUE DILIGENCE

Due diligence is divided up into three areas:

1. The *Business Aspects* of the park (NOI)
2. The *People* that live there *and the Laws* surrounding them
3. The *Infrastructure*

These areas are listed in the order of how you will gather the information. The *business aspects,* or NOI, will show you if the park is or can be made profitable. If it's not going to be profitable, there is no sense in continuing. The *people and the laws* will reveal the management needs of the town in which you will be the mayor. Once you have determined that you will be able to manage the town well, the *infrastructure* research will show the quality of the utilities and services that you will be supplying and maintaining for the townspeople who live there.

Ways to Gather Due Dilly and Due Dilly Decision Points

The process we have created allows you to spend as little of your own time and money as possible so you can quickly make a decision about parks you don't want to buy and concentrate on the ones you do. There are three ways to gather due diligence for each of the areas of three due diligence:

1. **Sitting down due dilly:** You will be given information from someone else. The understanding of it can be accomplished anywhere—sitting at a desk. The only cost to you is your time.

2. **On your feet due dilly:** The information is gathered by you when you are on site. The cost to you is time and your travel expenses if the park is a long distance from where you live.

3. **Due dilly you pay for:** This is information reported by others that costs you money to obtain.

There are four main decision points in the process of gathering due diligence (see the inset on page 320). At each point, you will decide one of three things: one, things look good so far and you want to continue to try to buy the park; two, there are problems that require stopping the due diligence and renegotiating the terms of the contract; or three, there are terminally serious problems with the park and you want to withdraw from the contract without renegotiation.

As mentioned above, there are several experts you are going to call in to give you reports. These reports will be about the title, the infrastructure, the laws, the licenses, the land, the buildings, and the market value of the park. Notice that your due diligence process puts paying for these reports towards the end of the due diligence period, so you won't waste your money if you decide you don't want to buy the park after some basic research.

DOIN' THE DUE DILLY

You have your starting list—the due diligence from the Seller, Schedule C, on the upcoming page. Don't worry. You will be more comfortable with this process as time goes on. Keep in mind that there is now a second list for you to research after you receive the Schedule C from the seller and/or broker. It's labeled "Due Diligence You Gather Yourself," and is shown on page 324.

You will find the information from a seller and/or broker is usually supplied in four stages, as you show increasing interest as a buyer:

1. The initial listing—usually just a few lines from an ad or on the Internet.

2. A one-page brochure with summary information and a few pictures.

3. A follow-up package centering around the rent roll, P&L and NOI.
4. A full package of due diligence with whatever is available, if there is anything more, after a buyer wants to make or has made an offer,

We have made the due diligence process as logical as possible and perhaps even a little dry and scientific. After you look at the two sets of information—seller supplied and your own research—I can almost hear your objections from here. Let's deal with them now.

The Four Main Due Dilly Decision Points

1. After you have the sitting down due dilly on the business aspects (NOI), and the people and the laws, you will decide: *Can the park be profitable and can you manage it well?* If yes, you will continue.
2. After you have gathered your on your feet due dilly by talking to residents, meeting with contractors, measuring and counting lots, driving around the area, and meeting with a local attorney, a mortgage broker and lenders from community banks, and so on, you will decide: *Is this is a park I want to keep, flip, or L/O?* If yes, go on.
3. Before you order all your experts' reports—the due dilly you pay for (see next inset) —and after meeting with lenders and mortgage brokers, you will decide: *Do I have a good chance of getting financing?* If yes, you will order the reports. If no, you will arrange for owner financing or withdraw. After you receive the reports, you will decide: *Do I still have any serious concerns?* If you do not, then you will continue on to financing. If you have serious concerns with any of the reports and the concern is terminal, you will withdraw. If the concern can be cured with a change in the contract, you will try to change it. If seller won't change it, then you will withdraw.
4. You will apply for financing, pay for the bank appraisal, and wait for the lender's answer. Your next decision: *Is the financing approved, and can I accept the financing terms?* If you can't accept them or you were turned down for financing, you will either get an extension to try another lender, ask for seller financing, or withdraw. If you like the financing terms, you will buy the park. *Congratulations!*

Yes, the due diligence list is a serious list. Yes, it will take time. Yes, Doin' the Due Dilly isn't as entertaining as other things you can do in your spare time. Yes, you will be responsible for running a small town. Yes, no property is perfect after you analyze it using this list. Yes, even though the list is extensive you could still miss something.

Okay, now let me add a few more yeses. Yes, even if you miss something, it probably won't be something major—the list has just about every major concern. Yes, when you pick your mobile home parks correctly, even when they are imperfect, you should still be able to grow wealthy. Yes, if you go into a park knowing the challenges that are facing you and you have a plan to fix them, you should still be able to gather wealth. These lists are your shield from misfortune. *They have been compiled by us, along with many others with years of experience. Much of them came as a result of mistakes we have made. It is our intention to protect you from making those mistakes.*

Knowing the Different Kinds of Sellers When it Comes to Due Diligence

There is an important fact of life to consider when you are gathering due diligence and doing inspections. We call this the *Step Inside Someone Else's Shoes Principle.* You've probably heard it said that to really understand another person and have compassion and empathy for his problems, you should step inside his shoes and walk a mile.

Well, the same is true when you buy a mobile home park. When you buy someone else's park, you have to *step inside his shoes,* because only then you will see the problems that go along with owning his park. There is an important difference here, though—when you walk a mile in someone else's shoes so you can understand his problems and challenges, his problems are still his problems after you take off his shoes. You are left with only the problems you had before. When you buy someone else's mobile home park, their problems become more permanent—you don't get to take their shoes off. You have to keep them on over your own shoes, adding any problems in the park to the problems you started out with.

Sellers generally fall into three groups when it comes to disclosing defects in a property:

Schedule C: Due Diligence from Seller

Business Aspects—NOI

- ***Annual Profit and Loss Statements*** (P&L) past three years and ***Monthly P&L*** current year
- ***Current Rent Roll*** with tenants' names, monthly rent, move-in dates, expiration, and balance
- ***History of Rent Increases and Legal Procedure to Increase Rents***
- ***Delinquency List*** for last three months
- ***Tax Returns*** (three years) of Seller (if available)
- ***Title Insurance Policy*** with current O + E showing marketable title and/or exceptions
- ***Hazard and Liability Insurance Policy***—riders, risk assessments, carrier—past claims
- ***Real Estate Tax Bills and/or Assessments***—last three years, tax amount after you buy property
- ***Service or Advertising Contracts*** assumed by Buyer—trash, extermination, maintenance, laundry, management, commission, union agreements, vending, billboards
- ***Payroll***—list of employees with name, position, wage rate, and entitled benefits
- ***Business License, Occupancy Permit, and/or Dock Permits***
- ***Utility Bills***—water, sewer, gas, electric, trash, street lights (two years monthly statements)
- ***Existing Loan Documents***—if you are assuming loans from Seller

People and Laws

- ***All Leases and list of Security Deposits***—entire copies plus any addendum or riders
- ***Rules and Regulations and Park's Eviction Procedure***—any prospectus for residents
- ***Litigation History***—any past or pending litigation; if none, an affidavit from owner

Infrastructure

- ***Physical Inventory***—furniture, fixtures, equipment, and supplies (see Schedule B)
- ***Sewage Treatment Plant Permit*** and maintenance records—letter from maintenance company on monthly costs, operating problems, lot capacity, capital expenditures needed
- ***Water Supply Permit*** and maintenance records—letter from maintenance company on monthly costs, operating problems, lot capacity, capital expenditures needed
- ***Natural Gas Permit*** and maintenance records—letter from maintenance company on monthly costs, operating problems, lot capacity, capital expenditures needed

If-Available Due Diligence

- ***Engineering Reports*** of sewer systems, water systems, gas, roads, electrical, and so on
- ***Environmental Inspection and Survey***—asbestos, lead paint, underground tanks, wetlands, and so on
- ***Appraisal for bank***
- ***Survey***—as-built, with legal description

1. The first group is honest and will disclose what is right and wrong with their property. In my opinion, this is not a large group.
2. The second group, the largest, plays "hide and seek." They won't hide problems but they won't volunteer information unless you seek it by asking specific questions.
3. The members of the third group are just plain hiders. They purposely mask defects and may not be honest when you point them out.

Again, like the first rule in boxing, protect yourself at all times from the second and third groups of sellers. *You must check out all information you are given by the seller or broker for validity—do not rely on their accuracy!*

After reading the above you might think that you will be so negative

Due Diligence You Gather Yourself

Business Aspects—NOI

- ***Inventory Lots***—count the number of lots, measure them, note what's on them, whether units are tied down- number of vacant lots, how many vacant mobiles and mobiles need to be removed, do vacant lots have utilities
- ***Utilities***—who (tenant or park owner) pays for water, sewer, gas, trash, lights, mowing, snow, common areas
- ***Your Own Market Survey***—comparable sales, lot rents in area, vacancies in other parks, prices of single family homes and mobile home/land deals, does owner have other parks, teaser ads, rent on three-bedroom apartments
- ***Current Management Ability***—have someone call to see how they handle prospects

People and Laws

- ***Interview Residents and Manage*r**—general feedback, opinions, and attitudes about the park and its future
- ***Find Out Pet Rules***—whether pets are allowed, any prohibitions by size or dangerous breeds
- ***Interview Local Mobile Home Dealers and Real Estate Brokers*** —current commercial outlook, prospects
- ***Visit Park***—go at different times, especially on weekend nights
- ***Check school districts and Demographics***—housing, income levels, population centers
- ***Letter from Chamber of Commerce or Planning Department***—job creation, population, and unemployment rate five years previous, now, next five years, companies moving in or out
- ***Letter from Police Department***—showing calls to park in last year and reason for the call
- ***Eviction Procedure***—visit attorney specializing in MHP evictions, go over procedure, and get legal opinion of mobile home park operating permit

Infrastructure

- ***Contractor Inspections***—of water, sewer, electric, gas, roads, and video of sewer lines
- ***Building and Termite Inspections***—on all buildings and park-owned or L/O homes
- ***Calculate Yearly Reserves for Replacements***—on buildings and infrastructure
- ***Environmental Inspection and Survey***—asbestos, lead paint, underground tanks
- ***Flood Plain and Wetland Information and Drainage Inspection***—check for problems with water lines near trees and buildings
- ***Physical Inventor***—check condition of furniture, fixtures, equipment, and supplies
- ***Potential for Lot Expansion***—check with building, zoning, fire, and health departments about rules and procedures and lot size, setbacks, age of mobile homes, types of homes
- ***Water, Sewer, Electric and Gas Lines***—potential for expansion
- ***Sewage Treatment Plant***—check for smells, appearance, verify condition with maintenance company
- ***Water Supply and Wells***—check for smells, appearance, verify condition with maintenance company
- ***Noise Problems and Tree Work***—check if needed
- ***Park Location***—whether it is easy to find, near jobs, schools, shopping, health care, church, and so on
- ***Survey and Plat Map***—check access, easements, encroachments; match the legal description to what is being purchased
- ***Aerial Photographs***—examine adjacent properties
- ***Letter from Zoning and Building Departments***—regarding current zoning, future zoning changes, permitted spaces, total allowed spaces, and procedures for filling empty lots or replacing homes
- ***Letter from Code Enforcement Department***—certifying no outstanding code violations

- ***Letter from Fire Marshall***—confirming that there are no outstanding violations and inspections are up to date
- ***Letter from Health Department***—confirming that there are no violations, water and septic systems are okay and permits are current
- ***Engineering Reports***—for sewer, water electrical, and gas systems, roads, and so on

The Due Dilly You Pay For

1. Contractor inspections on water, sewer, electrical, gas, and road systems.
2. A meeting with an attorney on eviction procedures and the park permit.
3. A sewer video made by a plumber.
4. A land survey.
5. A phase one environmental report.
6. A property and termite inspection of all buildings and park owned units.
7. An engineering inspection of the whole park.
8. A bank appraisal if you decide you can secure financing.

and suspicious about buying someone's mobile home park that you won't buy anything at all. Actually I am more worried about the reverse. I don't want you to be so excited about the future cash flow and profit you will make that you lose sight of the time you will be spending and the problems you will be accepting in the process. I want you to remind yourself that you are providing value to the community—don't sell yourself, or the business of being a mobile home park investor, short. You deserve to have cash flow and make a profit, but you also deserve to know how much to pay, given the issues contained in the property you are buying.

That being said, let's consider the three areas of due diligence—the business aspects, the people and the laws, and the infrastructure—and learn about Doin' The Due Dilly. For each of the three areas, we will obtain what the seller provides and then extend it with our own research.

The Business Aspects of the Park (NOI)—Supplied by Seller

Most lenders will want *annual profit and loss statements* (P&L) for the past three years and *monthly P&L statements* for the most current year. Three years of P&L will show a trend in cash flow and profit, while the monthly P&L will show the most up-to-date trend. To figure the NOI you will adjust the P&L by removing mortgage payments, interest, and depreciation. You should do a check of the gross rents actually received by multiplying the total occupied lots by the average lot rent per year. You will be amazed by how many times the total lot rent received can not be substantiated by that simple check.

You should also go over the expenses reported with the list of typical park expenses, as shown again on the next page. You may want to modify the list of expenses to include lawn care and/or snow removal or to take out water and sewer if the park is submetered, and make other revisions to more closely reflect the park under consideration. Then see how the seller-supplied expenses match up to your list. Remember, you should expect the total expenses before mortgage to be in the 30–40 percent range of total rents for a land-lease community, while 50 percent or more is common for park-owned units. You should be suspicious if the information you have been given shows expenses of 20 percent or less of the rents received. Typically, the seller will be doing the management or maintenance himself or is just "forgetting" some expenses.

Is it possible that an owner will have little or no useful information available on the P&L and NOI? Yes, I have seen it more than a few times. In that case, you will have to figure this out from your site inspection of the park: determine the actual number of occupied units and multiply that number by the average lot rent per year to get the approximate total rents received. Then approximate the expenses using the 40 or 50 percent rule, adjusting according to how utilities are paid.

The *Current Rent Roll* with tenants' names and each tenant's monthly rental rate, date moved in, lease expiration date, and current balance owed will also be required by most lenders. It is a good thing if there are many tenants with move-in dates many years ago. It shows the park has a strong retention of residents and the income is stable. A red flag is lots of new tenants in the last year. Some sellers pack the empty lots in their parks with undesirable tenants when they know they are going to sell,

MOBILE HOME PARK EXPENSES TABLE	
Categories	**% Gross Revenues***
Administrative Expenses	
Management Fee	5.0
Wages	4.5
Administrative Costs	2.5
Telephone	0.5
Advertising	0.5
Operating Expenses	
Supplies	0.5
Heating	0.5
Electric	1.0
Water/Sewer	9.0
Maintenance Expenses	
Repairs	5.0
Wages	3.0
Taxes & Insurance	
RE Taxes	6.5
Other Taxes, Licenses	0.5
Property Insurance	1.0
Total Annual Expenses	**40.0**

*Percentages based on a model by Lawrence Allen, MAI, author of *How to Find, Buy, Manage, and Sell a Manufactured Home Community.*

just to increase the NOI and the price. Then the new owner is stuck with the new problem tenants.

The *History of Rent Increases and Legal Procedure to Increase Rents* is important when you are looking for ways to increase the NOI. If the park has not had a rent increase in the last two to three years or even longer, that is a good thing. You should be able to increase the rent after you buy it, and that *money drops right down to the bottom line and into your pocket.* You should also check the comparable park rents in the area, and also use the formula for rents on three-bedroom apartments (on page 332) to see if an increased lot rent can be justified. The legal procedure to raise rents may vary from state to state. Most states let the market determine lot rent, and when increases can be made. Some states, like Florida, require that parks can only have one lot rent increase each year, with ninety days prior notice, and the increase must be approved by a state regulatory agency. Check what the seller provides in the way of information on raising rents, as well as with what an attorney tells you later when you interview her on eviction procedures for your area.

The *Delinquency List* for last three months is a useful tool to see how the residents are paying, how much they are behind, and if there are problems looming with evictions. Don't be surprised if many sellers don't have such a list available, but the more professional ones will.

It may be difficult to get *Tax Returns* for three years from the seller. (I personally would not give mine.) If a seller doesn't want to supply this, it shouldn't be a deal killer. Some investors feel the actual tax returns for a mobile home park tell the true story about income and expenses, while the P&L supplied by the seller is only a best-case scenario.

You want to get a *Title Insurance Commitment* as soon as possible. You should order one as soon as you have an effective contract for two reasons: one, you want to make sure you are not spending time and money inspecting a park that you will not be able to close on because the title is unmarketable and will take too long to clear up; and two, you want to make sure all the people who own the park are included in your contract.

The *Hazard and Liability Insurance Policy* is nice to have so you can be aware of any special riders or risk assessments on the park, and what past claims there have been. Further, you want to check out the actual cost of the insurance against what is shown on the P&L, and if the current insurance is sufficient to cover everything.

You will also need the *Real Estate Tax Bills and/or Special Assessments* for the last three years. You want to see if there is a trend in these costs—are they going up or down—and why. You also want to contact the tax collector or property appraiser to see what your taxes will be *after* you purchase the park at the new contract price. Some areas are slow to adjust real estate taxes to the current market value of a property and do it when the property is transferred to new owners. For instance, if the park you buying is assessed for tax purposes at $500,000 but you are purchasing it for twice that at $1 million, it might be reasonable to assume that the real estate taxes will double. *Be sure to adjust the NOI of the park for this.* If you are buying a park at a 10 percent cap rate, and the taxes are going to increase $5,000 per year after you buy it, that means $5,000 will come off the NOI, and 10 times that amount—$50,000—should come off your purchase price.

You will need to view the *Service and Advertising Contracts* for trash, pest extermination, maintenance, laundry, management, commissions, union agreements, vending, billboards, and so on, to see if they will be assumed by you as the new owner of the park and whether you will be required to continue them. We bought a mobile home park and a motel with onerous laundry machine contracts. We were lucky to get out of one but were stuck with the other for seven years because the previous owner 'neglected" to mention it. Also, we could not get a maintenance contract on the sewer lift station because the only maintenance company in town would not do business with anyone associated with the property due to the previous owner's terrible payment history with them.

On larger parks, it is important to have *Payroll* information with a list of employees by name, along with position, wage rate, and entitled benefits. Take this information and see if it conforms to what you are given on the P&L.

It is extremely important to obtain copies of the *Business License, Occupancy Permit,* and/or *Dock Permits.* Make sure there is a valid license to do business, that the park is allowed to be occupied, and that any docks on the property have been legally constructed. Check the licenses with the appropriate government agency to make sure that they are active and in good standing. You will confirm this information later with the local attorney when you meet to discuss eviction procedures and rent increases. There are parks that do not have a business license or are in violation of the occupancy laws, and the sellers will "forget" to tell you. You can then find yourself in a situation where the new inspections to get active licenses trigger some unpleasant effects, and you want to avoid them. I can not overemphasize how important this step is. *You do not want to buy a park that has problems with its business license or occupancy permit.* If you discover there are problems and the seller gets angry, that's okay. You are contracting to buy an ongoing business. If it's not ongoing, it's the seller's fault, not yours. Make sure the problem can be fixed before you own the park, or withdraw.

You want to see the *Utility Bills* for water, sewer, gas, electric, street lights, and trash for at least two years, directly from the monthly statements. You want this for two reasons: one, to see who is paying for what in the park; and two, to take this information and see if it is accurately represented in the P&L and NOI. You can assume the average household will use 5,000 gallons of water per month, and the sewer charges are billed from the water usage.

You will only need the *Existing Loan Documents* if you are assuming the loans from seller. Otherwise they will not apply.

The Business Aspects—Due Diligence You Gather Yourself

Doing an *Inventory of Lots* is one of the most basic and most important forms of research you need to do. First and foremost, count the lots and measure them to see what size mobile homes they will safely hold. You would be surprised how often the actual number of lots differs from the number you were given by the seller. While you're counting and measuring, you should note what type of mobile home is on each lot—is it a single-wide or double-wide, an RV, and so on, who owns the home (the resident or the park), whether the home is tied down or not, and whether it has skirting or not. Then you should examine the condition of utility connections. Next you are going to inventory how many vacant mobiles there are and whether any of them need to be removed from the park. If you want them to stay, find out who has title to them, how much is owed on them, and how you will get title to them. Finally, you will inventory how many vacant lots there are and whether there are utilities on those vacant lots.

While you are doing the lot inventory, you should note all information about the *Utilities* on each lot, such as who pays the water, sewer, gas, trash, lighting, lot mowing, and snow removal. You also want to note who pays for utilities in the common areas and how much it costs. Note who is paying to maintain, repair, and supply utilities to the clubhouse, pool, shuffleboard courts, playgrounds, and so on, if these are present. It is reasonable to assume the park owner is, but there are cases where a mobile home association may be billed directly.

Doing *Your Own Market Survey* can be as involved or as basic as you want to make it. You certainly want to know if there are any comparable sales of other parks in the area and what their cap rate was relative to the park you are buying. It's extremely important to find out what other mobile home parks in the area are charging for lot rents, and how the parks compare to the one you are buying in terms of size, utilities supplied as part of rent, amenities, location, and so on. You will also want to know how the other parks are faring in terms of vacancies. If there is a short supply of vacant lots and high occupancies, that speaks well for the demand for affordable housing. A great resource is JLT Associates (http://jlt-associates.com/) They supply market surveys on a county-by-county basis all around the country.

You also want to know about the cost of single family housing in the area, and if there are mobile home/land deals available, and at what price. If the cost of housing and the mortgage payment on it is much higher than your lot rent plus the mortgage payment on a reasonable three-bedroom mobile home, that is good. In other words, if the lot rent is $200 per month and the payment on a three-bedroom mobile home is $300 per month, then the total cost of living in the park is $500 per month. If a typical single family home in the area costs $200,000 and PITI (Principle, Interest, Taxes, and Insurance) of living in it is $2,000 per month, then living in the park has a real price advantage. However, if local developers are offering mobile home/land packages to buyers, say three-bedroom mobile homes on a half an acre of land for $59,900 and the PITI of living there and owning the land is $500 per month—the same as the cost of living in the mobile home park—then be careful. Most people will prefer ownership of the mobile home and the land for a price that is close to owning a mobile home and leasing the land.

There is also a formula for showing the comparable affordability of a three-bedroom mobile home versus a three-bedroom apartment. You want the lot rent plus the monthly payment on a reasonably attractive three-bedroom mobile home to be less than the rent on a three-bedroom apartment. The lower the mobile home plus lot rent is, the better. You also want to know if the seller has other parks in the area to which she could be siphoning off your residents after she sells the park. If the seller does have other parks you should get a written a noncompete agreement on the tenants in the park you are buying to protect yourself.

If you are buying a park that is a turn-around with many vacancies, place a teaser ad in the newspaper during the inspection period to see if there is a strong or weak demand for your vacant lots and/or the BBs you will bring in to do a Triple Zotz. If you receive many phone calls from the ad, that's good, but if you receive very few inquiries, you should find another park, because the demand for BBs and/or vacant lots is not there. There are some mobile home parks in which you can not fill up vacant lots profitably, because there aren't enough potential new residents interested in them.

If you are deciding whether to keep the *Current Management*, especially on a turn-around park for which you will need new residents to fill empty lots, have someone call to see how they handle prospects.

The People and Laws—Information Supplied by Seller

You will want, and need, a copy of *All Leases*—entire copies plus any addendum or riders. Lenders required a copy of every lease in every park we have purchased, and in the case of parks with a hundred lots or more, the paperwork ran to a thousand sheets. Read the leases, and pay particular attention to the leases of friends and relatives of the owner. Make sure you are not inheriting leases that are special deals and unprofitable for you. If you are buying a land-lease park, chances are there are few, if any, *Security Deposits*. You want a list of security deposits if you are buying park-owned units or other types of real estate along with the mobile home park, like houses, duplexes, warehouses, stores, and so on. Go over the list with the tenants and have them to sign off agreeing to the amounts of the deposits. Again, you would be surprised how many times a tenant gave a security deposit and the owner "forget" to give us credit for it at closing, and then we had to chase her to get it later—if at all.

You also want a copy of the *Rules and Regulations* for the mobile home park to make sure every resident has signed and agreed to be bound by them. You want to know the *Park's Eviction Procedure*. Their eviction procedure may or may not be legal, which you will ascertain later with a local attorney. Also, there are states, like Florida, which require that every resident in a land-lease community receive a "prospectus" agreed to by the state's mobile home park governing board that lists rules and regulations.

Last, you will want a *Litigation History* of the park to see if there is any history of lawsuits and, if so, what they have been. You want to make sure you will not inherit liability for current outstanding lawsuits should you take over as the entity that owns the park. Most people create a new entity to take ownership in a mobile home park so they don't inherit any liabilities from the former owner. At the very least, you want an affidavit from the owner stating what lawsuits, if any, are outstanding, and you should go over it at your meeting with an attorney.

The People and Laws—Due Diligence You Should Gather Yourself

Generally speaking, the residents of mobile home parks are gregarious, which means they are a social bunch. Parks residents are usually friendly and like to share news and opinions, so by all means, *Interview Residents.* Approach a few of them and ask what it's like living in the park, because you (or someone you know) are thinking of moving in there. They will usually be helpful. They will tell you the good points and negative points of living in the park. This information will be useful when it comes to improving the social atmosphere in the park after you own it. Don't mention that you are thinking of buying the park at this time. Park residents tend to be skittish about changes in ownership because they are worried the lot rent will go up and the new owner will not treat them fairly.

Next, *Interview the Manager.* The manager of the park is going to have some of the most valuable information about the park—which residents are good and which ones she would like to encourage to leave. She also knows where the maintenance problems are within the infrastructure and who to call to fix problems that arise. Some sellers will forbid you to talk to the manager because managers can also be skittish about changes in ownership. She may be worried about losing her job, getting her salary or benefits lowered, or having to work more and being appreciated less. Some sellers are worried that the manager will leave as soon as she finds out about a possible change in ownership. Then the seller will be without a manager and have to find a new one if the buyer doesn't complete the purchase.

We would not buy a park without talking to the manager. We explain to the seller that we are hands-on owners and we need to know all the important information a manager knows about the people and the infrastructure of the park. If the seller forbids us to tell the manager we might be buying the park, we will honor the seller's wishes in the beginning of the inspection period. However, speaking to the manager is critical to our decision as we near the end of the due diligence period and are interested in buying the park, and we will insist on doing so. We will add that when we speak with the manager and inform her of our intention to buy the park, we will stress we will not be making any unpleasant changes to the park or to her job description. We won't be lying. When we buy a park, we consider it a powerful benefit if it already has a good manager. Even if we do contemplate changing managers because the current manager is not doing a good job, we will wait until we find a new manager before we let the current manager go.

When we were doing the due diligence on the Jefferson Mobile Home Park, the previous manager (who is still our manager and doing a great job) would stop from time to time during our inspections and stare at me with a worried look on her face. Each time she did that, I said to her, "I promise, we're not going to fire you. Why would we do such a thing? You're doing a good job now, and I'm sure you'll do a good job for us, too." I must have said it at least ten times before we bought the park. After we owned the park, we increased the manager's salary, benefits, and responsibilities, and she blossomed into an important part of our business.

While you are inventorying the lots, doing your inspections, and talking to residents, note if there are *Pets,* specifically those that are dangerous breeds. Yes, I know people who have Dobermans, pit bulls, chows, German shepherds, Rottweilers, and so on, and they are sweet, well-behaved members of the family. However, some insurance policies will not cover you as the owner of the park if you allow what they call dangerous breeds of dogs into the park. If you have no insurance coverage and one of those sweet, well-behaved dogs bites someone, guess who will also be sued? That's right, you guessed it. Even though it's not your dog and you had nothing to do with the dog-biting incident, bite victims can get an attorney to sue you. You will have liability for the accident, just like when you lend someone your car and they get into a accident—the driver will be sued and you will also be sued as the owner of the car.

If you have the time, it could be important to *Interview Local Mobile Home Dealers and Real Estate Brokers* about the park. Be careful about what you say to them. The safest way to ask questions is to mention that someone you know is thinking of buying or renting a mobile home in the park, and would they have any information or advice about it. You can also get information from dealers and Realtors about the price of single-family homes and mobile home/land packages in the area.

In order to know more about the people and the social life in the park, you should also *Visit the Park at different times, especially weekend nights*. Friday night and Saturday night are party nights to many people, and you will get valuable information about what is going on in the park by driving through the park at those times. If you notice one particular location, or several locations with a lot of cars coming and going, there may be drug dealing. Drug dealers can be removed, so don't think they will be a permanent fixture. If there is so much drug dealing going on that you are squeamish about handling it, you should find another park without the problem.

Among the strongest magnets for attracting new residents in family parks are good schools. *Check out the School Districts* if you are buying a family park. We have seen low-quality family parks achieve high lot rents and occupancy because they were in superior school districts.

You should also get a *Demographic Report* showing housing, income levels, and population centers for the area where the park is. You will find that most population centers are close to where the jobs are. You can find information about the demographics of any area on government census websites on the Internet, such as www.bestplaces.net, or by calling the Chamber of Commerce.

Speaking of the Chamber of Commerce, job outlook is one of the most critical elements in an area's economics. You should get a *Letter from the Chamber of Commerce or Local Planning Department* detailing job creation, population levels, and the unemployment rate for the past five to ten years, the current levels, and what is expected in the next five to ten years. Ask if any large companies are moving into or leaving town. If jobs increase, real estate increases. If jobs decrease, residents start moving away, and that spells bad times for an area. Jobs, jobs, jobs. They are critical to investing.

It is also important to get a *Letter from Police Department* showing calls to the park for last year and the reason for the call. If a letter is not possible, ask for a report. Police departments are well organized now and use statistics and computers as an integral part of crime fighting. A few visits to the park by the police are no reason for alarm, because usually they concern excess noise or domestic disputes. If there are many calls of a serious nature, however, you need to be aware of it.

While we are discussing the more serious problems with the people living in the park, you should also go over the legal *Eviction Procedure*, which may not be the one the park actually uses. You should visit a local attorney who specialized in mobile home park evictions and go over the procedure, in terms of time and costs. You can ask the seller, the broker, or the local bar association for referrals to attorneys who specialize in this area. If they are not available, go down to where evictions are filed and ask the clerk of the court which attorneys do the most evictions, either on mobile home parks or on rentals in general. It usually follows that those attorneys have the most experience and are the most affordable. Don't ask which attorneys are the best, because the clerks can't answer that.

The Infrastructure—Supplied to You by Seller

First, you need to get from the list on Schedule B of your offer, for the personal property that is accompanying your purchase. You will go over this list, the *Physical Inventory* of furniture, fixtures, equipment, and supplies, and the contract is subject to both you and the seller agreeing to it.

Next, you will be getting the basic infrastructure information. As you know, responsibility for the property's infrastructure distinguishes mobile home park investors from other real estate investors. Some of you might feel intimidated by this, but don't worry—help is on the way. There are experts, contractors and civil engineers, who will inspect the park and then give you valuable advice about repairs and maintenance. There may also be maintenance companies that have been servicing the infrastructure. They will give you letters detailing their experience and costs while they have been maintaining it.

We are first going to check the waste disposal and treatment system, or sewer system. Sewage is handled in three ways, listed here from the best down to the most basic in terms of cost and time to maintain it:

1. Gravity-fed pipes connected to the municipality's sewage treatment plant
2. An on-site sewage treatment facility
3. On-site septic tanks and drain fields

It is best to have gravity-fed sewer pipes leading out of the park to the municipality's sewage treatment plant. This is common in urban areas. A subset of this is to have gravity-fed sewer pipes on site leading to an on-site sewer lift station, which then pumps the waste under pressure to the municipality's plant. The next type of system, an on-site sewage treatment facility, is common in rural areas for bigger mobile home parks. The most basic type of system is septic tanks and drain fields.

If you have a lift station and/or a sewage treatment plant on site, you will want the seller to supply you with the *Sewage Treatment Plant Permit* and/or *Lift Station Permit,* along with maintenance records. You should also require a letter from the maintenance company detailing the monthly costs, operating problems, the lot capacity, and any expected capital expenditures that will be needed in the near future to run it. *Pay particular attention to lot capacity if you are going to be filling in vacant lots or adding more lots in the future in a park with an on-site system.* You may be in for some expensive additions if the capacity of the system is exceeded. Have your engineer check this for you.

Next is drinking water, also known as potable water. There are two ways of supplying this, from the local municipality, or from a well onsite that pumps water that you may have to treat. If there is a well, the seller needs to supply you with a *Water Supply Permit* and the maintenance records for the well equipment. *You should also conduct a water test to examine the quality of the well water before and after it is treated.* Again, you will want a letter from the maintenance company as to monthly costs, operating problems, lot capacity, and any capital expenditures needed in the near future. *Pay particular attention to lot capacity when you are going to be filling in vacant lots in the park or adding more lots in the future in a park with an on-site well system.* If the capacity of the system is exceeded, you may be in for some expensive well additions. Have your engineer check this for you.

If you have natural gas lines on site, you will want the seller to supply you with the *Natural Gas Permit,* along with any maintenance records. You should also require a letter from the gas maintenance company detailing the monthly costs, operating problems, the lot capacity, and any capital expenditures needed in the near future. *Pay particular attention to lot capacity if you are going to be filling in vacant lots in the park or adding more lots in the future.* If the capacity of the on site system is exceeded, you may be in for some expensive gas additions. Have your engineer check this for you.

It will be rare that you will have the information described in the next section—the *If Available Due Diligence*—including Engineering

Reports, an Environmental Inspection, a recent Survey, and a bank Appraisal, supplied to you by the seller. It would usually only be available if another buyer had been interested in the park, had performed his or her due diligence, and then for some reason, did not go forward with the purchase. This could be due to a failure to secure financing, or perhaps something they felt was wrong with the inspections, or for any of the reasons people have for not finishing what they start. It could also be the even rarer case in which the seller, as a true professional, knew that other professional investors would want those reports before purchasing the park and therefore paid for them and had them ready to facilitate the process of selling the park. (However, some buyers might be suspicious that there could be some arm-twisting going on and would order their own reports anyway.)

We covered the seller-supplied information on the infrastructure fairly rapidly because you are mainly looking for letters. The bulk of your due diligence on the infrastructure will be your inspections, which are described next, and then, even more important, the inspection of a qualified civil engineer and licensed contractors.

The Infrastructure—Due Diligence You Gather Yourself

We are going to be very careful gathering information on the infrastructure of the park. The reason for this extra care is because major infrastructure problems can be expensive and they can have an unpleasant effect on the profitability of a park. The difficulty in evaluating infrastructure stems from the fact much of it is buried underground and difficult to visually inspect. You were already made aware of how one of our parks could have needed $600,000 in unforeseen sewer repairs, which would have made it into a loss situation. We have met other investors who needed expensive repairs on their parks' water and sewer systems and electric and gas lines, which also had a major effect on their profit from their parks. We want to protect you from this and strongly recommend that you go with the contractors and civil engineer who will do the bulk of your infrastructure inspections so you can learn what to look for in the future.

First, we are going to start with *Contractor Inspections of Water, Sewer, Electric, Gas, and Road Systems*. If possible, you are going to meet with two contractors for each of these areas—the contractor who maintains and repairs that system now and a new contractor, who will bring in a fresh point of view. You are also going to get a video of the sewer system lines from a plumbing contractor who specializes in snaking out and clearing sewer clogs. They can use equipment that snakes a line with a small video camera on the end through the sewer pipes to record a video showing whether there are any collapsed sewer lines or lines that have bellied and hold water.

Next, you will want to have *Building and Termite Inspections* on all buildings and park-owned or L/O homes that come with the park, as well as on the swimming pool if there is one. You may be able to do some or all of the inspections yourself if you have experience in the building trades or contracting, but I would not recommend it because you might have the same problem I have. When I am excited about purchasing a park, I become a little blind to its defects. It is a benefit to have a professional whose only concern is protecting you, and it is worth the expense. You will be shown how to inspect park-owned homes later on in this chapter, so you will have knowledge of what to look for. If you are hiring a professional inspector and there are a large group of park owned homes, say twenty or more, you should try to work out a volume discount. If the inspector charges a fee of $250 to $300 per mobile home, which is common, then it will total $6,000 for twenty park-owned home inspections, which is costly.

While you are doing the above inspections, you should *Calculate the Yearly Reserves for Replacements*. Every time you see a piece of machinery, like an air conditioner, a water or sewer pump, electrical apparatus, a golf cart, kitchen equipment, necessary furniture and fixtures, and so on, you should estimate the useful life left in it and the cost to replace it when it wears out. Roofs on structures should also be included in this calculation. Divide the cost to replace it by the years of life left, and that will give you an amount you should put away each year as a reserve. *This is considered a valid expense and should be subtracted from the NOI,* but it is rarely given or even considered by a seller.

Given the concern in recent years over the environment and the liability for damage to it, you need an *Environmental Inspection and Survey* done by an expert to search for pre-existing asbestos, lead paint, underground tanks, wetlands, and so on. The first report is called a Phase I. If the Phase I shows contamination, it will lead to Phase II and III reports, but only if you are still interested in the property. While it is rare to have environmental challenges, they do crop up and are critical in today's world. Most lenders will mandate an environmental inspection report, and even if they don't, you should do one anyway. By the way, just because the land was previously used for agriculture doesn't mean you are exempt from problems. Some farmers have contaminated their fields with outlawed pesticides and even buried environment hazards rather than pay the high cost of moving them offsite. Part of the environmental inspection is a *LUST Survey,* which stands for leaking underground storage tanks. These have become a major problem in the last few decades, especially when petroleum or its products were stored underground. Environmental specialists can also determine if there are any protected wetlands or protected species that can cause you problems. Along this line, your surveyor should supply you with *Flood Plain Information and Possible Drainage Problems,* but I want to add a little test you can do yourself. This comes from two parks we made offers on, as a result of seeing how floods can have a serious effect on the profitability on a mobile home park. Both parks were on lakes and both lakes flooded over their natural banks and into the parks. In one case, the park was perilously close to being shut down and the residents evacuated by the Health Department because the on-site sewage treatment plant was in danger of failing. In the other case, the lowest portion of the park was shut down, which affected fifty of the residents. In each case, *the flooding left water stains and lines on the trees, buildings, and fences in the flooded area.* As my son, who went with me on both inspections, says, "Flooding leaves clues." Look for them.

You should inspect the *Physical Inventory* of the personal property that you are purchasing with the park, specifically the furniture, fixtures, equipment, and supplies in the manager's office and clubhouse, and other common amenities.

You should only be concerned with the next area if you are anticipating expanding the park onto surrounding vacant land. To check the *Potential for Lot Expansion,* you will need to check with the building, zoning, fire, and health departments about the rules and procedures, the minimum lot size, required setbacks, and the age and types of mobile homes that can be placed on those future lots. You will also need to speak to the water, sewer, electric, and gas utility companies about their requirements.

Now we are going to do a simple inspection of the sewage system. There is not much to do if the park just has underground lines leading to the county sewer plant. However, you should pay particular attention to any noxious smells and appearance of deferred maintenance if the park has its own *Sewage Treatment Plant* or *Lift Station.* If the park has septic tanks and drain fields, you should have a septic company inspect each one to see how they are performing. Drain fields can be expensive and difficult to repair or replace. You should also go over the letter the seller supplied from the septic maintenance company with the company's personnel, even meeting with them on site to go over what is performed on a routine basis.

The procedure is similar for the *Water Supply Equipment.* If there are just underground lines leading from the county water lines, great. If there is well equipment, however, you should pay attention to any noxious odors and the appearance of deferred maintenance. It would be advisable to go over the letter the seller supplied to you from the water maintenance company with the water company's personnel, perhaps even meeting with them on site to go over what is performed on a routine basis.

While you are walking around, keep your ears open for any *Noise Problems* from the surrounding area, like trains, loud machinery, and of course, traffic. Also, keep an eye out for any *Tree Work Needed.* Falling tree limbs can be a liability to the park owner if it can be proved they were dead and rotted and the owner did not remove them in a timely manner. A park owner is not responsible if a live limb falls down—it is considered an act of nature. Because of this, many park owners trim trees back so they don't overhang residents' mobile homes.

Now that we've finished looking inside the park as much as possible, let's start looking at the outside perimeter. You need a *Survey* containing all the as-builts (a fancy term for showing where the buildings and improvements are on the property) and the legal description, which you will compare to the legal description for the park that is on your contract. *Make sure they match!* You should get a survey even if you are getting seller financing and not using a third-party lender. It is definitely worth the expense because it will show easements, encroachments, access, and title problems that could dramatically affect a future sale. It would also be nice to have a *Plat Map* from the county zoning department that shows how the lots are laid out.

Now that we're heading outside the park, you should inspect the *Park Location.* First and foremost, how easy is it to find? If it is difficult, you will always have problems finding new residents because they will give up after they get lost. Also, try to imagine from the eyes of potential new residents what they will see when they inspect the park—how near is it to jobs, schools, shopping, health care, churches, and so on. Drive around the neighborhood and see who the neighbors are. When you do that, it would also be helpful to have an *Aerial Photograph* showing adjacent properties. You can easily print one from the Internet using web sites such as Google Earth.

The next part of your due diligence concerns letters from various agencies. You need a *Letter from the Zoning and Building Departments* describing the property's current zoning, any future zoning changes that will affect the property, the number of currently permitted spaces, and the total allowed spaces. You also want to know the procedures for filling empty lots or replacing homes. I have seen cases where changes in zoning laws prevented replacing mobile homes in a park or filling empty lots. Whatever mobile homes that were there before were allowed to remain and were "grandfathered in" but no new mobile homes were allowed. You also want to know the procedures for adding lots on excess land. In almost every park I have contracted that had vacant excess land, the seller or broker made the addition of lots sound simple, easy, quick, and inexpensive. Then when we researched the process, we discovered it was complicated, difficult, time consuming, and expensive.

You also want a *Letter from the Local Code Enforcement Department* certifying that there are no outstanding building code violations in the park, a *Letter from Fire Marshal* certifying that there are no outstanding fire code violations and the inspections are up-to-date, and a *Letter from Health Department* certifying that there are no outstanding health code violations and the septic system and water supply are both in good working order and the permits are up-to-date. The reason you want a letter from the above agencies is because in many municipalities, these agencies don't answer to anyone other than authorities within the agency *and they don't record any violations, liens, fines, or outstanding lawsuits in the public records.* This happened to us on the Palm Frond Mobile Home Park. There was an outstanding fine and violation from the Health Department on the sewer system. This was recorded only in their records, so it did not show up in our title search. We learned about this only after we bought it on the courthouse steps and were ordered to pay a fine of thousands of dollars or the park would be shut down. We did not cause the violation or the resulting fine but we were responsible for it. We had a similar situation in the Calm Lake Mobile Home Park, a park we almost bought, but the residents exercised their first right of refusal and bought it out from under us. In that park, the fire marshal closed down a section containing seven valuable lots right on the waterfront because part of the road had washed away in a hurricane and he was concerned that fire trucks could not reach the residents there. The only papers detailing the closure of those lots were in the fire marshal's files—not the county public records.

The *Engineering Report* of the sewer systems, water systems, gas transmission lines and/or tanks, roads, electrical transmission lines, and so on, is your main reference point for the infrastructure due diligence, even after the contractors inspections. An engineer will tell you if you have any major design defects in the systems and the costs to cure them. Depending on the size of the park, it could take the engineer part of a day or part of a week to do the necessary inspections and research. Naturally, the cost of the report will depend on the time involved. To find a good engineer, ask the lender if he has any firms to recommend. Lacking that, call around and ask other park owners, Realtors, and investors who they would recommend. There are also national engineering firms who specialize on infrastructure inspections.

As mentioned before, once you have an engineer, you should accompany him on the inspection so you can learn more about how to identify problem areas or areas in the infrastructure that may be of concern in the future. If he locates problems or areas of concern, find out the solution to the problem and get an estimate of the cost. If there are corrections that must be taken, you can bid out the solution with local contractors and then bring this up at the end of the due diligence period with the seller. Any and all problems should be handled this way—bring them up with the seller at the end of the due dilly period. Don't stop your due diligence if you encounter a problem, unless it is a major deal killer. In that case, call a time out in the contract, and meet with the seller to discuss solutions and/or price adjustments. See the upcoming section on *Negotiating When Due Diligence Has Surprises* for ways of handling this.

We have not included an *Appraisal* on the property here because an appraisal usually won't be available until after the due diligence period, when you decide to go forward and purchase the park. In that case, you should examine the appraisal for any additional information it may contain, and learn about the comps and cap rates the appraiser used in generating the report.

Site Inspection at Mobile Home Park

You want to have firmly set in your mind what you will be doing on site. If the park is close by, the inspections can be done at different times on different days, depending on your time schedule. If the park is long-distance, your inspections will have to be done at set times because you will you have time constraints on your availability. As you know, the sitting down due diligence can be done by you anywhere. The on your feet due dilly must be done when you are physically inspecting the park—and if you miss something, it will mean another expensive visit. This will lead us to the next topic, doing the due dilly when the park is long-distance.

We have created a site inspection list for you gleaned from all of the due diligence so far. It will remind you what you have to physically inspect in a park and serve as a checklist later on if you are inspecting many parks in one period of time.

THE DUE DILLY FOUR-STEP

We created this process when we were buying mobile home parks that were a long distance from where we live to have a due diligence procedure that was as efficient as possible. We discovered it could be used to buy parks that are close by as well, so it became our main procedure for due dilly. When it takes you a day or two to visit a prospective purchase, plus the expense of plane tickets, hotel rooms, and restaurants, you don't want to make the trip unless the park is worth it. Think about how you will feel after missing days of work, losing time with your loved ones, and spending hundreds, even thousands of dollars or more, only to discover the following:

1. You had no interest in the park and would not have gone if you had better information beforehand.

2. Another offer was accepted while you were traveling or into your due diligence.

3. You required seller financing or other terms that the seller would not consider.

4. The seller changed his mind and took the park off the market.

You have two ways to stop these four unfortunate occurrences from happening:

1. Get enough preliminary due diligence and lots of pictures from the seller beforehand to make a good determination about buying the park.
2. Make an offer, which is accepted, *before you visit the park.* The offer is contingent on your site inspection within a week—or whatever is comfortable—or the offer is null and void.

If a seller absolutely refuses to consider an offer before you visit and conduct an inspection on the park, and the park is long distance and will take up a lot of your time and expense, then our advice is to move on to another park until the seller agrees. It may sound harsh and arbitrary, but we wish we had done that because of all the lost time and money that otherwise resulted. We would not buy a park long distance anymore without an accepted offer beforehand. You will have decisions to make whether to continue, or withdraw at the end of each step, based upon your due diligence. This process is heavily weighted with respect to *your* time and money.

The First Step, Part A: Checking out the Numbers

This step is all sitting down due dilly. It should take you no more than two or three days once you have all the information from the seller. You should order a title commitment immediately upon the contract being approved by both sides, to be delivered to you within one week and before you make your visit. You should have received all the due diligence from the seller, Schedule C, and your contract stated that the due diligence period did not begin until you have received all of this. In this step, your main concern is going over the P&L, the rent roll, and the expenses, and comparing *the numbers you get for the NOI* with what was supplied by the seller or broker.

Does the park really make the gross income you were given? A simple test of this is to take the total amount of occupied lots and multiply by the average rent received. Are the expenses accurate? Compare the expenses you are given on the P&L with the chart of expenses for the average land-lease park, which is 40 percent, and for park-owned units, 50 percent. Are there areas of expenses missing, like management and ground maintenance, as a few examples? Do the insurance documents, the real estate taxes, the service contracts, the payroll, and the utility bills agree with the P&L you were given?

Now you will check the leases, delinquency report, and rent roll. Are there too many residents that are late and owe more than a month's rent? Are there too many new residents? Are the leases in order, or are there sweetheart leases with friends and family of the seller? When was the last time the rents were increased? Do the rules and regulations make sense?

Next you will check Schedule B, the inventory of personal property included in the sale. Is all the equipment you need there? Are all the park-owned units listed, and do they have titles?

Your final step is checking the licenses of the park to see that they are in order, such as the business license, occupancy permit, dock permit, and the water, sewer, and natural gas permits. You will call the agencies and ask if the licenses are current with no violations.

Decision One, Part A: *Are there large discrepancies in the P&L and NOI, and is there any doubt about the ability of the park to earn a reasonable profit? Are the permits in order—is the park a going business?*

If you have doubts, you will need to discuss them with the seller and rectify the doubts or withdraw. If everything looks okay for now, you will proceed to Part B of the First step, all of which is information you gather.

The First Step, Part B: Your Own Market Survey

If you made it to Part B, then the park is capable of turning a profit and the permits appear to be in order. Now you are going to do the *Due Diligence You Gather Yourself,* which involves your own market survey and checking for problems with regulatory agencies. This should take three or four more days. This is still sitting down due dilly, with lots of phone calling and Internet research.

You can see from the list that you will be getting comps and checking out the affordable housing market, calling brokers and dealers, and

Due Diligence You Gather Yourself

- ❏ ***Your Own Market Survey***—comparable sales, lot rents in area, vacancies in other parks, prices of single-family homes and mobile home/land deals, learning whether the owner has other parks, teaser ads, and rent on three-bedroom apartments. A great resource is JLT Associates (http://jlt-associates.com/).
- ❏ ***Current Management Ability***—have someone call to see how management handles prospects
- ❏ ***Interview Local Mobile Home Dealers and Real Estate Brokers***
- ❏ ***Check School Districts and Demographics***—housing, income levels, population centers
- ❏ ***Letter from Chamber of Commerce or Planning Department***—job creation, population, and unemployment rate for previous five years, present rate, and next five years, companies moving in or out of area (potential employers of residents)
- ❏ ***Letter from Police Department*** showing calls to park in last year and reason for the call
- ❏ ***Potential for Lot Expansion***—check with building, zoning, fire, and health departments about rules and procedures, required lot size, setbacks, age and types of mobile homes
- ❏ ***Potential for Expansion of Water, Sewer, Electric and Gas Lines***
- ❏ ***Park Location***—easy to find, nearness to jobs, schools, shopping, health care, churches, and so on
- ❏ ***Aerial Photographs***—showing adjacent properties
- ❏ ***Letter from Zoning and Building Department***—current zoning, future zoning changes, permitted spaces, total allowed spaces, procedures to fill empty lots or replace homes
- ❏ ***Letter from Code Enforcement Department***—certifying that there are no outstanding code violations
- ❏ ***Letter from Fire Marshall***—certifying that there are no outstanding violations and inspections are up to date
- ❏ ***Letter from Health Department***—certifying that there are no violations, and that water and septic systems are okay and permits are current

getting the prices of single-family homes and any land/home mobile home packages. You will also be ordering letters from the Health, Code Enforcement, Fire Marshall, Zoning and Building, and Police Departments. You will be talking to the Chamber of Commerce and/or Planning Department about the growth and/or loss of jobs and population.

Decision One, Part B: *Is the park priced right relative to the market? Is there too much competition? Are there serious violations? Are the area and the park good investments?*

If you have doubts, you will need to discuss them with the seller and rectify the doubts or withdraw. If everything looks okay for now, you will proceed to step two, setting up your on-site inspection, the on your feet due dilly. Before you leave you should have a title commitment showing that the title is clean. You will arrange the following for your on-site inspection:

1. Meetings with electrical, plumbing, sewer, gas, and road contractors—two of each type of contractor, the one used by the park owner and a new neutral party.

2. A meeting with a local attorney to go over the law, to review eviction procedures, rent raising procedures, permits, and other such information.

3. A plat map or previous survey and aerial photographs of the park and the surrounding area (which you can get from the Internet).

The Second Step: Site Inspection—Off the Desk and On Your Feet

This should be happen a week after the due diligence period started. There is going to be a day or two of using your own senses to evaluate the park and meet people who will be important in helping you discover and overcome any problems. The first people you will meet will be the residents and the manager. You will be asking them questions as if a relative or a friend needs a place, and you're wondering about them moving into the park. That won't be a lie—when the park is running well under your management you will recommend it as a place to live when it is appropriate for a friend or relative.

At this time, you can't say that you are buying the park because that will upset everyone: the residents, the manager, and the owner. Every-

Inspection Checklist When Visiting a Property

- ❑ ***Interview Residents and Manager***
- ❑ ***Check Pets***—look for dangerous breeds
- ❑ ***Inventory Lots***—count lots, measure them, note what's on each lot (type and age of mobile homes), whether units are tied down, count how many vacant lots, how many vacant mobile homes, whether there are mobile homes that need to be removed, and if there are utilities on vacant lots
- ❑ ***Type of Mobile Homes***—single-wides, double-wides, age, condition, size
- ❑ ***Type of Residents***—blue collar, middle class, retired, family; whether there is any criminal or drug activity
- ❑ ***Utilities***—who pays water, sewer, gas, trash, lights, mowing, snow, and common areas
- ❑ ***Flood Plain and Drainage Problems***—water lines on trees and buildings
- ❑ ***Noise Problems***
- ❑ ***Tree Work Needed***
- ❑ ***Survey***—check access, easements, encroachments; match the legal description against description of what you are buying; obtain a ***Plat Map***
- ❑ ***Physical Inventory***—note and check condition of furniture, fixtures, equipment, and supplies
- ❑ ***Building and Termite Inspections***—arrange for your own inspections
- ❑ ***Calculate Yearly Reserves for Replacements***—for buildings and infrastructure
- ❑ ***Contractor Inspections of Water, Sewer, Electric, Gas, and Roads; obtain a Video of Sewer Lines***
- ❑ ***Sewage Treatment Plant***—smells, appearance, verify with maintenance company

- ❑ ***Water Supply and Wells***—check smells, appearance, verify condition with maintenance company
- ❑ ***Current Management Ability***—perform your own assessment
- ❑ ***Visit Park***—at different times, especially weekend nights
- ❑ ***Park Location***—is it easy to find, near to jobs, schools, shopping, health care, churches, and so on
- ❑ ***Aerial Photographs***—showing adjacent properties
- ❑ ***Inspect Neighboring Properties and Their Character***
- ❑ ***Eviction Procedure***—visit attorney specializing in mobile home park evictions, go over procedure, get a legal opinion on the mobile home park operating permit and rent raising procedure
- ❑ ***Interview Local Bankers and Mortgage Broker***—viability of getting financing
- ❑ ***Interview Local Mobile Home Dealers and Real Estate Brokers***

one is going to see you measuring lots, inspecting the utilities, and meeting contractors shortly. That is not what someone who is looking for a mobile home for a friend or relative does. *It would be best to say that the owner has asked you to do a report on the insurance for the park—which will not be a lie. You will ask the owner to ask you to do that, and put it in writing.*

Next, you will meet the utility contractors, a mortgage broker and community banker, your attorney, local Realtors, and mobile home dealers. You will be following the Inspection Checklist When Visiting a Property, the on your feet due dilly, starting from inside the park and working your way outside.

As you can see, there are many people to meet and a lot of things to see, touch, feel, and smell. You may want to make the first site inspection over two days or more, rather than one, depending on everyone's schedule. The highlights of this visit are your inspection of the lots, the residents, the mobile homes, the buildings, and the infrastructure inside the park. Then you will be evaluating the neighboring area and the legal considerations with your attorney. You will be walking around and driving the park and the area both night and day.

DECISION Two, Part A: *Is this a park that you want to buy? Are there serious problems to be overcome regarding NOI, residents, the community and its laws, or the infrastructure?*

If you have doubts, you need to discuss them with the seller and rectify the doubts or withdraw. If everything looks okay, you must make a decision on the availability of financing from the lenders and/or mortgage broker.

DECISION Two, Part B: *Is third party financing available?*

You are going to spending a lot more money on the due dilly you pay for, so you need to be reasonably sure now that you can get financing. You don't want to purchase a lot of expensive reports on a park you can't buy because you couldn't get a loan. If third party financing is possible, you will proceed. If financing is not possible, you will have to ask for owner-financing or withdraw.

If you proceed because financing appears available, you will be ordering the following:

1. Phase I Environmental

2. Sewer video

3. Land survey—updated if already available

4. Engineering inspection of infrastructure

5. Building and termite inspections on park owned homes and buildings

6. Placing test ads in newspapers

You should be present for these inspections if possible, and in the beginning, you should come back a second time to meet the people who perform your reports.

The Third Step: Completed Due Diligence

It's the end of the due diligence period. You should have finished all your due diligence and have all the reports from the due dilly you pay for.

DECISION Three: *Are there still serious problems to be overcome regarding the NOI, the residents, the community and its laws, or the infrastructure?*

You are either ready to go forward, or you have a list to talk to the seller about, or you want to withdraw. If you go forward, you will start the financing process.

The Fourth Step: Financing

In Step Two you got a good indication from a community bank or mortgage broker that they could finance the property. You will now pay for the appraisal and wait for your loan approval. If you arranged for all-owner financing, proceed to closing and skip Decision Four—congratulations!

DECISION Four: *Is financing approved?*

If you get acceptable financing, you buy the park. Congratulations!

If you are turned down by the lender, even after they led you to believe that financing was possible, or you don't like the lender's terms, you can still ask for an extension to find another lender. If that is not possible, you ask the seller to give owner financing, or the deal is over.

NEGOTIATING WHEN DUE DILIGENCE HAS SURPRISES

No park is perfect—every park has problems and challenges. Some are small and easily handled, and the park will still create wealth for you. Others parks can have challenges that are costly, time consuming, and aggravating. Don't assume that the contract is null and void because your due dilly turned up challenges. The deal may still be completed, given the right circumstances.

Keep in mind— you contracted to buy a park that was in good working order, not perfect, and you priced it accordingly. An adjustment in price is reasonable and expected if your due diligence revealed that the park had serious challenges and problems that meant it was not in good working order. Sometimes you will find out the following from the due diligence:

- The NOI is incorrect
- The Management is different than what you expected
- The infrastructure has problems
- The long-term outlook of the park is different from what you expected

Now—first and foremost—you need to have a helpful mindset, not an angry and defensive one. You should act as if it was just human error even if you are sure the seller knew about the problems, lied about the information, or committed out-and-out fraud. There is nothing wrong with buying a good park from a marginal person if the price and terms are right. Isn't it better to have a good park, owned and managed by a good caretaker, namely you?

With that in mind, if the due diligence showed serious challenges at any point, you need to set up a meeting with the seller and/or broker to go over the problem with them with an eye toward getting adjustments to the contract and an extension to the inspections. You should not tell the seller that. Just say you want to have a meeting to go over some concerns before you agree to buy the park. You should go into the meeting prepared, with each problem documented, and knowing the cost to solve it, who is going to fix it and when, and how much you want deducted from the price.

At the meeting, approach each problem as if you are puzzled about it and are asking the seller for help. Say something like, "Mr. Seller, you said the NOI was $100,000 for the park, but my analysis shows the NOI is only $80,000. Could you help me out here and show me what I did wrong?" or "Mrs. Seller, you told me the sewer system worked perfectly but I have an inspection report that shows otherwise. Could you explain this to me and show me what I am overlooking?"

Yes, you probably didn't do anything wrong or overlook something—the seller did. But if you have a spirit of cooperation, then you can explain to the seller that price and NOI go hand-in-hand, and you won't be able to get a bank loan, and neither will others, based on an NOI of $100,000 when the NOI is really $20,000 less. The solution is a lower price. You can also explain that when you have to spend $10,000 after you buy the park to fix something, then that money should be rebated to you from the seller at closing.

Perhaps the above sounds wimpy to you, but the aggressive way of doing it, like: "Mr. Seller, you lied to me and misstated the NOI by $20,000, which translates into a $200,000 higher price, and there is no way in hell I am paying for the park using your overinflated numbers! You better give me an adjustment in price or I am suing you for fraud!" is probably not going to get you anywhere and will shut down the transaction.

Most sellers will be cooperative and will adjust the contract so that both sides can proceed forward. When that happens, you will add an additional addendum, marked "D," to modify the previous terms. Some sellers, however, will insist on the original terms of the contract, regardless of whatever your due diligence shows. In that case, you either decide the park can still be a good deal and stay with the contract, or walk away. Again, you should walk away nicely, as you were shown in the chapter on negotiating. *It's critical to walk away nicely when you are trying to buy a mobile home park, because we have seen contracts that were negotiated for years before both sides could agree on terms.*

Preparing Due Diligence When You are Selling

The kind of information you now know you want when you are interested in buying a park will also guide you when it becomes time to sell one of your parks. You will want to provide this information to your prospective buyers in five stages:

1. Initial listing—usually just a few lines in an ad or on the Internet
2. Color brochure—summary NOI and P&L information and a few pictures when prospective buyers inquire from the ads
3. Follow-up package—with detailed information on the rent roll and P&L and lots of pictures, given to buyers who respond favorably to the brochure.
4. Physical inspection of park
5. Complete package of due diligence—containing everything a professional investor in mobile home parks would want, after the buyer indicates that he or she wants to make an offer

If the buyer is a long distance away, the fifth step will replace the fourth step, with an inspection to follow within a week after an agreed contract.

The better real estate brokers will spend a lot of time at the beginning of the listing, preparing the three packages of information before they start the marketing—the color brochure, the follow-up package, and the complete final package. Some brokers may not even put the property on the market until all the information is completed and the price of the listing is fully justified to a professional mobile home park investor. The best real estate brokers will refuse to list a park at anything other than a justifiable price—they don't want to waste their time or advertising money on overpriced listings and undermotivated sellers.

INSPECTIONS OF INDIVIDUAL MOBILE HOMES

You can get a professional mobile home inspector to do a complete inspection on individual park-owned mobile homes that you are considering buying for around $250-$300. Should you spend the money or do it yourself? The answer is yes, and yes.

If you have extensive well-rounded experience in the building and construction trades, then by all means, save the money and do the inspections on the individual mobile homes yourself. If you don't have experience—and most people don't—then spend the money and hire a professional home inspector. It will be the best money you spend until you become experienced in spotting the problems that you will face.

We are going to discuss doing the inspections yourself in the next part of this chapter, but again, you would be much better served by hiring a professional home inspector if you are inexperienced. Then follow him or her around during the inspection and take notes. Study the inspection sheet on the next page with that in mind. It lets you to inspect two mobile homes at a time and lists the parts of the home, the foundation, and the yard.

Inspecting Simplified

The simplest way to inspect a mobile home is to picture yourself starting at the top and then working your way down and all around. Starting at the top means you will begin with the roof. Then check out the attic or crawlspace, if there is one that is accessible, then the mobile home itself. Then look under the mobile home to see how it is supported and how the utilities are connected, including the water, septic, and electric lines. Then work your way around the mobile home to the outside yard. Let's take these steps one point at a time.

The Roof

It all begins with the roof. If the roof is faulty, the damage to the home can be catastrophic over time. Therefore, you must make sure the roof is

INSPECTIONS

	Property 1	Property 2
Address		
Type		
Location		
Curb Appeal		
Yard		
Style House		
Construction		
Roof Soffit		
Chimney		
Septic/Water		
Foundation		
Garage		
# Bedrooms		
# Baths		
Living Area		
Plumbing		
Electric		
Heat/Cool		
Hot Water		
Attic		
Basement		
Windows		
Doors		
Walls		
Ceilings		
Kitchen		
Appliances		
Bath 1		
Bath 2		
Master Bedroom		
Bedroom 2		
Bedroom 3		
Laundry		
Bugs/Termite		
REPAIRS		
Paint		
Carpet		
Other		
Notes		

functional. There are usually two kinds of roofs on ...tal and shingle. Older mobile homes are usually metal ...ly called "metal on metal" homes because the roof and ... metal. Newer mobile homes are usually "shingle and vinyl" with the common three-tab roofing shingle and lapped vinyl siding. There is a third type of roof, called a "roof over," which is used when an older mobile home needs a replacement roof. A roof over is a whole new metal roof, with new insulation under it, attached in place over the old metal roof.

There are three inspections you should do when you check for roof leaks. The first is to get a ladder and climb up and look. Even better—if you are light and athletic—you can walk around the roof and inspect it closely. After a visual inspection of the top of the roof, you should then look inside the crawl space, if it is accessible. Look for leaks that show up as stains on the trusses and also for water and/or termite damage. The last roof inspection is on the ceiling inside the mobile home. Anytime you see stains, or stains that are covered over with paint, or any new paint on a ceiling, it is a sign that you should inspect the roof carefully. Unscrupulous sellers will hide active ceiling leaks by painting them with a primer (like Kilz) over the stains, and then match up the ceiling with new ceiling paint. If you happen to notice a change in color—however slight—in the ceiling paint, point it out to the seller. An unscrupulous seller and an honest seller may both follow up with, "There used to be a ceiling leak, but we fixed it." Do not take a seller's word that a leak has been fixed. The best way to test the truth of whether a roof leaks on a mobile home is to run a hose over a wide area of the roof where you suspect there is or was a leak. If there is still a leak, you will hear or see a drip or see a fresh new stain.

Don't think it is the kiss of death on buying a mobile home if there is a roof leak. Fixing a mobile home roof is usually easy. On metal roofs—if you get to any damage soon enough—you will first clean and bleach the roof to remove dirt, leaves, mold, and mildew. If there are rust spots, use rust-treatment paint that chemically changes the rust to a dark, solid coating. If there are holes, take a piece of sheet metal, put roofing cement underneath it, and screw the patch to the roof. Whether there are rust spots or holes, finish the repair by covering the effected area with a thick, white, elastomeric coating. We usually go one step further and cover the whole roof with Kool Seal, which is an elastomeric white coating that is applied with a roller, like paint. Kool Seal stops the leaks and protects a roof for five years or more before you have to clean it and apply another coating. Kool Seal comes in five-gallon pails and costs about $60 per pail. One to three pails will be needed, depending on the size of the mobile home. We prefer using Kool Seal instead of doing a complete "roof over" because a roof over can cost $2,000 to $4,000, while a complete coating with Kool Seal will cost between $200 to $400.

On shingle roofs, the solution to leaks is the same on mobile homes as it is on site-built homes—replace the worn or damaged shingles or the whole roof if it is required. On shingle roofs that only need repair you should hammer back down any nails that have popped up and recoat the roofing cement around any of the perforations in the roof such as plumbing vent stacks. No matter what kind of roof is on the mobile home, chances are the perimeter of the vent stacks need to be recoated with roofing cement if you see ceiling stains in the bathroom and/or kitchen. Roofing cement lasts from three to five years before it loses its elasticity and begins to crack and leak. It is also a good idea to run rain gutters along the front and back, or wherever the longer sides of the roof are, because many mobile homes have short roof overhangs or no overhangs at all. By putting on a rain gutter you can keep a driving rain from coming in along the seam between the roof and sides of the home and then rotting the wood on the inside of the exterior walls.

The Crawlspace

Most older mobile homes have a small, completely enclosed crawlspace between the roof and the inside ceilings, so an inspection can not be accomplished without cutting out parts of the ceiling. This is not recommended unless you suspect a major problem is hidden there. However, there are some mobile homes that have an accessible space between the roof and the ceiling where you can examine roof trusses, ceiling joists, wiring, plumbing, or air conditioning (A/C) ducts. If you have an accessible crawl space, you can spot roof leaks more easily, and also see any termite damage in the joists or trusses and leaks in the A/C ductwork.

The Inside of the Mobile Home

The bulk of your inspection time is going to be spent on the inside of the mobile home. When you inspect the inside, you should go from the top down once again. Begin with the ceilings, then run your eyes down along the walls, and finish up on the floor. If there are plumbing fixtures or electrical appliances between the wall and the floor, detour to them and then continue your inspection downward.

When you inspect the ceilings, look for changes in color or patches that indicate a past or present roof problem above. As we discussed before, the problems may have been fixed by the owner or just covered up. The only way to determine if the problem lingers is to take a hose and run water over the roof above the area where the problem is or was, and listen or watch for leaks. You should also look for sagging, bulging, or changes in the level of the ceilings. This indicates a structural problem in the joists or trusses, which will require an inspection of the crawlspace. Once we bought a vacant RV park model at a foreclosure sale that had a sag in the ceiling in the kitchen. The neighbors warned us that there had been a leak in that area, but there were no patches or changes in ceiling color indicating a prior leak. We had our handyman take down the ceiling tiles during the renovation—a major job requiring two days—and we discovered that one of the ceiling joists had cracked and another had bowed over the years. We replaced both of them with two-by-fours and reattached the tiles, and the sagging was eliminated. When we sold that RV park model, those same neighbors informed the new buyer of the problem during her inspection, so we showed her pictures of what we found in the ceiling and how we repaired it.

The walls are easy to inspect. There are five problems you are most likely to find: The first is that the windows are no longer operable and have to be replaced. Second, the wallboard or paneling under the windows is discolored or needs to be replaced because the window was left open in the rain. Third, there are leaks along the top edge of the ceiling because of a short or nonexistent overhang between the roof and the exterior walls (as I said above, this can be corrected by installing rain gutters between the roof and the top of the exterior walls). Fourth, the doors are damaged and need to be repaired and/or replaced. Last but not least, there are active termites, in which case there will be a sawdustlike material, discarded wings, or mud tunnels deposited on the floor along the bottom of the walls.

Permit me to add a word about termites here. Mobile homes get termites with the same frequency and intensity as site-built homes. There are basically two kinds of termites—airborne, which have wings, and subterranean, which come up from the ground through mud tunnels they construct. There are two ways to treat airborne termites—either by enclosing the entire home with a tent and then emitting a poison gas inside, or by spot-treating an infestation with chemicals. Subterranean termites are treated by injecting the ground with poison so they die when they return to the ground to get water. I have spent hundreds of thousands of dollars to treat termites and correct the damage they have caused. There were two very bad cases. The first case involved a site-built house in which 75 percent of the exterior walls had been destroyed by subterranean termites and had to be rebuilt. We were amazed that the house had continued to stand before we started, considering all the structural damage. In the second case, we had a mobile home in one of our parks that was so weakened by termites that we feared for the life of the owner. After he ignored our warnings and refused to replace the mobile home, we evicted him and threw it away. In every case you should inspect a mobile home thoroughly to be sure of what termite damage lies in wait for you, but don't panic. You can fix almost any infestation—it's just a matter of time and money.

Plumbing fixtures and electrical appliances are easy to inspect—you turn them on, and if they run, they work. You can also call in an appliance expert to get a more in-depth picture of how much life is left in the stove, refrigerator, air conditioner, heater, dishwasher, washer, and/or dryer, if you want. On the plumbing side, bathroom and kitchen sinks have common replacement parts. Many times the bottom on the inside of the cabinets has been destroyed by a water leak; this is easily fixed by replacing it with a new piece of plywood and painting it. Bathtubs can be problematic because many older mobile homes have odd-sized plastic tubs that develop cracks. We have tried patching over the cracks with fiberglass repair kits, but this proved to be a temporary fix that just postponed total replacement. When we replace an old plastic tub, we try to adapt the space to accept a common five-foot long metal bathtub, as these are more durable and easier to find than the old plastic tubs.

Test all of the outlets along the walls to see if they are working or have problems. A simple way to test them is to plug in a drill and see if it runs, or you can purchase a tester that lights up if the outlet works. It is not unusual to have a few dead outlets in mobile homes, but it is usually not a big problem to have them fixed.

Floors are the last part of the inspection and are one of the areas where you will find the most problems. Somewhere between 1960 and 1990, mobile home manufacturers discovered that particle board—composition board made from sawdust and glue—saved them about $50-$100 over using good quality plywood. This decision cost us, and every other owner of older mobile homes, thousands of dollars in repairs. Particle board is strong only as long as it remains dry. As soon as it gets wet it absorbs the water, swells, and then has the strength of a pile of sawdust. Therefore, when there are particle board floors in a mobile home, you will find weak spots or even holes in the floor in bathrooms, around the kitchen sink, in front of the doors, and underneath windows. Many times, the only thing that will keep you from falling through a floor is the rug or linoleum covering it. There is an easy but time consuming fix. You have to cut out the area that is weakened, square it off between floor joists, perhaps add cross bracing between the floor joists, and then replace the particle board with good quality plywood. You may have to shim the replacement board to compensate for height differences. If the floor needs so many repairs that cutting out and replacing each weak spot will be very time consuming, then you may want to completely cover the old particle board with half- or three-quarter-inch plywood and screw it down into the floor joists underneath.

The Exterior

When you examine the exterior of the home, look for dents and holes in the siding and leaks around the windows and doors. It is easy to repair old siding on mobile homes with metal siding. Simply unscrew the panel from the home, replace it with a new panel, and paint it to match. Windows and doors are also easily unscrewed and replaced. Putty should put around window and door flanges to insure a watertight repair.

Let me say this about old mobile homes and paint. If you clean the exterior walls well and then paint them with good-quality semigloss paint, it will make a world of difference in the mobile home. It is simply amazing how good an old mobile home will look after it gets a paint job. We paint all of our mobile homes white with a green or brown trim. They seem to look better than if you paint them all one color, like blue or brown or red. If the home has vinyl siding, that also is easy to repair and even paint if the siding is old and faded.

The Foundation Underneath the Frame

The foundation of a mobile home is usually made up of cement blocks placed under the metal chassis of the home. A plastic plate is placed on the ground underneath the blocks, and wooden or plastic shims, which are used to level the home, are placed on the top block under the metal chassis. The mobile home is tied down with metal straps that extend from the metal chassis to ground anchors, which are dug about four or five feet into the ground and either cemented in or placed at an angle. The straps are placed at intervals, usually five feet apart, along the chassis. Recently in Florida, building departments have required mobile homes have two large metal straps—one in the front and one in the back—running completely around the sides and over and around the roof. The straps are anchored and tied down to the ground for additional protection against the mobile home being blown over.

If the mobile home is attached to a permanent cement or mortared foundation, or stem wall, instead of the more common cement block, inspect for shifting or cracking of the walls, and how the mobile home is attached to the foundation (straps or tie-downs).

In some parts of the country mobile homes are blocked and leveled but not tied down. We strongly recommend against this practice. If there is a sudden windstorm or a vehicle accidentally hits the home, without tie-downs the mobile home could fall off its foundation blocks, possibly causing serious damage and human injury.

No matter how the mobile home is tied down, skirting must be placed between the bottom of the mobile home and the ground to make the space underneath inaccessible to animals. Some of our tenants, mostly native Southerners, like to take off the skirting and chain their dogs to the tie-down straps so the dogs can rest underneath the trailer, out of the sun. But then the dogs chews up the A/C duct work, or whatever else is chewable, when they are bored. In hot climates without freezes, use ventilated skirting to cool off the home. In freezing climates, use skirting that provides insulation to keep pipes and ductwork from freezing.

Utilities

While you are under the mobile home checking out the foundation, check the utility hookups—water, sewer, electric, gas, A/C ductwork, and telephone and cable lines.

Make sure there is a main water shutoff so you can work on the plumbing without calling the water company to turn off the water. If you are in an area prone to cold temperatures and freezing, make sure that functional heat tape is wrapped along the aboveground portion of the water pipe. Determine how water is supplied to the mobile home—whether by a public utility or your own private well. If there is county water, check the condition of the meter can and the water lines entering and leaving it. If there is a well, you may want to have an expert check out the equipment and the volume of the water supplied, because wells can be very expensive to replace—$1,000 to $5,000 or more. You should avoid any unpleasant surprises by having an expert inspect the system.

Septic systems are as important as water systems. If you have county septic, check that the pipes are not leaking into the ground and that they run free when the toilets are flushed. If there is a septic tank, have it pumped and inspected. This inspection will show if the tank is cracked or damaged and also if the drain field is operational. The drain field has failed and should be replaced if you hear water leaking back into the tank from the drain field when the tank is pumped with the house water shut off. Drain fields can also run from $1,000 to $5,000 or more, so you might want to call in an expert for an inspection.

The electric system should be, at a minimum, 100 amps. If the system produces fewer than 100 amps, you can still get along if you use a gas stove, a gas dryer, and a gas hot water heater. If there are fuses, you probably will want to replace the box with circuit breakers for convenience. If the wiring is aluminum, make a note of this. Some manufacturers decided to use it to save short-term money—and, as with particle board, gave investors long-term aggravation. Let me issue a warning if the wiring supplying the trailer is underground and is aluminum: when someone digging close by nicks aluminum wiring with a shovel, the wiring will eventually short out into the ground. In this case it will either supply only 110 volts instead of 220, or supply 220 volts when it should supply 110, which will burn up all the 110 volt appliances. We have had this problem numerous times in our mobile home parks, and it drove us crazy until we figured it out.

Test all gas lines for leakage by using a soapy solution at the joints. Please do not use a match to test for gas leaks, as one of my handyman used to do before I stopped him. You should also find out who owns the tank and who supplies the gas.

Phone lines, cable lines, and satellite dishes are usually taken care of by the companies themselves, but you should test them to make sure they work. When it comes to satellite dishes, we insist that the companies attach them on their own poles, not to the roofs or sides of our mobile homes, where we can sustain damage that they will not repair.

Last, but not least, check the A/C ductwork underneath to make sure it is in good shape, doesn't leak, and hasn't been chewed up by a dog or cat or possum. It usually is inexpensive to buy new flexible ductwork if it needs to be replaced.

The Yard

When you inspect the yard, look for deep holes that could cause someone to break an ankle if they step into it and for abandoned septic tanks or deep wells that aren't filled in. Also, it is very important to look for signs of flooding or soil erosion from flooding. Most mobile homes are set three to four feet off the ground, providing ample protection from severe flooding, but the less serious kind of flooding that covers the ground with six inches of water or more for long periods of time can also cause serious damage, and if you are renting out the mobile home, could cause a tenant to move. Ground-level septic tanks and drain fields will not operate if there is water covering the ground above them. Flooding leaves stains, so the easiest way to tell if there has been flooding is look for stains on the blocks, trees, and steps. In South Florida, we have areas that flood so badly in the summertime that people have to park their cars down the road and then paddle a canoe to their home.

SETTING UP A MOBILE HOME FROM SCRATCH

If you are like me, you will be as nervous as a cat on a hot tin roof the first time you install a mobile home on a vacant lot. You'll worry about all sorts of things. Will the mobile home fall off the blocks? Will the utility connections break loose? Will the well go dry or the septic system back up? And so on. But after you do your first install and see how easy and logical it is, you will laugh at yourself and feel a deep sense of empowerment. Turning a vacant parcel of land that produces no cash flow into a mobile home ATM feels just plain good!

I'm going to talk you through the full setup listed in the inset for installing a mobile home on a parcel that never had one before. First, you will need to secure a permit if your local zoning department requires one—and most will. You may also need engineered drawings that show how the mobile home will be placed on a foundation or blocks and then tied down. Your county or municipality may require that you pay impact fees, which are taxes charged to cover the impact that new development will have on future infrastructure such as roads, schools, parks, libraries, and so on.

Once you secure a permit, get the site ready for your mobile home. You may have to clear the land of trees and vegetation, add or remove dirt or fill, and provide proper drainage so rain and snow drains away from the home. You will also have to figure out where utilities should go and put marking stakes into the ground.

Next, you will mark the corners where your mobile home will be placed. Most mobile homes are rectangles, so this is easy to do. Make sure the home will actually fit on the site, conform to the zoning setbacks and regulations, and be compatible with the utility hookups. If so, install your utilities—the well, the septic, the electric, and so on, to make sure everything is functioning before you move the home in.

Anatomy of a Mobile Home

1. End rail
2. J rail
3. Top starter panel
4. Exterior metal panel
5. Double hung (egress) window
6. Mobile home exterior door
7. Bottom starter corner
8. Wall sheathing
9. Carpeting
10. Carpet pad
11. Heat duct system
12. Furnace base
13. Running gear (wheels, tires, axles)
14. Bottom plate
15. Gusset
16. Water supply lines
17. Drain line/Sewer pipe
18. Fiberglass flooring insulation
19. Bottom barrier (blackboard, belly board, shepherd board, etc.)
20. Junior I-beam (main rail)
21. Outrigger
22. A-frame
23. Hitch & jack
24. Front cross member
25. Floor joists (16" on center)
26. Stringer
27. Vapor barrier
28. Floor underlayment
29. Bottom sill
30. Vinyl floor covering
31. Fiberglass insulation in exterior walls
32. 2" x 4" studs (16" on center)
33. Header
34. Top plate
35. Belt rails
36. Second layer of fiberglass roof insulation
37. Ceiling panels
38. Second roof vapor barrier
39. Truss rafter
40. Tie rail (cross rafter)
41. First roof vapor barrier
42. First layer of fiberglass roof insulation
43. Galvanized steel roof
44. Furnace roof stack
45. Electrical outlet box
46. Electrical wires

Illustrations represent typical mobile home construction and components which sometimes vary by manufacturer.

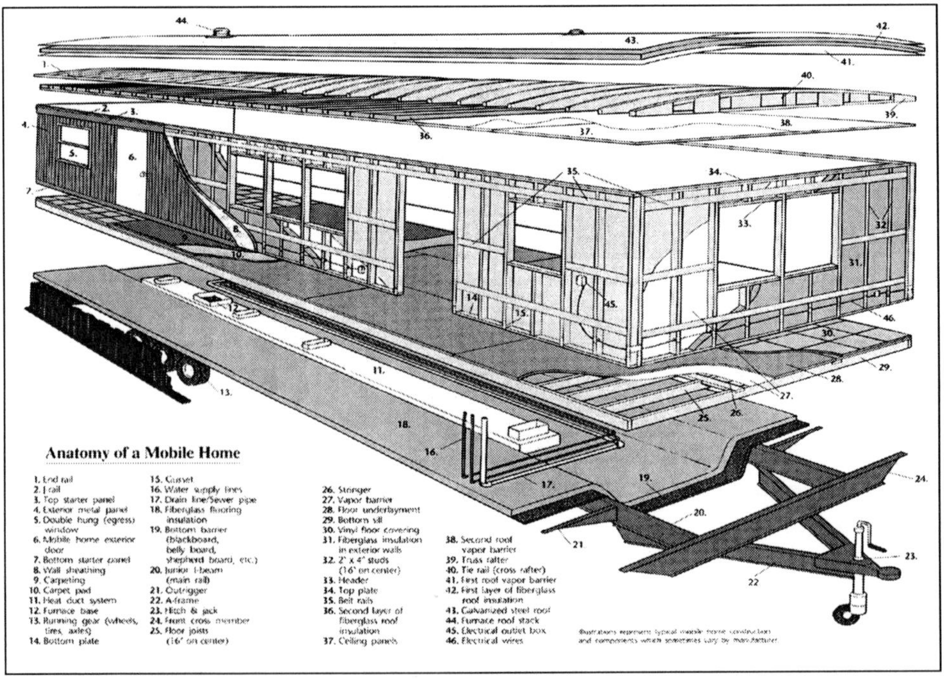

Setting Up a Mobile Home

- Get a move-on permit (this may require engineered drawings), pay impact fees
- Prepare the lot by clearing, adding fill, and providing adequate drainage
- Locate the utility hookups and stake them out—make sure the mobile home (M/H) will fit
- Stake out the corners of the M/H
- Install new utilities—water, sewer, electric, gas, phone, cable, etc.
- Move the M/H onto the site, if it is a double-wide, move in the second section and attach it
- Block and level the M/H at a desirable height, install tie-downs
- Install steps and/or porches
- Hook up the utilities to the mobile home, call for inspections
- After tie-down and utility inspections, put on skirting
- Pave the driveway, carport, sidewalks, etc.
- Install additions like sunroom, carport, storage sheds, etc.
- Put in sod and landscaping; call for the final certificate of occupancy (C/O) inspection

Now you will move the home in, set it on blocks or a foundation, level it, and tie it down. If it is a double-wide, do the same to both sections after connecting them securely, and do any necessary finish work on the roof ridge and on the interior and exterior connections. When the home is blocked, leveled, and tied down, install the steps and porches and make all the connections to the utilities. When everything is completed, call for an inspection to be sure you comply with all the applicable building codes.

Once the inspections are finished, put the skirting around the home and finish the exterior, including the driveways, carports or garages, sidewalks, sunrooms, storage sheds, and so on. Before you call for a final inspection for a certificate of occupancy, place the sod and landscaping.

Replacing an Existing Mobile Home

As you can see, replacing an existing mobile home has fewer steps—eight instead of thirteen. You still need permits and drawings, but you won't have to pay impact fees because there already was a mobile home on the site. You still have to locate the utility connections and stake out the corners of the new mobile home to insure it is going to fit and comply with any required setbacks. You won't have to install the utilities because they were installed for the previous mobile home, and this will save you time and money.

One again, you will block, level, and tie down the replacement mobile home and then attach the utilities and install the steps and porches. When you are finished, you will call for tie-down and utility inspections. Successfully completing these inspections will result in a certificate of occupancy. Then you can skirt the home and you are done. Driveways, sod, and landscaping do not need to be added.

As you can imagine, the actual work of replacing an existing mobile home can be done in a matter of hours. However, depending on the zoning and building departments' schedules, the time you will need to obtain permits and inspections could add weeks to the timeframe.

Replacing an Existing Mobile Home

- Get a move-on permit (this may require engineered drawings)—*no* impact fees
- Locate the utility hookups and stake them out—make sure the M/H will fit
- Stake out the corners of the M/H
- Move the M/H onto the site, if double-wide, move in the second section and attach it
- Block and level the M/H at a desirable height, install tie-downs
- Install the steps and/or porches
- Hook up the utilities to the mobile home; call for inspections
- After tie-down and utility inspections, put on the skirting, install any additions, call for final C/O

SUMMARY

We have covered the essentials of doing inspections on mobile home parks and individual mobile homes. For mobile home parks, we have laid out a logical method to evaluate the future little town over which you may become mayor. There are three important areas to be concerned with: the profitability of the town, the people who inhabit it and the laws they live by, and the infrastructure that supplies the little town's basic needs. You are excited about the wealth that little town creates, but you have been cautioned about potential problems with infrastructure that you need to be aware of *before* you accept ownership. If there are problems, that is okay, because no mobile home park is 100 percent perfect. You just have to be able to solve the problems and take the cost and time into account in your due diligence.

When it comes to individual mobile homes, you have learned there is very little difference in the inspection of a mobile home or a site built house. If anything, it is easier to do a mobile home inspection because it is usually easier to get access underneath the home and the utility connections are simple. If you don't feel comfortable yet with your level of expertise in inspections, then hire a licensed home inspection company. It is well worth the expense. In many cases it won't be an expense but will save you money in the long run if the inspection company finds something that needs to be repaired. Also, if you have a handyman who can do the work instead of hiring a subcontractor, there can be enough cost-savings to pay for the inspection report.

Last, but not least, you learned how to fill a vacant lot with a mobile home and convert it into an ATM, and how to replace an existing mobile home when it is time to do so.

HOMEWORK

I'm giving you some homework that is due now and some that will not be due until you read the next chapter on financing. First, I want you to revisit the two best land-lease mobile home parks you have seen for sale, and the two best parks for sale where all or part of the mobile homes are park-owned units. If you don't want to invest in mobile home parks with park-owned units, then only concern yourself with land-lease parks. (We will show you how to convert park-owned units to land-lease and how to calculate what you will pay for parks with park-owned units that you will convert to land-lease in Chapter 17, which deals with advanced topics. For now, just note in the back of your mind that there is a way to buy parks with park-owned units and convert them to the easier to manage land-lease type.) I want you to do your own initial inspections, with an inspection sheet on a clipboard. If something does not make sense to you, just note it on the sheet, and continue.

Now I want you to read the next chapter and then come back to this assignment. If you are comfortable after you read that chapter, then I want you to—sound of trumpets for type 3s—make offers on the four properties (or only on two if you don't want to invest in mobile home parks with park-owned units). Don't worry if all of your offers get accepted or if none of your offers get accepted. If more than one is accepted, you can decide which one is the best, and go with that one. You can try to wholesale the other ones or simply not go forward on them. If none of your offers are accepted, then negotiate to see if you can get something accepted that will still give you a profit and create wealth. If you still have nothing accepted, no big deal. Go out and look at more properties and make more offers. That's right. If you feel comfortable after the next chapter, make offers! You should be ready if you have been paying attention.

You should also get the name of several good engineering inspection companies from your Realtor contacts, your banking contacts, your REIA contacts, your title companies, or just the yellow pages. Do the same for inspectors of individual mobile homes. Find out what they charge, interview them, pick the best, and schedule an appointment with them to inspect your accepted mobile home park offers. I want you to follow them around during the inspection so you can learn. If they are the kind of people that don't like to be interrupted while they are working, write down your questions and ask them at the end.

If the inspections are clean, move forward to secure financing (the next chapter shows you how). If the inspections show defects, negotiate with the sellers about how much they are willing to pay to fix them. If the deal still looks profitable, go forward with the financing. If the defects will keep you from making enough money, then move on to the next property, but move on nicely.

Congratulations—you've made your first offers and gone on your first inspections!

COMING ATTRACTIONS

Now it's time to learn one of the most important aspects of being a successful investor—how to arrange financing. Real estate revolves around financing—if buyers can't finance their purchases, real estate activity stops dead in its tracks. You're going to learn what it took me more than two decades to learn, so you will be supercharged for success—you are going to learn about multiple places to find financing and how to secure the best kind of financing so that no matter what the banks think of you, no matter what your credit history has been, you will be able to buy mobile home parks and be on your way to financial independence and wealth.

Excited? You should be. Let's go!

11

Financing and No Money Down: Finance It

Congratulations again! You *found* a good deal, *figured* the price you wanted to pay, stuck your *flag* in front of it with an accepted contract, and inspected it so you know what you will have to *fix,* if anything. Now it's time to *finance* it. In this chapter, you are going to learn something that took us years to discover—and it supercharged our investing when we applied it.

Financing is the part of the process that usually intimidates beginning investors—it sure intimidated us. We went into banks thinking something was lacking in us because we wanted to borrow money. It almost felt like we were begging for a loan to help us get out of desperate situation, a situation we had been foolish to get ourselves into. We were intimidated by the tall buildings and the vice presidents inside them. In the back of our minds, we were worried about failing and not being able to pay our loans back. If you feel this way too, be honest about it. Let's begin this chapter, and every chapter, by being honest with each other and ourselves.

Now drive those negative thoughts and feelings about borrowing money right out of your head!

First, borrowing money to purchase investment real estate is an accepted practice. The vast majority of people borrow money to buy their homes and the same is true for income-earning real estate investments.

And as for being intimidated by lenders, how do you think we feel now—when lenders call us up and ask if we want to borrow money? That's right, they call *us* and ask if they can come over to *our office* to convince us that we should borrow from them and explain why they should be our favorite lender. I want you to imagine right now a bank vice president calling you up and saying, "Hi, Mr. or Ms. So and So, this is Charles (or Charlene) down at First Community Trust. I was wondering . . . do you need to borrow any money right now for your investments?"

Is such a thing possible for you? Why not? If it happens to us, why can't it happen to you? But is it happening to you now? Probably not. So what is the difference between us, right now? The difference is that we have a track record in investing, and to a lender, that makes us a good customer. We also know that lenders need us more than we need them—because we know their deep dark secrets. Do you want to know what their deep dark secrets are?

THE THREE DEEP DARK SECRETS OF LENDERS

Here's the first one: not only do lenders *want* to lend money, they *have to* lend money. They need to make loans with a higher interest rate than what they pay out on short term savings or money market accounts and also make a profit, or they will go out of business. If lenders don't make loans, they will not have enough income to keep their doors open.

Here is the second secret: lenders need the collateral for their loans to be secure, and real estate is one of the most secure forms of collateral. What are lenders' choices when it comes to lending money? They can lend on credit card balances, personal loans, car or boat loans, business loans, and real estate loans. Look at that lineup of choices and ask yourself: Which is the safest form of collateral if the loan goes bad? What if a borrower declares bankruptcy? What will be left for the lender after it repossesses the collateral? Real estate looks pretty good compared to the others, doesn't it?

The third and last secret will probably knock your socks off. The people who are responsible for making loans at lending institutions have quotas, and if they don't lend out enough money, they will lose their job. That's right. Lenders need to lend out a minimum amount of money each month, and if they fall below that amount, their jobs are in jeopardy. And if a lending officer lends out more than his or her quota, that person becomes eligible for bonuses and pay raises.

You should understand and take to heart the fact that lenders need you because they need to make real estate loans, and they like repeat customers, which is what an investor is. A lender will strongly prefer someone who is an expert in investing with a proven track record, because even if a loan officer reaches quota and makes enough loans, the loan officer's job is at risk if too many of those loans go bad when the borrower stops making payments.

You've already learned from this book how to become the kind of investor that banks and mortgage brokers call to see if they can lend you money. We've also shown you how to be the kind of investor people will want to partner with to supply the money and capital you need. What you need to do at this point is to develop a track record that proves you are an expert. When you are an expert with a track record, you're going to be able to get the financing you need. Then you will learn what every skilled investor knows—*you don't have to have money to make money.* You have to have moneymaking knowledge and strategies, which you will demonstrate by your track record in finding good deals. Then you can get the money you need from the people who already have it and want to make more.

But, you may ask: *What if I am a beginner and don't have a track record? How do I create a track record when I have no investing experience and the banks only want to lend to investors with experience?* Well, first off, I didn't say banks *only* want to lend to experienced investors, I said they *prefer* to lend to them as repeat customers. We're going to show you in this chapter how to start on your mobile home investing career, with one mobile home park at a time. Then, after you create a track record, you will have banks and people with capital coming to you. A journey of a thousand miles begins with the first few steps, and you are already starting the first steps of your journey.

THE SIX BASIC KINDS OF LENDERS—A BANKER'S HALF DOZEN

There are six basic types of lenders for mobile home parks. You need to understand the different types of lenders, how each type lends, and how to approach them. We are going to give you a script and then take you by the hand to show you how to approach each type of lender, develop a long-term relationship, and be a favored customer. Here are the *Banker's Half Dozen:*

1. Large money-center banks
2. Community banks
3. Subprime lenders
4. Hard money lenders (HMLs)
5. Conduit lenders who securitize
6. FHA

The fifth and sixth types of lenders, conduits and FHA, are used primarily for very large transactions of one million or more, and preferably three million or more. We will talk more about them at the end of this discussion.

We will concentrate first on the first four types of lenders: large money-center banks, community banks, subprime lenders, and hard money lenders (HMLs) after we discuss what kind of borrower you are. This will identify which lenders will be easiest for you to work with. After we determine what kind of lender and financing you will qualify for, you be given a plan of action showing you how to get the money you need to invest.

What Kind of Borrower Are You?

To determine what kind of financing you need and what kind of lender you should seek out, you need to know what kind of financing you will qualify for. Specifically, you have to determine three things:

1. What is your credit score?
2. Do you have any money to put down?
3. If you are lacking good credit or money, do you have a partner who isn't?

If your credit score is high enough—a score of 600 or above—to approach a bank or a mortgage broker that works with prime lenders, then you should start with that plan of action because it is the simplest and easiest. If you don't have a good credit score now, please don't think you will be ineligible for this plan of action forever. After you become a successful investor, you can fix your credit problems, and then you will be able to walk into a lender's office with confidence.

How do you find out your credit score? There are several sites on the Internet where you can find out for free or a small fee. Two main sites are www.creditreport.com and www.annualcreditreport.com (the official, free site set up by the credit reporting agencies). You can also go to the websites of three major credit reporting agencies, which you will learn about shortly. You can also go to a mortgage broker or lender that you intend to work with and ask them to run your credit report for you.

After you determine whether you have a sufficient credit score, then you have to determine if you have enough money for a down payment, usually 20 percent of the purchase price. If not—if you are "down payment challenged"—you are still not left out. We will show you *no money down strategies.*

By the way, do not skip the section on no-money-down strategies if you aren't "down payment challenged" right now. If you are like most investors (ourselves included), there will probably be times in your career when the cash you have available for down payments will be limited. This will happen after you discover the exciting fact that there are a tremendous number of good deals available—and sometimes they appear in bunches. There are so many good deals that eventually you will use up all your down payment money buying them. Then what? What do you do when you have used up all your capital and another great deal presents itself? Should you forget about the deal and stop investing until you save up more down payment money? No-money-down strategies will let you to acquire wealth no matter how much money you have at any one time. They will be essential tools during your entire career in real estate.

Last, we will discuss taking on partners who can put down the credit and money that you are lacking. When partnerships work out, they are wonderful. The opposite is also true. When partnerships turn sour, they can be as bitter as a bad divorce. We've had many partnerships, and all but one was great. Even with that one we earned back our initial investment many times. Based upon our experience, we will show you what to look for, and what to watch out for, when finding partners.

Lenders and Credit Scores

You need to understand what is going on in the minds of your lenders so they can help you. To start, lenders are trained to lend based upon the Six Cs:

1. Cash—how much *cash* the borrower has readily available.
2. Credit—what the borrower's *credit* history is.
3. Capital—how much *capital* or net worth the borrower has.
4. Collateral—what the loan is for, and if the *collateral* is sufficient to cover any loss in case of default.
5. Conditions—what the current and future economic *conditions* are.
6. Character—what the general *character* of the borrower is.

If you ask seasoned loan officers what the most important C is, they will usually tell you that character is the razor's edge—they look the borrower in the eye and asked themselves the question, "Is this borrower going to do everything in his power to pay off this loan according the terms, or will he default on the loan agreement when times get a little tough?" Credit scores are the banking world's answer to quantifying the elusive and subjective component called human character.

People have fought for the right and the freedom to be considered a human being with unique attributes and qualities, not just a number. Yet, the lending and credit industry has slowly but surely tried to convert everyone to a number, and that number is called a *credit score.* There are three major credit agencies as I write this—TransUnion, Equifax, and Experion—and each has its own way of reducing a human being's prior financial experience to a number that reflects his financial character and predicts the reliability of his *future* financial dealings. Some lending institutions average the numbers from the three agencies, others throw out the highest and lowest, and some just use their favorite agency's number. Whatever method is used, just about everyone has been reduced to a number somewhere between 300 and 850, similar to the SAT college boards. (Someone with no credit score number available—who has flown below the financial radar screen—is considered a bad risk.)

Keep in mind that the credit agencies not only report on the past actions of people but also make *predictions* about their future actions, and this is part of your credit score. This makes lending process more efficient, so parts of it can be automated using computers. However, the computer is at a disadvantage when it comes evaluating the character of the borrower. It can't reach into the heart of the borrower and determine if he has strong or weak character traits that will affect his behavior towards his future obligations.

Credit Scores and the First Four Lenders

The current state of the lending industry is characterized by a lender's dependence on credit scores. There are (1) lenders that rely very strongly—almost exclusively—on the credit scores from the three credit agencies, and their lending officers don't give much weight to character judgments when it comes to granting loans, (2) lenders that want their loan officers to evaluate the character of potential borrowers along with their credit history, and use that judgment in their lending decision, (3) lenders that are willing to look at borrowers who don't have sufficient credit scores but still have some good credit history and a reasonable character, and (4) lenders that lend strictly based on collateral, which is the value of the property, so credit scores and character are almost irrelevant.

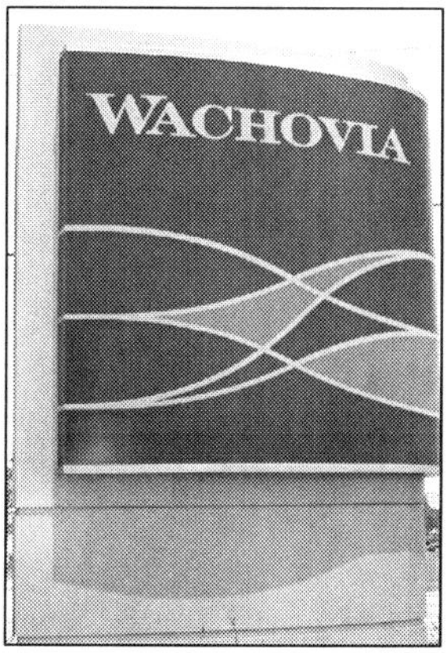

The first group of lenders relies strongly on credit scores, and they are usually the *large money-center banks.* You know who they are—they are on almost every street corner with a small local branch. They are regional, national, or even multinational in market base, with assets in the billions or trillions. The benefit of using these lenders is that your loan should be processed faster and the rates and terms are usually a little better. If you have a credit score above 650, they want you as a customer. If you have a credit score above 700, they will fast-track you and bend over backwards to keep you happy. This group generally will not consider no-money-down loans.

The second group of lenders is more willing to personally evaluate the character of their borrowers. *Local community banks* generally require that borrowers have credit scores above 600 or 620, depending on the particular lender. You should concentrate on these banks, because they are the most flexible lenders. They are more concerned with long-term relationships and more creative in their loan plans, and they are also more interested in developing their local community. *They may also look at no-money-down loans.*

The third group consists of *subprime lenders.* Borrowers turn to this group when they are turned down by the large money-center banks and the community banks. Borrowers may have credit scores in the 500s and may be using no-money-down or low-money-down strategies. As of this writing, this group of lenders terribly mismanaged their loans and the money entrusted to them. They were very popular in the real estate market run-up of the early 2000s, but they got hurt with defaulting loans when the market retraced its steps. Many of them have gone bankrupt at the time of this writing, but I believe some of the best will survive, because there is huge market for this type of loan product. Subprime lenders can be capricious in judging loans, so you have to be flexible and patient when dealing with them. They may be your only alternative if you have challenged credit and previous credit problems. *They may also look at no-money-down loans.*

The remaining group of lenders is known as the *hard money lenders,* or HMLs. As a rule, HMLs lend based on the value of the property and not on the borrower. They usually don't care about credit scores, credit history, previous bankruptcies, or foreclosures. They will only lend 50 to 70 percent of the value of the property, with 60 percent being the average, and they tend to use the quick sale value of the property, which is a lower value than the market value. They charge high interest rates (in the 12 to 18 percent range depending on market conditions) and high loan closing costs (in the range of 3 to 10 points, or percentage points, of the loan). I think they earned the name "hard money lenders" because the interest rates and closing costs on their loans are so high that the loans are hard to pay back. You could almost say they lend with the mindset that the borrower is probably going to default on the loan and they will have to foreclose and take the property to get paid. (We have seen hard money loans go bad within the first two or three months!) When they are lending only $60,000 on a $100,000 mobile home park, they have $40,000 worth of protection if the loan goes bad. *This group may also look at no-money-down loans* (you will see an example later in this chapter).

Mortgage Brokers

Mortgage brokers are a varied group, and you can use them no matter what your credit score is. Some specialize in borrowers with credit scores above 600, and others specialize in credit scores below that. The powerful advantage of a mortgage broker is that once your completed loan file is created, they will put it together to your best advantage and submit it to ten or twenty lenders for no extra cost and time. They can comparison shop for your best rate and closing costs. Also, if one lender should happen to turn you down, the mortgage broker can usually find another lender that will welcome you with open arms within a few days. When you find a good mortgage broker, you have struck gold.

That being said, there are many unscrupulous mortgage brokers who will fill your head with dreams and schemes, but show up empty handed when it comes time to produce results, and you wind up losing the deal as well as your time and money. The unscrupulous ones act under the premise, "Let's throw as many deals up against the wall as we can and see what sticks." Ask your Realtor contacts and REIA members for the best mortgage brokers, ones they have used and who produced results. You don't want just a name—you want to know who has actually performed well. Then judge carefully and interview the mortgage broker. Make sure they specialize in finding loans for investors and have done mobile home park loans in particular. Don't worry about the balance of power in this relationship. They are working for you. You are their customer.

Conduit Loans and FHA Loans

We discovered conduit loans and FHA loans by accident when we were pursuing financing on the Jefferson Mobile Home Park. If you remember, we contracted to pay $2.2 million for the park. At that time we were willing to put 20 percent down, or around $500,000. The reason we had so much money to put down is that after we discovered investing in land-lease mobile home parks, such as Happy Trails, we sold off most of our duplexes and triplexes at a nice profit. We strongly preferred owning mobile home parks—the costs, repairs, and management intensity was much greater for duplexes and triplexes.

We approached a local community bank to arrange the financing of

$1.7 million but the vice president of commercial lending balked at the amount. His bank was being cautious about accepting large loans—anything over $1 million—at that time. He suggested that we try the conduit loan route and he would help us put together the loan package. (In the Appendix there is a list of bankers and mortgage bankers who will put together a conduit loan package for you.)

The question in your mind is probably the same as the one that was in ours. "What is a conduit loan?" The banker explained that there were five or six large investment banks on Wall Street that made big commercial loans, typically $1 million or more, with $2 million being the preferred minimum. They put together a large pool of the loans, in the $100 million dollar to billion dollar range, and securitized them into CMBSs (Commercial Mortgage Backed Securities). Securitizing them meant they made them into a security like a stock or bond and then sold them to investors in smaller pieces of $10,000 or more. The fact that there was a pool of loans on many different properties, and therefore diversification, made the investors in these CMBSs feel secure about the quality of the securities. It was believed no one bad loan could adversely affect their investment's returns in a big way.

The investment bankers, the "conduits," provided liquidity for big commercial real estate deals, some of which were mobile home parks. Their rates were the lowest around—at the top of the market, they were supplying loans to the highest quality mobile home parks at 4 percent. Then they turned around and offered the loans to investors in $10,000 chunks at approximately 3.5 percent. Money market accounts were paying less than 2 percent at the time, so there was an incentive for investors to buy them. The big conduit lenders on Wall Street made their profit on the fees and the spread between what they received as payments from the mobile home parks (4 percent) and what they offered to investors (3.5 percent). These were some of characteristics of the conduit loans for mobile home park investors looking to finance mobile home parks:

- Lowest rates
- *Huge* loans, the bigger the better
- Nonrecourse loans (meaning the lender cannot go after the borrower for any assets other than those agreed to by the loan), but usually the borrower must put 20 percent down

- Wouldn't allow second mortgages of any kind, now or during the loan
- Thirty-year amortization, with five-, seven-, and ten- year balloon payments, with a possibility of fifteen and twenty-year full amortization mortgages

FNMA (Federal National Mortgage Association, commonly known as Fannie Mae), the largest mortgage lender in the world, also packages conduit loans and is still involved in these today. Their terms were more flexible than the Wall Street conduits but they were more restrictive in the types of properties they would lend on, and typically lend only on the higher-quality parks. While we were deciding whether to go the conduit route or not, we learned that the FHA (Federal Housing Administration), the federal agency that does home and apartment house financing for individuals and guarantees part of the mortgage, also did mobile home park loans. These are the characteristics of FHA mobile home park loans:

- Will do forty-year fixed rate loans
- Will lend up to 97 percent—a low-money-down situation
- Will finance parks with park-owned units
- Will give assumable and nonrecourse loans
- It is a very long process to get loan—six months to a year

We never completed the conduit loan or FNMA or FHA conduit loans. Time was becoming short, and we found a local banker who provided the benefits of the conduit loan without the long processing time and costs, and was willing to accept the quality of the Jefferson Mobile Home Park. We did not go with the FHA loan because we did not have that much time to complete the transaction.

As I write this, conduit loan financing has all but dried up due to the credit crisis that involved Wall Street in the early 2000s. Securitization of loans stopped, except for loans provided by FNMA and FHA. When Wall Street gets back to sound lending processes—which it most surely will—then these loans will be viable once again.

HOW TO APPLY FOR A LOAN

Now we are going to show you how to approach a lender or mortgage broker to obtain an investment loan. We are going to take you by the hand and give you a script to follow, specifically when it involves a local community bank—which we believe will be your best alternative when borrowing—and then we will show you how to modify the script for big money-center banks, HMLs, mortgage brokers, and hard money lenders.

The smiling gentleman in the picture on the left is a good friend of mine, and a great community banker as well. For the last ten years and to this day, he has loaned us money on various properties, including mobile home parks. We worked together in the seminar on how to become wealthy investing in real estate, and his section on finance was the highest rated among the students. With the assistance of the CEO of the seminar company, we put together the banking script you are about to receive.

Some of you may be thinking, "What's the big deal about applying for a loan? You walk into a bank, find out who the loan officers are, and fill out some application papers, after which you either get the loan or you don't." If you do that, you will do what 99 percent of borrowers do, and you will appear unprepared and unprofessional. Then, in addition to having no track record, you will also have no advantage and your character will not stand out from the other applicants.

Instead of using a haphazard approach, you are going to do something that sets you apart. *You are going to be prepared. Preparation will make up for your lack of experience, so your character will shine.*

You are going to prepare a formal package for the lender, a report that includes almost all the information that the lender needs in order to evaluate you and your loan. Your formal loan package will include the following:

1. Purchase contract

2. Pro forma sheet on the income and expenses for the property

3. Estimate of repairs (if necessary)

4. List of comparable sales, your appraisal estimate, and pictures of the park
5. Two years of tax returns, or W2s, and your two most recent pay stubs
6. Your personal financial statement
7. Your credit report, with explanations of any credit glitches

The good news is that you already have most or all of this information. The numbers and estimates in the first four items were all part of the process you followed when you figured out the value of the property and whether it was a flipper or keeper. The first is your contract, which came from the *flag* part of the Five Green Fs. (We don't recommend going into a bank without a signed and accepted contract, unless you are making a pilot trip to find out if the lender has any loan plans available for the property you are looking to invest in. In that case you would need to structure your offer with respect the down payment, interest rates, and closing costs. You did this during the second step in your due dilly.) The income and expenses come from the *figure* part of the Five Green Fs. The estimate of repairs comes from the *fix* part of the Five Green Fs. The comps and appraisal also come from the *fix* part, the due diligence, and also from the *figure* part of the Five Green Fs. You should include pictures of the park you want to buy along with your appraisal and comps, so it would be to your benefit to invest in a digital camera and a computer.

The fifth item simply includes copies of your tax returns for the past two years as well as your two most recent pay stubs.

The sixth item can give people who are unfamiliar with accounting a little trouble. A personal financial statement is merely a list of what you own—your *assets*—followed by a list of what you owe—your *liabilities*. The difference between the total of what you own and the total of what you owe is called your *net worth*. A personal financial statement is critical, but it is not brain surgery, so don't worry. An example of a personal financial statement is in the Appendix. If you have any doubts at all on how to prepare one, get help from your accountant.

The last item is your credit report, which you should have already obtained from either the Internet or a credit agency. Provide an explanation for any glitches or dings in your credit history. Don't think that you are hurting yourself by doing this because the lender may not be found out about them otherwise. The lender will most certainly find out about them, and if you try to hide them it will it will reflect poorly on your financial character. Get someone who is an expert in credit to help you with the explanations of your previous credit glitches so that you appear human but not lacking in character. Don't lie, but give yourself the benefit of the doubt.

The Lender Script

Now, let's take you by the hand and show you how to apply for a loan. You should prepare two copies of your loan package: one copy for the loan officer and the other copy for you to follow along with him as he reads. Remember, you are going to be prepared when you go to the lender, and that preparation will make you stand out in the lender's mind.

Once you have prepared your loan package, identify which community banks or lenders in your area are interested in mobile home park loans. Get their names from your Realtors, your REIA contacts, or again, by looking in the yellow pages under banks and lending institutions.

When you get the names and addresses of the three best lender candidates, put on your best business clothes and go visit them. *We are going to assume you are visiting the main branch of a local community bank,* which may also be the only branch. We will show you how to modify the script depending on whether you are approaching a big money-center bank, a mortgage broker, or a hard money lender. Again, *we prefer community banks because they have a lot of freedom in the loans they underwrite, and they are interested in the community and having long term relationships with its residents.*

If you or your partner has a credit score above 600, proceed with the script. If you have no money to put down, it's okay—proceed with the script, because community banks are easier to deal with in this regard. If you or your partner does not have a credit score above 600, it doesn't make sense to go into a community bank at this time. Instead, go to a mortgage broker that specializes in subprime lending or a hard money lender, or work with seller financing.

When you walk into the community bank, ask where the president's office is and go there. Yes, that's right. Go right to the top—you'll see why. When you are directed to the president, chances are you are not

The Lender Script

1. At the president's office: "Hello. I'm a real estate investor and I'm looking to establish a new banking relationship, and perhaps move over some of my accounts to this bank. Could you please direct me to the vice president of the Commercial Loan Department?"
2. With the vice president of the Commercial Loan Department: "I was directed to you by the office of the president of the bank, Mr./Mrs./Ms. _____. I'm a real estate investor and I'm looking to establish a new banking relationship and perhaps move over some of my accounts to this bank."
3. "At the present time, are you lending on mobile home parks?"
4. "Mr./Mrs./Ms. _____, how long has this bank been in business? How long have you been here? May I ask what your lending limits are?
5. "Here is the contract I have on the property. The next sheet is the pro forma on the property's income and expenses. The next list shows the contractor repairs that will be needed (*if you need to do any fix up*). And the next page has my appraisal and the comps and pictures of the property.
6. "Here is the debt service coverage ratio, based upon my estimate of the current lending terms"
7. "What loan programs do you have available?"
8. "Here are my last two years' tax returns and copies of my most recent pay stubs. The next sheet is my personal financial statement. The next page is a copy of my credit report (*if you have credit glitches, explain about them*). Please don't run a new credit report on me unless you are fairly certain you will be making the loan. (*This is because credit inquiries lower your credit score—not a lot, but who needs any lowering?*)
9. "How long do you think it will take you to make a decision?"
10. "Would you like to drive by and see the property with me?"

going to speak to him or her. The person you really want to see the president's assistant, who knows and is respected by everyone in the bank. You are going to smile and then say:

"Hello. I'm a real estate investor and I'm looking to establish a new banking relationship and perhaps move over some of my accounts to this bank. Could you please direct me to the vice president of the Commercial Loan Department?"

The commercial loan officer is the lending officer in the bank who makes loans with the bank's own portfolio and he or she has a great deal of flexibility in determining which loans to approve. You want to have a long-term relationship with this person. Remember, loan officers need to make loans, and they need repeat customers to fill their quotas.

The nice part of dealing with a community bank is that the assistant to the president will probably do one of the following:

1. Call the loan officer and say he or she is sending you over

2. Walk you over to the loan officer personally

Therefore, you will have a personal introduction from the president's office when you approach the loan officer. You will say the following:

"Hello, Mr./Mrs./Ms. __________, I was directed to you by the office of president of the bank. I'm a real estate investor and I'm looking to establish a new banking relationship and perhaps move over some of my accounts to this bank."

Using this reference will give you status, and you deserve this status. You are going to be so prepared and professional looking that you will shine compared to most loan applicants, and this just adds a little sizzle to your presentation. After you introduce yourself and make a little human contact in your conversation, you will ask:

"At the present time, are you lending on mobile home parks?"

If the answer is yes, great, continue on with the script. (If the answer is no, ask the loan officer if he or she knows any other banks that do lend on mobile home parks. Then shake hands, leave your business card, and ask the loan officer to call you when the bank changes its lending policy.) If the bank does lend on mobile home parks, ask the following:

"Mr./Mrs./Ms. __________, how long has this bank been in business? How long have you been here? May I ask what your lending limits are?

Establish a personal dialogue with the three questions, but in a friendly manner let the lender know that you are conducting the interview, not the loan officer.

After these questions are answered, hand the lender your loan package. He or she will follow along with you as you review your copy of the package. Be prepared for the loan officer to be surprised at your preparation. Remember less than 1 percent of borrowers do this, and 99 percent look like "tire-kickers."

"Here is the contract I have on the property . . . the next sheet is the pro forma on the property's income and expenses . . . the next list shows the contractor repairs that will be needed (*if you need to do any fix up*) . . . and the next page has my appraisal and the comps and pictures of the property . . .

You have gone over the first four items in the loan package. Now, you are going to let the vice president know that you know how lenders gauge the risk on lending on mobile home parks (and for any income producing real estate):

"Here is the debt-service coverage ratio for the property, based upon my estimate of the current lending terms"

Don't let this term scare you. The *Debt Service Coverage Ratio* (DSCR) is the basic first measurement for a lender. It shows how much breathing room, or profit, there is above the mortgage payment on a property. The formula is:

Debt Service Coverage Ratio = NOI ÷ Yearly Mortgage Payment of P&I

You are going to take the NOI, which is the net income produced by the property *before* you pay any mortgages, and divide it by the total mortgage payment on the property for the year at the current rates, using only the principal and interest payments, *not* the insurance and real estate taxes (those have already been subtracted to get the NOI).

To envision how to apply this formula, let's assume you are buying a $500,000 mobile home park. The NOI is $50,000, and the mortgage payments will be $3,000 per month on a $400,000 mortgage at 8 percent for thirty years, or $36,000 per year. Here is the formula:

Debt Service Coverage Ratio = NOI ÷ Yearly Mortgage Payment of P&I
= $50,000 ÷ $36,000 = 1.4 (Approximately)

That means the NOI covers the mortgage 1.4 times, so there is 40 percent extra coverage to pay the mortgage if the income should slide. Bankers feel a ratio of 1.2 to 1.25 is good, so anything above that is even better. If you have a property that is below 1.2 times coverage, you need to have a good strategy showing how you are going to raise it to at least 1.2 in the very near future, or the lender will balk at giving you a loan. In this case, 1.4 is a superb coverage ratio that would give lenders a stronger feeling of comfort than they would have for most of the properties they are asked to lend on. This is the reason that lenders who understand mobile home parks like lending on them. They are known as cash cows.

As this point, you have completed the first part of your package, the property part. You now turn to the lender and ask:

"What loan programs do you have available?"

If the lender has loan programs for your property, you are in! (If the lender doesn't, then once again ask the loan officer if he or she knows any banks that do lend on your type of property, leave the loan officer with a business card, and ask him or her to call you when the bank changes its lending policy.)

At this point, the loan officer has been *fully qualified by you*. However, he or she knows little about you other than that you are a real estate investor who is well prepared and professional. Now, you are going to reveal your financial information.

"Here are my last two years' tax returns and copies of my most recent pay stubs . . . the next sheet is my personal financial statement . . . the next page is a copy of my most recent credit report . . . (*if you have credit glitches, explain about them*) . . . Please don't run a new credit report on me unless you are fairly certain you will be making the loan (*This is because credit inquiries lower your credit score.*)

Now you have reached the climax of the script. You are going to look the lender in the eye, and ask:

"How long do you think it will take you to make a decision?"

Remember, we developed this script as a result of working with a banker. I tested it out first by putting together a *handwritten* loan package for myself and applying at a community bank. My loan package looked amateurish, yet *I received loan approval within twenty-four hours.* In over twenty years of experience, the banker I handed it to has had maybe three or four people come in as prepared as I was. His underwriter, by the way, said it was one of the most complete loan packages he had ever seen, even though it was handwritten.

At this point, if you have had a real meeting of the minds with the lender, and feel that this is a person you want to have a long-term banking relationship with, then add:

"Would you like to drive by and see the property with me?"

This is the best situation—to be able to spend some time outside the bank with the lending officer. You can become friends as well as business associates. This combination will make the borrowing process comfortable and easy. Believe it or not, what you have learned in this book about investing in mobile home parks is still foreign to most lenders, and the more you can educate them about mobile home park investing, the more comfortable the lender will be making repeat loans to you.

If you like to do flipping, ask the lender after the first few loans to arrange a special kind of loan for you, in which you just have to give the lender the contracts and pictures of a property, and he or she will lend you the initial purchase price and fix-up costs with a minimum of time and paperwork. After all, the lender has experience with you now and your financial character has not changed. With this special loan, you should be able to close within a week or two—a capability that can get you big discounts from sellers who want a quick deal.

How You Will Modify the Script for Different Types of Lenders

This Lender Script is for community banks, which are interested in long-term relationships and the local community. Now we are going to modify the script so you can use it when you are approaching a big money-center bank, a mortgage broker, or a hard money lender.

When you approach a large *money-center bank,* the president of the bank is not going to be accessible. Start with No. 2 in the script (skip the first sentence), forget No. 4, and you'll be fine. At the end of the script, No. 9, if you can get a vice president of commercial loans to get in your car to view the property, more power to you. It is possible to strike up a warm and friendly relationship with a money-center bank.

For *mortgage brokers,* when it comes to the script, eliminate No. 1 and follow through on the other eight items. It doesn't hurt to promise to bring them all your future deals if they do a good job for you on this one. They are also interested in repeat business, and you are interested in doing more deals with a professional company that produces results.

Last, but not least, let's discuss *hard money lenders*. Usually your contact with a hard money lender will be through a mortgage broker, but some hard money lenders do deal directly with borrowers. You can find them the same way you found a good mortgage broker—through REIA and Realtor contacts. The process is usually informal, and the usual reason you are dealing with them is because your credit score is low or you haven't been able to find anyone else who will lend on the property you want to buy. Start with No. 3 on the script and forget No. 4. You can try asking the hard money lender to come with you in your car to view the property, but don't be taken aback if he or she declines any form of personal contact. Hard money lenders are a tough bunch—they have to be. People run to them when they need money, usually because of their own carelessness and immaturity. Then they revert back to the behavior that got them in trouble in the first place after they get their loan. Hard money lenders are used to foreclosures, and many have had sympathy and pity driven out of their characters through bitter experience. In other words, to them it's just business, nothing personal.

The Difference Between Real Estate Loans and Personal Property Loans for Individual Mobile Homes

Believe it or not, it is usually faster and easier to borrow money on an individual mobile home without the land. It is almost exactly like buying a car, and you don't need to use a title company to create deeds. However, because of the negligence and corruption that took place in the chattel lending business in the early 2000s, these lenders have become very careful. A list is given in the Appendix.

If you are going to a bank for a personal loan, whether it is a community bank or a big money-center bank, you can try talking to the vice president of commercial loans, but chances are the vice president will simply direct you to the *Consumer Finance Department*. That department lends on personal property, like cars, boats, RVs, motorcycles, snowmobiles, and so on, and they feel comfortable lending on mobile homes because it has a title like a car or boat.

You can also try going to the Consumer Finance Department of the bank when you own the land under the mobile home. I have done it successfully for tenants who wanted to convert their lease option with me into ownership. You can start out in the *Mortgage Department* of the bank, but if you're told they don't lend on mobile homes, go to the Consumer Finance Department. When you go to large money-center banks, don't be surprised if the two departments don't know about each other or the other's lending practices.

When it comes to financing individual mobile homes with land, there are also government loans available from the Federal Housing Administration in addition to mortgage brokers and community banks. Usually the FHA wants to lend only on mobile homes built in the last ten or fifteen years, however, so you may need to do more research and scouting around to find a good lender if you have an older mobile home and land combination, but they are out there.

Partner with Someone with Good Credit and Capital and Private Money

Partnerships are like marriages. When they are good, they are very good. We have seen partnerships create great wealth for some people who would not have been able to become wealthy any other way. When a partnership turns bad, however, it can lead to bitterness, and we have also seen partnerships that hurt the people involved. You should look for the key elements of responsibility, respect, and trust when you form a partnership. You should also create a plan to end the partnership when the partners no longer see eye to eye—in other words, you should have a "prenuptial" agreement.

The best partnerships occur when each partner brings a needed skill and talent to the endeavor. Those unique skills will be appreciated by all, so there will be mutual respect among the partners. The typical successful partnership involves an "inside" and an "outside" person. The inside person takes care of the marketing and the office work, ensuring the smooth operation of the business. The outside person takes care of getting the product to the marketplace, making sure the product is topnotch and attractively priced, and that the customers are satisfied.

When it comes to real estate, sometimes the initial partnerships do not have inside and outside people, but instead one person who does all the work and the other who has all the money and financial credit. Typically, on a flipper, the working partner finds the deal and the money partner pays for it. The working partner improves the property, using the money partner's capital and the working partner markets it and sells it. The first moneys received go towards reimbursing the money partner for the purchase and improvement outlays and then the profits are split fifty-fifty, or however the partners arranged. On keepers, the first profits typically go to reimburse the money partner for the interest on any down payment, then the working partner is paid a management fee (usually 10 percent), and then the remaining profits are split fifty-fifty. The sale of a keeper is handled like the sale of a flipper.

There is a new term making its way called *Private Money.* This is when you go to an individual or corporation for either all the purchase money or for the down payment. Typically, the private money lender charges a higher interest rate, sometimes along with an "equity kicker" —a piece of the profits when the park is sold. The way the private money investor is paid can vary widely, but usually it is similar to how the nonworking money partner above is rewarded. (That is the reason it was brought up in the section on partnerships.)

We have been the nonworking money partner with working partners, and we understood right from the beginning that these would probably not be long-term relationships. As soon as the working partner accumulates enough borrowing ability, there is no longer a need for the partnership. After all, the working partner is doing all the work and the talent and responsibilities are not equally distributed.

When partnerships go bad, things can get ugly, so your partnership agreement should always include an arrangement to handle this possibility. Partnerships usually go bad because one of the partners loses interest, or thinks he or she can replace the other partner with a salaried employee and keep a larger share of the profits. The trust and respect are gone. When this happens, you need an agreement already in place for splitting up the partnership assets that is quick and fair. In our partnership agreements, we have the partner who wants to dissolve the partnership come to the others, and offer a price in writing to the other partners. The other partners then have the right to either buy the assets, *or sell them,* at the price named, to the partner who wants to dissolve the partnership. Either action must occur within 60 days. If the transaction cannot be completed, then the remaining assets are put up for absolute auction, at which the public and the partners can bid under the same terms. You should have an attorney prepare your first partnership agreement along with the terms of dissolution (even in the case of death of one of the partners) and then reuse it when you partner with someone on a property.

Different Types of Loans

When we first invested in real estate many years ago, there were only fixed rate, long-term loans at interest rates of 10 percent or more. Then, in the early 1980s we experienced inflation like we had never seen before, 15 to 20 percent per year, and the adjustable-rate mortgage was introduced.

The mortgage industry then recognized that some people had "creative" ways of computing their income taxes, and the "limited docs" or "no doc" loans were born. As long as the borrower put 20 percent or more down, they did not have to verify the yearly income they claimed. The home equity loan was born a short time later, as the value of people's homes escalated and homeowners needed a way to tap into their newfound equity without disturbing their original mortgage. (Actually, a home equity loan is just a second mortgage, only with a nicer name. In the "old days," a second mortgage was an embarrassment, an indication that the borrower was headed for financial ruin. Once the name changed to a home equity loan, it became more attractive to the public.)

In the early 2000s, lenders became even more creative, offering subprime loans for borrowers with low credit scores. Subprime loans were also used to finance property purchases with low-money-down loans and two simultaneous mortgages—a standard first mortgage and a subprime, high-interest second mortgage.

Develop a strategy for how you borrow. If you are buying a long-term keeper and you borrow from one of the middle four types of lenders, your loan is typically going to be for 20 to 30 years with an adjustable rate that will be fixed for the first three or five years and after that will change to reflect the current interest rates. These loans adjust every three or five years. You can refinance if the property goes up in value and you want to pull out the equity to invest in more property without paying income tax on the gain.

If you are buying a flipper, you can borrow short-term or with a longer-term adjustable, but always keep in mind that *sometimes a flipper don't flip.* You may have to hold the property longer than you figured. For that reason, try to have at least a five year due date on your flipper mortgages—which brings us to the topic of balloon mortgages.

With a balloon mortgage, mortgage payments are amortized, or calculated based on the assumption that the payments will continue a long time—like fifteen to thirty years—but the loan "balloons," or comes due, after a shorter time, typically one to five years. Since the principal (the actual amount borrowed) of the loan is paid down very slowly in the beginning, typically the balloon payment at the end of the loan is not much less than the total amount you borrowed in the first place. *Be very careful* of getting balloon loans. You may wind up in the terrible situation where the lender does not want to renew the loan and you can't find a new lender. In that case, you will face foreclosure and the loss of the property and your good credit standing. (I believe part of the reason they are called balloon loans is because when the loan comes due, it can burst in your face.)

The ultimate form of financing to arrange is a *pooled mortgage* for your flippers with, as mentioned before, an *automatic take-out mortgage* capability for when you decide to turn a flipper into a keeper. In other words, once you have a track record, arrange with your lender to have a pool of mortgage money ready and waiting for you so that all you have to do is submit a contract, a list of repairs, and how much you need to borrow. The banker frees up the money quickly and you can close quickly, allowing you to get big discounts from sellers who need a fast and guaranteed closing. When you sell the property, you repay the up-front and fix-up costs back to the pool loan you have set up, to be used on the next property. You will also pay the bank interest and fees for the use of the money. You pocket the profits. (This type of loan arrangement replaces the non-working money partner once the working partner has developed a track record with a banker.) If the flipper doesn't flip or you change your mind and want to hold it as a keeper, then the bank arranges a separate, long-term loan for the property and replenishes the up-front and fix-up money that was taken from the pool loan.

If you want to make this even better, make an arrangement with your lenders to bring them the buyers of your flippers, so they can set up the buyers' new long-term mortgages. Lenders are in the business of lending, and when you bring them new customers, you are creating a mutually beneficial relationship.

SELLER FINANCING AND NO MONEY DOWN

When we discovered seller financing and no-money-down deals, it was love at first sight. For many years, we had bought foreclosures and tax deeds on the courthouse steps, so cash reserves were very important to us. Then we discovered how to put together deals without money out of our own pockets. We still borrowed the first mortgage from a bank, but the down payment money came from a second mortgage from the seller. (This will be detailed later for you.)

Suddenly the investing world opened up for us. We were no longer bound by cash reserves. We could buy all the property we wanted since we didn't need any cash to buy them. All we were bound by was our ability to manage the properties we bought profitably. (We will discuss managing properties in Chapter 13.)

The ultimate experience was walking out of closing with cash, *after we bought a property.* This turned all our preconceived notions about investing upside down. A buyer was supposed to bring money to the closing, and the seller was supposed to get money, yet there we were, buying property and walking out of closing with a check and no money taken from our pockets. (We will detail this later also.)

When my son-in-law started investing in real estate, I mentored him. At the time, he didn't have good credit—or any credit for that matter—and no money to put down. I wanted to teach him to stand on his own two feet instead of always relying on me to be his partner, so we created five simple and easy ways to buy property with no credit and no money. *If you don't have a partner with good credit, and you don't have good credit or any down payment money, then seller financing is essential to start your investment career.* When you learn how to obtain seller financing you will feel incredibly empowered because now you have a way to invest that doesn't require lenders, and you can work strictly with sellers.

In almost all cases, trust is an absolutely key ingredient when you are looking to obtain seller financing and/or create no-money-down deals. *The seller must trust you,* the buyer, because if you don't do what you are supposed to, the seller may get hurt. (We'll discuss this more in the next section.) When my son-in-law put together deals, he worked very hard to get the seller to see him as someone with good character, who was going to "walk the talk." He brought along a "brag book" to his contract negotiations. In this loose-leaf book, he had "before and after" pictures of the properties he bought and fixed up as well as letters of recommendation from sellers who gave him financing, detailing how pleased they were with the results of their transactions together.

The first no-money-down strategy we are going to learn is the easiest and the most common. It involves a buyer who has good credit but little or no money to put down. When we train people who have good credit but little money to put down, we tell them this should automatically be their first offer whenever they buy property.

You Have Good Credit, But Little or No Money to Put Down

With this technique, you are going to a bank for a first mortgage on the property you are buying. In all probability, it will be a *local community bank* where the property is located because the major money-center banks do not like to finance no-money-down deals. Community banks, on the other hand, can lend from their "portfolio" —the funds they accumulate from their own deposits. Portfolio lenders have their own unique terms when they are not going to sell the loan in the "secondary market" to FNMA or Freddie Mac, who have rigid loan terms.

There are wide differences in terms among banks that lend from their portfolio, and you may have to shop around at a few community banks until you find the one with terms that are the most flexible and beneficial for you. Once you know their terms, you can structure the financing in your contract. For instance, most banks will lend up to 80 percent of the contract price or appraised value, *whichever is least*. That is why we added the following clauses in Chapter 9 on making offers:

1. If the Buyers wish to continue with the transaction after Due Diligence, Buyers will have 60 days from the end of the due diligence period to secure third-party financing, and contract is subject to Buyers' approval of financing terms. If Buyers do not secure financing or do not approve of the terms, Buyers' escrow deposit will be returned immediately.

2. If Buyers approve of third party financing, Sellers will give a purchase-money second mortgage on the property at the following terms: ____________________ amount of seller financing, ______% interest rate, _____________ amortization years, balloon in ____ years, payable monthly, assumable and nonrecourse.

For instance, if you are buying a mobile home park for $200,000, then you will set it up this way:

Purchase Price:	**$200,000**
First Mortgage (from Community Bank):	**$160,000**
Second Mortgage (from Seller) 7 percent, 30 years:	**$40,000**
Down Payment from You:	**$0**

You will adjust the amounts depending on the purchase price of your particular contract. Also, if your community bank wants to lend only 75 percent of the purchase price, then the second mortgage amount will be for 25 percent of the purchase price. The first and second mortgages must add up to 100 percent of the purchase price to achieve a no-money–down transaction.

Keep in mind that as the buyer, *you will still have closing costs,* which you must pay out of your pocket in cash. If you want to make this a completely no-money-down deal, then you should insert the following clause:

*Seller will pay Buyers' closings costs, up to $*____________________.

No Money Down, Trust, and Human Nature

You may think that trust and human nature have no place when it comes to financing mobile home parks, but in reality, they have everything to do with it, especially when you are buying with no money down.

First, the seller must trust you, the buyer. Why? Because if you don't do what you are supposed to do, which is pay both of your mortgages on time, then the seller will be forced to start a foreclosure, which is a time-consuming and expensive legal exercise. If you, as the buyer, continue to pay the first mortgage, but not the seller's second, then the foreclosure is somewhat simpler. The seller just has to sue to get the property back, and then continue to pay the existing first mortgage, until the seller finds a new buyer who will refinance the property. If you stop paying on both mortgages, which is more common, then the seller must keep the first mortgage current while completing foreclosure on the second. In the event the first mortgage lender does not accept mortgage payments and being kept current, then the seller must have enough money to buy the property when the first mortgage comes to foreclosure or risk being wiped out completely. As you can see, all the possible choices the seller will have if the buyer does not make payments are time consuming and aggravating. There will probably be times during the transaction when the seller will look at you the same way a banker would, and will ask himself, "When push comes to shove, is this buyer going to pay me back or run for the hills?"

The trust issue extends to human nature. Banks that refuse to do no-money-down deals believe implicitly that if the buyer uses his own money for the down payment the chance that he will run for the hills is reduced because he has some "skin in the game." Keep in mind that *when the seller gives you a second mortgage, the bank still has a down payment, but it's coming from the seller instead of the buyer.* Take the previous example:

Purchase Price:	**$200,000**
First Mortgage (from Community Bank):	**$160,000**
Second Mortgage (from Seller) 7 percent, 30 years:	**$40,000**
Down Payment from You:	**$0**

Now, let's look at the same transaction, but with your money down:

Purchase Price:	**$200,000**
First Mortgage (from Community Bank):	**$160,000**
Your Down Payment (Skin in the Game):	**$40,000**

The bank's risk is exactly the same on paper—they have lent 80 percent of the value of the property, verified by an appraiser, and if they have to foreclose, they have 20 percent of the property value as protection against loses. *The difference is who has put up the down payment, not whether the down payment exits.* Some banks just feel that the risk of foreclosure is lessened when the buyer has some skin in the game, and they want to limit the foreclosure risk as much as possible.

Also keep in mind that some sellers, bankers, and Realtors may try to treat your no-money-down offer like it's coming from a deadbeat. Don't let their opinions sway you one bit! In our experience, we have had wealthy, experienced investors submit no–money-down contracts on our flippers, and these investors had more than enough money to pay cash for our property and not use financing at all. Why did they not feel like deadbeats, nor get treated as such? The answer is that savvy investors understand that cash in hand can be a powerful resource sometimes, and they don't like to give up that power unless they absolutely have to.

Walking Out of Closing with Cash When Buying

The best deal in no-money-down financing is when you can walk out of a closing with cash in your pocket—*when you buy.* Let's consider two of the easiest ways to accomplish this.

1. Getting part of the commission
2. Having the seller rebate the proposed fix-up costs to you

The easiest way to get part of the commission is by being a Realtor yourself. Then, when you buy, you take the selling commission, which is usually half of the total commission. In this case, you are the selling broker and your client is yourself. This is a powerful reason to become a Realtor—to get the usual 3 percent selling commission when you buy a property. Since about 85 percent of properties sold are through Realtors, you have an 85 percent chance of getting this discount every time you buy. This is also a powerful reason to become a Realtor when you sell property, because you will only pay half of the usual 6 percent to the selling Realtor, because you will be the listing Realtor on your own property. Even if you are not a Realtor, you can still get the Realtor who is selling you the property to give you part of his or her commission at the closing. This is legal and acceptable, as long you state that you are not receiving part of the commission as a licensed real estate person but rather as a rebate on the sale.

You can also have the seller rebate the proposed fix-up costs at closing. This rebate is to be used for repairs once you own the property. Some lenders put restrictions on the amount of this fix-up rebate, usually around three to five percent of the selling price—but others may not. As long as the property appraises for the price you are paying without fix-up, most lenders feel comfortable with a fix-up rebate. These rebates can be written as follows:

1. Seller will rebate 5 percent of the purchase price at closing to the buyer for renovation of the property.
2. Selling Realtor will rebate 50 percent of his commission to the buyer at closing. This is not a real estate commission paid to the buyer, but a rebate.

Seller Financing—When You Don't Need Credit or Money Down

Seller financing represents the best of times and the worst of times. It represents the best in that the following five no-money-down techniques allow you to avoid the traditional lending world's rules and you are bound only by the amount of property you can profitably manage. With seller financing, you don't have to go to lenders, (with one exception, and this lender is the easiest lender to deal with) and you don't need to use your own savings. If you have the choice of avoiding banks and down payments, it is a nice choice to have. Alternatively, if you really don't have good credit or money to put down or any partners who do, then you have little choice if you want to grow wealthy.

Seller financing can also represent the worst of times, because you will usually have to make many more offers before you find sellers who are motivated enough to allow you to use these five techniques. When you are in a hot market and sellers can demand full-price cash offers, no-money-down offers will be put on the bottom of the pile. If you are in a slow or even a retreating real estate market, you have a much better chance of getting these no-money techniques accepted. On the positive side, in every market, hot or slow, there are slow deals—properties that aren't moving and have an owner who is motivated to do something quickly. Slow deals are excellent opportunities for no-money-down offers.

In each of the five strategies that follow, the seller is going to have to trust you. If you don't do what you are supposed to do, then the seller

Five Techniques for Investors with No Credit and No Money Down

1. Seller gives whole mortgage
2. Assume the first mortgage "subject-to," and seller gives a second mortgage or accepts boat, car, lot, or promissory note for the balance
3. Wrap-around mortgage
4. Hard money first mortgage, seller second mortgage if any balance
5. Sandwich L/O

will suffer some aggravating and possibly painful results. The best-case scenario in this domain is when you are fortunate enough to find a wealthy seller who would rather take back financing because he will receive a better rate than the banks are paying on deposits, or when the seller doesn't mind taking back the property if you don't do what you are supposed to.

1. Seller Gives Whole Mortgage

This is the most difficult no-money-down technique to apply because it requires the seller to have no existing mortgages on the property, in other words, the seller owns the property free and clear. The seller gives the buyer a mortgage and receives only the mortgage payments that come due each month—no cash up front. Nevertheless, it was the first technique my son-in-law and I used. Why? Because we got lucky. There were motivated sellers in a neighborhood where we were one of the biggest investors (we owned more than fifty units there). The sellers sought us out through a broker and offered us their property for $250,000 with $250,000 seller financing. That's right—no money down, and they came to us. We didn't go to them.

The sellers had sold the property to another investor and had given seller financing, but the new buyer put in terrible tenants, stopped making mortgage payments, kept all the rent, and then disappeared off the face of the earth, leaving a big mess. The sellers were wealthy, older, and didn't want the hassle of eviction and renovation and finding new buyers. They wanted to remain retired and play tennis seven days a week. They trusted us because we owned a lot of property in the same area, and they had confidence that we knew how to solve the problems. It was a marriage made in heaven.

We bought the property in a land trust and then transferred the beneficial ownership to my son-in-law. (You will learn more about this in Chapter 16, on protecting your assets.) My son-in-law got a great education. He learned how to evict bad tenants, renovate, find renters, and manage property. I was watching him and making sure he didn't make any major mistakes because my reputation was on the line. When we had some money to invest two years later, I bought the property back from my son-in-law for a $50,000 profit, to his surprise and glee. Two years later, the market unexpectedly exploded and we sold the property for an additional profit.

When I ask if anybody in my trainings has ever used this technique, I am surprised to find a few others have also done it. In most cases, the seller was extremely motivated, usually elderly, and looking to salvage something from an investment that had become very aggravating to manage. The buyers were usually younger with little starting capital, but lots of energy and desire. In many cases, the results were successful.

2. Assume the First Mortgage "Subject-to" and Seller Gives a Second Mortgage or Accepts a Boat, Car, Lot, or Promissory Note for the Balance

This is another of those best-of–times-worst-of-times techniques. It is the best because there are so many mortgaged properties out there with motivated sellers who just want out. Many times, they will just give you a deed and walk away. In this situation, you write a contract showing you are buying the property *subject to* the mortgage that is on it—in other words, you don't assume legal responsibility for the existing mortgage (you agree with the seller to pay it, but you are not liable to the lender if you don't pay it). If the seller wants more than the mortgage amount owed, so there is a difference between the price you are paying and the outstanding mortgage, then the seller will give you a second mortgage for that difference. Alternatives to getting a second mortgage from the seller would be giving the seller a boat, car, lot, or promissory note for the difference.

Let's detail this to make easier to understand. Assume that you are buying a mobile home park for $200,000 and it has an existing mortgage for $180,000. Here is the way you will set the deal up:

Purchase Price:	**$200,000**
First Mortgage Taken Subject-To:	**$180,000**
Second Mortgage (from Seller):	**$20,000**
Down Payment from You:	**$0**

If you have a boat or car worth $20,000, you could offer to give the boat or car to the seller instead of getting a $20,000 second mortgage. Or you could offer the seller a promissory note for $20,000, for which only your credit and good name serve as collateral.

So how could something so easy and accommodating as this technique represent the worst of times? In order to understand the downside, you need to understand the principle of being a "lame duck" as well as the "due-on-sale clause."

The lame duck principle arises when the buyer is unscrupulous and unethical. When a buyer purchases a property subject to the outstanding mortgages, he is not responsible for the mortgages as far as the lender and the courts are concerned. If the buyer decides to rent out the property, keep all the rent, and not make mortgage payments, the previous seller is going to have his credit ruined in a foreclosure that he can't stop, because he doesn't own the property any more. Any payments he makes will accrue to the benefit of the new owner and will not help his credit. He will literally have to make all of the payments on the mortgage to keep it out of foreclosure, and he still will not own the property. This doesn't make any sense. He is a lame duck in this situation. For this reason, some states have ruled that buying real estate subject to existing mortgages is illegal and they will prosecute such buyers. Make sure that subject to deals are not illegal in your state before you use this technique. We have used it, because it is not illegal in Florida. We always were ethical in handling them and made sure the mortgage didn't go into default, and when it came time to sell the property we made sure the mortgage was paid off before it was transferred to a new buyer.

This technique also goes around the due-on-sale clause, which is used in the vast majority of mortgages nowadays. This clause states that if the property is sold or transferred in any way, the existing mortgage becomes due and payable in full. If the lender finds out the property is transferred without the mortgage being paid off, the lender can start a foreclosure action and take the property away from the owner. In actual practice, the due-on-sale clause is rarely enforced by lenders if the mortgage is being paid on time. Lenders have enough trouble keeping track of who is paying and who is not paying. Typically, if a mortgage is being paid regularly, lenders do not go looking for problems by checking to see if the property has been sold and someone new is making the payments.

3. Wrap-Around Mortgage

Once you understand this complicated technique, you can overcome the main negative point of the previous subject-to technique, in which the seller becomes a lame duck. In this technique, the seller gives a new mortgage that wraps around and includes the previous mortgage on the property. Then, the buyer pays the seller one payment each month that includes the old mortgage payment plus any difference a second mortgage would have added. When the seller receives the payment from the buyer, the seller pays the outstanding mortgage to the lender and then pockets any additional money. This way, if the buyer does not pay the previous seller the payment on the new wrap-around mortgage, the seller can keep the old mortgage current while he starts a foreclosure to take the property back.

Let's look at an example of this. Suppose you want to buy a mobile home park for $200,000 with an outstanding mortgage of $180,000 and a payment of $1,800 per month. You write a contract in which the seller gives you a new wrap-around mortgage for $200,000 with a monthly payment of $2,000 per month. This is the way it works out:

Purchase Price:	**$200,000**
Wrap-Around Mortgage (Wraps Existing $180,000 Mortgage with Additional $20,000)	**$200,000**
Down Payment from You:	**$0**

Each month, you will send the seller $2,000 as payment for the new wrap-around mortgage. The seller will then send $1,800 to the existing first mortgage holder and will keep the $200 difference.

Like the previous technique, this technique circumvents the due-on-sale clause, so the lender could foreclose upon a property sold in this way. But, as mentioned above, lenders usually do not go looking for problems and checking to see if the property has been sold and someone new is paying the mortgage if it is being paid regularly,. Be sure to check and make sure that wrap around mortgages are not illegal in the state where you are buying property if you are going to use this technique.

4. Hard Money First Mortgage, Seller Second Mortgage on the Balance

This technique is the only one that requires going to a lender, but in this case, the lender is only lending on the property, not on your credit or down payment. You will remember from our previous discussion that hard money lenders will only lend 50 to 70 percent of the value on the property—and many times, that is the quick sale value, not the market value.

It may be possible to borrow the whole mortgage amount from the hard money lender if your contract price is equal to 50 to 70 percent of the appraisal. In other words, if you are buying a property for $60,000 and the hard money lender gets an appraisal of $100,000, the hard money lender may lend you the whole purchase price because 60 percent of the appraisal of $100,000 is $60,000, which is your contract price. Here is how it looks:

Purchase Price:	**$60,000**
Appraisal	**$100,000**
First Mortgage—60 Percent of Appraisal	**$60,000**
Down Payment	**$0**

The more common occurrence is when someone purchases a park for $100,000 and the appraisal is for $100,000. Then the hard money lender will still lend 60 percent of the purchase price, so the arrangement would like this:

Purchase Price:	**$100,000**
Appraisal	**$100,000**
First Mortgage from Hard Money Lender at 60 Percent	**$60,000**
Second Mortgage (from Seller):	**$40,000**
Down Payment from You:	**$0**

As you can see in the more common case, a seller would be required to give a large second mortgage (40 percent) when a hard money lender is involved because hard money lenders only lend around 60 percent of the value of the property.

5. Sandwich L/O

You already learned this technique in Chapter 5, when we discussed lease options. The Sandwich L/O is used when you buy using a L/O with terms favorable to you as a buyer and you then turn around and sell to a prospective buyer using a L/O with terms favorable to you as a seller. This is a very powerful technique that can give you immediate cash out and everything else you desire as an investor—a monthly cash flow as well as profit when the property is sold.

SUMMARY

Real estate revolves around financing—if buyers can't finance their purchases, real estate activity stops dead in its tracks. You've now learned what took us more than two decades to learn, and you're supercharged for success. You have multiple places to find financing, and you know how to secure the best kind of financing—seller financing with no money down. No matter what the banks think of you, no matter what your credit history has been, you will be able to buy mobile home parks and be on your way to financial independence and wealth.

You've now learned what every skilled investor knows—you don't have to have money to make money. You have to demonstrate with your experience that you have knowledge and strategies to make money, and then you can get the money you need from the people that already have it and want to make more. Your skills are knowledge and methodology. You know how to make a profit (Part One—The Four Basic Profit Strategies: Flippers, Keepers, L/Os and BBs) and you also have the methods to do it (Part Two—The Five Green Fs: Find It, Figure It, Flag It, Fix It, and Finance It). You will demonstrate with your experience that you can find good deals and make money.

In other words, when you have learned what we have taught you so far in this book and what you will learn in the next section and apply it with demonstrable results, money will flow to you naturally. It always does. It flows from the wealthy, who don't want to work too hard, if at all, to the *working wonderful,* and you will be one of the *working wonderful.* Don't look down at your profession because you have to work at it while the people who are lending you money only have to lend it. You will have the special pride that comes when you are a creator of wealth, not a salaried employee living paycheck to paycheck. If you do your work well and accumulate success, you or your children can become one of the wealthy who lend money to the working wonderful.

HOMEWORK

First, find out your credit score. Go to the websites listed in this chapter, the credit rating agencies, or to a banker or mortgage broker and have your credit report run. Based upon your credit score, decide how you are going to proceed with the different types of lenders.

If you have a credit score above 600 and you have the money needed to put down, take the best effective contract you have (one that is agreed to by both you and the seller) and put together a loan package for the lender, like we showed you. Then work on your lender script. Try to understand what you doing instead of just memorizing the words. It's okay to make a copy the script to follow when you visit the lender. Also make a copy of your property package to give to the lender. If you do all of this you will be prepared, more prepared than 99 percent of the investors out there, so imagine your success. Go ahead and imagine it. Now go visit the lenders in your area and use what you have learned.

If you have a credit score above 600 but little or no money to put down, then put together a contract like you were shown that uses a community banker and no money down. If this is accepted by the seller, put together your loan package and go see a community banker or a mortgage broker.

If you have a credit score below 600, you are going to need a hard money lender or a mortgage broker that specializes in subprime loans. If these options don't work you may have to use one of the five seller financing techniques. If you are limited with down payment money, then write the contract for no money down. But if you do have some cash and don't mind using it, then substitute your cash for the second mortgage shown in one of the five seller financing techniques.

Congratulations are probably going to be in order—you should get financing on your first property! If you followed the instructions in this book, you probably saw looks of admiration on the faces of the lenders and/or mortgage brokers you visited. They should have lent you whatever was reasonable once they saw how prepared you were and how much profit the property earned.

COMING ATTRACTIONS

Part Three of this book is coming up next. In this part you will mostly learn people skills. There are two chapters after that: the first involves understanding the principles of long-term wealth (in a humorous format), and the last part is your road map to earning an additional $100,000 per year, part-time, and having a net worth of one million dollars or more.

The next skills you will learn will show you how to close the deal, manage your business, and create your Power Team for maximum profit, efficiency, and *fun*. Don't ever forget to have fun. If you work hard—and there is nothing wrong with working hard—make sure you have fun while you do it. It will help you let off steam and enjoy your career. You are working for yourself now, with no boss scowling at you because you're having a good time at work. For some of you, just the simple act of inviting your family to work along with you as you begin to succeed will make it fun, as well as a meaningful experience.

Let's go!

Part Three

Reap Your Profits

Congratulations again! You've studied Part One, the Four Basic Profit Strategies, and learned the formulas for making money with mobile home parks. Then we combined that knowledge with Part Two, Getting the Deal Right, using the Five Green Fs, and you learned how to get each individual deal in shape to make money. In your homework, you picked out areas to invest in for mobile home parks, found good deals, and wrote contracts —either real or imaginary—on a few of them. If you "made the deal real," you then negotiated to your best advantage and, if possible, arranged an effective contract between you and the seller. Then you did your due diligence, your research, and if the deal was a "go," found bank or seller financing.

In Part Three coming up, you will learn how to close the deal and buy the park. Then, after you close, you will learn how to reap your profits. There are going to different things to do and overall strategies for running your business for each one of the Four Strategies, so you can repeat the steps to make profits over and over again. Here is how Part Three is set up:

Chapter 12: Closing the Deal. This is the finalization of your contract—the end of the path that changes the ownership of the property from the seller to you. Now your name is going to go on the deed, the title to the mobile homes, or both.

Chapter 13: Managing Your ATM and Building Your Power Team. If you are *keeping* the property, you will get it into top-notch rentable condition and learn how to find and qualify tenants to fill any vacancies. You will learn how to manage your tenants and enhance your relationship with them. If the relationship is not working out with some tenants, you will learn how to terminate it with an eviction and find better customers. We are also going to discuss building a Power Team, a contact file of professionals who will assist you in your mobile home investing career.

Chapter 14: Selling Like a Pro. If you are *flipping*, then you are going to get the property in prime condition, given time and price constraints. You are going to learn how to market the property like a professional for maximum profit and quick turnover. You will also learn how to build investor contacts to wholesale your mobile home park flippers to.

Chapter 15: Developing Your Own Mobile Home Park. You will learn how to take vacant land—in our example five acres—and place ten mobile homes on it to create your own mobile home park. You can then keep it for cash flow, sell off individual lots, or do both. We will also show you ways to grow from one park with ten units to parks with multiples of ten units—40, 60, even 100 units—while limiting your risk.

Chapter 16: Protecting Your Assets. You are going to learn the basics about protecting your wealth from people who want to take it away. You will also learn how to minimize your taxes—something that the government has made easy for you when you own real estate.

Chapter 17: Advanced Topics. We saved some of the more advanced topics for the end, where we will cover subjects like unusual mortgage financing, empty lots and their effect on NOI, buying mortgages on mobile homes along with the park, pricing a park to convert park-owned units to all land-lease units, plus a few more interesting subjects.

SUMMARY

We are going to show you how to be an effective and profitable business person who can manage people as well as properties. You can do most, or all, of the work yourself in the beginning, if you want keep costs down and have complete control. Or you may wish to grow the business to involve your family. As your business grows, you can involve more people or remain a family business. How, when, and how much you want to grow will be up to you, once you have the knowledge we are going to give you in Part Three.

HOMEWORK

No homework for now, but there's still some coming up in the next chapters.

COMING ATTRACTIONS

Let's get your first deal closed and some money in your pocket. Money has its own unique way of inspiring people, don't you think? Let's go!

12

Closing the Deal

Congratulations! It's now time to pull together everything you have been doing up until now: tie up all the loose ends regarding the contract, due diligence, and financing, and get your deal closed. Getting the deal closed simply means getting the ownership of the property transferred from the previous owner, the seller, to you, the buyer. It may seem too obvious to point out, but let me give you a dialogue we use at our auctions to motivate the bidders and get a laugh at the same time:

"Folks, I'm going to stop right now and give you the secret to investing. Is there anyone here who wants to make money, lots of money investing in real estate? Let me see a show of hands . . . Good! I hope you appreciate this secret because it took us years to discover it. Are you ready? Well, here it is. If you want to get rich in real estate . . . drum roll please . . . you must buy some first. We know that did not occur to you—that's why it is such a closely guarded secret. And where is one of the best places to get a good deal when you buy real estate? At auction, of course. Now let's get back to getting this property bought."

Right now we are going to discuss closing the deal when you are the buyer. Later we will talk about closing the deal when you are the seller completing a flip, an L/O, or a BB. Once you learn how to close a deal when you are buying, it will be easy for you to monitor a buyer when you are doing the selling.

STEPS TO A COMPLETED CLOSING

Think of a closing as if it were the gathering of crops by a farmer before he takes them to market. In your case, as a mobile home park investor, you're gathering the papers you will need to get a deed. You will need the following, in sequential order, to complete your purchase:

Some of you might be thinking, "Twelve things! Why do I have to jump through a dozen hoops just to buy one thing!" Well, calm down. We'll go over them one step at a time. You will discover that the process is set up according to good old common sense, and it ensures that each party's needs are met and that their interests are protected.

Steps to a Completed Closing

1. Fully Executed Contract
2. Escrow Deposit
3. Due Diligence Inspections, Including Termite Inspection
4. Loan Application
5. Appraisal
6. Lender "Clear to Close" Commitment
7. Title Commitment
8. Survey
9. Insurance
10. Final Walk-Through
11. Closing Statement
12. Closing—Deed Signed, Mortgage Signed, Funds Transferred

1. Fully Executed Contract

When both you and the seller have agreed to the terms of the deal, signed on the dotted line, initialed next to all the changes, and agreed upon an effective date, then you now have what is called a *fully executed contract*. You will need *four copies* of the contract—one for you as the buyer, one for the seller, one for the lender when you apply for the loan, and one for the title company. It would be nice if all four were originals with original signatures, but this is rarely the case. Typically, the contract with the original signatures goes to the lender, and everyone else gets an exact copy.

Speaking of original signatures, some attorneys and banks insist on contracts with ink on them—not copies or faxed copies. We have never had anyone commit forgery or fraud with copies or faxed copies, but attorneys, and thus their banker clients, live in mortal fear that this might happen. It is not uncommon for a contract to be faxed from the buyer to the seller or their broker and then back and forth a few times during negotiations, in which case the faxes are progressively more unreadable. Typically, when the contract has become fully executed, the broker will recopy the contract on a new original, mail it out for original signatures, and then send everyone fresh readable copies. Recently, the problem of legibility of faxes has been corrected by scanning contracts into a computer and then sending them as email attachments. In that case, all the copies are readable.

2. Escrow Deposit

Once the contract is fully executed you must place the good faith deposit—the escrow—in the agreed location, which is usually the escrow account of a broker, an attorney, or a title company. Remember to never allow a seller to hold your escrow deposit personally, and make sure that there is a clause in your contract that specifies that you will make the escrow deposit only *after* you have a fully executed contract. When you make your deposit, make a copy of your signed check and then have the escrow agent give you a copy of his deposit receipt when he deposits it into his account. Many times the seller will want to see a record that you made your escrow deposit in a timely fashion.

3. Due Diligence Inspections, Including Termite Inspection

You did a preliminary inspection of the property before you had a fully executed contract to ensure that you were interested in the property in the first place. Remember, you didn't want to spend a lot of time or money until you were sure you could buy it under the terms you wanted. Well now you are sure, so it's time to do the official due diligence inspections we discussed in Chapter 10.

Follow the "due dilly four-step" we described earlier to make the process as efficient as possible with respect to your money and time. Lenders will usually insist upon a licensed engineer, environmental specialist, and termite inspector to document their inspections. You can find competent inspectors through recommendations from your lender, Realtor, contacts in the local REIA, or a title company. It will take anywhere from a week to ten days to have the inspection reports completed. Once you receive them, share any "surprises," with the seller immediately and try to work them out. Attach an addendum to the contract stating what both of you agree to. Don't worry that your property has a few "dings." The important thing is arranging the time and money to fix them. If you can get the seller to pay for them and they won't chew up a lot of time to repair them, then go forward. Your lender almost always wants an appraisal, a termite inspection report, and an environmental report, but may not require the engineering, building, and mobile home inspections. Keep in mind—you are responsible for paying back the loan, and you probably guaranteed it with everything you own, so you need to be even more careful than the lender. Keep a file of your due diligence reports, along with your closing papers.

If the inspections do not present any unsolvable challenges, move forward to the next step. If, however, there are problems that stop the deal and won't be addressed by the seller, then stop at this point and tell the seller what you were advised to say whenever a negotiation is not successful. Then walk away, nicely, with the door still open, and go out and find another good deal.

4. Loan Application

Congratulations! You made it through the mobile home park due diligence inspections. Now you must apply to a lender for a loan. You have learned what paperwork you will need, where to go, and how to apply for your loan in Chapter 11. Complete the papers your lender needs and make sure you will be able to get a firm clear-to-close commitment from the lender within the time allowed in the contract. At this time, the lender will collect the money needed for your full credit report, property appraisal, and environmental report (if these are not already completed.) You should be careful of putting up any more money than this. You have a copy of your credit report and should have gone over it with the lender already, so you should be aware of any challenges you will face. If the lender feels you will not be able to overcome the challenges in your credit report, apply to another lender.

5. Appraisal

The lender, not you, must order your property appraisal. The appraisal can take anywhere from a few days to a few weeks, with two to three weeks being the average time. At this point you have to wait, because the transaction depends on the appraisal value. If the value is equal to, or greater than, your contract price, that's good. If the value is lower, you have a problem. The bank is only going to lend based upon a percentage of the appraisal, and if it is lower, that means you have to come up with a bigger down payment, which is not what you agreed to. You are going to need to meet with the seller and work this out or the contract is dead. The solution is usually to lower the contract price of the property to the appraised value. If you work it out, you will add an addendum to the contract stating the terms of the new agreement. If you can't work it out, walk away from the deal nicely, leaving the door open.

6. Lender "Clear to Close" Commitment

There are many types of commitments from lenders, but you are interested in the kind with no contingencies. At some point, you will get a "firm" commitment, which is subject only to the title report and survey. This is good. This means the property and your credit have met the lender's standards. You should have already ordered and received the title report and survey during your due diligence. If the lender's attorney agrees that these reports are okay, you will get a "clear to close" commitment, which means the lender is ready with the funds and is waiting for you to sign all the closing documents. Remember, you really aren't sure you will have a closing until you get the "clear to close" from the lender.

7. Title Commitment

The title commitment was one of the first things you ordered from a title company when you were considering buying the mobile home park, because you didn't want to spend thousands of dollars on due diligence only to find out the seller can't give you *clear* or *marketable title*. Most title companies won't charge you if a single contract does not go through. If you have many contracts that don't get completed, however, they might charge you around $150 to $200 for each report. You will need to go over the "exceptions" page in the title commitment with the title company to make sure all of those exceptions will be cleared up by the closing. An unscrupulous title company will offer to insure title as marketable, "subject to exceptions" that will still not be cleared up after the closing. This is not marketable title, and is not what you want.

8. Survey

Order a survey near the end of your due diligence period, but before the loan application when you are buying a mobile home park. In terms of time and money it's best to get a previous survey and have it updated. You want to know about the boundaries of the property, where the mobile homes sit on their lots, as well as the details about any accessory buildings such as clubhouses and storage places. The survey will also reveal any easements or encroachments from neighbors. You should go over the survey with the surveyor to make sure the land is the size that you were told and that the mobile homes are legally placed on the lots and are not too close to the boundaries or even on your neighbor's property. The title company and the lender will also go over the survey to make sure there is nothing that will affect the value of the property or its marketable title.

9. Insurance

Arrange for liability and property insurance for the park. This can take up to a week for a mobile home park, so order the insurance right after the appraisal has been completed and looks good. Ask the surveyor if the mobile home park is on a flood plain, because you will need flood insurance if it is. You may also have to arrange separate windstorm insurance if you are in a hurricane-prone area near a coastline.

10. Final Walk-Through

This is the inspection you do right before the closing, perhaps within an hour or two beforehand. Make sure that the buildings, the mobile homes, and the land are in the same condition they were originally, and that the personal property—appliances, air conditioning, furniture—are still there.

If you are retaining tenants and residents, make sure the rent is paid up and that the same tenants and residents are still there. Sometimes a seller may put an unqualified tenant in a vacant mobile home before closing just to collect some rent, leaving you with the problem later. You should require the seller and/or manager go with you to the property and introduce you to the all the tenants and residents. Inform them that you are the new owner, where to pay the rent, and how to contact you if there any problems. You and the seller should try to calm down any fears they have. Tenants can be skittish when the ownership of the park changes, and you should show them you will be an excellent and professional landlord.

11. Closing Statement

The closing statement shows how much money you will need to bring to the closing, how much the lender is lending you, all the different closing costs, and who pays what. *Go over the closing statement carefully!* It is not unusual for there to be mistakes on the closing statement that would cost you additional money. *Try to have at least one full day between receipt of the closing statement and the actual closing.*

Title companies and attorneys are notorious for handing out the closing statement an hour before the closing. They do that for two reasons. The first is that some lenders wait until the very last minute to give them all the figures and costs for the loan. The second reason is that it takes less time for title companies and attorneys to correct a closing statement when everyone is rushing through it at the last minute. Don't allow this to happen. Insist on going over the closing statement for at least one day before you close, and if you don't get it before then, then delay the closing until you have examined the closing statement without the "rush rush" pressure from others to do the closing as soon as you are done.

A sample closing statement is included in the Appendix. If you want to go over the closing statement, the title company will usually be more than happy to explain it on a line by line basis.

12. Closing—Deed Signed, Mortgage Signed, Funds Transferred

Okay, you're sitting at the closing table. If you have applied for a bank loan, the number of forms you are going to have to sign is formidable—there may be a pack of papers an inch or two thick. Most of the papers are to protect the lender and the title company from getting sued.

The most important papers are the deed, the mortgage, the note, and the closing statement. The *deed* is signed only by the seller, not the buyer, and it contains the legal description of the land. It may include a description of the mobile homes if you are buying park-owned units and the mobile homes are permanently attached to the land, or these may be covered by separate titles from the Department of Motor Vehicles. You want one or the other for park-owned units—something showing you now own the mobile homes in addition to the land. It's best to have DMV titles, because you then have a title to convey if you decide the move the mobile homes off the property or sell them in the future. If you don't have a title from the DMV for a park-owned mobile home you can usually get the DMV to give you a new one, but this involves a little time and expense.

The *mortgage* is the lender's lien on the property, and the *note* is the evidence of the debt. Sometimes the two are combined, and sometimes they executed separately.

When the papers are signed, you will slide a check to the closing agent for the funds required for closing. This must be a certified check or a cashier's check. Title companies and attorneys will usually take personal checks only up to a certain small amount, usually less than $500. *Make sure you receive a copy of all the papers you signed and a receipt for your check.* Make a permanent file for these papers as well as your due diligence papers. After all of the papers are signed, you are the proud owner of a mobile home park. The seller will give you the keys, all the park's files, and the original copies of the tenants' leases. Congratulations!

CLOSING WHEN YOU ARE SELLING

If you have completed a flipper, an L/O, or a BB, there is less to do. Basically, when you are selling, you are making sure that the buyers are completing the dozen steps they must take in order to close. Make sure all of their required deposits are securely placed in an escrow account, and that they are performing their inspections on time, applying for financing, getting appraisals, and moving ahead with their loan as expected.

It usually is not enough to sign a contract and then sit back and wait for the closing. You must interact with the buyers, or their real estate agent, to make sure they are doing everything necessary to get the transaction to the closing table. The good news is that this involves only a few phone calls every now and then.

DIFFERENCE IN CLOSING WHEN YOU ARE BUYING OR SELLING PERSONAL PROPERTY AS OPPOSED TO REAL ESTATE

If you do not own the land under the mobile home, and only the mobile home, the process is simpler. You will still need a contract, but the contract is the Personal Property Contract (in the Appendix), and is shorter and easier to fill out. There will still be escrow deposits and inspections. The loan process will be much simpler and faster, and will usually only take a week or two. The appraiser will contact the park manager or sales associate to get the necessary comps. The lender will issue a clear-to-close faster because there are fewer contingencies—there is no title commitment, no title insurance, and no survey. The final walk-through inspection will remain the same.

The closing will probably be done in the lender's office, using an abbreviated closing statement. You will need to bring the down payment in certified funds. You won't get a title, because the lender will probably hold it as the lien holder. If you are paying cash for the mobile home, I would recommend doing the closing at the Department of Motor Vehicles so the title can be transferred from the seller to you directly. This will ensure that there are no problems with registering the mobile home as yours. You will get a DMV title instead of a deed. All that is left is to get the keys or a copy of the tenant's lease and take ownership.

RICK'S RULE

I discovered Rick's Rule early in my real estate investing career, and it has made a big difference ever since. Rick was one of my first partners in real estate development, and everything we have done together has been successful, ranging from good to great. When we partner up, Rick usually brings "a great deal" —a piece of property we both would love to own. He finds these deals through his contacts and real estate networking ability. My part in the partnership is to manage the deal and ensure that we make money. I'm the "nuts and bolts" partner, and he is the "dealmaker." We respect and admire each other's abilities and different talents and we trust each other implicitly. These are the important components of a lasting partnership.

Sometimes, even when we are not working on a deal together, we will seek each other's counsel when we need to discuss a problem and get an unbiased viewpoint. This happened once when I already had a deal under contract for a warehouse foreclosure that was going to require lots of nuts-and-bolts fix up. I didn't invite Rick into the deal because I already had his part taken care of—I had found the deal and gotten it under contract. He didn't mind not being included because Rick understands that we both have to fulfill a need in any joint venture in order for the partnership to make sense, or it could lead to bad feelings later.

I felt uncomfortable about the deal, and he graciously listened to me describe it. When I was done, he said: "Zalman, you don't sound *excited*."

"Yeah, Rick, you're right," I responded. "I'm not sure if the profit is going to be zero, $5,000, $10,000, or more, because there are so many variable costs."

"Do you have a closing contingency?" he asked.

"Sure. I still have a few days left under the inspection period, and then I have to close a week after that. I don't have to buy it. Why?"

"One thing my dad always taught me is this: *If you're not excited to close, something's wrong with the deal. Buying or selling, you should come to the closing table with a smile on your face.*"

I dubbed this Rick's Rule, because his dad had the same first name. Rick's dad was one of the brightest and most respected real estate brokers in our area. He had a long history of accomplishments in many different areas of real estate investment. I always paid attention to the wisdom he gave his son, and you should, too. Rick's Rule means you should know that you will get a good profit from the deal when you buy. This will make you smile when you sit at the closing table. It also means you should be collecting a good profit when you sell, or be glad to be rid of the property, which should also make you smile.

I thanked Rick for the advice and then called the seller of the warehouse. After the opening pleasantries, I got down to business. This is how the conversation went:

"Mr. Seller, I've been studying the property, and the cost to repair your warehouse is going to be more than I first thought, and I can't pay you the $70,000 we agreed to on the contract."

I expected the seller to get angry and hang up on me. Instead, there was a pause, and then he asked: "So you don't want to buy it?"

"Well . . . no," I answered. "I just can't pay you $70,000. It's too much."

There was another even longer pause. Then he said, almost in a whisper: "How much can you pay me?"

"$60,000," I answered.

There was an ever longer pause, and he said, "Okay."

And then I was excited to close.

SUMMARY

Being an investor is like quarterbacking on a football team. You bring your deal down the playing field by using the Five Green Fs and then line up on the goal line, waiting to score. You've now know how to cross the goal line for a touchdown.

If you are the kind of person who is impatient, you need to keep calm and take your transaction one step at a time. Don't worry—it won't take all of your time to get the transaction closed. You still need to keep looking at properties, fitting them into one of the four Profit Strategies, and making more offers. You'll see why when we go over your road map to $100,000 in extra income in Chapter 19.

HOMEWORK

Take your best deal to closing. You've got it under contract, you've had it professionally inspected, and you went to a lender, applied for financing, and were approved. The lender may already have a title company or attorney to use for the closing. This is all right as long as you check them out and make sure they are a reputable firm and that they charge reasonable fees. If the lender is setting up the closing he will send the contract over to the closing agent. If the lender is not setting up the closing, then you should give your closing agent a copy of your contract. Make sure the title commitment gives you marketable title. When you have your clear-to-close, get your copy of the closing statement and go over it. Go over it line-by-line with the title company, your attorney, or your real estate agent. Set up the closing time when you are sure the closing statement is correct, get your down payment and closing costs from the bank, and do your final walk-through.

At closing, save all your papers, get copies of everything you signed, get the tenant files and leases, and get your keys. Your keys are your trophy.

COMING ATTRACTIONS

Now you own a park. Congratulations! If want to keep if for cash flow, you will learn how to manage it with a minimum of aggravation and a maximum of cash flow in the next chapter. The chapter after that will show you how to sell it like a pro if you want to flip it. It's getting exciting now. Money is on the way!

13

Managing Your ATM and Building a Power Team

Congratulations! You now own a mobile home park—your own ATM—and its primary accessory, an attractive mailbox where the rent checks are sent. This chapter is going to show you how to manage your rentals and the tenants/residents who live in them responsibly and efficiently, while receiving a nice profit at the same time. We're also going to show you how to set up your Mobile Home Park Power Team—your team of professionals who will assist you on your path towards wealth, no matter which of the Four Profit Strategies you use to gain wealth.

As we discussed in Chapter 2, there is a world of misinformation out there about tenants and mobile home park residents, and we will dispel these myths here the best way I know how, with good old American dollars. You applied the *Cash Flow Formula* prior to buying your first keeper, so you already know how much profit you can expect each month. Now you can go out and harvest it. Each morning, you will go out to your mailbox and find checks waiting for you, instead of only bills and junk mail. What's even better is when the value of the checks you receive each month exceed the cost of your bills, you have money left over at the end of the month to enjoy, save for a rainy day, or to invest so you can accumulate even more wealth.

The problems with tenants or residents can be solved once you learn how to manage them intelligently. This means learning how to find them and qualify them once you find them, and how to then maintain a mutually beneficial relationship. The former landlords who give rentals a bad name are almost always the same people who never learned how to manage tenants or residents and stumbled along hoping to find their way, but instead ended up with hurt feelings and shrunken wallets. The rental business is a business like any other; it involves customers, the services you provide to them, and the money you receive from them that becomes your profit. Most people would never think of buying a MacDonald's or Subway franchise without getting training from the company on how to run it, yet many people start a mobile home rental business without any training on being a landlord. We are going to outline the fundamentals of being a landlord in this chapter. How to be a landlord is the sole subject of many excellent books and I recommend that you get them and read them. This chapter will provide your primary training for now.

MANAGING YOUR MANAGER

Ordinarily, the mobile home parks you purchase will have a competent, experienced manager already in place. However, you might experience one of the following situations at some point:

- There is no manager transferring with a mobile home park purchase
- A manager unexpectedly leaves or needs a long leave of absence
- You have to let a manager go and find a replacement

You need to know the manager's job functions so you can train the new manager when one of the above situations occur. You may have to be prepared to manage the park yourself until you hire one, so we are going to show you how to manage a mobile home park yourself. This will be an insurance policy for the time when a manager is not available for your park, and you have to find a new one, train that person, and then evaluate his or her performance.

It's important to keep in mind that one of the main advantages of buying a mobile home park over purchasing individual mobile homes is that the costs you incur for having a manager are considered an accepted mobile home park expense, just like insurance and real estate taxes. It is not considered when pricing individual mobile homes because they are priced based on their shelter value, not their income-producing ability. The manager's salary and other expenses associated with managing were subtracted from the NOI of the mobile home park when you used the Magic Formula to compute the price you were prepared to pay for it, so in effect, the manager is free. When we discovered this fact and then saw how we spent less time managing a mobile home park with ninety land-lease residents and a manager than we did managing five individual mobile homes ourselves, the green light went on for us and we wanted to own more mobile home parks. It was so much easier than managing individual mobile homes spread out over an area. The same is true for managing single-family home and duplex rentals. When you combine the ease of management with the advantage of having mobile home park residents who maintain their own homes, mobile home parks become a very attractive form of investment compared to apartment buildings and other multifamily rentals.

If you want to own many mobile home parks, you will set up a system in which you manage your managers, with a site visit to your parks on a monthly or every other month basis. As your holdings grow in an area, you can hire a regional manager who will take over managing the managers and making regular site visits. Your function will become managing the regional managers and studying weekly and monthly reports to make sure your parks are functioning properly and profitably. Then you will perhaps make only quarterly, semiannual or annual visits to your parks. At the highest level, you can attain a yearly income in the seven figures (yes, that's right, in the millions of dollars) and a new worth in the eight or nine figures (I'll leave it to you to get excited after you figure out how much that is.)

How to Find and Hire a New Park Manager

When we train, we often get asked four questions about managers:

1. Where do you find a new mobile home park manager?

2. What qualities do you look for in a manager?

3. How much should you pay a manager?

4. Should the manager live on-site in the park?

In answer to the first question, *the best place to find a new park manager is right under your nose—in the park itself.* Identify the best tenants or residents—the ones who take the best care of their mobile homes and lots—and interview them, looking for the qualities we will talk about next. If there is no suitable person, then checking the help-wanted section in the classifieds, running an ad in mobile home park magazines, or putting a sign in front of the park can work well.

As to the second question, the qualities we look for in a park manager are, in approximate order of importance:

- Tenant/resident management experience
- Someone who will exhibit pride of ownership in the park
- Trustworthiness
- Hard working (and sales ability if the park is a turn-around situation)
- Fairness when dealing with residents and applying rules
- Someone who can grow with the job and become a regional manager

Finding someone who has experience managing tenant/residents is an advantage because it saves you time training her in doing her job. However, a park manager's job is not so difficult that she can't be trained in a reasonable period of time, and sometimes it's better to start with a beginner who can be molded to manage the park the way you want, rather than someone who has always done things in "this other way" and refuses to change, and her "other way" makes your teeth grind and even loses you money.

The next important quality might surprise you, but our managers look at *our* parks like *they* own them. When they speak about the mobile home parks they manage, they say, "I want *my park* to be this way, and I don't want *my park* to be that way." Believe it or not, we encourage them to think like that. People come with both a body and a mind. When you can engage their mind and their passions and not just their physical presence they will make you proud and wealthier, along with themselves. They improve your park because they take pride in being the managers of little towns that they can influence and improve. We have found that managers like the respect and power they have, and they will shine if they are shown by you, the owner, how to use their power well and for everyone's benefit.

Trust is important in a manager's position, because there will be times when the manager has to take in cash, pay bills from petty cash, arrange for repairs, hire outside contractors to fix things and get paid, and so on. We try to limit the cash our managers take in by not having them accept cash payments for rents. We also have the manager set up his or her own checking account that he or she controls to pay unforeseen bills (usually at the petty cash level) and then we reimburse that account when the manager provides the payment receipts.

We want our managers to work reasonably hard, but the job of a manager is not unusually demanding. If you have a turnkey park that is fully rented out and running well, a manager primarily functions as your eyes and ears. It is a full-time job in that the manager's presence is important, but many times she will not be busy full-time. If she needs to run a personal errand every now and then, it is not critical to the functioning of the park, and for this reason, it is an attractive career to single parents. This is not true for a turn-around park, however, where you will need to buy mobile homes, set them up on empty lots, and then sell BBs. In that case, organizational and sales ability are important in a manager. Setting up a mobile home is simple and not brain surgery, but it does require more job skills. Selling BBs requires some sales skills, but managers don't have to be super-salespeople. The terms of the BB and the marketing you put in place to promote it will normally pre-sell BBs for you, but your manager has to be able to show the BBs and feel comfortable presenting the terms to customers.

A good manager will also have to be fair to all the tenants/residents and can not apply the park rules in an arbitrary manner. If a manager shows favoritism it escalates tensions in a park and it affects profitability when people move out as a result. You can monitor the impartiality of your manager if you perform an exit interview with tenants/residents when they leave. When it becomes apparent your manager is upsetting the tenants/residents, he or she must be guided into being more impartial or be replaced.

If your vision is to own many mobile home parks and have regional managers, it is a benefit to have managers who are competent in their duties and can grow, manage, and train others to manage your other parks. Hiring and training from inside is a benefit.

The third question we get asked is about the salary and benefits of a manager. The answer is: it depends on the size and type of the park—the number of tenants/residents, and whether the park is in a turnkey or turn-around situation. Being a manager of turnkey parks of twenty units or less is a part-time job and usually can be paid by offering either a discount from the manager's rent, or free rent. As the number of units increases, you may want to offer free lot rent and a small salary of around $100 per week. You will need a full time manager when the number of units approaches fifty or more. Every situation is different, but in our area, for a turnkey park of eighty units or more, it is common to give the manager free rent on a mobile home or a site-built home in the park, perhaps include utilities, pay a salary of $300 per week or more, and perhaps include some medical benefits. Again, different areas and different parks will call for difference pay packages. If you want to know the common practice in your area, visit or call some neighboring mobile home parks and ask the manager or owner about it.

The last question we are asked is, "Should you require the manager to live on premises?" We have seen parks where the manager works in the office like a regular nine to five job and then leaves the park at the end of day, and his or her weekends are free. We require, however, that our managers live in the park and be around part of the weekend, even though they do not have working hours on the weekend. Many emergencies happen after business hours and on weekends, and having a manager present is a tremendous benefit. Having the park's handyperson live there is also a benefit for the same reason.

Now, you're going to learn how to perform a park manager's functions, so you can do it if needed, train someone how to do it, and knowledgeably evaluate the managers who work with you.

MANAGING TENANTS/RESIDENTS

You must have noticed that we have been referring to the people that rent from you as tenants/residents. The reason we have been doing that is to remind you that you have a choice—you could either be renting out a park-owned unit in which the *tenant* has no ownership and leases both the mobile home and the land from you, or you could be leasing out the lot only and the *resident* owns the mobile home. As we discuss management we will point out when there is a difference between managing a tenant or a resident.

When you bought your park, the lots were either all rented or there were some vacancies. If the lot was rented, you should have already met the tenant/resident when you went around with either the previous owner or the park manager. You should have given the tenant/resident new contact information for when repairs or problems happen and the new address for where to send the rent. In addition, you should have the following for each tenant/resident:

1. The tenant/resident's name and contact information
2. An original or copy of the lease for the resident's lot, or on a park-owned unit, the tenant's lease for both the mobile home and the lot
3. If it is a park-owned unit, a copy of your title and a set of keys, or if it is a resident-owned unit, a copy of the resident's title
4. A security deposit transferred to you at closing if it is a park-owned unit
5. Prorated rent for the remainder of the month after the closing date

You should get a separate phone number to give to tenants/residents. They can, and will, call with a problem, regardless of the day or the time.

If some of the lots were vacant or had vacant mobile homes on them when you bought the park, you must do one of two things:

1. If it was a vacant park-owned unit, you must get that mobile home into proper shape to rent it out or, if it will require too much rehab, dispose of it and place another unit on the lot. In either event, you will then need to find a new tenant.
2. If the lot was empty, you must tidy it up and make sure all the utility connections are functioning. Then you can either move on a BB if you want residents or try to find a new resident who will move his mobile home onto the lot. If you have only park-owned units, then you should move on another mobile home to rent out.

Rehabbing Park-Owned Mobile Home Rentals

Most of your park-owned mobile home rentals will probably be in the middle to upper end of affordable income segment or the lower end of the middle income segment, because that is usually where the greatest cash flow per dollar invested is. In these market segments, we have become more interested in safe, clean, and healthy accommodations rather than rehabbing until the property is perfect and beautiful. We are interested in durability, so the components will stand up to long-term wear and tear. We still want curb appeal, but most of this appeal is going to come from a fresh coat of paint on the outside of the mobile home and a mowed and tidy yard. The appeal on the inside is also going to come from a fresh coat of paint, a clean rug, and a clean mobile home. We select components like cabinets, faucets, bathroom and kitchen fixtures, and rugs for their sturdiness and ability to take abuse. Many times, fancy and pretty components are not built this way.

We do not rent furnished mobile homes, but we know some investors who do. If you can get used furniture for pennies on the dollar, get a premium for renting furnished mobile homes, and have very few vacancies and turnovers, then by all means try renting out your park-owned mobile homes furnished. We are interested in finding long-term tenants, not transients. Long-term tenants usually have their own furniture and transients usually do not.

When you get a turnover—when a previous tenant moves out and a new one is going to move in—you may have to do a light rehab, so don't get upset by any carelessness on the part of the previous tenant. You have a security deposit and you have been allocating part of your rents for this eventuality or vacancies. This may be the time to pay out some of this money.

In the beginning when we had only sixteen rentals, I used to do my own turn-around rehabs. Then I hired a handyman because I spent half the time cursing the previous tenant's carelessness and the other half actually doing the work. It took half the time to get the work done, and was cheaper in the long run, to hire a retired guy who appreciated getting the work. Our motto now when we have a tenant leave is: "Clean 'em up, fix 'em up, paint 'em up . . . Next!" Doing a light rehab after a tenant leaves is part of the cost of doing business. Take your emotions out of it, or you will get upset. The careless tenant that you lost will probably still be renting twenty years from now, while you will be wealthy and have a profitable business. Who is really better off?

On-Site Handyperson

Whether you have park-owned units or a land-lease park, you will need someone to do maintenance and repairs. If you have fifty park-owned units or more, chances are you will need a full-time handyperson to do park maintenance, repair the mobile homes, and do turnover rehabs. As I said before, that person should be required to live in the park because many emergencies will occur after business hours and on weekends.

If you have 100 land-lease units, you will need a full time maintenance person to pick up trash, mow lawns, do snow removal, maintain common areas, and make occasional infrastructure repairs. If you have less than 50 park-owned units or 100 land-lease units, you will only need a part-time handyperson, and you will have to figure out the best way to pay him and have him nearby for emergencies.

Vacancies

Whether you bought the mobile home park with vacancies or fully occupied with tenants/residents, there will come a time when a tenant/resident will leave and you will have find another. You should have a list of your current tenants/residents, in lease expiration date order. It should include the addresses and the dates each lease expires, the soonest ones first. We call this our expiration list.

You should check and update your expiration list on a monthly basis. Contact each tenant/resident at least six weeks before the expiration of his lease—eight weeks is even better. Call and ask if he wants to rent again, and after give him the terms of renewal (any rent increase and/or rule changes). If the tenant/resident wants to lease again, or is unsure, give them a deadline by which point the new lease must be signed—about a week—or you will start to advertise for a new tenant/resident. If the tenant doesn't contact you by the end of that deadline, try to reach him again, and if you still don't get a new lease signed immediately, assume the tenant is not staying.

The Difference between a Tenant Vacancy and Resident Vacancy

There is a basic difference when dealing with lease renewals for tenants on park-owned units and residents on land-lease lots. A tenant in a park-owned home can, and will, leave at will. The tenant has no ownership and no ties to your property. In a land-lease park, the resident has three choices when desiring to move:

1. Sell the mobile to some else or to the park owner

2. Abandon the mobile home

3. Move the mobile home to another park

If the resident sells their mobile home to some else, you have no rent risk. In fact, you will make money by charging the new owner for application fees. If they sell their home to you, you will make money on the resale, like we showed you in the section on BBs.

If the resident abandons the mobile home, you will claim it, retitle it in your name, and once again you will make money on the resale as with a BB. Even in the case the home is in terrible shape, you can probably sell it to someone who will rehab it.

In the rare case that a resident wants to move the mobile home out of the park, you should first determine if it is a newer or older home. If it is older, there is only a slim chance the resident will move it—it will cost too much, and many other parks won't allow older mobile homes in. If it is a newer mobile home and the resident is serious about moving it, you will suffer serious consequences as the park owner. You have a reverse Triple Zotz—a *Triple Whammy.* You will lose lot rent, you will have to pay to move in another mobile home and set it up, and your park will be worth less in the meantime because your NOI will go down. Try to avoid this, even at the cost of buying the home yourself. If you can't avoid it, then it's BB time again.

Finding Tenants/Residents

Always leave yourself at least a month to find a new tenant/resident when it that looks like one of your mobile homes will be vacated—and don't wait for the current tenant to sign a new lease on the last day of his rental period. Some tenants will leave you in the lurch when they inform you at the last minute that they have changed their mind, leaving you with a vacancy and at least a one-month loss of rent. We have plenty of painful experience with that sort of situation, so take my advice to your "wisdom bank" and deposit it in your safe deposit box. Also, when a tenant/resident wants to renew a lease, you should usually raise his rental rate at least a $10, just to get him used to paying more each year to cover inflation and the other cost increases that come with it.

When you have a vacancy, speed is very important—you want to rent it as fast as possible to the best available tenant. Every day or month that the park-owned mobile home or the lot is vacant is a day or month you will never be paid for—it's gone forever. In some areas, vacancies may routinely be filled in a week, while it may take a month or more in other areas. The following are the ways we find new tenants/residents, in order of their speed and effectiveness in our market. You may find that some of our ways to fill vacancies are more or less successful in your market, so fine-tune your own strategies accordingly.

- Classified ad in newspapers
- For Rent sign outside of park
- Internet websites such as Craig's List
- Rental agents/Realtors
- Word of mouth/finder's fee to other tenants
- Bulletin boards

Classified ads in newspapers are the fastest way we've found to fill vacancies. In our area, we have also found the paper of major distribution to be better than the local *Pennysaver*—it generated better leads, and is worth the greater expense. You may find the opposite is true in your market. When we first became landlords in Staten Island, New York City, *The Village Voice,* rather than *The New York Times,* was excellent at getting us new tenants—we filled a vacancy within three days, and the ads were cheaper. In your ad, put the location, the number of bedrooms, the rent, any restrictions, your phone number, and one line designed to sell the property. Here are two sample ads we might run, the first for a family rental, the other for retirees:

North—3 Bedroom Mobile
Clean and Quiet, Fenced Yard
$695/mo 555-1234
www.zalmanvelvel.com

South—2 Bedroom Mobile
Great Golf & Clubhouse
Adult Park
$695/mo 555-1234
www.zalmanvelvel.com

The good old standard *For Rent sign* is in second place with us, although as of this writing, signs are gaining in effectiveness compared to classified ads. You can't beat a sign for cost, but we have also found that it is slower to produce new tenants. That being said, we know landlords that only use For Rent signs, and they say their vacancies fill right up. If you have lots of drive-by traffic, that is possible. However, we have seen those landlords' signs sitting out for months, so we're not sure they were being truthful. Or perhaps "filling right up" means "sometime in the next three months" to them. They would rather be vacant an extra month or two than pay for an ad, and judging by our experience, that is being foolishly cheap. If you are getting $500 per month in rent and an ad costs $100 per week but saves you two weeks of vacancy time, or $250, then it is better to pay for an ad. Even if the ad only saves you a week of vacancy, it is still better to spend $100 on an ad if your mobile home rents are $500 or more each month or $125 per week.

We have also found that the tenant who responds to a For Rent sign can sometimes be less qualified than one who responds to a classified ad. Some substandard tenants drive around looking for For Rent signs and nonprofessional landlords, who won't check them out and qualify them. From our twenty-seven years of experience, we can state that someone who buys a newspaper and spends the time to go through the classifieds is usually a better qualified tenant. Again, these are just rules of thumb from our experience, not rules carved in stone. Your experience may be different, so adjust your methods accordingly. We always still set out a For Rent sign on a vacant property in addition to the newspaper ad, to double our efforts.

The *Internet* has risen dramatically on our list, and as of this writing, we have discovered tremendous benefits from using Craig's List. Using the website is free. (We wonder how long it will remain that way, given its usefulness.) It is primitive in appearance, but it does the job. The listings expire automatically after about fifteen or thirty days, and we reenter all our ads every other day because of a rule about repetition. Up until recently most of our affordable housing tenants didn't use the Internet that much, but this has changed. And, *if you have seasonal tenants in desirable recreational areas, the Internet is one of the best ways to find tenants.*

Using *rental agents* and/or *Realtors* can be excellent ways to fill vacancies, but you may have to pay for them. In our market, the landlord pays the rental agent to find a tenant, and rental agents charge a full month's rent. For an absentee landlord, they are worth the expense. Since we are hands-on landlords with over 500 rental units, rental agents are not worth the expense for us. When we were landlords on Staten Island, the rule in that area was the tenant paid the rental agent, and in that case, we used them more often.

Word of mouth is great when it happens, because it shines a positive light on you as a professional landlord. If your tenants are recommending you to their family and friends, you are doing a good job. You can try giving word of mouth a little shot in the arm by offering finder's fees to your current tenants if they send someone your way.

The good old free *bulletin board* comes in solid last for us, but by the time you build up an inventory of rentals—and by that, I mean 50 to 100 or more—you should be everywhere you can. Even if you only get one vacancy filled from it, a bulletin board posting is free, so it's worth using.

Okay, you have made your phone ring with prospective tenants/residents. If your experiences is like ours, you will receive about twenty phone calls per week for each vacancy. This can be a lot of calls, if you spend too much time on each one. You have to know how to qualify your tenants quickly and easily, and this is extremely important. *All of the failed landlords we have met had one thing in common—they did not qualify their tenants.* They rented to the first person who had a security deposit and the first month's rent. You should not do this.

Qualifying Tenants/Residents

You begin qualifying renters on the phone, *with their first call,* to see whether they meet your minimal standards as the type of people you want on *your property*. You don't want to spend a lot of time filling out paperwork and showing rentals to people you are not going to rent to. We patiently answer one or two of the caller's questions, and then we ask the following questions, nicely but firmly:

There is a flow to these questions, and they are important. In the Appendix there is a copy of one of our tenant call-in sheets. You should adapt it to your market and personality. If the caller gives an answer that shows he or she is not who you are looking for, end the call on that question. For instance, if the caller has the right amount of people for the rental but has five pit bulls, you might want to stop there and say you only allow one pet, and no pit bulls, because of insurance regulations.

1. *How many people will be moving in?* This should be the first question. You don't want a family of ten in a one-bedroom/one-bath mobile home. They will wear the place out if is park-owned, or create larger expenses if they are residents and you pay for utilities and trash. You also don't want to create a zoo. About half of the people who call us have pets, so if you have a "no pets" policy you will be eliminating half of your rental market. We have found it is a toss-up whether pets or children do more damage. Eliminating people who have either pets

Tenant Qualification Questions

1. Besides yourself, who else will be living with you? Any pets?
2. When do you need to move in?
3. How long will you need the property for?
4. If you like the property, do you have the deposit and rent now?
5. Are you employed? Is another member of household also employed?
6. How long have you been working there? What is your take-home pay?
7. Where are you living now? How long have you been there?
8. Is there anything in your background, such as a criminal or eviction record?

or children severely cuts down on our pool of qualified tenants and increases the time, effort, and expense for re-renting turn-arounds. We allow pets more now because renters sneaked them in anyway even when we didn't allow them. So, we monitor the number, type, and size of the pets instead. We have found that new tenants who have pets don't smell the pet smells left by previous tenants, while people without pets do.

2. *Next, you need to know if they need the rental right away.* If they need it in two months, and the unit is vacant now, politely tell them you'll call back in a month if the rental is still available or if another one becomes available.

3. *You also want to know how long a prospect will need the rental for.* When we ask the question, it is common for people to answer with, "Well, how long do you want to rent it for?" Don't answer their question until the prospect answers how long they want to rent. If you want a one-year lease and the people only want to rent for a month or so, explain nicely that you're sorry, but you need a longer-term tenant/resident. Then move on to the next call. People who only want to rent for a month or so know that short-term rentals are much more expensive than long-term rentals because motels and hotels are usually the only short-term rentals around. If you tell them up front that you are looking for a long-term rental they will lie and tell you they want to stay longer. Then they will leave after a month or so and not pay the last month's rent, and allow you to keep the security deposit for that last month. Meanwhile you have to go through the time and expense to start an eviction and get another renter.

4. *Next you want to find out if they have any money now.* You would be positively amazed how many people need a home or lot to rent right now and want to see yours, yet have no money to rent it. They are real time wasters.

5 and 6. *Now, get to facts and figures about their employment.* There is a strong correlation between how long people have been at their jobs and how long they will be renting from you. People who jump around from job to job also jump around on rentals, while steady employees tend to be steady renters. We also want to make sure they take home

enough money to afford living in our park. Again, you would be surprised how many renters call to rent something from you, and after you run through a budget for their rent and home expenses, they have only $100 left over each month for food, gas, clothes, and unforeseen problems that will crop up—which clearly isn't enough.

7. *You also want to know where they are living now, and how long they have been there* to see if they are coming from a high crime area and, again, whether they jump around frequently.

8. Last, *ask the "trick" character question—have you ever been convicted or evicted?* If the renter is a career criminal or evictee, he is going to lie. It's okay. You will find out—you almost always will—and then you can turn them down. If the tenant has some black marks from five or more years ago that he divulges completely, and has evidence that he has reformed, you might give him a second chance. If he lies, move on to the next caller.

As you get further along in the questions, the caller is becoming more and more qualified. If at some point the caller balks at answering so many questions, explain nicely you are really trying to save him time, so that he can find out with just this phone call whether you will rent to him. If he hangs up or gets huffy, then he is probably not serious and is just looking, is hiding something, or is looking for a more desperate and unskilled landlord.

Once the prospective tenant passes your phone qualification, give them directions to the property if he is calling in response to your ad so he can do a drive by and see if he is comfortable with the area and the home. If he is calling from a For Rent sign in the yard or has driven by and seen the property, then have him come in to the office and do the following:

1. Have the prospective tenant fill out a rental application, make a copy of his pay stub and driver's license, and collect the application fee

2. Run a credit check

3. Run a local and national criminal check

4. Run a local eviction check

5. Call employers—check job dates and salary

6. Call previous landlords—be careful about the truthfulness of the current landlord

7. If you have doubts, pay a surprise visit to the applicant's current residence

One of our rental applications is in the Appendix in the back of the book. Check everything the prospective tenant/resident writes on it and get a copy of his most recent pay stub and driver's license. We collect an application fee of $35 to $75, which we use to run a credit check and a national criminal check. We belong to the Experion credit service; you should consider joining Experion, TransUnion, or Equifax. For around $10 you can run a check on a tenant's credit history, and for about $5 you can run a national criminal check from another service. The local criminal and eviction check is free in our county and on the Internet. You should call the employer to verify the dates of employment and current salary.

Calling the current landlord or park manager is a mixed bag—some will be honest, but many will not be truthful if the renter is a problem the landlord wants to get rid of. For this reason we prefer to call the next-to-the-last landlord or park manager. They have no reason to lie because the renter is long gone.

The final item, paying a surprise visit to the prospective tenant's current residence, is the best insurance against renting to an undesirable tenant. Call the applicant and tell him there is something else you need to go over in his rental application, and insist on seeing him right then at his current home. If he absolutely refuses to invite you over after you tell him it is absolutely essential that you see him right away, he is probably hiding something—extra people, pets, a pig palace, or drugs. It's better to find another tenant.

The problem with this tactic is it takes time—as much as an hour or more. In the beginning, I heartily recommend it to all new landlords, because an hour or two spent eliminating a bad renter is worth it—a bad tenant will chew up many times that in hours of aggravation once they move in.

Try to qualify a tenant while he is sitting in your office after filling out the application. If he qualifies, show him the lot or the inside of the mobile home. If he is satisfied, sign the lease, collect the security deposit and the rent for the first month or first week, give him the keys, and let him move in.

If the renter does not qualify, either because of bad credit, undisclosed criminal violations or evictions, or an untruthful application, tell them you can't process him right then and that you will call him later. Then, when you call, gently explain that he had a credit problem. Almost everyone who lies on an application or has a criminal or eviction record has bad credit and knows it.

We had only one case in twenty-seven years where a career criminal applied to rent in one of our parks and had good credit. When we told him we were turning him down due to credit issues, he became surly. Then we told him that he had also lied on his application, and that we knew he had been arrested recently for cocaine possession and sales. At that point he went away quietly.

Filling Out and Signing the Lease

To have a written lease or not? That is the question. We have heard landlord acquaintances assert that they do not sign leases because a lease only protects the tenant, not the landlord. We run our rental business differently. The lease is our way of stating who pays for what, what the rules are, and when the lease is over. It also states that we have the right to cancel the lease on a park-owned unit with sixty days prior notice. We have never had a problem with the clause, and feel it is the ultimate answer to a bad landlord/tenant relationship. If we are not getting along—for any reason—the tenant has to be gone in sixty days. In twenty-seven years I think we've used it once or twice.

When it comes to our park residents who are only renting a lot from us, Florida law states that the land-lease is automatically renewed every year at the resident's choice. The only way the resident can be terminated is if he doesn't pay the lot rent or doesn't comply with the rules, or if we sell the park and the new owner changes its use from a mobile home park to something else. This automatic renewal law does not apply to park-owned units in which the tenant does not own the mobile home or the land.

One of our park-owned unit leases is shown in the Appendix. We took it from a book I read many years ago on how to be a good landlord and modified it over the years. As you can see it is only one page long and written simply so it is easy to understand. We go over every word on the lease with new tenants so they will understand what they are responsible for, what the rules are, and what their costs are. Our rules are all common-sense restrictions. As simple as it is, *we have never had a problem with our lease!*

We know landlords who have ten-page leases, created by attorneys, that list just about everything that can go wrong. The plain fact is that *the only time we have to refer to a lease is when the tenant doesn't pay or breaks the rules.* You do not need to be a Philadelphia lawyer to deal with affordable-income tenants—you just have to be fair, respectful, and firm.

We also have a copy of our land-only (lot) lease in the Appendix. The rules of the mobile home park are an important part of this lease. In Florida, the land-lease lease refers to the prospectus on the park, which is another Florida requirement. The park prospectus gives the rules and regulations of the park, the dimensions of the lots, and some additional legalese. All new residents in a land-lease community in Florida must be given a park prospectus.

Information to Keep in the Tenants'/Residents' File

When we are finished qualifying a tenant/resident, we keep the following in his file for reference:

1. Copy of the lease—park-owned or land-lease
2. Copy of application
3. Copy of credit report
4. Copy of criminal and eviction reports
5. Copy of driver's license
6. Copy of pay stub
7. Copy of title on mobile home if a resident
8. Copy of sales contract and note if for a BB

How to Maintain Tenants/Residents

When you were renting, what did you want from your landlord? Chances are that your tenants'/residents' answers to that question will be the same as yours. They want you to maintain and repair their mobile home or lot so it will be safe and healthy, and they want you to treat them with respect. Now, what do you want from them? You want them to pay the rent on time and treat you and your property with respect. It really is that simple. Let's discuss some common strategies that we use to make sure these basic principles are met on both sides.

- The initial move in, and how you are paid
- The security deposit and the first month and last month's rent
- Where and how to collect rent
- Late payments and penalties
- Repairs and maintenance
- Tenant/resident leaving early
- The tenant/resident is not working out, in spite of everything

At the *initial move in,* we do not take personal checks—only cash, bank cashier checks, or money orders. The tenants can pay their rent with a personal check after that, but the first time their check bounces is the last time we will accept a personal check. After that they will have to send in a bank check or money order.

The *security deposit* is nonnegotiable for park-owned units. We must have it in hand, in the form of cash, a cashier's check, or a money order, before the tenant can move into our mobile home. We usually charge a $500 security deposit, or a month's rent, whichever is lower. In Florida, you cannot evict a tenant for nonpayment of a security deposit, so we make sure that we get it up front. We also require a pet deposit, of around $250, if we deem it necessary. The question prospective tenants ask most often is, "How much to move in?" If you are lenient about the security deposit, later on you will probably find out what it is like to lose money. If a tenant can not manage his life so he has $500 in savings, he probably is not going to be able to pay his rent when an unexpected bill comes in, and you will have no financial protection when you have to evict him.

My wife came up with a clever way for securing the last month's rent, which is really like getting a second security deposit. She allowed tenants to pay the last month's rent in installments over a period of five months by paying an additional $100 each month after the first month. The extra payment was credited towards the last month's rent. This arrangement saved us a lot of money over time on early moveouts and unexpected damage.

We do not ask for a security deposit in our land-lease parks because the mobile home becomes the security deposit in the event that we have to evict the resident. Yes, that's right—we wind up taking away the mobile home if a resident is evicted. You will learn more about that later on in this chapter when we discuss evictions.

Our tenants *pay their rent by mail.* We send them a bill with a return envelope around the twentieth of each month, just like the phone company and electric company. They then write us a check, put it in the return envelope, put on a stamp on it, and send the payment back by the first of the month. *We do not collect rents in person* nor do we have our managers do it, because it would take too much time with over 500 rentals. There also would be some risk in carrying around that much money at certain times of the week or month. We know landlords who collect all their rents in person so they can inspect their properties regularly and take cash. When you have more than fifty rentals, though, this becomes time consuming. The choice is yours, however.

How do you collect rents if you own a long-distance park? We do it the same way we do for parks in our area—we send out a bill with a return envelope. We know some park owners who have the managers in their long-distance parks collect rents and deposit them in a local bank. When you collect rents this way, the manager has to copy the deposit slips and the individual rent checks and then fax or email them to the main office, to be entered into the accounting system.

For park-owned units, *sometimes we break up the rent into weekly payments.* This results in more rent for the same mobile home. This is how we do it:

Monthly Rent = $500
Weekly Rent = Monthly Rent Divided by Four, Plus $15
Weekly Rent = $500 ÷ 4 = $125 + $15 = $140 per Week

Weekly Rent Converted to Monthly Rent
$140 per Week × 52 Weeks = $7,280 per Year
$7,280 ÷ 12 Months = $606 per Month (Rounded)

In other words, when we allow someone to pay weekly, we collect $106 per month more per mobile home that would otherwise rent for $500 per month. Collecting weekly rents definitely involves more time and expense, though. We have about fifty weekly rentals, so collecting weekly gives us fifty times $106—about $5,000 per month more in income—making it worthwhile. It more than pays for the manager we hire to manage all of our park-owned mobile homes. By the way, we own about seventy mobile homes on individual lots in one area, where we have a little office with a mail slot in the door. Our tenants drop their rents off by putting them in the mail slot (with a strict warning to not put cash in the envelope), and our manager goes by a couple of times each week to collect the envelopes.

Our policy on *late payments and penalties* is: $15 per week extra on weekly rents and $50 on monthly rents—strictly enforced. If you do not strictly enforce late-rent penalties, tenants will pay you whenever they feel like it and you will be doing bookwork and deposits every day of the month. You want to get all of your rents in by the first week of the month and then move on to other important duties. If a tenant balks at the late penalty when we sign the lease together, we simply ask, "Do you intend on paying your rent late?" We have never had a tenant say yes, so we add, "Well, then we guess the late fee is not important since you will always be paying on time." If the tenant ever says yes, they will be paying their rent late, then we would say, "Well, perhaps you will be better off renting from someone else."

For *repairs and maintenance,* we tell our tenants that, in order to keep the rents low, they are going to have to do certain things like mow their own lawn and maintain their fridge and stove. We give them a working fridge and stove when they move in, and they have to leave us a working fridge and stove when they move out, and in between they are responsible for the repairs. We do this because, in owning and renting out around 100 mobile homes, we found that the majority of the repair calls were for appliances, and we didn't like being in the appliance-repair business. We used to make our tenants responsible for the first $100 of repairs every month, but that didn't work because then they just let problems deteriorate until the repairs cost many times that amount to correct.

We handle the plumbing, electrical, and carpentry repairs, and we make repairs promptly. We learned early on that if you take care of a tenant's problems promptly, they have no reasonable excuse when it comes time to pay the rent. If you repair late, they will tend to pay you late. We do make the tenant responsible for any broken windowpanes, regardless of how the glass got broken. We did this because the tenants had been responsible for the broken window 95 percent of the time. We didn't want to get into discussions regarding who broke it or how it was broken, especially when the tenant lost their key or left it locked up inside our mobile home.

There will also be times when a *tenant will want to leave early*, before the lease is up. Our policy is that we will advertise and try to re-rent the mobile home, but the tenant must pay for the ad and continue paying rent until we find another tenant. Sometimes the mobile home is rented quickly, at which point the tenant is only out the $50 or $100 cost for the ad. We return their security deposit if the mobile home is left clean and undamaged.

Last, there will be times when *it's not working out, in spite of everything*, between you and the tenant. You should never get into wars with your tenants because, as the saying goes, "When you go to war, dig two graves, one for your enemies, and one for yourself." If things are not working out between the both of you, you should call the tenant and simply say, "Things are not working out. You don't like renting from me, and I am not satisfied with our relationship. Let's come to an agreement as to when you will move out and how we will handle the rent and deposits."

Collecting Rent, Victor's Comeback, and the Dead Baby Story

When you are a landlord, you will hear every excuse imaginable for why a tenant can not pay the rent. The majority of these excuses are pure fiction or lies, in my opinion. Some of the excuses will tear at your heart strings and will make you feel like Scrooge when you demand payment. Try *Victor's Comeback* when that happens.

I met Victor on a bus tour of properties when I was conducting the class on investing in real estate. He came on the bus and showed us his duplexes, which were for sale in a rough part of town. I had seen these duplexes years before and passed on buying them because I didn't like the area and they were in bad shape. Victor bought them and did a great job turning them around. As he showed them to us, he told us how he handled the sob stories tenants gave him about not paying the rent. Victor said he listened patiently to their story, and then responded:

"I really sympathize with your situation, but let's not add homelessness to your list of problems. Now, when can you pay me the rent?"

I will leave it to you to decide whether you think this is a good response. Sometimes, when I am a particularly philosophical mood, I will tell a new tenant, "I want you to know that the only way I will excuse you from paying any late penalty on the rent is if you come up with a better excuse than The Dead Baby Story." I explain that, in the annals of excuses that tenants have used on me over the years, this one stands out as a work of art. Then I move on to another topic. At this point, the tenant will usually beg me to tell them the Dead Baby story. Again, if I am still in a particularly philosophical mood, I might tell it to them. You can find it on my web site, www.ZalmanVelvel.com, under the link "Stories from Your Father's Heart."

Raising Rents

Raising rents is good for you, but not so good for your tenants/residents. It's good for you because every penny of a rent increase goes right to your bottom line NOI. We showed you how we raised rents on the Jefferson Mobile Home Park, and that is the way we recommend you do it. Send a letter to every tenant/resident in the park in which you are raising the rent, explain why are you doing it (to create a better park for them), and provide a list of the other parks in the area and what they charge (naturally, only the ones that charge the same or more as the new rent). Do some inexpensive, yet easy to see, improvements to the park before you send the letter.

We usually follow the letter up by having a meeting with the tenants/residents after work on a weekday. We limit our meetings to an hour and since we have clubhouses, we hold them there. We start the meeting by going over all the improvements we have made to the park since our last meeting and then discuss any new business and the rent increase. At the end we ask for questions and comments, which means we create a new list of reasonable improvements. Be very careful about your lot rent increases if your park is age-restricted and over fifty-five. Retired people are on fixed incomes and have a lot of time on their hands. *Remember—be very careful about getting into disputes about lot rent increases with people who have nothing but time on their hands.*

Paying Bills

Pay your bills on time and in full. The bills you can expect on a monthly or yearly basis are:

- Mortgage payments
- Insurance payments
- Real estate taxes
- Utility bills
- Repair and maintenance bills
- Payroll, if you have employees
- Trash bills
- Advertising bills
- Legal and accounting fees

Most of these bills are self-explanatory. When it comes to utility bills, if your park is submetered you have to read the water meters and/or electric meters for the individual lots so you can send them a utility bill along with the monthly rent statement. We read the meters monthly in some parks to help the tenants better manage their expenses, and in other parks, we read the meters every two months to limit our time and expenses.

Evictions

Evictions are the result of a breakdown in the relationship between you and your tenant/resident. In one typical case, your renter fails to tell you he has been having financing difficulties until the problem becomes insurmountable. In another typical case, you had explained the rules about living on your property, but at some point the tenant decided those rules did not apply to him or his family anymore.

It is very important in a mobile home park to make examples of bad tenant/residents because, due to their close proximity, other tenant/residents will copy their bad habits. The way you make an example is by following through with evictions.

There is good news and bad news regarding evictions. The good news is, evictions usually take less time than the street wisdom says they take. In Florida, we can get a nonpaying tenant out within thirty days of taking action. In New York City, it used to take us forty-five days, but we had two months' security deposits, so there we suffered little or no financial loss.

The bad news is that evictions cost money even if you do them yourself, and if you hire an attorney, it costs even more. In the beginning we did all our own evictions. The process was not difficult, the forms were

Florida Eviction Procedure

1. The landlord gives the tenant/resident a three-day notice for nonpayment or a seven-day notice for noncompliance
2. If noncompliance occurs again in seven days, the landlord sends a notice of termination
3. If payment not made in three days, or noncompliance results in a notice of termination, the landlord files a complaint and the tenant has five business days to answer
4. If the tenant doesn't answer the complaint, the landlord files a default and requests final judgment. If tenant does answer, the judge sets a hearing convenient to both sides
5. If the judge finds in the landlord's favor at the hearing, the landlord gets a final judgment. If the tenant defaults (does not show), the judge will also sign a final judgment
6. The landlord takes the final judgment to the clerk, who issues a writ of possession
7. The landlord brings the writ to the sheriff, who serves the tenant with a twenty-four-hour notice to vacate
8. The sheriff shows up twenty-four hours later, the landlord changes the locks on the mobile home, and the tenant's belongings are put out on the curb. If tenant is still in the mobile home, the tenant is forcibly removed by the sheriff to the curb

easy to fill out, and in the majority of cases the renter moved out, rather than show up in court or pay an attorney to defend him.

If you want to learn how to do an eviction in your area, go down to your county clerk's office and ask one of the assistants for the names of the three attorneys who do the most mobile home or mobile home park evictions in your county. Don't ask who is the best attorney to do your evictions, because most government employees can't answer questions like that. When the clerk's assistant gives you the names of the three attorneys, go through the courthouse records and pull the case file for one of their completed evictions—which is public record. Make copies of the forms in the file, and use them as a starting point to create blank forms for yourself. Be sure you change some of the wording so you don't run into copyright infringement problems, but keep in mind that many attorneys go to a book of standard forms and modify them just as you are doing. You might even be able to get one of the county clerk's assistants to give you the forms, if they are available.

If you want to hire one of the attorneys to do the eviction for you—and I strongly recommend this in the beginning—then contact the three attorneys the clerk listed as doing the most evictions and find out their costs and experience. It's probable that these attorneys are busy because they charge reasonable fees and have created an efficient system. They also have the most experience in dealing with the judges. We have seen family lawyers—lawyers who handle all the legal affairs for a family—charge clients $1,500 in fees for an eviction for which an attorney specializing in evictions would have charged $300.

There are three basic types of evictions:

1. Nonpayment of rent
2. Noncompliance with lease terms—violation of rules
3. Holdover (staying past the end of the lease)

Probably 95 percent of all our evictions are for *nonpayment*. We start the eviction with a three-day notice to pay up or quit renting, and we wait no more than five days after the rent was due to post the notice and start the eviction, with almost no exceptions.

Noncompliance with the rules occurs less than 5 percent of the time and these cases rarely reach the point of a hearing in front of a judge.

When the tenant starts getting the eviction notices, they usually shape up or ship out.

A *holdover* eviction is rare. It happens when a tenant/resident does not leave at the end of the lease. The rent doubles during the holdover period, which is a strong incentive for the tenant to leave. We have never had a holdover go all the way to the sheriff.

On page 452 we listed a simplified outline of the paperwork and procedures involved in a typical eviction in Florida for either nonpayment or noncompliance. The system will vary in each state and possibly in different counties in the same state, but the logic will be similar.

As I explained before, you will really know and understand the power you have as a landlord when you see an eviction go to term. You will see the sheriff escort the tenant off your property or arrest him if he fails to comply, and the tenant and all of his belonging will be placed out on the curb. Be judicious in your use of this power. If your other tenants witness this they will respect the legal process and avoid testing you in the future.

By the way, if the eviction does not go to full term but the renter moves out, you have the option to inform all the credit rating services that the tenant owes you money due to an eviction. You can also place a flag in that renter's credit report for other landlords to see. This will negatively affect your former tenant's ability to rent another property, and might give him motivation to pay off any judgment you have against him.

Management Reports

I used to sit in the office of the owner of the largest real estate seminar company in this country and marvel at how he kept track of his many companies and hundreds of employees. When I asked him how he did it, he said he used good management reports. When I asked how he knew where to put his time and energy, he said that the struggling companies got most of his attention, while the profitable ones got less.

I did not understand his answers until years later, when we owned more than five different income-producing real estate companies. Then I became aware of how important management reports are to an owner who is unable to be present at all his mobile home parks all of the time. (I do not agree with his answer about time allocation, but that is a different topic.)

In 1981, when we first got started as landlords with ten units, we used a computer program I created to manage the accounting. Slowly but surely the program became less and less useful as our rentals exceeded 100 units, and we had to keep more information on hand-written sheets. We tried using a general accounting program with frustrating results. Then we discovered Rent Manager, software that was specifically developed to manage rentals, and it was love. It was not love at first sight, because Rent Manager was not inexpensive, but a stronger love developed as it helped us over the years. While Rent Manager was not inexpensive to purchase, it has made everyone in my office at least 50 percent more efficient. Therefore it became very inexpensive when we factored in the amount of time and expensive labor it saved. Also, it gives me a way to get a report when I want it without having to wait for one of my managers to give it to me. The following are reports I refer to on a weekly or monthly basis:

- Profit and Loss
- Lease Expiration
- Delinquency
- Vacancy
- Eviction
- Checking Account
- Rent Roll

The *Profit and Loss Report* shows how much rent is coming in, and how much money is going out in expenses. We have a separate checking account and separate LLC for each mobile home park and we do everything on a cash basis, so we normally can see this right in the checking account. We monitor the checking account on a weekly basis. When the park is making money there are excess funds in the checking account at the end of the month, which we move to a savings account. When we do our taxes at the end of the year we run a P&L report for the whole year to give to our accountant, and he uses it when he prepares our income tax returns.

The *Lease Expiration Report* lists when our properties' leases are coming up for renewal, so we can be proactive in renewing them with the current tenants/residents or finding new renters if the current ones do not want to re-rent. This report is printed in date order, with the leases coming up for renewal soonest appearing first.

The *Delinquency Report* shows who still owes us money in each park, how much they owe, and how late they are with their payment. We go over with the Delinquency Report with the property manager after the second and fourth weeks of the month to determine collections, or evictions, or both.

The *Vacancy Report* shows which lots or mobile homes are vacant and need to be filled up or re-rented.

The *Eviction Report* is an Excel spreadsheet we get from our attorney, usually on the second and fourth weeks of the month. It shows the current status of the evictions we are currently doing with a timeline of what stage it is in, so we can get ready on the turn-around and re-rent the mobile homes quickly.

We are lucky that I can see the action in our *checking accounts* on a timely basis because we run our parks on a cash basis. A separate checking account for each mobile home park lets us evaluate their performance on a property-by-property basis.

The *Rent Roll* is the list of the people in a park renting from us. This is usually created in lot-number order, showing how much the rent is, when the lease started and when it expires, and any other related information. I usually look at this report once a month.

SETTING UP AND NURTURING YOUR POWER TEAM

You will need a group of professionals to assist you as you climb up the ladder of success in the mobile home park investment field. We refer to them as your *Power Team* because they give you the power to create wealth for both you and them. You are all on the same team, pulling together to become successful. You will find you will need the following professionals in your mobile home park investment career.

Your Power Team

1. Realtor who specializes in mobile homes
2. Mortgage Broker who specializes in mobile homes
3. Home Inspector who specializes in mobile homes
4. Appraiser who specializes in mobile homes
5. Vice President of Commercial Lending at Community Bank
6. Vice President of the Consumer Loan Department at Community Bank
7. Hard Money Lender
8. Real Estate Attorney
9. Insurance Broker
10. Surveyor
11. Title Company
12. CPA/Accountant
13. General Contractor
14. Mobile Home Installation Contractor
15. Tradesmen—Plumber, Electrician, Painter
16. Well and Septic Repair Companies
17. Classified Ad Representative
18. Sign Contractor
19. Credit Reporting Company
20. Tenant Checking Company
21. Property Manager

Some of you might be thinking, *twenty-one people!* Yes, that is the major portion of your list. There will be even more, and that's okay. The more people whose services you engage, the more people you will have out there giving you referrals that will help you climb your ladder.

Think about yourself when you look at this list. You will be paying fees to over twenty different professionals—you are employing them to work on your business. How does it feel to be a creator of wealth for others? How does it feel to be on the top end of the food chain instead of down below, getting devoured by those above? That said, let's look at how to select the members of your Power Team, how to keep them satisfied, and how to use your team to grow your business.

Selecting a Team Member

The typical rules apply. Interview three people in each field, get a list of their fees and costs, and choose those who offer you the best deal and have personalities that work well with your own.

How to Keep Your Power Team Satisfied

The best way to keep the members of your Power Team humming along is to give them business so they can go to work for you. In the beginning, when you have a limited amount of work to give out, it is better to have the loyalty of one professional from a field at a time, so you can receive better service. As your business grows bigger, though, it's good to have a substitute or two to do business with in case one of the members of your team starts to slack off or leaves the business.

How to Use Your Power Team to Grow Your Business

You should openly ask members of your Power Team for referrals and recommendations, since you will give referrals and recommendations to them when you can. Attorneys, accountants, and bankers are especially good sources of referrals. Any time a member of your Power Team refers some business your way, you should thank them personally and make a greater attempt to refer business their way. That is basic networking.

TO HAVE A MANAGER OR NOT

We began this chapter describing how important a park manager is, and then spent the rest of the chapter showing you how to manage your own properties so you can train and evaluate any new managers you hire. A valid question at this time might be, *should I hire someone else to manage my properties?* Now that you know how to do it, should you hire someone, train him on your methods, and place your properties in his care? If you look at the Power Team you'll notice that the last member in the list is the Property Manager. Why?

The answer as to whether you should hire someone else to manage your properties is—it depends. It depends on how wealthy you want to get, how much time you want to spend on your ATM, and how much control you want to exert. Remember, the best use of your time in the field of mobile home investment is in finding new deals and then managing your managers. If you are spending the majority of your time managing your tenants/residents, then that is time you will not have to find new deals.

Let's assume you have two mobile home park keepers, each giving you $6,500 per month in positive cash flow, which is $13,000 per month or $156,000 per year. Here are three alternatives for managing your parks:

1. Manage everything yourself or with your family and be satisfied with a steady and great cash flow of $156,000 a year, adding with some flippers, L/Os, and BBs for dessert.

2. Hire two managers, pay each $25,000 per year or $50,000 total annually—which is a reasonable salary as I write this—and spend an hour daily to monitor the managers, while you earn $100,000 per year. You spend the majority of your time accumulating more keepers, flippers, L/Os and BBs to make even more money.

3. Hire two property managers, pay them $50,000 per year, and spend an hour daily to monitor them, while you earn $100,000 per year and spend your time doing whatever else you feel like.

The first choice is for someone who wants to grow and maintain a family business, which is what we wanted up to about eight years ago.

The second choice is for someone who wants to accumulate greater wealth, with their family and others. This is the choice we made eight years ago and we continue to use this model today.

The third choice is typical for artists, clergy, or people who want to semiretire and spend the majority of their time not working. I have trained many musicians, ministers, artists, and actors who wanted to pursue their passions without having financial worries.

The choice is yours to make, and each choice is a winner.

Please understand this. *To run a mobile home park without a manager has not worked for us.* It was suggested in a book I read, which was written by someone with a lot of experience in mobile home parks. We tried this once—when we first bought the Happy Trails Mobile Home Park. The manager at the park quit, with about an hour's notice, because he was offered a free mobile home by one of his relatives. I told Crazy Gersh that the people in the park were adults and they owned their own mobile homes, so why couldn't they just get along like adults should? Crazy Gersh said that he didn't think the park would manage itself, but he was willing to try it out and monitor it.

We recognized the foolishness of my idea after two weeks of monitoring the park and having the police summoned every other day. We hired another property manager pronto.

SUMMARY

In this chapter you have learned how to manage your park manager, and how to manage a park so you can train your manager to do it well. You learned how to market and advertise for tenants and how to qualify them when they call. On this point, you learned that the best way to overcome the problem of bad tenants is to qualify them right up front. Establish systems that make you as efficient as possible, while you still provide good, safe, healthy, affordable housing. You also learned about the reports you will need to efficiently monitor your parks.

You also learned how to build and maintain your Power Team, the group of professionals you manage on a part-time basis, who are on your team when it comes to building your wealth.

HOMEWORK

Go out and buy a fancy mailbox to impress your postal carrier, and be prepared to fall in love with cash flow. Money is on the way!

Let's get your park rented out, if it isn't already. If you have vacant park-owned units, put them in clean, safe, and healthy shape, add a fresh coat of paint if they need it, and clean the carpets. Put an ad in the paper and stick a For Rent sign in the front yard. If you have vacant lots in a land-lease community bring in a BB, set it up, and advertise it or find someone who will bring in his or her own mobile home and rent the lot from you. You can also contact mobile home dealers and see if they will set up a new or used mobile home on one of your vacant lots and sell it, and then you can collect lot rent from the new owner.

Use the tenant call-in sheet in the Appendix when prospective tenant/residents call, and join one of the credit rating agencies. When they make it through your initial qualification process, have them fill out an application and check them out like you were shown. If they check out okay, fill out a lease, collect the first month's rent and security deposit, and give them copies of the keys. Give them some self-addressed envelopes to send in the rent if you want to collect that way, and give them a phone number so they can reach you when problems arise.

Congratulations! You are now a landlord.

If you like your new profession, go out and buy another park. If you don't have any money, buy it with no-money-down seller financing. Make sure to get all the contact information to build your Power Team while you are doing all this.

COMING ATTRACTIONS

You are about 95 percent trained on your new mobile home park investment career. You should have had fun getting here and learned a lot along the way. You should feel a sense of power now that you are in control of your life. The good news is that this good feeling will keep getting better as you become more comfortable with the business. It's not brain surgery, as you will learn. You are providing a valuable service and product and will get well-paid for doing so.

You might want to collect some quick cash on a flipper or an L/O now or in the near future, so we're going to teach you how to sell a park like a pro in the next chapter.

Let's go!

14

Selling Like a Pro

Congratulations! You own a mobile home park that you want to sell or flip. You worked hard to get to this step. You looked at properties for sale, fit them into your Four Profit Strategies, and then went through the Five Green Fs to find the best candidate. You financed it and got the deal closed.

Since many—or probably most of you—wanted to buy a keeper first to get your Mobile Home ATM going, we discussed keepers first, in the previous chapter. Now we're going to talk about how to sell a flipper property. Keepers were covered first because one of the advantages of mobile home park investing is the "Refi Bonanza" it provides, in which you can cash out 80 percent of the increase in value of a park and still hold onto it when it is producing a great income and is easy to manage.

This chapter is designed for the times when you do not want to own a particular park anymore. You want to sell it as quickly as possible, for as high a price as possible. Selling involves four stages, in sequential order:

1. Rehabbing—getting your park in condition to sell

2. Marketing—letting the buyers know that your park is for sale

3. Contracting and negotiating with prospective buyers

4. Closing the sale

You already know about the third stage, contracting and negotiating. We discussed that in Chapter 9 when you learned about making offers and negotiating afterwards. The difference is now you are on the other side of coin, trying to get a good price for your property from a new buyer.

You also know about the fourth stage, closing the sale. We discussed that in the Chapter 12. When you are a selling, you are acting more like a timekeeper and a coach, making sure the buyer is completing the steps required to have your property close on a timely basis. This leaves only the first two stages to discuss—getting the property in condition to sell, and then letting the buyers in your market know that your property is for sale. We'll discuss both.

REHABBING—GETTING A PARK IN CONDITION TO SELL

First, remember to take pictures of all your parks in the worst possible state before you improve them. Don't forget this, like I did. These will be your "before" pictures, for you to use later in your "brag book" of accomplishments. When you are finished repairing the property, take "after" pictures. If you want to show how you arrived at the "after" condition, take pictures in between. You will use your brag book to illustrate your experience and expertise when you seek out money partners, lenders, or seller financing. This is very important, so don't forget to do it. I guarantee there will be a time when you regret not doing this—like me. Now let's discuss the different processes involved in wholesaling versus retailing when it comes to flipping.

To Wholesale or Not to Wholesale, That is the Question

Just as there are two kinds of parks, turnkey and turn-around, there are two kinds of investors. Whether the property is in an affordable-, middle-, or upper-income area, you have to decide whether you are going to wholesale the property to a turn-around investor and move quickly through the process, or get it into prime condition for a turnkey, retail investor. If wholesaling is your strategy, then you will be spending a minimum of time and money fixing it up. You will also receive smaller profits, but they will come at an accelerated pace.

Wholesalers generally want to do lots of deals and take a slice off the top of each one. They don't want to deal with the time and details of intensive remodeling. Wholesalers buy property cheap, clean it up right away, and then get a brochure of the property out to their list of investors and Realtors. If you are going to wholesale the property, the minimum you should do is de-trash it, both inside each park-owned mobile home and outside on the grounds. That means get it in broom clean condition inside and mow the lawn outside. I know some wholesalers who also pressure-spray the outside and perhaps paint the front side of the mobile homes and buildings.

Retailing—Getting the Property in Prime Condition

If you elect not to wholesale—and we usually don't wholesale because we want a greater profit margin—then you must get the mobile home park in prime condition for its market segment. Affordable-income parks should be in good condition—clean and freshly painted at the very least. Middle-income parks have to be in excellent condition. Upper-income parks have to be attractive and in perfect condition. The tastes of potential buyers become more stringent the further they are up the income chain. The type of property you tend to flip will usually reflect your own personal tastes in the same way.

There are two major areas to concentrate on when you renovate a flipper—the outside appearance and the inside living area. That probably sounds so elementary that it seems obvious, but it is not. What we mean is you must first brighten up the "curb appeal" of the park, so it will look as attractive as possible on the outside. If your park looks grungy and unattractive on the outside, prospective buyers will not want to get out of their cars to take a look, even if it will show beautifully on the inside. If you see buyers pull up in their cars, look around, and then leave, that is a good indication that you need to pay more attention to the curb appeal. The good news is that a mobile home park's curb appeal primarily involves the signs, landscaping, and fences at the park's entrances and exits. These are not expensive improvements. After you have the "front door" and "back door" of the park looking good, then improve the interior of the park. This involves painting the outside of park-owned mobile homes and creating attractive landscaping around them. These curb-appeal renovations are some of the lowest-priced improvements you can make, but they have the highest returns. I've said it before and I'll repeat it now—the difference a coat of paint and some bushes and flowers can make to the appearance of a mobile home and a mobile home park is positively amazing. In some of our parks, we have even painted resident-owned units at our own expense—mobile homes we didn't own—just to improve the overall appearance of the park. (In some cases, the residents complained and didn't want us to paint their dirty, ugly, trailers. We persisted, saying they were violating the rules of the park by not maintaining their mobile homes, and would face eviction if we couldn't make them look better.)

When it comes to the inside of park-owned mobile homes and common areas like clubhouses and bath houses, there should be fresh paint on the walls and clean—or even better, new—carpets. You can probably get away with cleaning the old carpets in an affordable-income area, but in middle- to upper-income areas, new carpets are more the rule. Many times we cleaned the carpets on a middle-income segment flipper and then sat on the property for longer than we would have liked. Then, when we tore out the clean carpets and replaced them with new carpet, the park promptly sold. Also, keep in mind that the rooms that create the strongest buying impulse on the part of retail buyers are typically the kitchen and the master bedroom and bathroom, so those areas should look particularly attractive.

There are many books available that detail the techniques for improving flippers. I strongly suggest you get some of the better ones and study them for ideas, because many contain excellent pictorial examples of how to improve your property and make it stand out from your competition. We only outlined some rules of thumb and some common-sense strategies. For those of you who love flipping, you will create your own sense of what to fix and improve, and you will place your own individual signature on the property. Remember to stay within the budget you set before you purchased the flipper, or you will be spending your profit before you receive it, on what will become someone else's investment.

MARKETING—LETTING BUYERS KNOW YOUR PROPERTY IS FOR SALE

When you are marketing a product, you have to ask the following important question: *"Who is the buyer of this product, and how do I reach that buyer and let him know this product is for sale?"*

Being auctioneers, we have often been asked to sell properties that were unique to a small market segment with few potential buyers. Usually, the typical Realtor sales process had not been succeeding so the seller became impatient and called us in to speed up the sales process. Over the years, we learned to ask the owners of unusual or unique property the following question: "Who do you think the typical buyer for your property is, where do we find that buyer, and are there any unique ways to reach that buyer—any special periodicals, magazines, or trade papers we can use to let buyers know that your property is for sale?" Combining this information with the auction method of marketing was a powerful tactic.

In this case, the property is yours, and your first choice for promoting it will be the same sources you used to find it when you purchased it in the first place—those in the list in Chapter 7 on finding deals. The Internet and various websites will probably be the best way to market your mobile home park, followed by your local MLS as a close second. After that, you might search for new and interesting ways to find additional buyers for your flippers. No matter how you market your mobile home park, your first decision is the traditional one—*do I use a Realtor or not?*

To Use a Realtor or Not to Use a Realtor

Whether you use a Realtor is an important decision, especially from the standpoint of profit. If you are not a Realtor yourself, it will usually cost you 5 to 10 percent of the final sales price in commissions to sell your property through the MLS, with 6 percent being the average. You can get away with a 5 percent commission if the property is worth $100,000 or more, 6 percent if it is in the $30,000 to $99,999 range and 10 percent if it is less than $29,000. These are not hard rules, just general practice. Commissions are negotiable—don't let a Realtor convince you otherwise.

We are Realtors and brokers, yet we use other Realtors to sell the majority of our properties. We act as the listing agent and offer a selling commission to other Realtors. Our reasoning is that it only costs us half of what it costs an investor who is not a Realtor, and that makes it very worthwhile. When Realtors sell our flippers, it costs us only 3 percent of the selling price. After we discuss the different ways to market your property (as listed in the following inset) you will become acquainted with how much time and money it takes to sell a property and will understand why we consider it a bargain to pay someone else 3 percent to locate and deal with the buyers of our properties. We would rather spend our time finding and managing deals. We believe finding deals is ultimately where our wealth starts, so it is more efficient for us to spend our time finding lots of good deals rather than finding buyers and then nursing them to closing. When we do buy from another Realtor, *we receive half of the commission*, which is usually means we get a 3 percent discount from the price. *When you consider the benefits of being a Realtor when it comes to investing for yourself, you might want to get your license, too.*

That said, we know investors who do not use Realtors when they sell because they want to keep as much of the profit for themselves as possible. Taking 6 to 10 percent off the top to pay a Realtor is not in their marketing strategy. We understand this, but we feel it is shortsighted. Statistics show that 85 percent of residential real estate is bought and sold through Realtors. It logically follows that if you eliminate Realtors from your marketing, you will probably eliminate 85 percent of your buyers.

How to Select a Realtor

One of the best ways to select a Realtor is to pick the ones on the Internet who have the most mobile home park listings in your area. Another option is to drive around your market area and write down the three Realtors with most signs. Most Realtors will have their company name plus their own personal name and cell phone number on the sign, so you can call to set up appointments to interview them. If the sign just lists the name of the brokerage firm, then call and ask for the broker. When you speak with the broker, ask for the agent with the most experience in mobile home parks and who gives the best service, and then make an appointment for an interview. You might want to ask the following questions during the interview:

- How long have you been in the real estate business?
- How long have you specialized in selling mobile home parks?
- Do you own any mobile home park investments yourself?
- Do you work full-time?
- Do you have any banking connections (mortgage brokers, lenders)?
- How many mobile home parks do you have listed currently?
- How long does it take you, on average, to sell a mobile home park?
- How many parks did you sell last year? The year before?
- How do you market your mobile home park listings?
- Where will you be advertising my property, and how often?
- What commission do you charge, and is it negotiable?

Based upon the answers to these questions, you can make an informed decision about whom you will choose for your Realtor. It's very important to have a meeting of the minds, and a meeting of the hearts, when you make your choice. You definitely want to be able to trust that person's ability and honesty, and you also want to enjoy working with them. You are going to be spending a lot of time together, so you should look forward to doing so without cringing every time you take her phone call.

When we use a Realtor to list and sell our parks, we give her the following incentives and conditions:

- If the total commission is 6 percent, make the listing commission 2 percent and the selling commission 4 percent.
- The Realtor can keep the listing "in their pocket" for two weeks to try to sell it herself to get the whole 6 percent, but if it is not sold after two weeks it must be placed in the MLS and on the most popular Internet websites so other Realtors can sell it.
- Either party (the Realtor or us) may cancel the listing after thirty days with two weeks prior written notice, if there is dissatisfaction for any reason with the arrangement.
- The Realtor will give us buyer feedback if the property is not moving.

THE STEPS TO MARKETING YOUR PROPERTY

If you use a Realtor, she will handle the marketing of your property. You will sit back and wait for offers, negotiate with the buyers, and have the Realtor monitor the progress of the buyer you selected, and give you reports. We will now discuss the different ways to sell your property so you can understand what your Realtor is doing, if you choose to use one, or handle the process yourself. It is worthwhile to repeat that a good Realtor earns their commissions with the time and expertise it takes to sell a property.

Marketing Your Property

1. Prepare a due diligence package
2. Erect a For Sale sign, a brochure box, and directional signs (optional)
3. Advertise on Internet websites
4. Add the property to the MLS
5. Create and submit newspaper and magazine ads
6. REIAs—networking with other investors and buyers

Preparing a Due Diligence Package

In Chapter 10, we discussed preparing due diligence when you are selling. In our experience, the better Realtors don't just write up a listing for a mobile home park with the seller and then advertise it. Instead, they spend a lot of time initially preparing a due diligence package before they begin to market the property. In the case of larger mobile home parks, it may take a few weeks or even a month to do this. Why do they do that? Is there anything you can learn from this if you choose to market your parks yourself?

The answer will become obvious to you when you sell your first mobile home park on your own. You will see that when buyers/investors respond to your marketing the second question they ask after "Hello, how are you?" is, "Do you have a package on the mobile home park that you can send me?" They are looking for a due diligence package, just as you were when you purchased the park. When we discussed this in Chapter 10, we suggested that you provide information to your prospective buyers in five stages:

1. Initial listing, usually just a few lines in an ad or on the Internet
2. Color brochure with summary information of P&L and a few pictures to give to prospective buyers who inquire from the ads
3. Follow-up package with more information on P&L, additional information, and lots of pictures to give to buyers who respond favorably to the color brochure—this will also help out-of-town buyers decide whether to make the trip
4. Physical inspection of park with the prospective buyer
5. After the buyer indicates that he or she wants to make an offer, the complete package of due diligence containing everything you would want as a professional investor in mobile home parks

Unfortunately, there can be an element of distrust on the part of prospective buyers when it comes to the due diligence they are given. When a Realtor supplies the due diligence the buyer might think that the Realtor is trying to puff up the property in order to earn a commission. The distrust deepens when a seller provides the due diligence. The seller will get 94 percent of the purchase price, so in some buyers' minds, this gives the seller more than ten times the motivation to puff up the numbers and the price. Even so, you still have to have a due diligence package available for investors or you won't get optimum results for your efforts. Just keep in mind that some investors will use your package only as a starting point and their own due diligence will be their major determinant of value.

For Sale Sign, Brochure Box, Directional Signs (Optional)

You will note we put "optional" on these methods. Perhaps you are curious why we did this after telling you that the best return on your marketing dollar is the sign on the property, a brochure box, and directional signs leading to the property from major roads. They are optional because many times mobile home park owners don't want their residents or manager to know that the property is for sale. The residents and the manager tend to feel defensive and insecure in this situation. The residents worry about rents going up or being evicted, and the manager worries about the job parameters changing for the worst or losing his or her job. While a sign is the best marketing tool for selling an individual mobile home, it may not even be used for marketing a mobile home park.

If there is a sign, we pay a lot of attention to the call when a buyer calls from it. This is a person who has seen the property, knows the neighborhood, and is interested. Furthermore, we attach a brochure box to the sign so prospective buyers can get all the pertinent facts about the mobile home park before they call. This way we don't have to repeat the same information over and over again. Directional signs with arrows leading off the main roads to the property are a great additional tool, if you are allowed to place them in your area.

A sign on the property will have diminished value if the mobile home park is on a back road and out of the way. In that case, it serves mostly as a landmark when you give directions to prospective buyers. If your property is on a heavily traveled road, however, a For Sale sign is a real marketing benefit for your property because so many people will drive by and see that the property is for sale.

Internet Websites

As we mentioned earlier, the Internet is starting a revolution in the marketing of properties. We listed several prominent websites for buying and selling mobile home parks. The two general sites are LoopNet.com and MobileHomeParkStore.com. You can use these to list your mobile home park as either a seller selling directly to the public or as a Realtor offering a selling commission to other Realtors as well as the public. There are also the websites of Realtors who specialize in selling mobile home parks. You can also use these websites to sell your flippers if you give the Realtor the listing or a co-op. The only way to gauge their results is to try them and see what happens.

The eBay auction website is just beginning to be used to market mobile home parks as I write this book. In many cases, the park is put up as a reserve auction with a minimum price, and then does not sell. The seller takes the list of bidders, who are all potential buyers, and then negotiates with them off the site.

Realtor.Com is a primary site when it comes to residential real estate, and it is just starting to come into its own for investment property sales. If your property is listed in your local MLS, it may be downloaded to Realtor.Com or another "sister" website that specializes in commercial rather than residential property. There is a time delay in this process, however, from several days to a week or more, so don't expect immediate results from it.

You can also use your own website to market your mobile home parks. If you do, be sure to have all your other advertising—signs, brochures, and so on—point to your website.

MLS

MLS is a powerful tool—85 percent of sales take place through it. The percentage of MLS sales goes down in hot markets, because when the market is hot you can just put a cheap ad in the paper and stick a sign in the ground and lots of buyers will find their way to you. Realtors and the MLS shine in slow markets, however, when the percentage of sales through the MLS goes up to close to 90 percent.

If you are not a Realtor, and do not use another Realtor to list your property, you will not have access to the MLS as a sales tool. You may have access to an abbreviated form of the MLS as an information tool, because you will be able to view all of the Realtor listings in your area through Realtor.Com or your local Board of Realtors website. If you want to cut your commission cost down to around 3.5 percent, some Realtors will place your listing in the MLS for about .5 percent of the price of the property; then you can offer the selling Realtor 3 percent to sell it for you. In this case, the listing Realtor is going to do little more than place your property in the MLS for another Realtor to see, and sell, for 3 percent. You know my thoughts on this—it is a bargain to have all those Realtors working for you, selling your property, when you only have to pay them 3 percent if they are successful, plus only .5 percent for the listing agent. If you go that route, you will have to prepare the due diligence yourself.

Newspaper and Magazine Ads

Newspaper ads work. They are also expensive. Newspaper advertising is undergoing a revolution as I write this because of competition from the Internet. For that reason, you should give your website address, if you have one, in all your newspaper ads. The important thing is this: you need to learn how to write an ad that works—one that brings in qualified buyers. Most newspapers will gladly teach you how to best use their advertising capability, if you ask for assistance.

When we place ads, we are usually looking to sell just one property, so we include a brief description of the property, the price, the location of the property, our phone number, and our website. We practice what we call *The Walmart Rule: If you are proud of the price, put it in the ad.* Nothing sells so well as a good price on a good product. We believe that, and Walmart, the world's number-one retailer, hasn't done too badly with that philosophy either, so maybe there is some value to it.

Newspaper ads also bring out lots of unqualified buyers, and when you answer the call, you have to give out the same information, over and over again, to people who have little desire or ability to buy your property. For that reason, try to be specific as possible in the ad, so you can avoid wasting the caller's time as well as your own. Specify the location of the mobile home park, how many lots there are, include one line aimed at selling the property, and then list the price, your phone number, and your website. This is what a typical ad would look like:

North—Mobile Home Park
5 Lots, $15,000 NOI
Reduced $25,000 for quick sale
$124,900
Let's Talk 555-555-5555
www.OurWebsite.com

Let me describe how this classified ad will work. First, most investors have areas they like and don't like, so identifying the area will qualify callers. Specifying the type of property and how many lots it has continues to qualify potential buyers, because people investing in parks have certain minimum and maximum sizes they will consider.

Now that you have narrowed the audience to qualified buyers, you may want to motivate them by offering a discount and a low price. The "Let's Talk" is positively magic to buyers—it says you are friendly, ready to listen to their needs, and willing to cut a deal. List your phone number so buyers can contact you, and your website so they can see all of the property you have for sale or rent, get a more complete description of the property, perhaps request a color brochure.

Here is how a generic ad would look if we had a few mobile home parks to flip that are located in different market segments at different prices and sizes:

Mobile Home Parks
From 5 Lots to 50
Priced to Sell
Let's Talk 555-555-5555
www.OurWebsite.com

We have found that advertising in the Sunday paper works the best. *A Sunday ad will typically bring in as many calls as the rest of the week combined.* After Sunday, Wednesday and Thursday seem to work equally well for us, and then in descending order, Saturday, Friday, Tuesday, and Monday.

There are also two magazines that specialize in mobile home parks for investors—*The Journal* and *The Manufactured Home Merchandiser.* Advertising in these publications is an excellent way to reach investors. There may be other magazines—usually the best way to find them is to do a Google search.

REIAs—Networking with Other Investors and Buyers

If you are wholesaling properties, you will definitely want to work with the REIA in your area as well as other investors and buyers who don't go to REIA meetings. If you want to retail mobile home parks, maintain a list of buyers who were interested in other properties you flipped, but for whatever reason, did not end up buying the property. Call it your waiting list of prospective buyers. When you establish a reputation for providing good, safe mobile home parks at good prices you will find that you have also built a network of interested investors. You are providing a valuable service through affordable housing, and there is a strong demand for it.

DIFFERENCES WHEN SELLING AN L/O OR BB

Realtors may or may not be interested in selling your L/Os and BBs, and you may or may not be interested in using them. On the plus side, Realtors can find you an L/O investor and will charge you a small commission up-front for the rental, and then will get another large commission if and when the L/O investor completes the option. On the negative side, they will be taking a portion of your up-front profit, which you may need. Another negative is that many Realtors don't want to wait for a commission that may or may not materialize in the future and prefer to work on a straight sale right now. For you as an investor, however, lease options are very easy to market and there is a strong demand for them. *You can usually get all the buyers you need for lease–options through your own advertising.* The initial ad can say something like:

North—50 Unit Mobile Home Park
Lease/Option
$25,000 down/$5,000 month
$2,000/mo cash flow after payment
Let's Talk 555-555-5555
OurWebsite.com

BBs have very similar advantages and disadvantages when it comes to using a Realtor. On a BB, Realtors will like getting a commission, because a BB is a straight sale. The problem is that the commission the Realtor receives is going to be paid from the buyer's down payment, which will probably leave little or nothing for you. Like the L/O, *you can usually get all the buyers you need for BBs from a yard sign, a brochure, and a simple classified ad.* The ad or the yard sign will probably say something like the following:

North—3 BR Mobile
$1,000 down/$195 month
Owner Finance—No Banks Involved
Let's Talk 555-555-5555
OurWebsite.com

ROTHSCHILD'S RULE

I learned the following statement, attributed to Baron Rothschild, early on in my investing career.

"You can never go broke taking a profit."

That rule is not entirely accurate, but it is close enough that it conveys some real wisdom. It means that the majority of time, you will look back on your flippers with a smile and say, "What a sweet deal that property was!" Nick's version of the same rule was:

"Don't fall in love with your inventory. There is always another trolley coming down the track."

SUMMARY

In this chapter, you learned some of the rules of thumb on how to rehab property to get it into shape to flip, and the basics of selling your mobile home park once it is ready. Many of the primary methods for selling your property are the same today as they were thirty years ago: the For Sale sign, newspaper and magazine ads, and the MLS. The Internet, REIAs, and networking are the new kids on the block.

HOMEWORK

Take the "before" pictures of the property you bought to flip. Then buy a brag book—a loose-leaf binder with clear plastic pages for inserting pictures. Then, pretty up the mobile home park's entrances and exits and de-trash the outside of the park and inside any park-owned units. In other words, clean it inside and outside, and mow the lawn. You can do this yourself or find people to do this for you. If you are going to "sub" out the work, try to get three different bids from contractors recommended by your Realtor, your REIA friends, or the listings in the good old yellow pages. Take "during" pictures while you rehab it and the final "after" pictures once the rehab is complete, and put them all in your brag book.

Now, if you are going to use a Realtor—and we strongly recommend you give this some serious thought when you are beginning—choose one the way you were shown in this chapter. Get the phone numbers of the three Realtors in your area who have the most signs or the most listings on the Internet. Interview them using some or all of the questions we gave you in this chapter.

Then, if you are going to use a Realtor, wait for the offers to come in, while you continue to look for more deals. Qualify the deals by trying to fit them into your Four Profit Strategies and Five Green Fs. Don't stop investing while you are waiting to sell your flipper. If you are short on money for a down payment, then work on your next deal using the no-money-down seller financing you were shown in Chapter 11.

COMING ATTRACTIONS

One of the strongest motivations for people who take my training is to learn how to develop their own mobile home park. They want to take a parcel of vacant land and turn it into their own personal cash register. You will be shown how to do that in the next chapter.

Excited? Good. So turn the page.

15

Developing Your Own Mobile Home Park

The first time we placed a mobile home on a vacant parcel of land, we were excited—and scared. We were scared because we worried that something would go wrong, and excited because we knew that if we could learn how to take a vacant parcel of land—like the one here—and turn it into an income producing asset, it would be a landmark in our journey to attain wealth.

Well, nothing bad happened —in fact, there were little or no problems whatsoever. It was a simple process once we went through it. Now, the fear is gone, but the excitement remains to this day. Land is a wonderful asset to own, but it can soon become an albatross around your neck when you realize that it has to be "fed" three times each day. Land eats a light breakfast of real estate taxes in the morning and it lunches on the principal paydown of the mortgage at noon. Finally, vacant land has a hearty dinner consisting of the interest on the mortgage loan. The bigger the parcel of land, the bigger its appetite.

In this chapter, we will show you how to take five acres of vacant land and develop it into a generic ten-unit mobile home park. When you have completed the development of your generic park, you will have the choice of selling off the mobile homes and making a hypothetical

$150,000 in profit or keeping the mobile home park and receiving $24,000 a year in positive cash flow. This can be accomplished with little or no money down to start, but will probably require making more offers and visiting more banks for financing.

If you want to keep the mobile home park, you will be shown how to expand it into 50 or 100 units or more—comfortably, 10 units at a time —with a minimum of risk. You will also be shown how to achieve two goals simultaneously—selling off some mobile homes and keeping some, which will get you quick cash while you set up an ATM for yourself.

HOW WE ARRIVED AT THE GENERIC MODEL

Originally we designed a plan for investors who wanted to "think big." We explained how to develop a mobile home park that contained hundreds of units and cost millions of dollars. That way, in one shot, an investor could create financial security for himself and his loved ones.

When we introduced the plan (which took us hours to develop with the help of a civil engineer and colleagues who were developers), the reaction of students was surprising. Their yawns were so wide that we could examine their old dental work. It was embarrassing . . . and frustrating. Finally, after three classes, I stopped right in the middle of training, put down my pointer, and asked:

"What's wrong?"

The class stared at me, but no one said anything.

"Come on. I'm not blind." I added. "Why are most of you ready to fall asleep?"

One brave person in the class raised his hand and said:

"Zalman, please don't think I'm a wuss, but I don't want to build a huge mobile home park costing millions of dollars right from the get-go. I just want to put some mobile homes on the five acres I have in Missouri."

I looked around, and saw some of the other students nodding in agreement.

"Is that what most of you want to do?" I asked.

The class nodded their heads.

"Okay, then let's do this together," I said. "You fill me in on your particulars, and we'll build us a mobile home park."

I polled the class to determine the approximate costs of what they needed, averaged them over the next three classes, and then wrote up the results. And, as a result of our discussions, what you are going to receive in this chapter are the average costs to construct a ten-unit mobile home park on five acres, according to various students around the United States. Please pay attention to the process rather than the dollar amounts, because the numbers can change dramatically depending upon where you are developing. Please consider the numbers to be a guide, not absolute costs.

A WARNING

Let's start with a warning: *This is the most difficult, the most time-consuming, and the most risky aspect of investing in mobile home parks. I believe it is easier to find an existing mobile home park that is "broken," buy it with good terms and then fix it than it is to develop your own park from scratch on a vacant parcel of land.*

If you are like some of the people we train, this warning will not faze you in the slightest. We have found that the drive to create something new upon the earth is very strong in some people, so we still see the light of creation shining brightly in their eyes after we give this warning.

Therefore, we will also mention the benefits of developing your own mobile home park: *It can be one of the most satisfying and profitable endeavors in mobile home park investing when it is successful.* Since some of you are going to do it anyway, no matter how many warnings we give, then we might as well show how to do it so you will limit your risks and maximize your profit, and have every chance possible to be successful.

IT ALL BEGINS WITH THE LAND

I don't know if you've ever seen what many believe is one of the greatest movies ever made, *Gone With The Wind,* but there is a line of dialogue that makes the heart of this real estate investor beat a little faster. (Aside from one of the last lines in the movie, "Frankly, Scarlett, I don't give a damn.") It's said in the beginning, when Scarlett O'Hara's father, Gerald, turns to her and tells her of his greatest love.

"Do you mean to tell me, Katie Scarlett O'Hara, that Tara, that Land, doesn't mean anything to you?! Why, land is the only thing in the world worth workin' for, worth fightin' for, worth dyin' for, because it's the only thing that lasts."

Why did I bring that up? Because when you are designing a neighborhood for people—and a mobile home park is a neighborhood that will serve those people for many years to come—you should start with a good parcel of land . . . Katie Scarlett O'Hara.

Things to Look For in the Parcel of Land

First, you have to decide what kind of park you are designing, and you have three choices—family, over-fifty-five, or RV park. You can also do any combination of these if you want to appeal to more customers. If you are designing a family park, there will be no age restrictions and children will be allowed. In this case jobs and access to employment is of paramount importance. After that comes proximity to schools, shopping, transportation, churches, and health care. It's a tremendous benefit to locate a park near major employers, factories, warehouses, army bases, or a bus or train stop that goes to areas of high employment.

If you are designing an age-restricted, over fifty-five community, then the order of priorities is reversed. Retirees are very conscious of their medical needs and the fact that distance to health care can mean the difference between life and death in the case of a heart attack or stroke. Therefore, if you are developing an age-restricted community, it helps if hospitals and doctors are reasonably close by. Next, look for houses of worship, public transportation, and shopping centers. Closeness to jobs, which is so important to young families, is not that important to retirees.

If an RV park is your preference, then choosing land in a recreational location such as a lake or a river, or close to an attraction like Disney World, a golf course, a skiing resort, or Las Vegas will go a long way towards the park's success. Closeness to interstate highways is also of prime importance to RV'ers.

No matter what kind of park you choose to develop, it will be an advantage if the property has frontage on a well-traveled road, so your signage will be productive when you advertise your mobile homes for sale or rent. A large sign on a good road is a major benefit when it comes to marketing your product. If you are thinking about long-term appreciation in a keeper mobile home park, road frontage will represent a higher and better use and increased values for the land in the future.

In addition to being aware of the positive factors to look for in a location, you should also be aware of negatives you should avoid. Low-lying lands are important to avoid. It's okay to have some wetlands or land in a flood plain on the edges of your property, but not close to the living areas. If any of the living areas of the park are in a flood plain, your park may become uninhabitable and a health hazard when there are floods—even if the floods only happen once in a hundred years. Don't think that a hundred-year flood event is not going to happen in your lifetime. It could very well happen six months after you buy the land and start development. It won't matter to you that the flood might not occur again for another century—your project will be ruined and the neighborhood will be ruined, and the lives of the people and families who trusted you and your engineer will be painfully disrupted.

Basically you want the topography, or the lay of the land, to be gently rolling or even flat, but not flooding. If you want to develop on the tops of hills or mountains, you will need expertise in this. Yes, the views of the valleys below can be breathtaking, but remember that in hilly regions, some mobile homes will have to be raised up and blocked more than eight feet on one side, and expensive tie-down procedures will have to be used.

You also want to avoid excessively noisy areas, areas with air pollution, and places that just plain smell bad. Locating a mobile home park next to a large dog kennel, a lumber mill, a meat-processing plant, or a drag strip, among other places, might not bode well for happiness of the residents of the park you are developing and could severely hinder your sales or rentals.

Given the above considerations when you pick a site, it must also be noted we have seen a few successful mobile home parks with none of these characteristics. They were far from jobs, health care, interstate highways, and recreation, but were beautiful, quiet, healthy place to live with lots of trees and fresh air. Personally, if I was looking for land on which to place a park I would place strong emphasis on job creation, population growth, and proximity to health care, and so on over simply a beautiful, quiet place to live with none of the other considerations, but it is possible to build a successful park that is out in the country. In this case the location should have a reasonable demand for affordable housing and a short supply of it, as well as a local government that understands the need for affordable housing and believes mobile home parks are a benefit. Chances are you will need to be patient if you choose a remote location because *the absorption rate*—the rate at which your product is bought or rented—may be two or three times slower than elsewhere, and you will incur greater carrying costs on your loans and a longer time period before you see your full profit. To professional developers, absorption rate and profitability are of critical importance.

After the Land, Then What?

First, you shouldn't run out and buy five acres just to get started. Get the land under contract with the seller with a suitable due diligence period of sixty to ninety days and a financing contingency, just as you would have on a mobile home park. Then contact a civil engineer to help you plan the park, itemize the costs in the area, and determine if it is feasible to develop the park or not.

What does feasible mean? It means you start your planning backwards, just like with a flipper or a keeper. You and the engineer will take the price you believe the market will pay to buy or lease one of the park's mobile homes and then you will work backwards, subtracting all of your costs, to see if there will be any profit left over for you. If there is going to be little or no positive cash flow after selling or renting out the homes in the park, then you will probably want to try developing somewhere else until the park becomes feasible in the area you originally chose.

Experienced builders know within reasonable limits what their buyers, or renters, will pay. Then they figure the cost of the dwellings they are going to supply, accounting for their time and unforeseen risks, and determine how much profit they need to stay in business. The basic variable to a builder is the cost of the land. If the cost of the land allows them to make a profit, then the project is a "go." If not, they try a different location or a different product. As mentioned above, one of the keys to a successful development is the absorption rate—how much of the end product can be sold or rented in a certain time period. Big developers hire financial experts to do expensive feasibility studies to arrive at those two critical factors—the marketability of the product at a certain price range, and how fast the product should sell or rent and be absorbed.

In your case, it probably won't be economically wise to spend tens of thousands of dollars on a feasibility study. You are going to have to do your own study by calling around and checking prices and rental comps and vacancies in other mobile home parks, by placing test ads to see if they generate any interest in a mobile home for sale on a half-acre lot or for lease at a certain rent, by networking with local residents, and by using a little of the old "gut feeling." If your project looks feasible—and we will assume for our example that it does—continue with your planning. At this point we are going to give the park a name, Pine Tree Acres, because the property has big pine trees and each lot is going to be almost a half acre.

We're going to employ a method we use when we teach the live three day classes to give you an idea of what you will be discussing about Pine Tree Acres with the engineer you select. This technique is called the Socratic Method, and it was developed by the ancient Greeks. Basically, it teaches by asking questions, so the student learns to think rather than just memorize facts and figures.

So—here is your first question: You chose the land, got it under contract, and did your own feasibility study to see if it will be a viable product within a certain price range. It looked viable, so you named it Pine Tree Acres and hired an engineer to figure your costs. What's next?

What's next is your first question: how many homes do you want to put on your five acres? The answer you would give to this question would be, "Ten." Okay, so now what? You have to draw up a plat, or schematic, showing how you would subdivide the land. It would look something like the drawing here. You will draw rough lines for now, and later, you will call in a surveyor to lay out the lines exactly. We will assume the survey and plat will cost you $3,000. By the way, we are also going to assume that the five acres we picked are the standard dimensions, 330 feet wide by 660 feet deep.

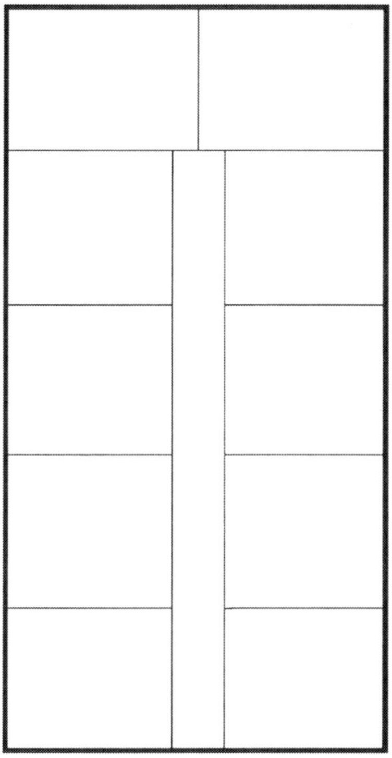

A plat, or schematic, shows how you will subdivide the land.

Now what? Well, do you want the people in your neighborhood to have to park out on the highway and walk several hundred feet to their front doors, or would they prefer to drive up and park their cars outside their homes? The answer is obvious—we now have to put in a road. (Most of the answers to the questions you will be asked here are obvious. What we are also trying to do with this exercise is have you realize that planning a neighborhood is mostly common sense, combined with engineering know-how. You have to take care of basic human needs before you can appeal to their other senses.)

You will find that road costs vary widely. In some areas you will just run a bulldozer down the middle of the property, and then put down base rock or gravel. In the South they call this "crush and run," and it can be accomplished for around $10,000. In other areas, you may have put in a paved road and build it to DOT (Department of Transportation) standards, which can cost many times crush and run. In this case, we're going to assume $20,000 for the road.

Next, do you want the people in your park to put out rain barrels to gather their drinking water and use outhouses for their restrooms, or do you think they will require indoor plumbing? This means that you will have to have discussions to find out whether city water and sewer systems are available, or if wells and septic systems are needed. We are going to assume city water and sewer are available at a cost of $10,000 each for the permits and the underground pipes and connections. If city water and sewer are not available, the costs could escalate from $10,000 to $20,000 or more, depending on what you and the engineer determine.

Next, do you want the residents to set up generators and use candles and wood stoves when the generators are off? How about phone and cable? We are going to assume that your customers want all the modern utilities they can get, and that the utility companies in your area are interested in growing and will put up the electric poles and power lines, phone lines, and cable at their own expense in return for having more paying customers. Again, you and the engineer will determine what the costs are and whether the utility companies will pay for all, part, or none of the costs.

Now that we have accounted for roads and utilities for the residents you should see that we have just been setting up the infrastructure—the very same infrastructure that we inspected so carefully when we were "doin' the due dilly" on other people's mobile home parks we were considering investing in.

Okay, now it's time to set up mobile homes. This is one of your most important decisions because the home is what your customers will focus on. Are you developing a keeper or a flipper? If it is a keeper, do you want park-owned units to increase your cash flow or a land-lease community in which the residents will own their homes and only lease the land? If you want to have park-owned units, you will probably want to use single-wide, three-bedroom, two-bath units, ranging in size from 14 x 70 to 16 x 80 feet. You might buy good quality repos, ten years old or newer—preferably newer, if they are available for $10,000 or less. (Remember that double-wides cost twice as much to buy and install, but don't return twice as much in rent.) If you want to create a land-lease community, you need to know early on if your customers will bring in their own mobile homes, if a dealer can bring in mobile homes and sell them on your leased land, or if you will have to bring in mobile homes and turn around and sell them to do a BB. (We'll come back to this when we discuss profits.)

If you are going to sell the mobile homes and land to buyers one at a time, then you will probably want to buy double-wides. We have found that owners greatly prefer double-wides and will pay the additional cost. You can plan on spending $20,000 for double-wide repos. (At this point, you may even want to think about selling new mobile homes, like a dealer. This will entail getting a mobile home dealer's license and a factory that will sell you their products—or doing a joint venture with a mobile home dealer. This is a topic best saved for another time and perhaps another book.)

Now, for the next question: Do you think your customers—either buyers or renters—would want to just leave the mobile homes sitting on the wheels with the front hitch blocked up, or do you think they would prefer to have their homes blocked, leveled, and tied down, with skirting placed around the crawlspace under the home and with stairs and landings to get to the doors? The answer is obvious once again, and we are going to assume that the setup cost of the homes will be $4,000 for each single-wide and $8,000 for each double-wide.

Last, but not least, we are going to expect the unexpected and account for it by allowing $10,000 for any miscellaneous surprises. (That number may be too optimistic, and your engineer may want it to be $25,000.) One such "surprise" might be that your absorption rate is less than you figured. In other words, instead of filling up your park with renters in three months, it takes you six months or longer. In the case of a flipper, instead of selling off all ten mobile homes in six months, it takes a year or longer, so the interest cost on your loan becomes important. Surprises on the cost side tend to be unpleasant rather than profitable.

We are done now with our accounting, except for marketing costs, the money you will spend reaching your customers and the commissions you will pay for inside or outside sales help such as Realtors and rental agents. A sign in front and a few ads may be sufficient for a mobile home park keeper with park-owned units, and your marketing costs may be less than $1,000. This can be absorbed into the miscellaneous column. You may have to do more marketing and spend more money on a land-lease keeper. For a flipper, marketing may be an even more substantial number, which we will account for later when we discuss selling and the costs of sales.

To Hire a General Contractor or Not?

In some areas, your engineer can act as your GC—your general contractor. He can apply for permits, bid out the different parts of the development, and hire the subcontractors to do the work. It may also be possible for you to do it yourself, with the engineer acting as a mentor and adviser for some additional fees.

If you have to add a GC, you might be able to work out a fee structure in which you fill out the paperwork before the GC checks and signs it, and you can bid out the job with the GC's assistance. This might add anywhere to a few thousand dollars to 10 percent of the total cost to your expenses. For now, we are going to assume you will be doing the vast majority of the paperwork and legwork, because you are impassioned by the idea of building your own neighborhood, and you have an engineer or a GC looking over your shoulder. We will take the costs and include them in the additional costs of the miscellaneous surprises.

The Costs to Set Up the Park as a Keeper with Park-Owned Units

To set up Pine Tree Acres as a keeper, with ten park-owned single-wide homes, your costs will be:

Five acres of land	$50,000
Engineer	$7,000
Survey and divide land into ten half-acre lots	$3,000
Put in road	$20,000
Put in water lines	$10,000
Put in sewer or septic	$10,000
Set up electric (free)	$0
Set up phone and cable (free)	$0
Ten mobile homes (single-wide repos)	$100,000
Block, tie down, and connect	$40,000
Miscellaneous surprises	$10,000
TOTAL COST	**$250,000**

Yes, we tried very hard to come in at a round number, so you would not be put off by a number like $267,913, which is difficult to visualize. And remember—the numbers in our generic mobile home park example are not as important as the numbers will be when you are actually developing your own Pine Tree Acres. The process of developing the park is what you need to retain.

The Costs to Set Up the Park as a Keeper with Land-Leased Units

To set up Pine Tree Acres as a keeper and land-lease community with ten *resident-owned* single-wide homes, your costs will be:

Five acres of land	$50,000
Engineer	$7,000
Survey and divide into ten half-acre lots	$3,000
Put in road	$20,000
Put in water lines	$10,000
Put in sewer or septic	$10,000
Set up electric (free)	$0
Set up phone and cable (free)	$0
Miscellaneous surprises	$10,000
TOTAL COST	**$110,000**

If you are expecting your residents to bring in their own mobile homes at their cost, or dealers to move homes into your park and sell them at their own cost, then $110,000 is all you will spend to create the park, which is very reasonable. If, however, you need to populate the park with mobile homes yourself—which is probably the case—then you will have to add the cost of the mobile homes because you are going to be doing BBs or lease options. For single-wides, the additional costs will be:

Ten mobile homes (single-wide repos)	$100,000
Block, tie down, and connect	$40,000
TOTAL COST	**$140,000**

For double-wides the cost would be double, or $280,000. You will have to decide whether single- or double-wides are better for your market and how you will be financing the homes. As you can see, the cost of the homes can easily exceed the cost of setting up the infrastructure of the park.

The Costs to Set Up the Park with Units You Will Flip

Now, to set up Pine Tree Acres as a flipper, with ten double-wide units that you will sell off, each with almost half an acre of land, your costs will be:

Five acres of land	$50,000
Engineer	$7,000
Survey and divide into ten half-acre lots	$3,000
Put in road	$20,000
Put in water lines	$10,000
Put in sewer or septic	$10,000
Set up electric (free)	$0
Set up phone and cable (free)	$0
Ten mobile homes (double-wide repos)	$200,000
Block, tie down, and connect	$80,000
Miscellaneous surprises (doubled)	$20,000
TOTAL COST	**$400,000**

The Profits for a Keeper with Park-Owned Units

Setting up Pine Tree Acres as a keeper, with ten park-owned single-wide homes, each renting for $500 per month (the average amount the classes thought was reasonable) is a common choice because this maximizes the cash flow. The profits will be:

INCOME	
Ten mobile homes rented at $500 per month	$5,000
EXPENSES	
$250,000 mortgage at 8 percent for 30 years	$1,835
Taxes (2 percent of value per month)	$417
Insurance (1 percent per month)	$208
Repairs, surprises, and other unexpected expenses	$540
TOTAL MONTHLY EXPENSES	**$3,000**
NET MONTLY CASH FLOW ($5,000 Income – $3,000 Expenses)	**$2,000**
NET YEARLY CASH FLOW ($2,000 x 12 Months)	**$24,000**

Again, we worked this and the next examples out so the numbers would be round and simple to understand. The monthly income for a park with park-owned homes will be $5,000 and the expenses will be $3,000. The net monthly profit will be $2,000 and the yearly income twelve times that, or $24,000. We are assuming that you will borrow all of the money to do the project—which we will discuss shortly under financing. Please note we did not add in many management costs because in the majority of the cases, our students wanted to manage their own Pine Tree Acres Mobile Home Park themselves and they didn't feel that only ten units at one location would take much of their time.

The Profits for a Keeper with Land-Leased Units

To set up Pine Tree Acres as a land-lease keeper, with ten resident-owned homes, each paying a lot rent of $250 per month (the average around the country) the profits are:

INCOME	
Ten mobile homes rented at $250 per month	$2,500
EXPENSES	
$110,000 mortgage at 8 percent for 30 years	$807
Taxes (2 percent of value per month)	$183
Insurance (1 percent per month)	$92
Repairs, surprises, and other unexpected expenses	$118
TOTAL MONTHLY EXPENSES	**$1,200**
NET MONTLY CASH FLOW ($2,500 Income – $1,200 Expenses)	**$1,300**
NET YEARLY CASH FLOW ($1,300 x 12 Months)	**$15,000**

The monthly income will be $2,500 and the expenses only $1,200. The net monthly profit will be $1,300 and the yearly income will be $15,000. We are assuming that you will borrow all of the money to do the project (which we will discuss shortly). We also are assuming that the residents will mow their own lawns and pay their own utilities, and that there will not be much to do in the way of management or costs. Again, most students wanted to manage their Pine Tree Acres Mobile Home Park themselves, and didn't feel that only ten units in one location would be taxing on their time.

Also note that we will spend less than half of the money to do a land-lease community—only $110,000 versus $250,000 for an all park-owned community—yet we received more than half as much income from the land-lease park. However, given my experience, I am skeptical about the success of filling up a new park with resident-owned units unless the owner of the park does it himself with BBs. Rather than complicate this already complicated process, let's leave that discussion for another time and accept the fact that many people are going to do all park-owned units when they build a small mobile home park with only ten units.

The Profits for a Park with Units You Will Flip

Now, to set up Pine Tree Acres as a flipper with ten double-wide homes, each selling for $60,000 ($59,900), the average price that the classes thought was reasonable, your profits will be:

INCOME	
Ten mobile homes sold at $60,000	$600,000
EXPENSES	
$400,000 mortgage at 8 percent for 30 years	$400,000
Commissions, closing costs, marketing (10 percent of average value of sale)	$50,000
TOTAL COSTS	**$450,000**
NET PROFIT = TOTAL SALES – EXPENSES ($600,000 – $450,000)	**$150,000**

The people I polled thought that a reasonable price for a double-wide on a half-acre was $60,000, and any more than that would meet buyer resistance. There will be ten mobile homes, so the total sales will be $600,000, and the expenses will be $450,000, leaving $150,000 profit. You should note that the cost will be $150,000 more than setting up all park-owned units because of the cost of the double-wides on the flipper homes versus single-wides on park-owned units.

Stepping Back to Understand

Now let's step back from all the calculations we have been analyzing and ask a very basic question: How would you feel about doing one flipper and one keeper Pine Tree Acres Mobile Home Park every year, for the next ten years?

Each year you would be creating a ten-unit mobile home park keeper and adding $24,000 a year to your net income. You would also be selling ten newly created units and adding $150,000 a year to your net profits. If you do a little math, at the end of ten years (assuming no increase in rents), you would receive $240,000 a year in annual cash flow from the 100 units that you keep and rent, and you would have amassed $1,500,000 in profits from the flippers that you sold. Is that another million dollar strategy? Or two?

Financing Pine Tree Acres

When you are a developer, which you are when you are take Pine Tree Acres from an idea to a real neighborhood with people living in homes, you will be dealing with financing in a way that is similar to what you did before but also different than before.

First, many banks feel more secure lending on already existing parks, not parks that haven't been created yet. They are concerned that if anything stops you from completing the development, they will get stuck trying to sell the property in its uncompleted condition. It will take them a long time to get their money back, and this situation may even represent a loss. Community banks are interested in developing the community they do business in so they are more inclined take the additional risk lending on new developments, but they also want adequate protection for their loans.

On the other end of the spectrum, many of you will be trying to borrow as much money as you can while putting out as little money as you can. If you fall into that category, you can try to get the seller of the land to take back a second mortgage to help you with the down payment. You can also try to get the dealer or lender you are buying the repo homes from to finance the mobile homes instead of requiring full cash payment on delivery.

At the end of the day, a bank may want to do the financing for only one mobile home at time until they feel comfortable with you and the project. They will lend on the land, and then when you bring in the first mobile home, and set it up, they will lend you the value of the mobile home plus set up costs so you can pay for the mobile home. In this case you need *random releases* on the mortgage if you are doing a flipper.

Random Releases

Random releases means the bank will remove their lien on part of the land, on individual lots, when they are paid a portion of the loan on the whole parcel of land. Let's describe how a random release works. In this case, you are paying $50,000 for the land plus $60,000 for the infrastructure, for a total of $110,000. We'll assume the bank lent you $90,000 and wanted $20,000 down (or a second mortgage from the seller). Since there are ten lots, each lot now has a one-tenth proportional share of the loan on it, or $9,000, but can't be sold unless the bank agrees to release the lot from the whole mortgage. Most banks will do this for a premium of 20 to 25 percent of the value of the proportional share of the land. In this case, therefore, the bank may require a release price of $11,250 for the land when the home on it is sold. You can see that after you have released eight lots in this way the bank's mortgage on the land will be paid off (eight lots x $11,250 per lot = $90,000), and at that point the remaining two lots will be free and clear of debt.

Making Money One Home at a Time

After the repayment of the loan for the land, you will have to repay any loans for the purchase and set up of the homes. The difference between the sale price that your buyer paid and the loans you paid off will be the return of money you put down, plus your profit.

After the first home is sold, you will move on a second home and sell it, and then a third home, and so on. The details of this process will vary from lender to lender. You should be aware that lenders have been burned in the past on construction loans, so don't be yet one more developer who burns them too, and ruins this opportunity for others who come after you.

Once again, when you go in to interview lenders, follow the script you were given in Chapter 11. Have two copies of a complete package, with engineered drawings and estimates, comparables, and pictures of the type of product you will be offering, what your income and expenses will be, and the resulting profits.

Coping with Success and Rolling Options

If Pine Tree Acres is a stunning success, you will have a big problem. You may think that statement was designed to get your attention, and it was. If your first development sells or rents quickly for as much or more than you estimated, many of you will want to do another ten units right away, and then another ten units . . . and then another twenty units . . . and then . . .

But then the problem will be that you ran out of land. Now you have to go out and find another parcel of land to create Pine Tree Acres II and III and so on, and this new parcel of land may be many miles away from the first Pine Tree Acres or even on the other side of the town, so all of the good will that you built while creating your first Pine Tree Acres will be lessened or possibly lost. Wouldn't it be nice to create a situation in which you have minimal risk if your development plans don't work out as well as you hoped—and maximum profit potential if your plans do? Of course it would.

What developers used to do was start small, like you are doing here. If they were successful, they went out and bought a bigger parcel of land and did more developing. If that development was also successful they went out and bought a huge parcel of land, and that is where they got into trouble. Real estate goes in cycles, and sometimes—even though your product is priced perfectly for your market—the absorption of your product (in this case, mobile homes) slows down or even stops. This may be due to some adverse act of Mother Nature, like a hurricane, a flood, or tornado, or an adverse act of human nature, like a recession, inflation, deflation, a terrorist incident, or another negative event.

If you bought a huge parcel of land and only developed a tenth of it before human nature or Mother Nature worked its ill effects on you, you would be stuck with a huge mortgage on the remaining 90 percent of the land. Then you would find out—in living color, up close and personal—how land needs to be fed three times each day. Many of the large developers around today have gone bankrupt in the past, some more than once, because they got caught in an unexpected downward trend in a real estate cycle while owning too much vacant land with large mortgages and large interest payments.

Then they discovered *rolling options.*

Rolling options are similar to a lease option, but are on land. They give you a chance to stay in one place and start small and then continue to build a bigger development if conditions are good. If conditions change due to no fault of your own—because of human nature or Mother Nature—you will be able to disconnect and move on with your profits and investment money still in your pocket. In other to accomplish this, you are going to start by writing a contract to buy a bigger tract of land than five acres, say one that is five times as big, or twenty-five acres. This will look like the figure shown on the following page.

You will still have a due diligence period and a financing contingency, and if conditions are good, you will "take down," or buy, the first five acres on the same terms we agreed upon in this chapter, namely $10,000 per acre for a total of $50,000.

What about the remaining twenty acres? Well, that is what you arrange to have an option to buy. You will put down nonrefundable

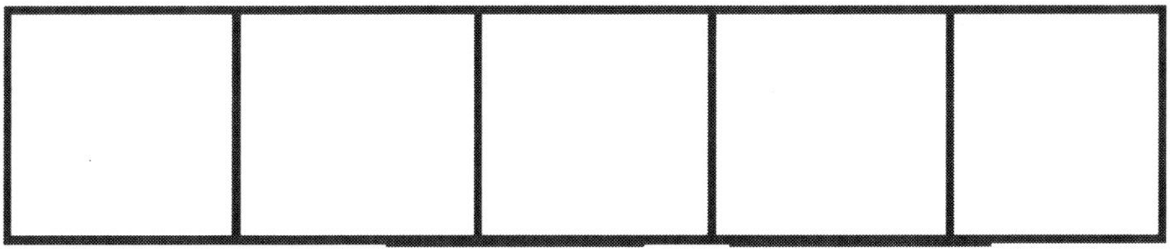

A 25-acre tract divided into five 5-acre parcels.

option money—say $2,000 for each additional five-acre tract, or a total of $8,000—for the remaining four five-acre tracts. You will also contract a set point in time by which you have to purchase the additional five-acre tracts or forfeit your deposit. For this example, let's assume that you establish a one-year option period for the next five-acre tract, a two-year period for the next five-acre tract, a three year period for the next five-acre tract, and a four–year period for the last one. In other words, every year you will be developing an additional five-acre mobile home park that is right next to the previous ones you developed so you can take advantage of the good will and networking you have already created.

You will also have to establish a price for each of these additional five-acre tracts that you will take down in the future. We paid $50,000 for the first one. For the second tract, we could add 10 percent and make the price $55,000. For the third tract, the price would be $60,000, the fourth, $65,000, and the final tract would be $70,000. What are we doing with this option that *rolls* from one five-acre tract to the next? We are creating incentives for the property owner to give us the option by offering non-refundable deposits and increased prices in the future. We are also giving ourselves the option to get out of the deal if conditions change due to no fault of our own. If we are successful, we would be still guaranteed a nice profit despite the additional cost of the land. If we have to stop developing, the costs of forfeiting the $2,000 deposits is a lot less than the interest-carrying costs of a mortgage on the additional land and is an insurance policy against failure. In other words, if in two years the market changes and developing is no longer profitable, you can stop. All you will lose are the three $2,000 deposits on the remaining three five-acre tracts.

The actual terms of the rolling option are between you and the owner of the land. You need to find someone who is motivated and reasonable, and work out together what best suits your individual needs. It would be best to find a landowner who understands that her land has to be fed three times each day. We have only outlined some of the terms that you would discuss with her.

Doing a Keeper and Flipper Simultaneously Using Rolling Option

What if you wanted to do both flippers and keepers—and still take advantage of the rolling option to protect yourself against unknown adverse problems while retaining local good will when successful?

You could do a rolling option on two big parcels of land, say two twenty-five-acre tracts. One tract would be used for flippers in which you would sell off mobile homes on half-acre lots, one at a time, for quick flipping profits. The second big parcel would be for keepers, in which you would develop ten lots at a time to keep for cash flow.

This would protect you against adverse conditions not under your control, and also—if for some reason the flippers were going well and the keepers were stagnating—you could stop developing your keepers and concentrate on the flippers, or vice versa. It's nice to have diversity when you are making money, with two pots cooking instead of one.

SUMMARY

In this chapter, you learned some of the basic principles for developing property. Please remember that this was only a generalized review. There are whole books written solely on the subject of developing neighborhoods, and it is a dynamic field that is constantly changing.

Again, we'll repeat the warning that this is a risky and time-consuming way to make money. I prefer buying existing mobile home parks that need tender, loving care to nurse them back to profitability. My opinion aside, I can also say that developers are some of the wealthiest and most contented people I have met. They love the act of creation and find the act of developing neighborhoods fulfilling. If you are like that, then you should look into this exciting field using affordable manufactured housing. But always, always, keep your eyes on the prize—you have to be profitable or face dire consequences. It's no fun going broke while you are creating.

HOMEWORK

If you feel that developing is something you would like to consider, go out and look at tracts of vacant land, put the best one under contract, and find an engineer. If the feasibility and costs are promising, try doing a rolling option on a bigger tract. Go ahead.

And remember to have fun while you are doing it.

COMING ATTRACTIONS

Now let's learn how to protect the assets you are buying and the business you are creating. Let's also learn about the different ways to own real estate and how to minimize your taxes. More good news! The government wants you to make money with real estate, and they offer some powerful tax advantages to encourage you to do so.

16

Protecting Your Assets

Congratulations! Now that you're on your way to creating wealth for yourself and your loved ones, you have to think about protecting the assets that you are accumulating and reducing your income taxes by taking advantage of the incentives Uncle Sam and Auntie IRS so generously provide to real estate investors.

It's a fact of life that once you have something, there are people who will try to take it from you—with lawsuits, for example—rather than working hard for it themselves as you did. You could also suffer onerous taxes. That's okay. You have the prize. But now you have to protect it.

We're going to give you some interesting things to think about in this chapter, but before we do, I have to give you a disclaimer. *I am not an attorney or a CPA, and you should seek professional advice from your attorney and CPA before you follow any of the information in this chapter.* Check out everything discussed here with the appropriate members of your Power Team. There may be differences in laws and regulations in different states, different cities, between the counties within a single state, and even because of your own unique circumstances. In this chapter, we are going to discuss the following topics:

1. The six ways you can own real estate

2. Threats from inside and outside your properties
3. Various tax reduction strategies
4. Risk reduction on mortgages

SIX WAYS TO TAKE TITLE TO REAL ESTATE

There are at least six different ways to take ownership of real estate. These are the most common:

1. Individual—in your own name
2. Partnership—general or limited
3. Corporation—either subchapter S or subchapter C
4. LLC—limited liability company
5. Land trust
6. Offshore corporation—in another country

Each of these has unique asset protection and liability characteristics. You are probably familiar with the first mode of taking title, taking it *individually in your name* or perhaps in your name along with your spouse's name. This is like being a sole proprietor. You have unlimited liability in case of lawsuits, but homestead laws in most states, and insurance, usually provide enough protection for your primary residence if you take title to your home individually in your name.

However, you don't have homestead laws protecting you when you own investment property in your own name, and this property is fair game. The people that sue you can come after everything you own, including the corporations, partnerships, LLCs, and land trusts you own, if they can prove you own them. But, as you will see later, it is difficult for these people to find out what property you own if it is not titled individually in your own name.

Most of you should own an investment property by now because you have been following the steps you've been given in this book. However, it's likely that asset protection and taxation have not been foremost in your mind just yet. At some point soon, if you are as successful as I think you will be, you are going to have to decide how you want to take ownership in the properties you accumulate, and there are better choices than taking title individually in your own name.

When you take title in the name of a *partnership,* you have two choices. In a *general partnership,* each partner will have complete and total liability for all of the actions of the partnership, regardless of the ownership percentage of each partner. This is not a good choice for asset protection. In a *limited partnership,* however, each of the limited partners risks only his contribution to the partnership and nothing more. Typically members of a limited partnership have a passive role and they hand over management and liability to general partners. This may not be a better choice for the start of your career, either, since you are probably be actively managing your properties.

When you take title under a *corporation,* either as a *"subchapter S" or "C corp,"* only the properties owned by the corporation are at risk when someone starts a lawsuit as the result of a liability associated with one of the properties owned by the corporation. None of the officers or shareholders is at personal risk (unless there is gross or criminal negligence involved, which is rare). This could be a good way to take ownership of your investment properties. One of the basic differences between the subchapter S and the C corp is that the profits in a subchapter S corporation flow to your individual tax return, while C corps are taxed as a separate entity.

An *LLC,* or *limited liability company,* is a relatively new type of corporate entity and is only a few decades old. It offers the same protection from personal liability as a corporation but the ownership and profit distribution percentage can be agreed by the corporate members instead of being based on the capital contribution made by members in the beginning.

A *land trust* is a very old legal entity that dates back hundred of years to old England and Europe. The land trust has two types of participants, a trustee and beneficiaries. The trustee may or may not have any ownership, but does the signing of important papers and is the only person the outside world deals with or even may know of. The beneficiaries own various percentages of the property and direct actions of the trustee, and often require that they remain anonymous to the outside world. Land trusts are an excellent way to own investment property, as long as you are not your own trustee. You will see why later, when we discuss public records.

Finally, you can take title in an *offshore corporation, located in another coun-*

try. This is an advanced form of asset protection and you should seek expert legal council before attempting it. In my opinion, it is a mixed bag. On the one hand, the individual stockholders can be almost completely invisible in the United States, and the corporation can be difficult to sue because the country the corporation is in may not easily give jurisdiction to the United States to pursue lawsuits or other legal procedures against its corporations. On the other hand, many foreign governments, and their property rights, may not be stable. In the past, some foreign countries have annexed the property owned by its citizens and corporations—they just took their property—which defeats the whole idea of asset protection. You should think about why many foreigners move their investments *to the United States, not out of it,* and whether this has something to do with the stability of our government and our basic property rights.

THE DIFFERENCE BETWEEN AN INSIDE THREAT AND AN OUTSIDE THREAT

You will need to protect your investment property from any lawsuit that can threaten to take it away from you. To do this, you must understand the difference between inside and outside threats, because threats can come from either source.

An *inside threat* occurs when someone sues you because of a liability connected with the property itself. For instance, let's say that someone trips and falls in a hole that a dog dug next to one of your investment mobile homes. That person breaks his ankle and sues you for damages, accusing you of being negligent for knowing of or allowing the condition that caused him to trip and fall. This is an example of an inside threat—it originated from the property itself. The person suing you will find any one of a number of attorneys who will take the case on a contingency basis, which means that he doesn't have to come up with any money at all. His attorney will pay for all the court costs, which she will be reimbursed for after the case is settled. If the court finds in favor of the person who broke his ankle, the court will assess damages against you, the owner of the property. The person who sued you will be paid first from your liability insurance on the mobile home. If he is awarded damages *in excess of your insurance,* he will probably demand the difference in cash from you. If you don't have the additional cash available, he will have his attorney file a lien against your mobile home and have the sheriff forcibly sell it at auction. He will then be paid the amount he was still owed from the proceeds of the sale.

However, what if after receiving the insurance and the proceeds from sale of the investment property itself, the plaintiff is still owed money? Well, then the attorney will try to find any other property you own and have it sold by the sheriff to pay off the remainder of the judgment. That is an *outside threat* to your other investment properties. Someone is threatening those properties based on a judgment that did *not* occur on them. The attorney will search public records to see what else you own. If your state has homestead laws to protect your home against a forced sale—and many do—the attorney will ignore your home and look for any other investment property you own. If the attorney finds other investment property, she will have the sheriff sell off that property, too, until the judgment is satisfied.

You should know that if, at any point in your life, someone gets a judgment against you for any reason—whether it is because of an unpaid debt or income taxes, or any other liability—he can check property records to see what else you own besides your home if you don't pay the judgment off with cold hard cash. He can then get an attorney to put a lien on it and then have the sheriff auction it off and give him the proceeds.

Let me tell you about a business acquaintance of mine named Arthur. Arthur owned a small private airport that was earning a good profit. Then a plane crashed on the runway. The attorney for the passengers sued Arthur and his airport. They were awarded a judgment in the millions of dollars, far exceeding Arthur's insurance. The attorney then proceeded to sell off the airport and took the proceeds for his clients. The judgment was still not satisfied, so he proceeded to take away every piece of property Arthur owned in sheriff's auctions, except for his homestead. Such threats are real, so you should be careful to protect yourself.

Insurance

You should see from the example above that your first line of defense against an inside threat to one of your properties is having *enough insurance* to protect you against lawsuits. That is why, as you become wealthier, you will be spending larger and larger amounts of money on insurance. The good news is that liability insurance is the most reasonably-priced insurance on real estate, and you can get additional umbrella policies that will cover all your properties for up to $10,000,000 or more to make sure you are protected if a lawsuit should result in a judgment greater than the coverage provided by your primary liability insurance. Don't worry about paying big insurance premiums. It is a sign you are successful. It's better to pay large insurance premiums out of the large profits you earn from investing than to have no investments, no profits, and no insurance.

Public Records

The first form of asset protection, insurance, protects the property you own from lawsuits that threaten to take it away. *A more advanced form of asset protection limits the number of people who even know you own a property,* making it difficult for outsiders to track down the ownership of your properties and pursue lawsuits against you. This is one of your best defenses against an *outside threat* to your properties.

How you take title directly affects how your property is recorded in the county *public records,* which are available for anyone to see. If you own all your property individually in your name, or in both you and your spouse's names, then anyone can go to the county public records and get a list of everything you own. If that person is an attorney who wants to sue you, she will be able to attach everything you own in her lawsuit easily after she does a simple search for your name. However, if you take title to your properties in the names of corporations, LLCs, or land trusts that you control, then there will be no direct linkage to your name. In our county, the clerk requires that the names of trustees in a land trust be recorded along with the name of the land trust; if this is the case in your area it is not a good idea to be the trustee of the land trust if you don't want your name attached to the property.

Here is an example of how public records work. Let's assume Bob and Nancy Johnson own their home at 123 Main St. In addition, they also own two mobile homes, one at 456 Second Street and the other at 789 Third Street. When an attorney wants to sue Bob and Nancy Johnson, she will do a search in the public records and find the following properties:

Address	Homestead	Owner
123 Main Street	Yes	Bob and Nancy Johnson
456 Second Street	No	Bob and Nancy Johnson
789 Third Street	No	Bob and Nancy Johnson

The attorney will see that 123 Main St is the Johnson's homestead, so she will skip past it. Then she will see that the 456 Second Street and 789 Third Street addresses are investment properties. She will then list them in her lawsuit and post a notice in the public records that she is starting a legal action against Bob and Nancy Johnson. This notice of impending legal action is called a *Lis Pendens,* and it will "color the title" of the 456 Second Street and 789 Third Street properties. This coloring of title will prevent the Johnsons from selling or refinancing the properties until the lawsuit is settled.

Now, let's assume that Bob and Nancy Johnson formed a new corporation called NanceBob Corporation and took title to the properties in the name of that corporation. Then, when an attorney wants to sue Bob and Nancy, she will find only the following in the public records under their name:

Address	Homestead	Owner
123 Main Street	Yes	Bob and Nancy Johnson

The attorney will not know about NanceBob Corporation, and will not know to attach those properties and attack them from outside the properties.

However, if someone trips and falls at 456 Second Street, Bob and Nancy's investment property and that person hires an attorney to sue the owners, the attorney will check the public records to see who owns the property. She will see that the NanceBob Corporation is the owner, will search for all the properties owned by NanceBob, and will find the following:

Address	Homestead	Owner
456 Second Street	No	NanceBob Corporation
789 Third Street	No	NanceBob Corporation

Then she will also attach 789 Third Street to the lawsuit. The attorney can attach all the properties owned by NanceBob Corp in a lawsuit that is associated with one of NanceBob's properties, but she cannot attach any other properties owned by Nancy and Bob Johnson under different legal entities. If, for instance, Bob and Nancy also own several properties in the MobileBob Corporation, the attorney cannot come after them because of the liability limits afforded to a corporation.

You could formulate three possible strategies from this example. Make sure that the public records have only your homestead property listed as directly owned by you and your spouse.

1. Place your investment properties into a corporation, an LLC, or a land trust, and limit each entity to a specific number of properties or to a specific total value, in order to limit the entity's liability. Start a new entity once you exceed the number or value of the properties. Keep in mind that each entity will need separate accounting and tax returns, which will increase your paperwork—but it's worth it.
2. Carry sufficient liability insurance as a first line of defense, and consider obtaining a large umbrella policy that will act as a backup to your primary policies.

WAYS TO REDUCE YOUR TAXES WITH REAL ESTATE

Uncle Sam and Auntie IRS generously offer four bonuses to real estate investors, in the form of tax advantages. There is also a fifth one that they give grudgingly—if at all. These bonuses are:

1. 1031 exchanges
2. Using your IRA to invest in real estate
3. $500,000 exclusion on gain for sale of primary residence
4. Depreciation
5. Offshore or foreign corporations

1031 Exchanges

My brother is an excellent CPA. He mentioned 1031 exchanges to me years ago and when I asked more questions about them he handed me one of his accounting manuals so I could read up on them. As I read it, my eyes opened wide in shock. I could not believe the government would be so generous. Let's go over the basics.

If you want to sell one of your real estate investments and use the proceeds from the sale to buy another real estate investment, you are in effect exchanging one piece of real estate for another. When you do this while following a few simple rules, the government will not charge you any income tax on the profits from the sale of the first property. The taxes will be postponed until you sell the exchanged property outright. If you continue to exchange property over and over, you can defer your income taxes until you die, at which point the taxes will be paid by your estate. The rules that must be followed are:

1. The property you sell must be investment real estate, not personal property, and cannot be your own residence at the time of sale. Investment real estate can be land, condos, mobile home parks, houses, apartments, warehouses, stores, and so forth.
2. You must state in your sales contract that you are contemplating a 1031 exchange.
3. When you sell the first property, all of the proceeds must go directly into an escrow account of a qualified intermediary, not into your account.
4. You must designate the potential replacement property or properties within forty-five days from the date of the sale of the original property and close on the specified property within 180 days of the original sale.
5. The replacement property must also be investment real estate, and cannot be your personal residence at the time of purchase.
6. If you take any cash out after the purchase is completed, it will be considered "boot," and you will pay taxes on the boot.
7. If your mortgage decreases from the first property to the replacement property, the difference is also considered boot and will be taxed.
8. You can add cash to the transaction or increase your mortgage indebtedness without owing additional tax.

Let me give you an example, my first exchange. I owned a property in Long Island, New York, a small carriage house that we rented out on half an acre. My cost was only $10,000 because I split it off from a much larger and more expensive property that it had been attached to. The next-door neighbor came to us and wanted to buy the property for $275,000. This was a $265,000 profit! At the time, my Federal and New York State income taxes would have been at least half that, or $132,500, leaving me only $132,500 to spend on another piece of real estate.

Instead of selling outright, we did an exchange. We wrote a contract with our next door neighbor for $275,000 and stated in the contract that we were contemplating a 1031 exchange. Then we went on a shopping spree, and found five duplexes in Florida on almost two acres of land for the same amount of money. We put the duplexes under contract subject to completing the sale of the carriage house in New York.

On closing day, we sold the carriage house in New York, holding the proceeds in the escrow account of a qualified intermediary. We then bought the five duplexes in Florida with the proceeds in the escrow account. When the smoke cleared, we no longer owned the carriage house on half an acre in New York, from which we collected $350 per month in rent, and we owned five duplexes in Florida on two acres from which we collected $3,000 per month in rent. Total taxes paid—zero! If we had not done an exchange but simply sold the carriage house, we would have had only $132,500 to invest after taxes and could have purchased only two-and-a-half duplexes instead of five.

By the way, I introduced the concept of 1031 exchanges to my real estate attorney at the time. After we did my exchange, he went on to specialize in handling 1031 exchanges for his other clients and gave me a reduction in his fees as thanks for teaching it to him. I fell in love with 1031 exchanges and have done many after that, each with wonderful results. How many situations are there in which you can take the money you should have paid in taxes and instead use it to continue to invest? It's like a free loan from Uncle Sam that doesn't have to be paid off until you die.

Maintaining a Separate Entity for Flippers

Now that you understand exchanging—and it should be a major part of asset protection—let me add one additional rule. You cannot exchange property that you use in your trade or business inventory, so you cannot exchange flippers. Furthermore, if you hold flippers and keepers within the same entity, Auntie IRS may determine that all of the properties in that entity were really flippers for tax purposes, and deny you the 1031 blessing on all of them. Therefore, you need to separate your keepers from your flippers. Your flippers are going to be taxed at ordinary income rates or possibly at long-term capital gains rates if you hold them for a year or more, and that's okay. But you should put a fence around your keepers by putting them in a separate entity so that you can take advantage of the 1031 exchange when it will work for you.

Using Your IRA to Invest in Real Estate

The rules have changed—you are no longer limited to CDs, stocks, bonds, or mutual funds as investments for your IRA. You can now direct your IRA to invest in real estate through all four Basic Profit Strategies, and the profits from the real estate transactions are not taxed until you retire and start drawing down on the money. You can even do this in a Roth IRA and never pay taxes on it if you wait until you retire to draw it down.

Seek advice on how to set up a self-directed IRA, what the rules are when it comes to investing in real estate for an IRA, and whom to use as the trustee. You can read an excellent book on this, *IRA Wealth*, by Patrick Rice.

$500,000 Exclusion on Gain of Sale of Primary Residence

This is another one of those "Pinch me, I can't believe it's true" favors Uncle Sam and Auntie IRS give to real estate investors. This blessing applies only to your own home, not your investment property. If you reside in your homestead real estate for two years or more before you sell it, you do not have to pay taxes on up to $250,000 of the profit if you are unmarried or $500,000 if you are married. None. And you can keep doing this every two years—buy a home, sell it, and not pay taxes on the profit, up to $250,000 or $500,000.

Think about this. It can be used as a simple strategy to become wealthy. You find a great flipper with your spouse, move into it, fix it up while you are living there, and then sell it two years later. When you sell it, you keep all the profit, tax-free, up to $500,000, and then you do it again . . . and again . . . and again. If you start this process with a medium priced home, you will escalate into the upper-income levels, using some of the proceeds from the sale to keep trading up. You will invest the remaining profits in more keepers to give you even greater cash flow. In the end, you will sell off your multimillion dollar home and buy a smaller one, use the profits to buy even more keepers, ensuring a great cash flow and retirement income. (The drawback to this strategy is that you may grow accustomed to the multimillion dollar home and not want to sell it. That's okay, if you have created sufficient cash flow from your mobile home park keepers.

Depreciation

This gift comes at the end of every tax year, like a birthday present from your Uncle Sam and Auntie IRS, only in this case your birthday present is delivered on April 15th. At that time each year, when you figure out the income taxes you owe on the positive cash flow from your keepers, your aunt and uncle will allow you to deduct one-twenty-seventh, or 3.7 percent, of the value of the mobile home portion of your property from your net positive cash flow. They call this the gift of *depreciation*. You can keep deducting this depreciation for twenty-seven-and-a-half years. If you sell the keeper and don't exchange it, your aunt and uncle are going to ask for this tax deduction back. If you exchange the keeper, over and over, you can keep delaying paying the depreciation back until you die.

Therefore, in order to get the most benefit from deprecation, it is to your advantage to claim that as much of the value of your mobile home keepers, as legally possible, resides in the infrastructure, buildings, and park-owned units and not in the land value. See your accountant to determine the amounts.

Let's take an example. You buy a mobile home park keeper for $500,000 and allocate $400,000 for the buildings, park owned mobiles, and infrastructure and $100,000 for the land. After expenses and mortgage interest, the park provides $2,000 per month cash flow:

Yearly Profit = $2,000 per Month × 12 Months = $24,000 per Year

$500,000 Mobile Home Park = $400,000 Mobile Home Structures + $100,000 Land

Yearly Depreciation = $400,000 × 3.7% = $14,800

Net Income for Park = $24,000 – $14,800 = $9,200

Instead of paying tax on $24,000 income, you will pay on $9,200 income. That's a 62 percent reduction in your income taxes. Thank you, Uncle Sam and Auntie IRS.

Offshore or Foreign Corporations

Your aunt and uncle are not really happy about this one. Some countries have no income taxes, and if you put your investment property ownership in corporations located in such a country and then manipulate your income accordingly, it is possible to avoid paying income taxes altogether in both this country and the foreign country. Again, you need to seek out legal and accounting advice before doing this, and also think about the risk that the foreign government could suspend personal property rights and take your property from you.

RISK REDUCTION ON MORTGAGES

Almost all your mortgages from banks and private lenders will involve a *full personal guarantee* from you to pay that mortgage back. This means that if you default on the mortgage for any reason, the lender can foreclose, take the property, and sell it. If sale generates less money than you were lent, the lender can come after you and all of your assets for the difference. This is called a *deficiency judgment.*

You may be wondering, *why should I care about this, when all of my properties are throwing off cash flow far exceeding my mortgages, so I will never default.* What you want to do is protect yourself against something catastrophic and unforeseen. Take, for instance, Hurricane Katrina, one of the most destructive natural events to occur in our country's history. Many of the properties destroyed by flood waters had not been required to have flood insurance because they were not in a flood plain. The regular insurance would not cover these properties because they were not destroyed by fire or wind but by flood. If you owned one of those properties, you would have a catastrophe on your hands. The land would still be there, but the mobile home would either be gone or completely destroyed, with no insurance coverage. Let's assume further that the government refuses to allow you to put another mobile home back on the land, and insists upon the construction of a new site-built home, costing $150,000. The new home would rent out for $800 and result in a negative cash flow for the foreseeable future. In the meantime, your old mortgage on the now long-gone mobile home will still have to be paid. This would be a catastrophe, and even worse if it happened to many of your properties.

What you want to do is limit the possibility of this happening by asking the lender to make your mortgages *nonrecourse,* which means that the real estate itself, not your personal guarantee, is the sole security for the loan. That means that if, for any reason beyond your control, you have to default on the mortgage, the lender do nothing more than foreclose and sell the property. There is no deficiency judgment and the rest of your assets cannot be taken. In the case of the example above, you would simply deed the flooded property over to the bank and walk away from it with no further loss, other than whatever equity you had in the property.

The clause in your mortgage that makes it nonrecourse is called an *exculpatory clause.* The simplest way to write it is, "In the case of default, this property shall be the sole security for the note and mortgage." We include that clause whenever we buy seller-financed properties, but it is admittedly difficult to get a lender to make a loan nonrecourse. The only way to get it is to ask for it. The lender will certainly not offer it automatically. When you become a prized borrower at a bank, you can start to demand this provision, and you might get it.

SUMMARY

In this chapter you have learned how to protect yourself and how to minimize inside and outside threats to your property. You also learned how to take advantage of the gifts offered you by your Uncle Sam and Auntie IRS in the form of 1031 exchanges, IRA real estate investments, the $500,000 tax deduction on the sale of your residence, and depreciation. You even learned how to protect yourself against the possibility that you may have to default on a mortgage due to a catastrophe.

When you examine all of the advantages real estate offers as an investment vehicle, both asset-protectionwise and taxwise, you have to love it.

HOMEWORK

You need to meet with the attorney and accountant members of your Power Team to go over what you learned in this chapter and apply it to your own circumstances. Ask them for guidance as to what type of entities you should establish and how you can prepare to take advantage of all the gifts from Uncle Sam and Auntie IRS. And you may want to order *IRA Wealth,* too.

COMING ATTRACTIONS

Now that you are ready to be a mobile home park investor, we want to raise you up to an even higher level and discuss some advanced topics.

17

The Magic Formula—Advanced

At the end of Chapter 1, we mentioned that there were advanced topics to discuss that would be postponed until you were more comfortable with investing in mobile home parks. Now we are going to assume you are comfortable.

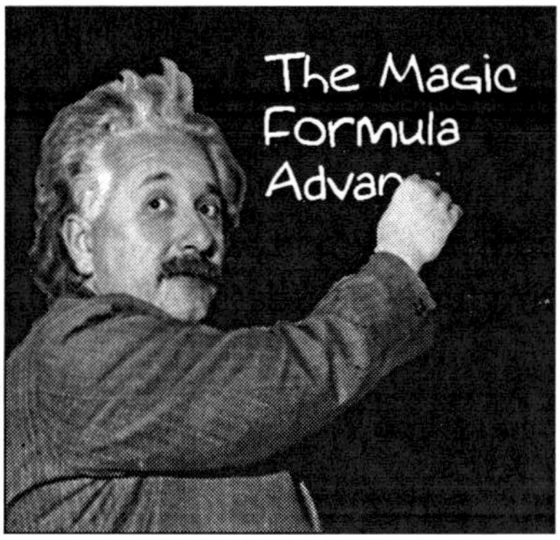

You may encounter situations that do not conform to the norm as you become a more experienced mobile home park investor. You will need additional strategies to arrive at a price for these investments, because they may or may not turn out to be profitable once you understand and analyze them. Don't worry. You won't have to be as smart as Einstein to figure them out. Some of these situations are:

1. Using a pro forma NOI in the future versus the current NOI

2. Unusual mortgage financing

3. Accounting for empty lots when calculating the NOI

4. Accounting for mortgage payments *received* on mobile homes that you buy along with the park when calculating the NOI

5. How to calculate the price for a mobile home park when you will be converting park-owned mobile homes into a land-lease community, or

the reverse—converting a land-lease community into park-owned mobile homes

6. Accounting for the highest and best use of the land today when it differs from its current use as a mobile home park
7. Accounting for the value of excess land

Each of the above situations will be explained, so you can evaluate them safely and understand any inherent risks they may hold.

1. USING A PRO FORMA NOI IN THE FUTURE VERSUS THE NOI THAT EXISTS TODAY

This topic was discussed in Chapter 8, but it bears repeating because it is one of the most common ways that owners and Realtors attempt to artificially inflate price, especially commercial Realtors who should know better. Don't allow yourself to be persuaded into paying a higher price now for income that *may be* received sometime in the future. If that income does not arise for any reason your return on the park will be substandard. Lenders will help you avoid this trap because they usually will base the amount of their loan solely upon the current, verifiable income of the park and the resulting debt service coverage ratio.

In our previous discussion you were told that you could use 20 percent of the pro forma increase in NOI to evaluate the park if the future income looks so sure and enticing that it is hard to turn down. *There is another way of treating the pro forma future income.* You can base your contract price on the income as the park sits now, and then add a "kicker" if the income should increase in the very near future (say less than two years). For example, if a park has a $50,000 NOI now, and the seller demonstrates that the NOI *should rise* to $60,000 in the near future—say in one year—and remain at least at that amount, here is how you could handle the price differential:

NOI as the Park Sits Now	=	**$50,000**
Price at 10% Cap Rate	=	**$500,000 Price**
Pro Forma NOI in Near Future	=	**$60,000**
Price at 10% Cap Rate	=	**$600,000 Price**
Increase in Price	=	**$600,000 – $500,000**
	=	**$100,000**

You could offer that if the NOI does increase within a year, and remains at the new rate for two years, then you would rebate half of the increase in price, at a 10 percent cap rate, to the seller by attaching an additional mortgage on the property for half of the increase at 8 percent interest for twenty-five years. If the NOI increase works out to be $10,000, then you would take half of that amount, or $5,000, which would represent a price increase of $50,000. The $50,000 payment would be $385 per month for twelve months, which is $4,620 per year. This means you would, in effect, be almost splitting the higher projected pro forma NOI between you and the seller, which is reasonable. You get $5,380 of the $10,000 increase, and the seller receives $4,620.

Let me repeat, though—my preference is to only pay for the NOI received by the mobile home park at the time you buy it, and to be consistent with this principle, you should expect to be paid only for your NOI today when you are selling.

2. UNUSUAL MORTGAGE FINANCING

Unusually good mortgage financing, especially seller financing, can turn a mediocre mobile home park investment into a superb one. Let me add that the financing must continue for a long enough time into the future, say five to ten years or more, so you will receive its full benefit. Let's look at an example that demonstrates this by continuing to use a mobile home park that has $50,000 NOI and a price of $500,000, which is a 10 percent cap rate.

Let's assume you are ambivalent about buying the park, your opinion being equally balanced between positives and negatives. Let's assume the bank will lend to you 80 percent of the market value at 8 percent interest, for twenty-five years, with the interest rate adjusting to market conditions every five years. In other words, your mortgage payment and cash flow will be:

Purchase Price = $500,000
Loan Amount = 80% of Purchase Price = $400,000
$400,000 Mortgage at 8% for 25 Years = $3,084 per Month × 12
= $37,000 per Year
NOI = $50,000 per Year
Cash Flow = NOI − Mortgage = $50,000 − 37,000 = $13,000 per Year

Now, let's turn your ambivalence into a positive by asking the seller to finance the deal instead of going to the bank. You ask the seller to provide a $400,000 no-interest mortgage for twenty-five years. If the seller does that, the mortgage payments will be $1,333 per month, or $16,000 per year, instead of the bank's $3,084 per month, or $37,000 per year. Now your cash flow is:

Cash Flow = NOI – Mortgage = $50,000 – $16,000 = $34,000 per Year

You have now increased your cash flow—the amount of profit you make—from $13,000 to $34,000, *almost tripling it!* Now you should be very positive and excited to own the property. If the seller counters your offer of a no-interest mortgage with a 5 percent mortgage due in thirty years, then the payment would be $2,147 per month, or $26,000 per year. Then your cash flow would be:

Cash Flow = NOI – Mortgage = $50,000 – $26,000 = $24,000 per Year

This is almost twice the current cash flow. Is it easy to find a seller willing to give a long-term no-interest mortgage, or a 5 percent interest mortgage, when bank rates are 8 percent? No. But there may be situations that favor this—for instance, an older seller looking ahead to retirement might want to create a stable monthly income for the rest of her life. It will add to the seller's motivation if she is fixated on getting a certain price for the park and is not as concerned with how that price is achieved.

3. ACCOUNTING FOR EMPTY LOTS IN THE NOI

This is an area of strong disagreement between buyers and sellers. Buyers don't want to pay for a lot that isn't earning any money, and sellers say, "But it's easy! Just bring in another mobile home and fill the lot . . . which I didn't have a chance to do." At which point, the buyer might respond, "Well, Mr. Seller, if was so easy to fill the lot, why didn't you do it, given how important it is and how much money you want now for the empty lots?" At which point the seller might respond, "I was busy, otherwise I would have."

You should understand, based upon the examples of the Happy Trails and Jefferson mobile home parks that mobile homes don't suddenly grow on empty lots. It takes time, money, and effort to fill in mobile home lots to make them earn money and add to your NOI. *The buyer should be paid for expending this time, money, and effort, not the seller.*

It is rare to buy a park in such a highly sought-after area with such a tremendous demand for empty lots that you can fill them simply through an ad in the paper or a sign advertising lots available. The more common case is that you will have to do a BB to fill the spaces. You are going to have to work to fill empty lots and use more of your own capital, so you should not have to pay for the lots.

That being said, if you placed test ads in the paper and found there was a strong demand for BBs in the park, and there were plenty of good, cheap, used mobile homes available for purchase, and you have money available to invest in BBs, then you might be persuaded to give some value to empty lots in a park you are buying. That number might approach 20 percent of the value of the lot after you bring in a mobile home that will pay rent. This is similar to our previous approach, when the seller wants to use pro forma NOI. We are talking about a case in which you are aggressively looking for mobile home parks to buy. Otherwise the value of an empty lot is exactly equal to the income it is bringing in today, as it sits—nothing.

Could you work out another compromise on payment for empty lots, like we did in the first situation we discussed—accounting for future income by adding a mortgage kicker to the property that will go to the seller? Yes. But again, the filling of the vacant lots would have to happen in the short-term future, say less than two years. And again, it would have to be a time when you are strongly pursuing an addition to your portfolio of mobile home parks.

4. ACCOUNTING FOR MORTGAGE PAYMENTS RECEIVED ON MOBILE HOMES YOU BUY ALONG WITH THE PARK

As you know, the BB is a powerful tool to use when you want to increase the NOI of a park that has vacancies. Now, what do you do when you want to buy a park in which the seller is including the notes for mobile homes he has sold to residents for his BBs? How do you value those notes? This is a fascinating area of discussion, and we have heard viewpoints on both sides.

One thing you do *not* do is add the mortgage payments received from residents to the NOI. We have seen sellers do this, so please don't fall for it. *NOI and cap rates are based upon the primary assumption that the income is received now and far into the foreseeable future.* How can you add the income from a note that will be paid off in five years to the lot rent income that will be received for the next thirty years or more? They are not the same types of income, and they won't be received for the same length of time. To come up with a price for this type of park, you will first restrict the evaluation of the NOI of the park only to lot rents and other long-term income that will be received far into the foreseeable future. Then you will come up with a way to add the value of the notes to this price. There are three ways to add the value of the notes on the BBs in a park:

1. Do not buy them—add no value, or get them for free
2. Buy them for the remaining principal balance on each note
3. Buy them at a discount from the principal balance remaining

The first case, to not buy them at all, is plausible. (Getting them for free probably isn't plausible, but you can ask, can't you?) Suggest that the seller keep the notes and collect the mortgage payments himself after you buy the park. If they are good notes, they will be an excellent investment. However, in many cases, the seller won't want to do this. She may want to separate herself from the park and move on to greener pastures after she sells it.

This brings us to the second case, in which the seller wants the full remaining principal balance of the notes, whatever is left to be paid. How much is still left on a note after so many payments is not a difficult number to calculate, yet many sellers have difficulty with it. All you need is the original face value of the note, the interest rate, the total number of payments needed to pay off the note, and how many payments have been received up until now. You should check all of the seller's numbers before you negotiate a price for the notes.

What's wrong with this second case? If you remember how we priced a BB, we took the price we paid in cash and then doubled it to get the price that would be financed, less a small down payment. Wouldn't it stand to reason, then, that if we were buying those same notes today we would halve the value of the outstanding balance to determine their cash price? Unfortunately, that may be different than what the seller is thinking. The seller may be hoping and dreaming how nice it would be to get paid cash now for twice the value he paid for the mobile homes when he financed them. Wouldn't it also be nice, when you did a BB, if the buyer paid off the note after two payments and you received all your profit right away, instead of waiting years for it? *So as a buyer, your first point of reference—the most you should pay—is half the value of the principal amount outstanding on the notes.*

Even better than paying half is going around and making a personal inspection of each mobile home that has a note on it. Calculate what you would pay, in cash today, for the mobile home as it sits, when you are looking to make a profit. We prefer using this figure. It usually is lower than 50 percent of the balance of the note because you are taking into account wear and tear on the mobile home since the loan started as well as the worst-case scenario, in which you get the home back and you have to sell it for fast cash.

Once you have an agreed-upon price for the notes, then that price is added to the price of the park using the lot rents and so on, from the NOI. Keep in mind that the bank will probably not lend to you on the value of these notes, so you will have to find a separate source of financing for them, like OPM or using your IRA.

5. HOW TO CALCULATE THE PRICE FOR A MOBILE HOME PARK WHEN YOU WILL BE CONVERTING PARK-OWNED MOBILE HOMES TO A LAND-LEASE COMMUNITY OR THE REVERSE

This is one of my favorite topics. It brings into focus one of the most powerful advantages of mobile home parks over other forms of investment real estate—the land-lease community. It also has a philosophical aspect to it, in terms of valuation, because most experienced mobile home park investment professionals favor land-lease communities. They don't like park-owned homes because of the additional management involved in maintaining and repairing tenants' homes. We are a spoiled lot. Investors who primarily buy single-family houses and apartments are used to maintaining and repairing their tenants' homes and consider it a normal expense of doing business. We should know—for many years, we were one of those investors. Now we have joined the group of mobile home park investors who smile when we encounter single family and apartment investors. We remember when we too didn't know any better and considered taking care of residences a fact of life.

Some of us bought our first parks with all park-owned units, enjoyed the cash flow and the low price, and thought nothing more about it. After all, mobile homes were just cheaper single-family homes that were blocked and tied down. The rule was that a landlord had to repair and maintain his rentals.

Then some of us bought our first land-lease community, and we wondered how we could have been so wrong for so long. Let me make this statement, based upon first hand experience:

It is at least three times easier to manage a land-lease mobile home park with only resident-owned homes than the same size park with park-owned units.

Now, are you ready for the catch? If this is true—and it is—then shouldn't the cap rate be much higher for parks with park-owned units? Shouldn't an investor earn a greater return, as represented by the cap rate, when he invests in a property with additional management headaches and risks? The answer to both of those questions is yes, but in practice it is not always the case. Many times land-lease communities sell at the same cap rate, 10 percent, as an all park-owned mobile home park. What is wrong with this picture?

What is wrong is that you have sellers and Realtors taking advantage of inexperienced buyers who don't know about the powerful advantage of land-lease communities. They assume that all mobile home parks are the same as apartments and houses and are run the same way.

A good question is: if a mobile home park contains all park-owned units, how much higher should the cap rate be when it is compared to a land-lease community of the same size that has a 10 percent cap rate? The answer is: nobody is sure! Some investors might want a 15 percent cap rate on a mobile home community filled with park-owned units; some more, some less. Appraisers would have an interesting job trying to determine and then justify that additional cap rate for a park filled with park-owned units.

Let's get practical. The following is the formula most mobile home park investors use to evaluate a park that contains park-owned units:

1. Figure the price of the park using only lot rent in the NOI—in other words, the NOI as if it were only a land-lease community.

2. Figure the wholesale price of the park-owned units. You would do this in the same way suggested before, when you evaluated the price of the notes on the BBs that came with the park. Figure out the wholesale cash price each park-owed mobile home would be today, assuming worst case scenario and you had to sell them off for cash right now.

3. Add the numbers from 1. and 2. above, and that is the price of the park.

Let's work an example. Assume you want to buy a fifty-unit mobile home park with all park-owned units, each paying $500 per month in rent. Let's also assume the owner is asking for a 10 percent cap rate, and the expenses are 50 percent of the gross rents (which is average). This is how the park would be priced:

Gross Rent	=	Total Lots	×	Monthly Rent	×	12 Months
$300,000 per Year	=	50	×	$500	×	12 Months

NOI = 50% of Gross Rent = 50% of $300,000 = $150,000

Price = NOI ÷ Cap Rate = $150,000 ÷ .10 = $1,500,000

The seller would price her park with fifty park-owned units, giving $150,000 NOI at a 10 percent cap rate, so she would consider $1,500,000 to be a fair price.

The professional mobile home park investor would convert the park to all land-lease units and would assume the expenses would come down to 40 percent when the park was converted. He would also know from the comps of other comparable land-lease parks in the area that the average lot rent is $250 per month, and after inspecting the park-owned mobile homes and checking the values in the area (perhaps using the NADA manual), that the average cash price for each park-owned mobile home is $5,000. Therefore, he would do the following pricing calculation:

Gross Rent	=	Total Lots	×	Monthly Rent	×	12 Months
$150,000 per Year	=	50	×	$250	×	12 Months

NOI = Gross Rent − 40% Expenses = $90,000

Price = NOI ÷ Cap Rate = $90,000 ÷ .10 = $900,000

Therefore, when the park was converted to all land-lease and the existing park-owned units were sold, it would produce $90,000 NOI and would be priced at $900,000.

Now the investor would evaluate the price he would pay for the park-owned mobile homes and come up with an average quick-sale cash price of $5,000 apiece, or:

Price of Mobile Homes	=	Number of Homes	×	Cash Value of Home
$250,000	=	50	×	$5,000 per Home

The price of the park as all land-lease, plus the discounted price of the mobile homes (as they are today) would be added together:

Price of Park	=	Price as Land-Lease	+	Value of Homes
$1,150,000	=	$900,000	+	$250,000

The buyer would want to pay a price of $1,150,000. The seller is asking $1,500,000, almost $350,000 more, or 30 percent higher!

The following assumption goes along with the above pricing formula: the buyer is going to convert all of the park-owned units to BBs and offer them to the current tenants on very easy terms. In other words, he is going to convert the park to all land-lease with profitable BBs. He is also going to test-market that plan by asking tenants in the park how they would feel about owning the mobile home they are now renting, if the total monthly cost—the lot rent plus the mortgage payment—is less than their current rent. This fact is a powerful incentive to most tenants and is usually easy to put into place.

Here is an example of how you would do this on that same fifty-unit mobile home park, with fifty park-owned units, each paying $500 per month in rent. We will use a lot rent of $250 per month and assume that the average cash price of a park-owned mobile home is $5,000. Therefore, the buyer of the park would work it out so: the tenants can purchase the mobile homes they are renting for $10,000, with a $1,000 down payment. They will sign a $9,000 note payable at 9.9 percent interest, at $195 per month for fifty-eight months. From the tenants' point of view, their cost is now:

Tenant Cost as Land-Lease Unit	=	Lot Rent	+	Mortgage Payment
$445 per Month	=	$250	+	$195

Tenant Cost as Park-Owned Unit = $500 per Month

Benefit to Tenant	=	Park-Owned Rent	–	Land-Lease Cost
$55 per Month Cheaper	=	$500	–	$445

Look at that. The tenant's cost before was $500 per month in rent. Now it is $445, so their total cost has gone done $55 per month! After eighteen months they have gotten their down payment of $1,000 back in rental savings (18 months x $55 per month), and they are money ahead after that. Even better, at the end of fifty-eight months—just a little less than five years—their mobile home is paid off. Their cost of living is now:

Tenant Cost as Land-Lease Unit	=	Lot Rent	+	Mortgage Payment
$250 per Month	=	$250	+	$0

Tenant Cost as Park-Owned Unit = $500 per Month

Benefit to Tenant	=	Park-Owned Rent	–	Land-Lease Cost
$250 per Month Cheaper	=	$500	–	$250

The tenant is now a resident who has reduced his monthly housing expense to $250 a month, or *half of what it was when they were a tenant!* In addition, they will own an asset worth $10,000. This is a powerful benefit. (In this discussion, we have ignored insurance, which might cost between $10 and $20 per month. This would not materially change the tenants' benefits.) Changing the park to land-lease units is also a powerful benefit to a mobile home park buyer, who will no longer have to maintain fifty mobile homes and will reduce management expenses and time.

Something had to give, though, in this pricing strategy. What gave was the price the seller wanted when the park was all park-owned units and priced at a 10 percent cap rate, to come up with $1,500,000. That 10 percent is the same cap rate as a land-lease park with three times less management, which does not make sense. If the seller had priced the park with all park-owned units at a 13 percent cap rate—a much fairer number—the price would have been the same for a fifty-unit park containing all park units at a 13 percent cap rate as an all land-lease park with 50 BBs at a 10 percent cap rate.

Price of Park	=	NOI as Park Owned	÷	Cap Rate as Park Owned
$1,150,000	=	$150,000	÷	13

So you can conclude that the cap rate for a park with all park-owned units should be 3 percent higher than for the same park as a land-lease community. You should still do the individual calculations for each park to determine the price more exactly than just using a 3 percent differential.

You may like working this strategy in reverse. In other words, you buy a fifty-unit land-lease park at a 10 percent cap rate for $900,000, move on fifty inexpensive park-owned units for $250,000, and experience a huge jump in NOI from $90,000 to $150,000 (along with more management costs). Then you would try to sell the park as all park-owned units at a 10 percent cap rate for $1,500,000, like so:

Profit	=	Price as Park Owned	–	Cost as Land-lease	–	cost of BBs
	=	$1,500,000	–	$900,000	–	$250,000
	=	$1,500,000	–	$1,150,000		
	=	$350,000				

You would make $350,000 profit when you found an investor who expects to manage fifty park-owned units to get a 10 percent return. We personally wouldn't do this, but there are other investors doing it as I write this. At least now you are the wiser.

6. ACCOUNTING FOR THE HIGHEST AND BEST USE OF THE LAND TODAY WHEN IT DIFFERS FROM ITS CURRENT USE

We see this situation occur frequently, especially in California and around major cities with hub airports. It happens when a mobile home park inherently is more valuable than just the NOI would account for, because the land can be used to develop something with a higher and better use, such as a condominium, high rise apartments, a shopping center, an office complex, or another similar project. We have seen cap rates on such offerings in the 1 to 2 percent range. Who would want to buy an investment that earns less each year than putting your money in a bank CD and just sitting back and collecting interest?

The answer is: land speculators or developers. These people are used to buying vacant land and "land banking it," paying the cost of a loan on the vacant land until they are ready to develop it—anywhere from six months to ten years in the future. In other words, it will cost them 8 percent or more per year to hold onto the land.

Look what happens when they buy a mobile home park at a cap rate of 2 percent. They will still borrow the money for the park, say at 8 percent, but now they have 2 percent coming in as NOI. Their borrowing cost is lowered by the NOI income to 6 percent (8 percent borrowing cost minus 2 percent cap rate). To land-banking developers, buying a mobile home park that is bringing in some income is better than vacant land with no income at all.

As you would infer from this, you should only be interested in parks that have very low cap rates because of the underlying value of the land if you are a developer or land speculator who understands the risks and values.

7. ACCOUNTING FOR THE VALUE OF EXCESS LAND

Typically, excess land is used as a teaser to buyers. Sellers make claims that there are some number of extra acres of vacant land—say ten acres—that come with the park and therefore so many extra mobile home lots can be added on this land—say fifty extra lots. Then the seller asks for the value of the land as if it has been developed as extra mobile home lots.

Almost every time we have encountered this, the seller was misinformed in some way. Yes, we could have added *some* lots on this extra land, but usually one-quarter to one-half of the number that the seller claimed, and for a cost many times what the seller claimed. The only way to figure out the additional value, if any, of excess land is to go down to the local Zoning Department to get a letter stating that you can use the land, how many lots you can add, and what you have to do to get permits to do this project. Then you will need to meet with a civil engineer, like you did when we discussed developing your own mobile home park, to find out how long it will take to get the permits, how much it will cost, and the total cost of infrastructure that will be needed so the added lots can be used. You may be shocked to find that just putting in the infrastructure for added lots may cost you $7,000 to $10,000 per lot or more, in addition to the extra land.

As an example from our own experience, The Jefferson Mobile Home Park was purchased with a vacant lot that was 100 feet wide and 1,000 feet deep on the north side. That is 100,000 extra square feet of land, almost two and one-half acres. After spending six months with the Zoning Department and our engineers, we found out the land was worthless other than for additional outdoor storage at the park. Adding mobile home lots on the strip of land, which would be the highest and best use, would cost $25,000 per lot—almost twice what it cost for the already usable lots when we purchased the park.

Further, even thought the land is on a major highway, setbacks precluded doing any commercial development—because of its narrow 100-foot width, we could only build a building that was fifteen feet wide. Luckily, we paid nothing extra for the land, but it has a cost even though it came for free. We get billed $4,000 each year for additional real estate taxes on this lot. Someday it will be worth it when the park is made into a commercial site, but how many years of $4,000 tax bills will it take before that happens?

As an additional example, we also contracted to buy a twenty-acre RV park that had 150 RV lots on half of the land. The sellers said we could add 100 more lots on the ten vacant acres. A meeting was set up between the Zoning Department, the seller, and us. At the meeting, it was explained that the park was only permitted for *100 lots on all 20 acres,* so the additional acreage was useless and that fifty of the current RV lots were illegal. The seller was flabbergasted. He said the previous owner told him 100 lots could be added, not that fifty lots had to be subtracted! We did not go through on our contract and the seller found another investor who did not do his due diligence. The conclusion you should take from this example is that you should be skeptical about any claims about the value of additional land, and do your due diligence on it.

SUMMARY

You are now equipped to handle just about every situation you will encounter on your path to being a mobile home investor. If any of this discussion felt like it was over your head, don't worry. You can do fine for many years simply by buying parks that are easy to evaluate and don't have advanced pricing strategies. Come back to this chapter later, once you are comfortable with simpler mobile home parks.

HOMEWORK

If you are comfortable with this discussion, go out and find parks that are examples of the seven advanced pricing strategies—pro forma income, unusual seller financing, empty lots, BB mortgages included in the sale, parks with park-owned units, low cap rate deals, and parks with excess land. Get into discussions with the brokers or owners about pricing and then make an offer that works for you, using the advanced pricing strategies in this chapter. If you are not comfortable, then stick to simple parks for now.

COMING ATTRACTIONS

You now have the skills and knowledge you need to make money on just about every type of park. The next chapter will get you thinking about the future, and how to make it even brighter for you and your loved ones. It's thrilling to think about the future when it's bright, isn't it?

18

Three Basic Principles of Wealth

One of the most interesting trainers I ever met, who is also the founder of the seminar company I subcontracted for, said "Money should come with a book of instructions." He said this because so many people he met didn't know how to manage it or grow and multiply it. That has also been my experience. Therefore, consider this chapter a set of instructions for managing money.

As a prerequisite to this discussion, it would be helpful if you read a book on the basic principles of managing your money, *Rich Dad, Poor Dad,* by Robert Kiyosaki. After I read that book, I said to myself, "Here is another person who shares my values, and he expressed them in such a way that he felt like a friend." In my opinion, the book stresses that in order to grow wealthy you must earn more than you spend, or simply spend less than you make, as this produces excess money. Then this excess money should be invested in places that will give you positive cash flow and a solid return on your investment. It will then grow into greater wealth and eventually allow you to work for yourself. He distinguishes clearly between what is an investment and what is not. (It's ironic that I trained many of his students through a strategic alliance with his company. I enjoy teaching his students because they feel that same sense of integrity and warmth from Robert Kiyosaki as I do.)

Moving forward from the principle of spending less than you earn and investing the excess, let's discuss some other basic principles. After living more than a half of a century and meeting thousands of people, a law of human nature has became clear to me: people are the beneficiaries—and the victims—of their values. Those who have long-term, solid values usually prosper and those whose values are short-term and false usually suffer. Therefore, this chapter also contains solid, long-term values that will result in prosperity.

I worked hard to get wealthy, as a way of strengthening my family. I knew wealth would provide jobs for my children and grandchildren, good health care, financial security for my wife and me in our later years, sound homes, well-built cars, and free time, among other things. My struggle to gain wealth did not take place overnight, it was decades long. When I finally achieved wealth, I wondered. "Is this the best thing I can leave behind to those I love so much and sought to strengthen?"

My honest answer to that question made me realize that wealth was not the most permanent of endowments, because many times I saw wealth squandered by those it was bequeathed to. This is evidenced by the statistic that 70 percent of the people who come into sudden wealth, either through lotteries or inheritance, are broke within a few years. Why? It's because the recipients have had no primer on how to handle money nor the values to manage, grow, and multiply it.

I have come to believe that love, solid values, and wisdom are the greatest endowment that we can pass along to our children. If you combine those three with wealth, then you will provide fertile ground for those that come after you, so they can take over where you leave off and live useful, satisfying, and full lives. (Keep in mind, everyone reading this book, including you and me, will not be around forever.)

When I was a young man in my thirties and working on Wall Street, I had the great fortune to work briefly with two business acquaintances, Nick and Ken. Both were in their mid-fifties and at the top of their careers. They owned a small securities firm and they were successful, pure traders—they made money for over thirty years, taking risks, buying and selling for their own positions. They didn't need customers, but because of their skill in timing and determining market direction, they had plenty of them.

During lulls in the market, Nick and I played chess. Nick knew I admired him, and I goaded him during these chess games into expounding on what he had learned during his thirty years of trading on Wall Street. He is the one who taught me the Three Principles, for no other reason than he liked me and I liked him. He was the son of a rabbi, and he used Yiddish terms to describe the Three Principles. I continue to use them to this day because Yiddish words are so expressive and humorous sounding. They are also easy to remember, and when you are training people you prize such words.

I didn't use these Three Principles until I left Wall Street and applied them to real estate. The reason the Three Principles worked not only on Wall Street, in the securities markets, but also on Main Street, in the real estate market, is that Wall Street is a market like any other market, only faster, smarter, and richer. What works there will work in slower and less sophisticated areas—like real estate—as well. I left Wall Street because no matter how much I read, or studied, or computed, the security markets made me uncomfortable. I knew the principles that wealth was built upon, but I felt that as a "little guy," I was competing against people who had better information, better political contacts, and greater wealth. The real estate market made me feel more comfortable, more in control of my own destiny. In other words, it was easier to get "into the game" and the competition was not as tough.

The Three Principles Nick taught me are:

1. The Shmata Principle
2. The Big Tuchus Principle
3. The Chicken Little, Blue Skies Forever/Buy for 1, Sell for 2, Make Your 1% Principle

THE FIRST PRINCIPLE: THE SHMATA PRINCIPLE

Nick received a phone call while he and I were playing chess. What I overheard sounded something like this:

"For 25,000 New York City 7s of 2010, I can offer them to you at 80 less 1/2." Nick then added, "No, I don't want to do any better because I just sold another 25,000 at the same price already today. I probably should raise the price, they are selling so well . . . Okay, 25,000 NYC 7s of 2010 are sold to Jimmy L at Merrill Lynch for 80 less $\frac{1}{2}$."

When Nick hung up the phone, I asked him, "Why do you sell that junk?" New York City was one of the lower rated municipal bonds.

Nick got annoyed. "Junk! They aren't junk. They are backed by the full faith and credit of New York City, and the bondholders are guaranteed to be paid before the police and firemen."

"Yeah, right," I answered back.

"I'll bet you have that lousy attitude, Zalman, because the fancy firm you used to work at didn't sell them. I'll bet they were interested in only the "high quality bonds," weren't they?"

"Well . . . yeah," I said.

"Just as I thought. Well, listen good, Mr. Fancy Pants. NYCs are not the best quality, but they give some of the best income, and many investors are willing to take a higher risk in order to get paid a much higher rate. For us, they have been a moneymaker because there is less competition from the big snobby firms, like the one you used to work for, so the profit margins are greater. That's why we make a market in them." He then started grumbling underneath his breath. "Junk . . . he calls my inventory junk . . . snot-nosed kid."

"Okay, okay. You don't have to be so touchy about it, Nick," I said, moving one of my pawns.

"If you saw the Shmata Man, you wouldn't be saying such foolish things," he said, moving his knight.

My next question was probably the one you were thinking.

"The who?"

"The Shmata Man. I grew up on the East Side of Manhattan during the Depression. Millions of people were out of work. People were standing in bread lines or selling apples on the corner. The richest man in our neighborhood was called the 'Shmata Man.'"

"What's a shmata?" I asked, countering his move with my bishop.

"It's Yiddish for rag," Nick answered, finally moving a pawn.

"And there was money in this? Were people so depressed during the Depression that they forgot how to tear up old clothes and make rags?" I asked, moving my queen.

"It was slang, wise guy," Nick answered. "Listen to how smart the Shmata Man was. He rented empty factories down South for almost nothing. He bought cloth at distress sales for pennies on the dollar. Then he contracted for piecework labor at very low rates because so many people needed jobs. He produced very cheap clothes, which he sold cheaper than just about anyone around. He shipped these clothes to poor neighborhoods around the country, ours being one of them. We called the clothes shmatas—we sneered at them in the stores . . . and when no one was looking, we all bought them."

"Why?" I asked.

"Think about it, you dummy," Nick said, taking one of my pawns. "We were poor, and it was all we could afford!"

"What did the Shmata Man wear?" I asked, with a sinking feeling. Now that Nick was one pawn ahead, we would evenly exchange chess pieces until we were down to a king apiece and his one extra pawn. Then he would march that pawn across the board until it became a queen. Checkmate was inevitable.

"The Shmata Man wore expensive silk suits. And every year he bought a brand new Cadillac," Nick answered, exchanging knights.

I fought on, hoping for a mistake, while Nick expounded further on the First Principle.

"I learned that if you sell enough shmatas, you can buy a new Cadillac every year. Believe me, you watch a rich man go happily about his life while your stomach is empty and growling, and you don't forget it. That lesson always stayed with me. So yes, I sell NYC bonds, the shmatas of the municipal bond market . . . and I have a new Cadillac sitting in the garage downstairs."

Please don't be misled by the English meaning of the word shmata. Making low-priced clothes is a valuable product, especially to people who cannot afford much. There are a lot of people who need clothes but can not afford to pay high prices for them.

Another way of stating the principle of the Shmata Man was attributed to Henry Ford: "If you serve the masses, you will eat with the classes. If you serve the classes, you will eat with the masses." He was smart enough to know that if you made the price of a Ford automobile within the reach of the working man, you would sell a lot of Ford automobiles. The bottom line is this: the more people you perform a service for, or sell a product to, the better your chances are that you will make a lot of money. There are a lot of people who can afford to spend only a small amount but only a few people who can afford to spend a lot.

Now, perhaps this discussion was interesting to you, but you are wondering, "What the heck do shmatas have to do with investing in mobile homes?"

Mobile homes, especially the older ones, are the shmatas of real estate. (Newer mobile homes—those built since 2000—are actually built better than many site-built homes, but they are still shmatas in the minds of the public. That will probably change over time.) When you invest in them, you will discover, as I did, that there is a huge demand for them. The mobile home market now goes by the label of "affordable" housing, which sounds better than shmata, but mobile homes are shmatas nonetheless. Twenty-seven years ago, when I first got started in real estate, there was a huge demand for affordable housing, and now there is even a greater need. As you have learned, this form of housing has the lowest prices, but it does *not* have proportionally lower rents, so it provides great returns to investors.

Therefore, *if you own enough mobile home parks, you can buy a new Cadillac every year.*

THE SECOND PRINCIPLE: THE BIG TUCHUS PRINCIPLE

"Why don't you sell?" I exclaimed, when Nick told me how much of a profit he was holding in one of his stock positions.

"Because the real money is not made by taking a quick profit. A merchant's profit is just day-to-day money. The real money is made by sitting on your big tuchus," he answered, pointing to his backside.

"But the price could go back down!" I said, excited about the money he would be losing. "Look, the quote just went down an eighth."

"Nah, it's going to go back up," he countered.

"You can never go broke taking a profit," I replied, quoting Nick to Nick.

"Don't be a wise guy," Nick replied.

"Seriously, Nick, you should sell now and wait and see what happens. If the market is still good, you can always buy it back."

"Why would I want to buy at fifty and sell at fifty-one, wait and see if the market gets better, then buy back at fifty-two and sell at fifty-three, wait and see again, and then buy back again at fifty-four, and sell at fifty-five? Isn't it easier to just sit on my big tuchus at fifty? Look, it went back up the eighth. "

"Yeah, but you don't know that's what's going to happen," I maintained.

"Zalman, if you want to make the really big money, you'll develop a big tuchus. Real wealth is created by buying quality when it's priced like a shmata, and then sitting on it and waiting while it gets better."

"You mean you never sell?" I asked, astounded.

"The only time you ever sell quality is when it's overpriced, and you can buy even more of something that is just as good."

He dubbed it *The Big Tuchus Principle.*

How does this apply to mobile homes? In my first book, *Mobile Home Wealth,* I discussed my first encounter with mobile homes in the first chapter, titled "The Adventure." In that adventure, I had ten acres out in the far reaches of the county I lived in. I thought that someday the land would go from being a shmata, at $2,500 per acre, to quality acreage at $10,000 when development came closer, and that is exactly what happened, enabling me to make a little more than $100,000. (I now wish I had sat even longer on my big tuchus to get the really big profits of $500,000.)

In other words, when you put mobile homes on vacant land so the land can earn a monthly income, or when you invest in a mobile home park already set up on land you also own, you can sit on your big tuchus and wait for the land to rise in value while your ATM sends you checks each month. This principle works extremely well when you buy mobile homes parks on acreage located in the path of development.

THE THIRD PRINCIPLE: THE CHICKEN LITTLE, BLUE SKIES FOREVER/BUY FOR 1, SELL FOR 2, MAKE YOUR 1%

The Third Principle has two parts. The first part states when everyone is crying that "The sky is falling!" like Chicken Little, or "The end of the world is near!"—*it's time to buy.* It's great to buy quality assets at that time, but only if you can buy them at large discounts. If you can get a great price on a shmata, then you should buy that, too.

The opposite is also true. When the feeling in the

air is that "It's blue skies forever!"—*it's time to sell,* if you can get a golden price for your shmatas. This principle came through loud and clear in 2005 in South Florida, when everyone was saying, "Real estate has gone up five years in a row, and it is going to continue to go up for the next five years, and forever." People actually said that. From 2000 to 2005, real estate appreciated 200 to 300 percent here. When we reminded the new real estate "wizards" about the stagnant period between 1991 and 1999, when there was almost no appreciation, they ridiculed me and walked away. As a result of the euphoria and the blue skies feeling, binge buying continued during all of 2005. Investors bought preconstruction houses and condos at prices that could only be justified if the music kept playing and another investor was waiting to buy at an even more foolish price. The cash flow from the preconstruction houses and condos was negative in the extreme, but no one was thinking about holding property long enough to collect any rent.

Suddenly the music stopped and all the musical chairs were occupied, and prices went down 50 percent or more over the following three years, bankrupting many of these new real estate "wizards." Mobile home park investors weathered the storm with their excellent cash flows and the continued demand for affordable housing. (As I write this, there are record numbers of home foreclosures, yet mobile home parks around the country are increasing occupancies and lowering vacancies. Why? Because many of the people who fell victim to foreclosure are starting over again in mobile home parks.)

You need strong nerves to follow the first part of the Third Principle and go contrary to public thinking and trends. There are always great reasons why public opinion and the markets it affects feel pessimistic or optimistic. You need to be *comfortable* with your current financial situation so you can take advantage of the difference between facts and the fear and greed that arise from public opinion.

Comfort is a subjective term. Some people will be calm and collected with $2,000 in the bank and a steady paycheck or income. Other people will need millions in cash to feel secure. Either way, you must discover what your comfort level is and stick to it. Without a feeling of comfort, you will be swayed by public opinion and confined to what the public earns and accumulates—which is barely enough to live on or retire with. Think back to a time when you were insecure about your financial situation—when a big bill came due, or you lost a chunk of your income, or you even lost your job. Didn't every piece of bad news throw you into a panic? Had you owned assets, wouldn't you have wanted to sell them at that time in order to salvage something?

What is the reality? The truth is our economy moves in cycles that last, on average, seven to ten years. You can count on a recession and fear of a depression at least once during every decade. When we're in a recession, doesn't it seem like it will never end? Doesn't it feel the worst right at the bottom?

You're probably wondering, how do you know when the real estate market is at its bottom and is about to improve? Does a bell ring, telling you the market is now going to go up? No, of course not. Basically, you have to use your intuition and gut feeling. If a piece of real estate seems so cheap that it's almost unbelievable, *go and buy it.* If you can buy a shmata for fifty cents on the dollar, or less, do it! Yes, it may get cheaper, but if you miss the absolute bottom, don't worry. Prices will eventually go up—they always do—and you will be delighted. In the meantime, you will have plenty of cash flow to keep you safe and secure.

Now, what about the up side? In every cycle, you can usually count on a boom every seven to ten years, where unbridled greed and speculation drive prices up to the point that something once considered a shmata is now priced closer to quality. When times are good, don't you look back at the recession, or the market crash, and wonder, "What was I worried about?" Don't you kick yourself for not buying back then? Don't shmatas go up in value during a boom?

The absolute rock-solid truth is that the United States is too strong to be destroyed by a minor annoyance like a recession or a boom. People the world over are coming here to live, and they will continue to come here, because our political and economic system is like paradise to them. They know hard work, guided by wisdom, will produce wealth in this country. In many third world countries, there is much less or no opportunity, no matter how hard you work. As you will see, there is only so much usable land in the population centers of the United States, and our population keeps increasing, particularly in those areas. It's an economic certainty that when you have a limited supply of land in population centers and a growing population with an increasing demand for it, prices will go up. This country and our economic system has already survived the worst threats to a country's existence: civil war, world war, depression, plague, oil embargoes, high unemployment, double-digit inflation, terrorism, and so on. Each time, we emerge changed, improved, and stronger.

Warrant Buffet explained the first part of this principle in an interesting way, when he described one of his basic investment strategies: "We become greedy when others are fearful, and fearful when others are greedy."

The Second Part of the Third Principle: Buy for 1, Sell for 2, Make 1%

If real estate cycles are seven to ten years between recessions and booms, what do you do in between, when the market is neither climbing or crashing but stable? The answer is, you *buy for one, sell for two, and make your 1 percent*. This is intended to be funny. When you buy for one and sell for two, you are really making 100 percent, not 1 percent. You already know the answer to what you do in between highs and lows, when markets are stable.

In stable times, you continue to do what you learned in the first part of the book about the Four Basic Profit Strategies—you find flippers, keepers, LOs and BBs. If you like flippers (we do), then you can become a merchant and make an additional short term profit to enjoy while you invest the excess in more keepers. We prefer to keep the larger mobile home parks we buy. If we want to pull out profits, we do a Refi Bonanza instead of flipping the property.

We do like flipping individual mobile homes and small parks with four units or less, making an additional $100,000 per year or more. I discussed this in my first book *Mobile Home Wealth*. After investing for twenty-eight years, I still find flipping fun and the additional profit like dessert after a satisfying meal. We have discovered that greater wealth comes from the Second Principle and the first part of this Third Principle, rather than just through flipping.

SUMMARY

In this chapter, you should have gained some wisdom to employ over the long term. When you find most investors in your market becoming greedy, you should sell some of your assets to take advantage of the tremendous price appreciation or do 1031 exchanges to sell your overpriced real estate and replace it with undervalued real estate while avoiding tax consequences.

The reverse is also true. When you see headlines screaming about recession and depression, and prices look rock bottom, you should add to your portfolio. Granted, this will require nerves of steel, but if you are comfortable and not stretched beyond your capacity, you can do it. Also, with positive cash flow, you have the ability to hold a property forever, if need be, and still be profitable.

If your real estate career spans twenty or thirty years, you should see two or three complete market cycles where you can take advantage of Chicken Little and blue skies forever. You can double or triple your net worth in each of those cycles if you follow these principles, which is an astonishing thing when it happens. Even if you don't believe in timing market cycles, just holding onto real estate is a good long-term strategy that will guarantee financial security for you and your loved ones.

HOMEWORK

Your only homework here is to convince yourself that the best time to buy is when everyone is scared and prices are low, and the best time to sell is when everyone is feeling euphoric and prices have risen to greedy levels. Think back to the times in your life when the newspapers printed headlines that made you greedy and want to get in on the "tech boom" and "the stock market boom" and the "real estate boom," and what happened to the price of assets. Then think back to the headlines that came later, the ones that scared the heck out of you, about the "tech wrecks" and "stock market corrections" and the "real estate bubbles."

COMING ATTRACTIONS

Now we're going to give you the road map to adding $100,000 per year to your income and $1 million to your net worth, on a part-time basis. You're ready for it, and you deserve it. Now let's do it!

19

The Road Map to $100,000 per Year and $1 Million in Net Worth

This chapter completes this book. In it you will be given the road map to earning an additional $100,000 per year on a part-time basis, to increase your net worth by $1,000,000 while you continue to work in your current career. It would be appropriate to give a disclaimer here: *Results may vary depending upon the individual following this roadmap and his or her location and situation. This roadmap is only a possible indication of the success you may have.*

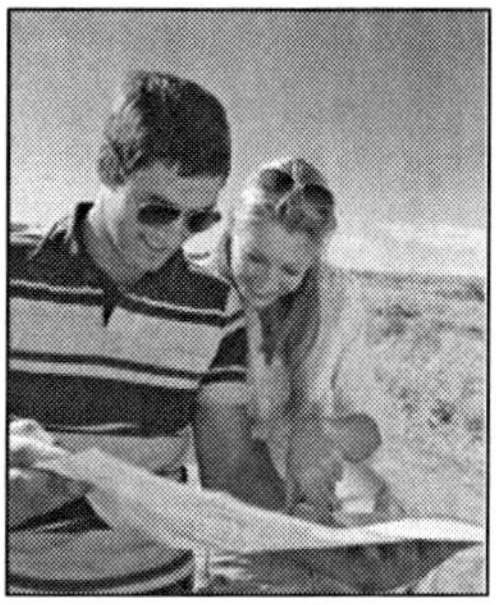

The goal of this plan is for you to accumulate savings and investment capital as well as additional monthly income. It is a simple, easy-to-follow, step-by-step approach whereby you will buy and manage at least one mobile home park every six months, each a keeper. Once you own and manage each new park you will improve the positive cash flow so it becomes at least $2,000 per month greater.

After two years, when you have four keepers, the positive cash flow should add up to an additional $8,000 per month, which is $100,000 per year.

$2,000 per Month Keeper Cash Flow per Park × 4 Mobile Home Parks = $8,000 per Month Additional Income
$8,000 per Month × 12 Months = $100,000 per Year

For those of you following along with your calculators, the income is actually $96,000, but once again we are going to use round numbers which are easier to visualize. If you purchase my first book, *Mobile Home Wealth,* you can learn how to flip individual mobile homes so if you do just one flip on one mobile home for at least $4,000 each year, you will get your total income up to the $100,000 mark or more.

HOW YOU ARE GOING TO REACH THIS GOAL

In order to follow this roadmap and reach your goal, assume you will be working two hours extra each weekday. Most likely this will be from six to eight in the evening, but it can also be from seven to nine in the morning or whatever two hours you decide to use. Also assume you will be working one full day on the weekend, either Saturday or Sunday. This is what was feasible for the average student we trained when he or she was beginning a new mobile park home investment career. You really have three alternatives in terms of the amount of time you are willing to invest in your new career.

1. Invest in mobile home parks full-time.

2. Invest the average way—two hours each workday, one full day each weekend.

3. Invest less than the average amount of time.

If you can invest in your real estate career full-time, then you are blessed with no time constraints, as I was. I knew I wanted a different career from the one I started with on Wall Street, and I worked hard and saved enough money to be able to start this new career when it was time to leave. *If you have no time constraints you can purchase turn-around parks that may require a full-time commitment but can also give superior results. You can also purchase parks that are either close by or long distance.*

Most of you will choose the average plan or even less hours, which is like pursuing a new part-time career while you are working and receiving paychecks at your current career. You should do this with a sense of appreciation that you now have a path to a better way to live your life. You know it has been made simple for you. You have the formulas for success, the strategies for getting the deal right, and the methods for managing your business. They're all here—but you have to put in the time and the work. That time and work will be focused on improving both the world around you and your own world. *With time restraints, you can buy close by or long distance turn-key parks and close by turn-around parks.*

I believe you can do it, and you must also believe you can do it. You will need motivation, especially when you have "one of those days," which we all have from time to time, the times when we think of chucking it all. When that happens, think of what you will do with the extra money. Think of how much your life will improve. Think of how wonderful it will be when you will only be bound by your own energy and talent, not stuck in a dead end career and dealing with job politics. Think of how great it will be to provide careers for your family and keep the people you love close to you. Think about helping out your favorite charity if that excites you. If you have a dream car, think of how good you will look behind it. What I'm saying is, "Go ahead and dream!" Dreams are good, especially if they give you the fuel to achieve more with your life.

You must create the motivation you need for yourself. Don't expect your family or your friends to give you a lot of encouragement in the beginning. It's difficult to say this, but many of them won't want to see you change, even if that change improves your life, because they may feel bad by comparison. It's okay. You can be the beacon, and they will follow in your light. When you are successful, they will definitely want to share in your success. They may not want to share in the time and work it will take for you to become successful, but that is what separates the achievers from the underachievers in life. Achievers don't complain much, and they do the best they can, each day, to improve themselves. Underachievers complain a lot and don't do much.

Above all, make your new mobile home investment career fun for yourself. It can be fun. It should be fun. If you have a family, try to involve them so you can spend time together. Mobile homes are an investment, and a people business. You can have fun with the people you meet and work with, while still being a prudent investor. *Repeat, have fun, or make it fun!*

WHAT ABOUT THE MILLION DOLLARS IN NET WORTH?

No, I didn't forget about the million dollars you are going to add to your net worth. I started with the goal of increased cash flow, $100,000 per year, because that is a basic goal for many beginning mobile home park investors. Now that we have discussed that goal, the next goal follows naturally.

You can flip mobile home parks and create a million dollars extra in net worth for yourself by simply buying parks and then selling them at a profit. Or, alternatively, you can improve the NOI in the parks you keep so your net worth increases by a million dollars. In our road map we will assume you are taking the second path and increasing the NOI on the parks you keep.

We will assume that the mobile home parks you buy have a minimum cap rate of 10 percent, on average. You are going to have to increase the NOI of each park by $2,000 per month to make each of the four parks you buy in the next two years worth at least $250,000 more than when you bought them, increasing your net worth by a total of $1,000,000.

Let me show you an example to make this clearer. Let's assume you are buying a forty-unit park for $500,000 because the cap rate is 10 percent and the NOI is $50,000.

Price = NOI ÷ Cap Rate = $50,000 ÷ 10% = $500,000

In order to get an NOI of $50,000, we assumed that the gross rents were $80,000 per year and the total annual expenses were $30,000.

NOI = Gross Rent – Expenses = $80,000 – $30,000 = $50,000

We also are going to assume that the lot rents are $200 per month and that there are only thirty-three lots rented and seven vacancies. You are going to raise the lot rents by $25 per month after you buy the park, because other comparable parks are getting at least that, and you are going to fill up the seven vacancies (with BBs, new residents moving their own homes in, or a dealer selling homes in your park) so that the increase in NOI is:

Increase in NOI = 33 Lots × $25 per Month Increase in Rent = $825 per Month

7 Vacant Lots Filled × $225 Month = $1,575 per Month
$825 + $1,575 = $2,400 per Month × 12 Months = $28,800 per Year

Therefore, when you increase the NOI from the $50,000 it was when you bought the park to $50,000 plus the $28,800 you received by raising the lot rents $25 and filling in the seven vacancies, the NOI will now be:

New NOI = NOI at Purchase + Increase = $50,000 + $28,800
= $78,800

The park is now worth:

Price = NOI ÷ Cap Rate = $78,800 ÷ 10% = $788,000

You increased the value of the park by $288,000, more than our $250,000 goal. When you do that on four parks over the next two years, you will get:

Increase in Net Worth = $288,888 per Park × 4 Parks = $1,152,000

If you want to see your improvement in net worth in cash, then you will do the Refi Bonanza and get up to 80 percent of that amount in tax-free cash:

Refi Bonanza	**=**	**Increase in Value of Parks**	**×**	**80%**
$900,000	**=**	**$1,152,000**	**×**	**80%**

That means you can put $900,000 of your $1,152,000 increase in net worth in the bank, in cash. If you do that you will have less positive cash flow, because you have increased your mortgage payments by the payment on the $900,000 you additionally refinanced, but you can use that cash in the bank to buy even more parks.

The Effect of No Money Down Deals on the Road Map

Some of you will not have much positive cash flow left over when you buy a mobile home park with little or no money down, at a 10 percent cap rate. Remember, the difference between cash flow and NOI is the mortgage payments on the mobile home park. All this means is that you will have bigger mortgage payments on the park when you buy through a no-money-down deal.

Therefore, you will have to increase your NOI by $2,000 per month to receive any substantial cash flow at all, and you will have to do this on all your parks to achieve both of your goals. So you will have to accomplish both of the above goals simultaneously: $100,000 per year in positive cash flow and one million in increased net worth.

Okay, Let's Get Your Objections out of the Way Right Now

I sense that some of you were upset when we suggested that you would have to work overtime to accomplish this roadmap if you were going to keep your present job. Yes, many of you want more time for yourself and your loved ones, not less. And I agree with those of you who say, "Hey wait a minute, this isn't easy!" Go ahead, complain and say it out loud: "This isn't easy!"

Good, now that you got it out of your system, let's face hard facts. What other alternatives do you have, with formulas that show you beforehand whether you can be successful, that let you add $100,000 to your yearly income and a million dollars to your net worth? The only way your life is going to change is if you change it, and to do that you need to work a little harder right now. No one else can do it for you.

If the extra hours we suggested are not reasonable for you, then cut the hours in half. Of course, your results may also be cut in half. Allocating half the time may mean it will take you four years to accumulate four keeper parks that give you the $100,000 year in extra cash flow. That's okay. Some improvement is better than no improvement, isn't it?

If you can only spare an hour here and there, or a day here and there, that's okay, too. Just doing *something* will still improve your life. Even if you only buy one mobile home keeper per year instead of a whole park—just one mobile home with $200 per month in positive cash flow—at the end of twelve years you will have $30,000 per year in additional income, which is still pretty good.

Have we gotten the negatives out of the way? Good. Because they weren't doing you any good in the first place, were they? Now let's move on.

SETTING UP YOUR OFFICE

By now, you should have an office somewhere in your home. If you don't, then make one, even if all you can afford right now is a desk in some corner of a room. There should be *a map on the wall near your desk* of your county or market area, and on that map you should circle the segment areas you want to invest in right now. Next to the map, put *a copy of the Business Plan* up on the wall. Next to the Business Plan, *put up two pictures of your dreams*, whatever they may be. Whether they include a new home, a new car, college diplomas for your children, fabulous trips and dream vacations, or charitable work, put those pictures up there for you to see on a daily basis.

On your desk you will need a phone, all of your forms (especially

The Business Plan

Step 1. *Buy one keeper every six months.* You must spend at least two hours every weekday and one full day every weekend calling, looking at properties, or making offers.

Step 2. *For every five properties you call about, look, at the least, at the best one.* For every three properties you look at, make an offer on, at the least, the best one. This is the 15-3-1 plan.

Step 3. *When you have an accepted offer, inspect the park carefully and do your due diligence well.* If the park looks okay, work on the financing while you call, look at, and make offers on other backup properties. If the first deal goes through and other properties also look good, either buy them, too, or flip them to another investor.

Step 4. *When you close on a property, take a "before" picture and start a folder for its paperwork.* Then get the property in shape and take "after" pictures.

Step 5. *Complete the Profit Strategy.* Every day, work on improving the park and increasing the NOI and cash flow while you continue to call, look at other properties, and make offers.

your contracts), a computer to access the Internet and keep track of your paperwork, a fax machine, and a printer. These days, with computers so much cheaper than they once were, you can have a laptop and a combination printer/fax/copier/scanner for less than $1,000. If you don't have these already, you will need them. If you can't afford them now, then that's okay. Just plan on buying them after you do your first flipper. In the beginning of my career, I used a computer only one or two hours a week and I still made plenty of money. Now, I need to use it more than four hours each day.

Last, but not least, get some business cards made up identifying you as a mobile home park investor, and get a magnetic sign for your car doors.

THE BUSINESS PLAN

The goal of this business plan is to keep your momentum going. You don't want to get bogged down on any one deal, and you don't want to get lazy and put off what you need to keep doing day by day. What you will be doing just about every day is calling, looking at properties, and making offers, or managing, fixing up, and improving the NOI of parks you have purchased. When an offer is accepted, you have to get the deal financed and to closing while you are still calling, looking at properties, and making offers, in case the deal does not go through for any reason.

In Step 1, you are affirming your goal of *buying one keeper every six months.* Therefore, you must spend at least two hours every week day, and one full day every weekend, calling FSBOs or Realtors about property, checking the different places you were shown to look for good deals. Then you should be looking at property and making offers. Remember, every weekday for at least two hours, and every weekend for one full day, you should be *calling, looking at properties, or making offers.* This goes back to our maxim, *if you're not making offers, you're not making money.*

In Step 2, you are establishing a benchmark to force you into making offers. *For every five properties you call and speak to the broker or the owner about, you must look at least the best one.* If there are two or three that look enticing, then by all means, look at all the enticing ones. But you must decide from every five phone calls you make to look at the best one of the bunch. Then, *for every three properties you look at, you must make an offer on at least the best one,* an offer that gets you excited. If there are two or three that you want to make offers on, then by all means, make more offers. But you must decide to make an offer on one out of every three properties you look at. In other words, after making fifteen phone calls where you talk to the seller or the Realtor, you must look at three properties and make at least one offer. You can look at more properties and make more offers, but *the bare minimum is the 15-3-1—fifteen calls resulting in three inspections and one offer.*

Remember, if you aren't making offers, you aren't making money! And don't forget to determine your profit strategy before you buy the property. You have four strategies—keeper, flipper, LO, and BB.

With Step 3, you now have an accepted offer. Great! When that happens, you will inspect the property carefully. Do not skimp on your due diligence, because when you buy a park, you will inherit the problems left by the former owner. If the due diligence is okay or within acceptable limits—remember, no park is perfect—you have to work on finding financing. If you are using all-owner financing, this is very easy. If you are going to lenders, then working on the financing means you will spend time *every day* to get the financing completed while you are still continuing to call, look at properties, and make offers. You do not want to stop your momentum by only looking at financing for one property. Continue to work your 15-3-1 plan. If your first deal goes through and you have excellent backup deals, you can either buy them too, or flip them to another investor.

In Step 4, you have closed on a property. Great! Now, you will take a "before" picture and open up a folder for all the paperwork and bills, and then start on getting the property in shape, managing it, and improving the NOI. When the park is in good shape, take an "after" picture. At this point in time, it is okay to allocate more of your time to getting the property in shape, but you must continue to call, look at property, and make offers to keep a steady momentum going.

Step 5 completes your Profit Strategy. This means your property is running smoothly with a park manager handling the park's day–to-day management. At this point in time, you are going to have to allocate some time each day, or every other day, to overseeing the parks you own. Never forget that you must also continue to call, look at property, and make offers with the remainder of your time, to keep your momentum going.

As time goes on, you will need to spend more time managing your keepers, and you will be well paid to do it. In other words, you will have to take care of the ATM that is providing you with your cash flow and increased wealth. You will also become more efficient in your prospecting. You will not need to spend as much time on it, but you must continue doing it if you want to grow more.

Something interesting will also happen to your motivation. The money coming in will provide you with strong motivation, and you won't need to look at your business plan that much. It will become second nature.

Momentum, Time for Results, and the Three Common Beginner's Mistakes

It should take about four to six months for results to appear, because it takes time to close a property with financing, it takes time to fix it up, and it takes time to improve your NOI after you close. Be patient in the beginning. When you get your mobile home park investment machine going, and you continue with the momentum of calling, looking at property, and making offers, a lot of money is going to come your way.

You may have to go back to step 1 of the Business Plan and make adjustments so it fits *your* life and is comfortable and realistic for your market area. That's okay—make it work for you. Then keep *calling, looking at property, and making offers* to achieve your goals.

We stress momentum because of the three most common mistakes beginners make:

1. *Spending too much time on any one deal in the beginning.* Beginners err by trying to make one of their early deals into a good deal by negotiating for months and months when it really wasn't a good deal to begin with. You will be better off if you continue to prospect, call, look at, and make offers on other, better properties.

2. *Buying a career fix–up early on.* Beginners can spend all their time bogged down with the one of these "projects." In the beginning, you should not buy career fix-ups, only cosmetic fix-ups. You simply don't have the time.

3. *Not making offers.* Don't be timid, make an offer. It never hurts to try. Remember—*if you're not making offers, you're not making money.*

Plan a Little More, Dream a Little More, Reap a Little More

Keep in mind: this is only a two-year plan. At the end of the second year, you will have approximately $100,000 in extra cash flow. You still have the same three choices at the end of the second year that you will have when you start this plan:

1. Invest in mobile homes full-time.
2. Invest the average way—two hours each workday, one full day each weekend.
3. Invest less than the average amount of time.

At this point, you can decide whether you want to switch over to full-time investing in mobile home parks, starting with $100,000 a year in keeper income and some serious savings if you do a Refinance Bonanza. It might be reasonable to expect twice the results you had in the first two years if you commit all of your time to investing in yourself. That means at the end of the third year, you would have eight keepers, or about $200,000 per year in keeper income and $2 million in net worth. It's up to you.

You also can take a more conservative approach by keeping your present career and continuing your third and fourth years as you did in your first two years. However, you will have to spend more of your two hours each day and one weekend day managing the parks you own, so there will be less time to prospect for new deals.

Or you can take an even more conservative approach and try to accumulate just one mobile home park keeper each year from now until you retire, with perhaps a flipper or two each year for some extra spending money. The choice is up to you. It's nice to have a choice that is up to you, isn't it?

Numerology—Three, Four, Five, and Now Six

At this point, you have *three* Basic Principles of Wealth, *four* Basic Profit Strategies, *five* Green Fs to get the deal right, and *five* Steps on Your Roadmap Business Plan. Now we will close with *six* of something—six wise things to remember. You should copy these and put them on your wall, next to your business plan, your map, and your motivational pictures.

Six Wise Things to Remember

1. Your first investment property is your education. It will *not* be the best deal you ever make, just another good one, so quit worrying about it. Do your calling, looking at property, and making offers, and buy something! When you own something, you will get smart—quickly.
2. Most people work their whole lives, living paycheck to paycheck, and have only a home and social security to show for it. So if one home is good, two homes are better. And three or more are even better, which means a mobile home park is better.
3. When a tenant drives you a little crazy, ask yourself, "Why did God make crazy tenants?" Then remember the answer—to pay off your mortgages, give you positive cash flow, and make you wealthy.
4. The definition of insanity is doing the same thing over and over again, and expecting a different result. If you change nothing, nothing will change.
5. From time to time, we all have "one of those days" when it comes to investing. Everyone does. Smile, forget it, and move on.
6. After air, water, and food, affordable housing is a basic need. As the population increases, the need increases. And nothing is more affordable than mobile homes. You are on the ground floor of a solid business with a great future.

Conclusion

Shalom for Now

My publisher and friend, Rudy Shur, said something poignant to me during the publishing of my first book, *Mobile Home Wealth.* He said, "Authors like saying hello to their readers, in their preface or introduction. Don't you think it would be nice if an author also said goodbye?"

So at this time, I want to wish each of you a good life, and a full one. Please take with you my sincere hope that you are fruitful and multiply your wealth, happiness, and success in all that you do.

If one of your goals is leaving the world a little better than when you found it, you will have the opportunity to do that when you are the mayor of your own small town, and people entrust their dwellings to you.

If you would like to go further in your mobile home education, you can visit my website, www.ZalmanVelvel.com, where you can discover other books I have written and additional training programs I'm involved in.

Now, before I say Shalom, I want you to take a deep breath and say something important to yourself . . . say, "I can do this."

Then go out and do it.

Goodbye . . . Shalom . . . for now.

THE END

Appendix

This Appendix contains many of the forms you will need as you embark on your path towards mobile home wealth. They are listed in the order in which they were mentioned, and the chapter or chapters that refer to each form are noted.

Remember, please consult an attorney or competent financial adviser before using these forms. Real estate practice and the law may vary from place to place.

Prepared by: ____________________
Property Appraiser's Tax Folio Number: ______________________

ASSIGNMENT OF CONTRACT

The Contract between ______________ (seller) and ______________ (original buyer) that became effective on _____/_____/20___, that is hereby attached, now has all rights and duties of the ORIGNAL BUYER assigned to ________________________ (assignee and new Buyer) for the total consideration of $___________. The earnest money deposit of $______ is now also the property of the assignee and new Buyer.

The contract is to purchase the following described property in ________ County, ________:

____

Address and/or legal description of property

____________________ ____________________________

Date ORIGINAL BUYER

____

Witness 1—Printed Name____________

____

Witness 2—Printed Name____________

STATE OF ______________
COUNTY OF ____________
The foregoing instrument was acknowledged before me this _____ day of _______, 20__, by ____________________________. __________________ is personally known to me, or produced ___________________________ as identification.

____
Notary Public Signature

____
Printed Name of Notary

Commission No.:

(SEAL) My Commission expires:

This instrument was prepared by: ______________________________
Property Tax Identification Number: ______________________________

MEMORANDUM OF CONTRACT

This Memorandum of Contract, executed this ______day of __________, 20 ______,
between: ____, herein known as BUYER,
and: ____, herein known as Seller.

WITNESSETH, that the said BUYER, for and in consideration of the sum of $25,000 and other good and valuable consideration, escrowed for SELLER, which said BUYER has equitable title in the following described parcel of land, situate, lying and being in the County of ________, State of ________________, to wit:

SEE ATTACHED LEGAL DESCRIPTION

TO HAVE AND TO HOLD the same together with all and singular the appurtenances thereunto belonging or in anywise appertaining, and all estate, right, title interest, lien, equity, and claim whatsoever of the said first party, either in law or equity, to the only property use, and benefit of the said second party forever.

IN WITNESS WHEREOF, the said BUYER has signed and sealed these presents the day and year first above written.

SIGNED, SEALED AND DELIVERED:

______________________________ ______________________________
Witness 1: Printed Name________________ Buyer on Contract Signature

____
Witness 2: Printed Name________________

STATE OF ______________ COUNTY OF ______________: (Seal of Notary)

The foregoing instrument was acknowledged before me this ____ day of _________, 20 ____, by ________________________. He is personally known to me, or produced ______________ as identification.

______________________________ ______________________________
Printed Name of Notary: Commission # ________ Notary Public Signature
Expires:________________

OPTION TO PURCHASE

THIS OPTION AGREEMENT is made and entered into this _____ day of __________, 20__, by and between __________________________, hereinafter referred to as "Seller," and __________________________, hereinafter referred to as "Buyer."

WITNESSETH:

(_______ Initials)

That in consideration of _________________ cash, which amount is nonrefundable, and other good and valuable consideration, the receipt and sufficiency of which are hereby acknowledged, the Seller hereby agrees to sell and deliver to the Buyer, under the terms and conditions set forth herein, the following described property:

Description of Mobile Home and Personal Property:

Size: ______________________________________

Make and Model: ____________________________

Identification Number: ______________________

Location: __________________________________

Personal Property: ___________________________

The Seller hereby grants to the Buyer, its successors and assigns, an irrevocable option to purchase the property upon the following terms and conditions:

1. **TERM:** The Buyer may purchase the property under the terms and conditions set forth herein at any time during the term of the Option granted herein (hereinafter referred to as the "Option"). The term of this Lease-Option shall be for a period of _______ months commencing on ________________, 20__, and ending on __________, 20__. The term will be automatically extended for __________ periods of _________months.

2. **EXERCISE OF OPTION:** This Option may be exercised upon written notice by the Buyer to the Seller at the address set forth below, given during the term of this Option. Such notice of Buyer's intent to exercise this Option may be delivered in person, by U.S. Mail, or by private overnight courier, and shall be deemed to have been given upon the day of the postmark of the mail or receipt by private overnight courier. Upon exercising this option, the Seller shall deliver title to the Mobile Home to the Buyer. All taxes and transfer costs will be borne by the Buyer.

3. **PRICE AND TERMS:** Upon exercising this Option, the purchase price for the premises shall be the sum of _________________________ in cash. As an alternative, the Buyer may elect to pay the purchase price in equal monthly payments, amortized over

_______________ at ____% interest per annum. In that event, the Buyer will have the right to prepay all or part at any time.

4. **OTHER CONSIDERATION:** As part of the consideration for this Option, the Buyer has entered into an agreement with the Seller to net lease the above-described Mobile Home. In the event the Buyer abandons the mobile home, is evicted, or fails to cure any default in the lease within three (3) days from receipt of notice of a default, this Option shall become null and void.

5. **EXPIRATION OF OPTION:** This Option shall expire automatically and be of no force or effect after the end of the term set forth in paragraph 1 above, unless notice has been delivered to the Seller, as provided for in paragraph 2 above. Upon expiration of this Option, the Seller shall retain any consideration paid as full liquidated damages and payment for this Option, and all obligations of each party shall terminate.

6. **RIGHT TO CURE:** In the event of a default in any loan payment on the above-described property, or in the event of any impairment to the title that reduces the value of the buyer's interest, the Buyer shall have the right, but not the obligation, to cure such default and receive full credit therefore against the purchase price set forth above.

7. **NOTICES:** Any notice to be given under this Agreement may be delivered in person, by U.S. Mail, or by private overnight courier and shall be deemed to have been given upon the day of the postmark of the mail or receipt by private overnight courier, or upon receipt, if given in person, at the following addresses:

BUYER: ____

SELLER: ____

8. **TRANSFER:** This Option may be assigned by the Buyer, provided, however, any assignment must first be approved by the park manager and the Seller, in which case a $100.00 fee will be charged for administration and documentation.

9. **BINDING EFFECT:** This Option is binding on the heirs, assigns, trustees, and successors of the Seller.

10. **VALIDITY:** This Option Agreement shall be governed pursuant to the laws of the state of _________________; and invalidation of any portion of this Agreement shall not invalidate the remainder.

IN WITNESS WHEREOF, the parties hereto have placed their hands and seals as of the date first above written.

Signed, sealed, and delivered in our presence as witnesses:

SELLER: ______________________________

BUYER: ______________________________

BUYER: ______________________________

WITNESS: ______________________________

WITNESS: ______________________________

Prepared by: ____________________
Property Appraiser's Tax Folio Number: ______________________

RELEASE OF LEASE OPTION

Be it known that the Lease and Option recorded on __/__/20__ by instrument number ____________ for the Optionee _________________________ on the following described property in ________ County, _________ :

See Schedule A attached

HAS BEEN RELEASED, ALL OPTION RIGHTS ARE REMOVED, AND NO FURTHER ACTION WILL BE TAKEN.

____
Optionee Signature

____
Witness 1—Printed Name ___________

____
Witness 2—Printed Name ___________

STATE OF ______________
COUNTY OF ____________
The foregoing instrument was acknowledged before me this _____ day of _______, 20__, by ____________________________. __________________ is personally known to me, or produced ____________________________ as identification.

____
Notary Public Signature

____
Printed Name of Notary

Commission No.:

(SEAL)

My Commission expires:

MOBILE HOME PURCHASE AGREEMENT

Date: ____________________

The undersigned Seller(s) agree to sell and the undersigned Buyers(s) agree to buy the following mobile home:

Make: ________________ Year: ________________ ID#: __________________

Located at: ____

Total Sales Price: $______________________ Deposit Paid: $____________________

Additional Payment Due: $__________________ Due Date: ___________________

Date of Possession by Buyer(s): ____

Appliances and Contents included in Sales Price: ____________________________

____

Unless otherwise noted, Seller(s) warrant that all appliances, A/C, electrical service, plumbing, and heating system to be in good working order at settlement, which is to be on_____________________________________.

Buyer(s) reserve the right to a walk-through inspection and approval on day of possession and settlement. Seller(s) agree to remove all trash and debris from premises and leave home in clean condition.

Seller(s) certify they are the legal owners of mobile home, appliances, and contents. Unless otherwise noted, Seller(s) certify that no liens exist on home, appliances, or contents. Any existing liens are to be paid and satisfied by Seller(s) prior to settlement and payment to Buyer(s). Upon approval and payment by Buyer(s), Seller(s) agree to deliver to Buyer(s) a clear title to mobile home.

Seller(s) certify that park lot rent is current through ________________________ and agree to furnish proof of same prior to settlement. Any delinquent rent or other charges by the mobile home park to be paid by Seller(s) prior to settlement. Seller(s) to furnish proof that all taxes on mobile home have been paid and current through __________________________ .

If for any reason mobile home is not allowed to remain on present lot, this agreement becomes null and void and Seller(s) agree to return all money paid by Buyer(s) and cancel this agreement.

This agreement is subject to verification of information necessary to complete this agreement, and subject to approval by Business Partner. Otherwise, this agreement becomes null and void and Seller(s) agree to return all money paid by Buyer(s) and cancel this agreement.

Seller(s) verify they have read, understand, and agree to this sales agreement and acknowledge a copy of this agreement.

SELLER:		BUYER:
______________________		______________________
Signature		Signature
______________________		______________________
Print Name		Print Name
______________________		
SS#	DOB	
SELLER:		BUYER:
______________________		______________________
Signature		Signature
______________________		______________________
Print Name		Print Name
______________________		
SS#	DOB	

___ Appliance inventory including serial numbers attached and signed by Seller(s) and Buyer(s)

___ Identification checked and compared with name(s) on title.

RENTAL APPLICATION—PROPERTY: ______________

NAME: ______________________________ DATE OF BIRTH: ________________

SOCIAL SECURITY #: ___________ VEHICLE (make, model, tag #): ______________

CURRENT ADDRESS: ____
PREVIOUS ADDRESS: ____

TELEPHONE #: HOME: ____________________WORK: _____________________

MARTIAL STATUS: ____________# OF CHILDREN AND AGES: ______________

PRESENT EMPLOYER: _____________________ POSITION: ________________

MANAGER/SUPERVISOR: ____________________ PHONE #: ______________
HIRE DATE: ___________

TAKE-HOME PAY: $____________________/MONTH

PREVIOUS EMPLOYER (If present employment less than one year):__________

____

CREDIT REFERENCES: TYPE OF ACCOUNT ACCOUNT# LOCATION

BANK ACCOUNTS (checking/savings): _____________________________________

OTHER (car loans, credit cards, etc.): ___________________________________

OTHER MONTHLY INCOME: $__________________ SOURCE: ________________

NAME, ADDRESS, AND PHONE # ____
OF PRESENT LANDLORD: ____

NAME, ADDRESS, AND PHONE # ____
OF PREVIOUS LANDLORD: ____

NAME, ADDRESS, AND PHONE # ____
OF NEAREST RELATIVE: ____

This information is, to the best of my knowledge, true and complete and contains no misrepresentation. I authorize ________________ to use this credit application and make any investigation deemed advisable or necessary before or after a contract is made. This application will remain the property of ______________ whether or not a contract or lease is consummated.

________________________________ ________________________________

Signature of Applicant Date

MOBILE HOME SALES AGREEMENT

Date ___________

Buyer(s): ______________________________

Address of Mobile Home Lot #____, _________________, ________________________

Make and Model: _________ Year: _____ VIN I.D.#: __________ Title #: ___________

Total Purchase Price: $ ___________

Deposit Paid: $ _______________ Date Deposit Paid: ___________________

Additional Cash Payment Due: $ N/A Date: N/A

Appliances And Contents Included In Sale: **AS-IS**

Date of Possession of Mobile Home: _______________

Total Price	$ ______
Sales Tax	$ ______
Title Fee	$ ______
Registration Fee	$ ______
Processing Fee	$ ______
Insurance	$ ______ (must have ins. and renew each year or we will place it for them)

Mobile Home & Contents Sold in "AS-IS" Condition

Subtotal $ _______

Deposit Paid – $ _______

Total $ _______

~~~~~~~~~~~~~~~~~~~~~~~~~~~~~~

ANNUAL PERCENTAGE RATE ____ %
The cost of your credit as a yearly rate.

AMOUNT FINANCED $ ________
The amount of credit provided to you.

FINANCE CHARGE $ ________
The dollar amount the credit will cost you.

TOTAL OF PAYMENTS $ ________
The amount you will have paid when you have made all scheduled payments.

Payable in ________ monthly installments of $ _____ each, beginning ________ and on the _____ day of each month thereafter. A $ _____ late charge is assessed for any payment not received within FIVE (5) days of due date, plus $ ______ each day thereafter until received.
~~~~~~~~~~~~~~~~~~~~~~~~~~~~~~

THIS NOTE IS FOR THE MOBILE HOME ONLY AND NOT FOR THE LAND UNDERNEATH IT, WHICH IS LEASED. BUYERS WILL BE RESPONSIBLE FOR REPAIRS AND MAINTENANCE OF MOBILE HOME, AND IT IS SOLD IN CONJUNCTION WITH A LAND LEASE AGREEMENT ATTACHED. BUYERS UNDERSTAND THEY MAY LOSE THEIR RIGHTS TO THE MOBILE HOME IF THEY DO NOT COMPLY WITH ATTACHED LAND LEASE.

Buyers acknowledge they have read, understand, and agree to the terms of this contract and have received a copy of this agreement.

Signed,

Buyer ____________________________ **Seller** ____________________________

____

____________________________ ____________________________

Printed Name____________________ Buyer - ____________________________

Witness 1

____

Printed Name____________________

Witness 2

STATE OF ___________

COUNTY OF ___________

The foregoing instrument was acknowledged before me this ______ day of ________________, 20_____, by ____________________________________. He/she is personally known to me _____, or produced ____________________ as identification.

(SEAL) Notary Public Signature______________________________

Printed name of Notary ____________________

Commission No.: ____________________

My Commission expires:____________________

______________________________ ___________________________________

Printed Name____________________ Seller - ______________________________

Witness 1

____

Printed Name____________________

Witness 2

STATE OF ______________________

COUNTY OF ____________________

The foregoing instrument was acknowledged before me this ____________ day of ________________, 20____, by ____________________________________. He/she is personally known to me, or produced ____________________ as identification.

(SEAL) Notary Public Signature _______________________________

Printed name of Notary ____________________

Commission No.: __________________________

My Commission expires:____________________

MOBILE HOME NOTE

$ ___________ (value of note) **Date** ____________

FOR VALUE RECEIVED, the undersigned, jointly and severally, promise to pay to the order _______________________at _____________________________, or at such other place as the holder of this note may designate in writing, in lawful money of the United States, the principal sum of $ ___________ with interest at the rate of _____%.

The principal and interest on this note shall be paid in _______ consecutive payments of $ ______ each, beginning ___________ and on the same date each month thereafter until fully paid. If not sooner paid, all principal and accrued interest shall be due and payable on __________.

Payments shall be applied first to any late charges or penalties owed, then to interest and the remainder to principal. Any payment not received within five (5) days of due date shall be assessed a late charge of $20.00, plus two dollars ($2.00) per day thereafter. Any check returned by Bank for non-payment, regardless of reason, shall be assessed a charge of twenty five dollars (*$25.00*).

This note is secured by a first lien on a year ______ mobile home model ________, VIN # _______________ Title # _________________
located at LOT _____________, ________________, ______________________. Title to remain in possession of Note Holder(s), _______________________, until satisfactory payment of this note is made, at which time title will be delivered to fee of liens of Note Maker(s). Note Makers(s) to pay all costs of transferring title.

THIS NOTE IS FOR THE MOBILE HOME ONLY AND NOT FOR THE LAND UNDERNEATH IT, WHICH IS LEASED.

This note shall, at the option of the Note Holder(s), be declared in default if any of the following occur:

- Failure to receive any payment within ten (10) days of due date.
- Failure to carry sufficient fire and extended coverage insurance on mobile home at all times, in amounts to cover the outstanding liens, and furnish Note Holder(s) with a copy of policy naming Note Holder(s) in a first lien position.
- Failure to pay lot rent and abide by Park rules.
- Moving mobile home from present location. It may not be moved.
- Failure to pay required taxes, insurance premiums, and water bills when due.

Should a default occur on this Note, the Note Holder(s) reserve the right to call all remaining principal and accrued interest due in full immediately, without further notice to Note Maker(s). If legal action is necessary to collect on this note, Note Maker(s) agree to pay all such cost, including reasonable attorney fees.

If the premises are left unoccupied for ten (10) days or more while payment is due and unpaid, property will be considered abandoned and Note Holder(s), at their option, are authorized to take immediate possession of abandoned property as liquidated damages, disposing of mobile home and owner's personal property as they wish, without recourse.

This note may be paid off at any time without penalty but cannot be assumed by another party without written consent of Note Holder(s). Note Maker(s) acknowledge a copy of this note.

____________________________ ____

Printed Name Note Maker - _______________________________

Witness 1

____

Printed Name

Witness 2

STATE OF ____________________

COUNTY OF __________________

The foregoing instrument was acknowledged before me this ________ day of _________, 20_________, by ______________________________________. He/she is personally known to me, or produced________________________ as identification.

(SEAL) Notary Public Signature___________________________________

Printed name of Notary _____________________

Commission No.: ___________________________

My Commission expires: ____________________

This instrument was prepared by: ______________________________
Property Tax Identification Number: ____________________________

NOTICE OF LIEN ON MOBILE HOME IN A MOBILE HOME PARK

Be advised that on this day of ___/_____/_____there is a lien on the mobile home on Lot # ________ at the street address known as ________________ in the Mobile Home Park named ___________________. The owner of the mobile home who has the lien placed upon it is ___________________.

If there is any problem with lot rent payment, or noncompliance with the rules, or any problem that may result in an eviction of the mobile home, please contact me at:

____
Name of Lienor

____
Address of Lienor

____
Phone Number of Lienor

A condition of the lien is that the owner of the mobile home is current on lot rent and does not have problems with eviction. If there is a problem, I will take all necessary measure to cure it and protect my lien.

____________________________________ ________________________

Witness 1: Printed Name__________________ Lienor Signature

____

Witness 2: Printed Name__________________

STATE OF _______________, COUNTY OF ______________: (Seal of Notary)

The foregoing instrument was acknowledged before me this ____ day of ______, 20 ____, by ______________________. He is personally known to me, or produced ______________ as identification.

____ _______________________

Printed Name of Notary: Commission # ________ Notary Public Signature
Expires: _______________

HISTORICAL CAP RATE FOR 55+ COMMUNITIES

Rating	Rating Criteria	Under 50 Units	50–100 Units	100–200 Units	200–300 Units	300 or more Units
A *****	Major amenities, public utilities, no rentals	0	0	7.25	7.00	6.75
B ****	Amenities, public utilities, no rentals	0	0	7.50	7.25	7.00
C ***	Amenities, on-site utilities, no rentals	0	8.00	7.75	7.50	7.25
D **	No or minimum amenities, on-site utilities, no rentals	8.50	8.25	8.00	7.75	7.50
E *	No or minimum amenities, on-site utilities, some rentals	9.00	8.75	8.50	8.25	8.00
F	No or minimum amenities, on-site utilities, many rentals	9.50	9.25	9.00	8.75	8.50

HISTORICAL CAP RATE FOR FAMILY PARKS

Rating	Rating Criteria	Under 50 Units	50–100 Units	100–200 Units	200–300 Units	300 or more Units
A *****	Major amenities, public utilities, no rentals	0	9.50	9.00	8.50	8.75
B ****	Amenities, public utilities, no rentals	0	10.00	9.50	9.00	9.25
C ***	Amenities, on-site utilities, no rentals	14.00	13.00	12.00	11.00	10.00
D **	No or minimum amenities, on-site utilities, no rentals	16.00	15.00	14.00	13.00	12.00
E *	No or minimum amenities, on-site utilities, some rentals	20.00	18.50	17.00	15.50	14.00
F	No or minimum amenities, on-site utilities, many rentals	22.00	20.50	19.00	17.50	16.00

WOODALL STAR MOBILE HOME PARK RATING SYSTEM

The Woodall Star Mobile Home Park Rating System is a rating system developed by the Woodall Publishing Company and published in their directory on an annual basis until the early 1970s. During this time, RV/Campground parks began growing and the Woodall Publishing Company began publishing a directory for them instead. In the Woodall Star Mobile Home Park Rating System, the stars were meant to be a guide for various levels of service, not to rank one park above another, such as used in rating hotels. The following ratings were taken directly from the 1970 directory.

Woodall One-Star Park

- Fair overall appearance.
- Patios on most lots. May be concrete, asphalt, wood, or some suitable material.
- Grass, rocks, or shell to cover ground.
- Streets fair to good. May be dirt, asphalt, or gravel in reasonable condition.
- Restrooms clean, if any.
- Adequate laundry or Laundromat nearby.
- If fences allowed, must be neat.
- Mail service.
- Homes may be old models, but show evidence of some care.
- Manager available some hours of each day.

Woodall Two-Star Park

In addition to the one-star requirements, a two-star park must have:

- Landscaping--some lawns and shrubs.
- Streets in good condition. Must be dust free of crushed rock, gravel, or shell minimum.
- Neat storage.
- Well equipped laundry or laundromat nearby.
- 220-volt electrical connections available.
- If children accepted, park should have play area.
- Park free of clutter, such as old cars and other abandoned equipment.
- Well-maintained and managed.

Woodall Three-Star Park

In addition to the requirements for one-star and two-star parks, a three-star park must have the following:

- Attractive entrance.
- All mobile homes must be in good condition.
- Awnings and cabana rooms on some homes in southern area.
- Some spaces for large mobile homes.
- Paved or hard surfaced streets.

Woodall Four-Star Park

Four-star parks are luxury parks. In addition to the requirements for one-star, two-star, and three-star parks, a four-star park must have the following:

- Good landscaping.
- Most homes skirted with metal skirts, concrete block, ornamental wood, or stone.

- Paved streets, edged, or curbed.
- Uncrowded lots.
- Underground utilities if permitted by local conditions and authorities.
- Most tanks, if present, concealed.
- Any hedges or fences must be attractive and uniform.
- Awnings, cabanas, or porches on most homes in southern areas. (Except double-wide units.)
- Most lots to accommodate large homes.
- Where row parking of homes exists, all must be lined up uniformly.
- Community hall and/or swimming pool and/or recreation program. (If a park is four-star in all but this requirement, the fourth star will be printed as an open star, indicating a four star park without recreation.)
- Excellent management.

Woodall Five-Star Park

Five-star parks are the best ones. In addition to the requirements for one-star, two-star, three-star and four-star parks, a five-star park must have the following:

- Well-planned and laid out spacious appearance.
- Good location in regard to accessibility and desirable neighborhood. In some locations park should be enclosed by high hedges or ornamental fence.
- Wide paved streets in perfect condition. Curbs or lawns edged to street, sidewalks, street lights, street signs.
- Homes set back from the street.
- Exceptionally attractive entrance and park sign.
- Patios at least 8 x 30 ft. (Except double-wide units.)
- Paved off-street parking such as carports or planned parking.
- All homes skirted.
- All hitches concealed. Any existing tanks concealed.
- Recreation, some or all of the following: swimming pool (except areas with long, cold winters), shuffleboards, horseshoe pitching, golf course, hobby shop, hobby classes, games, potlucks, dances, or natural recreation facilities.
- Beautifully equipped recreation hall with kitchen. Room for community gatherings. Tiled restrooms, etc.
- Uniform storage shed or central storage facilities.
- All late model homes in excellent condition.
- At least 60% occupancy in order to judge quality of residents which indicates park's ability to maintain a five-star rating between inspections.
- All empty lots grassed, graveled, or otherwise well maintained.
- If pets or children allowed, there must be a place for them to run and play without cluttering the streets and yards. Most five-star parks are for adults only.
- Superior management interested in comfort of residents and maintenance of park.

LIST OF CONDUIT LENDERS

Union Capital Investments	404-812-4800		
Wells Fargo	248-833-2613	858-509-2122	
Collateral Mortgage	800-366-1840	407-772-0750	
GMAC Commercial Mtg	602-912-8952	205-991-6700	
GE Real Estate	949-477-1545	949-477-1554	312-441-7685
Onyx Capital	310-442-8400		
Column/Credit Suisse	212-538-6267		
Northwestern Mutual Live	813-229-0135		
Tremont Realty Capital	312-236-0960		
First Bank of Illinois	847-654-4443		
Universal Bank	626-654-2818		
Security Mortgage	585-423-0230		
Monroe & Giordano	813-229-5055		
UBS	212-713-8871		
Industry Mortgage Assoc	800-429-6766		
Local Oklahoma Bank	405-841-2914		
Sterling Financial Mtg	480-446-2600		
First United Mortgage	212-332-3457		
Santiago Financial	714-731-8080		
Baker Mortgage	503-390-4914		
ValueXpress, LLC	800-650-2627		
Green Park Financial	301-215-5578		
ARCS Commercial Mtg	248-740-0353		
Intervest Mortgage Co	800-508-8568		
Crown Capital	407-767-9553		
Consultants Resource Group	813-661-5901		
Manufactured Housing	303-442-4402		

SAMPLE FINANCIAL STATEMENT

Assets		Liabilities	
Home at 123 Friendly Dr.	$200,000	Loan on Home	$180,000
Furniture	15,000		
2001 Ford Pickup	10,000	Loan on Pickup	5,000
2002 Toyota Camry	12,000	Loan on Toyota	8,000
Investment Mobile on Main St.	50,000	Loan Main St. Mobile	40,000
Investment Mobile Grassy Par	10,000	Loan Grassy Pk. Mob.	8,000
Savings Account at First Federal	10,000	MasterCard Balance	1,500
Checking Account	3,000	Visa Balance	2,000
Total Assets	**$310,000**	**Total Liabilities**	**$244,500**

Net Worth = Total Assets – Total Liabilities

$310,000 – 244,500 = $65,500

LIST OF LENDERS SELLING REPOS

Lender	Website
Vanderbilt Mortgage	vmfrepos.com
21st Mortgage	21stmortgage.com
Triad Financial	riadfs.com
Tammac	ammac.com
GreenTree	Gtservicing.com

A. **Settlement Statement**

U.S. Department of Housing and Urban Development

OMB Approval No. 2502-0265

B. Type of Loan

1. ☐ FHA 2. ☐ FmHA 3. ☐ Conv. Unins. 4. ☐ VA 5. ☐ Conv. Ins.	6. File Number:	7. Loan Number:	8. Mortgage Insurance Case Number:

C. Note: This form is furnished to give you a statement of actual settlement costs. Amounts paid to and by the settlement agent are shown. Items marked "(p.o.c.)" were paid outside the closing; they are shown here for informational purposes and are not included in the totals.

D. Name & Address of Borrower:	E. Name & Address of Seller:	F. Name & Address of Lender:

G. Property Location:	H. Settlement Agent:	
	Place of Settlement:	I. Settlement Date:

J. Summary of Borrower's Transaction		**K. Summary of Seller's Transaction**	
100. Gross Amount Due From Borrower		**400. Gross Amount Due To Seller**	
101. Contract sales price		401. Contract sales price	
102. Personal property		402. Personal property	
103. Settlement charges to borrower (line 1400)		403.	
104.		404.	
105.		405.	
Adjustments for items paid by seller in advance		**Adjustments for items paid by seller in advance**	
106. City/town taxes to		406. City/town taxes to	
107. County taxes to		407. County taxes to	
108. Assessments to		408. Assessments to	
109.		409.	
110.		410.	
111.		411.	
112.		412.	
120. Gross Amount Due From Borrower		**420. Gross Amount Due To Seller**	
200. Amounts Paid By Or In Behalf Of Borrower		**500. Reductions In Amount Due To Seller**	
201. Deposit or earnest money		501. Excess deposit (see instructions)	
202. Principal amount of new loan(s)		502. Settlement charges to seller (line 1400)	
203. Existing loan(s) taken subject to		503. Existing loan(s) taken subject to	
204.		504. Payoff of first mortgage loan	
205.		505. Payoff of second mortgage loan	
206.		506.	
207.		507.	
208.		508.	
209.		509.	
Adjustments for items unpaid by seller		**Adjustments for items unpaid by seller**	
210. City/town taxes to		510. City/town taxes to	
211. County taxes to		511. County taxes to	
212. Assessments to		512. Assessments to	
213.		513.	
214.		514.	
215.		515.	
216.		516.	
217.		517.	
218.		518.	
219.		519.	
220. Total Paid By/For Borrower		**520. Total Reduction Amount Due Seller**	
300. Cash At Settlement From/To Borrower		**600. Cash At Settlement To/From Seller**	
301. Gross Amount due from borrower (line 120)		601. Gross amount due to seller (line 420)	
302. Less amounts paid by/for borrower (line 220)	( )	602. Less reductions in amt. due seller (line 520)	( )
303. Cash ☐ From ☐ To Borrower		**603. Cash ☐ To ☐ From Seller**	

Section 5 of the Real Estate Settlement Procedures Act (RESPA) requires the following • HUD must develop a Special Information Booklet to help persons borrowing money to finance the purchase of residential real estate to better understand the nature and costs of real estate settlement services; • Each lender must provide the booklet to all applicants from whom it receives or for whom it prepares a written application to borrow money to finance the purchase of residential real estate; • Lenders must prepare and distribute with the Booklet a Good Faith Estimate of the settlement costs that the borrower is likely to incur in connection with the settlement. These disclosures are manadatory.

Section 4(a) of RESPA mandates that HUD develop and prescribe this standard form to be used at the time of loan settlement to provide full disclosure of all charges imposed upon the borrower and seller. These are third party disclosures that are designed to provide the borrower with pertinent information during the settlement process in order to be a better shopper.

The Public Reporting Burden for this collection of information is estimated to average one hour per response, including the time for reviewing instructions, searching existing data sources, gathering and maintaining the data needed, and completing and reviewing the collection of information.

This agency may not collect this information, and you are not required to complete this form, unless it displays a currently valid OMB control number.

The information requested does not lend itself to confidentiality.

Previous editions are obsolete

Page 1 of 2

form **HUD-1** (3/86)
ref Handbook 4305.2

L. Settlement Charges

	Paid From Borrowers Funds at Settlement	Paid From Seller's Funds at Settlement
700. Total Sales/Broker's Commission based on price $ @ % =		
Division of Commission (line 700) as follows:		
701. $ to		
702. $ to		
703. Commission paid at Settlement		
704.		
800. Items Payable In Connection With Loan		
801. Loan Origination Fee %		
802. Loan Discount %		
803. Appraisal Fee to		
804. Credit Report to		
805. Lender's Inspection Fee		
806. Mortgage Insurance Application Fee to		
807. Assumption Fee		
808.		
809.		
810.		
811.		
900. Items Required By Lender To Be Paid In Advance		
901. Interest from to @$ /day		
902. Mortgage Insurance Premium for months to		
903. Hazard Insurance Premium for years to		
904. years to		
905.		
1000. Reserves Deposited With Lender		
1001. Hazard insurance months@$ per month		
1002. Mortgage insurance months@$ per month		
1003. City property taxes months@$ per month		
1004. County property taxes months@$ per month		
1005. Annual assessments months@$ per month		
1006. months@$ per month		
1007. months@$ per month		
1008. months@$ per month		
1100. Title Charges		
1101. Settlement or closing fee to		
1102. Abstract or title search to		
1103. Title examination to		
1104. Title insurance binder to		
1105. Document preparation to		
1106. Notary fees to		
1107. Attorney's fees to		
(includes above items numbers:)		
1108. Title insurance to		
(includes above items numbers:)		
1109. Lender's coverage $		
1110. Owner's coverage $		
1111.		
1112.		
1113.		
1200. Government Recording and Transfer Charges		
1201. Recording fees: Deed $; Mortgage $; Releases $		
1202. City/county tax/stamps: Deed $; Mortgage $		
1203. State tax/stamps: Deed $; Mortgage $		
1204.		
1205.		
1300. Additional Settlement Charges		
1301. Survey to		
1302. Pest inspection to		
1303.		
1304.		
1305.		
1400. Total Settlement Charges (enter on lines 103, Section J and 502, Section K)		

Previous editions are obsolete

form **HUD-1** (3/86)
ref Handbook 4305.2

RENTAL CALL SHEET

Date: ____________________ Time: ____________________
Called about _________________ property from ________________ (sign, paper, etc.)

As you know, we have very reasonable rents, and very nice rentals. In order to get you approved, and not waste your time, I'll need some simple info. OK?

1. What is your name? _________________ (first) _________________ (last)

2. Besides yourself, who else is living with you? _________________
   a) Ages of children _________________
   b) Pets _________________
   c) Your age _________________

3. When do you need it? _________________

4. How long do you need it for? _________________

5. If this rental works for you, are you ready now with deposit? YES NO

6. Employed? YES NO
   How long? _________________
   How much take home 2 weeks? $ _________________

7. Anyone else employed? YES NO
   How long? _________________
   How much take home 2 weeks? $ _________________

8. Where living now? _________________ How long there? _________________

9. Is there anything in your background that would preclude the owners from renting to you, for instance, a conviction or eviction in the last six years? YES NO

WOULD YOU LIKE ME TO GET YOU A QUICK APPROVAL NOW? YES NO
[CHECK CRIMINAL/EVICTION RECORD WHILE TALKING]

10. IF PROPERTY NOT YET SEEN:
Before I give you directions to drive by, please give me your cell phone so I can reach you: _________________. Call us when you want to come in and apply, and please don't wait because our rentals go quickly.

11. IF PROPERTY SEEN BECAUSE OF SIGN OUT FRONT:
Want to come in today and fill out an application and get started? YES NO
Before I give you directions to our office, please give me your cell phone so I can reach you: _________________.

MOBILE HOME LEASE—WEEKLY

Agreement between _______________, Owner, and _______________, Tenants, for a dwelling located at ________________________________. Tenants agree to lease this dwelling for a term of __________, beginning __________and ending __________ at 5 PM for $_____ per week, payable in advance on each Friday of every calendar WEEK to Owner at ____________________. When rent is received after each Friday of every calendar WEEK, Tenants must pay a $_____ late fee. In addition, there will be a $<u>10.00</u> late charge for every day after the rent is seven (7) days late, and the rent must be delivered in person at ______________________.

Tenant will pay Pet Deposit in (2) equal pays of $ ________ on ________ and ________. The first week's rent for this dwelling is $________, plus Trash. The entire sum of this lease is $______________________. The security/cleaning deposit on this dwelling is $_______. It is refundable if Tenants leave the dwelling reasonably clean and undamaged and if, at the end of the full lease, keys are returned and a forwarding address given. Owners will refund deposits within <u>15</u> days after Tenants have moved out and returned their keys.
Only the following persons and NO PETS are to live in this dwelling: ______________

____

No overnight guests and no overnight pets. No other persons or PETS may live there without Owner's prior written permission, and it may not be sublet.
Owner pays for the following, which is included in the rent: ____________________
Tenant pays for and must maintain the following in addition to rent: <u>**Electric, Water, Trash, Cable, Telephone, Lawn,** ***blinds, stove, fridge, (2) A/Cs that belong to Owners. Tenant must leave working appliances when lease is over.***</u> **NO CABLE DISHES ATTACHED ANYWHERE ON BUILDING.
Trash charges, utility charges, lawn mowing, and late charges will be considered additional rent.
REMARKS: <u>*Tenant responsible for Bug Exterminating every 3 months, and tenant must purchase and install own Smoke Detector and Batteries. Tenant must purchase own garbage cans and pay for air conditioning filters.*</u>

TENANTS AGREE TO THE FOLLOWING

1. To keep yards and garbage areas clean. Inside of house to be kept neat and tidy at all times.
2. To keep from making loud noises and disturbing neighbors. Any noise heard outside home is a loud noise.
3. Not to paint or alter dwelling without first getting Owner's written permission.
4. To park their motor vehicle in assigned space and to keep that space clean of oil dripping.
5. Not to repair their motor vehicle on premises.

6. To allow Owner to inspect the dwelling and show it at any and all reasonable times.

7. All vehicles must have current tags and be in working condition. All others will be towed at tenants' expense.

8. Not to keep any liquid-filled furniture in this dwelling.

9. To pay rent by check or money order payable to Owner. (Bad check means late charge will be applied).

10. To pay for all repairs, including drain stoppages, they or their guests have caused.

11. To pay for **ANY** broken windows and window parts in their dwelling while they live there.

12. To be responsible for cleaning or replacing A/C filter and repairs caused by neglecting this.

13. Tenant is responsible for the first $75 per month of any other repairs.

14. Tenant is responsible for lawn mowing. If not done, tenant will be billed $ ________ per cut (or rate increase, per lawn service), billed with rent statement and due immediately with rent, considered additional rent.

15. Tenant is responsible for garbage and trash fees and water and sewer bills, considered additional rent.

16. Owner is not responsible for tenant's personal property. Tenant must get renter's insurance.

17. Owner may cancel lease with 60 days' prior notice.

18. Tenant has received Lead Base Paint pamphlet EPA747-K-94-001.

19. If tenant vacates premises by surrendering, abandonment, or eviction, landlord shall not be liable or responsible for storage or disposal of the tenant's personal property [F.S.83.67(3)].

20. There will be no open containers of alcoholic beverages outside of the home.

Violation of any part of this agreement or nonpayment of rent when due shall be cause for eviction, and the prevailing party shall recover court costs and attorney's fees. Tenants hereby acknowledge that they have read this agreement, understand it, agree to it, and have been given a copy.

Owner: ______________________________ Tenant: ______________________________

Date: ______________________________ Date: ______________________________

MOBILE HOME LEASE—MONTHLY

Agreement between ______________________, Owner, and, ____________________, Tenants, for a dwelling located at ____________________________. Tenants agree to lease this dwelling for a term of ___________ beginning ___________and ending _________ at 5 PM for $___________ per month, payable in advance on the _____ day of every calendar month to Owner at ____________________. When rent is received after the _____ day of every calendar month, Tenants must pay a $**50.00** late fee. In addition, there will be a $**10.00** late charge for every day after the rent is seven (7) days late, and the rent must be delivered in person at ____________________________.

Tenant will pay Last Month's Rent in five (5) equal pays of $ _____ from _______ to _______. The first month's rent for this dwelling is $___________, plus Trash. The entire sum of this lease is $___________.

The security/cleaning deposit on this dwelling is $_______. It is refundable if Tenants leave the dwelling reasonably clean and undamaged and if, at the end of the full lease, keys are returned and a forwarding address given.

Owner will refund deposit within ______ days after Tenants have moved out completely and returned their keys.

Only the following persons and NO PETS are to live in this dwelling:

____

____.

No overnight guests and no overnight pets. No other persons or PETS may live there without Owner's prior written permission, and it may not be sublet.

Owner pays for the following, which is included in the rent: ________________

Tenant pays for and must maintain the following in addition to rent: **Electric, Water, Trash, Cable, Telephone, Lawn,** ***blinds, stove, fridge, (2) A/Cs that belong to Owner. Tenant must leave working appliances when lease is over.*** **NO CABLE DISHES ATTACHED ANYWHERE ON BUILDING.

Trash charges, utility charges, lawn mowing, and late charges will be considered additional rent.

REMARKS: *Tenant responsible for Bug Exterminating every 3 months and tenant must purchase and install own Smoke Detector and Batteries. Tenant must purchase own garbage cans and pay for air conditioning filters.*

TENANTS AGREE TO THE FOLLOWING

1. To keep yards and garbage areas clean. Inside of house to be kept neat and tidy at all times.

2. To keep from making loud noises and disturbing neighbors. Any noise heard outside house is a loud noise.

3. Not to paint or alter their dwelling without first getting Owner's written permission.

4. To park their motor vehicle in assigned space and to keep that space clean of oil dripping.

5. Not to repair their motor vehicle on premises.

6. To allow Owner to inspect the dwelling and show it at any and all reasonable times.

7. All vehicles must have current tags and be in working condition. All others will be towed at tenants' expense.

8. Not to keep any liquid-filled furniture in this dwelling.

9. To pay rent by check or money order payable to Owner. (Bad check means late charge will be applied).

10. To pay for all repairs, including drain stoppages, they or their guests have caused.

11. To pay for **any and all** broken windows and window parts in their dwelling while they live there.

12. To be responsible for cleaning or replacing A/C filter and repairs caused by neglecting this.

13. Tenant is responsible for the first $75 per month of any other repairs.

14. Tenant is responsible for lawn mowing. If not done, tenant will be billed $_____ per cut (or rate increase, per lawn service), billed monthly with rent statement and due immediately with rent, considered additional rent.

15. Tenant is responsible for garbage and trash fees and water and sewer bills, considered additional rent.

16. Owner is not responsible for tenant's personal property. Tenant must get renter's insurance.

17. Owner may cancel lease with 60 days' prior notice.

18. Tenant has received Lead Base Paint pamphlet EPA747-K-94-001.

19. If tenant vacates premises by surrendering, abandonment, or eviction, landlord shall not be liable or responsible for storage or disposal of the tenant's personal property [F.S.83.67(3)].

20. There will be no open containers of alcoholic beverages outside of the home.

Violation of any part of this agreement or nonpayment of rent when due shall be cause for eviction, and the prevailing party shall recover court costs and attorney's fees. Tenants hereby acknowledge that they have read this agreement, understand it, agree to it, and have been given a copy.

Owner: ______________________________ Tenant: ______________________________

Date: ______________________________ Date: ______________________________

MOBILE HOME COMMUNITY LEASE

This Rental Agreement is entered into by ____________ Mobile Home Community, herein called "Park Owner", and __________________, herein called the "Mobile Home Owner."

WITNESSETH

That in consideration of the premises, the rents, covenants and agreements to be paid and performed by Mobile Home Owner, Park Owner agrees to rent to Mobile Home Owner that certain mobile home as herein described upon all covenants, terms, conditions, restrictions, and limitations set forth or otherwise provided by law.

1. Mobile home located on lot #_________.

2. Year of Mobile Home: _______ Make: __________ Title Number:______________ VIN:________

3. Only the following people are living in Mobile Home: _________________________ ____ .

NO OTHER PERSON(S) OR PET(S) .

4. Only the following pets are allowed:______________________________________ .

5. Only the following vehicles are allowed: __________________________________ .

6. The term of this Rental Agreement shall commence on __/__/20__ and terminate on __/__/20__. In the event the Mobile Home Owner wants to vacate the leased premises at the end of this lease, then the Mobile Home Owner will give at least 60 days prior written notice.

7. The monthly rent that the Mobile Home Owner shall pay to the Park owner is $ _______ per month, which shall be due and payable on the 1st day of each month. If rental payments are not received at the park office by the 5th of the month, there will be a $25 late charge. If a rental payment is returned due to insufficient funds, there will be an additional $25 charge in addition to the late charge, and both charges shall be considered as additional rent. Rents will be paid by check or money order. CASH WILL NOT BE ACCEPTED. The monthly rental rate may be increased or refrained from being increased at the sole discretion of the Park Owner with 30 days prior notice to Mobile Home Owner, and Park Owner's failure to increase rent shall not be deemed a waiver of Park Owner's right to do so.

8. RESPONSIBILITIES OF MOBILE HOME OWNER:

A. Mobile Home Owner agrees to fully comply with all the terms and conditions of this Rental Agreement and the attached Rules & Regulations of the ____________ Mobile Home Community and the laws of the State of ________________.

B. Mobile Home Owner agrees to pay all rental payments when due.

C. It shall be the responsibility of the Mobile Home Owner to make and maintain all connections to utilities, including but not limited to water, sewer, electrical, cable and telephone at Mobile Home Owner's sole expense. Any problems or repairs to utility connections shall be the sole responsibility and cost of the Mobile Home Owner.

D. Mobile Home Owner and guests and invitees shall comply with all rules and regulations of the Park attached hereto, which shall be amended from time to time. Mobile Home Owner agrees that he or she understands said Rules and Regulations and violation of said Rules shall be grounds for eviction from the mobile home park.

E. Mobile Home Owner shall maintain its mobile home in good and proper condition. Mobile Home Owner shall NOT make an alteration, addition or modification to the interior or exterior of the mobile home or make any changes to the premises without prior WRITTEN permission from Park Owner.

F. Mobile Home Owner is responsible for maintenance of all landscaping on the leased lot. In the event that any tree or other vegetation shall require removal, in the sole estimation of the Park Owner, then the Mobile Home Owner shall pay all costs of removal.

G. Mobile Home owner and its guests and invitees shall not make any improper or offensive use of the subject home or any property or facility of the mobile home park. All shared facilities shall be used for the purpose for which it was designated and in a reasonable manner.

H. Mobile Home owner shall be responsible for any damages caused to the property or facilities of the mobile home park by the Mobile Home Owner or his guests or invitees.

I. Mobile Home Owner may NOT sub-lease or rent the mobile home without prior written permission of Park Owner.

J. Mobile Home Owner shall provide his own liability and casualty insurance.

9. PAYMENT OF UTILITY AND SERVICE CHARGES AND MOWING: Mobile Home Owner is responsible for mowing their own individual lot. If Mobile Home Owner does not mow their lawn and the Park Owner has to provide lawn service, the Mobile Home Owner will be charged $10.00 each time the Park Owner has to provide service to cut the lawn. In any event, all charges for electricity, telephone, cable, etc. shall be the responsibility of the Mobile Home Owner. Mobile Home Owner will be responsible for trash, water and sewer charges as additional rent and will be billed monthly for trash, water and sewer charges along with the monthly rental charges. Trash, water, sewer and monthly rental charges are due payable on the 1st day of each month.

10. DEFAULT: In the event the Mobile Home Owner defaults under any term of this Rental Agreement, any rule or regulation of the park, or upon conviction of the Mobile Home Owner for violation of federal, state or local law which is detrimental to the health, safety or welfare of other residents of the mobile home park, the Park Owner may evict the Mobile Home Owner in accordance with ___________ Law, and Park Owner shall other rights as permitted by law or in equity. Mobile Home Owner agrees to pay Park Owner all of Park Owner's costs, expenses, and fees, including attorney's fees which may incurred in pursuing the Park Owner's rights on account of any default of the Mobile Home Owner.

11. ASSIGNMENT/SUBLET: Mobile Home Owner shall NOT have the right to assign this Rental Agreement or sublet all or any part of the home without express WRITTEN Park Owner's permission.

12. GENERAL PROVISIONS:

A. This Rental Agreement can not be changed, cancelled, amended or modified except by express WRITTEN agreement of both parties.

B. This Rental Agreement is construed in accordance with Florida law.

C. This Rental Agreement is binding upon parties, their heirs, successors and assigns.

D. All notices by Mobile Home Owner to Park Owner shall be sent to ___________ Mobile Home Community c/o ________________________________.

E. All notices by Park Owner to Mobile Owner will be delivered to Mobile Home Owners lot.

F. This agreement is entire and not divisible. If any of the provisions of this Rental Agreement are held invalid or non-enforceable by any Court or tribunal, then all the other terms and provisions shall remain in full force and effect.

G. **By execution of this agreement, Mobile Home Owner acknowledges that he/she has read and understands the foregoing, and was offered the foregoing prior to occupancy. Mobile Home Owner further acknowledges he/she has received a copy of Rules and Regulations, and has read The Prospectus of the Park.**

_______________________________________ _______________________

Mobile Home Owner (Resident) Date

_____________ Mobile Home Community (Park Owner)

By ____________________________________ _______________________

Manager or Park Owner Date

MOBILE HOME COMMUNITY RULES & REGULATIONS

1. **APPLICATION:** Prospective residents must fill out an application and be approved in writing by management BEFORE residing in the park. The $25 application fee is NON-REFUNDABLE. **No one can lease, sub-lease, or sell his home in our park without our prior written approval.**

2. **RENTAL PAYMENTS:** All rents are due by the 1st of the month. If rental payments are not RECEIVED by the 5th, there will be a $25 late charge. If a rental payment check is returned due to insufficient funds, there is an additional $25 charge. CASH WILL NOT BE ACCEPTED. Please pay by check or money order.

3. **OCCUPANCY:** Only the family who rents the lot may reside on it. Each adult tenant is responsible for his children and visitors and any lessees or sub-lessees.

4. **PETS:** All pets must be kept indoors. Each household is allowed 1 cat or 1 dog under 30 pounds. If a resident has very small dogs, then the total poundage of all the dogs taken together must be less than 30 lbs. All pets must be on a leash when outdoors and you MUST pick up their waste. No pet is allowed to be tied up outside at any time. If a pet causes damage, the owner must pay for it or face eviction. If a pet is deemed a nuisance by management, it must be removed or owner will face eviction.

5. **BUSINESS:** Absolutely no type of business may be conducted within the park without the prior written approval of management.

6. **NOISE:** Excessive noise is not allowed and is grounds for eviction. If your neighbor can hear you, no matter what time, that constitutes excessive noise.

7. **SIGNS:** No signs are allowed on lots in the park. A small resident name and address sign is permitted on the home. Current year license tags must be displayed in the front window and only one 9" x 12" FOR SALE sign is permitted in front window.

8. **UNDERSKIRTING:** Management approved skirting must be installed on your home within 30 days of moving in.

9. **SPEED LIMIT:** The park limit for all vehicles is 5 MPH and is strictly enforced. Posted regulations and traffic signs must be observed.

10. **VEHICLES:** Vehicles must be parked off the street and ONLY on resident's lot. Only one vehicle is allowed per lot, unless there is a carport, and all vehicles fit under the carport. All others must be parked at ________________. Commercial vehicles, boats, boat trailers, and untagged vehicles are not allowed. No mini-bikes, dirt bikes, or ATV bikes are allowed. There is no parking on the grass, and no washing of vehicles.

11. **WATER CONTROL:** Use of a hose is permitted only if used with an on-off nozzle at the end that allows water to be shut off when not spraying to avoid wastage.

12. **STORAGE:** No outside storage is permitted unless in a metal or wooden shed, and all new or replacement storage sheds must have prior written management approval. There will be no storage on lanai's or patios, or under trailers. If a storage shed is a deemed a nuisance by management, the owner must remove it.

13. **REPAIRS:** Repairs of cars, boats, motors, motorcycles are not permitted in park.

14. **EXTERIORS & TRASH COLLECTION:** All homes, lots & drives must be kept neat and clean. No additions of any kind can be built on any mobile home without prior written management approval. No fences are allowed. Each mobile home is required to have at least two 32 gallon garbage cans with tight fitting lids that are to be kept at the rear of the home, except on garbage collection days. All garbage placed in cans must be in plastic bags. Garbage pickup days are Tuesday & Friday, except holidays. Brush and shrubbery must be cut into 3 foot lengths and tied. Clippings must be bagged and tied. All large items that can not be fit into cans, like furniture, couches, air conditioners, frigs, etc. must be called into the manager to be hauled away. DO NOT PUT LARGE ITEMS NEXT TO THE DUMPSTER. THEY WILL NOT BE PICKED UP. No laundry is to be hung anywhere outside.

15. **LOT CARE:** Residents must maintain and mow their own lots, and all planting must be around the perimeter of home. No flower beds or gardens are allowed in yards, and all bushes, plants and shrubs must be kept neatly trimmed. Grass over 3" high is required to be mowed, and if tenant does not mow, management will do it for $20.

16. **ANCHORS:** Hurricane anchors are required at set-up according to county code.

17. **MOVING HOME FROM PARK:** Any tenant planning to move his mobile home from the park is required to notify management in writing 60 days prior to moving. If we are not notified, then 60 days lot rent will be due. NO TOW TRUCK MAY ENTER OUR PROPERTY TO REMOVE A HOME UNTIL IT IS CLEARED IN WRITING PRIOR TO THE REMOVAL.

18. **OPEN CONTAINERS:** Residents are not allowed outside or walking around with open containers of alcoholic beverages, or to be publicly intoxicated.

19. **DISTURBANCES:** Any tenant or guest of a tenant who causes a disturbance that necessitates law enforcement officials to be called to the scene of our park must appear at our office the next day with a written explanation. At that time, a determination will be made as to whether that tenant will be evicted or not. In any case, after the second time law enforcement officials are called for a tenant, that tenant will be evicted.

20. **WATER METERS:** Management may arrange to have water meters installed to measure tenant's water and sewer usage. Tenant agrees to pay for such usage and it shall be considered as additional rent. If tenant does not pay for water and sewer usage when due, it shall constitute non-payment of rent and will result in an eviction.

21. **EVICTION:** The owner may evict a resident to any of the following reasons:
    a Nonpayment of lot rent or additional water and sewer usage in full.
    b. conviction of a violation of a federal, state, or local ordinance which is detrimental to the health, safety and welfare of the residents of the park.
    c. Violation of a park rule or regulation, the rental agreement, or Chapter 723 F.S., as prescribed by Section 723.061 F.S.
    d. a change in the use of land comprising the mobile home park or portion thereof.
    e. Failure of a purchaser of a mobile home situated in the park to be qualified and obtain approval to become a tenant, such approval being required by the Rules and Regulations attached hereto.

I HAVE READ THE ABOVE RULES AND AGREE TO ABIDE BY THEM:

Date: ____________________ Resident: ________________________________

Lot: ____________________

Manager: ________________________________

Date: ________________________________

Index

About the Author

Zalman Velvel has been a full time investor for more than 28 years. His family owns and operates eleven mobile home parks, as well as duplexes, warehouses, miniwarehouses, offices, and motels. Zalman holds the coveted CCIM designation, and he is licensed as a real estate broker, mortgage broker, auctioneer, mobile home dealer, and former real estate appraiser. Zalman is also licensed as a real estate trainer, and has trained more than 5,000 people in real estate investing.

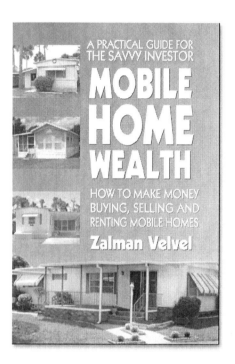

Printed in the United States
221031BV00003B/1/P

9 780982 353103